FOREIGN AFFAIRS
AND THE UNITED STATES CONSTITUTION

DATE DUE

FOREIGN AFFAIRS AND THE UNITED STATES CONSTITUTION

Second Edition

LOUIS HENKIN

University Professor Emeritus
Columbia University

CLARENDON PRESS · OXFORD
1996

at Clarendon Street, Oxford OX2 6DP
ord New York
land Bangkok Bombay
Town Dar es Salaam Delhi
Florence Hong Kong Istanbul Karachi
Kuala Lumpur Madras Madrid Melbourne
Mexico City Nairobi Paris Singapore
Taipei Tokyo Toronto
and associated companies in
Berlin Ibadan

Oxford is a trade mark of Oxford University Press

Published in the United States
by Oxford University Press Inc., New York

© *Louis Henkin 1996*

British Library Cataloguing in Publication Data
Data available

Library of Congress Cataloging in Publication Data
Henkin, Louis.
Foreign affairs and the United States Constitution / Louis Henkin.—2nd ed.
p. cm.
Rev. ed. of: Foreign affairs and the Constitution. Mineola, N.Y.:
Foundation Press, 1972.
Includes bibliographical references (p.) and index.
1. United States—Foreign relations—Law and legislation.
2. United States—Constitutional law. I. Henkin, Louis. Foreign
affairs and the Constitution. II. Title.
KF4651.H45 1996 342.73'0412—dc20 [347.302412] 96–17202
ISBN 0-19-826099-7.—ISBN 0-19-826098-9 (Pbk)

1 3 5 7 9 10 8 6 4 2

Typeset by Hope Services (Abingdon) Ltd.
Printed in Great Britain
on acid-free paper by
Bookcraft Ltd., Midsomer Norton, Avon

For
Alice and Josh and David and Daniel

PREFACE TO THE FIRST
EDITION (excerpt)

Volumes about the American Constitution and about American foreign relations abound, but they are two different mountains of books. Those that deal with the Constitution say little about American foreign relations; the others expound, scrutinize, dissect, and criticize the international relations, foreign policy, and the 'foreign-policy-making process' of the United States, but the controlling relevance of the Constitution is roundly ignored. A constitutional crisis in the conduct of foreign relations besets every generation and fills the journals for a brief time, but how the Constitution governs the conduct of foreign relations does not receive sustained attention or extended exposition.

This was not always so. In earlier days, the constitutional law of American foreign affairs was one, important, integral part of constitutional debate and study. The foreign relations of the future republic were prominent concerns in the deliberations of the Constitutional Convention and in the debates that raged during ratification. They were the subject of essays by Madison, Hamilton, and Jay when they wrote the Federalist Papers to promote acceptance of the new Constitution, and of heated polemics later when Hamilton and Madison (and Hamilton and Jefferson) came to see so differently the Constitution and the government it had established. Constitutional issues in the conduct of foreign affairs were disputed learnedly in Presidential messages, Congressional debates, opinions of attorneys-general and writings of leading lawyers. The Supreme Court Reports carried frequent, extended essays on national sovereignty, the law of nations, executive and legislative powers, the Treaty Power, the special role of the courts in foreign affairs. The law of foreign relations received many pages from early commentators on the Constitution (e.g., Story) and in the nineteenth and early twentieth century treatises (Cooley, Willoughby).

Perhaps the constitutional law of American foreign affairs began to suffer scholarly neglect when, for reasons I suggest later, constitutional lawyers increasingly concerned themselves only with what the Supreme Court was doing, while the Court's contributions in foreign affairs became less frequent. Perhaps it suffered when 'public law' expanded to claim much besides constitutional law and international law, and these two fields themselves grew apace and developed into separate expertises of different experts. The constitutional law of foreign affairs, together with international law, became the special domain of those few lawyers who advised the Government in its foreign relations, and it is they who produced the classic treatises and digests—Wharton, Moore, Malloy, Crandall, Hyde, Hackworth and, most recently, Marjorie Whiteman. For the rest, the law of foreign affairs fell somewhere between the constitutional lawyer and the international lawyer, perhaps nearer to the latter, but his credentials in constitutional law were not universally accepted and he was himself less than wholly comfortable with its matter and manner.

. . . . .

Volumes devoted to the law of foreign affairs in particular have not appeared to fill the void. There was indeed an excellent study by the late Professor Quincy Wright[1] to which I am much indebted, but it is now 50 years old and much has happened since—in the Constitution, in the institutions and processes of government, in American foreign relations . . . Not only have there been at least a dozen innovating Supreme Court decisions since his publication, but its constitutional universe is not ours: the distributions of power between Nation and State and between Congress and the President look different; the safeguards for individual rights have become central; and we have had new problems raising new constitutional questions or framing old questions in new contexts so as to render them effectively new. There have been more recent studies of individual segments,[2] of the powers of the President or of the Congress: in particular, I have drawn heavily on Corwin's study of the Presidency[3] in which the President's role in foreign relations is the subject of one chapter and pervades several others. The particular focus of these studies, however, permits only peripheral vision of the other actors and of the rest of the scene, and some of them are also redolent of an earlier mood, concentrate on earlier problems, antedate several constitutional crises and the latest self-searchings and re-examinations. Most of them reflect the perspectives and insights of the political scientist rather than of the constitutional lawyer.

This volume is designed to begin to fill the need. It is a legal study, although I have attempted to make the text accessible also to those not trained in the law, most of it even to the 'general reader'. In that cause I ask the indulgence of scholars whom I condemn to turning to the back of the book for citation of authority as well as for the longer illustrative and complementary notes.

. . . . .

LOUIS HENKIN

November, 1972

PREFACE TO THE SECOND
EDITION

The 20 years and more that have elapsed since the publication of the previous edition have seen revolutionary change in international relations and in the foreign affairs of the United States, yet none in the U.S. Constitution* and little in the constitutional jurisprudence directly related to foreign affairs. But developments in U.S. foreign affairs have uncovered constitutional questions not previously addressed, and have raised again, in new guises and in new circumstances, issues that continue to cry for understanding even if not susceptible to ready resolution.

The great unknowns and the perplexing issues in the constitutional law of foreign affairs continue to lie between President and Congress—the definition of their respective constitutional domains, the consequences of interference or failure of cooperation in the exercise of their separated powers. In particular, in the wake of the Vietnam War and the Watergate scandal, an aroused Congress imposed the War Powers Resolution on a resistant President. Still in draft when the first edition of this work appeared, the Resolution has now had more than 20 years of troubled life (and essential neglect), and has released a small flood of academic writing. The end of the Cold War and the resurrection of the United Nations Security Council made possible U.S. involvement under United Nations auspices in the Persian Gulf crisis and war (1990–91); in Somalia (1993); in the former Yugoslavia (1993–96); and in Haiti (1994), and roused dormant questions about the constitutional relevance of Security Council resolutions. During the past 20 years, constitutional controversy simmered also when Congress asserted authority to regulate executive conduct of intelligence activities. Differences between the Executive branch and the U.S. Senate as to the interpretation of the Anti-Ballistic Missile Treaty (1987) revealed hidden implications in the

* The Twenty-Seventh Amendment, limiting the power of Congress to 'vary' its compensation, adopted by the Congress in 1789, finally received the necessary ratifications in 1992. The Equal Rights Amendment for women, twice adopted by Congress, did not receive the required ratifications by three-fourths of the states.

speciously clear, simple, and uncontroversial constitutional dispositions of the treaty power.

The Supreme Court and the federal judiciary have continued to develop the law of foreign relations as they develop aspects of constitutional jurisprudence generally. What the Supreme Court has said in addressing issues of 'separation of powers'—the power to appoint and remove officials, 'legislative veto', Executive privilege—though in focus on internal matters, presumably applies to foreign affairs as well. Individuals have asserted, and courts have adjudicated, claims of constitutional right against invasion by Congress and especially by the Executive branch, including some that are particular to or implicate foreign affairs, such as denial of a passport; detention of undocumented aliens; searches and seizures in foreign countries; interdiction of vessels and refugees at sea. Reluctantly, without confidence, courts have attempted to locate international law, notably the law of international human rights, in the hierarchy of U.S. law.

The analysis and restatement in this work 20 years ago remain pertinent in impressive measure. But further consideration, and further elaboration by judges and scholars, have suggested nuances in analysis and refinement in exposition. Even where the text seems to require no change, the end notes—the bountiful back pages of this volume—have been enriched and brought up to date by reference to intervening cases, legislation, executive and administrative actions.

Scholarship and literature in the constitutional law of foreign affairs have flourished, modestly, in the last quarter-century. General works on constitutional law have blossomed and have included some pages on foreign affairs.[1] *The Restatement of the Foreign Relations Law of the United States*, including some constitutional law, appeared in 1987 in a new edition.[2] Volumes on Congress and on the Presidency have addressed also their constitutional roles in foreign affairs; some books have addressed in particular the 'tension in the twilight zone' where the constitutional powers of Congress and the President confront and compete.[3]

I remain grateful to those who assisted me in preparing the previous edition on which this version builds.[5] I have continued to teach and write about the subject, and have learned from colleagues, notably Professor Lori Damrosch at the Columbia University School of Law. She has also generously read this work, saved me from error and made many valuable suggestions. In the preparation for this edition I have had the invaluable research assistance of a number of students at the Columbia Law School, notably Eric Schnurer, class of 1986; Melissa

Spatz, class of 1991; David Parish, class of 1992; Kevin Hughes, class of 1993; Katherine Mulhern, class of 1994; Paul Savage, class of 1995; Nick Bourtin, class of 1996, and, not least, Laura Guthrie and Robert Phay, class of 1997, who helped bring the new edition to completion. Elizabeth Martin (B.A. Columbia 1989, M.S.S.W. Columbia 1993) and Sally Otos (later J.D. Columbia 1995) were indispensable along the way to the production of this edition.

LOUIS HENKIN

1996

CONTENTS

Contents

III. COOPERATION WITH OTHER NATIONS UNDER THE CONSTITUTION

Chapter VII. Treaties, the Treaty Power, and Executive Agreements

ABBREVIATIONS

A.B.A.	American Bar Association
A.B.M.	Anti-Ballistic Missile
F.A.O.	Food and Agriculture Organization
F.C.N.	Treaty of friendship, commerce and navigation
F.I.S.A.	Foreign Intelligence Surveillance Act
G.A.T.T.	General Agreement on Tariffs and Trade
I.C.A.O.	International Civil Aviation Organization
I.C.C.P.R.	International Covenant on Civil and Political Rights
I.E.E.P.A.	International Emergency Economic Powers Act
I.C.J.	International Court of Justice
I.L.O.	International Labor Organization
I.N.F.	Intermediate Nuclear Forces
I.N.S.	Immigration and Naturalization Service
L.N.T.S.	League of Nations Treaty Series
N.A.F.T.A.	North American Free Trade Agreement
N.A.T.O.	North Atlantic Treaty Organization
O.A.S.	Organization of American States
P.L.O.	Palestine Liberation Organization
R.U.D.'s	reservations,understandings and declarations to treaties
S.A.L.T.	Strategic Arms Limitation Talks
S.D.I.	Strategic Defense Initiative
S.E.A.T.O.	Southeast Asia Collective Defense Treaty
T.I.A.S.	Treaties and Other International Acts Series
U.N.E.S.C.O.	United Nations Educational, Scientific and Cultural Organization
U.N.R.R.A.	United Nations Relief and Rehabilitation Administration
U.N.T.S.	United Nations Treaty Series
U.S.T.	United States Treaties and Other International Agreements
W.H.O.	World Health Organization

TABLE OF CASES

TABLE OF STATUTES

(including references to U.S. Constitution,
other Constitutions and other public documents)

CONSTITUTIONS

STATUTES

United States

RESOLUTIONS

United Nations General Assembly

TABLE OF TREATIES, INTERNATIONAL INSTRUMENTS

INTRODUCTION

Constitutional government has come to suggest limited government, and the Constitution of the United States is commonly thought of as an edict of limitations on the government of the United States (and of the states) to protect individual liberty. In fact, in largest part, the Constitution is not a charter of liberties but a blueprint for a federal system of government and for dividing authority among branches of the national government.[1] Limitations are implied, of course, in these allocations, divisions, and distributions, and in the principles of federalism and the 'separation of powers' they reflect.* There are also some express limitations on the national government and on the states, including important safeguards for individual liberty, notably in the Bill of Rights and in later amendments**.

* The separation of powers was designed also to safeguard the people's liberties. See Justice Brandeis, quoted, n. 3 to Intro. to Pt II.
** The original Constitution contained a few express limitations and prohibitions on the national government, most of them (in Art. I, sec. 9) to protect State interests (rather than individual freedom); the express limitations on the states also principally protect national (not individual) interests (Art. I, sec. 10). There are some safeguards for individual rights in the original Constitution, for example, provisions prohibiting double jeopardy and *ex post facto* laws, and those requiring a jury trial in criminal cases (Art. III, sec. 2), or prescribing requirements for conviction for treason (Art. III, sec. 3). The principal limitations in favor of the individual are in the Bill of Rights, added by amendment immediately after the Constitution came into force, and those imposed on the states in the wake of the Civil War, in the Thirteenth, Fourteenth and Fifteenth Amendments. See Ch. IX.

Study of the U.S. Constitution tends to neglect—or assume—the constitutional blueprint and to concentrate on the limitations and prohibitions it contains, largely because these are the focus of cases and controversies in the courts. A student of the Constitution learns to distinguish between two kinds of limitations: since the federal government has limited powers, since each of its branches has defined authority, one asks first whether an act is within the power of the federal government and of the branch that claims authority to exercise it. (This is often a single inquiry since almost all the grants of power to the federal government take the form of grants to a particular branch of that government.) A distinct and subsequent question is whether an action within the domain of the federal government, and of the particular branch,

The constitutional blueprint, of course, shapes the activities of government, not least the conduct of the nation's foreign relations, and constitutional prohibitions and limitations inhibit foreign affairs as they do other governmental action. And yet, neither they who are concerned with the Constitution nor those who deal with foreign affairs attend regularly to the applicable constitutional law. The student of U.S. foreign relations is aware, no doubt, that officials who conduct affairs with other nations derive their authority from the Constitution and perform their functions in a framework of institutions and processes determined by it: the President appoints a new ambassador; Congress appropriates billions for foreign aid; the Senate consents to the Nuclear Non-Proliferation Treaty, the North Atlantic Treaty, or the International Covenant on Civil and Political Rights; or, the Secretary of State announces a different U.S. policy in the Middle East or in the former Yugoslavia; a Congressional committee holds hearings on the desirability of joining a new World Trade Organization. But few ask where in the Constitution their authority derives, what constitutional prescriptions, if any, they are carrying out, and under what restrictions, if any, they act.

In part, no doubt, students of foreign affairs share the common, citizen's unease with legal inquiries and legal documents. In this instance, I believe, lack of interest reflects, too, the impression that the Constitution and its law do not matter, or perhaps that, like other mechanisms that 'work' smoothly, it can be taken for granted. The conduct of foreign relations seems long and far removed from constitutional origins, confronting no constitutional limitations and generating no constitutional issues. When, recurrently, foreign affairs explode in constitutional controversy, it comes as a surprise, and the participants themselves, and other foreign affairs 'experts,' fumble and mumble in discussing the issues.[2] Only recurrent recriminations when Presidents claim (and Congresses deny them) authority to deploy U.S. military forces in foreign hostilities—the Gulf War (1991), Haiti (1994)—ring with constitutional tones and undertones, and even these rarely rise to constitutional debate honoring constitutional text, and history, and doctrine.*

Indifference—I dare add ignorance—is not limited to those who might claim lack of legal expertise. Students of constitutional law know that there are clauses in the Constitution that pertain more or less

---

is nonetheless prohibited by the Constitution, for example, because it violates the Bill of Rights.

* See Ch. IV.

foreign affairs, but they can tell you little more. They too, perhaps, have the sense that the constitutional law of foreign affairs weighs and matters little. But there is much else to deter or deflect them. Students of constitutional law have long been students only of the cases of the Supreme Court, and constitutional issues of foreign affairs rarely come to court.* The courts consider only cases, and cases require proper parties and proper issues; and foreign affairs do not ordinarily provide them to the courts' satisfaction. Other judicial doctrines and practices also preclude constitutional suits and discourage constitutional suitors. Claims that would limit the freedom of government to conduct foreign relations, in particular, usually receive short shrift, and some have been declared 'political questions' and get no shrift at all. The Supreme Court's jurisdiction is now almost wholly discretionary and the occasional foreign affairs cases that come to its door are not all welcomed. As a result, the Court has not developed any confident expertise,** further encouraging judicial abstention and further discouraging might-be litigants.

For other reasons, too, the constitutional issues that trouble the conduct of foreign relations are not those with which constitutional lawyers are familiar. Federalism—once a staple of constitutional litigation—rarely raises its head in foreign relations,[3] since for these purposes the United States is virtually a unitary state. Because the constitutional allocations of power to conduct foreign affairs are different from those for domestic matters, issues between the President and Congress in foreign affairs are not the same 'separation-of-powers' controversies that have roiled the governance of domestic affairs. A principal Presidential power, 'to make Treaties,' has no counterpart in domestic affairs. Even the modest role played by the courts in foreign affairs is different, asserting different judicial authority, maintaining different relations with the political branches, monitoring different limitations on the states.

The fields of constitutional controversy, and the protagonists and the causes represented there, are also different. Since the courts are not the

---

* See Ch. V.

** A few of the Justices of the Supreme Court had some exposure to foreign affairs. Chief Justice William Howard Taft had been President from 1909–13; a few had served as Secretary of State—John William Day (1898), Charles Evans Hughes (1921–25), John Marshall (1800–1), and John Jay (Secretary of Foreign Affairs, 1784–86). A few others had other experience in public office e.g., Hugo Black (Senator, 1927–37), Harold Burton (Senator, 1941–45), Salmon P. Chase (Governor, Ohio, 1856–60), John McKinley (Senator 1826–31), Sherman Minton (Senator, 1935–41), George Sutherland (Senator 1905–16). Some 30 others had served as representatives or other public servants.

principal arena, the contests are fought within and between the political branches of government and are political rather than juridical. Since, usually, private interests are not directly at stake, the causes behind the issues tend to be 'political' rather than economic or libertarian. Charges of Presidential usurpation, for a recurrent example, come principally from those who oppose the politics of the President's policies, from isolationist critics between World Wars and again after the Cold War, or from other anti-interventionist critics who opposed or remember Vietnam. Constitutional limitations on the Treaty Power are asserted to keep the United States free of foreign entanglements, or to preserve remnants of 'states' rights'.

The constitutional law of foreign affairs is also removed from the mainstream of constitutional studies and the focus of constitutional lawyers for yet another reason: the lawyer wants answers and this law often fails to provide any. Generally, all now know, the Constitution is what the Supreme Court says it is,[4] but since the Court has not said much about foreign affairs and promises to say little more, many issues have no final, 'infallible', arbiter and expositor,* and are 'resolved' only *ad hoc* without resolution in principle. Powerful Presidents and determined Congresses (or members of Congress) take constitutional positions and provide precedents to encourage their successors, but the issues remain to be fought again some new day. If old and not-so-old Supreme Court constitutional decisions do not escape re-examination,[5] there is even less *stare decisis* for what former Presidents and earlier members of Congress asserted in word or action. And so, major constitutional issues of foreign policy today are at bottom the same struggles for constitutional power of our early history. The world is changed, the United States is changed, the institutions of government are changed, the Constitution itself is changed, but the constitutional materials, the Federalist Papers, the debates of Hamilton versus Jefferson or Hamilton versus Madison, remain fresh and relevant and are played back again and again by new voices in new contexts.

I believe—obviously—that the neglect of the constitutional law of foreign affairs is unwarranted and unfortunate. The foreign relations of the United States cannot be understood without that law, for it continues to shape the institutions and the actions that determine those relations. If the conduct of foreign affairs seems beset by politics rather than governed by law, it is the law of the Constitution that gives the politics its

* 'We are not final because we are infallible, but we are infallible only because we are final.' Justice Jackson concurring in *Brown* v. *Allen*, 344 U.S. 443, 540 (1953). Compare *Cooper* v. *Aaron*, 358 U.S. 1 (1958).

form and much of its content. Even the extra-constitutional institutions and processes that often seem to dominate the conduct of foreign relations are offspring of the Constitution and of needs created by its blueprint for government. If the Constitution says nothing about the President as leader, as 'representative of all the people', as chief of his party, as hero or scapegoat, if it says nothing about Congressional committees, seniority, or Senatorial courtesy, much of these can be traced to the Constitution, some to its special treatment of foreign affairs.

The constitutional issues of foreign affairs are alive and important. In our day, as with not-infrequent regularity since the beginnings of the nation, foreign relations have echoed and re-echoed with constitutional controversy and have continually generated constitutional law. The public official, the lawyer, the student of foreign affairs, the citizen, cannot afford to ignore them. That the courts are often not available to resolve them renders it more, not less, important that they be understood and publicly debated. Did President Bush have constitutional authority to invade Panama (1989) or to send troops to fight the Gulf War (1990–91); and did President Clinton have authority to send troops to restore legitimate government in Haiti (1994), or to keep the peace in Bosnia (1995–96)? Could President Reagan commit the United States to the 'Reagan doctrine', as earlier Presidents—Monroe, Eisenhower, Truman—committed the United States to doctrines that bore their names? Could President Reagan bomb Libya for allegedly supporting terrorist activities; or President Clinton bomb Iraqi intelligence headquarters for an alleged attempt to assassinate former President Bush? Could the President promise hundreds of millions of dollars to the Ukraine to persuade it to give up its nuclear arms, or to the Palestine Liberation Organization (PLO) to support peace in the Middle East? Should U.S. adherence to the new World Trade Organization have been achieved by treaty with the consent of the Senate rather than by resolution approved by both houses of Congress? Could Congress prevent President Carter's recognition of Communist China or his termination of a defense treaty with Taiwan? Can a U.S. citizen be forbidden to travel to Castro's Cuba? Could states (and municipalities) apply their own sanctions against the Republic of South Africa when it practised apartheid? Did President Reagan have authority to dispose of private claims against Iran by an executive agreement to resolve the 'hostage crisis'? Does a person have any recourse when his (her) suit is dismissed because the defendant enjoys sovereign or diplomatic immunity?*

* One asked similar difficult questions in earlier times: Could President Roosevelt constitutionally give away U.S. destroyers to the British fighting Hitler, or President

These and many other questions are discussed—I do not say answered—in this volume. Its subject is Foreign Affairs and the U.S. Constitution, and it attempts to illuminate the constitutional provisions that deal with foreign relations and the special significance for foreign relations of general constitutional clauses and extraordinary constitutional theories. Implied, of course, is that for this purpose 'foreign affairs' can be defined, isolated, distinguished. That is hardly obvious. In many aspects of national economic life, for example, the domestic and the foreign are thoroughly mixed. Domestic influences—say, the political power of particular industries or ethnic groups—shape foreign policy, and foreign relations have deep domestic consequences even when they do not involve us in war. For constitutional lawyers as for others, the line between domestic and foreign affairs is increasingly fluid and uncertain, sometimes unreal, always at most a division of emphasis and degree.* Yet the distinction is basic: for the lawyer, constitutional theories and doctrines depend on it; students of government and politics build generalizations on that difference; and government officials in every branch, and citizens less or more sophisticated, accept and act on it.

This volume is an essay in law, not in legal history, and it concentrates on where we stand with an eye to where we are going, rather than on where we were or even how we got here. As an essay in constitutional law, it must attend particularly to what little the Supreme Court has

Truman give other matériel to allies of the United States fighting in Korea? Could the President's sole acts—the Truman Proclamation on the Continental Shelf, or Franklin Roosevelt's agreement with Litvinov—have the effect of law in the United States? Could Congress disown the President's post-Second World War commitments at Potsdam or Yalta; or compel President Truman to lend millions to Franco Spain? Could Congress deny foreign aid to countries that expropriate U.S. properties, or tell the courts not to give effect to such expropriations? Could the United States adhere to the international covenants on human rights? Could the State of Oregon refuse an inheritance to a resident of East Germany because his Communist government did not allow an American to inherit there? What was the constitutional effect of a Senate resolution declaring that commitments to use U.S. troops abroad can effectively be made only by treaty with the advice and consent of the Senate? Could a person be deprived of his citizenship for voting in a foreign election? *Et al.*

* Some may find utility in a 'definition' that domestic activities are those about which we do not recognize the right of other governments to complain. But compare the fate of Art. 2(7) of the United Nations Charter which purported to deny authority to the United Nations 'to intervene in matters which are essentially within the domestic jurisdiction of any state': it has not kept the United Nations from at least discussing virtually anything members wished to discuss.

held or said, and what it has held and said recently, rather less to cases which, although never reconsidered, smell of doctrine of a past day. Where the Supreme Court has not spoken directly, I sometimes attempt to read and extend its mood. But usually I ask more questions than I attempt to answer, and array opposing arguments often without deciding between them. Although what is current is not necessarily new, or abiding, or important, I have given perhaps undue and distorted emphasis to issues that have agitated our times—the constitutionality of the President's actions in the Vietnam War; or in Haiti (1994); the authority of the courts to deny effect to Cuban expropriation of U.S. investments; the use of the Treaty Power to promote international human rights. Such issues having particularly engaged my intellectual interest and sometimes drawn me into intellectual controversy—I have not always refrained from asserting strong convictions or giving confident answers that are not universally shared.

The plan of the book is simple and, because it attempts to focus separately on parts of a web that has few seams, inevitably somewhat artificial. The larger part of it reflects the fact that, even in our federal system, foreign affairs are national affairs, and that the constitutional law of foreign affairs is principally the law of the allocation of authority within the federal government. I consider first (Chapter I) insufficiencies in the constitutional blueprint and attempts to explain them, including special theories about the constitutional status of the nationhood of the United States and of the powers of the federal government in foreign affairs.

Chapters II to IV describe the distribution of federal political power in foreign affairs, the powers of the President and of Congress, singly and together, in conflict and cooperation. This part is most important and probably least satisfying. Here are the major issues, real and hypothetical, and the large and abiding uncertainties. Some will ask whether there is constitutional 'law' where constitutional text is inadequate, where the Supreme Court is silent, where 'constitutional scripture' and theoretical argument are invoked by one branch or the other to buttress political power, without any means or hopes for resolution. But if the constitutional law of these chapters is different, it is still constitutional law. The Constitution is not *only* what the Supreme Court says it is, not only what appears in cases. Presidents and members of Congress are under oath to support the Constitution, and undoubtedly, generally, they take their oath seriously. Some issues have been resolved, others have been narrowed. Self-serving constitutional argument can reach far, but it is not without limit—in language, and logic, and history, and good sense, and acceptability, and national interest. If the arguments on two (or more) sides are sometimes equally persuasive, if the constitutional lawyer has few confident answers, he has the same blocks with which the Supreme Court itself must often build, and it usually builds according to the advice of counsel.

Chapter V examines the powers of the judicial branch of the federal government in foreign affairs. References to the courts abound in every chapter, when they have spoken on what the political branches have done; in this chapter I bring the courts center stage to consider whether in foreign affairs they play their usual role, whether they play it differently, whether they have additional parts. Chapter VI rounds out national authority in foreign affairs by reflecting on the small but abiding relevance of the states.

A substantial portion of the book (Chapters VII and VIII) is devoted to the constitutional law governing international agreement and cooperation. The Constitution lists treaty-making among the President's powers, but some prefer to see 'the treaty-makers' (the President and two-thirds of the Senate) as a special branch of the federal government with special processes raising special questions, including issues about its relation to the other branches. Here, of course, is law particular to foreign affairs and there are some judicial decisions, dicta, and substantial 'hard law'. Here there is contemporary controversy rooted in differences as to the kind of international cooperation that is appropriate and desirable for the United States in today's world. It has seemed reasonable to include here (rather than in the President's chapter) international agreements that are not treaties, whether made by the President on his own authority or in cooperation with Congress. Also in this part is a chapter dealing with issues (some real, some hypothetical; some weighty, some flimsy) engendered by U.S. participation in the special phenomenon of international society since the Second World War, the proliferation of international organizations, some of them dormant during the Cold War (1947–89), now aroused, but confused.

Essentially, Chapter IX constitutes a discrete, smaller part of the volume, setting forth the limitations on national power in foreign affairs imposed by the constitutional rights and freedoms of the individual. Constitutional law generally has become less and less a study of the limitations of federalism and separation of powers, more and more of the safeguards for individual rights against governmental power. I consider how the constitutional law of individual rights applies to the conduct of foreign affairs, which rights are of particular relevance and weight, and whether there are on the horizon new human rights safeguards to limit government in its international relations.

Finally, I venture words of summary and evaluation: what is clear and what is uncertain; what is settled and what is in flux; how satisfactory is the whole; what can be done about deficiencies in and dissatisfactions with an eighteenth century Constitution already in its third century.

I

FOREIGN AFFAIRS AS NATIONAL AFFAIRS

Chapter I

THE CONSTITUTIONAL AUTHORITY OF THE FEDERAL GOVERNMENT

Foreign affairs are national affairs. The United States is a single nation-state and it is the United States (not the states of the Union, singly or together) that has relations with other nations; and the United States Government (not the governments of the states) conducts those relations and makes national foreign policy.[1]

As the proverbial schoolchild knows, the Constitution established a 'more perfect Union' on pillars of federalism and the separation of powers. It delegated authority and function to the federal government* by vesting legislative powers in Congress, the executive power in the President, the judicial power in a federal judiciary. 'The powers not delegated to the United States by the Constitution . . . are reserved to the States respectively, or to the people.' (The Tenth Amendment.)

From the beginning, it was clear, this 'more perfect Union' was one sovereign nation, and from the beginning the federal government has maintained the relations of that nation with other sovereign nations. But the Constitution does not declare the United States a single sovereign nation, expressly or even by indisputable implication. Indeed, where foreign relations are concerned the Constitution seems a strange, laconic document: although it explicitly lodges important foreign affairs powers in one branch or another of the federal government, and explicitly

---

* The Constitution speaks only of forming 'a more perfect Union', not of creating a new government. The powers it vests are the executive, legislative and judicial powers 'of the United States', not of the United States government. (Compare Art. III, sec. 1.) The Constitution contains one reference to 'the Government of the United States' (in the 'necessary and proper clause', Art. I, sec. 8, cl. 18), and several to 'the United States'; the latter seems to denote the national entity rather than its government. In the Articles of Confederation, 'the United States in Congress assembled'—'united' apparently an adjective modifying the noun 'states'—seemed to refer to the states acting together in a kind of partnership-entity, and the term 'United States' commanded the plural form of the verb. Whether in the Constitution 'the United States' is a singular or plural noun is not clear.

denies important foreign affairs powers to the states, many powers of government are not mentioned.

Constitutional lawyers have been troubled by these lacunae and have struggled to explain and to fill them. No explanation has been universally accepted, and no proposed principle of constitutional construction has supplied what is missing to universal satisfaction. Different doctrines that have been suggested have different legal and political consequences. Under all of them, however, foreign affairs remain exclusively national.*

In preparing the Constitution, 'the draftsmen could not often assemble the words of a sentence without some reference to the foreign affairs of the little republic to be',[2] but very much about foreign relations went without or with little saying. The Constitution does not delegate a 'power to conduct foreign relations' to the United States or to the federal government, or confer it upon any of its branches. Congress is given power to regulate commerce with foreign nations, to define offenses against the law of nations, to declare war; and the President is given the power to make treaties and is authorized to send and receive ambassadors, but these hardly add up to full power to conduct foreign relations. Where—for random examples—is the power to recognize other states or governments; to maintain or rupture diplomatic relations; to open consulates in other countries and permit foreign governments to establish consulates in the United States; to acquire or cede territory; to grant or withhold foreign aid; to proclaim a Monroe Doctrine, an Open-Door Policy, or a Reagan Doctrine; indeed to determine all the attitudes and carry out all the details in the myriads of relationships with other nations that are 'the foreign policy' and 'the foreign relations' of the United States? The power to make treaties is granted, but where is the power to break, denounce, or terminate them? The power to declare war is there, but where is the power to make peace, to proclaim neutrality in the wars of others, or to recognize or deny rights to belligerents or insurgents, or to address the consequences of the United Nations Charter and other international agreements regulating war? Congress can enact laws to define and punish violations of international law, but where is the power to assert U.S. rights or to carry out its obligations under international law, to help make new international law, or to disregard or violate law that has been made? Congress can regulate commerce with foreign nations, but where is the power to make other laws relating to U.S. foreign relations—to regulate immigration or the status

* The abiding significance of federalism for U.S. foreign affairs is discussed in Ch. VI.

and rights of aliens, or activities of citizens abroad? These 'missing' powers, and a host of others, were clearly intended for, and have always been exercised by, the federal government, but where does the Constitution say that it shall be so?

Traditional interpreters of the Constitution have attempted to find the missing powers by traditional modes of constitutional construction. Foreign affairs powers expressly granted have been held to imply others: for example, the power to make treaties implies the power to terminate or break them. And several powers taken together have been found to 'result' in others: for example, the authority to appoint ambassadors and to receive foreign ambassadors 'results' in the power to recognize governments and to do all else that may be involved in maintaining diplomatic relations with a foreign country.[3] Foreign affairs powers, we shall see, have been spun also from general grants of power and from designations read as grants; for example, the power of Congress to do what is 'necessary and proper' to carry out other powers (Art. I, sec. 8), or the provision vesting in the President 'the executive Power' (Art. II, sec. 1). Additional powers for the federal government might be inferred from their express denial to the states.*

Attempts to build all the foreign affairs powers of the federal government with the few bricks provided by the Constitution have not been widely accepted. Such constitutional 'interpretation' requires considerable stretching of language, much reading between lines, and bold extrapolation from 'the Constitution as a whole';[4] in the end, it still does not plausibly account for all the foreign affairs power that the federal government claims and that it exercises in fact.** For that reason, perhaps, some have suggested finding constitutional foundations for plenary federal power in foreign affairs in the grant to Congress of the power to regulate commerce with foreign nations (Art. I, sec. 8); others would find it in the provision vesting in the President 'the executive

---

* Art. I, sec. 10. See Ch. VI.

** Nor does it explain why a particular foreign affairs power devolves upon a particular branch of the federal government. In one of the examples given, the explicit power to make treaties is in the President-and-Senate, but the Senate has achieved no role in a resultant power to break treaties, and both the President and the Congress have claimed authority to do that alone. See Ch. VII. Similarly, the Senate has a part in appointing ambassadors, but none in controlling their later activities. Perhaps, it might be argued, the powers in question belong to the President, the Senate's role being only ancillary, and therefore the powers implied in them also belong to the President but not necessarily with a corresponding ancillary power in the Senate. See also Ch. II, p. 51.

Power' (Art. II, sec. 1). Such generous readings of particular grants may indeed support plenary power in the federal government, but they thereby support also plenary (and exclusive) power for the particular branch, whereas the Constitution clearly contemplated a division of authority among the branches in foreign affairs as in domestic matters.*

Faced with lacunae in the constitutional text, the Supreme Court long ago concluded that, in addition to the enumerated powers and their 'derivatives', the federal government enjoys some powers not rooted in the Constitution, but inherent in the nationhood and sovereignty of the United States. In *The Chinese Exclusion Case*, for example, the Court found that Congress could legislate to exclude aliens because:

Jurisdiction over its own territory to that extent is an incident of every independent nation. It is a part of its independence . . . [T]he United States, in their relation to foreign countries and their subjects or citizens are one nation, invested with powers which belong to independent nations, the exercise of which can be invoked for the maintenance of its absolute independence and security throughout its entire territory.[5]

We are not told where in the Constitution the Court found support for such powers, or how they are to be justified in the face of the provision in the Tenth Amendment that the powers not delegated to the United States are reserved to the states. We are not told which are the powers that 'belong to independent nations'; how they are to be determined, by whom they can be exercised on behalf of the United States,** or how they relate to the powers expressly conferred upon one branch or another of the federal government.

These difficulties, and the anomalous, 'spotty' treatment of foreign relations in the Constitution, as well perhaps as an impression that the Constitution assumes rather than confers foreign relations powers, probably inspired a singular constitutional theory: the powers of the United States to conduct relations with other nations do not derive from the Constitution! Although this theory did not spring new and full blown from the mind of Justice Sutherland, it found authoritative expression, almost 150 years after the Constitution was adopted, in his opinion for the Supreme Court in *United States* v. *Curtiss-Wright Export Corp.*[6]

* See Ch. IV.

** That other 'independent nations' have a particular power may argue that the United States has it too, but does not of itself show that it belongs to the federal government; even the governmental powers reserved to the states under the Constitution would, in a unitary system of government, also be powers inherent in national sovereignty.

In that case, a Joint Resolution of Congress had authorized the President to embargo arms to the countries at war in the Chaco, and imposed criminal penalties for violation of the embargo. President Franklin Roosevelt proclaimed such an embargo and the defendant company was indicted for violating it. The company challenged the Resolution and the Proclamation as entailing an improper delegation of legislative power by Congress to the President. Sustaining the indictment, the Supreme Court held that the principles that limit delegation of legislative authority in domestic affairs do not apply equally in foreign affairs.*

To reach that conclusion, Justice Sutherland's opinion begins by declaring a historical proposition: with independence the former colonies became, not thirteen independent countries, but a single sovereign nation. From independence, whereas the powers of 'internal sovereignty' lay with the individual states, 'external sovereignty' passed directly from the British Crown to the Union of States as a collective entity. The Articles of Confederation, and later the Constitution, conferred upon the Union some of the powers of internal sovereignty enjoyed by the individual states after independence; but neither the Articles nor the Constitution conferred upon the new Union the powers of external sovereignty, for these already belonged to the collectivity since independence. The Constitution did not declare or enumerate the Union's powers of external sovereignty; it assumed them. And, in general, the Constitution dealt with powers of external sovereignty only where there was some reason for doing so, principally to allocate particular powers to one or another branch of the new government, particularly where the locus of the power within the new federal government reflected change from the Articles, or had been the subject of controversy or compromise—for example, which of the branches of the new government should make treaties.**

* The issue of delegation in foreign affairs is discussed in Ch. IV, at pp. 96–7.
** Perhaps also to remove doubt, especially as it is not always obvious whether some power is an aspect of external or internal sovereignty, e.g., the power to establish rules of naturalization. Sutherland might have added that although the states did not have powers of external sovereignty, the Constitution expressly denied these to them (Art. I, sec. 10) out of abundance of caution and to assure doubly against practices that had troubled the Confederation and were among the principal motivations for the Constitutional Convention.

Sutherland does not explain why the Framers did not list all the foreign affairs powers of the President, an office that did not exist under the Articles. Perhaps Sutherland thought they were subsumed in 'the executive Power'. See Ch. II.

'It results', Sutherland summed up:

that the investment of the federal government with the powers of external sovereignty did not depend upon the affirmative grants of the Constitution. The powers to declare and wage war, to conclude peace, to make treaties, to maintain diplomatic relations with other sovereignties, if they had never been mentioned in the Constitution, would have vested in the federal government as necessary concomitants of nationality. . . . As a member of the family of nations, the right and power of the United States in that field are equal to the right and power of the other members of the international family. Otherwise, the United States is not completely sovereign. The power to acquire territory by discovery and occupation . . ., the power to expel undesirable aliens . . ., the power to make such international agreements as do not constitute treaties in the constitutional sense . . ., none of which is expressly affirmed by the Constitution, nevertheless exist as inherently inseparable from the conception of nationality. This the court recognized, and . . . found the warrant for its conclusions not in the provisions of the Constitution, but in the law of nations.[7]

Since, as Justice Sutherland saw it, the powers of the United States to conduct its foreign relations, and other powers inherent in its national sovereignty, do not derive from the Constitution, one cannot identify them by construction of, or by inference and extrapolation from, constitutional language. In particular, foreign affairs powers (though some of them are mentioned) are not 'enumerated powers' and are not denied to the federal government (or reserved to the states) because they are not enumerated; one must look elsewhere—to political philosophy, to international law and the practices of nations—to determine their full array. And these powers are not subject to principles of interpretation and limitation applicable to powers granted by the Constitution, for example those deriving from commitment to 'separation of powers' or 'federalism' (such as limitations on delegation of Congressional authority, the issue in the *Curtiss-Wright* case).

Sutherland invoked *The Chinese Exclusion Case* and others, but his theory seems different from and more embracing than theirs. The earlier cases found powers inherent in sovereignty to be vested in the federal government 'by the Constitution'; Sutherland apparently thought them to be extra-constitutional.* The earlier cases seemed to consider that external sovereignty provided powers supplementary to those

---

* Sutherland does not say explicitly that the foreign affairs powers of the federal government are extra-constitutional, only that they 'did not depend upon the affirmative grants of the Constitution'. But the thrust of his history, and his insistence that the states never had powers of external sovereignty, seem to imply my reading.

expressly granted; Sutherland apparently considered sovereignty the principal source of foreign affairs power. Sutherland insisted that these powers were not delegated by the states in the making of the Constitution; the earlier cases said nothing on the matter.[8]

Justice Sutherland's theory has not been unanimously acclaimed or accepted.[9] His history, in particular, has been challenged, and surely it is not manifestly all his way. There is disagreement as to whether the Declaration of Independence declared a single sovereign entity or thirteen independent nation-states. There is evidence that, after independence, at least some of the erstwhile colonies, at least for some time and for some purposes, considered themselves sovereign, independent nations. Even under the Articles of Confederation, it is not wholly clear that 'the United States' was a sovereign entity rather than a band of sovereigns 'confederating', acting together through the agency of the Congress.[10] But Sutherland's view of the locus of sovereignty between 1776 and 1789 has strong support;[11] and—what Sutherland's critics have largely overlooked—challenging his history does not necessarily destroy his constitutional doctrine. Even if it were assumed, contrary to Justice Sutherland, that the states were each independently sovereign up to (and even during) the regime of the Articles of Confederation, the crux of Sutherland's theory might yet stand: the states irrevocably gave up external sovereignty, and the United States became one sovereign nation, upon adopting the Constitution but outside its framework and its scheme of enumerated delegations.[12] The Constitution, Sutherland might point out, does not explicitly terminate the sovereignty of the states, or declare or recognize the United States a nation; it does not confer upon the federal government the powers of national sovereignty generally, or specify many of the powers implied in sovereignty. It is reasonable to conclude, he might say, that the Framers intended to deal in full with the governance of domestic affairs because as to them the distribution of power between the central government and the states was new, and critical, the states retaining most of the powers of internal sovereignty and the new central government acquiring only what was given it; but, with a few explicable exceptions, the Framers did not deal with or enumerate powers in foreign affairs because the federal government was to have all.

Other criticisms of *Curtiss-Wright*, some of which apply as well to the earlier cases looking to sovereignty as an additional source of federal power, are not as readily avoided. That the new United States government was to have major powers outside the Constitution is not intimated in the Constitution itself, in the records of the Convention, in the

Federalist Papers, or in contemporary debates. The Sutherland theory,
like the earlier cases finding additional power in sovereignty, carves a
broad exception to the historic conception, often reiterated, never questioned, and explicitly reaffirmed in the Tenth Amendment, that the federal government is one of enumerated powers only.[13] The Sutherland
theory requires that a panoply of important powers be deduced from
unwritten, uncertain, changing concepts of international law[14] and practice, developed and growing outside our constitutional tradition and our
particular heritage.*

Students of the Constitution may have to accept Sutherland's theory,
with its difficulties, or leave constitutional deficiencies unrepaired.[15] His
opinion, containing far more than necessary to the Court's decision,**
was joined by six other Justices,† has been cited with approval in later
cases, and remains authoritative doctrine.[16] If one hesitates to accept its

* The Sutherland theory also lent itself to the argument that these powers, inherent in sovereignty and not deriving from the Constitution, are not subject to constitutional limitations, but that argument has not had wide appeal. See Ch. IX. That
international law determines the powers inherent in national sovereignty may suggest that international law might also limit those powers. It has been held, for example, that international human rights law limits the federal government's power
(rooted in its external sovereignty) to exclude aliens. Also, this suggestion may not
comport with the accepted view that the federal government has constitutional
authority to breach international law. See, e.g., Ch. VIII, pp. 234 *et seq.*

** Sutherland was not looking for new power for the United States or for either
the President or Congress, but for a theory that would uphold a broad delegation
of power by the Congress to the President. In domestic affairs, such delegation
would have raised serious constitutional questions for Sutherland and for most of
the Justices; Sutherland needed to show only that foreign affairs were different in
this respect. Today, the limitations on delegation are much relaxed even in domestic
affairs. See Ch. IV, p. 123.

† Only Justice McReynolds dissented, with an opinion of one sentence. Justice
Stone did not participate in the case. Six months earlier Sutherland had written the
opinion of the Court in *Carter* v. *Carter Coal Co.*, 298 U.S. 238 (1936), a 5–4 decision, in which he denied the existence of any unenumerated, 'inherent' federal powers in domestic matters; the question of inherent power over external affairs, he there
said, 'is a wholly different matter which it is not necessary now to consider'. *Id.* at
295. Sutherland also joined the opinion of the Court declaring unconstitutional
Congressional delegation in two famous domestic cases decided the previous year.
See n. 111 to Ch. IV.

One may wonder how Sutherland's *Curtiss-Wright* theory received almost unanimous concurrence in a Court so sharply riven by fundamental constitutional differences. Of course, in foreign affairs, states' rights were not an issue and other
philosophical differences that divided the Court were also irrelevant. Individual
rights had not yet had their luxuriant growth and in any event did not seem

suggestion that foreign affairs powers are extra-constitutional, or that sovereignty and nationhood are principal sources of power, surely *Curtiss-Wright* at least reaffirms the earlier cases finding in sovereignty an additional source of foreign affairs power.* Before *Curtiss-Wright*, the Court had looked to sovereignty as a source of federal 'power to acquire territory by discovery or occupation . . . to expel undesirable aliens . . . to make such international agreements as do not constitute treaties in the constitutional sense',[17] to control immigration, to regulate some conduct of U.S. nationals abroad;[18] since *Curtiss-Wright*, the Court has found in sovereignty additional powers—to register aliens, and to regulate travel by U.S. citizens and their activities outside the United States.[19]

'Sovereignty' remains available to assure that no federal exercise of power in foreign affairs will fail for want of constitutional support, but sovereignty need not be doctrine for every day. Usually, a power in question could plausibly be inferred from one of the powers explicitly conferred upon Congress or upon the President, to which the Court has given imaginative, liberal, expansive (some will say far-fetched) readings, say, the Commerce Power, or the War Powers of Congress or of the President, the limits of which are yet to be found. For, beginning with the judicial revolution in the year following *Curtiss-Wright*,[20] the Constitution has largely ceased to limit the powers delegated to the federal government, in domestic as in foreign affairs, and federalism, as a limitation on national power, largely survives only by grace of the federal government and the political forces it reflects.** The formal safeguards against tyranny and abuse of governmental power† lie in the specific prohibitions of the Bill of Rights and these apply to the conduct of foreign as well as domestic affairs, whether the powers invoked are deemed to come from within or without the Constitution.‡

Whatever the theory, then, there is virtually nothing related to foreign affairs that is beyond the constitutional powers of the federal government. Reliance on sovereignty, however, brings a particular difficulty; for, whereas the few foreign affairs powers specifically mentioned in the Constitution are clearly assigned—the President makes treaties (with the

threatened by broad foreign affairs powers. Perhaps, too, the divided Justices were content, even eager, to find one area of agreement.

   * See Ch. III.
   ** See Chs. III and IV. For intimations of revival of limited state's rights, see pp. 65–6, 165–9.
   † Apart from those inherent in the separation of powers. See Ch. IV.
   ‡ See Ch. IX, p. 284.

advice and consent of two-thirds of the Senate), Congress regulates commerce with foreign nations or declares war—we are not told how the undifferentiated bundle of federal powers inherent in sovereignty is distributed among the federal branches. It seems to have been assumed that they are distributed 'naturally', those that are 'legislative in character' to the Congress, those 'executive' to the President, with apparently, also, a judicial foreign affairs power lodged in the federal courts.[21] Perhaps that assumption is 'natural' and 'logical', but its principle of division is hardly self-defining.*

A similar difficulty, however, is not wholly avoided by more traditional theories as to the sources of federal power in foreign affairs. Of course, if a foreign affairs power is derived by inference or extrapolation from some express power, both lie in the same hands: if the authority to receive ambassadors, for example, includes the power to recognize foreign governments, the President who is expressly given the one has the other as well.** But many foreign affairs powers are not clearly implied in particular enumerations, and it is often less than obvious whether some power runs with one of the President's or with one belonging to Congress: e.g., did the power to proclaim neutrality as regards the wars of other nations belong to Congress by virtue of its power to declare war and to regulate foreign commerce, or to the President as part of his authority in foreign relations and as Commander in Chief? Major struggles for power between the President and Congress, then, are equally intractable under every theory of constitutional power in foreign affairs.

I deal with these and other questions in the following chapters, according to the scheme which the Constitution itself ordained, by inquiring into the powers of each branch of government.

---

* In addition, Sutherland's theory requires (whereas traditional views avoid) a definition of, and sharp distinction between, domestic and foreign affairs. Compare e.g., n. 12 to Ch. IV.

** But sometimes, apparently, not identically so—as when the President claims the power to terminate treaties on his own authority though he needs the consent of the Senate to make them. See Ch. VII, p. 211.

II

THE DISTRIBUTION OF
CONSTITUTIONAL POWER

Curtiss-Wright declares that the basic constitutional doctrine, that 'the federal government can exercise no powers except those specifically enumerated in the Constitution', does not apply to foreign affairs.[1] But the doctrine of enumerated, delegated powers is an aspect of federalism, designed to reserve states' rights, and there are few states' rights in foreign affairs. The Constitution reflects also other political principles, in particular 'constitutional legitimacy', 'separation of powers'[2] and 'checks and balances',* and these were not primarily safeguards for federalism but postulates of 'constitutionalism' and bulwarks against tyranny.[3] Whether one finds the mantle of national authority over foreign relations buried in the Constitution or more or less outside it, separation and checks and balances govern the conduct of foreign affairs also, but here they look different, have different consequences, raise different issues.

Behind the principle of enumerated powers for the federal government is the tacit but axiomatic general principle of constitutional legitimacy: all governmental authority derives from the Constitution; every action by President or Congress, by any official or institution of government, must find justification and show authority in the Constitution.[4] In domestic affairs, the requirement of constitutional legitimacy combines with the principles of federalism that permeate the Constitution: unless Congress or the President (or the U.S. courts) can find constitutional authority to act, their action is *ultra vires*, beyond their power, indeed beyond the power of the federal government (and left to the states). In foreign affairs, we have seen, the federal government has undisputed monopoly, and it has plenary powers rooted in its 'sovereignty' beyond those expressed in the Constitution. But in foreign affairs, too, constitutional legitimacy requires Congress, the President, and the courts to justify any authority they would exercise in some constitutional grant or implication; the Constitution must be deemed to have conferred upon the institutions it established authority to exercise the unenumerated powers of sovereignty as well.

* 'Separation of powers' and 'checks and balances' are not identical but they are often confused and indeed are intimately related. Separation lodges executive, legislative, and judicial functions in different branches of government. That, of course, results in government that is 'balanced' rather than concentrated in one body; because different powers are in different hands, they can check each other by failing to cooperate. But the Constitution establishes also explicit checks and balances, special devices engrafted on, indeed modifying, separation—the President's veto, the need for Senate consent to the President's appointments and treaties. See below, p. 26. A principal 'check' has been judicial review to determine the constitutionality of governmental action, discussed in Ch. V.

Constitutional authority to act is unquestionable where the Framers expressly conferred it: the power to declare war to Congress, the treaty power to the President-and-Senate. But constitutional jurisprudence assumes that the foreign affairs powers of the federal government that are unexpressed (and therefore not clearly distributed and allocated) were intended for either the President or for Congress* in accordance with that other major constitutional theme, the 'separation of powers', a principle also not explicit but clearly reflected in the constitutional blueprint.[5]

In domestic affairs, the principle of separation is more or less clear and its constitutional consequences more or less agreed. The Constitution gives legislative power to Congress, executive power to the President, judicial power to the courts. In a word (though requiring many qualifications), the laws and policies of the federal government are made by the Congress (even if largely, now, on Executive initiative), are carried out and enforced by the President, and applied by the courts in particular cases. Constitutionally, the branches are independent of each other, their provinces, generally, have defined, separate, 'natural' outlines, and no branch may usurp the functions of another: in the *Steel Seizure Case* (1952), for a famous instance, the Supreme Court seemed to think that seizure of steel mills to prevent disruption of their operations by a labor dispute obviously and inherently required authorization by a legislative act and was therefore not to be done by the President on his own authority.[6] Separation has also been held to imply that one branch may not abdicate any of its functions by delegating it to another.** Separation provides checks and balances, since each branch is master of its own essential contribution to the common government, checking and balancing the other branches. In addition, there are explicit checks derogating from separation: the President has a check on Congress by his veto, which Congress in turn can override by two-thirds vote of each of its houses. (Art. I, sec. 7.) There is a check on the President in the requirement of Senate consent to his appointments. (Art. II, sec. 2.)

In the governance of foreign relations, too, the political authority of the United States is lodged in the President and Congress, and one or the other, surely the two together, can do on behalf of the United States† whatever any other sovereign nation can do.[7] The foreign rela-

---

* Or, in some respects, perhaps for each, or both, concurrently. See Ch. IV.

** See Ch. IV, p. 123. I speak here of the political branches, of the courts in Ch. V.

† Subject to the Bill of Rights. See Ch. IX. The Constitution may also impose some limitations to preserve the integrity of the states, even against attempts to invade it by treaty. See Ch. VII, p. 189.

tions powers too reflect commitment to separation and checks and balances, but what each branch can do alone, when the other is silent or even in the face of its opposition, is not determined by any 'natural' division. As they have evolved, the foreign relations powers appear not so much 'separated' as fissured, along jagged lines indifferent to classical categories of governmental power. Whether they are theoretically legislative, executive, judicial, or administrative, some powers and functions belong to the President, some to Congress, some to the President-and-Senate; some can be exercised by either the President or by Congress; some require the joint authority of both. Irregular, uncertain division renders claims of usurpation more difficult to establish, and the courts have not been available to adjudicate them. Delegations by Congress to the President have been extensive and continuing, and *Curtiss-Wright* tells us that in foreign affairs the principle of separation does not bar them. The special 'checks' established by the Constitution are also modified: the President has his usual veto on foreign affairs legislation, but some insist, for example, that he could not veto a declaration of war; the Senate can check the President's treaties as well as his appointments; treaties and acts of Congress, we shall see, can supersede each other in domestic law.*

The constitutional distribution of foreign relations powers is rooted in the antecedents of the Constitution, and grew out of dissension, vacillation, and compromise at the Constitutional Convention. Under the Articles of Confederation, there was no executive, and Congress was all: it appointed ambassadors, instructed them, received their reports, followed their activities, and approved the treaties they negotiated.[8] In the Congress, each state had one vote, and major decisions—e.g., engaging in war or concluding treaties—required the assent of nine of the thirteen states.[9] Outside the Congress—*pace* Justice Sutherland**—the states were not above some frolics of their own, sometimes sending their own agents abroad, often disregarding the treaties concluded by Congress (even treaties to which they had assented).[10]

In allocating political authority, the Constitutional Convention decided to deny to the states powers which they had, but it was also taking powers from Congress, powers which it had exercised under the Articles. The emergence of the Presidency reflected both the felt need for an Executive generally, and dissatisfaction with multiheaded diplomacy in particular.[11] But the Framers were hardly ready to replace the representative inefficiency of many with an efficient monarchy, and unhappy

* See Ch. VII.   ** See p. 25 above.

memories of royal prerogative, fear of tyranny, and reluctance to repose trust in any one person kept the Framers from giving the new President too much head. In the process of constitutional negotiation different formulae were considered—different allocations and combinations of authority, different divisions and partitions of function between Congress and President. In the end and overall, Congress clearly came first, in the longest article, expressly conferring upon it many, important powers; the Executive came second, principally as executive-agent of Congressional policy. Every grant to the President, including those relating to foreign affairs, was in effect a derogation from Congressional power, eked out slowly, reluctantly, and not without limitations and safeguards. Major functions were retained for Congress—'legislative' authority generally, and the power to declare war. Some powers taken from Congress and given to the President were to be checked by the Senate, a part of Congress, to prevent autocratic power (and to give strong voice to the states). Some powers—perhaps they were thought of as merely 'duties' or 'functions'—were the President's alone, but what they included and how significant they were to be was perhaps not wholly agreed and appreciated, and are not wholly agreed and appreciated today.

How well the blueprint was conceived is still debated more than two centuries later, and how well the machine has worked is a living issue. Perhaps the 'contraption'* was doomed to troubles from the beginning, for although the Framers ended the chaos of diplomacy by Congress and of state adventurism, the web of authority they created, from fear of too much government and the need for contemporary political compromise, virtually elevated inefficiency and controversy to the plane of principle, especially in foreign relations.

For the Framers, moreover, foreign relations seemed to consist wholly of making or not making war and making or not making treaties. They built magnificently, perhaps better than they knew, but they could not foresee what the United States would become, what the world would become. Even in domestic affairs, there are gaps between the 'paper powers' and the real powers, between the patterns of separation and checks and balances conceived and those later realized. That in foreign relations the division of power was irregular and uncertain has made it the more susceptible to shaping, even distortion, by evolving institutions and by the realities of foreign relations for an expanding, transforming country in a changing world.

* See Ch. X, p. 319.

Irregular partition has encouraged rivalry and, since the respective allocations are not 'natural', well-defined or explicit, has led both President and Congress to tug for more of the blanket under claim of constitutional right. Concurrent jurisdiction has led to competition for initiative, sometimes to inconsistent policies, without an accepted constitutional principle for resolving them. Division of a common enterprise between independent, competing branches has begotten intrusion, interference, or failure of cooperation and, for the lawyer, issues as to whether cooperation is constitutionally prescribed and interference constitutionally forbidden. Realities have further modified the theoretical divisions, for in the competition between the political branches the President has had most of the advantages and Congress has not always been able to maintain its prerogatives.

Constitutional legitimacy requires that both Congress and the President, when exercising authority in foreign affairs, justify their actions in constitutional text or implication. Presidential claims have proliferated and expanded during the twentieth century, but particularly in the wake of the Vietnam War and the Watergate scandal, when the Presidency was on the defensive, Congress acted to limit Presidential authority by 'organic statutes' such as the War Powers Resolution, and the Hughes-Ryan and the Boland Amendments on covert intelligence activities.* As a result, constitutional debate and controversy have focused on the power of Congress to limit or regulate Executive activity, but, inevitably, both proponents and opponents of Congressional 'activism' have had to revisit constitutional foundations.

I address the constitutional claims of each branch in the following chapters. The Constitution begins with the powers of Congress; the constitutional law of foreign relations, I believe, should begin with the President. I deal with his constitutional authority in Chapter II, the power of Congress in Chapter III. In foreign as in domestic affairs, the division of political authority between Congress and the President has required cooperation and non-interference and has produced doctrine and dogma commonly subsumed under the vaguenesses of 'separation of powers'; foreign affairs, where the respective powers of President and Congress are less than explicitly conferred and less than sharply delineated, has also engendered claims to concurrent authority, raising issues of primacy and supremacy. These are the subject of Chapter IV. As the potential, and often unwilling, arbitrator of contests (between the

* See Chapter IV.

President and Congress, the federal government and the states, foreign states and U.S citizens, foreign nationals and the U.S. government), the courts have preferred to read their own constitutional role in foreign affairs narrowly—the subject of Chapter V. Similarly, the states have enjoyed a smaller role in foreign affairs, discussed in Chapter VI.

Chapter II

THE PRESIDENT

Students of United States government, and newspaper-readers generally, know that U.S. foreign relations are in the charge of the President. Foreign governments believe that it is principally he who determines United States policy towards them. Long ago, the Supreme Court of the United States described 'the very delicate, plenary and exclusive power of the President as the sole organ of the federal government in the field of international relations'.[1]

A stranger reading the Constitution would get little inkling of such large Presidential authority, and the general reader might comb the Constitution yet find little to support the legitimacy of large Presidential claims. The powers explicitly vested in him* are few and appear modest,[2] far fewer and more modest than those bestowed upon Congress. What the Constitution says and does not say, then, can not have determined what the President can and can not do. The structure of the federal government, the facts of national life, the realities and exigencies of international relations (particularly in the age of nuclear weapons and during the Cold War and its aftermath), and the practices of diplomacy, have afforded Presidents unique temptations and unique opportunities to acquire unique and ever larger powers.

* I refer to the President as 'he', as does the Constitution. The constitutional qualifications for the office of President are gender-neutral. ('No person . . . eligible for the office' Art. II, sec. 5). The Framers were well acquainted with women heads of state in history, including several in Europe, such as Queen Elizabeth. But doubtless reflecting legal and literary usages of the time, perhaps also its prejudices and expectations, the Constitution uses the masculine pronouns exclusively in its references to the President, e.g. 'He shall hold his office . . .', Art. I, sec. 1; and 'He shall have power . . .'

Following the Constitution's example, the constitutional opinions of the U.S. Supreme Court also use the masculine pronouns. That usage corresponds to the facts of U.S. history, there having been no woman President to date. Before long, no doubt, any references to the President as 'he' in constitutional texts and constitutional jurisprudence and literature will have to be read as 'he/she'. It has been suggested that the Constitution be amended to make the change, even before the United States elects its first woman President.

In domestic matters, the political powers of the federal government are divided between Congress and the President along reasonably clear lines, and the principle of separation of powers has been held to imply that their respective powers are exclusive. In foreign affairs, we shall see, the allocation of authority to the two branches is sometimes disputed, and there may be concurrent powers as to which President and Congress strive for priority or preference.* In that competition, the President's advantages have been many, some general (for example, those deriving from his national constituency, as the only official selected by the country at large, from party leadership and from control of patronage), others particular to foreign relations. From the beginning, the President has been the organ of communication with foreign governments and has had control of the principal channels of information—making the President the voice as well as the eyes and ears of the United States. As Commander in Chief he has been also its ever stronger arms. The President has been one, and the Congress many and increasing. Diplomacy by Congress was ineffectual even under the Articles of Confederation, when international relations were few and limited and Congress was unicameral and small; under the Constitution, an enlarging Congress could not begin to master the proliferating, complex affairs of a growing country with interests flung far about a growing international society. Unlike Congress, the President is always 'in session'. He can act quickly, informally, and secretly. Whether as a matter of international law or the 'laws' of international politics, he can effectively commit the United States,** and Congress cannot lightly or effectively oppose or disown him.

As a result, in addition to powers which were indisputably the President's by explicit enumeration in the Constitution, many more came to him by accretion, some will say by usurpation never effectively recaptured. Powers claimed by the President that Congress has continued to dispute without resolution have been exercised by the President as though the disputes had been resolved in his favor. And Congress itself has found it necessary to delegate to him enormous additional power.

In the second half of the twentieth century, the President's control of information and expertise has loomed overwhelming, as military technology and foreign intelligence have become more complex and the need for secrecy appeared more compelling. Congress, however, also became

---

* See Ch. IV.
** On the President's power to commit the United States by treaty or other international agreement, see Ch. VII.

more expert, and more assertive. In foreign affairs as elsewhere, members of Congress with seniority of service sometimes gained sophistication greater than that of rotating Presidents and cabinet members, enabling Congressional representatives to discuss and dispute with Presidents and diplomatists, with military commanders and arms experts. Congress acquired a huge and knowledgeable staff which could compete with the Executive branch in expertise and often even in information, and Congressional committees mustered citizen experts to match the Executive's. Erosion of the Executive monopoly, and long periods during which one or both houses of Congress were dominated by the political party other than the President's, increasingly encouraged Congress to challenge Presidential assertions of constitutional authority.

If constitutional language has not determined Presidential pre-eminence, it has not been without importance in achieving it. Much of the authority that the President has attained may indeed lie in or between the lines of the Constitution, and all of it has been shaped by what is there. Presidents did not achieve their powers at one blow, and respectable claims to constitutional legitimacy have been compelling weapons in the struggles to acquire and retain it. Despite his predominance, moreover, the President is never wholly independent of Congressional cooperation or at least acquiescence, and these are more forthcoming when he holds firmer constitutional ground. Constitutional legitimacy is important to the President also in maintaining a principal source of his power: the confidence of his national constituency, the people of the United States. And, though the courts have not been generally available to check alleged Presidential usurpation in foreign affairs, Presidents know that judicial review lies in wait and might yet strike them down. (The ultimate Congressional sanction of impeachment, too, is not wholly a paper weapon.)* Presidents, finally, take a solemn oath to execute their office faithfully and to preserve the Constitution (Art. II, sec. 1, cl. 7), and all of them, we must assume, have taken that oath seriously.[3]

Like the Constitution, I speak of the President as an individual occupying a single office. Today, all know, the President is the chief officer of the Executive branch of millions of employees, of whom many thousands are directly involved in the conduct of foreign relations and many thousands more shape them in important ways. The vast majority of Executive decisions are made, and the vast majority of its actions are taken, without the participation or even knowledge of the President, as

* As in the case of Richard Nixon, who resigned the Presidency under threat of impeachment.

we learned to our dismay in the 'Iran-Contra' scandal.[4] In principle, however, the authorized acts of the President's 'foreign affairs establishment' are the President's acts, claim his constitutional power, and are subject to his constitutional limitations.* But constitutional theory and law, too, cannot blink the realities of the process, and one may expect that the Supreme Court would pay greater respect to the President's own decision than to one taken by a 'middle-level' officer of the Department of State.[5]

THE SOURCES OF PRESIDENTIAL POWER

For the constitutional lawyer, inquiry into the President's powers in foreign affairs begins with the language of the Constitution. Of course, if, as Justice Sutherland taught, the authority of the federal government in foreign relations derives from national sovereignty and is essentially extra-constitutional, the powers of the President might also have to be sought elsewhere. One would nonetheless seek in the Constitution some guidance as to which of the nation's sovereign** powers are the President's to exercise.

One general theory of Presidential power might eliminate this avenue

* The authority of the President to delegate to subordinates has not raised significant constitutional questions, none that matter in foreign affairs. The Constitution does not expressly limit Presidential delegation of authority. But it is accepted that, in principle, some Presidential authority and functions are not to be delegated, for example, his power to pardon, or to appoint officials. The President can delegate authority to negotiate, sign, and ratify a treaty, but the President himself 'makes' the treaty. As Commander in Chief he can appoint generals and give them authority, but he retains ultimate authority. The Secretary of State, the Attorney General, and other cabinet officers can be authorized to speak and act for the United States, but they do so by the President's authority, subject to his continuing control and continuing responsibility.

Congress has legislated to regulate Presidential delegation of authority conferred upon him by statute. See 3 U.S.C. § 301 (1994).

** The U.S. Constitution does not refer to national sovereignty and does not tell us where it lies. (Compare article 3 of the French Declaration of the Rights of Man and of the Citizen (1789), which declared that 'the source of all sovereignty lies essentially in the Nation'.) That the U.S. Constitution was ordained by 'We the People of the United States' suggests that the Framers thought of sovereignty as in 'the people', and U.S. constitutionalism is commonly associated with popular sovereignty.

A news report of an interview with President Nixon quoted him as referring to himself as 'The Sovereign'. See Newsweek, March 22, 1976.

of inquiry, or at least radically change its focus. In his autobiography, written after he left office, Theodore Roosevelt said:[6]

The most important factor in getting the right spirit in my Administration . . . was my insistence upon the theory that the executive power was limited only by specific restrictions and prohibitions appearing in the Constitution or imposed by the Congress under its constitutional powers. My view was that every executive officer, and above all every executive officer in high position, was a steward of the people bound actively and affirmatively to do all he could for the people, and not to content himself with the negative merit of keeping his talents undamaged in a napkin. I declined to adopt the view that what was imperatively necessary for the Nation could not be done by the President unless he could find some specific authorization to do it. My belief was that it was not only his right but his duty to do anything that the needs of the Nation demanded unless such action was forbidden by the Constitution or by the laws.

This 'stewardship theory', surely, would apply to foreign relations as to other responsibilities of national government, and one might therefore move immediately to consider what the Constitution expressly forbids to the President and which powers of Congress support limitations on his authority. But, although Theodore Roosevelt's theory might be reflected in how some Presidents have sometimes acted, it has not been accepted in principle. His immediate successor, William Howard Taft, for example—also writing after he was out of office—expressly rejected that 'unsafe' notion,[7] and the Supreme Court's opinion in the *Steel Seizure Case*[8] could hardly be squared with it. Even the 'stewardship theory', moreover, would no doubt seek some support in constitutional text.

THE PRESIDENT'S FOREIGN AFFAIRS POWER

What the President can and cannot constitutionally do in foreign affairs has been in issue from President Washington's day. The enumerated components of his foreign affairs power are undisputed; the President's explicit power to make treaties (with the advice and consent of two-thirds of the Senators present) is beyond question.* His authority to appoint ambassadors (with Senate advice and consent), and to receive foreign ambassadors, in themselves raise only small issues and need little elaboration, and these are better considered in the context of a broader 'foreign affairs power'. As to unenumerated Presidential powers, the

* It has its own extensive law. See Ch. VII.

Supreme Court has decided little (and most of that long ago), and precedent, partisan debate, and scholarly speculation have yielded only partial resolution. But Presidents continue to act, sometimes to applause, sometimes to grudging acquiescence, sometimes to bitter condemnation and challenge; action and reaction are also stuff of constitutional law and jurisprudence. With time, the area of uncertainty has shifted. Except where the Constitution expressly allocates power to Congress and implies that it is exclusive of the President, there is increasingly less disposition to deny the President power to act where Congress had not acted. But initiative by the President does not foreclose action by Congress, and, except where the Constitution implies that Presidential authority is exclusive of Congress, there is greater disposition to accept that the President is subject to regulation and control by Congress.

In law as in politics, what matters is the total of Presidential power, rather than the shape and size of its individual components. Constitutionally, every Presidential act stands on all his powers together (as well as on authority delegated to him by Congress). Presidents do not, and need not, 'plead' their powers with precision, or match particular act to particular power, and the lawyer is often hard put to determine even the President's own appraisal of the various resources of his constitutional authority. But the constitutional sum of Presidential power depends on its parts, and, however imprecisely, analysis measures them singly.

Enumerated and Implied Powers

Article II provides that the President 'shall have the Power, by and with the Advice and Consent of the Senate, to make Treaties'. The following clause declares that the President 'shall appoint Ambassadors, other public Ministers and Consuls'—the agents of U.S. diplomacy. A subsequent provision states that the President 'shall receive Ambassadors and other public ministers'.

The treaty power

For the Framers, treaties were an essential element in international relations and an indispensable means for safeguarding and realizing the vital interests of the United States. The Framers did not wish to make it too easy to make treaties, but they were not content to leave them to clumsy, ineffectual diplomacy, negotiations, and drafting by the Congress (as under the Articles of Confederation). In the end, after struggling with various possibilities, the Framers gave the authority to make treaties to the President—but subject to the advice and consent of the Senate, indeed of two-thirds of the Senators present.* It is the President who makes treaties, if the Senate consents; the Senate cannot make a treaty. The President need not make a treaty, even if the Senate, or Congress, demands it.

Making treaties has remained an essential vehicle in U.S. foreign relations. The treaty-making process has engendered few constitutional issues, but there have been important uncertainties as to the reach of the treaty power, and as to the power of the President to make international agreements other than as treaties.**

Appointing and receiving ambassadors

As in the case of the power to make treaties, the President requires the advice and consent of the Senate to his appointments, but here he requires only a majority of the Senators voting, not two-thirds of the Senators present. Neither the President's authority to appoint diplomatic and consular personnel, nor the requirement of Senate consent, has raised important constitutional issues.

The Constitution provides also that the President 'shall receive Ambassadors and other public Ministers'. Like the authority to appoint ambassadors, the authority to receive ambassadors is not described as a 'power' of the President,† but whereas the authority to appoint

---

* The Constitution requires consent of two-thirds of the Senators present, not two-thirds of the total membership of the Senate. Effectively, the President needs consent to a treaty by two-thirds of a quorum of the Senate, the number necessary for it to do business. The Constitution declares a quorum for each House to be a majority of the members. See U.S. Constitution Art. I, sec. 5, and the discussion in *Missouri Pac. Ry. Co.* v. *Kansas*, 248 U.S. 276, 283–4 (1919).

** See Ch. VII.

† Ambassadors, public ministers and consuls are included with judges and other officers as those whom the President 'shall appoint'. Authority to appoint ambassadors is not characterized as a 'power' but appears in the section that lists various Presidential powers. Art. II, sec. 2. Receiving foreign ambassadors is in a subsequent section (sec. 3) which does not speak of 'powers' but lists what the President 'shall' or 'may' do.

At least while they were urging ratification of the Constitution, both Hamilton and Madison claimed little for the 'power' to appoint and receive ambassadors: 'This, though it has been a rich theme of declamation, is more a matter of dignity than of authority. It is a circumstance which will be without consequence in the administration of the government . . .' THE FEDERALIST, No. 69 at 448 (Hamilton) (B.F. Wright, ed. 1961). Compare *id.* No. 42 at 302–3 (Madison). Hamilton later saw this and other clauses in Art. II, sec. 3, as sources of power. Compare the 'Pacificus-Helvidius' exchange, n. 10 to this chapter; and see Jefferson, n. 19 to this chapter.

ambassadors is included among Presidential powers, the authority to receive foreign ambassadors is in a subsequent section, and seems to be couched rather as a duty, an 'assignment'.

On the face of it, this is all the Constitution empowers the President to do in regard to other nations. It is strikingly little. The making of treaties is important, but it is only an occasional activity; the appointment of ambassadors is ordinarily routine, not consequential, and even more infrequent. Both are powers which the President can exercise only with the consent of the Senate (treaties requiring even a two-thirds majority). Receiving ambassadors seems a function, an assigned duty, a ceremony that in many countries is performed by a figurehead. It seems incredible that these few, meager grants support the most powerful office in the world and the multi-varied, wide-flung web of foreign activity of the most powerful nation in the world.

Since no one believes that the President's powers are only what, on their face, these clauses seem to say, those who resist looking beyond the enumerated grants have had to insist that they are not as flimsy as appears.[9] The authority to appoint and receive ambassadors, they would say, implies power to recognize (or not to recognize) governments; to establish (or not to establish) relations with them; and to modify or terminate relations by withdrawing the U.S. Ambassador or having a foreign ambassador recalled. It does not fetch too far to infer also power to do all that is involved in relations with other nations: establishing and maintaining channels for intercourse and communication; instructing and informing our ambassadors and receiving their reports, inquiries and recommendations; exchanging information and views with foreign governments. For some, it is only another step to conclude that the President must be able to decide also the contents of communications to his ambassadors and to foreign governments, including the attitudes and intentions of the United States that constitute U.S. foreign policy. Similarly, some will say, the power to make treaties implies also the power to interpret and implement treaties, scrutinize their operation, even denounce or break them. And if the President can determine the nation's foreign policy by treaty, is it not reasonable to infer that foreign policy is his responsibility even when formal international commitment is not involved?

Such arguments are not intrinsically more extravagant than other, established constitutional constructions and interpretations, but some of them seem strained and unpersuasive. Those deriving from the power to make treaties or to appoint ambassadors suggest, at most, authority in the President and Senate acting jointly. What is more, one can with equal plausibility suggest extrapolations and inferences from the enumerated powers of Congress that would lodge control of U.S. foreign policy and U.S. foreign relations in that body rather than in the President.*

If constitutional clauses are to support, justify, and explain the growth of Presidential power, more must be found. Additional support, we shall see, was found in two other clauses to which Presidents have turned as sources of power in the conduct of foreign relations: the President is 'Commander in Chief of the Army and Navy of the United States' (Art. II, sec. 2), and he 'shall take Care that the Laws be faithfully executed' (Art. II, sec. 3). Perhaps because these too seemed insufficient, others sought, and found, cleaner, larger grants of Presidential power.

'The Executive Power'

Alexander Hamilton early insisted that, by the clause vesting in the President 'the executive Power', the Constitution expressly conferred upon him all authority over foreign relations, subject only to few explicit exceptions.[10] Article I, he noted, gives to Congress '[a]ll legislative Powers *herein granted'* (emphasis supplied), but Article II begins: 'The executive Power shall be vested in a President of the United States of America'. The President, then, is not limited to the powers that are expressly enumerated; he has the whole of 'the Executive Power'.[11] That includes, of course, the authority and responsibility to execute the laws enacted by the legislature; it includes, in addition, said Hamilton, a recognized congeries of independent, major, substantive powers 'to determine the condition of the nation' in its foreign relations.** The enumerations that follow that grant provide emphasis; some of them, indeed, are designed to modify and limit the general grant: for example, the powers to appoint ambassadors and make treaties are part of the Executive Power and would have been within the President's sole authority, had the Constitution not made that authority subject to the advice and consent of the Senate.[12]

If the 'Executive Power' clause constitutes a large grant of power, the accumulation by the President of vast powers in foreign affairs is neither surprising nor improper (and the Constitution ceases to be as

---

* See Ch. III, pp. 64 *et seq.*

** The executive power, Hamilton might have added, was not defined because it was well understood by the Framers raised on Locke, Montesquieu and Blackstone. See n. 11 to this chapter.

strangely inarticulate about foreign affairs as appears).* But that view, often stated, has been as often challenged; when Hamilton launched it, Madison lashed out at him for attempting to import into the Constitution British monarchical prerogatives.[13] The Supreme Court has not considered the 'Executive Power' clause as a possible source of constitutional authority to conduct foreign relations,[14] and its use to support other Presidential claims has had a mixed reception. Earlier in the twentieth century, the Court drew on the 'Executive Power' clause to support the President's authority to remove a postmaster in disregard of an act of Congress requiring the Senate's consent for such removal.[15] Later, in the *Steel Seizure Case,* the Court's opinion pointedly refrained from looking to it.[16] Indeed, Justice Jackson—who as Attorney General had justified extended Presidential powers**—said[17] 'I cannot accept the view that this clause is a grant in bulk of all conceivable executive power but regard it as an allocation to the presidential office of the generic powers thereafter stated.'

Here too, then, the constitutional lawyer will have the hard choice between the theory that the conduct of foreign affairs, undefined, was indeed 'granted in bulk' to the President as executive power, and the need to scrounge among, and stretch, spare constitutional clauses to eke out full powers which the President has in fact commanded and many of which he was probably intended to have.[18] The choice will turn in part on 'general principles' and general theories of constitutional inter-pretation, in part, no doubt, on political disposition, even on taste; it will probably not decide concrete issues of Presidential power. 'Executive power' to 'transact business' with foreign nations is hardly self-defining and may seem large, but constitutional history is witness that inference and extrapolation from enumerated powers also support broad conceptions of constitutional authority. Either line of constitu-tional construction will have to accept that some power is denied to the President by implication in what is granted to others, principally to Congress. All will agree that by constitutional exegesis, by inferences and extrapolations small and large, at least by sanctifying reference to the express grants and the mantle of 'executive power', Presidents have achieved and legitimated an undisputed, extensive, predominant, in

---

* This interpretation would also provide Justice Sutherland a ready answer as to how the powers inherent in sovereignty are distributed: on this view, except as otherwise provided, the Constitution lodged those sovereign powers of the United States in the President.

** See especially his famous opinion upholding the 'destroyers for bases' agree-ment, Ch. VII, p. 219.

some respects exclusive, 'foreign affairs power', though—like its constitutional underpinnings—its scope and content remain less than certain.

'Sole organ'

Undefined and undifferentiated invocations of a Presidential 'foreign affairs power' alternate with, and may derive from, innumerable references to John Marshall's early characterization: 'The President is sole organ of the nation in its external relations, and its sole representative with foreign nations.'[19] It is not apparent that either 'foreign affairs power' or 'sole organ' aspires to legal precision, or that they imply different measures of constitutional authority; both have come to describe a constitutional 'power', supplementing if not subsuming the powers specified, supporting a variety of Presidential actions not expressly authorized by the Constitution.

In terms and in context, Marshall was characterizing the President as 'spokesman', perhaps also as 'representative', to make or receive communications on behalf of the United States. Spokesman, even 'representative', does not necessarily imply that the President has authority to determine the content of what he should communicate, to make national policy. Even as narrowly conceived, 'sole organ' implies some legal authority in the President and some legal limitations on others: only he (not, notably, Congress) may communicate with foreign governments.*

In legal principle as in practice, the President's monopoly of communication with foreign governments derives in large part from his control of the foreign relations 'apparatus'. By Article II he appoints 'Ambassadors, other public Ministers and Consuls', subject to Senate approval; he fills other offices created by Congress, and does so in many instances without need of Senate approval.** In general, those whom he appoints report and are responsible to him; he directs and instructs them, and determines what they shall communicate and what they shall

---

* I deal with the limitations on Congress in Chs. III and IV, pp. 80, 88.

** Art. II, sec. 2, provides that the President shall appoint, with the consent of the Senate, 'all other Officers of the United States, whose Appointments are not herein otherwise provided for, and which shall be established by Law; but the Congress may by Law vest the Appointment of such inferior Officers, as they think proper, in the President alone, in the Courts of Law, or in the Heads of Departments'. Much of the President's 'foreign affairs establishment' is appointed by the President alone, and while many, including all Foreign Service Officers, are subject to Senate consent, approval is largely perfunctory. For issues arising out of Senate or Congressional control of executive personnel, see Ch. IV, beginning at p. 121.

withhold.[20] Those officials whose functions are purely 'executive' can be removed by the President.[21]

Beginning with George Washington, Presidents have also appointed innumerable 'agents' without asking the Senate, and in some cases have purported to give them the 'personal rank of ambassador'.[22] For the most part, these have been sent for particular missions, as John Jay by Washington to negotiate a treaty, or Harry Hopkins by Franklin Roosevelt to develop 'lendlease', or Henry Kissinger by Richard Nixon to negotiate in Vietnam and the Middle East, or former President Jimmy Carter by President Clinton in Haiti. Many such agents have been delegates to international conferences, and some have gone on fact-finding errands. The constitutional requirement of Senate consent was considered inapplicable because these agents, whatever they were called, were not appointed to permanent 'offices', did not serve indefinitely, did not have emoluments of office (often not even compensation), or perform duties prescribed by the Constitution or by Congress. The practice has not been effectively challenged and is doubtless irreversible, but from time to time the Senate will probably object to particular appointments made without its consent.

As 'sole organ', the President determines also how, when, where, and by whom the United States should make or receive communications, and there is nothing to suggest that he is limited as to time, place, form, or forum.* He receives 'Ambassadors and other public Ministers' by explicit authorization in Article II, but he also determines how many lesser diplomats shall come and be accredited; and he 'receives' heads of state or of government, foreign ministers, and special envoys.[23] He also decides whom he will not receive and who shall go home, as when, in a celebrated first instance, Washington demanded the recall to Paris of Citizen Genêt.**

That the President is the sole organ of official communication by and to the United States has not been questioned and has not been a source of significant controversy. Issues begin to burgeon when the President

* Once, Congress purported unsuccessfully to control the President's participation in international conferences. See Ch. IV, p. 118. Congress has sometimes directed the President as to how to vote in international organizations on particular issues. See Ch. VIII, p. 249. In 1995, Congress enacted legislation directing the President to move the U.S. Embassy in Israel from Jerusalem to Tel Aviv. See Ch. IV, p. 119.

** 'thereby establishing a precedent followed by later Presidents again and again, and more than once in the face of impending war.' CORWIN, THE PRESIDENT (n. 5 to Intro. to Pt. II) 212.

claims authority, as 'sole organ', to be more than an organ of communication and to determine also the content of the communication, or when, under his 'foreign affairs power', the President presumes to determine also the attitudes, decisions, and actions which are the foreign policy of the United States. It has sometimes been said that the President has power to conduct foreign relations but not to make foreign policy;[24] in fact, a President could not conduct foreign relations without thereby making foreign policy. But if the division were feasible and meaningful, it is contradicted by what Presidents have done and do daily beyond challenge. It is no longer questioned that the President does not merely perform the ceremony of receiving foreign ambassadors but also determines whether the United States should recognize or refuse to recognize a foreign government, for example, the People's Republic of China before 1979, and whether to maintain or terminate relations with it, for example, Castro's Cuba.[25] Presidents have also established their authority to determine other policy which international usage, one must regret, captures in the same, ambiguous word, 'recognition'—whether to recognize (or not to recognize) new states (e.g., Bangladesh in 1971–72, but not Biafra (1967–70), or Bosnia in 1992); the conquest and incorporation of territory (Japanese authority over conquered Manchuria in 1932, or Soviet incorporation of the Baltic republics in 1940); especially, in earlier times,* the status of belligerency, neutrality or insurgency (as for Franco's forces in the Spanish Civil War).[26] Hamilton's celebrated exposition of the executive character of foreign relations was designed to support the constitutionality of Washington's proclamation of U.S. neutrality in the war between France and Great Britain. Later, 'neutrality' was generally proclaimed pursuant to Congressional resolution, but Presidents have not admitted that they could not act on their own and have sometimes deviated from Congressional neutrality policy.[27]

The President asserts rights and assumes duties for the United States. In addition to treaties (requiring Senate consent), he makes international agreements of varying importance and formality on his sole authority,** and he acts and speaks the part of the United States in the subtle process by which customary international law is formed. He claims reparation when another state violates our international rights—when it invades our territory, harasses our ships at sea, infringes our sovereign or

---

* The continuing vitality of 'neutrality' in contemporary international law is uncertain. See n. 26 to this chapter, and Ch. VIII.

** See Ch. VII. Sole agreements may also be law of the United States, subject to the President's express duty to see that the laws are faithfully executed, and enforceable in the courts. See Ch. VII, p. 199.

diplomatic immunities, violates treaty obligations to us, abuses our citizens or confiscates their property; he calls foreign governments to account when they violate the human rights of their inhabitants in breach of obligations under international covenants or under customary international law. He has staked out new claims for the United States, for example, to acquire territory by discovery or prescription, or to proclaim rights to the mineral resources of our continental shelf, or rights in the Exclusive Economic Zone off our shores.[28] He can also waive U.S. rights, as President Eisenhower did when he canceled the debts of our allies arising out of the Korean War. And he can sometimes fail to meet our obligations and commit other violations of international law.*
It is to the President that other nations turn with claims that the United States has violated their rights, and he can give or deny satisfaction.[29] He responds to other overtures by foreign governments, for example, requests for extradition.[30] He has admitted foreign officials and foreign troops and vessels into the United States.[31] The President acts for the United States at its borders even in ways and for purposes that, at least indirectly, involve 'foreign policy' or communications and relations with foreign governments: he can admit or exclude individual aliens—President Carter admitted many thousands of Cubans in 1980;[32] President Grant admitted undersea cables and President Wilson electric current from Canada.[33]

The President surely 'makes foreign policy', too, when he declares the attitudes and intentions of the United States in matters that concern other nations. The celebrated 'Doctrines' (Monroe's or Truman's or Eisenhower's, and others less celebrated, Nixon's or Reagan's), or the 'China Open-Door Policy', are only famous and dramatic examples;** the President also makes and expresses foreign policy, say, by inviting a head of state to visit, or 'hosting' an international meeting-event (such as the Rabin–Arafat handshake towards peace between Israel and its neighbors (1994)), or by smiling upon a request for a loan, and daily (through his many representatives) in small deeds and words and gestures showing and promising more or less friendliness or hostility toward other nations. It is foreign policy when Presidents encourage or

---

* On the power of the President to interpret and implement treaties, react to their violation by others, or terminate them, see Ch. VII. As to whether the courts will enjoin the Executive branch from violating international law, see Ch. VIII, p. 241.

** Presidents have sometimes sought Congressional approval for such doctrines even when they believed they did not need it. See n. 65 to Ch. IV; compare n. 44 to this chapter.

discourage other governments, or assert pleasure or displeasure about their policies or actions.

That Presidents have asserted these (and other) powers related to foreign affairs is not conclusive evidence that they were entitled to do so under the Constitution, and some of their acts and claims have been challenged—by Congress, in the courts, by scholars, by citizens. Some Presidential actions can be sustained without acknowledging independent Presidential power because they draw authority from an act of Congress or from a treaty. But the broader theories I have set forth, and recurrent practice, lend support to the view that the President's powers in foreign affairs are 'plenary'—Justice Sutherland's word—which may mean that matters relating to U.S. foreign relations are plausibly, presumptively, within his authority and that nothing is inherently outside his domain.[34] His powers are limited, of course, by implications in constitutional grants to Congress, by Congressional legislation that is within its constitutional authority, and by the prohibitions applicable to all acts of government; in particular, some of what Presidents have done in the past might today be successfully challenged under the Bill of Rights.*

RELATED PRESIDENTIAL POWERS: THE COMMANDER IN CHIEF

The President has more than one hat, he wears them at the same time, and he can act under one or another, or under all of them together. In addition to his 'foreign affairs power', the President is 'Commander in Chief of the Army and Navy of the United States', and that clause, too, has inspired assertions of independent Presidential authority and initiative in foreign relations.**

There is little evidence that, by that designation, the Framers intended more than to establish in the Presidency civilian command of the armed forces during wars declared by Congress (or when the United States was attacked)—the lesson learned from their unhappy experience with 'war by Congress' after independence and under the Articles of Confederation. In the Federalist Papers, Alexander Hamilton (later a leading

---

* See Ch. IX.

** I explore here the independent constitutional authority conferred upon the President by that clause. Ch. IV addresses the play between Presidential power and Congressional power, including the authority of Congress to limit or regulate military action by the President.

proponent of large Presidential powers) depreciated the significance of the Commander in Chief clause:[35]

It would amount to nothing more than the Supreme command and direction of the military and naval forces, as first general and admiral of the Confederacy; while that of the British king extends to the *declaring* of war and to the *raising and regulating* of fleets and armies—all which, by the Constitution under consideration, would appertain to the legislature.

Explicitly, Hamilton was denying to the Commander in Chief only those powers expressly granted by the Constitution to Congress. But his depreciation of the significance of that designation seemed to go farther and deeper: generals and admirals, even when they are 'first', do not determine the political purposes for which troops are to be used; they command them in the execution of policy made by others. Later, however, Presidents claimed to find in that clause substantive, 'policy-making' authority. They have claimed authority to make rules for the government and regulation of the land and naval forces,[36] although that power was explicitly given to Congress (Art. 1, sec 8, cl. 14); they have invoked their authority as Commander in Chief to legitimate using troops for political purposes, even to justify actions not involving use of the armed forces that the President wished to take for 'military' reasons.*

Presidential War Powers

Some of the 'military' powers that Presidents have asserted, deriving from or relating to the 'Commander in Chief' clause, supported the growth of Presidential 'war powers'. President Lincoln, in particular, in an unprecedented emergency, claimed unprecedented powers, and though he asserted them temporarily, pending ratification by Congress, later Presidents have claimed them independently of Congress. Lincoln's powers were exercised during civil war and largely vis-à-vis the domestic enemy;[37] later Presidents claimed them as well, perhaps *a fortiori,* during foreign wars and in relation to foreign nations. As Commander in Chief in war declared by Congress, the President has exercised full and exclusive control of the conduct of the war** claiming to act by authority of Congress as well as his own. The President has also been able

* See nn. 43, 44 to this chapter.
** Including powers to act within the United States in relation to U.S. citizens. See CORWIN, THE PRESIDENT (n. 5 to Intro. to Pt. II) 277 *et seq.* See generally C. BERDAHL, WAR POWERS OF THE EXECUTIVE IN THE UNITED STATES 31–4 (1921). As to competition between the President and Congress in the control of the conduct of war, see Ch. IV.

to rely on Congressional authority in wars not declared by Congress, since usually he had broad delegation in advance, as in Vietnam by the Tonkin Gulf Resolution (1964) and in the Gulf War (1991), or ratification after, as, I believe, in Korea (1950).* In war, the President exercised the rights that the state of war accords the United States under international law in regard to the enemy as well as to neutrals.[38] He has authority to enter into armistice agreements terminating hostilities, although some armistices have had long duration, some have determined the later peace treaties (as with Germany after the First World War), and one armistice—in Korea (1953)—has never been replaced by a political peace treaty.** Presumably as Commander in Chief (though perhaps with other supporting authority) Presidents have concluded wartime agreements, as at Yalta and Potsdam (1945), which not only prescribed the conduct of the war but determined major post-war political and territorial dispositions. Presidents have occupied and governed enemy territory long after hostilities ceased, and courts established under the President's authority as Commander in Chief have tried even U.S. citizens.[39]

In response to an attack upon the United States, the President has constitutional authority to defend the United States.† Without awaiting a Congressional declaration of war, or other authorization from Congress,‡ the power of the President to use the troops and do anything

---

* See Ch. VIII, p. 255.

** Wilson expressed the view that the armistice he concluded in 1918 was within his constitutional powers and obligated the United States to conclude a peace treaty in accordance with its terms. See S. Doc. No. 120, 66th Cong., 1st Sess. 173 (1919). But compare Q. WRIGHT, THE CONTROL OF AMERICAN FOREIGN RELATIONS 41 (1922). As to the President's power to end a state of war, see n. 21 to Ch. IV.

† In the event of an armed attack upon the United States, the rights of the United States under international law to act in self-defense and the constitutional powers of the President come together. Under international law since the United Nations Charter of 1945, a state may use force against another state only in self-defense against an armed attack, UN Charter Arts 2(4), 51 (unless in collective action pursuant to authorization by the U.N. Security Council, see Ch. VIII). See, e.g., Military and Paramilitary Activities in and Against Nicaragua (Nicaragua v. United States of America), 1986 I.C.J. 14.

International law is the law of the United States, and where international law forbids the use of force by the United States, such use of force would seem to be a violation of the President's constitutional duty to take care that the laws be faithfully executed. (Art. II, sec.3; see p. 50 below). As to whether the courts will enjoin the President from violating that duty, see Ch. V, pp. 241–5.

‡ In the War Powers Resolution of 1973 (sec. 2c), Congress declared that 'the Constitutional powers of the President as Commander in Chief to introduce U.S.

else necessary to repel invasion is beyond question.[40] Congressional authorization to respond to an attack upon the United States is assumed. In such circumstances, the President has power not merely to meet the invasion but to wage in full the war imposed upon the United States.[41] In our day of instant war, and the ever present threat of such war during the decades of the Cold War, everyone has assumed that the President would have power also to retaliate against a nuclear attack.*

The Commander in Chief clause has also provided the President important authority as regards the wars of others. Washington's Proclamation of Neutrality in the war between England and France, and Franklin Roosevelt's deviations from Congressional neutrality policy to aid those fighting Hitler in 1939–41 (before the United States was itself at war), built in part on the President's power as Commander in Chief.[42] Before the United States entered the First World War, President Wilson closed a wireless station which would not undertake to abide by naval censorship regulations,[43] and armed merchant vessels for protection against German submarines.[44]

Most controversial have been Presidential assertions of the right to use the armed forces for purposes short of war. Since Jefferson sent the Navy against the Barbary Pirates to protect U.S. shipping, Presidents have asserted the right to send troops abroad on their own authority in hundreds of instances[45] differing widely in purpose and magnitude. The President has frequently directed naval vessels to 'show the flag'; he used the Navy to 'open up' Japan; he sent troops to protect U.S. lives and other interests in China early in the century; he stationed troops in the Philippines for common defense; he sent marines to Nicaragua in the 1920s to fight 'bandits', to Lebanon in 1958 to discourage external intervention, and to the Dominican Republic in 1965 to prevent an undesirable government; he imposed a naval 'quarantine' in 1962 in the Cuban missile crisis;[46] U.S. participation in hostilities in Korea and in Vietnam began on the President's sole authority. Later, President Carter sent

armed forces into hostilities' are exercised only pursuant to 'a national emergency created by attack upon the United States, its territories or possessions, or its armed forces'. It has been argued that, in view of the awesome character and implications of nuclear weapons, the President ought not respond to a conventional attack with nuclear weapons unless authorized by Congress. See n. 50 to Ch. IV.

* Presumably, the President has constitutional authority to retaliate even if the motive was retribution only. The moral issues raised by such retaliation have not been widely considered. But see the National Conference of Catholic Bishops, 'Pastoral Letter on War and Peace—Challenge of Peace: God's Promise and Our Response', reprinted in CASTELLI, THE BISHOPS AND THE BOMB 274 (1983).

marines into Iran in an abortive attempt to extricate U.S. hostages; President Reagan invaded Grenada (1983), bombed Libya (declared to be responsible for a terrorist attack in Germany in which U.S. servicemen were injured), sent naval vessels to protect oil tankers and other shipping during the Iran–Iraq war (1987); President Bush invaded Panama in 1989 to depose and capture General Noriega, and sent troops to deter an attack on Saudi Arabia early in the Persian Gulf Crisis. President Clinton bombed Iraq's Intelligence Headquarters in response to an attempt to assassinate former President Bush.*

By repeated exercise without successful opposition, Presidents have established their authority to send troops abroad, probably beyond effective challenge, *where Congress is silent*, but the constitutional foundations and the constitutional limits of that authority remain in dispute. Such authority no doubt resides somewhere in the government of a 'sovereign nation'; in the United States, constitutional scripture does not explicitly grant (or deny) such authority to either Congress or the President. Presidential authority has to be found—if it can be—within his larger powers. Some have argued that as Commander in Chief the President can use the forces he commands as he will, but that view of the constitutional design is highly dubious.[47] It is more plausible to urge that, although as Commander in Chief the President's policy initiatives are limited, he can sometimes use the troops he commands in support of his other substantive powers.[48] In modern instances, one can say, President Truman stationed troops in Europe pursuant to his authority to carry out the obligations of the North Atlantic Treaty; President Eisenhower sent marines to deter intervention by others in Lebanon under his foreign affairs power; President Kennedy sent airplanes to save civilians in the Congo; and President Carter sent marines to extricate U.S. citizens held hostage in Iran, under their authority to protect U.S. citizens abroad.[49]

In these and other instances, the President can be seen as using the forces under his command to carry out purposes within his 'foreign affairs powers'.** In the result, since a military mission abroad generally supports a foreign affairs purpose, the President's 'plenary' foreign affairs power may support uses of troops 'short of war' as largely as

* That action might have been seen as an aftermath and still part of the Gulf War authorized by Congress and the U.N. Security Council. See Ch. VIII, p. 256.

The legality of Presidential uses of force after 1973 has to be considered in the light of the War Powers Resolution. See Ch. IV.

** Presidents Reagan, Bush and Clinton claimed analogous foreign policy purposes for military action, see p. 48 above.

would an unlimited Commander in Chief power. That he must rely on another 'substantive' power, however, is not only more palatable in constitutional theory, but may make a difference. It rejects the notion that the armed forces are the President's 'private army', and requires that their use be for a national purpose within the President's constitutional authority. And the President's inexplicit, undefined foreign affairs power, we shall see, is not immune to Congressional regulation.*

GENERAL PRESIDENTIAL POWERS

Among the President's hats are others that provide authority for his conduct of foreign affairs. As head of the Executive branch, the President appoints ambassadors and officials who conduct foreign relations. The President has yet another hat implied in the common understanding of 'executive': he has authority to execute the laws. Article II expressly adds: 'He shall take Care that the Laws be faithfully executed.' Although the words suggest duty and responsibility, they have served as a source of power in ways relevant also to foreign affairs.

'He shall take Care that the Laws be faithfully executed'

The principal purport of the clause, no doubt, is that the President shall be a loyal agent of Congress to enforce its laws. For our purposes, then, he is required—and has the necessary power—to assure that Congressional legislation affecting international relations (say, a regulation of foreign commerce) is carried out as law of the land. U.S. treaties and customary international law that have domestic normative quality, we shall see, are also law of the land, and Presidents have asserted responsibility (and authority) to interpret such international obligations and to see that they are 'faithfully executed', even when Congress has not enacted implementing legislation.** In the past, Presidents invoked

---

* See Ch. IV. Perhaps the President has acquired authority to deploy U.S. forces short of war only by tacit delegation from Congress, or at least by Congressional acquiescence. (Compare the President's authority to settle international claims by executive agreement, p. 43 above.) If so, we shall see, the President's authority is subject to Congressional control.

** See Ch. VII, p. 200. That interpretation was accepted by both Pacificus (Hamilton) and Helvidius (Madison), n. 10 to this chapter, despite their otherwise sharp differences. Pacificus wrote: 'The executive is charged with the execution of all laws, the law of nations, as well as the municipal law which recognizes and adopts those laws.' Helvidius agreed. 'The first sentence is a truth.'

that authority to carry out U.S. obligations to send troops to various parts of Latin America when required by treaty;* to extradite persons to a foreign country;[50] to suppress piracy and slave trade;[51] to restore to a foreign government its vessels or other property;[52] to compel U.S. citizens to honor the obligations of neutrality; to intern foreign insurgents when the United States was obligated to do so under an international convention.[53]

The principle is clear and unexceptionable; its implications are sometimes misunderstood. For example, President Truman asserted authority to go to war to defend the Republic of Korea against aggression, pursuant to a recommendation of the United Nations Security Council.** In 1990, spokesmen for President Bush asserted Presidential authority to go to war to liberate Kuwait from Iraqi aggression pursuant to authorization by the United Nations Security Council.† In both instances, apologists for the President argued that he had that authority since he was carrying out U.S. responsibilities under the United Nations Charter, a treaty of the United States. The argument has substantial plausibility when the President acts to carry out a legal obligation of the United States under a treaty. But in both Korea and in the Persian Gulf, the Security Council *recommended* or *authorized* the military action;‡ it did not purport to order states to take such action, and there was no legal obligation for the United States to take such action. It is difficult, then, to derive a constitutional power for the President to act to take care that a U.S. legal obligation under the Charter be faithfully executed in circumstances where there is no legal obligation.§

* For example, to Panama to maintain the guarantee in the Colombia Treaty of 1846, to Mexico (1882–94), Cuba (1903), Haiti (1916); see Q. WRIGHT, THE CONTROL OF AMERICAN FOREIGN RELATIONS 217, 227 (1922). More recently Presidents claimed authority to send troops to Korea and Vietnam, in part pursuant to their responsibility to carry out obligations under the United Nations Charter and the South-East Asia Treaty. Compare the debates about sending troops to Europe pursuant to the North Atlantic Treaty, Ch. IV, p. 100.

** See Ch. VIII.

† In the end, in both cases, the war was authorized by Congress. In Korea, Congress quickly ratified the President's action. In the Gulf War, the President in fact asked for and obtained Congressional authorization.

‡ Under Chapter VII of the Charter, the Security Council may *decide*, and what it decides is mandatory and creates a legal obligation. The Security Council may also *recommend*, and states are expected to give such recommendations great weight, but they are not legally binding. See Ch. VIII, p. 253.

§ Presidents have sometimes claimed a 'responsibility' to 'respond' to U.N. resolutions, but it is difficult to find power to do so within his authority to execute 'the laws'.

The 'take care' clause, it has been argued, would also justify Presidential action in relation to other states, to vindicate rights of the United States under international law.[54] The argument seems to be that since 'the Laws' which the President is required to execute include treaties and international law, the President has the duty and the power to see to it that foreign nations observe these laws, and he can do so by every means including the use of force,* as, for example, early against the Barbary Pirates,[55] recently during the Iran–Iraq War. The argument is not compelling. Surely, authority to see that the laws shall be executed means that the President shall enforce the laws of the United States[56] (including international law and obligations that constitute United States law) where U.S. law applies, that is, within the United States, or elsewhere as to U.S. law that governs the U.S. authorities or its citizens;[57] there is nothing to suggest that the 'take care' clause was intended to extend to violations of international obligations to the United States, committed outside the United States, by those not subject to the laws of the United States.** In such cases, stronger and more persuasive support for Presidential action might be found in a broad foreign affairs power (supplemented by authority as Commander in Chief), but reasonable men and women continue to differ as to whether those powers are strong and persuasive enough.

The responsibility to take care that the laws be faithfully executed is sometimes invoked to support Presidential initiative to exercise rights granted to the United States by treaty, to pursue general policies established by treaty, or to act on discretion in foreign affairs delegated to him by Congress. That such initiatives were contemplated by the 'take care' clause is less than obvious,[58] but that the President has such authority is not now questionable.†

---

* In 1985, in the Achille Lauro incident, President Reagan sought to seize individuals carried on an airplane of a friendly foreign state in order to bring them to trial in the United States for murdering hostages. Some such argument was made to justify invading Panama in 1989 to capture General Noriega to bring him to trial in the United States, or to abduct Dr. Alvarez-Machain from Mexico to bring him to trial in the United States. See n. 91 to Chapter IX.

** Compare the argument that United States courts should refuse to give effect to foreign acts of state which violate international law because international law is part of the law of the United States, Ch. VIII, p. 245.

† Provided he pursues those purposes by means short of war and subject to any limitations imposed by Congress.

NATIONAL SECURITY AND EMERGENCY POWER

The President can act under all his hats and invoke all his sources of constitutional authority at the same time. Often he cites generally 'the President's powers under the Constitution',* or, only somewhat less generally, his 'executive power', his 'Foreign Affairs power', his 'authority as Commander in Chief'. Sometimes instead of invoking constitutional sources of power, Presidents claim areas of responsibility, for example, 'to protect the national security'. Presidents have sometimes claimed 'emergency powers'.

'National security' is not a constitutional term, and it is a concept too uncertain to support authority beyond what can be distilled from the responsibilities and powers bestowed on the President by the Constitution.** Congress has recognized the President's constitutional power to protect the United States against attack, as well as against 'other hostile acts or intelligence activities of a foreign power'.[59] Presidents have asserted authority to exercise electronic surveillance over foreign governments or agencies, and to do so without a warrant, pursuant to the Fourth Amendment or authorization by Congress. The courts have not had occasion to rule definitively on these claims.

The Constitution recognizes no 'emergency powers', whether for the President, or for other branches of the federal government. 'Emergency does not create power. Emergency does not increase granted power or diminish the restrictions imposed upon power granted.'[60] Even in 'emergency', then, the President has only the powers granted him by the Constitution, or others delegated to him by act of Congress. But where security needs or emergency are claimed, the Court is likely to interpret the powers of the President generously† and even to reduce the restrictions and safeguards of the Bill of Rights.[61]

---

* Increasingly, Presidents invoke their authority 'under the Constitution and laws of the U.S.' to include the sum of all authority delegated to them by Congress. And Congress has given the President broad authority; Presidents have interpreted Congressional delegations generously, and the courts have often acquiesced.

** 'The word "security" is a broad, vague generality [the contours of which] should not be invoked to abrogate the fundamental law embodied in the First Amendment.' *New York Times Co.* v. *United States*, 403 U.S. 713, 719 (1971) (Black, J. concurring). See Ch. IX.

† The courts have been more scrupulous in invoking the safeguards of the Bill of Rights than in limiting the scope of the Constitutional authority of the political branches. See n. 61 to this chapter, and Ch. IX.

PRESIDENTIAL 'LAW-MAKING'

Making law in the United States, in foreign as in domestic matters, is a legislative function, therefore for Congress, not the President;* for example, only Congress can regulate commerce with foreign nations or adopt laws to define and punish piracy. Some of the President's international acts we have been discussing, however, also have domestic effect as law or have legal consequences in the United States. The President makes domestic law, we shall see, when he makes a treaty or an executive agreement which becomes the law of the land, and he unmakes domestic law when he denounces or otherwise terminates an international agreement and thereby also its effect as law of the land.** There may be domestic legal consequences when the President decides to recognize or not to recognize a foreign state or government.[62] President Truman made law when he proclaimed the right of the United States to exploit the resources of its continental shelf. It was law by almost any definition when, on his sole authority, he promulgated law and established courts during U.S. occupation of Germany and subjected even U.S. citizens to their authority.

In these instances, law is made, or modified, as a by-product of international action by the President. No one has suggested that under the President's 'plenary' foreign affairs powers he can, by executive act or order, enact law directly regulating persons or property in the United States.† In at least one regard, however—sovereign and diplomatic immunity from the jurisdiction of courts in the United States—the courts have given effect to declarations by the Executive branch as to an act of Congress or of a legislative agency.

Understanding the cases and their constitutional implications requires background and context. The courts, we shall see, ascertain and apply international law 'as often as questions of right depending upon it are duly presented for their determination';[63] for a common example, courts in the United States have given effect to the principles of international law that give foreign states and their accredited diplomats immunity from suit in national courts.‡ Until 1976, when Congress established a legislative regime, if a court found that under international law the defendant in a case before it (or his property at stake in the case)

* See Ch. III, p. 64, and Ch. IV, p. 89.   ** See Ch. VII, pp. 212 *et seq.*

† Even Wilson's closing of the Marconi station (n. 43 to this chapter) might be seen as executing neutrality rather than 'legislating'. On the President's power to 'legislate' by authority delegated him by Congress, see Ch. IV, p. 123.

‡ See Ch. VIII, p. 239.

enjoyed immunity from judicial process, the court gave effect to international law and dismissed the proceeding. In deciding whether international law accorded immunity in the circumstances, the courts often sought (or received) from the Department of State 'suggestions' as to the international identity and status of the defendant or of the property before the court. Sometimes the courts received, too, Executive expressions of opinion as to what international law required in the circumstances, but while these were accorded 'great weight', the courts decided the question of immunity on the basis of their own conclusions* as to what international law required.[64]

In 1943, in *Ex parte Republic of Peru,* the Supreme Court struck a different note. In that case, the Department of State had 'recognized and allowed' the immunity of a merchant vessel owned and operated by the Peruvian Government. The Court said:[65]

The [Department of State's] certification and the request that the vessel be declared immune must be accepted by the courts as a conclusive determination by the political arm of the Government that the continued retention of the vessel interferes with the proper conduct of our foreign relations. Upon the submission of this certification to the district court, it became the court's duty, in conformity to established principle, to release the vessel and to proceed no further in the cause.

Two years later, in *Republic of Mexico* v. *Hoffman,*** the Court went on:[66]

But recognition by the courts of an immunity upon principles which the political department of government has not sanctioned may be equally embarrassing to it in securing the protection of our national interests and their recognition by other nations. . .

We can only conclude that it is the national policy not to extend the immunity in the manner now suggested, and that it is the duty of the courts, in a

* In 1926, in *The Pesaro,* for example, the Supreme Court concluded that under international law a ship owned and operated by the Italian Government was immune from the jurisdiction of the courts even though the ship was used in the carriage of merchandise for hire. In doing so, the Court disregarded the views of the State Department which had for some time urged a 'restrictive theory' that would accord immunity only for 'governmental', not 'commercial', activities of foreign governments. See n. 64 to this chapter, and Ch. V.

** In that case a libel *in rem* for collision damage was filed against a vessel owned by the Government of Mexico but operated by a private company under a profit-sharing arrangement with the Mexican Government. The Mexican Ambassador filed a claim of immunity but the State Department's communication only confirmed the facts and expressed no opinion as to the immunity claimed.

matter so intimately associated with our foreign policy and which may profoundly affect it, not to enlarge an immunity to an extent which the government, though often asked, has not seen fit to recognize.

The doctrine announced by the Court seems clear and inescapable: the courts would decide the question of immunity in accordance with international law if the Executive wished them to (or if the Executive was silent);[67] but if the Executive announced a national policy in regard to immunity generally, or for the particular case, that policy was law for the courts and binding upon them,* regardless of what international law might say about it.[68]

In the immunity cases, the Supreme Court did not say (or intimate) that issues of immunity are unique, or that the Executive had special powers in regard to them; to support its doctrine the Court invoked only general Executive powers in foreign affairs. During the same judicial era, the Court also decided the *Belmont* and *Pink* cases,[69] leading cases giving legal effect to a 'sole executive agreement', an international agreement concluded by the President on his own authority.** In those cases, the Court did not appear to give any weight to the fact that Executive policy was contained in an international agreement rather than, as in the immunity cases, in a unilateral Presidential act. In *Pink,* for example, the Court described in broadest terms 'The powers of the President in the conduct of foreign relations'; it concluded that 'We would usurp the executive function if we held that that decision was not final and conclusive in the courts'; that 'Effectiveness in handling the delicate problems of foreign relations requires no less'.[70] During those years, too, Judge Learned Hand (of the U.S. Circuit Court of Appeals) was prepared to treat as binding also an Executive policy modifying the doctrine requiring courts to give effect to the 'Act of State' of a foreign government in its own territory. He asked whether 'our own Executive, which is the authority to which we must look as the final word in such matters, has declared that the commonly accepted doctrine . . . does not

---

* In 1976, Congress adopted the Foreign Sovereign Immunity Act which in effect defined the international law of sovereign immunity for courts in the United States and effectively terminated Executive branch involvement in the process. See n. 64 to this chapter. But that legislation applies only to the immunity of states or their instrumentalities, not to cases raising issues of diplomatic or consular immunity. In such cases, the Executive branch has continued to 'suggest' immunity, for example, in a suit against the Prince of Wales in 1978; against Marcos when he was head of state of the Philippines in 1982; against President Aristide of Haiti in 1994, and the courts seem to have given binding effect to these suggestions of immunity.

** I deal with these cases at greater length in Ch. VII.

apply'. Later the Court of Appeals concluded that the doctrine indeed did not apply, 'in view of this supervening expression of the Executive policy'.[71]

Those cases left many questions unanswered. Principally, do they recognize the President's power to make special law in special circumstances, or do they represent some broad principle of Presidential 'legislative power' in foreign affairs?[72] If so, how broad is it, and what are its limitations? If not, how are these cases to be distinguished from others where executive action would not be given effect as law binding on the courts?[73] The Supreme Court has not told us. Indeed, although it has never retreated from either the immunity or the executive agreement cases, it has not extended or even reaffirmed them.* And a generation after they were decided, in the *Sabbatino* case,[74] the Court took pains to refrain from following Judge Hand's lead to give the Executive the controlling 'say' as to the Act of State doctrine. In that case, the Court held that the doctrine required courts in the United States to recognize and give effect to Castro's title to U.S. sugar which he had expropriated, even if the expropriation was in violation of international law. Although that was the rule requested by the Executive branch, the Court went to lengths, in novel constitutional doctrine, to re-establish 'Act of State' not as national policy promulgated by the Executive but as law created by the federal courts on their own authority for their own guidance.[75] Was the Court merely seizing an occasion to aggrandize judicial power? Or was it now reserving its position as to the earlier view that the President can declare national policy in foreign affairs with legal effect binding on the courts?

Perhaps the Court feared the implication, beyond Act of State, that the Executive could legislate; especially, that the courts were subject to *ad hoc* determination by the Executive branch directing the decision of particular cases. Perhaps the Court was reluctant to have the judiciary appear less than independent, its power less than 'separate', particularly

---

* Both the law as to executive agreements and the Act of State doctrine came back to the Supreme Court in recent years. See Ch. V. The Supreme Court upheld the President's agreement settling the Iran Hostage crisis, giving it the effect of law affecting claims of U.S. citizens. See n. 71 to Ch. IX. But the Court did not assert large constitutional power in the President to make executive agreements with legislative effect, preferring to rely on a long history of particular executive agreements to settle international claims, a practice in which Congress had long acquiesced. In Act of State cases after *Sabbatino*, too, a divided Court continued to refine the doctrine; the Justices expressed respect for Executive communications but hardly suggested that they deserve legislative effect.

in regard to the Executive. Perhaps the Court was reluctant to establish the power of the political branches to determine, define, and modify a doctrine that had been judicially developed. Perhaps it was moved by the probability that the policy invoked was not that of the President but of lesser Executive officials.*

What was perhaps buried in *Sabbatino* surfaced somewhat in *Zschernig* v. *Miller*.[76] In that case,** the courts of Oregon, applying a state statute, had denied an inheritance to a resident of East Germany (then a Communist country not recognized by the United States) because he did not prove that he would enjoy the inheritance 'without confiscation', and that U.S. citizens had a reciprocal right to inherit in his country. The Supreme Court reversed, holding that the Oregon statute as applied was 'an intrusion by the State into the field of foreign affairs which the Constitution entrusts to the President and the Congress'.[77] In that case, the Solicitor General of the United States had informed the Supreme Court that 'the Department of State has advised us . . . that State reciprocity laws, including that of Oregon, had little effect on the foreign relations and policy of this country';[78] yet the majority of the Court did not feel bound by that view. Even Justice Harlan, who rejected the majority's constitutional doctrine, did not suggest that the Court had to defer to the Executive branch. Justices Stewart and Brennan 'would go further':[79]

We deal here with the basic allocation of power between the States and the Nation. Resolution of so fundamental a constitutional issue cannot vary from day to day with the shifting winds at the State Department. Today, we are told, Oregon's statute does not conflict with the national interest. Tomorrow it may. But, however that may be, the fact remains that the conduct of our foreign affairs is entrusted under the Constitution to the National Government, not to the probate courts of the several states.

---

* What seems clear is that the Court which had established Executive power to dictate to the courts in the immunity cases or to make law by executive agreement would not have been reluctant to conclude that judicial authority to declare and apply Act of State is derivative, auxiliary, and subordinate to policy declared by the principal architect of foreign policy, the President. Indeed, in *Pink*, the Court had said incidentally that the considerations that required giving legal effect to executive agreements also explain the Act of State doctrine. See 315 U.S. at 233.

In the 1990s, lawyers were asking what would happen if the Department of State were moved to tell the courts to dismiss a case, if the defendant insisted on it as the price of agreeing to a peace settlement, e.g., in the former Yugoslavia. See n. 73 to this chapter.

** Discussed more fully in Ch. VI, pp. 163 *et seq.*

The Court did not have before it a formal act of the Executive branch. The friendly interventions of the Solicitor General, the informal statements of State Department views, did not assert that national policy required upholding Oregon's statute, only that such statutes did no harm to the national interest. In the result, however, the Court disregarded the State Department's view and substituted its own judgment on an issue of foreign policy. Inevitably, it was holding—at least—that the State Department cannot informally legitimize state incursions into foreign policy which, in the Court's view, were forbidden by the Constitution.*

In 1972, the Supreme Court had another opportunity to speak to the Executive's 'legislative' authority when the State Department sought to modify the Act of State doctrine as the Court and Congress had established it. The Cuban Government had sued to recover assets held by the First National City Bank; the Bank counterclaimed for the value of its properties which Cuba had confiscated. While the case was in the courts, the Department of State communicated 'a determination by the Department of State that the Act of State doctrine need not be applied' in given circumstances, and its belief that the 'doctrine should not be applied to bar consideration of the defendant's counterclaim'. The Court of Appeals in effect disregarded the State Department and applied the Act of State doctrine to dismiss the Bank's counterclaim.[80] The Supreme Court reversed,[81] but only three of the five Justices in the majority did so on the ground that the courts should give effect to State Department policy; two Justices who concurred in the judgment of the Court, as well as the four dissenting Justices, explicitly rejected the view that the courts are bound to follow the Executive in such cases.[82]

---

* Compare the power of Congress to permit state burdens on interstate or foreign commerce, Ch. VI, p. 160. Perhaps an 'activist' Supreme Court was less impressed with Executive expertise and more confident of its own, including its ability to see the long-term needs of the nation which constitutional doctrine represents. Perhaps the Court believed that the courts could better protect the national interest, particularly at some times and in some cases: in *Zschernig* itself, for example, the State Department—long a target of accusations that it was 'soft on Communism'— might not have felt free to object to laws and practices directed primarily against the Communist states and involving criticism of Communist ideology and practice.

The end of the Cold War has changed the national security interests of the United States and may well cause the courts to reconsider their implications for executive-judicial relations. But the new world order (and disorder) may yet give rise to new issues of Executive authority and judicial independence. See, e.g., n. 73 to this chapter.

Neither *Sabbatino* nor *Zschernig* overruled either *Ex parte Peru* or *Belmont:* the older cases were not strictly in point and were not mentioned. In the *First National City Bank* case, a majority in effect refrained from reconfirming the immunity cases and refused to extend them to Act of State, but no Justice in the case rejected those cases.[83] Nor was the Executive's 'legislative power' clearly in issue when the Court in 1971 denied the Government's request for an injunction against publication of the classified 'Pentagon Papers'.[84] But one reader at least would guess that to the Justices in that case the older cases may have represented undue deference to the political branches by the 'New Deal' Court, in reaction to undue restraints upon those branches earlier which had led to accusations of 'government by judiciary', to Franklin Roosevelt's 'court-packing plan', and the greatest crisis in the Court's history. The later opinions of the Court seem to reflect further thoughts, at least about the language in the older cases, perhaps about the acceptability of law-making by informal, *ad hoc* State Department intervention, possibly about Executive legislation generally;* it might portend re-examination—some day—of executive finality even in the immunity cases themselves.

If such change indeed comes, the practical consequences need not be radical. The President and the State Department have not been eager to 'legislate', or to intervene *ad hoc* in particular cases. In regard to sovereign immunity, at least, the Department has often seemed unbelieving of the power which the Supreme Court said it had,[85] and it has been generally disposed not to inject itself to suggest immunity and thereby deny a U.S. plaintiff his (her) day in court. In general, the Executive preferred to leave issues of immunity in particular cases to the courts, guided by general policy established through Congressional legislation; indeed, the Executive branch encouraged Congress to enact the Foreign Sovereign Immunities Act so as to be relieved of that responsibility. Similarly, though Congress has given the President express authority to make exceptions to the limited Act of State doctrine which Congress enacted, the Executive branch has not been eager to assume the onus of doing so and thereby perhaps defeating the claim of a U.S. citizen against a foreign government.[86] The Supreme Court's reception of the State Department's effort to modify the Act of State doctrine in *First National City Bank* was not likely to encourage further efforts. But every

---

* At least where, as in *First National City Bank,* the Executive acts not by formal Presidential order. And might even State Department policy have been given effect had it not sought to modify a doctrine which the Supreme Court had legislated and which Congress had arguably reaffirmed? See n. 85 to this chapter.

now and then the Executive branch is pleased to be able to assert the power the Supreme Court once said it has, and to intervene in a particular case for what seems to the Executive to be an important foreign policy reason. And if that does not happen often, neither Congress nor the Supreme Court may be moved to deny the Executive power, however uncertain its constitutional foundations.

More 'conservative' Supreme Court attitudes have included also deference to the political process, notably to the Executive in foreign affairs, not in the name of any new constitutional doctrine but rather by broad—sometimes extravagant—interpretations of Congressional delegations of authority. Sometimes the Courts have deferred by avoiding adjudication.

The cases that struggled with issues of Presidential 'law-making' dramatize the special quality of the constitutional law of foreign affairs and the vagaries of judicial incursions which are infrequent and develop no confident mastery. The 'New Deal' Supreme Court, abjuring the earlier 'judicial activism' and espousing self-restraint, moved from deference to Congress to deference to the Executive, indeed to deference to unidentified officials of the State Department. A later Supreme Court turned its back on the earlier attitude but could not be too 'activist', since its opportunities to intervene were limited (and the dangers of 'inexpert' intervention uncertain). The result has been to tear down old guideposts without erecting new ones. The Court seems disposed to follow an earlier precedent but not necessarily to reaffirm its underlying constitutional doctrine or to go where it would seem to lead.* The law student's distinctions between principle, holding, and dictum become critical: we have judicial guidance only on the few issues which the Supreme Court has actually decided, and not always there, since *stare decisis*—adherence to precedent—in constitutional cases means less than elsewhere.** Issues of Presidential power, in particular, remain to be fought out in the consciences of the Executive branch and in the political arena.

LIMITATIONS ON PRESIDENTIAL POWER

The broader theories, and extensive—even extravagant—Presidential claims suggest that the President's powers in foreign affairs are 'plenary',

* It has avoided confirming doctrine that would uphold law-making by executive agreement generally. See Ch. VII.
** See n. 5 to Introduction.

and that they can be exercised even to make law in limited contexts within the United States. Of course, the President cannot do what is forbidden to him, as to all of the United States government, by the Bill of Rights, and those safeguards have been increasingly invoked and frequently vindicated, even where foreign relations are affected.* Even the broadest theories, moreover, accept that there are major limitations on the President implied in or flowing from grants of power to Congress or the treaty-makers, that some powers can be exercised by the President only when Congress is silent (or subject to Congressional control or guidance), some only jointly with Congress.**

THE POLITICAL INFLUENCE OF THE PRESIDENT

In addition to the President's powers—both enumerated and implied—grounded in the Constitution, and those constitutional powers derived 'extra-constitutionally' from U.S. international 'sovereignty', the President has acquired political power from his unique political position. He is the only official elected by all the people,† the only official with a national constituency. He is the leader of his political party. He controls official and party patronage. Presidents can represent, commit, and inspire the people of the United States as neither Congress nor any member of Congress can. Political power married to constitutional powers strengthens the President's hand, provides justification, induces Congressional cooperation and sometimes compels Congressional acquiescence in actions already undertaken.‡ Political power, too, however, is not without its limits; Congress has its own political as well as constitutional advantages, as we shall see in Chapter IV.

---

* See Ch. IX.

** I deal with the limitations deriving from Congressional power in Ch. IV (after we consider the powers of Congress), and those that derive from the Treaty Power in Ch. VII.

† In fact. Technically, under Art. II of the Constitution and the Twelfth Amendment, the people vote for electors who then elect the President.

‡ For example, in 1991, in deploying U.S. armed forces to help defend Saudi Arabia prior to the Persian Gulf War, President Bush achieved popular support for the action; having put the nation behind the effort, he in effect forced the hand of Congress to approve and authorize U.S. participation in the Gulf War.

Chapter III

THE CONGRESS

If in the competition for power in foreign relations the President has had inherent practical, political advantages, Congress has had other, enormous strengths, not least the history, the conception, and the generous grants of the Constitution.[1] The President had to contend for power in a novel office furnished with few, inarticulate constitutional phrases, compelling him to reach outside the Constitution (as per Justice Sutherland) or for special meanings (as in 'the Executive power'). Congress has needed no extravagant, uncommon constitutional interpretations to support the legitimacy of its exercises of power; even its authority deriving from national sovereignty has been secondary to the impressive array of powers expressly enumerated in the Constitution, not least the sole charge of an indispensable and ample purse.

CONGRESS AS LAW-MAKER

The Constitution confers upon Congress 'legislative Powers,' set forth principally in Article I, section 8.[2] Those directly related to foreign affairs are the powers:

To regulate Commerce with foreign Nations, and among the several States, and with the Indian Tribes (clause 3).
To define and punish Piracies and Felonies committed on the high Seas, and Offences against the Law of Nations (clause 10).
To declare War, grant Letters of Marque and Reprisal,[3] and make Rules concerning Captures on Land and Water (clause 11).*

And, although explicitly the Constitution gives Congress only 'All legislative Powers herein granted', Congress, we know, has also an

---

* One might add the power 'To establish an uniform Rule of Naturalization' (cl. 4) in which the Supreme Court has seen authority for 'specialized regulation of the conduct of an alien before naturalization'. *Hines* v. *Davidowitz*, 312 U.S. 52, 66 (1941). In other respects, too, foreign relations are not unaffected by our naturalization and nationality laws. See also Ch. IX. Also relevant to foreign relations is the power of Congress to govern territory (Art. IV, sec. 3), including territories acquired by conquest or treaty, see n. 53 to this chapter. The power of Congress to

unenumerated 'foreign affairs power', the legislative derivative of the powers of the United States inherent in its sovereignty.* Congress also has general powers that are indispensable to the conduct of foreign relations, e.g., the power to tax and to spend for the common defense and the general welfare, to do what is 'necessary and proper' to carry out other powers, to appropriate funds from the Treasury.**

The powers of Congress are denominated 'legislative', as distinguished, in particular, from those 'executive'. Most of the enumerated powers of Congress are indeed legislative, i.e., they provide authority to enact domestic law in the matters indicated. The power to declare war is authority to perform an international act, but it has legislative implications and consequences as well. Congress has also claimed authority to make foreign policy by resolutions and other actions, not least by authorizing spending and appropriating funds, which strictly do not 'legislate,' do not enact law in the United States.

Enumerated Foreign Affairs Powers

For some 150 years the meaning and scope of the enumerated powers of Congress were a principal fare of constitutional adjudication. Since 1937, the Court has given Congress the broadest scope, and some of its powers, including some particularly relevant to foreign affairs, have known few limits.† Other powers of Congress have been little used, but

establish federal offices and to authorize the President to fill them without Senate consent (Art. II, sec. 2) has also been used for foreign affairs purposes. See this chapter, p. 73.

    * See Ch. I. Under the Articles of Confederation, whatever executive powers there were had also been exercised by the Congress.

    ** 'The Congress shall have Power to lay and collect Taxes, Duties, Imposts and Excises, to pay the Debts and provide for the common defence and general Welfare of the United States . . .' (Art. I, sec. 8, cl. 1). The power to impose duties on foreign goods might also have been inferred from the power to regulate foreign commerce.

The 'necessary and proper' clause is in Art. I, sec. 8, cl. 18, quoted this chapter, p. 73.

The power to appropriate funds from the Treasury is implied in Art. I, sec. 9, cl. 7: 'No Money shall be drawn from the Treasury, but in Consequence of Appropriations made by Law . . .'.

    † And every broad power of Congress is extended yet further by the additional broad power to make laws 'which shall be necessary and proper' for carrying out the enumerated powers, see p. 73 below.

In 1995, the Court gave some evidence that it may be reconsidering the boundaries of the Commerce Power. See p. 65, this chapter.

prevailing judicial deference to Congress would doubtless extend to these as well.[4]

The Foreign Commerce Power

From the beginning, the foreign trade of the United States was near the core of its foreign policy, and the power to regulate commerce with foreign nations gave Congress a major voice in it.* As intervening years brought radical growth and enhanced importance to the international trade of the United States, they brought enhanced importance and radical growth to the Commerce Power of Congress, but in the history of constitutional jurisprudence power to regulate foreign commerce was, in the main, the incidental beneficiary of the explosion of the power to regulate interstate commerce.

Long ago Chief Justice John Marshall told us that commerce is not merely trade, 'it is intercourse'.[5] Today, we know, Congress can regulate every aspect of intercourse among the states of the United States and of an interdependent interstate economy; it can regulate what is in interstate commerce and, largely, what will be or has been in interstate commerce, as well as other intra-state matters that substantially affect interstate commerce; it can regulate intra-state matters when necessary for the effective regulation of interstate commerce.[6] No longer subject to serious constitutional challenge, Congress has embarked on unprecedented, far-reaching regulation of trade and finance, transportation and communication, labor and management, crime and punishment, manners and morals, even in respects that might have seemed remote from 'commerce' and from 'interstate' considerations.[7] Between 1936 and 1995 Congress was not found to have crossed the limits of its Commerce Power[8] and many have wondered whether there are any limits other than those resulting from Congressional self-restraint reflecting the restraints of political forces.** In 1995, in *Lopez*, the Court invalidated a provision in an act of Congress on the ground that Congress had not demonstrated a significant link between the activity prohibited by

* In addition to direct regulation of foreign commerce by statute, as in tariff laws, Congress has also authorized executive trade agreements. Trade can also be regulated by treaty. See Ch. VII.

** In 1976, the Supreme Court carved a narrow immunity from Congressional control for traditional governmental activities of the states, and invalidated Congressional regulation of wages and hours of state employees. The Court reversed itself and canceled that immunity in 1985. Then, in 1992, it re-established a small part of that narrow immunity, invalidating laws that purport to command state legislatures to do Congressional bidding. See n. 7 to this chapter.

Congress and interstate commerce, but it remains to be seen whether that case signals only more meaningful judicial scrutiny of the established limits of the Commerce Power, or also re-evaluation, re-interpretation or redrawing of those limits.*

There have been fewer occasions for Congress to act on so broad a conception of the Commerce Power in regard to foreign commerce, but there is no reason in principle (or in politics) why it could not do so.[9] With perhaps some differences of degree which do not appear constitutionally material, the international economy is as interdependent as our own interstate economy. Many local activities impinge on foreign commerce and require regulation to make control of foreign commerce effective. There is room for 'police power' regulation in foreign commerce and of local matters that affect foreign commerce and intercourse.**

The Commerce Power, then, might be sufficient to support virtually any legislation that relates to foreign intercourse, i.e., to foreign relations.[10] It is principally in the Commerce Power that Congress has found authority to regulate international shipping, aviation, and old and new media of communication; to impose tariffs and authorize reciprocal trade agreements; to grant or deny 'more favored nation' treatment or other preferences; to impose embargoes on unfriendly countries;† to deny the sale of arms to gross violators of human rights. With a small assist from the powers 'to borrow Money' and 'to coin Money, regulate the Value thereof, and of foreign Coin', the Commerce Power supports the part of the United States in a worldwide network of finance and

* See n. 8 to this chapter.

** Often interstate and foreign commerce are inextricably intertwined, and local activities that impinge on foreign commerce often impinge also on interstate commerce and could be regulated on that ground as well.

Indeed, the power of Congress over foreign commerce might be seen as even broader than that over interstate commerce since the latter was effectively carved out of state powers, whereas states were not intended to regulate foreign commerce. See Art. I, sec. 10; n. 9 to this chapter.

† 'Most favored nation' treatment has generally been granted by treaty, but, for example, Congress legislated to condition such treatment for Soviet bloc countries in the Jackson-Vanik Amendment of 1974, 19 U.S.C. §2462(b), and later legislated to repeal that denial. See Ch. IV, note 96. Congress has also legislated authority to impose sanctions, invoked, for example, for the embargo against Iraq following its invasion of Kuwait in 1990 Ch. V, n. 54. Congress could support that embargo also by its power to enact laws necessary and proper to carry out U.S. obligations under the U.N. Charter, a treaty of the United States, and plausibly also by its power to define offenses against the law of nations. See Ch. VIII. Increasingly, trade is the subject of executive agreement pursuant to Congressional authorization. See Ch. VII, p. 219.

banking.[11] At one time the Commerce Power was seen also as the basis for Congressional regulation of maritime and admiralty affairs[12] and its control of immigration.[13] Only the availability of other powers (discussed below) made it unnecessary for the courts to rely exclusively on the Commerce Power or to explore its reaches for other legislative regulation of the international relations of the United States.

The War Power as legislative power

To the Constitutional Fathers, one might guess, the most important power in foreign relations was the power to declare war, and they gave that power to Congress. I deal later with the power of Congress to decide for war or peace and to limit or regulate military activity by the President;* here I consider the War Power as a source of domestic legislative authority. For, the Supreme Court has ruled, the power to declare war implies the power to wage war and supports what is necessary and proper to wage war successfully.[14] We have, then, that congeries of 'war powers' under which, during the Second World War, for example, Congress mobilized the manpower and the resources of this country and regulated the minutiae of the lives of the people.[15]

Legislative war powers, moreover, are not born with the declaration of war, nor do they die with the coming of peace. The power to declare and wage war implies power to prepare for war and to act to deter or prevent war; hence, to establish elaborate peacetime defense programs—as during the Cold War**—entailing not only huge expenditures but detailed regulatory programs,† including, for a few examples, compulsory military service, control of activities related to atomic energy, comprehensive security programs affecting millions of employees of the federal government and of government contractors.[16] Congress also has the power to deal with the aftermath and the consequences of war, for example, by providing for the renegotiation of wartime contracts, or the control of prices and rentals for years after the fighting ended.[17] The Supreme Court has never declared any limit to the war powers of Congress during war or peace, or even intimated where such limits might lie.‡

* See this chapter, p. 75, and Ch. IV.   ** Dated, approximately, 1946–89.

† Defense expenditures are also within the express power of Congress 'to lay and collect Taxes . . . to pay the Debts and provide for the common Defence and general Welfare of the United States . . .' Art. I, sec. 8, cl. 1. But that clause provides authority only for spending, not for regulatory legislation. Compare *United States v. Butler*, 297 U.S. 1 (1936).

‡ Presumably, in principle, the regulation must be related to the power invoked and must be reasonable. See Ch. IX.

Inevitably, what Congress does to wage war, to anticipate or prevent war, to recover from war, has importance for international relations. Directly, the war powers enable Congress during war to regulate the rights and obligations in the United States of enemies, allies or neutrals, their ships and airplanes, their citizens and their properties, as well as communication, trade, and every form of intercourse with them.[18] In differing degrees in respect of different countries, such regulations could be supported also during the consequences of war that long endure, and during the chronic state of 'less than peace' and eternal defensive vigilance that was our lot during the Cold War and is with us even after the Cold War has ended. In our day, at least, trade and embargo, transportation and communication, arms programs and foreign aid, indeed whatever might be reached by the power to regulate foreign commerce and intercourse, seem plausibly also within the war powers of Congress.[19]

The power of Congress over war and peace is 'plenary'.* The thorny issues of Congressional War Power arise from suggestions that the power of Congress is exclusive, that even if Congress has not exercised its powers the Constitution precludes any exercise of War Power by the President. In our time, since Congress has acted to limit and regulate Presidential 'war-making', notably in the War Powers Resolution of 1973, issues of War Power have become issues of conflict and cooperation in a 'twilight zone' of uncertain or perhaps concurrent power.**

'To define and punish offences'

The rule of law in relations between nations and at sea loomed large in the minds of the Constitutional Framers, hence the explicit grant to Congress of the power to define and punish piracies, felonies on the high seas, and offenses against the law of nations.[20] Congress has made it a federal crime to commit piracy as defined by international law and has prescribed punishment for offenses committed at sea, as on U.S. vessels, and more recently in the air, as on U.S. airplanes.[21]

The power to define and punish offenses against the law of nations has been little used, and its purport has not been wholly clear.[22] In the past, in general, traditional international law imposed duties upon states only, not upon individuals, and it was not obvious how an individual could commit an offense against the law of nations.[23] Presumably, however, the clause would support laws that would provide punishment of

---

* But limitations inherent in individual rights are not without significance, even in time of war. See n. 36 to Ch. IX.

** I address these in Ch. IV.

U.S. officials for acts or omissions that constitute violations of international law by the United States, e.g., when they deny fundamental 'justice' to an alien, arrest a diplomat, violate an embassy, fail to carry out a treaty obligation (as under human rights covenants or conventions to which the United States is party), or violate the growing customary law of international human rights.[24] The clause would also authorize Congress to enact into U.S. law any international rules designed to govern individual behavior, for example, the humanitarian laws of war relating to the treatment of prisoners of war.[25] Today, when international law or a treaty of the United States may apply directly to acts by individuals,[26] Congress could implement that law by providing for punishment under this clause, as, for example, pursuant to the Genocide Convention or the Convention against Torture.*

But Congress apparently, and the Supreme Court explicitly, gave the clause a broader meaning. In upholding a statute that made it a crime to counterfeit foreign currency, for example, the Supreme Court said:

A right secured by the law of nations to a nation, or its people, is one the United States as the representatives of this nation are bound to protect. Consequently, a law which is necessary and proper to afford this protection is one that Congress may enact, because it is one that is needed to carry into execution a power conferred by the Constitution on the Government of the United States exclusively . . .

This statute defines the offence, and if the thing made punishable is one which the United States are by their international obligations to use due diligence to prevent, it is an offence against the law of nations.[27]

It is perhaps under such an interpretation of the 'Offences clause' that Congress long ago made it a crime to harass diplomats, to impersonate them, to damage the property of foreign governments, or to initiate activities directed against the peace and security of foreign nations.[28]

---

* But it could also do so amply under other powers discussed below, e.g., under its power to implement treaties, or its Foreign Affairs Power, this chapter, p. 70.

The 'Offences clause' presumably contemplated legislation rendering such offenses violations of the laws of the United States and punishable as such. The power to make such offenses international crimes punishable under international authority is discussed in Ch. VIII, p. 268. Congress has also given jurisdiction to the federal courts to afford civil remedies to aliens for torts in violation of the law of nations, and to any victim under the Torture Victims Protection Act. That legislation has been interpreted by some as not only providing a federal forum for adjudicating such claims under international law, or under state law, but also as creating a federal tort, in exercise of Congressional power under the 'define offences' clause. See nn. 20, 23, 44 to this chapter.

That power, then, would enable Congress to enforce by criminal penalties any new international obligations the United States might accept, say that U.S. companies shall abide by a new international regime for the sea.*

Powers Deriving from National Sovereignty

Whether under Sutherland's theory in *Curtiss-Wright*, or the narrower implications of the *Chinese Exclusion Case*,** Congress derives additional legislative authority from the powers of the United States inherent in its sovereignty and nationhood;[29] the same (or a similar power) has been invoked as a 'power of Congress to deal with foreign relations'.[30]

The Foreign Affairs Power

It is this 'Foreign Affairs Power', presumably, that supports legislation regulating and protecting foreign diplomatic activities in the United States,[31] providing for cooperation with foreign governments, e.g., by giving facilities to foreign consuls;[32] or imposing restrictions on foreign governments, e.g., by freezing their assets, or forbidding those in default to sell bonds in the United States.[33] Probably under this power, Congress enacted the Foreign Sovereign Immunities Act, and modified the judicial Act of State doctrine to require courts in some circumstances to deny effect to acts of foreign governments.[34] Although other powers have been suggested,† the Foreign Affairs Power might best support Congressional assertions of U.S. national sovereignty in territory or in air-space, and special authority in special zones at sea.[35] It is presumably under this power that Congress has authorized or approved international agreements on matters that may not be within its enumerated powers.[36]

The Foreign Affairs Power also supports the network of immigration laws regulating the entry, sojourn, and departure of aliens,[37] and, in the past, laws requiring aliens residing in the United States to register.[38] The Supreme Court has not expressly held so, but presumably this power supports other regulations of aliens, and laws giving them equality, advantage or disadvantage in comparison with citizens.[39]

---

* Again, Congress could also implement such undertakings under other powers considered below.

** See Ch. I, p. 16.

† For example, that the power to acquire territory is implied in the expressed power to govern territory; see n. 53 to this chapter.

The Foreign Affairs Power reaches also conduct of U.S. citizens that affects foreign relations. It is presumably that power that at one time justified a statute depriving a woman of her U.S. citizenship if she married an alien,[40] or a law withdrawing U.S. citizenship from one who voted in a foreign election.[41] It apparently permits Congress to provide for extradition to a foreign country of a person in the United States, even when no treaty requires it.[42]

It is probably the Foreign Affairs Power also that is involved in various statutes governing the conduct of U.S. nationals abroad. Nothing in the Constitution prevents Congress from exercising its powers outside the United States, and, under the applicable enumerated powers, Congress can tax the income of a U.S. citizen living abroad, or require him to return for military service, or to testify before a U.S. court.[43] But Congress has also regulated abroad actions that it could not regulate in the United States because they are not within any enumerated powers and are therefore reserved to the states. For example, Congress established an extensive criminal code, to be enforced by court-martial, for dependents of U.S. service personnel and for civilian employees of the military forces living abroad. The Supreme Court struck down the provisions subjecting such civilians to court martial because such provision denied the accused a jury trial and other constitutional safeguards,[44] but it has been commonly assumed, and the Supreme Court intimated, that Congress could have such persons returned for trial in civilian courts in the United States.[45] Yet the power to punish, say, homicide committed by a U.S. citizen abroad is not within any enumerated power of Congress; the most plausible basis on which Congress might reach that conduct is the Foreign Affairs Power, on the theory that the right to regulate the conduct of nationals abroad is inherent in sovereignty, or that such conduct implicates or might affect U.S. foreign relations.[46]

No one knows the reaches of the Foreign Affairs Power of Congress. In a bold (perhaps too-bold) article, I wrote with confidence* that the Foreign Affairs Power would support legislation on any matter so related to foreign affairs that the United States might deal with it by treaty:[47] the rights in the United States of foreign governments and their officials, diplomats and consuls; the rights of foreign nationals in commerce, friendship and navigation in the United States; extradition;

* Less confidently, I argued that, just as the Commerce Power reaches all, no matter how local, that is or affects interstate or foreign commerce, perhaps the Foreign Affairs Power reaches any matter, no matter how domestic, which in our interdependent world affects our foreign relations, including our 'image' and influence abroad, even, say, race, or poverty, or the alienation of youth.

taxation and trade rights of U.S. nationals abroad; the status of U.S. military forces stationed in friendly countries and of foreign forces in the United States; and a host of reciprocal rights, or rights conditioned on reciprocity.[48]

In *Missouri* v. *Holland,* Justice Holmes said: 'It is obvious that there may be matters of the sharpest exigency for the national well being that an act of Congress could not deal with but that a treaty followed by such an act could. . . .'[49] But Holmes wrote more than 70 years ago, before the explosion of Congressional powers. Today, there is surely no warrant for confident assertion that there is any matter relating to foreign affairs that is not subject to legislation by Congress.

General Congressional Powers

The vast legislative powers of Congress that relate particularly to foreign affairs do not begin to exhaust its authority to make law affecting foreign relations. Congress has general powers that, taken together, enable it to reach virtually where it will in foreign as in domestic affairs,* subject only to constitutional prohibitions protecting individual rights.**

'To lay . . . Taxes . . . to provide . . . for the general Welfare'

The power to tax (Art. I, sec. 8, cl. 1) has long been held to permit Congress to regulate through taxation, and could be used to control, say, foreign travel, as it has gambling or narcotics.[50] The power to tax is linked in the same clause to the power 'to provide for the common Defence and the general Welfare of the United States', commonly known as the 'Spending Power'. Major programs, domestic and foreign, depend wholly on this Spending Power, and it has been used in our day for many billions of dollars in foreign aid.[51]

Other general powers also have their international uses: Congress has authorized a network of international agreements under its postal power (Art. I, sec. 8, cl. 7), and there are international dimensions to the regulation of patents and copyrights.[52] The express power to govern territory (Art. IV, sec. 3) may imply authority to acquire territory, and Congress determines whether territory acquired shall or shall not be incorporated into the United States, giving us the different histories of The Philippines, Hawaii, Guam, and the continuing drama of Puerto Rico.[53]

---

* Subject to what may come of *Lopez,* p. 65 and n. 8 to this chapter.
** The protection of individual rights in foreign affairs is discussed in Ch. IX.

Congress can exercise 'exclusive Legislation' in the nation's capital, its diplomatic headquarters (Art. I, sec. 8, cl. 17). The power to acquire and dispose of property was used for lend-lease during the Second World War and since then has supported multi-varied arms programs and sales or gifts of nuclear reactors or fissionable materials.[54] The passing assertion in the Constitution that the President can make appointments to offices 'which shall be established by Law' (Art. II, sec. 2, cl. 2) gives Congress the power to create and control the Executive bureaucracy, including the foreign service establishment, and the independent agencies, including several with major significance for international relations.* By implication in the Constitution's grant of maritime jurisdiction to the federal judiciary (Art. III, sec. 2), Congress can legislate maritime law,[55] and it can doubtless extend that law in, under, or above the seas, a power that has had new importance as the seas became increasingly hospitable to human activity. The authority in the Thirteenth Amendment to implement the abolition of slavery enables legislation cooperating in international suppression of slavery and the slave trade. The Fourteenth Amendment enables Congress to maintain the equal protection of the laws and the due process of law required of the States, and supports laws that have given to aliens in the United States basic rights that more than satisfy what international law requires and other nations ask of the United States.[56]

'Laws which shall be necessary and proper'

The final clause of Article I, section 8, gives Congress the power 'To make all Laws which shall be necessary and proper for carrying into Execution the foregoing Powers, and all other Powers vested by this Constitution in the Government of the United States, or in any Department or Officer thereof'.

Through most of our history, and in most respects, the courts have interpreted that clause in the light of John Marshall's celebrated dictum: 'Let the end be legitimate, let it be within the scope of the Constitution, and all means which are appropriate, which are plainly adapted to that end, which are not prohibited but consist with the letter and spirit of the constitution, are constitutional'.[57]

The 'necessary and proper' clause has loomed large in Congressional authority, justifying varied, imaginative initiatives for carrying out the many powers of Congress, whether enumerated or 'inherent'.[58] For the conduct of foreign relations, the clause has additional significance since

* See Ch. IV, pp. 121, 128.

it empowers Congress to carry out not only its own powers but also all those vested in 'the Government of the United States, or in any Department or Officer thereof'. In that clause, Justice Holmes found the basis for his landmark opinion in *Missouri* v. *Holland* upholding a statute implementing a treaty, legislation that, it was assumed, Congress could not have enacted in the absence of treaty.[59] Laws for carrying into execution the President's powers might include also those that support the President's foreign affairs establishment, that punish interference with his freedom of action (as by the old Logan Act forbidding 'private diplomacy'), that protect foreign diplomacy in the United States.* Indeed, one can readily build a plenary power of Congress to enact laws in regard to foreign affairs as necessary and proper to carry into execution the President's 'plenary powers' to conduct foreign affairs.**

One necessary and proper power of Congress, as important as any for the conduct of foreign relations, is that implied in the provision that 'No Money shall be drawn from the Treasury, but in Consequence of Appropriations made by Law'. (Art. I, sec. 9, cl. 7.) As we shall see,† Congress ordinarily feels legally, politically, or morally obligated to appropriate funds to maintain the President's foreign affairs establishment and to implement his treaties and other foreign undertakings. But Congress can readily, and properly, refuse to appropriate money to pay for what the President has done or wishes to do when it thinks the President has exceeded his powers. Even when the President seeks appropriations for activities clearly within his powers, Congress decides the degree and detail of its support: it determines ultimately the State Department's budget, how much money the President shall have to spend on the armed forces under his command, how much he can contribute to United Nations programs.‡ Since the President comes to Congress for money for innumerable purposes, domestic and foreign, Congress and Congressional committees can use appropriations and the appropriations process to bargain also about other elements of

---

* See nn. 28 and 31 to this chapter.

** Some might argue that when Congress acts to carry out the President's powers it ought not to be able to enact legislation he does not approve of, for example by overriding his veto. Congress might reply that it acts in support of the power of the Presidency not of a particular President, and that the views of the present incumbent are not controlling.

† See Ch. IV, p. 112, Ch. VII, p. 204. Congress is not bound by the President's views of his own powers, unless the courts have confirmed that what the President has done is constitutional. See Ch. V.

‡ For distinctions between voluntary and obligatory contributions to international organizations, see Ch. VIII, p 254.

Presidential policy in foreign affairs. Because the President usually cannot afford to veto appropriations acts, they are favorite vehicles for conditions and other 'riders' imposed on unwilling Presidents.*

NON-LEGISLATIVE POWERS OF CONGRESS

Congress can mold if not determine the foreign policy of the United States through its vast legislative powers, including the 'quasi-legislative' powers to spend and appropriate funds. In addition, the Constitution leaves to Congress the most momentous non-legislative decision in foreign policy, the power to declare war.[60]

To Declare War

For the Framers, surely, war or peace was the paramount decision in foreign policy.[61] Traditionally, war terminated relations and abrogated or suspended treaty obligations and the bulk of rights and duties between belligerents under international law.** Traditionally, war also altered relations between belligerents with all other nations, often modifying their treaties, and imposing on them the choice of neutrality or belligerency, and the consequences of that choice.[62] The United Nations Charter (1945) was designed to outlaw war and to transform, if not eliminate, the traditional law of war; it has not importantly affected war powers under the U.S. Constitution.† Constitutionally, war suspends some provisions and gives others a different cast,[63] and, we have seen, provides Congress (and the President) with a formidable arsenal of powers to mobilize the lives and other resources of the country for war.

The Founders considered the power to declare war too important to entrust to the President, or even to him and the Senate; they gave it to

---

* Presidents had sought, but failed to obtain a 'line item veto', the right to veto one item without vetoing the whole enactment. Congress finally gave the President a limited line-item veto, effective in 1997. See p. 119, note.

** For the effect of war on treaties, see n. 141 to Ch. VII. But war brings into play the international laws of war and humanitarian laws. See Ch. VIII.

† As a matter of constitutional law, Congress can decide for war even in violation of the U.N. Charter. See n. 64 to this chapter; Ch. VIII, p. 258. For the suggestion that the President can take the United States into war (without Congressional authorization) pursuant to a resolution of the U.N. Security Council, see Ch. VIII, p. 256.

Congress (or left it there, as under the Articles of Confederation).* The Constitution gave Congress the power to decide the ultimate question, whether the nation shall or shall not go to war.⁶⁴ It is true that the five declarations of war by Congress were requested by Presidents and that no such request has been denied; it is true that Presidents can pursue policies and conduct foreign relations in ways that might lead to war; it is true that the hand of Congress may be forced, or a declaration of war become academic, if the United States were attacked.** Nonetheless, the constitutional power to decide whether to go to war lies with Congress. There have been suggestions that the power of Congress was intended to be a formal power to declare a formal war, but that the President can fight a war on his own authority without 'declaring' it.† That view is without foundation. Others—some critics during the Vietnam War and some during the Persian Gulf Crisis of 1990–91—expressed the view that Congress can decide for war only by formal declaration; there is no foundation for that view either. Congress can decide, and has decided, for war, formally or informally, expressly or by implication, in advance or by subsequent ratification, by legislation or resolution, even merely by appropriating funds for the conduct of war. The Supreme Court recognized undeclared war against France in 1800, as well as our undeclared Civil War. Congress has on numerous occasions asserted the power to authorize the use of force by resolution rather than by declaration.⁶⁵

The power 'of determining on peace and war' surely implies also a corollary power to decide that war should end. Ordinarily, wars are ended by treaty, but Congress declared an end to both World Wars by resolution.⁶⁶ Congress can decide when war should end by imposing a time limit on its duration when it authorizes war, or by defining the purposes of the war in terms that imply that it shall end when those purposes are achieved. Congress in effect ordered an end to the Vietnam War by denying appropriations for continuing it.

To Make Other Foreign Policy

That Congress was expressly given the powers of war and peace, power to regulate commerce-intercourse with foreign nations, and other large

* Under the Articles of Confederation, Art. IX, Congress had 'the sole and exclusive right and power of determining on peace and war'. That statement of plenary and exclusive power was not designed to preclude Presidential power—there was no Presidency—but to deny war powers to individual states.

** Discussed in Ch. IV.   † See Ch. II, p. 47, Ch. IV, p. 99.

legislative powers pertaining to or affecting foreign affairs, early led to claims that Congress had all the powers of the nation in foreign relations other than those explicitly conferred on the President (alone or with the Senate). Congress, not the President, it was said, or at least Congress as well as the President, can determine 'the condition of the nation',[67] the grand designs of its foreign policy as well as the attitudes that shape day-to-day relations with other nations.

Especially in earlier times, Congress in fact declared national policy other than by legislation or declaration of war. In 1794, and on several occasions thereafter, Congress proclaimed the neutrality of the United States in regard to the wars of others.[68] In 1798, Congress resolved 'that the United States are of right freed and exonerated from the stipulations' of treaties with France, and on other occasions it directed the President to terminate treaties.* In the nineteenth century, one or both Houses pretended to some part in recognizing the independence of several Latin American republics, and Congress did in effect recognize the independence of Cuba in 1898.[69] After treaties to that effect had been negotiated but not ratified, Congress resolved to annex Texas, and later Hawaii.[70] Congress issued directives to Presidents and instructions to delegates to international conferences; and in numerous cases it sought to control or influence foreign relations by 'riders' and other conditions.** Congress has authorized or approved international agreements on matters not within its enumerated powers.† In one famous instance, in 1864, the House of Representatives resolved sweepingly:

Congress has a Constitutional right to an authoritative voice in declaring and prescribing the foreign policy of the United States, as well in the recognition of new Powers as in other matters; and it is the Constitutional duty of the executive department to respect that policy, not less in diplomatic negotiations than in the use of national forces when authorized by law; and the propriety of any declaration of foreign policy by Congress is sufficiently proved by the vote which pronounces it.[71]

The best known, farthest reaching argument for a plenary Congressional power is probably that made by 'Helvidius' (Madison) in his challenge to 'Pacificus' (Hamilton) who had supported President Washington's power to proclaim neutrality in the war between France and Great Britain.[72] Basically, with variations, the argument is that

---

* 1 Stat. 578 (1798). The power to terminate a treaty internationally is to be distinguished from the power of Congress by legislation to make law for the United States in disregard of existing treaty obligations. See Ch. VII.

** See Ch. IV, p. 119. † See Ch. VII, p. 216.

Congress is the principal organ of government and has all its political authority, in foreign affairs as elsewhere, except where (and to the extent that) the Constitution explicitly granted authority to the President (alone or with the Senate). The determination of foreign policy and the control of foreign relations lay with Congress under the Articles of Confederation and, with particularized exceptions, the Constitution left them there. The powers of Congress are not limited to domestic 'law-making', narrowly conceived: witness, the Constitution gives Congress the most important foreign affairs power, the power to declare war, which can effectively terminate all relations with the enemy and modify relations with other nations. That power surely includes the power to decide not to go to war, as by a proclamation of neutrality; it must include also the power to determine national policy generally, for these might determine war or peace.

Adding to Madison's arguments, one might note too that (even war apart) the enumerated powers of Congress are not in fact limited to domestic law-making. Congressional regulations of foreign commerce are not exclusively domestic laws;* and Congress can authorize or approve international agreements that are not legislative in character.** Is it not significant also that the power to consent to wars or compacts between a state and a foreign government was given to Congress, not to the President?† Building on Sutherland, one might add that the powers of the United States inherent in its sovereignty—which include the authority to make foreign policy—properly reside in Congress, the principal repository of the sovereign power;[73] indeed, when the Court invoked the sovereignty of the United States it was usually to support an act of Congress.‡ In sum, the argument concludes, in foreign affairs as elsewhere, the President is only the executive agent of Congress:

* The powers to spend, to borrow money, to support an army and navy are also not plainly 'legislative' in character.

** See Ch. VII, p. 216.

† 'No State shall, without the Consent of Congress, lay any Duty of Tonnage, keep Troops, or Ships of War in time of Peace, enter into any Agreement or Compact with another State, or with a foreign Power, or engage in War, unless actually invaded, or in such imminent Danger as will not admit of delay.' Art. I, sec. 10, cl. 3.

‡ See p. 70 above. In what is perhaps dictum, however, the Supreme Court found in sovereignty also Executive power to exclude aliens, n. 32 to Ch. II

The implication of popular sovereignty—'We the people'—might also be invoked to support Congressional authority since Congress appears to be the more representative body, elected directly, whereas the President is chosen by unrepresentative 'electors'. See Art. II, sec. 1.

Congress makes foreign policy and the President conducts foreign relations in the light of that policy. At least, Congress has concurrent power to 'resolve' foreign policy, and its power is superior and should control inconsistent Presidential action.

The merits of arguments for 'plenary' Congressional authority in foreign affairs—including powers claimed by the President as within his 'executive Power' or as 'sole organ'—are debatable and continue to be debated.[74] That Congress is the principal repository of the external sovereignty of the United States is not obvious and would surely be denied by Presidents;* surely, they would deny that any national sovereignty Congress might represent includes full authority over foreign relations. The grant to Congress of power to decide for war gives it respectable claim to related authority, say to end war, or determine the status of territory gained in war; perhaps, too, to decide to stay out of the wars of others and proclaim national neutrality; arguably, Congress can also regulate Presidential foreign policy or his conduct of foreign relations insofar as they plausibly threaten to lead to war. But, as a matter of constitutional construction, control of war and peace will not (*pace* James Madison) obviously reach to give Congress blanket authority 'to make foreign policy'. The fact is that, increasingly, the large part of foreign policy is less than intimately related to 'war and peace'.** Fortunately, war has not been common in the life of the United States, and foreign policy has not often brought us close to war, or tempted Congress to legislate in order to reduce the likelihood of war. In theory, the power to declare war can give Congress great influence even when it is not exercised, but one cannot say that Congress has importantly shaped the foreign policy of the United States through the unexercised 'uses' of the war power.

In the end, the theoretical arguments for Congressional primacy, or at least for concurrent authority in Congress, are not less persuasive than those for the President, but in our history Congressional claims have often collided with and recoiled before the President's claims to paramount if not exclusive authority.† The President prevailed in part

---

* Compare Richard Nixon's declaration of Presidential sovereignty, Ch. II, p. 34 note.

** Even the common invocations of 'national security' during and after the Cold War were often rhetorical.

† Congress did win, early, the battle of neutrality proclamations, and since President Washington's day neutrality has been determined by Congress—perhaps because proclamation of neutrality is in substantial measure a decision not to go to war, perhaps, too, because neutrality was addressed also to U.S. citizens and

because, in the nineteenth century surely, U.S. foreign policy did not readily court war and its relation to war became increasingly hypothetical; even more, because foreign policy depended effectively on communication and commitment, expressed or tacit, to other nations, and the President was effectively 'the sole organ' of the United States, whereas Congress, vis-à-vis other nations, long remained effectively 'deaf and dumb'.[75] Congress itself effectively reduced its claims, and early precedents for Congressional authority to make policy other than by legislation have been limited or abandoned and explained away.[76] Resolutions of policy are indeed adopted by one or both Houses of Congress but usually they are only 'sense resolutions' (discussed below) not purporting to establish or declare the policy of the United States or to direct or control the President. No doubt, wider claims will again be made and power might be effectively redistributed, but at the end of the twentieth century Congress can assert with confidence, in addition to its spending and law-making powers, only the power to go to war and the rimlands of that power.[77]

Especially with the changing character of war, the allocation to Congress of the power to decide for war while foreign relations are conducted largely by the President has led to competition for power and has engendered doubts about the viability and wisdom of the constitutional distribution.*

LIMITATIONS ON CONGRESSIONAL POWER

Like the powers of the President, like domestic powers of Congress, Congressional authority related to foreign affairs is, of course, limited by the Bill of Rights. Congressional powers are subject also to limitations on Congressional power expressed in the Constitution, some of which have relevance to foreign affairs: for example, Congress may not impose a tax or duty on articles exported from any state, or give a preference to the ports of one state over those of another.[78] Limitations on Congressional power are implied in grants of power to the President, to the courts, some even in powers reserved to the states.

The principal limitations on Congress are those implied in Presidential power and in the principle of separation of powers. But the changed

---

depended directly on legislation to make it effective. The power of Congress to resolve an end to war can also be accepted as a necessary implication of its authority over 'war and peace'.

* See Ch. IV.

character of U.S. foreign relations has enhanced the powers of both President and Congress; it has not made them independent of each other, nor has it made it easier to separate their powers or determine their respective limits.

THE POLITICAL INFLUENCE OF CONGRESS

Assuming that Congress has little power in that narrowing area that does not involve legislation, or spending, or the implications of its war powers, it can nonetheless exercise tremendous influence even on such policy: by non-legislative riders to legislation or appropriations, by 'sense resolutions', by the formal and informal actions of Congressional committees, by the interventions and expostulations of individual members of Congress. For Presidents need Congress, have to get along with it, must take its views into account; and individual members of Congress often reflect public opinion and can create opinion for or against Presidential policies.

Since the President is the *sole* organ of communication with foreign governments, Congressional resolutions directly addressed to foreign governments are technically objectionable: once, President Grant even vetoed a resolution by Congress saying thanks to foreign governments for their congratulations upon our First Centennial as a nation![79] But resolutions by one or both Houses of Congress expressing the 'sense' of the Congress about some international matter, or calling on the President to do something, have long been with us, and Presidents cannot lightly disregard them.[80] They are particularly significant when they reflect national public opinion, or when they imply that Congress might support its 'sense' by adopting or refusing actions or appropriations that are indisputably within its powers. Presidents and Secretaries of State have had to tell other governments that even members of Congress have freedom of speech, but that singly, or even together in non-legislative resolutions, they do not speak for the United States nor are their statements of any legal effect: Secretary Seward disowned a House Resolution attacking French activities in Mexico during our Civil War;[81] Secretary Dulles disowned an address by Senator John F. Kennedy promoting Algerian independence.[82] On the other hand, the President has been known to encourage, even inspire, sense resolutions in order to strengthen his position vis-à-vis other nations, claiming that he must take account of the views of Congress and of public opinion which Congress reflects.

The power of Congress to investigate and to conduct hearings is implied in its power to legislate and should be related to that function, but there is no way of keeping Congress close to its legislative last, and Congress can investigate virtually any subject to determine whether legislation *might* be desirable or even whether it is permissible.[83] In any event, whether in connection with particular legislation, appropriations, appointments, or under undefined and undifferentiated investigative power, Congressional committees and individual members of Congress have opportunities to inquire, cross-examine, expose, criticize, even harass and threaten executive officials engaged in the conduct of foreign policy, and the need to justify to members of Congress is a not insignificant influence on Executive policy.

Informal, extra-constitutional powers also give Congress—or some members of Congress—important influence. The heads of important committees, party leaders, other influential legislators, are not to be ignored, and, especially if their support should later be needed for formal action, the Executive will inform and consult them.[84] Members of Congress engage in making foreign policy when they are appointed to delegations to international conferences.* In our times, ready travel, instant international communication and foreign 'monitoring' of our Congressional processes bring Congressional voices into foreign offices and to foreign homes. Spending programs give members of Congress official reasons for investigation around the world, and neither foreign officials nor U.S. diplomats will deny them access or refuse to talk with them.

The legal and political influence of Congress in the conduct of foreign affairs is sometimes met with Executive compliance, at other times, with resistance. The result, of course, is hardly to prevent conflict or assure cooperation, the subject of the following chapter.

---

* The practice no longer raises constitutional questions under Art. 1, sec. 6, cl. 2.

Chapter IV

SEPARATION OF POWERS: COMPETITION, CONFLICT, AND COOPERATION

Both the President and Congress command vast powers in foreign affairs, but the distribution of constitutional authority between them, even as originally conceived, surely as now realized, is not what it is in domestic affairs. The classic separation of executive from legislative functions obtains in some measure in foreign affairs as well, but we have seen also a division of the power to 'legislate' foreign policy between the two political branches, and some concurrent authority.* The President makes foreign policy by his conduct of foreign relations generally; by international acts as 'sole organ' or as Commander in Chief (including some deployments of U.S. forces); by concluding international agreements; by asserting rights for the United States or responding to claims by others against the United States; by proclaiming 'doctrines' that announce national intentions; by occasional domestic regulation; in a few circumstances even by direction to the courts.** Congress makes foreign policy by regulating foreign commerce and intercourse, and by other legislation that impinges on U.S. foreign relations; by spending for the common defense and by some of its spending for the general welfare; by declaring and making war; by adopting statutes or resolutions† (such as the War Powers Resolution) defining Executive authority; by authorizing or approving executive agreements. In a sense, there is also a division of executive function: the President carries out the foreign policy that he makes as well as that made by Congress, but Congress 'executes' the President's policies, too, by enacting legislation to implement treaties and by appropriating funds to pay for Executive programs and activities.

* I deal here with conflict and cooperation between Congress and the President. Conflict and cooperation between Congress and 'the Treaty-makers', and the relation of Congress to executive agreements are discussed in Ch. VII.
** See Ch. II.
† Both joint resolutions and statutes have legislative character and effect as law.

The respective powers of President and Congress are established in the large, but the division I have described has not been accepted in all respects by all Presidents and all Congresses (or all members of Congress) at all times; in any event, the generalizations leave ample areas of uncertainty. In principle as in fact, recurrent competition for power has punctuated relations between President and Congress, raising the dominant, least tractable constitutional issues of U.S. foreign relations. That the Constitution is especially inarticulate in allocating foreign affairs powers; that a particular power can with equal logic and fair constitutional reading be claimed for the President or for Congress; that the powers of both President and Congress have been described in full, even extravagant adjectives ('vast', 'plenary'); that instead of a 'natural' separation of 'executive' from 'legislative' functions there has grown an irregular, uncertain division of each—all have served and nurtured political forces inviting struggle. Recurrent disputes have resulted in particular from the separation of power to conduct foreign relations and make foreign policy generally, which the President has acquired, from the power to decide for war or peace, lodged in Congress.* Conflict has been compounded also by the blurry bounds of 'Executive power' and the uncertain reach of the authority of the Commander in Chief, in war or in peace. Since, generally, these 'boundary disputes' between Congress and the President have not been resolved in court,[1] they remain unresolved in principle; if the President has succeeded in winning most of them in fact, Congressional 'irredentism' runs deep and erupts in almost every Congressional generation, and Congress has powerful weapons—the power to enact laws and to regulate, its control of the Executive bureaucracy, the 'power of the purse', political clout.**

Practice—and sometimes even constitutional doctrine—have been shaped by personal, or partisan, relations between particular Presidents and particular Congresses (or particular members of Congress), sometimes, too, by passions generated by particular issues. Lincoln and both

---

* Shades of Clausewitz! '[W]ar is not merely a political act, but also a real political instrument, a continuation of political commerce, a carrying out of the same by other means'. 1 CARL VON CLAUSEWITZ, ON WAR (1832) Bk. 1, Ch. 1, § 24, at 23 (8th Rev. edn. 1966). Compare John Quincy Adams, n. 43 to this chapter.

** For decades after the Second World War, and especially during the Cold War, it was often said that party politics 'stops at the waters' edge' and do not trouble U.S. foreign relations. That was only more or less the case, and was sometimes rhetoric not principle, aspiration not fact. Even in foreign policy, the respective powers of Congress and the President have been exercised differently when the two branches are controlled by the same political party or by opposing parties.

Roosevelts effectively took power from fearful, or friendly, or careless Congresses. In the 1970s, national malaise caused by the Vietnam War bestirred an unhappy Congress, and the 'Watergate' scandal weakened the Presidency and emboldened Congress to reclaim and assert authority. As a result, Congress confronted and challenged the Presidency by enacting the War Powers Resolution to prohibit, discourage or contain Presidential war-making, but Presidents have challenged its constitutionality and have sometimes flouted its restrictions.[2] Later, Congress forbade the use of appropriated funds to aid the 'Contras' in Nicaragua, but the Executive branch violated the restrictions, leading to the 'Iran–Contra' scandal.[3] Congress enacted laws providing that there shall be no foreign assistance or arms sales to countries guilty of consistent patterns of gross violations of internationally recognized human rights, but Presidents have taken less than scrupulous care that these laws be faithfully executed; when Congress also provided Presidents some 'escape' clauses, it did not respond firmly when the Executive branch exploited or abused them.[4]

The division in the Constitution of a seemingly indivisible process requires peaceful co-existence if not active cooperation between the political branches, and in innumerable ways every day the conduct of foreign relations reflects and depends upon their combined powers and actions.[5] Routine cooperation, of course, goes unnoticed and raises neither political nor constitutional issues.* But joint operations by substantially independent branches cannot wholly escape conflict; the exceptional prerogatives of the President and the exceptional acquiescence of the Congress in foreign affairs during long periods of our history, followed by resurgent bouts of 'activism', have bred tendencies that engender controversy.[6] The Executive is sometimes carried away by ready opportunity and initiative, by expertise, by responsibility, and by the security of secrecy, to invade where Congress has its claims—for example, when the President 'goes it alone' to the brink of war and beyond, as some think happened in Vietnam in the 1960s, later in Grenada (1983), and Panama (1989), and threatened to do so in the Gulf War (1991), and perhaps in Haiti (1994). Congress, frustrated by separation and secrecy from the means and channels of diplomacy, distrustful of executive assertions of expertise, sensitive to domestic implications or responding to domestic 'pressures', is sometimes tempted

---

* Sometimes there have been complaints of 'excessive cooperation' in the form of undue delegation of authority to the President by Congress. See p. 124 below, this chapter.

to tie the President's constitutional hands.* Sometimes the President claims authority from 'the Constitution and the laws', but Congress rejects his constitutional claims and denies that it had authorized what he had done or would do.

Particular allocations of power have evoked particular resistance. Congress has not been content merely to make domestic laws and to pay the President's bills; it has especially resented Presidential *faits accomplis* committing the United States before the world and compelling Congress to rubber-stamp the President's initiative. Presidents, in turn, have resented control by Congress of their foreign affairs establishment, their dependence on Congress for money and for implementing legislation, and Congressional efforts to exploit that dependence to limit Executive prerogative. There have been claims by each branch that the other has refused cooperation which the Constitution commands, or has actively hampered the exercise of constitutional powers. Presidents have challenged the constitutionality of special, extra-legislative devices developed by Congress to oversee Executive activity, such as the legislative veto.**

EXCLUSIVE AND CONCURRENT AUTHORITY

The Constitution assigns powers to the federal government by allocating powers to one or another branch of that government. In principle, the Framers, in allocating federal powers, separated them, giving some to each of the three branches exclusively.† Exclusivity of authority is

---

* Frequently, controversy between President and Congress is not strictly constitutional. Much Presidential power is his by delegation from Congress and issues arise when members of Congress deny that a Presidential action was within the authority delegated to him, or that a Presidential commitment or expenditure of funds was within the scope of a Congressional appropriation, as, for example, the loan to Mexico to bail out the *peso* (1995). See n. 6 to this chapter. Of course, Congress can clarify the scope of its delegation for the future.

** See pp. 125, 126 below, this chapter.

† In principle, it was accepted, the Constitution did not contemplate 'concurrent authority'. Madison, in his second Helvidius letter (see n. 10 to Ch. II) said: 'The same power cannot belong, in the whole to both departments, or be properly so vested as to operate separately in each. Still more evident is it that the same specific function or act, cannot possibly belong to the two departments and be separately exercisable by each . . . . A concurrent authority in two independent departments, to perform the same function with respect to the same thing, would be awkward in practice, as it is unnatural in theory.'

implied in the structure and the language of the Constitution. Each of the three first articles of the Constitution allocates a major 'category' of governmental powers to a different branch of government. 'All legislative Powers herein granted shall be vested in a Congress' (Article I). 'The executive Power shall be vested in a President' (Article II). 'The judicial Power of the United States, shall be vested in one supreme Court and in such inferior Courts . . .' (Article III). The exclusivity of allocated powers is implied also in the apparent recognition of certain powers as inherently legislative in character, and therefore within the powers of Congress, others as executive, therefore within the powers of the President. Congress shall have power to *regulate* commerce, a legislative act; the President shall have power to *nominate* ambassadors, an executive act. No legislative act, no act identified as legislative, can be exercised by the President; no executive act, no act identified as executive, can be exercised by Congress. But some acts may be ancillary to either a legislative or an executive power and therefore within the authority of either branch, and some acts may require cooperation of both branches.

Because in domestic affairs the respective powers of President and Congress are allocated explicitly and according to an expressed principle, they are generally recognized as 'exclusive', denied to the other branch.[7] Even with this clear division, issues have arisen as to where some power lies, whether a particular action lies within one of the powers explicitly allocated to Congress or one granted to the President, or whether it is legislative or executive 'in character' and vested accordingly.* In foreign affairs, much of the authority of the federal government is not explicitly allocated to either branch, and even the explicit division of power between President and Congress conforms to no 'natural' separation of executive from legislative powers; nevertheless, the domains of President and Congress are, for the most part, distinct and exclusive (as they are in domestic matters). Congress, we have seen, can determine national foreign policy in respects expressly confided to it by the Constitution or by the plausible penumbra of these explicit grants. Congress can make foreign policy by enacting laws within the legislative powers granted to it, or within the legislative component of national authority inherent in U.S. sovereignty. Thus, Congress can decide to go to war, or end war, or abstain from war and proclaim neutrality, or act to prevent war as by regulating activities that might lead to war. It can

* In the famous *Steel Seizure* case, p. 91 below, a divided court held that President Truman could not seize private steel mills to help settle a labor strike, because such an action was an exercise of legislative power. See also nn. 7, 15 to this chapter.

make foreign policy by taxing and spending for the common defense or the general welfare. It can join the President in making international agreements.

For the constitutional lawyer the principal questions include: What are the inherent limits of particular powers? What limitations upon the powers of one branch are implied in those granted to the other? Are all powers of each branch 'exclusive', or is there some overlapping domain so that a particular action might lie within the authority of either branch? If so, which branch should prevail if their acts conflict?

Exclusive Powers of the President

Even for champions of maximum Congressional authority,* the expressed, unambiguous grants to the President leave no doubt that he—he alone, not Congress—can make treaties, appoint or receive ambassadors, command the armed forces, and take care that the laws be faithfully executed. Since the early years, too, Congress has not seriously doubted that the President is the sole organ of communication with foreign governments: Congress does not speak or receive communications on behalf of the United States, or negotiate with foreign governments, or 'conduct foreign relations'.[8] Congress cannot itself (and cannot direct the President to) recognize foreign states or governments,** or establish or regulate or break relations with them, or terminate treaties, or determine present and future policies or attitudes of the United States, though it may express its 'sense', and can request or exhort the President.

Presidents have also claimed 'war powers', as part of their 'foreign affairs powers', to which they join their authority as Commander in Chief.† And they have insisted that such powers are exclusive, so that Congress may not interfere with or regulate Presidential actions within such powers, and indeed must cooperate to support such actions (as by appropriating funds). Until the 1970s, it was ordinarily not important

* See Ch. III, pp. 77 *et seq.* As Madison did, members of Congress—usually in rhetoric and declamation—sometimes continue to claim that Congress can 'make foreign policy' concurrently with the President, but that view has not prevailed.

Some of the express limitations on Congress in the original Constitution (as distinguished from those in the Bill of Rights and later Amendments), notably those in Art. I, sec. 9, also have relevance for foreign affairs. See n. 78 to Ch. III.

** See, e.g., the 1995 resolution directing the President to move the U.S. Embassy in Israel from Tel Aviv to Jerusalem, footnote on p. 119.

† See Ch. II.

whether such Presidential 'war powers' were 'exclusive'. Formally, at least, Congress was silent, and Presidents could claim authority to act even if Congress had concurrent authority; sometimes they might claim Congressional consent or acquiescence. In 1973, Congress adopted the War Powers Resolution regulating Presidential introduction of armed forces into hostilities, and Presidents have challenged the Resolution as unconstitutional and have resisted it in fact.*

Exclusive Powers of Congress

Broad assertions and extravagant adjectives, some of them supported by careless rhetoric in opinions of the Supreme Court, might leave the impression that the President can exercise virtually all the national political power in foreign affairs, at least concurrently with Congress, so that in foreign affairs no powers of Congress are exclusive. That is not so. In fact, large areas have never been claimed by any President. In principle, it would be difficult for a President to dispute that by vesting in Congress 'all legislative Powers herein granted', and then granting Congress a comprehensive array of specific powers, the Constitution barred the President from exercising the powers specified, even those that relate to, or impinge on, foreign affairs.** Whatever, then, the President might have authority to do by treaty or other international agreement, he cannot unilaterally regulate commerce with foreign nations,[9] or make domestic laws punishing piracy or defining offenses against the law of nations,† or declare war.‡ Similarly, he cannot exercise, even for foreign affairs purposes, the general powers allocated to

---

* I discuss the constitutional ramifications of that controversy below, beginning on p. 105.

** Even theories such as Theodore Roosevelt's that the President can do anything not forbidden by the Constitution or by the laws, Ch. II, p. 35, have not been pressed that far.

Additional limitations on the President's powers are clearly implied: he can make treaties or appoint ambassadors with the consent of the Senate, but not without that consent. But compare Ch. VII, p. 217, and Ch. II, p. 35.

† In the Nuremberg Charter and its counterparts, the President in effect joined to define new offenses against the law of nations, but he did that by international agreement, and he did not purport to make them offenses in the United States punishable as criminal laws in U.S. courts. Compare Ch. VIII, p. 266. See also n. 26 to Ch. III on the implementation of the Genocide Convention and the Convention against Torture.

‡ The relation of the President's powers to those of Congress as regards making war is discussed at p. 97.

Congress:[10] he cannot lay and collect taxes, duties, imports and excises, to pay the debts and provide for the common defense and general welfare of the United States. He cannot, on his own authority, spend money for foreign assistance. He cannot regulate patents or copyrights or the value of money, or establish post offices, or dispose of U.S. territory or property;* he cannot enact necessary and proper laws to carry into execution the powers of Congress or even his own powers, for example, criminal laws to enforce respect for treaty obligations.[11] The limitations imposed in Article 1, section 9, generally addressed to Congress, also contain at least one exclusive grant to Congress: only Congress, by law, can appropriate funds; no President can draw funds from the Treasury—without Congressional appropriation—even to pay his Secretary of State's salary or to build an embassy.[12] Presumably, also, the law-making component of the powers of the United States deriving from its national sovereignty are vested in Congress and generally denied to the President: for example, he cannot enact general immigration laws by executive order.**

Even beyond the established 'hard core' of exclusive Congressional power—legislation, war, spending, and the appropriation of funds—some powers have been authoritatively denied the President though Congress was silent. In 1936, the Supreme Court† held that the President did not have authority to extradite a U.S. citizen when not required to do so by treaty or statute.[13] One might ask whether the later Supreme Court, which gave effect to Executive policy in the immunity cases and upheld various sole executive agreements,[14] would have refused to honor a Presidential agreement providing for extradition, perhaps even a President's decision *ad hoc* to extradite a particular person. Since then the tides of governmental power in general, and of executive power in particular, have again receded, unmistakably if in unknown degree, especially before the rising claims of individual rights and the realities of the bureaucratic process. A contemporary Supreme Court, too, might insist that extradition of a person for criminal trial abroad should be based on national policy, not on the possible caprice of a

---

* As regards the President's power to dispose of United States property by executive agreement, see Ch. VII, p. 219 and n. 164 to this chapter.

** But apparently the President (as well as Congress) can sometimes exclude aliens. See n. 32 to Ch. II.

† By Justice Sutherland, in the same year in which, in *Curtiss-Wright,* he wrote of 'the very delicate, plenary and exclusive powers of the President as the sole organ of the federal government in the field of international relations'. See n. 1 to Ch. II.

'working-level' official of the State Department signing the name of the Secretary of State.

Perhaps the most famous Presidential 'defeat' in the Supreme Court during the second half of the twentieth century occurred in 1952, in *Youngstown Sheet & Tube Co. v. Sawyer,* the *Steel Seizure Case.*[15] President Truman had seized the steel mills in order to compel resolution of a labor dispute and to resume production of steel needed to prosecute the Korean War. The President claimed authority to do so under the 'Executive power' and his authority as Commander in Chief. The Supreme Court ruled that to establish national policy for resolving labor disputes by such means in such circumstances required a legislative act by Congress, and could not be done by the President on his own authority.*

There is also *Kent v. Dulles,* decided in 1958. In that case, the Supreme Court held that Congress had not authorized the Department of State to withhold a citizen's passport (and thereby deny his right to travel) because of his alleged Communist beliefs and associations. The majority of the Court said:[16] 'If that "liberty" is to be regulated, it must be pursuant to the law-making functions of the Congress.'**

Later cases upheld Executive power to limit travel, finding that the President's action had been authorized by Congress;[17] there was no suggestion that the President could impose such limitations on his own constitutional authority.

There are other matters as to which Presidents, without conceding exclusive powers to Congress in principle, have accepted in fact. President Washington proclaimed neutrality on his own authority but later Presidents have in practice conceded to Congress the power to decide to be neutral, as equivalent to a power to decide not to go to war.† Similarly, Presidents have not claimed the power unilaterally to declare peace, as distinguished from an armistice.

In all, then, whatever the President might do by delegation of authority from Congress or by international agreement, only Congress can spend, authorize war, legislate, and regulate generally within the United

* The *Steel Seizure Case* was decided by a narrow majority, and two of the Justices in the majority joined the judgment (and the Court's opinion) on the ground that Congress had in fact addressed the issue and decided against authorizing the President to seize companies. For those Justices, apparently, the case involved not Presidential usurpation of an exclusive Congressional authority but a case of concurrent power; but, when Congress acted, the President could not act contrary to its wishes.

** Citing *Youngstown Sheet & Tube Co. v. Sawyer,* n. 15 to this chapter.

† See Ch. II, p. 47; Ch. III, p. 76. See 'War Powers', p. 97 below.

States, even in matters regarding foreign affairs. The courts will be particularly reluctant to uphold unilateral executive acts that impinge on individual rights.* They might be less unsympathetic to unilateral acts of some urgency that impinge only on economic activities and property rights, particularly of corporations. But the *Steel Seizure* case suggests that even the economic rights of corporations will be protected against unilateral Executive action, at least if it appears that the President was acting contrary to Congressional wishes.** *Ad hoc* 'legislation' by the Executive for particular individuals and circumstances, and 'suggestions' to the courts in particular cases, have also become suspect, and have given way to Congressional regulation, as in the Foreign Sovereign Immunities Act.† Where such *ad hoc* Presidential 'law-making' survives, it may be limited to matters such as diplomatic immunity which directly involves a foreign government and relations with it, and which are particularly the concern of the Executive.

Concurrent Powers

The President and the Congress each have large exclusive powers which each alone can exercise, but there is also clearly some undefined zone of concurrent authority in which each might act, at least when the other has not acted. For the reasons favoring Executive initiative generally, Presidents have successfully asserted authority to act instead of Congress‡ more often than Congress has ventured to act in what is indubitably the President's domain.

* If so, courts might have denied President Wilson power to impose censorship in support of neutrality, unless supported in legislation, Ch. II, p. 48. Presidential decisions to admit cables or electric current (Ch. II, p. 44) might pass as a form of control of communications with the outside world, only indirectly regulating domestic private rights; one might distinguish them also because they affect only economic rights, not personal liberties which rank higher as constitutional values. The Supreme Court has elsewhere built constitutional doctrine distinguishing between economic regulation and intrusions on 'preferred' freedoms. See Ch. IX, p. 289. A lower court denied the President authority to impose restrictions on foreign investment by U.S. nationals. See n. 6 to this chapter.

** See this chapter, p. 90.

† See n. 64 to Ch. II, and the cases in Ch. II, p. 55.

‡ Exactly how much Congressional power Presidents exercise on their own authority cannot readily be determined since they exercise so much by delegation from Congress.

In a large sense, all the legislative power of Congress may be concurrent with the President's Treaty Power, since the President can make a treaty on matters as to which Congress may legislate. See Ch. VII.

The absence of a comprehensive, 'natural' division of political authority in foreign affairs which would indisputably exclude the other political branch has been a strong invitation to compete for power, and to claim at least a concurrent authority. Recurrent cries of 'imperial Presidency' have been countered by voices decrying an 'imperial' or 'activist' Congress. In the competition for power in foreign affairs, the principal issues have resulted from Presidential initiatives invoking one or more of his 'plenary' powers, resisted by Congress citing its 'plenary' powers; but Presidents have also accused Congress of 'trespassing'. Sometimes each has claimed exclusive power, sometimes each claimed the power to act as well as the other; occasionally the branches have acted differently if not inconsistently, and each has sought to prevail.

Concurrent power often begets a race for initiative and the President will usually 'get there first'. When the President acts and Congress is silent, there is often a justifiable presumption that Congress has acquiesced in, even approved, what the President has done; if so, the action can be seen as supported by the constitutional powers of both branches.* A President is less likely to remain silent when Congress acts in what he considers his domain, but his failure to veto Congressional legislation or to protest other Congressional initiatives might also imply acquiescence and mute any objection that Congress lacks constitutional authority.

Cases and precedents offer some guidance. The Supreme Court, we have seen, has recognized the authority of the President to direct the courts in regard to sovereign and diplomatic immunity, and some Justices thought the courts must bow to the Executive also as to Act of State, subjects which are also appropriate for Congressional legislation.** The President, it has been held, can apparently exclude aliens at least in some circumstances, as Congress surely can generally.† Presidents have also 'legislated', as no doubt Congress could, 'at the border', e.g., to admit international cables or electric power. President Truman claimed rights for the United States in the Continental Shelf, and President Reagan in an Exclusive Economic Zone, which Congress could have done, just as it declared fishing rights and national sovereignty over air space.[18] Presidents have abstained but have not conceded in principle that they could not proclaim or implement neutrality in the wars of others. For its part, Congress has not admitted that it could not terminate treaties or direct the President to do so.[19] Concurrence results

---

* Compare the suggestion that when Congress is silent the President always acts by tacit acquiescence of Congress, n. 18 to Ch. II.
  ** See Ch. II, p. 54 and n. 63 to this chapter; also p. 96 below.
  † See n. 32 to Ch. II.

in particular from the President's authority as Commander in Chief, which authority overlaps the explicit power of Congress to make rules for the government and regulation of the land and naval forces. No one, we shall see, can disentangle the war powers of the two branches,[20] including their powers to act towards the enemy, toward neutrals, and towards foreign nationals; there are suggestions that Presidents, like Congress, can determine to end hostilities.[21] The Supreme Court held that Presidential courts in occupied Germany after the Second World War could exercise jurisdiction over a U.S. civilian for whom Congress had in effect provided trial by court-martial.[22]

That there is some concurrent authority is now accepted,* and the zone in which both Congress and the President may act may be larger than has been recognized. What lies within that zone is hardly agreed, and the courts have provided little guidance. Concurrent authority inevitably carries the possibility of conflicting assertions of power, and the constitutional lawyer must consider who prevails as a matter of law. Justice Jackson, in a concurring opinion in 1952, provided a suggestive formula, which has been cited in later opinions of the Court and has become a starting point for constitutional discussion of concurrent powers. Jackson wrote:[23]

1. When the President acts pursuant to an express or implied authorization of Congress, his authority is at its maximum, for it includes all that he possesses in his own right plus all that Congress can delegate . . .
2. When the President acts in absence of either a Congressional grant or denial of authority, he can only rely upon his own independent powers, but there is a zone of twilight in which he and Congress may have concurrent authority, or in which its distribution is uncertain . . .
3. When the President takes measures incompatible with the expressed or implied will of Congress, his power is at its lowest ebb, for then he can rely only upon his own constitutional powers minus any constitutional powers of Congress over the matter . . . .**

---

* Contrary to James Madison, p. 86 note, above.
** Jackson's formula does not address the antecedent, underlying questions: Does the President in a particular case have 'express or implied authorization of Congress?' (clause 1). Under clause 2, which are the President's 'independent powers', and what is their scope? The allocation of which powers is 'uncertain' and must it remain uncertain, or might uncertainty be resolved by the courts or by experience and precedent? Which powers are concurrent, and how does the Constitution resolve conflict between President and Congress in the exercise of such concurrent power? When, in case of conflict, one 'subtracts' the constitutional power of Congress from that of the President (clause 3), how does one perform the

The Jackson formula was written from the President's perspective; a parallel formulation might address the powers of Congress in relation to those of the President, and might be somewhat different.* Jackson suggests that there may be concurrent constitutional authority for President and Congress in a 'twilight zone',** and his third category, where the President takes measures incompatible with the will of Congress, also assumes, I think, that each branch is acting within its constitutional authority, implying an area of overlap of concurrent power.†

Jackson wrote in the *Steel Seizure Case*, which the Court treated as domestic, not as involving foreign affairs.[24] Even in domestic matters, Jackson implies, there is a 'twilight zone' clearly within the constitutional domain of Congress in which the President could also act. In foreign affairs, surely, where the President admittedly has large power, the fact that Congress can act does not, of itself, prove that the President could not; Presidents, we have seen, have acted unilaterally in foreign affairs matters which Congress might undoubtedly have regulated, where Congress had not in fact done so.

Justice Jackson did not tell us, or offer a principle that might help us determine, which powers are concurrent. Nor does the Jackson 'arithmetic' suggest which branch prevails in case of conflict between them.‡ The area of concurrent power seems to involve principally Presidential pretensions where Congressional authority is clear, which might suggest that Congress should usually prevail in case of conflict, no matter which branch acted first.[25] So, surely, the President was considered bound to follow Congressional directives in regard to neutrality or the landing of

---

subtraction, how much Presidential power remains, and what actions does it justify? Jackson's formula also does not address the case in which a President has no authority to act and improperly invades an area of exclusive Congressional power; in that circumstance, the President is usurping Congressional authority and violating the separation of powers.

* The first element in Jackson's formula addresses delegated authority: Congress delegates authority to the President; Presidents do not delegate authority to Congress.

** Where, according to Jackson, the locus of authority as to some matters in the twilight zone is uncertain, resolution of that uncertainty may decide either for exclusive authority for one of the branches or for concurrent authority.

† Jackson's second category may refer to areas where the authority of each branch is uncertain, and may be determined—eventually, by the courts—to be either exclusive or concurrent; Jackson's third category seems to assume that both branches have authority, and addresses how to resolve conflicts of authority.

‡ Or, in Jackson's arithmetic, how much power is left for each branch when the subtraction is completed.

submarine cables.[26] Even where the President's authority is clear and perhaps primary, for purposes of domestic law his acts will bow before Congressional legislation that is within its constitutional authority: the President is bound by, and the courts will give effect to, Congressional legislation modifying the Act of State doctrine, or regulating the extradition of inhabitants of the United States, or the admission of foreign forces, perhaps even sovereign or diplomatic immunities.* The Foreign Sovereign Immunities Act (1976),[27] for example, superseded executive authority and responsibility to determine sovereign immunity, authority which the Supreme Court had recognized. In that instance, the Executive branch desired to shed such responsibility and encouraged Congressional legislation to that end; presumably, however, the Executive has retained control of decisions as to immunity in matters not covered by the statute, a concurrent authority which Congress might (or might not) regulate in future.

Other areas of concurrent authority may yet produce conflict and may require a principle to resolve it. In general, except where the President has primary responsibility—some aspects of diplomatic relations, regulation of the armed forces—Congress should prevail, particularly when Congress acts under its explicit authority to legislate for matters within the United States, or to spend for the general welfare.**

COMPETITION FOR POWER

Beginning in the 1970s, constitutional relations between President and Congress in foreign affairs underwent a change in character, and consequently constitutional issues changed focus. Earlier, Congress had rarely gone its own way in foreign affairs matters, and Presidents, therefore,

---

* For purposes of domestic law, even a treaty can be superseded by a later act of Congress, and a self-executing treaty can effectively repeal an earlier statutory provision, Ch. VII, p. 209. And, perhaps, the immunity cases mean that even when Congress has legislated, the courts should follow the President's instructions, at least *ad hoc*, to dismiss a proceeding which he says would jeopardize relations with the country involved. See, e.g., n. 73 to Ch. II.

** Perhaps there are foreign affairs matters in which neither President nor Congress can claim primary responsibility; if so, perhaps the later in time should prevail, as in the case of conflict between a statute and a treaty.˙See Ch. VII, p. 209. But it would be anomalous that the President, acting wholly on his own authority, should be able to 'repeal' an act of Congress. Compare Ch. VII, p. 228 on conflict between a sole executive agreement and a statute.

rarely took (or contemplated) 'measures incompatible with the expressed or implied will of Congress'.* But Presidents increasingly claimed authority to act when Congress was silent, and indeed claimed to find in such silence Congressional acquiescence in, if not tacit authorization for, Presidential action. In the 1970s, Congress ceased to be acquiescent and Presidents began to claim additional independent authority to act, not rooted in Congressional consent or acquiescence. Indeed, Presidents began to assert constitutional limitations on Congressional power, or, if they admitted concurrent authority in Congress, claimed Presidential supremacy where Congress and President acted inconsistently. In particular, Presidents denied that Congress has constitutional authority to limit or regulate the President's use of the armed forces and his covert intelligence activities.**

War Powers, Exclusive and Concurrent

The most dramatic powers of the federal government are its 'war powers', an undefined category, politically or constitutionally. War powers are divided—unevenly—between President and Congress. Some are exclusive with Congress, some are exclusively the President's. Some may be concurrent. Some may be joint, requiring action by both branches. Others are disputed between them. The division of authority between the President and Congress is the most controversial and intractable issue in the constitutional law of U.S. foreign relations.

The Constitution gives Congress the power to declare war. That, it is accepted, confers on Congress the power to decide for war or peace, and whether to wage total or limited wars; Congress has the power also to legislate, tax, spend, and do all that may be necessary to wage war successfully. The war power of Congress is exclusive.[28] No President has claimed the authority to decide for 'war' on his own authority. Even the accepted exception—that the President has authority to wage war if the U.S. were attacked—can be seen either as requiring no Presidential decision, since war is forced upon the United States by the enemy, or as

---

* Jackson's formulation, p. 94 above.

** Some began to suggest even that Congress cannot act in foreign affairs except in support of Presidential policy, for example, that Congress cannot use its spending power to provide foreign aid other than in conformity to Presidential wishes. Some even suggested that Congress is obligated to appropriate funds for foreign policy purposes as the President ordains. Such Presidential claims have not prevailed and have not received wide support.

based on implicit authorization from Congress to resist attack and wage war in self defense.*

The President, too, has 'war powers' and at least some of them are exclusive. He is Commander in Chief of the armed forces of the United States and has constitutional authority inherent in such command which Congress may not invade.

What is 'war'?

The term 'war', enshrined in the Constitution by the Framers, was at the time a fundamental concept in public international law, and it is not implausible to conclude that for the Framers the power given to Congress to make war referred to war as understood in international law.** But in the intervening centuries, war changed radically in life, in international relations, in law. The United Nations Charter, designed to abolish war, eschewed the term. The Charter outlaws the *use of force* against the political independence or territorial integrity of another state, whether or not in an earlier day such use of force would have been *casus belli* (an act of war or a cause of war).

The status of war in international law at the end of the twentieth century is confused, and the implications of that confusion for U.S. constitutional jurisprudence are less than certain. But it is not implausible to conclude that, however a use of force may be characterized for purposes of international law under the United Nations Charter, its character for constitutional purposes remains what it was: extended hostilities involving large numbers of military personnel are acts of war for constitutional purposes and require Congressional authorization, consent or approval. Even an 'easy' invasion against a weak target, that is (or traditionally would have been) an act of war, requires Congressional consent: President Kennedy's abortive invasion of Cuba at the Bay of Pigs; President Johnson's deployment of troops to the Dominican Republic; President Reagan's invasion of Grenada (1983); President Bush's invasion of Panama (1989). Such military acts appear to be treated by

* See Ch. II, p. 47. The exclusive power of Congress to decide for war or peace is not in doubt. It should not be confused with other issues: whether in a particular case—say, in Vietnam—the President had received authorization from Congress and had conformed to the authority delegated to him; whether a use of force in particular circumstances is 'war' within the meaning of the Constitution and therefore within the exclusive power of Congress; whether the war power of Congress empowers it to regulate hostilities or military deployments 'short of war', and if so whether the power of Congress to address them is also exclusive; whether, if it is a concurrent power, Congress or the President prevails in the event of conflict between them.

** See Ch. III, p. 75.

Presidents (and sometimes even by Congress) as something less than, or other than, war. They have been brief and 'inexpensive', and members of Congress disposed to object or protest did so briefly and without provoking constitutional crisis. But their constitutionality, I am persuaded, depends on Congressional authorization, consent, or ratification.*

As regards what is indisputably 'war', the realities of national life have rendered constitutional issues hypothetical, for it is increasingly difficult to make an authentic case that the President had taken the country into war without Congressional authorization in advance or ratification soon after. Presidents could not use the armed forces for long in substantial operations without Congressional cooperation; surely, any action that could properly be called war depended on Congressional appropriations and other forms of approval, expressed or implied. Presidents who fought these wars—in Korea, in Vietnam, in the Persian Gulf— inevitably sought Congressional approval (and obtained it).

Military deployments and hostilities 'short of war'

That there are accepted zones of exclusive authority for President and Congress respectively has not prevented political controversy and constitutional confusion in 'frontier areas', particularly between the President's conduct of foreign relations, including the deployment or use of force for foreign policy purposes,** and the power of Congress to decide for war. Perhaps because Presidents of both major political parties have repeatedly asserted large power and sometimes commanded Congressional and public support, it has become commonly accepted, usually also by many members of Congress, that the President deploy U.S. forces for foreign policy purposes, even to court or engage in hostilities short of war.

* Even an isolated use of force—a bombing in Libya by President Reagan (in retaliation for a terrorist attack in Germany charged to Libya and apparently aimed at U.S. servicemen); a bombing of intelligence installations in Iraq by President Clinton (in response to an alleged attempt to assassinate former President Bush)— would seem to be an act of war which the President cannot do on his own authority (and which are 'hostilities' for purposes of the War Powers Resolution). Perhaps because such actions require secrecy and surprise, and seeking the formal approval of Congress would be impractical; perhaps because such actions do not ordinarily lead to extended hostilities, Presidents have felt freer to engage in them without seeking Congressional authorization, and Congress is usually presented with a *fait accompli*. Members of Congress might protest, but Congress does not act formally, with the result that Presidents consider Congressional failure to act to be 'acquiescence'. But such 'acquiescence' would seem not to be 'ratification'.
** See Ch. II, p. 48.

During our national history, Presidential deployments of U.S. military forces abroad have differed widely in magnitude and significance and have evoked different Congressional reactions. There were strong objections in 1940 when President Franklin Roosevelt sent troops to Greenland and Iceland in the face of legislation that seemed to forbid it.[29] Following the North Atlantic Treaty, in the extended 'Troops to Europe' debates in 1950–51, Congress considered, and the President resisted, limitations on the number of troops the United States could station in allied countries in time of peace. Members of Congress cited Congressional authority to raise armies and to spend money for the common defense, and saw troops in Europe as intimately related to its powers of war and peace. The President, invoking authority as Commander in Chief and his foreign affairs powers, argued, in effect, that troops were to be stationed abroad, not for making war, but for not making war, i.e., for deterrence, or for general political influence. In the end, the limitations were not formally imposed, and the constitutional issue was not resolved.[30] More recently, however, Congress has adopted *ad hoc* restrictions on Presidential deployments of U.S. forces, as in Somalia (1993).[31]

In sum, however, as a result of opportunity, temptation, and initiative, Presidents have in fact deployed U.S. armed forces beyond U.S. borders hundreds of times* without authorization or subsequent ratification by Congress, and in many of these cases they engaged in 'hostilities' of varying significance, intensity and duration. Members of Congress sometimes demurred, though not for long, but their objections did not lead to formal action by Congress—to legislation, to denial of funds, or to measures of censure against the President. What Presidents did, they justified, and their justifications may have hardened into principle. But what they claimed, what Congress can be said to have acquiesced in, was Presidential deployment of forces for purposes short of war. There was no claim of a Presidential power to go to war;** there was no serious claim of Presidential power to deploy forces when Congress told him not to do so.

---

* Different numbers are cited, depending on the kind and degree of deployment. See n. 45 to Ch. II.

I address later presidential claims that resolutions of the U.N. Security Council recommending or authorizing war—in Korea in 1950, in the Persian Gulf in 1990—empower the President to go to war without authorization by Congress. See Ch. VIII, p. 255.

** Suggestions in a brief filed in a lower court that the President has a concurrent power to go to war on his own authority were summarily rejected by the court. See *Dellums* v. *Bush*, 752 F.Supp 1141 (D.D.C. 1990).

In general, then, no President has disputed that, unless war is thrust upon the United States, Congress alone has the authority to decide that the United States shall go to war.[32] Unfortunately, the line between war and lesser uses of force is often elusive, sometimes illusory, and the use of force for foreign policy purposes can almost imperceptibly become a national commitment to war. Even when he does not use military force, the President can incite other nations or otherwise plunge or stumble this country into war, or force the hand of Congress to declare or to acquiesce and cooperate in war.[33] As a matter of constitutional doctrine, however, one can declare with confidence that a President begins to exceed his authority if he willfully or recklessly moves the nation towards war, and a responsible President, loyal to his constitutional oath, should stop, or seek the authorization of Congress—as, in the end, President Bush did before entering the Gulf War, as President Clinton considered doing when he contemplated incursion into Haiti in 1994.[34] Some might ask, even, that the President seek Congressional approval for policies that might conceivably lead to war,[35] but foreign policy and international relations do not permit infallible prescience or fine judgments, and a President can insist that the 'line' between war and foreign policy by means short of war is the constitutional imperative delimiting his domain from that of Congress.

Did Congress authorize war?—Vietnam.

In substantial measure, I believe, failure to accept political realities and their relevance for constitutional principle confused a major controversy of the twentieth century, the national division over the Vietnam War.[36] In the light of piles of precedent hardening into doctrine, it is difficult to fault on constitutional grounds the Presidents who began to support South Vietnam by various forms of aid short of war.* Even with sad hindsight to show how these early steps were 'inevitably' to lead the United States into war, one cannot make a case that the Presidents usurped Congressional authority, especially since those early measures too, in fact, had the approval of Congress. In time, however, Vietnam—like Korea a decade earlier[37]—became what was surely a war within the meaning of the Constitution, and it was not for the President to wage it on his sole authority. He needed the approval of Congress, and the question—a different question, with different constitutional undertones—was whether he had it. For constitutional purposes it seems indisputable that he did—in the 'Tonkin Gulf Resolution', in repeated Congressional

---

* See Ch. II, p. 48.

appropriations, and in an express declaration by Congress of 'its firm intentions to provide all necessary support for members of the Armed Forces of the United States fighting in Vietnam'.[38]

That, as some later claimed, Congress did not appreciate what it was doing, or that its hand was forced to do it, was constitutionally immaterial. (In other cases, too, Presidents have been charged with forcing the hand of Congress or misleading Congress into declaring or authorizing war.)[39] It would be constitutionally material if, as some claimed, the resolution did not authorize full-scale war, but the President misinterpreted it and exceeded the authority it granted; there is no evidence, however, that Congress (as distinguished from some members of Congress) thought so,[40] and Congress had the power and many opportunities to tell the President so, and did not seize them.* (The Tonkin Gulf Resolution itself expressly reserved the power to withdraw the authorization it granted by concurrent resolution.)[41] Congress also had the power to withhold appropriations, or at least to make them with disclaimer and protest, and to check the President in other ways; and surely Congress could readily and justifiably have done so if it believed he had exceeded the authority granted him. Similarly, that Congress could not muster a majority to terminate or redefine the President's authority;[42] that it could not openly break with the President without jeopardizing major national interests; that it could not discontinue support for the war because it 'could not let the troops down'—these do not indicate that Congress did not authorize or continue to support the war; rather, they show that, and why, Congress did.**

For the constitutional lawyer, as for the citizen, then, it is important to distinguish in these controversies between appeals to the Constitution and complaints against it.[43] As regards Vietnam, the complaint, properly, was not that the President usurped power or that the Constitution gave him 'excessive' power; rather, the proper claim was that the constitutional distribution of authority did not work because, in the end, Congress and the President did not exercise their authority as intended, and the restraints on the President were not effective. Many asked whether, in essential respects, our system for conducting foreign relations was what we wished it to be.

---

* As a matter of constitutional doctrine, Congressional inaction cannot always, or usually, be deemed consent, but in general consent once given remains effective unless it expires or is terminated.

** I deal later with Congressional authority to limit the President's conduct of the war, at p. 103.

Exclusive and concurrent powers during war

Constitutional conflict between President and Congress in time of war was virtually unknown until Vietnam.* In every U.S. war, Congress had either delegated virtually unlimited powers in advance, or later ratified what the President had done, and Congress had not otherwise attempted to limit or regulate the President's conduct of the war; nor were there strong differences between Congress and the President as to when war should end. But issues of Congressional authority over the conduct and duration of war agitated political discourse in the latter part of the Vietnam war. In 1970, when President Nixon sent troops into Cambodia, he claimed that he was not engaging in a new war (requiring new Congressional approval) but pursuing the same war, and acting realistically—as well as literally—within the terms of the original authorization.[44] But members of Congress, unhappy with the spread of the war and fearful of further extensions—and some members indeed desiring to terminate the war—sought to repeal the original Tonkin Gulf Resolution authorizing war in Indochina, and to forbid expenditures for certain purposes and beyond prescribed dates.[45] The President purported to acquiesce in the repeal of the Tonkin Gulf Resolution, claiming that he could continue planned operations under his authority as Commander in Chief, and challenged the right of Congress to control the conduct of war once authorized, whether directly or by imposing conditions on expenditures.

As a matter of constitutional law, in my view, the President was wrong. The power of Congress to declare war is the power to decide for war or peace, and should imply the power to unmake war as well as to make it.[46] In the political context of Vietnam–Cambodia, however, repeal of the Tonkin Gulf Resolution did not in fact constitute (or imply) a Congressional decision to end the war;[47] but a clear resolution to that effect would have bound the President,[48] and he could not properly have insisted on prosecuting the war thereafter.

Less confidently, I believe also that in war the President's powers as Commander in Chief are subject to ultimate Congressional authority to 'make' the war, and that Congress can control the conduct of the war it has authorized. (One might suggest, even, that the President's powers during war are not 'concurrent' but delegated by Congress, by implication in the declaration or authorization of war.)** It would be unthinkable for

* Congress has never declared a war which the President did not wish to fight. See n. 28 to this chapter.
** Compare *Brown* v. *United States*, n. 51 to this chapter, and accompanying text.

Congress to attempt detailed, tactical decision, or supervision, and as to these the President's authority is effectively supreme. But, in my view, he would be bound to follow Congressional directives not only as to whether to continue the war, but whether to extend it to other countries and other belligerents, whether to fight a limited or unlimited war,[49] perhaps, even, whether to fight a 'conventional' or a nuclear war.[50]

The respective powers of the political branches during and in relation to war have not been addressed by the Supreme Court in many decades and on some issues the Court's latest words appear in aged cases, still authoritative but likely to be revisited. In 1814, the Supreme Court (by Chief Justice Marshall) held that the President could not confiscate the property of alien enemies in time of war without authorization from Congress, and that a Congressional declaration of war alone did not constitute such authorization.[51] In issue was the President's power as Commander in Chief during war, not his foreign affairs powers; the property was seized in the United States, there were no relations with the enemy, and relations with other nations were not involved. Marshall wrote long before Lincoln established virtual Presidential autonomy in war and before other aggrandizements of Presidential power; later, during the Civil War, the Supreme Court in effect rejected much of what Marshall had written when it upheld seizure of vessels pursuant to Lincoln's blockade.[52] A principal theme of Marshall's opinion, moreover, was that war between nations did not ordinarily engage their civilian nationals and the private property of such nationals.[53] Since that era, however, nations have learned total war, and have recognized the importance to the conduct of such war of new kinds of property controlled by new kinds of aliens, particularly large alien companies; in the two World Wars, Congress authorized comprehensive confiscations of enemy property.[54] If, then, a war-time President some future day proceeded to seize alien enemy properties without Congressional authorization, it is unlikely that the courts would interfere, and surely they would not write as Marshall did about the narrow limits of Presidential war-power. The Supreme Court might again reject, however, what Marshall in fact rejected—the seizure of a private vessel by a local U.S. attorney claiming the mantle of Executive authority but apparently acting without Presidential decree or authentic Presidential decision.

In 1851, the Supreme Court (by Chief Justice Taney) held that the President, as Commander in Chief, could temporarily occupy and control conquered territory, but that only a treaty or an act of Congress could annex it to the United States.[55] Taney, too, spoke of Presidential war-power still in its infancy, of a subordinate President and a dominant

Congress. In the twentieth century, the President's powers as Commander in Chief in declared wars have known few constitutional limits, and the Supreme Court did not find any on his power in occupied territory.* The President's matured foreign affairs powers, too, might well give him authority to claim for the United States what the forces he commands had conquered.[56] But the power to determine the permanent constitutional status of acquired territory, with its far-reaching irreversible consequences, might still be for Congress alone, to which are expressly granted related powers to govern territory and admit new states (Article IV, sec. 3).**

The War Powers Resolution

Unhappiness about the Vietnam War led Congress to seek remedies for what some thought to be the constitutional problems the war had revealed. In 1973, Congress transformed the field of constitutional controversy between President and Congress by enacting the War Powers Resolution.[57] With that resolution, chronic uncertainties as to the President's constitutional 'war powers' became entangled with new questions of hierarchy between concurrent Presidential and Congressional powers in the 'the twilight zone'. Henceforth, any action by the President that came within the terms of that resolution was action not under alleged Presidential authority when Congress was silent, but rather Presidential action which Congress has prohibited, limited, regulated. That left the President's power only—in Justice Jackson's terms— 'at its lowest ebb . . . his own constitutional powers minus any constitutional powers of Congress over the matter'.†

In the War Powers Resolution, Congress began by declaring its understanding of the President's constitutional authority:

---

* The President's constitutional power to seize, occupy and govern enemy territory in the course of war is well established. See Ch. II, p. 47. Compare p. 94, this chapter.

After 1945, the Court would have to consider the relevance of the U.N. Charter, a treaty of the United States, designed to outlaw war. The Charter has also been construed to render it unlawful to retain territory acquired by conquest in violation of the Charter. See Declaration of Principles of International Law concerning Friendly Relations and Co-operation among States in accordance with the Charter of the United Nations, U.N. General Assembly Res. 2625 (XXV 1970).

** The President could, of course, annex territory by treaty (with the consent of the Senate). See Ch. VII. Compare the power of Congress to decide whether territory acquired by the United States shall be 'incorporated' into the United States or remain 'unincorporated'. See n. 53 to Ch. III.

† See p. 94 above.

The constitutional powers of the President as Commander-in-Chief to introduce United States Armed Forces into hostilities, or into situations where imminent involvement in hostilities is clearly indicated by the circumstances, are exercised only pursuant to (1) a declaration of war, (2) specific statutory authorization, or (3) a national emergency created by attack upon the United States, its territories or possessions, or its armed forces.[58]

Congress's definition of Presidential power, insofar as it addresses Presidential actions that constitute going to 'war',* conforms to constitutional text, to the Framers' intent and to our constitutional history. The case for Congress's declaration is less strong to the extent that it denies the President constitutional authority to engage U.S. forces in hostilities 'short of war' for foreign policy purposes. To that extent, Congress would be denying the President authority he had acquired by history (with Congressional acquiescence.)**

Congress's declaration of the scope of the President's constitutional authority does not purport to legislate, or otherwise to bind the President.† A judgment by Congress as to what actions by the President, in what circumstances, would be constitutionally legitimate, implies that in Congress's view Presidential actions beyond those limits usurp Congressional power and are unconstitutional, but that judgment of Congress does not bind the President.‡

The sections of the War Powers Resolution that follow are legislative in character and intend to bind the President. The Act requires that the President 'in every possible instance shall consult with Congress before

* The Framers intended the President to have authority to go to war to defend the United States in the event of an attack on the United States. In the War Powers Resolution, Congress apparently recognized the authority of the President to go to war also in the event of an attack on U.S. armed forces (even if they are stationed in a foreign country or on the high seas). Congress may have been accepting an extension of Presidential power in the spirit of the original exception, since, after the Second World War, large numbers of U.S. forces were stationed in foreign countries and were seen as being there for the protection of the United States. Congress's declaration that the President has authority to resort to hostilities in the event of attack on U.S. forces may also be construed as, or as tantamount to, Congressional authorization for the President to act in those circumstances in the future.

** Perhaps Congress was thereby terminating its historic acquiescence, but it did not purport to be legislating to do so.

† Unlike the version of the section previously adopted by the Senate, which would have enacted that understanding of limited Presidential power into law. See n. 58 to this chapter.

‡ But it might form the basis for impeachment, as a 'high Crime and Misdemeanor'. (Art.II, sec.4).

introducing U.S. armed forces into hostilities or into situations where imminent involvement in hostilities is clearly indicated by the circumstances' (section 3). The Resolution provides that if U.S. armed forces are introduced into hostilities, the President shall report to Congress in writing within 48 hours (section 4). Congress also requires the President to terminate any U.S. involvement in hostilities after 60 days* unless Congress has declared war or otherwise authorized the President to continue. Congress reserved the right to terminate hostilities at any time by concurrent resolution (which is not subject to Presidential veto) (section 5). Congress also declared that authority to introduce U.S. forces into hostilities shall not be inferred from any law or treaty unless that law or treaty specifically authorized introduction of U.S. forces into hostilities (section 8).

The War Powers Resolution has been subject to criticism from, and before, its adoption. President Nixon insisted that it was unconstitutional and vetoed it. (It was adopted over his veto). Subsequent Presidents also questioned its constitutionality. The Resolution is poorly drafted. It is not clear whether the provisions requiring consultation, reporting, or termination apply only when the President involves the United States in hostilities without having constitutional authority to do so (as that authority was defined by Congress), or even in cases where the President is acting within his constitutional authority or by authority delegated by Congress. The Resolution does not define 'hostilities', and may apply to circumstances that constitute 'war' under the Constitution, as well as hostilities that are far 'short of war'. It has been suggested that the resolution is impractical, even impossible, to comply with: for example, the consultation requirement seems to require formal consultation with both houses of Congress (not merely with designated leaders or Committee members). Some have argued that instead of limiting Presidential authority, the Resolution indeed enlarges it by giving legislative sanction to Presidential hostilities, even to war, for 60 days.

The War Powers Resolution indeed suffers serious deficiencies, some of which may explain recurrent Presidential evasion, if not violation of, its provisions. But I do not perceive any constitutional objections to the Resolution in principle.** In vetoing the resolution, President Nixon

* The 60-day period is extended to 90 days if the President certifies in writing that 'military necessity respecting the safety of United States forces require the continued use of such armed forces in the course of bringing about a prompt removal of such forces'. Section 5(b).

** The legislative veto provision in section 5 reserving the power of Congress to terminate hostilities by concurrent resolution (not subject to Presidential veto) has

declared that it was unconstitutional, but did not specify which provisions he considered unconstitutional and on what grounds. His veto message contains only a conclusory declaration that the Resolution 'would attempt to take away, by a mere legislative act, authorities which the President has properly exercised under the Constitution for almost 200 years'.[59] But the message does not indicate which of the relevant powers Presidents have in fact exercised, and which constitutional provisions made such exercise 'proper'. The veto message did not address why a Presidential action, that may have been proper when, and because, Congress was silent and may be deemed to have acquiesced in it, cannot be regulated by Congress if Congress decides to do so. The message seems to suggest that by acquiescing in Presidential resort to hostilities in the past, Congress has sacrificed its authority to regulate such activities now. Since in fact Presidents have not gone to war or claimed authority to go to war on their own authority, the veto message seems to suggest that Congressional acquiescence in Presidential hostilities short of war implied also Congressional acquiescence in hostilities that constituted war.

In my view, Congress is clearly within its authority to regulate hostilities that constitute 'war' under the Constitution. Under general principles of constitutional jurisprudence, Congress, under its War Powers, can regulate also hostilities short of war which plausibly might lead to U.S. involvement in war. Congressional acquiescence in Presidential military engagements (of varying significance in varying circumstances over the years) did not atrophy Congressional power and deprive it of authority to regulate for the future. Presidential authority as Executive, as Commander in Chief, or as 'sole organ', may confer large powers on the President to act with Congressional authorization; or independently, with Congressional acquiescence; or even during Congressional indifference or neglect. Presidential authority does not preclude or limit Congressional action, its legislative authority, including its war powers and its spending powers. Even hostilities resulting from attack on the United States, which the President clearly has authority to wage without awaiting Congressional authorization,* are (in my view) subject to regulation by Congress under its authority over war and peace. But unless the Supreme Court finds occasion to speak, and speaks clearly, Presidents are likely to continue to resist Congressional regulation of Presidential hostilities 'short of war'.

presumably been declared unconstitutional in the sweeping invalidation of all legislative vetoes in *I.N.S.* v. *Chadha*. See pp. 125, 126–7 below, this chapter.

* See pp. 97, 106n. above.

War powers issues under the Constitution and under the War Powers Resolution emerged soon after the Resolution was enacted, simmered again in the 1980s, and boiled during the Persian Gulf crisis (1990). President Ford seized *The Mayaguez* (1976); President Carter sent marines in an unsuccessful attempt to extricate U.S. hostages from Iran (1980); President Reagan sent marines to Lebanon (1983), invaded Grenada (1983), bombed Libya (1986), and sent naval vessels to protect shipping in the Persian Gulf (1987); President Bush invaded Panama in 1989. Members of Congress challenged the President's authority to invade Grenada (1983), but the brevity of hostilities (and their successful outcome, from the U.S. perspective) early mooted opposition and discouraged constitutional challenge by Congress. Quick success and the popularity of the action also discouraged Congressional criticism of the invasion of Panama.*

In 1990, following Iraqi aggression against Kuwait, President Bush deployed U.S. forces to Saudi Arabia and the Persian Gulf. He did not bow, or even nod, to the War Powers Resolution. Presumably, he claimed authority to do what he did under his foreign affairs power and his power as Commander in Chief; not implausibly, he could claim that U.S. forces were deployed not for war, but to deter further Iraqi aggression in the area. Later, President Bush expressed the view—a far more radical view—that he did not require authorization from Congress to send U.S. troops into war to liberate Kuwait, if only because the United Nations Security Council had authorized it.** In the end, however, President Bush requested and obtained Congressional authorization[60] to use the armed forces for the purposes indicated by the United Nations Security Council.† The President's request and the Congressional

* See *Crockett* v. *Reagan* and *Sanchez-Espinoza* v. *Reagan*, n. 60 to Ch. V; *Holtzman* v. *Schlesinger*, n. 67 to Ch. V; *Dellums* v. *Bush*, p. 100; *Ange* v. *Bush*, n. 48 to Ch. V. Quick success and the popularity of the action also discouraged criticism of the bombing of Libya in 1986, in response to imputed terrorist activities against U.S. soldiers in Europe, or the bombing of intelligence installations in Iraq (1993) in response to an alleged attempt to assassinate former President Bush. The authority to bomb Iraq may have claimed justification in the original authorization by Congress and in the resolutions of the U.N. Security Council, since Iraq remained under a kind of 'probation' long after the Gulf War ended. See Ch. VIII, n. 55, above.

** See Ch. VIII.

† President Clinton also declared that he had the power to send forces into Haiti to help restore democracy there; he too claimed authority from the United Nations Security Council, but when members of Congress insisted, he too considered seeking Congressional authorization. See n. 60 to this chapter.

In 1995, President Clinton and some members of Congress disagreed as to

response lent confirmation to the constitutional tradition: the President does not have authority to go to war without Congressional authorization.

Whether legislation—such as the War Powers Resolution—effectively restrains the President is a different question. Presidents have continued to challenge the constitutionality of that Resolution, in gross or in detail, and have repeatedly flouted its requirements. Presidents wishing to mitigate confrontations with Congress could exploit ambiguities and uncertainties, notably the meaning of 'hostilities', and when 'imminent involvement' in them is 'clearly indicated'. Perhaps such legislation serves to promote policies of non-action, to discourage a hesitant President and enable him to shift the responsibility for action (or inaction) to Congress. In fact, the War Powers Resolution appears not to have figured significantly in Executive planning. Members of Congress have sometimes objected, but the Congress has not acted to secure Executive compliance—by new legislation,* by exerting its power over the national purse, or by threat of impeachment.[61]

whether he had authority to deploy U.S. forces to Bosnia for 'peace-keeping'. Presumably, the President took the position that the troops were not being introduced into 'hostilities' within the meaning of the War Powers Resolution. In the end, Congress accepted deployment, with some conditions.

Presidential claims of authority deriving from U.N. Security Council resolutions are discussed in Ch. VIII.

* There have been periodic proposals to repeal or amend the War Powers Resolution, but even some who are unhappy with the Resolution have resisted efforts to repeal it outright: Congress should not abdicate its constitutional responsibility and should do nothing that might be interpreted as bowing to Presidential denials of the constitutional authority of Congress. But many would rewrite the Resolution to remove its ambiguities and its impracticalities. They would attempt to distinguish levels of hostilities and regulate accordingly. They would have Congress assert and assume responsibility for war and peace, determine whether there are circumstances in which it is prepared to grant the President authority to engage U.S. armed forces in hostilities and to delegate such authority for such circumstances in advance, explicitly. In addition (or instead, if Congress concluded that it is not politic, or practical, or desirable, to attempt to regulate Presidential war-making by normative prescription), Congress might establish a standing, joint Executive-Congressional body to determine or recommend national policy on war and peace, and define the authority of such a body and the procedures it should follow. I see no basis for questioning the constitutional power of Congress to maintain a War Powers Resolution with such 'ingredients'. See n. 61 to this chapter. And see Ch. X.

'*Cold war*'

During the several decades of the Cold War, the changed character of war, and the extraordinary acerbity of international relations, gave a new cast to competition between the President and Congress. 'Cold war' was a metaphor carrying all the dangers of metaphor, but the phrase inevitably stirred echoes of older constitutional controversies. Was cold war sufficiently like 'hot war' so that major decisions as to whether to 'declare' it, wage it, or end it, belonged to Congress? Or is what was constitutionally crucial about the Cold War that it was not war and was not even likely to lead to war, that it was, by definition, foreign policy short of war and therefore the responsibility of the President, except to the extent that its 'conduct' depended on domestic legislation and spending? Or, perhaps, was it constitutionally, as some have thought it was politically, *sui generis*, calling for extraordinary Presidential leadership but demanding special forms of cooperation with Congress, rather than checks and balances? The broad constitutional issues were not debated but they colored particular issues of conflict and cooperation, discussed below.*

The end of the Cold War transformed the international order; its implications for the competition between President and Congress remain to be seen.

Regulating Intelligence Activities

From our national beginnings, Congress has recognized the President's exclusive responsibility for gathering intelligence, as an extension of his role as 'sole organ' and his traditional function as 'the eyes and ears' of the United States. Gathering intelligence sometimes led to related intelligence activities. After the Second World War, and especially during the Cold War, the Executive branch developed far-flung programs of 'special intelligence activities' (including some denominated 'dirty tricks').

After the Vietnam War and the War Powers Resolution, Congress began also to regulate the Executive's intelligence activities. By legislation, and by conditions on appropriations, Congress required findings and certifications by the President, and provided for oversight by Congressional committees, including requirements of prior notice and some reporting to such committees.[62] Congress also imposed conditions and limitations to bar, notably, the use of appropriated funds to support military or paramilitary activities in Nicaragua.[63] Respect by the

* Compare pp. 112 *et seq.* below, this chapter.

Executive branch for Congressional restraints has been uneven. In a famous instance, executive failure to abide by Congressional restrictions led to the 'Iran–Contra' scandal in 1987–89.[64]

Presidents have resisted Congressional regulation of intelligence activities in principle, insisting that Congress was invading the President's constitutional domain. In principle, it is difficult to accept Executive objections on constitutional grounds. Congress has continued to respect a line between intelligence gathering and 'special intelligence activities'. Covert intelligence activities are actions by 'the United States' as to which Congress has primary if not exclusive responsibility. When such activities involve foreign assistance they carry out decisions by Congress under its Spending Power, 'to provide for the common defence and general welfare of the United States'. (Art. I, sec.8) When covert activities involve providing or selling arms they constitute commerce with foreign nations or the disposition of U.S. property, both of which are within express constitutional powers of Congress. Under its power to create executive offices and determine their functions, Congress has created agencies such as the National Security Council and the Central Intelligence Agency, and has defined and circumscribed their functions and responsibilities. In these matters, the President acts to execute laws of Congress, by authority delegated to him by Congress, and Congress can regulate and control such activities by law or by conditions on appropriations.

ISSUES IN COOPERATION

Division and separation of powers were not designed to make the political branches—the Legislative and the Executive— completely autonomous, independent, and self-sufficient, and the conduct of foreign relations surely depends on their continuing cooperation. There have been doctrinal differences about the character and limits of that cooperation and on the obligation to accord it.

The Obligation of Congress to Cooperate: Implementing Legislation and the 'Power of the Purse'

The President requires funds to maintain the foreign affairs establishment, to defray the expenses of conducting foreign relations generally, and for special foreign policy actions and programs which the President undertakes under his constitutional authority (including the use of troops for purposes short of war), or for carrying out obligations of the United States under international agreements. Establishing and maintaining the foreign policy bureaucracy, the implementation of foreign policy and foreign relations generally, and international agreements in particular, sometimes also require implementation and support by domestic legislation.[65] But the Constitution forbids the President to take even a penny from the Treasury except pursuant to an appropriation 'made by law',* and only Congress can enact laws, even laws to implement foreign policy. Is there a constitutional obligation on Congress to provide the money or the legislation, or was Congress intended to exercise an independent 'checks and balances' judgment and possible veto?

The issue arose early as regards the obligation of Congress to implement a treaty, and members of Congress periodically assert their independence in this regard in principle.[66] In fact, Congress has rarely refused to adopt the laws or appropriate the funds required to implement an international undertaking,** though Congress might differ with the President as to how much money or what laws were required.†
Congress has also generally refrained from drawing its purse strings to frustrate other activities that are clearly within the President's prerogative, as by refusing to appropriate for the salary of an Ambassador or the expenses of an embassy, for participating in international conferences, or even to pay the costs of sending the Navy on a foreign policy mission far removed from war.[67] But, especially since Congress resists the suggestion that the President can 'make foreign policy' without the consent of the Senate or the approval of both Houses, Congress would surely deny that it has no choice but to pass laws or appropriate funds to implement Presidential policy generally.

The 'power of the purse'

Presidents have sometimes expressed their discontent with Congress, and have supported it with constitutional argument, in respects that acquired increased significance during the second half of the twentieth century, and especially during the Cold War. Invoking the President's

---

* Art. I, sec. 9.
** See Ch. VII, pp. 204–5. Infrequently, Congress has enacted legislation inconsistent with international obligations of the United States, thereby compelling the United States to dishonor them. See n. 98 to this chapter.

† And Congress might sometimes delay, as it has for years, to appropriate funds to pay U.S. dues to the United Nations, or to enact laws to implement U.S. obligations under Human Rights conventions.

authority as Commander in Chief and his duty to defend the United States, some have claimed for him a greater voice in the development and acquisition of armaments. In the second half of the twentieth century a similar issue has arisen in the special context of foreign assistance. It has been argued[68] that foreign policy increasingly takes the form of spending programs; that bilateral aid (and contributions to multilateral assistance programs) in particular are essential elements in contemporary foreign policy, and—for the United States—essential indicia of friendly relations with many countries; that decisions as to aid are therefore properly the President's responsibility, and therefore Congress can no more refuse the President's request for appropriations for foreign assistance than for maintaining an embassy.

The arguments for the Presidency reflect a fundamental misunderstanding, a confusion of two different powers and functions of Congress: the 'spending power'—the power to provide for the common defense and the general welfare—and the power to appropriate funds necessary and proper to carry out the functions, activities, policies, and programs of all branches of government.

The President can surely claim a strong voice in decisions as to defense expenditures, and perhaps also as to foreign assistance. But under the Constitution the ultimate decision is for Congress. Explicitly, Congress has the 'spending power', 'the power to lay and collect taxes to provide for the common defence'. Congress also has the power 'to raise and support armies', and 'to provide and maintain a navy'. (Art. I, sec. 8). And nothing in national history, in the history of the Constitution, in the transformed international political system or in the radically-changed character of weaponry and warfare, suggests that power has moved, or should move, from Congress to the President.[69] Similarly, foreign assistance entails not merely an appropriation of funds to implement policies that are primarily the President's responsibility; constitutionally they are justified as within the 'spending power', the power to provide for the general welfare of the United States. It is difficult to accept that the President should command a power expressly conferred upon Congress. Congress can exercise its other expressed powers—for example, to regulate foreign commerce—in ways inconsistent with Presidential designs, and favorable trade terms have loomed at least as large in contemporary foreign relations as direct financial assistance. Whether and how much to spend, moreover, depends inevitably on national resources, presumably from taxes (determined by Congress), and on choices and priorities in the national budget that go far beyond foreign affairs and are admittedly for Congress ultimately to determine.

However unfortunate the consequences of division of authority here (as elsewhere), one must conclude that Congress could insist on its spending power as on other express powers, and in foreign as in domestic matters can spend (or not spend) according to its views of what would promote the general welfare of the United States.[70]

In constitutional principle, then, loose references to Congress's 'power of the purse', require refinement and qualification. Congress is constitutionally free to spend or not to spend for the common defense or the general welfare as Congress sees them.* Congress has the power also to appropriate funds as necessary and proper to defray the costs of governance. That power to appropriate, however, reflects also a constitutional duty. Congress is required to appropriate funds for the activities of other branches of government that are within their independent constitutional authority. It is not free, for example, to refuse to appropriate funds to carry out treaty obligations, or independent decisions of the President. If Congress has authority under the Constitution to reject, regulate or terminate a Presidential activity it can do so by legislation or by refusing to appropriate funds** (or by terminating funds previously appropriated). But what it cannot constitutionally regulate by legislation, it may not properly do by exercise of any 'power of the purse'.

The President's Obligation to Cooperate: Executive Privilege

Presidents have been frequently charged with failure to cooperate when they deny to Congress or its committees information or documents, whether in order to preserve 'confidentiality' within the Executive branch, or because the Executive believes that the information should be 'classified' and concealed in the national interest.[71] In regard to foreign relations in particular, Presidents often claim that disclosure would jeopardize national policies, offend some friendly nation, or otherwise embarrass the United States in its relations with other nations. Congress, in turn, has insisted that it needs information which the Executive may possess in order to decide whether to legislate and how

* Subject, of course, as are all powers of Congress, to the Bill of Rights.

** To do so by withholding appropriations rather than by legislation engenders additional constitutional concerns, since legislation requires action by both houses, subject to presidentail veto, whereas withholding appropriations circumvents the President's veto and can be effected by one house of Congress refusing to approve an appropriation of funds.

Similar constitutional issues were raised by Congressional failures in 1995–96 to adopt a budget, causing temporary shutdown of governmental activities.

to legislate, and that it has constitutional authority to command information in the President's possession as it can subpoena information from private citizens. Congress has insisted that it recognizes some need for confidentiality but that the Executive often abuses it, and in any event Congress can respect any necessary confidentialities as well as the Executive branch can.

The issue is as old as the Republic. 'Executive privilege' was asserted by President Washington to withhold from the House of Representatives papers relating to the negotiation of the Jay Treaty.[72] In that case, the President justified his refusal in part on the ground that the House had no constitutional function in the making of treaties. But later Presidents have refused documents and information that were indisputably relevant to legitimate Congressional concerns.[73] This issue, too, has not been resolved in principle,[74] but in fact Presidents have often prevailed.[75] Congress has not sought to enforce its demands by threat of criminal sanction against executive officials, or citation for contempt of Congress.[76] In foreign affairs, in particular, Congress has itself recognized some limitations as necessary, for though it has long demanded reports of all executive departments, it has requested them of the State Department only 'if not incompatible with the public interest'.[77] But Presidents have been careful not to deny Congress lightly, or too often.[78] They have often given information to Congress under injunction of secrecy, which Congress has generally respected.

The courts recognized executive privilege but found some limitations on it during the extended controversy between Congress (and the special prosecutor) with Richard Nixon prior to his resignation from the Presidency in 1974. In that case, the Supreme Court ruled that the President enjoys an 'executive privilege' but that it must sometimes bow to the demands of the administration of criminal justice. The Court considered only executive privilege to protect confidentiality within the Executive branch; it explicitly reserved the question of executive privilege in the courts in cases involving confidentiality for reasons of diplomatic or military necessity. And the Supreme Court considered only executive privilege in relation to the needs of the administration of justice; it has not considered whether a President could withhold information from Congress.[79] In the 'Iran–Contra' scandal, Executive officials sought to invoke Presidential autonomy and privilege to claim exemption from Congressional regulation,* but the courts rejected their claim.[80]

* During the trial of Oliver North for pursuing a foreign policy contrary to law, and for withholding information from Congress, the Justice Department filed an

The President's Obligation to Execute the Laws

A somewhat analogous issue as to obligation to cooperate would arise
if a President refused to execute Congressional laws relating to foreign
affairs, laws which he could not afford to veto or which were repassed
over his veto (or had been approved by a predecessor President). Early
Presidents sometimes claimed that the constitutional provision that 'He
shall take Care that the Laws be faithfully executed' gave them discretion not to execute a Congressional enactment that, in the President's
view, was unconstitutional;[81] in respect of legislation affecting foreign
affairs, a President might raise the particular objection that Congress
was invading his domain. More recently, it has been asserted generally
that the constitutional independence of the President, the complexities
of government, and limited executive resources permit the President discretion at least as to which laws he should execute first,[82] and even
whether some laws should be executed at all. Presidents long claimed, in
particular, that authorizations and appropriations of funds are not
mandatory and that the Executive is free to 'impound funds' and spend
less, or not to spend at all.[83]

In general, as regards impoundment of appropriated funds, the President
appears to have lost the argument. In 1974, Congress enacted the Budget
and Impounding Control Act,[84] which requires legislative approval of
Executive decisions to reduce or terminate programs for which Congress
had authorized funds. Presidents have apparently accepted this legislation
but some President may yet reopen the issue or may insist that it is not
applicable to expenditures and appropriations for foreign affairs.*

No doubt, many laws, including laws that authorize or appropriate
funds (especially for programs initiated by the President), can properly
be interpreted as leaving the President discretion as to whether or not to
act, or to spend; surely, he need not spend all that is appropriated if
the job can be done for less. But other laws, including some spending

---

amicus curiae brief in which it argued, *inter alia*, that 'the President has plenary
power which Congress cannot invade to conduct diplomacy, including covert diplomacy that seeks support (including financial contributions) for the foreign policy he
articulates on behalf of the Nation'. Memorandum of Law of the United States,
United States v. *North*, No. 88-0080-02 (D.D.C. filed Nov. 18, 1988). The court
rejected that argument, as well as the argument that the case involved a non-justiciable political question. See Ch. V. North and others were convicted of, *inter alia,*
withholding information from Congress and destroying documents but the convictions were reversed in part, on grounds of immunity. See n. 80 to this chapter.

* In 1996, however, Congress granted the President a limited 'line-item' veto. See
p. 119 n.

programs, are clearly intended to be mandatory and, as to these, it is difficult to build a persuasive argument that 'He shall take Care that the Laws be faithfully executed' gives him discretion not to execute them.[85] There is little to support the view that the President's duty is weaker, or different, in respect of laws that govern or impinge on foreign relations.* Presidential authority not to execute some Congressional mandates would have to be found in some other constitutional power: the argument might be that Congress cannot impose foreign policy on the President, and that the President's 'primacy' in foreign relations gives him special discretion as to whether and how to execute laws or spend money[86] relating to foreign affairs.** The argument goes against explicit, unambiguous constitutional text; it is not persuasive.

INTERFERENCE BETWEEN BRANCHES

Separation of powers has also contributed to charges of unconstitutional 'interference', usually by the President against Congress. Differing conceptions of their respective constitutional authority have sometimes led Congress to enjoin the President in matters which he deemed not its business: Congress has directed Presidents to negotiate or to denounce treaties;† once Congress directed the President (President Grant) to tell certain diplomatic and consular establishments 'to close their offices'.[87] A known dead letter, still on the statute books (since 1913), provides:[88] 'The Executive shall not extend or accept any invitation to participate in any

* Congressional 'weapons' to see to it that the President does his duty to execute the laws are not always effective, and sometimes Congress is reluctant to use them. In the 1970s, Congress enacted laws to deny foreign aid or the sale of arms to states guilty of gross violations of human rights, but Congress later turned a blind eye to evidence that the President was not enforcing the law or was abusing 'loopholes' in the law provided him by Congress. See p. 120, this chapter. When members of the Executive branch apparently violated the law in the Iran-Contra scandal (1987), Congress was largely frustrated in its desire to remedy the violations, and the courts were not notably successful in punishing the violators. The judicial process was frustrated also by Presidential pardon of Executive officials prior to their indictment. See Grant of Executive Clemency, Dec. 24, 1992, Pres. Proc. No. 6518.

The courts have been reluctant also to see to it that international law—part of the laws of the United States—is faithfully executed. See Ch. VIII.

** That may be what President Truman had in mind when he declared that a provision directing him to make a loan to Franco's Spain was unconstitutional and he would treat it as only an authorization to do so. In fact, he lent Spain the money. See n. 86 to this chapter.

† See Ch. VII, pp. 194, 212.

international congress, conference, or like event, without first having specific authority of law to do so.' Presidents have been sensitive to such encroachments,* have usually protested, and often disregarded them.**

'Unconstitutional Conditions'

Congress has attempted to influence the conduct of foreign policy by the President, and the behavior of other governments, by imposing 'conditions', especially on spending and appropriations. Favorite vehicles for various such 'riders' (to which they are not always germane) have been the foreign assistance acts and the annual appropriations acts, which Presidents usually cannot 'afford' to veto even if they object to incidental provisions.†

The constitutional lawyer would distinguish between different appropriations and between different conditions. If Congress cannot properly withhold appropriations for the President's activities, it ought not be able to impose burdensome conditions‡ on such appropriations.[89] Even when Congress is free not to appropriate, it ought not to be able to regulate a Presidential action by imposing conditions on the appropriation of funds to carry it out, if it could not regulate that Presidential action directly. So, should Congress provide that appropriated funds shall not be used to pay the salaries of State Department officials who promote a particular policy or treaty, the President would no doubt feel free to disregard the limitation,[90] as he has not felt bound by 'riders' purporting to instruct delegations to international conferences.[91]

The constitutional answers might be different as regards the conditions that Congress has been imposing in the annual foreign assistance

* Sometimes, too sensitive, even to harmless Congressional resolutions. Compare President Grant's protest when Congress adopted a resolution thanking certain foreign nations for their congratulations upon the centennial of the United States. See Ch. III, p. 81 and n. 79 to Ch. III.

** In 1995, Congress adopted a resolution directing the President to move the U.S. Embassy in Israel to Jerusalem (from Tel Aviv). There is strong constitutional argument that the resolution would not be binding on the President. Cutting-off funding for particular consulates is also constitutionally questionable if done for foreign purposes opposed by the President. Jerusalem Embassy Act of 1995, Pub.L.No. 104-45, 109 Stat. 398 (1995).

† Recurrent attempts, to give the President a line-item veto did not succeed. In 1996 Congress finally granted the President a line-item veto for appropriations (and some tax) legislation, effective in 1997; see Pub. L. No. 104-30, April 9, 1996. Its constitutionality (and its effectiveness) remain to be determined.

‡ In every appropriation there is, of course, an implied condition that funds be used for the purpose for which they are appropriated.

acts. There are in effect 'conditions' in every such act, when Congress designates countries to receive aid (implicitly denying aid to other countries), allocates foreign aid by categories, or limits the number of countries to be assisted. In several acts, Congress has also imposed qualifications and other requirements for designated recipients. In 1954, for example, Congress provided that none of the funds authorized shall be used to assist a government 'committed by treaty to maintain Communist rule in Asia'. That year Congress declared also that there shall be no delivery of military goods bought with U.S. foreign aid funds to signatories of the European Community Defense Treaty until they had all ratified the treaty.[92] The Foreign Assistance Act of 1961,[93] as amended, barred or restricted: aid to Cuba; to any country that assisted Cuba; to Communist and unfriendly countries; to those that traded, or that permitted ships flying their flags to trade, with Cuba or North Vietnam; to those that sold certain materials to the Communist Bloc; to the United Arab Republic; to countries that seized U.S. fishing vessels in international waters; to countries whose military expenditures materially interfered with their development. In 1963, the First Hickenlooper Amendment forbade foreign assistance to any country that nationalized American properties without prompt, adequate, and effective compensation.[94] Beginning in 1973, Congress has denied foreign aid and arms sales to governments guilty of consistent patterns of gross violations of internationally recognized human rights, and such limitations have been maintained though sometimes with 'loopholes' or 'strings', such as directions to the President to continue aid to such countries only if he certified that there was 'significant improvement' on human rights.[95] For years Congress denied 'most favored nation' treatment in trade to Communist countries if they failed to permit emigration,[96] and in 1994 there was controversy as to whether to deny 'most favored nation' treatment to China because of dismal human rights conditions there.

Presidents have resented many of these conditions and sometimes resisted them, challenging their validity. Surely, to give to some nations and not to others, to use aid to extract concessions from recipient nations, to terminate or threaten to terminate assistance or other spending programs as a sanction, can seriously affect relations with the 'target' nations, and Presidents deplore such Congressional 'interference'.* But Congress has insisted, and Presidents have reluctantly accepted, that in foreign affairs as in domestic affairs, the spending power is expressly entrusted to Congress and to its judgment as to which spending is for

---

* Congress has itself sometimes recognized the President's claims and authorized him to waive the conditions in some circumstances. Compare nn. 75, 91 to this chapter.

'the general welfare' of the United States, and Congress can designate the recipients of U.S. largesse and impose other conditions upon it.[97]

The distinction I have drawn between obligatory appropriations and voluntary spending would apply also to appropriations to international organizations. If Congress is obliged to implement treaty obligations it must appropriate what the United States is obliged to pay, for example its share of the regular budget of international organizations, and ought not be able to impose conditions on such appropriations.[98] Repeated failure by Congress in the 1990s, despite urgent pleading by the President that it appropriate funds to pay arrears in U.S. obligations to the United Nations, has political explanation but no legal justification. On the other hand, voluntary contributions by the United States to special programs require an exercise of the Spending Power of Congress and it can spend or not spend, or spend on conditions.[99] But Congress cannot impose conditions that invade Presidential prerogative to which the spending is at most incidental, or which violate individual rights; for example, in contributing to a special program of an international organization, Congress ought not be able to instruct the Executive as to how to vote on issues before the organization unrelated to that contribution, or insist that certain persons be denied employment there.[100] Sometimes Congress has escaped political conflict and has attenuated constitutional objections by giving the President authority to waive the conditions or limitations it has imposed.[101]

Congressional Control of the Foreign Affairs Establishment

One source of conflict and confusion, in foreign as in domestic affairs, has been Congressional control over the organization and personnel of the Executive branch. The Constitution (Art. II, sec. 2) provides that the President:

shall nominate, and by and with the Advice and Consent of the Senate, shall appoint Ambassadors, other public Ministers and Consuls, Judges of the supreme Court, and all other Officers of the United States, whose Appointments are not herein otherwise provided for, and which shall be established by Law: but the Congress may by Law vest the Appointment of such inferior Officers, as they think proper, in the President alone, in the Courts of Law, or in the Heads of Departments.

That provision is evidence that despite commitment to the Separation of Powers, the Constitution 'mixes'* as well as it separates powers, and

* See Madison in the Helvidius letter, quoted in the footnote on p. 86.

Executive independence is modified by the requirement of Senate consent to appointments, and by broader Congressional regulation and control.

The quoted provision has raised questions, real or hypothetical, many of which apply also to officers conducting foreign affairs. It seems accepted that the Senate can only consent or refuse to consent to the President's appointments; it cannot consent with conditions (as it can in consenting to treaties).[102] That view apparently reflects the assumption that germane conditions could only invade the powers of the office or limit its term, and these are either prescribed by the Constitution, established by law, or reserved to the President's discretion. But it is not obvious why the Senate should not be entitled to grant consent on other kinds of conditions, for example that the appointee divest himself (herself) of certain financial holdings, or that she or he learn French or Swahili. In the realities of political life, or course, the Senate can informally impose any conditions, simply by withholding consent until the President gives satisfaction, but it would not be surprising if the Senate began also to impose conditions formally. If so, there would be no consent if the conditions were not met, and Presidents would probably accept them as the price of consent, rather than consider the appointment rejected.[103]

The constitutional requirement that appointment to offices not expressly provided in the Constitution be 'established by Law', means that although it is the President who appoints the members of the Executive branch engaged in foreign affairs, many of the offices to which they are appointed are created by Congress. 'Ambassadors, other public Ministers, and Consuls', are expressly mentioned in the Constitution and would appear to occupy offices not 'established by Law', and arguably not subject to legislative regulation. But Congress has in fact acquired control of the entire foreign service and has subjected it to detailed regulation, determining the number of its members, prescribing its table of organization, defining functions, setting qualifications and terms of employment.[104] Presidents are probably entitled to disregard qualifications that are so detailed as to constitute virtually a direction to appoint particular persons.[105] The Supreme Court has upheld the President's power to remove officers who exercise the President's 'Executive power',* even if they were confirmed by the Senate, even within the term of office fixed by Congress, even if

---

* But Congress can insist on a voice for itself, or for the Senate, and impose conditions on the removal of officials who are part of the 'Fourth Branch', the independent agencies. See p. 129 and n. 106 to this chapter.

Congress purported to forbid their removal without Senate consent.[106] Officers protected by Civil Service laws and other legislation cannot be discharged by the Executive without cause, but could no doubt be assigned to other duties.

Controversy has also flared when Congress purported to direct the actions of members of executive departments, claiming the power to decide what is necessary and proper to see that its laws are executed, even if the President directed them otherwise. In the nineteenth century, in the *Kendall* case,[107] the Supreme Court ordered the Postmaster-General to pay out money as directed by Congress although President Jackson told him not to pay. The Court said:

There are certain political duties imposed upon many officers in the executive department, the discharge of which is under the direction of the President. But it would be an alarming doctrine, that Congress cannot impose upon any executive officer any duty they may think proper, which is not repugnant to any rights secured and protected by the constitution; and in such cases, the duty and responsibility grow out of and are subject to the control of the law, and not to the direction of the President.

In the conduct of foreign affairs the lines of authority are tangled, since executive officials carry out both laws enacted by Congress—for example, tariff or immigration legislation—and 'political duties' under the direction of the President.[108] It has long been accepted, for example, that the authority which Congress gives consular officers to issue visas pursuant to the Immigration Laws is not reviewable by the Department of State, or, presumably, even by the President, though if that view conforms to the theory of the *Kendall* case it does not necessarily reflect the realities of foreign service in the Executive branch.[109]

ISSUES IN DELEGATION

The conduct of foreign relations is permeated by a special form of 'cooperation', involving not the conjunction of separate powers of President and Congress, but Presidential actions pursuant to Congressional power delegated to him. When the President acts by Congressional authority he has the sum of the powers of the two branches,* and can be said 'to personify the federal sovereignty',[110] and in foreign affairs, surely, the President then commands all the political authority of the United States. But earlier in our history the separation

* See Justice Jackson's formulation, p. 94, above.

of powers was held to forbid abdication by one branch to another and to imply, therefore, limitations on delegation. Uneasy Congresses themselves sought to mitigate the dangers of delegation by special devices to revoke or limit delegated authority, or to oversee the President's discretion in carrying it out, some of which Presidents have challenged as impermissible.

'Excessive' Delegation

That the separation of powers forbids excessive, unguided, uncontrolled delegation by Congress, even to the President, is doctrine that still has some life in domestic affairs.[111] In foreign affairs it has never had much: whatever else *Curtiss-Wright* said and may stand for, it specifically held that 'within the international field' Congress may 'accord to the President a degree of discretion and freedom from statutory restriction which would not be admissible were domestic affairs alone involved'.[112] If, as we saw, some parts of Sutherland's essay are not compelling,* one might nonetheless find sufficient reasons for the Court's conclusion about delegation in the realities of the foreign affairs process. For, from the beginning, reluctant Congresses have felt compelled to delegate to Presidents the largest discretion, with minimal guidelines, to carry out the most general legislative policy. That the President's own powers are 'plenary' and include some legislative authority, that the division of authority to make foreign policy is irregular and uncertain, tend to reduce any doctrinal objections to delegation: often, a strong argument can be made that what Congress has delegated to the President was in fact within his power to do on his own authority. If there remain some theoretical limitations on Congressional delegation even in foreign

---

* That the foreign affairs powers of the federal government derive from national sovereignty, and are perhaps extra-constitutional, does not tell us whether one branch can delegate its component of that sovereign power to another. Indeed, since it seems agreed that the sovereign foreign affairs power is divided between President and Congress along lines not unrelated to those expressed in the Constitution, one might conclude that the principle of the separation of powers and the constitutional limitations it implies are not irrelevant. At least, one should ask whether the reasons that support Separation generally apply in some measure to the conduct of foreign affairs. Sutherland treated the issue in *Curtiss-Wright* as one of delegation; he did not consider whether the arms embargo could be imposed by the President on his own authority, with Congress enacting criminal penalties as necessary and proper to carry out the President's embargo. But perhaps that is what he had in mind. See n. 11 to this chapter.

affairs, no one has persuasively stated what they are and apparently no actual delegation by Congress has approached them.

In practice, however, Congress has increasingly sought to limit delegation and to scrutinize Executive implementation of delegated authority by requiring reporting, consultations, and certifications to Congress or to Congressional committees, even in foreign affairs. The Supreme Court has seemed disposed to consider the propriety of delegation where the delegated power impinges on individual rights, for example the right to travel abroad.* In such cases, the pre-New Deal limitations on delegation in domestic matters may be alive and well and applicable even in regard to foreign affairs.[113]

Controlling Delegated Authority: The 'Legislative Veto'

The need to delegate vast powers to the President has often left Congress uneasy, and it has sought to circumscribe the powers delegated, supervise and impose conditions on their exercise, limit their duration, and require the President to seek renewal of his mandate. Sometimes Congress has insisted on making explicit what is not being granted to the President, perhaps implying an opinion that he does not have such power on his own authority either. In the United Nations Participation Act of 1945, for example, Congress provided:

[N]othing contained in this section shall be construed as an authorization to the President by the Congress to make available to the Security Council . . . armed forces, facilities or assistance in addition to the forces, facilities and assistance provided for in [an agreement subject to the approval of Congress].[114]

A different limitation was expressed in the Trade Agreements Extension Act of 1951:

The enactment of this Act shall not be construed to determine or indicate the approval or disapproval by the Congress of the executive Agreement known as the General Agreement on Tariffs and Trade.[115]

In the War Powers Resolution (1973) Congress provided that:

Nothing in this joint resolution . . . shall be construed as granting any authority to the President with respect to the introduction of United States Armed Forces into hostilities or into situations wherein involvement in hostilities is clearly indicated by the circumstances which authority he would not have had in the absence of this joint [resolution].[116]

---

* See p. 91 above and Ch. IX, p. 291.

Sometimes Congress has provided that executive action pursuant to delegation shall lie before Congress for a time before going into effect, so as to give Congress the opportunity to reject it by new legislation; such 'waiting periods' have not been seriously challenged.[117] Constitutional controversy was generated, however, when, to avoid the difficulties of repealing or modifying delegations by ordinary legislative process (requiring a majority of both houses and subject to Presidential veto), Congress developed extraordinary machinery. Especially with the increase of Congressional activism in recent decades, Congress inserted 'legislative veto' provisions in legislation and in appropriation acts dealing with the export of arms to foreign governments, foreign assistance, foreign trade, the provision of nuclear power facilities, and Presidential action in emergencies. Congress inserted such legislative veto provisions not only where it might wish to recoup authority it had delegated to the President, but also where it sought to restrain claims of Presidential authority under the Constitution, as in the War Powers Resolution. Sometimes Congress provided for veto by concurrent resolution of both houses, sometimes for veto by one house or by Committee* or even by a committee chairman.[118]

Such 'infra-legislative' controls of the Executive were challenged on various grounds. Presidents objected to any repeal or modification of legislation other than by the normal legislative process. Concurrent resolutions for legislative purposes (as distinguished, say, from 'sense' resolutions) would seem to violate the express constitutional requirement of Presidential approval for every 'Order, Resolution, or Vote to which the Concurrence of the Senate and the House of Representatives may be necessary'.[119] 'Legislative veto' in any form was said to violate the separation of powers in that either it seeks to legislate by less than both houses of Congress and Presidential approval, or it arrogates to Congressional bodies executive functions including the President's express power to take care that the laws are faithfully executed.[120]

In 1983, in *I.N.S.* v. *Chadha*,[121] the Supreme Court invalidated the legislative veto. In that case, the Court struck down a provision whereby Congress reserved authority to either house of Congress to invalidate a decision of the Executive branch to allow a particular deportable alien to remain in the United States. The Court held that a scheme that in effect provided for legislative action by less than both houses violated the constitutional requirement of legislation by a bicameral Congress, as

---

* Some legislation required the Executive to give notice to Congress (or to a Committee) and to delay action for a specified time.

well as the 'presentment clause' which subjected legislation to Presidential veto.

In *Chadha* the Court spoke in sweeping terms and seemed to tolerate no exceptions. Its terms and its reasoning would seem to apply to all legislation, in foreign as in domestic affairs. Arguably, the case against the legislative veto is even stronger when, as in regard to war powers, the President often claims to act on his own authority, not by delegation from Congress.*

In the realities of national and international life, of course, these issues of constitutional power are often not drawn sharply. Lawyers' arguments about the implications of Separation sometimes reflect as much as they determine conflict or cooperation between President and Congress; but they test the respective bargaining powers of the two branches and shape the compromises that emerge. Since the courts are usually unavailable to define or circumscribe the powers of either branch, their joint powers are virtually without limit except in self-restraint, while their respective powers depend on what each can seize, and on relations between them. The President has won most of the battles, not because his constitutional arguments are necessarily stronger but because his temptations and opportunities have been greater, because he has had all the advantages of 'sole organ', and because foreign policy is often, effectively, what he communicates to other nations. If increasingly Congress can also see and hear for itself, its means are even now not wholly effective; today, Congress succeeds in being heard around the world, but its voice is diffuse, and restrained by historic limitations, by the customs of international life, and by the reluctance to have the United States speak uncertainly and in a confusion of different voices. Even in circumstances where Congress can effectively frustrate national attitudes and intentions expressed or intimated by the President, Congress cannot—without making our international life impossible—readily 'repeal', contradict or derogate from what the President said.

In reality even more surely than in principle, then, Congress is not free to refuse to appropriate funds for an embassy to a country which the

* On the other hand, it has been argued that, under the War Powers Resolution, if Congress acts to terminate hostilities, it is not legislating but is exercising authority not subject to Presidential veto; therefore, there should be no constitutional objections to Congressional action by concurrent resolution. The argument that a declaration of war is not within the Presentment Clause and therefore not subject to veto has never been authoritatively accepted (or rejected); even if a declaration of war is not subject to Presidential veto the argument that a decision to end war is also not subject to veto is plausible but not compelling. See n. 28 to this chapter.

President insists on recognizing; to prevent the President from using the armed forces for limited foreign policy purposes; to fail to implement formal or informal undertakings to other nations. But neither can the President take Congress wholly for granted or disregard its known sentiments and those of its constituents, for he needs the cooperation of Congress generally and for his foreign policy in particular, and Congress has been known to convert that need into power, creating a check and a balance not provided by the letter of the Constitution. In the end, while insisting on its constitutional autonomy, Congress has generally sensed that in the strange contraption which the Fathers created for conducting foreign policy,* the Congress is the rear wheels, indispensable and usually obliged to follow, but not without substantial braking power.

THE INDEPENDENT AGENCIES

The U.S. Constitution divides the federal government into three branches, but for more than a hundred years there has been a 'fourth branch', the independent agencies that saw their big growth in the New Deal of the 1930s and are now a permanent part of our governmental landscape and our national life. Independent agencies are created by acts of Congress, and they exercise rule-making and other 'quasi-legislative' power by delegation from Congress. Their officials, however, are appointed by the President with the consent of the Senate, and they are sometimes called 'executive agencies', yet the constitutional relation to the President of the Federal Trade Commission, or the Nuclear Regulatory Commission, is not the same as that of the Department of Education or the Department of Agriculture. Independent agencies have also adjudicated and resolved claims. In different measures and ways, their status, powers, and activities have been denominated 'quasi-executive', 'quasi-legislative', 'quasi-judicial'.**

---

* See Ch. X.

** 'Administrative agencies have been called quasi-legislative, quasi-executive or quasi-judicial, as the occasion required, in order to validate their functions within the separation of powers scheme of the Constitution. The mere retreat to the qualifying 'quasi' is implicit with confession that all recognized classifications have broken down, and 'quasi' is a smooth cover which we draw over our confusion as we might use a counterpane to conceal a disordered bed.' Jackson J., dissenting in *Federal Trade Commission* v. *Rubberoid Co.*, 343 U.S. 470, 487–8 (1952). And see n. 122 to this chapter.

The independent agencies have never fit comfortably into the constitutional blueprint and have been described as a 'constitutional sport'. Presidents especially, committed to the idea of a 'unitary executive', have found these agencies hard to swallow. There have been continuing issues as to the President's power to remove members of these agencies, and his right to direct, coordinate or guide them. The Supreme Court has distinguished between the constitutional status of the President's 'Departments', and that of the anomalous, hybrid 'agencies': the President has the power to remove officers of Departments without the consent of Congress, but Congress can regulate and require Congressional (or Senate) consent for the removal of a member of an independent agency.*

The anomalous constitutional existence of the independent agencies brings particular uncertainty in foreign affairs, especially in their relation to the President as the 'sole organ of the federal government in the field of international relations'. Increasingly, such agencies act on the international scene, and they have established links to comparable bodies in other countries and to international organizations. In field after field—aviation, communication, nuclear regulation, drug control, energy policy, environmental control, securities regulation, trade regulation—agencies in the United States regularly cooperate, exchange information, and coordinate activities with counterpart agencies abroad. They have also negotiated agreements of international character, sometimes without the participation, scrutiny or even awareness of the President or the Department of State.

The foreign affairs activities of independent agencies have not been examined by the courts from a constitutional perspective. Under general constitutional principles, insofar as the agencies act under legislative mandate, they impinge on foreign affairs by authority of Congress. Congress can authorize the Nuclear Regulatory Agency to negotiate and conclude agreements with foreign counterparts, or with the International Atomic Energy Agency, as it has long authorized international postal agreements, which the Supreme Court upheld as early as 1838.[122]

Nevertheless, in foreign affairs, surely, the President as 'sole organ' and as Chief Executive is entitled to insist on a 'unified executive'. Especially since what the independent agencies do with foreign counterparts cannot be isolated from U.S. foreign policy generally and inevitably affects relations with other countries, especially since these agencies also carry out executive functions which the President might

* See n. 106 to this chapter.

also claim as his own, the President is entitled to insist that he (generally through the Department of State) be fully informed, and participate in any negotiations at least as an observer.[123] In some instances, the President might be entitled to insist that inter-agency agreements be made by the President as treaties or by Congressional-Executive agreement between the United States and the foreign governments (or the international organization) involved.*

Constitutional issues of conflict and cooperation abound also but take special forms as regards the special power of the President to make treaties and other international agreements. I deal with them in the course of the following chapters.

* And usually requiring consent by the Senate or approval by both Houses. See Ch. VII.

Chapter V

THE COURTS IN FOREIGN
AFFAIRS

Foreign relations are political relations conducted by the political branches of the federal government. At times, however, they come into court. The ordinary business of courts, too, sometimes involves or affects U.S. foreign relations.

An independent judiciary applying the written Constitution is a hallmark of government in the United States. The courts have successfully established 'judicial review' and 'judicial supremacy', their final and 'infallible'* authority to impose their readings of the Constitution on the political branches of the federal government as well as on the states,[1] to monitor the separation of powers and the divisions of federalism, to protect individuals, minorities, even majorities, against governmental excesses.**

Judicial review is the most dramatic function of U.S. courts, but it is not their principal or their most important activity; and even judicial review is incidental to the real business of the courts—to decide cases between parties, to administer civil and criminal justice, to regulate the complex administration of government. In the course of that business, the judges interpret and apply law made by the federal political branches and by the states. In interpreting law, they make law—of course. They also make law explicitly. The common law, woven magnificently over centuries by the judges of England, was received by the colonies and maintained by the states, their judges continuing to add and change. When legislatures intervened to codify or modify, the judges continued to apply their art to carry out and fill out legislative policy and purpose. The federal courts, too, applied the common law, as they saw it, in the federal territories, and as the states saw it in cases between citizens of different states.[2] The courts have also found in the Constitution or in

---

* See Justice Jackson's remark, Introduction, p. xiii.
** The 'anti-majoritarian', 'undemocratic' character of judicial review, and its relation to constitutionalism and popular sovereignty, continues to be a subject of rich debate. See n. 5 to this chapter.

acts of Congress directives to them to develop law—sometimes called 'federal common law'—for given subjects and purposes.[3]

That courts make law, once radical 'realism', is now commonplace; now it is necessary realism to emphasize the limits of judicial law-making. The law the judges make is still only 'interstitial':[4] even in interpreting the Constitution, even the Supreme Court cannot be heedless of the constraints of language, history, and politics,[5] not least of the presumption that the political bodies whose acts the courts monitor have themselves interpreted the Constitution and have acted within its limitations. Judicial review and judicial legislation render the courts in the United States probably the most independent and powerful in the world, but 'government by judiciary' is a polemical exaggeration.[6] The judiciary is still 'the least dangerous branch',[7] having principally braking power, and even that cannot always be applied and is not always effective, especially in matters of transnational import. The powers of the courts, including judicial review, are also contained by the character of the judicial function and by particular constitutional limitations: under Article III, the courts of the United States exercise only the judicial power of the United States, carry out only judicial functions, decide only 'cases' or 'controversies' and only those committed to their jurisdiction by the Constitution or by law. Political forces further curtail in fact the part courts might play in theory.

The Constitution vests 'the judicial power of the United States' in the Supreme Court and in 'such inferior courts' as Congress may establish. But the federal courts are in a judicial network that includes also the courts of the states, which in effect also exercise 'judicial power' for the United States. State courts are created by state legislatures pursuant to state constitutions, and their jurisdiction is prescribed and circumscribed by the state constitution and by state law. In the U.S. constitutional system, the state courts also apply the U.S Constitution and give effect to federal law. For constitutional and other federal purposes, state courts are subject to the final authority of the Supreme Court of the United States and state court decisions on federal questions are subject to review by the Supreme Court.[8]

The scope and the limitations of judicial power largely apply in foreign affairs as elsewhere. But foreign affairs make a difference. Here, the courts are less willing than elsewhere to curb the federal political branches, are even more disposed to presume the constitutional validity of their actions and to accept their interpretations of statutes, and have even developed doctrines of special deference to them.* The courts have

* See page 134 below, and n. 11 to this chapter. Compare the courts' view that they are bound by Executive assertions of immunity (Chapter II, p. 54) and will give

asserted judicial power to develop doctrines to safeguard the national interest in international relations against interference and invasion by the states. The courts have a special role, acting on behalf of the nation, to give effect to obligations of international law.

THE JUDICIAL ROLE IN FOREIGN AFFAIRS

The judicial part in foreign affairs is an aspect of the judicial power of the United States generally prescribed in Article III, section 2:

The judicial Power shall extend to all Cases, in Law and Equity, arising under this Constitution, the Laws of the United States, and Treaties made, or which shall be made, under their Authority;—to all Cases affecting Ambassadors, other public Ministers and Consuls; . . . to Controversies . . . between a State, or the Citizens thereof, and foreign States, Citizens or Subjects.

In all Cases affecting Ambassadors, other public Ministers and Consuls, and those in which a State shall be Party, the supreme Court shall have original Jurisdiction. In all the other Cases before mentioned, the supreme Court shall have appellate Jurisdiction, both as to Law and Fact, with such Exceptions, and under such Regulations as the Congress shall make.[9]

As there contemplated, the federal courts have exercised jurisdiction over suits by foreign ambassadors (and over suits against them, when not inconsistent with international law), over cases to which foreign consuls are parties, and suits by states against foreign nationals.[10] The principal participation by courts in foreign affairs, however, is in cases arising under the Constitution, laws or treaties, involving various parties and diverse matters:* a company challenges the validity or

---

great weight to Executive interpretations of treaties (Chapter VII, p. 206) or determinations of international law. And see the 'political question' doctrine, p. 143 below.

Judicial review, the political question doctrine, the respect generally given by the courts to executive actions and determinations, can be seen as aspects of 'separation of powers' between the Executive and the Judiciary. Judicial–Executive 'separation' is sometimes modified by Congress. Compare *La Abra Silver Mining Co.* v. *United States*, 175 U.S. 423, 459-61 (1899), where the Court held that Congress could ask the courts to decide a question of fraud underlying a claim against Mexico which the Executive might have decided. See also the Second Hickenlooper Amendment and the Helms-Burton Act of 1996 on Cuba, n. 36 to this chapter.

* The cases in U.S. courts that have some transnational import are legion. Indeed, in our 'one world' in trade, finance, and communication; in an age where every occurrence may be known elsewehere, instantly—any case in any court in the United States might become grist for transnational mills and become of interest to U.S. foreign relations.

applicability of a tariff; an airline invokes the Warsaw Convention to limit its liability to the victim of an accident; an alien challenges state laws that deny him (her) employment or inheritance; a soldier seeks to enjoin the Secretary of Defense from sending him to fight in Vietnam or in the Persian Gulf; a citizen asks the court to invalidate a law denying him (her) a passport, or an executive order prohibiting travel to Cuba; Haitian refugees challenge the validity of Coast Guard interdictions of their vessels on the high seas; a citizen of Mexico objects to trial in the United States on the ground that he had been abducted from Mexico by U.S. officials. The courts review actions of federal administrative agencies whose reach includes or impinges on U.S. foreign relations (e.g., the Immigration and Naturalization Service, the Federal Trade Commission or the Federal Communications Commission), the foreign activities of the Department of Commerce and the Treasury, of coastal and border states relating to foreign neighbors, or those of New York State and New York City to the United Nations.

JUDICIAL REVIEW

In principle, judicial review applies to foreign affairs as elsewhere, but practice reflects differences. Without the guidelines of enumerated powers, in foreign affairs—courtesy of *Curtiss-Wright*—the Separation of Powers doctrine is less meaningful as an interpretive principle for the courts. Similarly, the obligations of federalism are relaxed, even reversed: instead of guarding principally against federal encroachment upon states' powers, the courts are more intent on watching and striking down state interference in the nation's foreign relations.

As in domestic affairs, the Supreme Court has been more willing to scrutinize foreign affairs actions alleged to violate individual rights, although national interest in foreign relations, as the Court sees it, no doubt weighs heavily in the balance of competing claims.* Here, too, however, judicial review rarely asserts or spends itself; foreign affairs 'are so exclusively entrusted to the political branches of government as to be largely immune from judicial inquiry or interference'.[11] Reluctant to invalidate political action, the courts are likely to stretch, narrow or bend words to avoid the rigors of a statute or an Executive order, or to find that it did not authorize what had been done under it.[12] Such gymnastic interpretation does not limit the constitutional power of the polit-

* The protection of individual rights under the Constitution in foreign affairs is discussed in Ch. IX.

ical branches, but it casts the onus on the Congress or the President clearly to authorize what has been challenged and warns them of possible constitutional difficulties.

Monitoring Federalism: The 'Dormant' Commerce Clause

In foreign affairs, the courts have had little to do in monitoring 'federalism' as a limitation on federal power, since there are hardly any such limitations: 'in respect of our foreign relations generally, state lines disappear. As to such purposes, the state of New York does not exist.'[13] On the other hand, the courts have been alert to protect the nation against imposition by the states, staunchly upholding the supremacy of treaties, and of acts of Congress or of the President that relate to foreign affairs, over inconsistent state law.

The judicial role is particularly significant in implementing the 'dormant' commerce clause.* Applying, even extending, the doctrine which the courts developed in respect of commerce among the states, the Justices have read the grant to Congress of the power to regulate commerce with foreign nations as implying limitations on the states, forbidding them to discriminate against foreign commerce or to burden it unduly. Here, the courts, acting without any guidance in text, find comfort and reassurance in the knowledge that their judicial review, and any invalidation of a state act, are only 'tentative',[14] since Congress can 'overrule' the courts and legislate to permit the states to do what the courts say the dormant commerce clause would forbid.

And in a rare case, the Supreme Court, reading no constitutional text, found in the federal monopoly over our foreign relations a basis for invalidating state 'intrusion into the field of foreign affairs'.[15]

Monitoring Separation of Powers in Foreign Affairs

I have discussed the Separation of Powers and 'checks and balances' in foreign affairs, but its certainties owe little to judicial resolution, and the courts have made only modest contributions to resolving its uncertainties. In foreign affairs, the limitations on the judicial power (discussed below) are only rarely overcome to permit resolution of inter-branch disputes: issues only infrequently find a plaintiff with a direct personal interest (as distinguished from a political interest) that qualifies to afford 'standing' and create a 'case or controversy'. And if the obstacles of case or controversy and standing do not preclude adjudication, the courts

* See Ch. VI, pp. 158–62.

might sometimes avoid decision by finding an issue to be a 'political question', and therefore not justiciable.* Moreover, the political branches have their own political weapons in their competition for power and would not necessarily seek judicial resolution even if it were available.

Monitoring Respect for Individual Rights

Only in monitoring governmental respect for the Bill of Rights do courts play their important part. Here the limitations on the judicial power are not a major obstacle. But unusual deference to the political branches (though not to the states), and the unusual weight given to 'the national interest' largely as perceived by the political branches, commonly outweigh even important individual rights. In foreign affairs, scrutiny of governmental actions by the courts results only infrequently in vindicating the individual's claim.**

JUDICIAL LAW-MAKING

In foreign affairs as elsewhere, the courts make law implicitly when they determine and interpret the applicable law to decide cases before them. Judicial law-making by interpretation is fundamental and dispositive when the courts develop the law of the Constitution,† and their constitutional constructions have importantly influenced foreign relations and sometimes built a continuing role for the courts, for example to monitor state burdens on foreign commerce or intrusions into foreign relations. The courts have ample scope and influence, too, when they read and apply statutes, treaties, other international agreements or executive acts, or, we shall see, when they determine customary international law.

The federal courts have made and developed law avowedly in several parts of the federal domain, claiming authorization to do so from Congress or from the Constitution,[16] and this judge-made law partakes of the supremacy of those sources over state law. In foreign affairs, apparently, Congress has not in fact delegated law-making authority to the courts,[17] but the Constitution itself readily supports, for example, the power of federal judges to make maritime law, since the judicial power of the United States extends 'to all Cases of admiralty and mari-

* See p. 143 below.   ** See Ch. IX.

† Some constitutional clauses, e.g., the due process clause, have been largely filled by the courts. See Chapter IX, p. 289.

time Jurisdiction'; and maritime law was (and has remained) largely judge-made.[18]

Federal courts have also made other law relevant to foreign affairs but, until recently at least, its constitutional basis and status have been unclear. The courts have determined the principles of customary international law* and the requirements of international comity;[19] the rules that decide which of differing laws of different countries should govern a transnational transaction; the rights of foreign governments to sue in domestic courts and the effect to be given here to judgments of foreign courts.** But unlike the maritime law and other law made by direct authority of Congress or the Constitution, this other law made by the federal courts was—for long—commonly deemed to be only their particular 'finding' of 'the common law' and did not enjoy federal supremacy, so that the states were free to go their own way.[20] Indeed, in cases involving suits between citizens of different states, where a federal court must apply the law of the state in which it sits, it appeared that the federal courts would have to apply the law as determined by the local state courts even on matters affecting foreign affairs.[21]

The Act of State Doctrine and the 'Federalization'
of International Law

All that changed when the Supreme Court decided the *Sabbatino* case.[22] In that case, a financial agent of the Cuban Government sued in the federal courts to recover the proceeds of a sale of sugar. The defendant denied the Cuban Government's title to the sugar, alleging that it belonged to a company largely owned by U.S. citizens and had been expropriated without compensation in violation of international law. The lower federal courts held that although, under the Act of State doctrine, courts were not to sit in judgment on the acts of a foreign state performed in its own territory, they did not have to give effect to

---

* See Ch. VIII, p. 232. Strictly, in applying international law, the courts are supposed to be finding rather than making the law and must look to what others consider the law to be. That was said, too, of the common law, e.g., by Justice Story in *Swift* v. *Tyson*, 41 U.S. (16 Pet.) 1, 18-19 (1842) (a view rejected in *Erie R.R.* v. *Tompkins*, 304 U.S. 64, 79-80 (1938)), but the judges have been substantially less free to follow their own bent in determining customary international law, in view of the authority of the Executive branch in the matter and the need to attend to the practices and opinions of many nation-states over many years.

** Local federal courts also determine the common law applicable in the District of Columbia and other federal territories.

Castro's expropriation of sugar belonging to U.S. nationals because it violated international law.[23] On appeal, the Supreme Court reversed, holding that the Act of State doctrine applied even as to acts that violated international law.*

What is of interest here is the basis on which the Court reached its decision, and what it said in reaching it. After concluding that the Act of State doctrine was not required by notions of sovereignty, by international law, by the 'political question' doctrine, or by anything in the Constitution, the Court said:[24]

The act of state doctrine does, however, have 'constitutional' underpinnings. It arises out of the basic relationships between branches of government in a system of separation of powers. It concerns the competency of dissimilar institutions to make and implement particular kinds of decisions in the area of international relations. The doctrine as formulated in past decisions expresses the strong sense of the Judicial Branch that its engagement in the task of passing on the validity of foreign acts of state may hinder rather than further this country's pursuit of goals both for itself and for the community of nations as a whole in the international sphere.

In addition to recognizing the authority of federal courts to make such law, the Supreme Court established the supremacy of that law to state law:

Whatever considerations are thought to predominate, it is plain that the problems involved are uniquely federal in nature. If federal authority, in this instance this Court, orders the field of judicial competence in this area for the federal courts, and the state courts are left free to formulate their own rules, the purposes behind the doctrine could be as effectively undermined as if there had been no federal pronouncement on the subject. . .

However, we are constrained to make it clear that an issue concerned with a basic choice regarding the competence and function of the Judiciary and the National Executive in ordering our relationships with other members of the international community must be treated exclusively as an aspect of federal law.**

---

* At least 'in the absence of a treaty or other unambiguous agreement regarding controlling legal principles'. 376 U.S. at 428. Compare RESTATEMENT (n. 2 to Preface) § 444.

** The Court also proceeded, in effect, to declare that international law, as law in the United States, was federal law, and that determinations of international law by the U.S. Supreme Court are binding on the states. See 376 U.S. at 425. See RESTATEMENT (n. 2 to Preface) § 111, Comment *d*, and Reporters' Notes 2 and 3. See n. 30 to this chapter.

The Court claimed no authorization from Congress to elaborate the Act of State doctrine, and seemed carefully to avoid seeking support for it in Executive authority;[25] the Court found, implied in the Constitution, an independent power for the federal courts to make such law on their own authority.[26] It was the federal judiciary that decided that the foreign relations of the United States required the Act of State doctrine; and it was the judiciary that was deciding, in *Sabbatino*, that the foreign relations of the United States did not require (or permit) exception for acts of state that violate international law.[27] And, of course, like other federal law, this is one of those 'enclaves of federal judge-made law which bind the States'.[28]

In the result, in the Court's reasoning and dicta and their implications, *Sabbatino* establishes foreign affairs as a domain in which federal courts can make law with supremacy. There ought to be little doubt, then, that in the established areas of judicial law-making, law that is substantially related to foreign affairs—the determination of customary international law and comity for judicial purposes;* guidelines for the interpretation of treaties and the meaning of particular treaty provisions; the principles of (international) conflicts of laws; rules as to access of foreign governments to domestic courts and the treatment of foreign judgments[29]—as to these, and others, the federal courts can make law for their own guidance and can decide also whether federal interests require that the states conform to them. It follows that state decisions regarding such supreme, judge-made, federal law raise federal questions subject to review by the Supreme Court if Congress so provides.[30]

Future cases will have to answer a different, difficult question, whether and which new subjects are also within the legislative power of the federal courts. The Court in *Sabbatino* noted that the Act of State doctrine 'concerns the competency of dissimilar institutions to make and implement particular kinds of decisions in the area of international relations'.[31] Act of State is a doctrine particularly for the guidance of the courts, and it is about its own 'engagement in the task of passing on the validity of foreign acts' that the Judicial branch felt competent and justified to express its 'strong sense' that such involvement may hinder rather than further national and broader interests in international relations.[32] Act of State is an element of the law of conflicts of law in multinational transactions where the political branches hardly tread and courts have never waited for the political branches to make law or to ask the judges to make it.[33] But can the courts make law, without

---

* See Ch. VIII, pp. 232 *et seq.*

invitation of the political branches, on foreign affairs questions that are not the specialty of courts, indeed on any matter in which the political branches could legislate?* Only the courts can tell us, but one may expect that, without limiting their power in principle, they will legislate sparingly.[34]

Still to be resolved also is the place of such judge-made law in relation to other sources of law in the United States. In *Sabbatino*, Congress was silent and the President and the Supreme Court arrived at the same conclusion;[35] power in the courts concurrent with the powers of the political branches here brought neither conflict, nor competition for initiative, nor a reach for new power to fill a vacuum of authority. But the legislative power of the courts in foreign affairs is concurrent,[36] not exclusive, and surely it is subordinate to that of Congress.** Judicial legislation would also bow to a subsequent treaty;† would it give less respect to executive agreements‡ or Presidential declarations of policy?

Foreign policy is largely made by the President, and the 'intrinsically federal' character of foreign relations on which the Court relied in *Sabbatino* is substantially Presidential. Judge-made law, the courts must recognize, can serve foreign policy only interstitially, grossly, and spasmodically; their attempts to draw lines and make exceptions must be bound in doctrine and justified in reasoned opinions, and they cannot provide flexibility, completeness, and comprehensive coherence.[37] In the *First National City Bank* case,[38] we know, most of the Justices expressed their independence of, and distaste for, *ad hoc* dictation or direction by the State Department, but a majority of the Court in fact reached the result the State Department asked for.§ Might the Court yet accept, even welcome, formal, general declarations of policy approved by the President, not in the context of a particular case?[39]

Supervisory Power of the Federal Courts

A half century ago, the Supreme Court asserted a power in the federal courts to supervise elements of the criminal justice activities of the

---

* If so, the courts might have some of the powers of both Congress and the President, but limited, as is all judicial legislation, by the *ad hoc,* random character of judicial law-making.

** Congress has in fact legislated to modify the Act of State doctrine and the courts have accepted and given effect to the statute. See n. 36 to this chapter.

† *A fortiori*, since even Congressional legislation bows to a subsequent self-executing treaty. See Ch. VII, p. 209.

‡ See Ch. VII, p. 228.   § See Ch. II, p. 59.

Executive branch; in particular, the Court said that, in order to discipline and deter the police, the federal courts would not bring to trial persons abducted or otherwise seriously mistreated by federal police officials.[40] In the intervening decades the Court has used that supervisory power sparingly, indeed hardly at all, but the power remains in the judicial arsenal. The supervisory power of federal courts might have lent itself—and might lend itself again—to sanctioning the Executive branch in foreign affairs cases, for example when federal agents are involved in kidnapping persons abroad in order to bring them back to the United States for trial. But in 1992, the Court maintained its refusal to use its supervisory powers to that end when it applied an old case* and allowed a federal trial of a person abducted by federal agents from another country.[41]

LIMITATIONS ON JUDICIAL POWER

United States courts derive their jurisdiction from the Constitution and from acts of Congress,** and both define judicial authority generally and in foreign affairs as well. The courts have also inherited and elaborated principles of judicial self-limitation,† and these circumscribe the judicial role in foreign affairs at least as much as in governance generally.

Thanks to both constitutional, legislative, and political limitations on the business of the courts, the paramount judicial prerogative of invalidating acts of the political branches has not loomed large in the conduct of foreign relations.‡

* *Ker* v. *Illinois*, 119 U.S. 436 (1886), discussed in Ch. IX, p. 306.

** Congress can regulate the jurisdiction of the lower federal courts and the appellate jurisdiction of the Supreme Court. See n. 10 to this chapter. Periodically, members of Congress have threatened to withdraw the jurisdiction of the Supreme Court to review certain cases; in fact that has rarely happened. Congressional regulation of federal jurisdiction is not likely to affect the role of the courts in foreign affairs.

† Since the courts interpret the Constitution, some of the limitations on the exercise of judicial authority which they have found there may reflect also judicial dispositions to limit their own role. But what they declare to be required by the Constitution is binding on the courts, and cannot be changed by Congress.

‡ The Judiciary is, of course, subject also to the limitations that govern all branches (and officials) of government, notably the Bill of Rights. See Ch. IX. The Supreme Court has not invalidated any statute, treaty, or executive act intimately related to foreign affairs on the ground that it was beyond the power of the federal

Constitutional Limitations: Case or Controversy

A major obstacle to judicial involvement has been the requirement of 'case or controversy': constitutional issues cannot be addressed by the federal courts unless raised by one who has 'standing' and makes a 'justiciable' claim in an actual case[42] against a proper, available defendant.[43] (It was in regard to a foreign affairs matter that the Justices told President Washington they could not give him an advisory opinion.)[44] The President himself cannot bring a judicial proceeding to challenge alleged usurpation of his authority by Congress, nor can Congress (or members of Congress) sue to enjoin an alleged usurpation by the President, for these would seek to vindicate political not personal interests and assert political not justiciable claims.* A state cannot complain in court of a breach by Congress or the President of the constitutional compact,[45] nor can a citizen, *qua* citizen, complain that an act of Congress or of the Executive** transgresses the separation of powers and distorts the constitutional system of government.[46] Only an individual aggrieved in his (her) person or property, or a company similarly affected, can challenge an act of the political branches (or of a state) as beyond the power of the federal government, or of the particular branch of that government (or of the state).[47] Most of foreign policy and foreign affairs, however, including most acts that have raised serious constitutional issues, do not impinge directly on private interests. It is difficult even to conjure up hypothetical cases in which the courts would decide whether Congress had constitutional authority, say, to recognize the independence of Cuba from Spain, or to direct that the U.S. Embassy to Israel be located in Jerusalem, or whether the President had

government or *ultra vires* a particular branch or organ of government; some have been struck down because they violated individual rights. See n. 49 to this chapter, and Ch. IX. But compare the *Steel Seizure Case*, discussed in Ch. IV, which the Court apparently treated as a domestic case despite President Truman's claims that he needed steel to fight the Korean War.

* Members of Congress sought to challenge Presidential action in Vietnam and involvement in El Salvador and Nicaragua on the ground that it usurped their legislative authority; some sought to enjoin the President from going to war to liberate Kuwait without Congressional authorization. None of these suits succeeded. See Ch. IV, p. 109.

The 'standing' of members of Congress to bring such suits has sometimes been accepted (or tolerated), but the Supreme Court has not thoroughly explored and expounded on the issue.

** A citizen's suit against state officials, too, cannot be brought in a federal court, or appealed from a state court to the U.S. Supreme Court. See n. 8 to this chapter.

the power to commit the United States to the Yalta and Potsdam agreements without Senate consent. In practice, surely, few 'boundary disputes' between Congress and the President in regard to foreign affairs have come to court: even the perennial issues as to the President's power to send troops abroad, which might perhaps have been challenged by an individual about to be sent, did not reach the courts during the 175 years before the bitter days of Vietnam, and those that knocked on court doors then and since have generally not been heard.[48]

Jurisdictional limitations apart, resort to the courts is unlikely if claimants and their lawyers see little hope of winning, and the courts have evinced no disposition to frustrate national foreign policy. Long before the constitutional revolution of the 1930s gave the federal government virtually full powers* in domestic matters,[49] its accepted monopoly in foreign affairs discouraged constitutional controversy based on states' rights, and the few claims made were quickly proved hopeless.[50] Issues of separation of powers fared little better. Usually, the President and Congress were in fact acting together and—as in *Curtiss-Wright*—the courts were not disposed to limit their cooperation.** Even when one branch—usually the President—was clearly acting alone, the courts have been loath to find 'usurpation', perhaps because they thought his powers 'plenary', perhaps because in the silences of the Constitution the Justices could find few standards to justify and guide judicial intervention; perhaps because in foreign relations in particular, they thought, cooperation and conflict had to be worked out between the President and Congress and the courts could not contribute much to their accommodation.† The Supreme Court itself has been able to avoid frustrating political action yet without affirming its validity, by exercising its discretion to deny certiorari and refuse to hear the case.[51]

'Political Questions'

Judicial review of the conduct of foreign relations has faced an additional obstacle: the courts have elevated judicial abstention to a principle that the courts will not decide 'political questions', and issues of foreign affairs have been cited as providing prime examples and a principal justification of the doctrine.[52]

* Whether *Lopez*, in 1995, signals the beginning of a 'counter-revolution' remains to be seen. See n. 49 to this chapter; n. 8 to Ch. III.
** See Ch. IV, p. 124.
† See Ch. IV; also *Goldwater* v. *Carter*, n. 60 to this chapter. But compare the cases finding lack of Presidential authority, Ch. IV, p. 104 and Ch. II, p. 40.

That there is a 'political question' doctrine is not disputed,[53] but there is little agreement as to anything else about it—its constitutional basis and scope; whether abstention is required or optional; how the courts decide whether a question is 'political', and which questions are. Some have insisted that the courts may abstain only when they must, when—as a matter of fair construction—the Constitution has denied the courts authority to review a particular case or kind of case. Others have seen in the doctrine 'something greatly more flexible, something of prudence', giving the courts a substantial measure of discretion to avoid a question.[54] Justice Frankfurter, the Supreme Court's leading modern proponent of the doctrine, inveighed against '[d]isregard of inherent limits in the effective exercise of the Court's "judicial Power" ' which 'not only presages the futility of judicial intervention' but may well impair 'the Court's position' and '[t]he Court's authority'.[55] It is not clear whether he was saying that in such cases the Constitution requires the courts to abstain, or that they have discretion to do so, if only the general discretion of a court of equity to deny relief.*

The Supreme Court took occasion to reexamine the doctrine in 1962, in *Baker v. Carr*.[56] Justice Brennan found that the doctrine has 'attributes which, in various settings, diverge, combine, appear, and disappear in seeming disorderliness'.[57] After discussing previous cases, he concluded:

It is apparent that several formulations which vary slightly according to the settings in which the questions arise may describe a political question, although each has one or more elements which identify it as essentially a function of the separation of powers. Prominent on the surface of any case held to involve a political question is found a textually demonstrable constitutional commitment of the issue to a coordinate political department; or a lack of judicially discoverable and manageable standards for resolving it; or the impossibility of deciding without an initial policy determination of a kind clearly for nonjudicial discretion; or the impossibility of a court's undertaking independent resolution without expressing lack of the respect due coordinate branches of government; or an unusual need for unquestioning adherence to a political decision already made; or the potentiality of embarrassment from multifarious pronouncements by various departments on one question.[58]

---

* In an appropriate case, the federal courts have authority to act as courts of equity and assume powers that such courts had traditionally, subject to corresponding limitations. For a famous instance see the Supreme Court's handling of the racial desegregation cases, *Brown* v. *Board of Education*, 349 U.S. 294 (1955). Unlike suits for money damages, a petition for an injunction seeks an 'equitable' remedy and is subject to equitable considerations. See n. 9 to this chapter.

The majority of the Court seemed to conclude, on the basis of the earlier cases, including notably foreign affairs cases, that the courts must abstain on some issues (where there is 'a textually demonstrable commitment of the issue to a coordinate political department'); and should, or may, abstain on others, when in its judgment abstention is required by limitations inherent in the judicial function, or for the sake of proper relations with the other branches, or of the national interest.* But the Court's selection and summary of the precedents did not reduce the confusion which they had engendered, for it failed to recognize that 'political question' had been used in different cases in different senses to describe different kinds of questions as to which the functions of the courts were different.

The doctrine of political questions is constitutionally significant only as an ordinance of extraordinary judicial abstention, particularly if it prevents judicial review of a claim that the federal political branches have failed to live up to constitutional requirements or limitations. In such a case the courts would say, in effect: 'It may be that, as the petitioner claims, the political branches have indeed violated the Constitution, but in this instance their action raises a question not given to us to review; only political relief is available.'[59]

Despite common impressions and numerous citations, there are in fact few cases, and apparently no foreign affairs case,[60] in which the Supreme Court ordained or approved such judicial abstention from constitutional review or from deciding some other question that might have led to a different result in the case.** In the foreign affairs cases commonly cited, the courts did not refrain from judging political actions by constitutional standards; they judged them but found them not to be constitutionally wanting. If the Court sometimes spoke of the special quality of foreign relations and the need for the nation to speak with

---

* Justice Brennan said: 'There are sweeping statements to the effect that all questions touching foreign relations are political questions. Not only does resolution of such issues frequently turn on standards that defy judicial application, or involve the exercise of a discretion demonstrably committed to the executive or legislature; but many such questions uniquely demand single-voiced statement of the Government's views. Yet it is error to suppose that every case or controversy which touches foreign relations lies beyond judicial cognizance. Our cases in this field seem invariably to show a discriminating analysis of the particular question posed, in terms of the history of its management by the political branches, of its susceptibility to judicial handling in the light of its nature and posture in the specific case, and of the possible consequences of judicial action'. 369 U.S. at 211–12 (footnotes omitted).

** In principle, presumably, courts may, or must, abstain on a 'political question' in any kind of case, not only where constitutional issues are raised.

one voice, it did so not to support judicial abstention but to explain why the challenged action was within the broad constitutional powers granted to the President or Congress. In no case did the Court have to use the phrase 'political questions', and when it did, it was using it in a different sense, saying in effect: 'We have reviewed your claim and we find that the action complained of involves a political question, i.e., one that is within the powers granted by the Constitution to the political branches to decide. The act complained of violates no constitutional limitations on that power, either because the Constitution imposes no relevant limitations, or because the action is amply within the limits prescribed. We give effect to what the political branches have done because they had political authority under the Constitution to do it.'[61]

Thus, for example, when the political branches asserted the sovereignty of the United States, or denied the sovereignty of a foreign power, in particular territory, the courts did not abstain, but followed the political branches on these 'political questions' because they had made decisions that were theirs to make.[62] To whom the territory in question belonged as a matter of international law was irrelevant: the President (or the Congress) was not constitutionally forbidden to make a claim contrary to international law or even to violate it, and his actions were 'law of the land' binding on the courts.* Or, when the President decides to recognize or not to recognize a foreign agreement, the courts do not abstain from reviewing his action; they give effect to it because recognition is a political act within the President's constitutional powers.[63]

There is, then, no Supreme Court precedent for extraordinary abstention from judicial review in foreign affairs cases.[64] Lower courts, however, invoked the political question doctrine to justify abstention from considering constitutional issues arising out of the Vietnam war. In several cases, plaintiffs raised two principal issues. One was whether the actions of the United States in Vietnam violated international law, in particular the treaty obligations assumed in the Kellogg–Briand Pact and in the United Nations Charter.[65] The courts properly refused to consider that question because it was immaterial, and would not control the disposition of the case: the Constitution does not forbid the political branches, acting within their powers, to disregard treaties or other obligations of international law.[66] Plaintiffs also claimed that the President had exceeded his constitutional power by engaging in war not declared by Congress; several courts held that the political question doctrine required or permitted them not to decide that question.[67]

* See Ch. VIII, p. 241.

The Supreme Court refused to review these cases. The constitutional issue which the lower courts refused to decide was, of course, 'political' in a deep sense, but so is every claim that the President (or Congress) has exceeded his (its) powers to a petitioner's detriment.[68] If the political question doctrine means that the courts must abstain only when, as a matter of fair construction, the Constitution says they must, there was no basis for refusing review in these cases. But if, as Justice Brennan seemed to say, the political question doctrine includes also a right (or an obligation) for the courts to refrain from deciding constitutional cases from 'prudence', the courts in the Vietnam cases could claim, in Justice Brennan's words, 'an unusual need for unquestioning adherence to a political decision already made', and 'the potentiality of embarrassment from multifarious pronouncements by various departments on one question'. On that view, courts should not consider issues of war and peace, or other questions as to which a decision adverse to the political branches could have grave consequences for the national interest, where indeed the President might feel compelled not to heed the courts.* Courts might refuse, in particular—as in the Vietnam cases—to step into major confrontation between the President and the Congress to protect the Congressional domain when Congress itself can but will not do it. This broader view of the political question doctrine would give the judiciary, in theory, discretion to 'sit out' major foreign affairs cases,** but it is not likely to be exercised often, and hardly to avoid a claim that a foreign policy action denies individual liberty or property under the Bill of Rights.[69]

The role of the courts in foreign relations appears likely to remain modest, even more modest than its constitutional role generally. But it may yet become less modest if President and Congress are again tempted—as they were during the Cold War—to tread on important individual rights in the name of national security. Overall, the contribution of the courts

* Or, as Professor Bickel suggested, n. 54 to this chapter, the Court's anxiety may be 'not so much that judicial judgment will be ignored, as that perhaps it should be, but won't'.

** In time, presumably the Supreme Court would lay down standards or lines to guide the discretion of the lower courts.

The political question doctrine is judge-made, but to the extent that it is not required by the Constitution, it can probably be modified or regulated by Congress. Compare the control of Congress over the jurisdiction and rules of the courts, nn. 10, 51 to this chapter. Congress has also modified the Act of State doctrine, n. 36 to this chapter, but there Congress merely determines the applicable law; modification of the political question doctrine would compel the courts to act where they do not deem it appropriate.

to foreign policy and their impact on foreign relations are significant but not large. The Supreme Court in particular intervenes only infrequently and its foreign affairs cases are few and haphazard. The Court does not build and refine steadily case by case, it develops no expertise or experts; the Justices have no matured or clear philosophies; the precedents are flimsy and often reflect the spirit of another day. But though the courts have only a supporting part, it is indispensable and inevitable, and if their competence and equipment for making foreign policy are uncertain, they can be improved by stronger, continuing guidance by Congress and, perhaps, by the President.

Chapter VI

THE ABIDING SIGNIFICANCE OF FEDERALISM: THE STATES AND FOREIGN AFFAIRS

The states are unknown to foreign nations; . . .

It was one of the main objects of the constitution to make us, so far as regarded our foreign relations, one people, and one nation; . . .

in respect of our foreign relations generally, state lines disappear. As to such purpose the State . . . does not exist.

So said three Supreme Court Justices known for their sensitivity to the claims of the states in the federal system, at different times during more than a hundred years;[1] similar views were expressed in different ways by justices and commentators before, between, and since, without dissent from even the most ardent champions of states' rights.[2]

Even in the Articles of Confederation, the states had left themselves little independent authority in foreign relations, and eliminating that little was a principal purpose of the Constitutional Fathers.* Whether, as *Curtiss-Wright* said, the states never had international 'sovereignty', or whether they had international statehood after they declared independence but gave it up when they agreed to Union, they have none under the Constitution.

Federalism, then, was largely irrelevant to the conduct of foreign affairs even before it began to be a wasting force in U.S. life generally—before we became one nation economically, and moved toward centralized welfare

---

* Under the Articles: 'Each state retains its sovereignty, freedom and independence, and every Power, Jurisdiction and right, which is not by this confederation expressly delegated to the United States, in Congress assembled'. (Art. II.) But the states were expressly denied the power, without the consent of Congress, to send or receive ambassadors, enter into agreements with any foreign state, or engage in wars; or lay imposts or duties that would interfere with any treaty made by Congress. (Art. VI.) The Congress was given 'the sole and exclusive right and power of determining on peace and war', of sending and receiving ambassadors and concluding treaties and alliances. (Art. IX.)

government disregarding state lines, before the power of the states was theirs only by grace of Congress, and by political realities rather than constitutional compulsion. Revolution in the national mood in the 1990s has tended to seek to take from the federal government and give to the states, but this trend is not likely to have impact on foreign affairs. At the end of the twentieth century as at the end of the eighteenth, as regards U.S. foreign relations, the states 'do not exist'.

Foreign relations are national relations. The language, the spirit, and the history of the Constitution deny the states authority to participate in foreign affairs, and constitutional construction by the courts has steadily reduced the ways in which the states can affect U.S. foreign relations. And yet, despite careless, flat statements to the contrary, the foreign relations of the United States are not in fact wholly insulated from the states, are not conducted exactly as though the United States were a unitary state. In constitutional theory, the states are not irrelevant or insignificant; they play a small part of their own, and even limit somewhat the plenary authority of the federal government. In political fact, states and state interests also help select those who conduct our federal relations and substantially shape the foreign policy they make.

That foreign affairs are national affairs means that ultimate, supreme authority over them is in the national government, and that states may not intrude upon them with initiatives and policies of their own. But, inevitably, the states touch foreign affairs even in minding their proper business, since foreign nationals live or do business in a state pursuant to its laws and seek the aid of its courts, and citizens bring transnational affairs within its jurisdiction. International concern for human rights has made a state's respect for the rights of its inhabitants a subject of international law and international politics, therefore a concern of U.S. foreign policy. In principle, all local contacts with foreign affairs might be brought under national control by federal law or international agreement, but Congress could not begin to do that in fact, and there has never been any disposition to attempt it. Federal authority in foreign affairs as in other national affairs, then, remains essentially interstitial, and the lives and affairs of foreign nationals and the transnational business of citizens remain largely subject to state laws and legal institutions.

The federal government has also given (or left) to the states a substantial part in the implementation of national foreign policy. Congress has left to the states at least concurrent authority to implement some U.S. obligations under international law,[3] and the Executive has left to the states some implementation of U.S. obligations under treaties.* Congress has never sought to deprive state courts of all jurisdiction of all federal questions, or to authorize removal of all such questions from state to federal courts, even of cases directly involving foreign governments, diplomats, treaties, or other international matters.[4] In fact, in the 1990s, sympathy for local authority and interests, favoring state rather than federal regulation, penetrated also into matters relating to foreign affairs. For example, the United States appended understandings to human rights conventions indicating an intention to leave much implementation of the agreements to the states.[5] In the Uruguay Round Agreements Act,[6] Congress left significant implementation to the states.

STATE EXCLUSION FROM FOREIGN AFFAIRS

By *Curtiss-Wright*,[7] the federal government would have all the foreign relations powers, and the states none, even if the Constitution had said nothing on the subject. In fact, the Constitution explicitly denies to the states the principal foreign affairs powers, and clearly implies other limitations on the states; still other barriers to state involvement in foreign affairs have been raised by the courts.

Article 1, section 10 of the Constitution, is a catalogue of prohibitions and limitations upon the states, and most of them relate or are relevant to foreign affairs:

No State shall enter into any Treaty, Alliance, or Confederation; grant Letters of Marque and Reprisal; coin Money; emit Bills of Credit; make any Thing but gold and silver Coin a Tender in Payment of Debts; pass any Bill of Attainder, ex post facto Law, or Law impairing the Obligation of Contracts, or grant any Title of Nobility.

No State shall, without the Consent of the Congress, lay any Imposts or Duties on Imports or Exports, except what may be absolutely necessary for executing it's [sic] inspection Laws: and the net Produce of all Duties and Imposts, laid by any State on Imports or Exports, shall be for the Use of the Treasury of the United States; and all such Laws shall be subject to the Revision and Controul of the Congress.

No State shall, without the Consent of Congress, lay any Duty of Tonnage, keep Troops, or Ships of War in time of Peace, enter into any Agreement or

---

* See nn. 3 and 5 to this chapter. But the United States remains responsible for any violation resulting from a failure by a state to implement or enforce the U.S. obligations. See, e.g. Ch. VIII, p. 232.

Compact with another State, or with a foreign Power, or engage in War, unless actually invaded, or in such imminent Danger as will not admit of delay.

Most of these restrictions are as clear as words can make them and have raised no issues, but some beg for interpretation and invite at least hypothetical questions; and a few have engendered controversies and cases.

The provision that a state shall not lay a duty or impost on imports or exports, except what may be 'absolutely necessary' for executing its inspection laws, has required interpretation of principal terms. The Supreme Court early decided that a tax on the importer was a tax on the import, that an import remained an import immune to tax while it remained the property of the importer in the 'original package'.[8] An export became an export when the article entered 'into the export stream that marks the start of the process of exportation'.[9]

That a state may not make a treaty, but may make a compact or agreement 'with a foreign power' with the consent of Congress,[10] requires distinguishing between the two categories of agreement.* No helpful, authoritative distinction has emerged. No agreement between a state and a foreign power has been successfully challenged on the ground that it is a treaty which the state was forbidden to make.[11] It might be sufficient to invalidate an agreement if the state were indiscreet enough to call it a treaty, or to conclude it with all the formalities associated with treaties.[12] Looking rather to the substance of the agreement, one early writer suggested that treaties deal with 'subjects of great national magnitude and importance, and are often perpetual, or for a great length of time', but Justice Story found this 'at best a very loose and unsatisfactory exposition'. His own suggestion, that the prohibition of the Constitution applies 'to treaties of a political character', also has not received unanimous acceptance.[13] Presumably, the Framers sought to preclude agreements likely to impinge on the interests of other states, or of the nation. One can perhaps do no better than to itemize kinds of agreement with a foreign power that the Framers probably considered

---

* Art. I, sec. 10 applied to treaties, compacts or agreements which are legally binding. States have freely concluded non-binding arrangements with foreign countries. For example, almost all states have promulgated 'parallel uniform policy declarations' on child support enforcement, under which the state will give effect to a child support order of a foreign jurisdiction if the foreign country has one and gives effect to support orders of the state's courts. See n. 29 to this chapter. The U.S. Department of State has been aware, and approving of, these arrangements. See federal reciprocal legislation, n. 93 to Ch. VII.

to be treaties forbidden to the states, e.g., agreements of alliance or confederation, war or peace, cession of territory.*

Whatever the distinction the Framers contemplated, whatever motiv-
ated them to prohibit some state agreements entirely but as to others
to entrust the national interest to Congressional surveillance,** the different constitutional treatment of the two categories of agreement has
lost all practical significance. It is difficult to believe that Congress
would withhold consent from an agreement of which it approved
because it deemed the agreement to be a treaty and therefore forbidden,
or that the courts would invalidate on that ground an agreement to
which Congress consented.[14] In fact, the states have asked, and
Congress has given, consent to few foreign agreements, and none that
apparently involved local intrusion on matters of national policy.
Congress has consented to an agreement by the State of New York with
Canada to establish a port authority to operate a bridge across the
Niagara River.[15] It authorized Minnesota to enter a highway agreement
with the Province of Manitoba.[16] It approved the Northeastern
Interstate Forest Fire Protection Compact among several states and
contiguous Canadian provinces.[17] During the Second World War
Congress authorized the Civil Defence Administrator to 'give all practic-
able assistance to States in arranging, through the Department of State,
mutual civil defense aid between the States and neighboring countries'.[18]
The St. Lawrence Seaway project, in which the federal government,
states, and Canadian authorities participated, may be seen as including
a state compact with Canada with Congressional consent, but federal
participation gives that agreement special character and directly safeguards national interests.[19]

The 'Agreement or Compact'† clause itself has also produced issues.[20]
In *Holmes* v. *Jennison*,[21] the only case in which the Supreme Court considered that clause in respect of a state agreement with a foreign power,
the Justices divided as to whether there had been any 'agreement'.
Holmes, a resident of Canada, was indicted there for murder, but fled
to Vermont. Although there was no effective extradition treaty between
the United States and Great Britain (which was then responsible for

---

* Compare the efforts to distinguish treaties from executive agreements, Ch. VII,
pp. 215–18.

** The Articles of Confederation, by contrast, did not draw this distinction and
forbade the making of treaties (and confederations or alliances) 'without the consent of the United States in congress assembled'. See Arts. VI, IX.

† On the difference—if any—between an agreement and a compact, see n. 13 to
this chapter.

Canada's foreign relations), the Governor of Vermont signed a warrant for Holmes's arrest and his extradition to Canada. On writ of habeas corpus, the Supreme Court of Judicature of Vermont upheld the Governor. Holmes's appeal to the Supreme Court of the United States was dismissed because the Court was equally divided,[22] but, among other arguments, Chief Justice Taney (for himself and three other Justices) said:[23]

The word 'agreement', does not necessarily import any direct and express stipulation; nor is it necessary that it should be in writing. If there is a verbal understanding, to which both parties have assented, and upon which both are acting, it is an 'agreement'. And the use of all of these terms, 'treaty', 'agreement', 'compact', show that it was the intention of the framers of the Constitution to use the broadest and most comprehensive terms; and that they anxiously desired to cut off all connection or communication between a state and a foreign power: and we shall fail to execute that evident intention, unless we give to the word 'agreement' its most extended signification; and so apply it as to prohibit every agreement, written or verbal, formal or informal, positive or implied, by the mutual understanding of the parties.*

Holmes v. *Jennison* dealt with extradition, historically a subject of national policy, usually made by reciprocal international agreement.[24] All the Justices seemed agreed that a clear compact or agreement on that subject between Vermont and Canada would have required Congres-

---

* Taney added: 'The Constitution looked to the essence and substance of things, and not to mere form. It would be but an evasion of the Constitution to place the question upon the formality with which the agreement is made. The framers of the Constitution manifestly believed that any intercourse between a state and a foreign nation was dangerous to the Union; that it would open a door of which foreign powers would avail themselves to obtain influence in separate states. Provisions were therefore introduced to cut off all negotiations and intercourse between the state authorities and foreign nations. If they could make no agreement, either in writing or by parol, formal or informal, there would be no occasion for negotiation or intercourse between the state authorities and a foreign government. Hence prohibitions were introduced, which were supposed to be sufficient to cut off all communication between them.'

In a separate opinion, Justice Catron seemed to agree that if the extradition had in fact been requested by Canadian authorities, the Governor's action would have constituted an agreement with Canada that required the consent of Congress. On the record in the case, however, he assumed (as Taney did) that there was no request by Canadian authorities, and there was therefore no agreement, only a unilateral action by Vermont which the Constitution did not forbid. Three other Justices concluded virtually without discussion that there was no agreement between Vermont and Canada within the meaning of Art. I, sec. 10.

sional consent. But neither Taney's essay nor any of the other opinions suggests that the subject or the particular disposition of it made any difference: an agreement between a state and a foreign authority on any subject is forbidden unless Congress consents.

Later, in a case involving an interstate (not a foreign) compact, the Court held that, despite the general constitutional language, state agreements or compacts require the consent of Congress only when they tend 'to the increase of political power in the States, which may encroach upon or interfere with the just supremacy of the United States'.[25] Since the same language applies to foreign compacts, one might extend and adapt the Court's distinction to such agreements as well. Congressional consent to an agreement between a state and a foreign government, then, is required only if the agreement tends to give the state elements of international sovereignty, interferes with the full and free exercise of federal authority, or deals locally with a matter on which there is or might be national policy.*

Whether by so narrowing the constitutional requirement of Congressional consent, or because consent was assumed, state and local authorities have in fact entered into agreements and arrangements with foreign counterparts without seeking consent of Congress, principally on matters of common local interest, such as the coordination of roads, police cooperation, border control.[26] The State and the City of New York have arrangements with the United Nations about the U.N. Headquarters and its personnel, and with permanent missions to the United Nations of various foreign governments.[27] An interstate compact to facilitate the interpleader of other parties to judicial proceedings, which contemplates adherence by foreign governments and their component units, also appears not to have sought the consent of Congress.[28] States have also enacted legislation giving rights to foreign nationals if the foreign province gave similar rights to state citizens, but such reciprocal legislation, it would seem, is not a compact requiring Congressional consent, since neither party is legally bound to maintain its law.[29]

Effectively, whether an agreement or compact requires Congressional consent will often be determined by the state.[30] If it proceeds without consent, and if Congress learned of it and were moved to act to reject it, Congress would doubtless prevail, but ordinarily the state's judgment would not be reviewed unless some aggrieved private interest challenged

* Congress, presumably, can determine whether a particular agreement or category of agreements requires its consent. See Frankfurter and Landis, n. 13 to this chapter. Congress can supersede a state compact by legislation. See p. 156n. below.

the agreement in court.* Where Congressional consent is required, it may be explicit or implied, sometimes assumed.** Congress may consent to a particular compact, or to a category of compacts. It may consent after the compact has been concluded, or in advance.[31] If Congress does formally consent to an interstate agreement, that agreement becomes federal law.[32]

EXCLUSION BY FEDERAL SUPREMACY

Additional limitations on the states are indisputably implied in the explicit prohibitions of Article I, section 10 of the Constitution, and some of the grants of power to the federal government also imply that the states do not have those powers.[33] Article I, for example, does not expressly forbid the states to appoint ambassadors to foreign nations, but such a prohibition can be inferred from the provision forbidding states to make treaties and those granting the President the Executive power and the power to appoint ambassadors.†

A major limitation on state action relating to foreign affairs is rooted in the Supremacy Clause of the U.S. Constitution. The Constitution itself, and treaties and laws of the United States, are expressly declared to be the supreme law of the land, and will supersede inconsistent state law. Innumerable federal statutes regulating interstate or foreign commerce, for example, have superseded state laws that would otherwise have been within the authority of the state. For a different example, laws denying employment to an alien, we shall see,‡ have been held to be inconsistent with 'the right to work for a living in the common occupa-

* Congress, or the treaty-makers, can presumably supersede a state's agreement or compact by statute, by U.S. treaty, or by another agreement, even when the state's agreement is deemed not to require Congressional consent. If the state's agreement is designed to have legal effect within the state, Congress can supersede that law as it can the domestic legal effect of a treaty. See Ch. VII, pp. 209 et seq.

** Congress, of course, can act to dispel that assumption and reject the agreement.

† That the exchange of ambassadors and negotiation with foreign powers are forbidden to the states by implication from the grants to the federal government, see Taney's opinion in Holmes v. Jennison, n. 1 to this chapter. But since the states may make foreign agreements with the consent of Congress (and some even without such consent, this chapter, p. 155), they must have the right to negotiate with foreign governments or with their subsidiary units to achieve such agreements. It has not been suggested that states must obtain Congressional consent to begin negotiations.

‡ See Ch. IX, pp. 293 et seq.

tions of the community' implied in the decision of Congress to admit the person to this country.[34] Treaties imposed on the State of Missouri an international regulation of migratory birds; invalidated Virginia's laws sequestering debts of its citizens to British creditors, or denying aliens the right to inherit local land; required Seattle to permit Japanese nationals to run pawn shops; the International Covenant on Civil and Political Rights and the Convention against Torture, and other conventions to which the United States is party, are binding on the states and supersede any inconsistent state law or policy.[35] Executive agreements on the President's sole authority, and law made by the courts under their judical power, also enjoy supremacy to state law: New York's policy to deny effect to Soviet confiscations was overturned by President Franklin Roosevelt's executive agreement with Litvinov; the Act of State doctrine promulgated by the federal courts binds state courts as well.* The states are also bound by public international law and, under the better view, now established, what international law requires is a federal question as to which state courts must follow the federal lead and their decisions are subject to review by the United States Supreme Court.**

Federal Preemption

The supremacy of federal law can do more than supersede inconsistent state law; often it 'preempts' or precludes even state regulation that is not inconsistent with the federal regulation. Congress can direct the states to desist even when Congress is not regulating in the matter or when its regulation is not inconsistent with what the states wish to do. The courts will interpret federal legislation to determine whether Congress intended to preempt state regulation. In numerous instances, the Supreme Court has found that a federal regulation barred even identical, consistent, or supplementary state regulations because the federal government 'occupied the field'. In such cases, the Court avoids finding that the state action violates some implied substantive provision of the Constitution or is inconsistent with a federal regulation: it finds instead a purpose in the federal regulation to exclude the state, and places the onus for invalidating state law on the federal political branches.[36]

Whether a federal regulation was designed to exclude consistent state regulation is not always obvious or easy to determine, but the Court has suggested some guidelines† for finding such a purpose:[37]

* See *Belmont*, Ch. VII, p. 220, and *Sabbatino*, Ch. V, p. 137.
** See Ch. VIII, p. 238, Ch. V, p. 131.
† In *Hines* v. *Davidowitz*, n. 57 to this chapter, the Court struck down

Such a purpose may be evidenced in several ways. The scheme of federal regulation may be so pervasive as to make reasonable the inference that Congress left no room for the States to supplement it . . . Or the Act of Congress may touch a field in which the federal interest is so dominant that the federal system will be assumed to preclude enforcement of state laws on the same subject . . . Likewise, the object sought to be obtained by the federal law and the character of obligations imposed by it may reveal the same purpose . . . Or the state policy may produce a result inconsistent with the objective of the federal statute . . .

To date, the Supreme Court has found preemption only in acts of Congress, but there is no reason why a treaty, an executive agreement, a judicial doctrine or any federal regulation might not also be construed as 'occupying the field', closing it even to state regulation that is not inconsistent.[38]

'Commerce with Foreign Nations'

International trade and intercourse are commonly regulated by federal statute or treaty, and these are supreme law binding on the states. A fertile source of limitation on state action in respect of foreign commerce has been the Supreme Court's early conclusion that, in conferring upon Congress the power 'to regulate commerce with foreign Nations, and among the several States', the Constitution also addressed words of prohibition to the states: the Constitution does not prohibit every state law or regulation that has some effect on interstate or foreign commerce,[39] but it does not leave the states wholly free to act upon or to affect interstate or foreign commerce until prevented by a supreme act of Congress, for Congress could not anticipate and deal with all the myriads of state actions that might infringe the national interest in commerce. Because Congress has not attempted to establish a comprehensive regulation of state burdens on commerce, or granted full authority to an administra-

Pennsylvania's alien registration law although it was wholly consistent with the federal alien registration law, because, the Court found, Congress had occupied the field, in effect telling the states to stay out. The Court said: 'Consequently the regulation of aliens is so intimately blended and intertwined with responsibilities of the national government that where it acts, and the state also acts on the same subject, "the act of Congress, or the treaty, is supreme; and the law of the State, though enacted in the exercise of powers not controverted, must yield to it". And where the federal government, in the exercise of its superior authority in this field, has enacted a complete scheme of regulation and has therein provided a standard for the registration of aliens, states cannot, inconsistently with the purpose of Congress, conflict or interfere with, curtail or complement, the federal law, or enforce additional or auxiliary regulations . . .'

tive agency to do so, the courts have become the guardians of the 'dormant' commerce clause, protecting commerce against 'undue' state burdens.[40] The prohibitions implied in the Commerce Clause, of course, are determined in the first instance by the states, but the power of the courts to protect the interests of the nation and of the other states in interstate commerce against 'balkanization' and self-seeking advantage, has long been accepted as a basic safeguard of the federal system.[41] Similar considerations have guided the interpretation of the Commerce Clause in its applications to commerce with foreign nations.

What the Commerce Clause forbids to the states and what it permits them has splintered the Supreme Court, and has filled volumes of law, not all of it clear or consistent. No one has claimed that the Commerce Clause denies to the states more than it grants to Congress: what is not within the Commerce Power of Congress is surely not forbidden by that clause to state regulation. But, it was agreed from the beginning, what Congress might do under the Commerce power is not *ipso facto* forbidden to the states;[42] surely, not all that Congress could reach today with the long, long arm of the Commerce Power is foreclosed to state regulation if Congress is silent. The Supreme Court, then, has had to develop doctrines to distinguish an area susceptible to federal regulation in which states will be tolerated, from one from which they are excluded.

Long ago, in the *Cooley* case,[43] Justice Curtis announced: 'Whatever subjects of this power are in their nature national, or admit only of one uniform system, or plan of regulation, may justly be said to be of such a nature as to require exclusive legislation by Congress.' The *Cooley* doctrine is still cited but it clearly has not proved an adequate touchstone: few 'subjects' are in their 'nature' either wholly 'national' or wholly local, and to many issues of state 'interference' with commerce the *Cooley* doctrine is simply irrelevant. Later, the Court attempted, and abandoned, distinctions between direct and indirect burdens on commerce.[44]

In the second half of the twentieth century, two 'doctrines' emerged but it was not wholly clear how they were related. One had it that 'reconciliation of the conflicting claims of state and national power is to be attained only by some appraisal and accommodation of the competing demands of the state and national interests involved'.[45] In other cases, the Court seemed to decide merely whether a state burden on inter-state commerce was 'unreasonable' or 'undue', weighing the effect on commerce but attending less to the character or weight of the local interests.[46]

In the end several principles seemed to be established.[47]

160 *The Distribution of Constitutional Power*

— Regardless of the magnitude of the burden on commerce, or the balance of national and local interest, the courts will not tolerate state regulations that exclude or discriminate against out-of-state commerce, or that otherwise favor local economic interests.[48]
— The states may regulate to protect some local interests, notably the health and safety of its citizens,* but not to promote their own economic welfare.[49]
— Even regulations for health or safety might not stand if the Court believes that a less burdensome means than that used was available, or that discrimination against out-of-state commerce lurks in the regulation.[50]

In 1990, the Supreme Court summarized** the applicable jurisprudence:

Where the Statute regulates evenhandedly to effectuate a legitimate local public interest, and its effects on interstate commerce are only incidental, it will be upheld unless the burden imposed on such commerce is clearly excessive in relation to the putative local benefits. If a legitimate local purpose is found, then the question becomes one of degree. And the extent of the burden that will be tolerated will of course depend on the nature of the local interest involved, and on whether it could be promoted as well with a lesser impact on interstate activities.[51]

In very large part, the cases defining the implied prohibitions of the Commerce Clause deal with state regulation of interstate rather than foreign commerce, since most states have greater opportunities and temptations to impinge on commerce with other states than with foreign countries. But nothing in the Supreme Court cases suggests, and there is no reason to believe, that these interstate cases and the various doctrines they have developed do not apply equally to foreign commerce.[52] The Court, then, will not tolerate state regulations that exclude foreign persons or foreign goods, that discriminate against foreign buyers or sellers, that set up tariffs or other obstacles to transportation or trade or to other forms of intercourse with foreign nations. Surely the Court will be as sensitive to burdens on foreign as on interstate commerce, and, in any balancing,† the Court might find even that the national interest

* The state may also protect its citizens against fraud or deceptive practices.
** This summary, in *Pike* v. *Bruce Church*, n. 51 to this chapter, has become the starting point for dormant Commerce Clause cases.
† Balancing state and national interests is easier to propose than to execute with confidence or consistency, and much depends of course on who balances and in what scales. Inherently, inevitably, constitutionality here depends on facts, perceptions, judgements.

in protecting foreign commerce has additional weight, that local regulation is particularly suspect when it impinges on the foreign commerce, foreign policy, and the foreign relations of the United States.*

The Court has also built into the Commerce Clause a complex, technical, not wholly rational edifice of limitations and permissions governing state taxation of interstate or foreign commerce.[53] The constitutional law implied in that structure can not be explained by any 'Cooley Doctrine' distinguishing subjects 'in their nature national' or local, by differences between substantial and insubstantial burden, or even by a general principle of balancing. But the Court obviously has been trying to achieve some accommodation between the principle that out-of-state commerce should 'pay its way' by contributing to the costs of state government, and the need to protect it from 'undue' burdens of taxation.** Here, too, discrimination against out-of-state commerce is forbidden, and here the Court has been sensitive also to burdens of multiple taxation on the same property or activity. But states, hungry for revenues, have been imaginative in developing complex formulae that would identify the state's particular 'contribution' and 'services' to the local activities of multi-state enterprises, and would justify an appropriate measure of taxation of the property or revenue of the enterprise.

Again, most of the relevant law has been made in interstate cases and, again, it doubtless applies also to foreign commerce.[54] The revenue needs of the states, and their entitlement to a fair return for 'services' rendered, will support a fairly-apportioned tax on earnings or property of companies engaged in foreign commerce.† But here one might expect

---

* In principle, the states may protect the health of their citizens against dangers from foreign commerce as well, for example, by quarantine laws. See n. 49 to this chapter. An old case also upheld state game protection laws even as to animals in foreign commerce. See n. 49 to this chapter. But such state laws, too, can be supplanted by Act of Congress.

Even when states law does not fall before the dormant Commerce Clause it may be precluded by 'preemption' because Congress intended to 'occupy the field' and exclude the states. See p. 157 above.

** Also, the state can raise revenue from other sources, and need not raise it from taxation that burdens foreign commerce.

† The Supreme Court laid down guiding principles in 1977, in the *Brady* case, n. 55 to this chapter. A state tax will not survive scrutiny if it applies to an activity lacking a substantial nexus to the states; or if it is not fairly apportioned; or if it discriminates against interstate (or foreign) commerce; or if it is not fairly related to the services which the state provides. In respect of foreign commerce the Court later identified two additional concerns—the enhanced risk of multiple taxation, and the danger that state taxation might interfere with the federal government's capacity 'to

that the courts would be especially sensitive to state taxes that might burden the foreign relations of the United States, and which are often tantamount to a duty or impost (or a tax on exports) which are expressly forbidden to the states.[55]

Under its power to regulate foreign commerce, Congress can, of course, bar state regulations which the courts would tolerate if Congress were silent. It is also established that Congress can permit the states to regulate commerce in ways that would not stand were Congress silent.[56] So far as the Commerce Clause is concerned,* then, in principle Congress could authorize the states to exclude foreign commerce, to discriminate against it, to impose heavy burdens upon it, to satisfy minor local interests at the price of major obstacles to such commerce, to establish a patchquilt of local idiosyncrasies.** But such concessions to localism have been infrequent domestically, and rare (if any) as regards foreign commerce.

State 'Intrusion' into Foreign Affairs

The limitations on state regulation or taxation of foreign commerce were found to be implied in the Commerce Clause. The Court never asked whether such state actions might run afoul also of some larger principle limiting the states in matters that relate to foreign affairs. Such a larger principle—how large is yet to be determined—has apparently become part of the Constitution.

Until 1968 there was no hint of such a principle.[57] In the governance of their affairs, states have variously and inevitably impinged on U.S. foreign relations. They regulate and tax commerce with foreign nations. They regulate the rights of foreign nationals resident or present in their territory. Even laws that apply identically to aliens and citizens might invite issues with foreign governments. But states have also singled out aliens for special treatment, subjecting them to registration, limiting their right to own or inherit property, to work, to engage in trade or professions, to direct or own stock in domestic corporations, to use state recreational and other facilities. In the absence of supervening federal

---

speak with one voice when regulating commerce relations with foreign governments'. See *Japan Lines*, n. 55 to this chapter.

   * But presumably Congress could not authorize the states to do what the Constitution expressly prohibits them, e.g., to coin money or emit bills of credit. See pp. 151–2 above and n. 40 to this chapter.

   ** Subject, however, to other constitutional doctrines, notably the due process clause and other provisions of the Bill of Rights. See Ch. IX.

law, state courts apply state law and policy in deciding whether domestic law or foreign law should apply to a transnational transaction; whether to give effect to a foreign act of state that imposed a tax or penalty, or was criminal in character, or that confiscated property outside its territory; whether to enforce the judgment of a foreign court.[58] Some of these state regulations have indeed been struck down because they violated the Fourteenth Amendment or other constitutional restraints applicable to the states—including the 'dormant Commerce Clause'—or because they were inconsistent with federal policy as expressed in a treaty, statute, executive act, or judicial decision. But it had not been suggested that they might run afoul of an implicit constitutional limitation barring state intrusion on the federal domain of foreign relations even when the federal government had not acted.[59] Indeed, in 1947, in upholding a California statute that allowed an alien to inherit in the state only if his (her) country permitted U.S. citizens to inherit, the Supreme Court rejected such a claim as 'far fetched'.[60]

In 1968, the Supreme Court decided *Zschernig* v. *Miller*.[61] Pursuant to state statute, the Oregon courts had denied an inheritance to a resident of then-independent 'German Democratic Republic' (East Germany) because he could not satisfy them that the laws of his (Communist) country allowed U.S. nationals to inherit estates in that country, and that the East German heir would receive payments from the Oregon estate 'without confiscation, in whole or in part'. In a brief *amicus curiae* before the Supreme Court, the U.S. Department of Justice said that the federal government 'does not contend that the application of the Oregon escheat statute in the circumstances of this case unduly interferes with the United States' conduct of foreign relations'.[62] The Supreme Court, however, reversed the state court, finding 'an intrusion by the State into the field of foreign affairs which the Constitution entrusts to the President and the Congress'.[63]

This was new constitutional doctrine. No doubt, an act of Congress or a treaty, probably an executive agreement, perhaps an official executive declaration, possibly even a rule made by the federal courts, could have forbidden what Oregon purported to do. Here there was no relevant exercise of federal power* and no basis for deriving any prohibition for the states by 'interpretation' of the silence of Congress and the

---

* The Supreme Court was not purporting to make federal substantive law. Compare *Sabbatino*, Ch. V, p. 137. In *Zschernig*, the Court found that the Constitution itself preempted the field for the federal government and told the states to stay out.

President. The Court told us that the Constitution itself excludes such state intrusions even when the federal branches have not acted.[64]

Zschernig v. *Miller*, then, imposed additional limitations on the states, but what they are and how far they reach still remain to be determined. Political branches might prescribe for particular cases or even provide some guidelines, as under the Commerce Clause, but it will be largely for the courts, and may take many years and many cases, to develop the distinctions and draw the lines that will define the *Zschernig* limitations on the states.[65] It may prove that *Zschernig* v. *Miller* excludes only state actions that reflect a state policy critical of foreign governments and involve 'sitting in judgment' on them.[66] Even if so limited, the doctrine might cast doubts on the right of the states to apply their own 'public policy' in transnational situations.* Or was the Court suggesting different lines—between state acts that impinge on foreign relations only 'indirectly or incidentally' and those that do so directly or purposefully?[67] Between those that 'intrude' on the conduct of foreign relations and those that merely 'affect' them? Difficulties with similar formulae in the Commerce Clause cases may yet lead instead to doctrines like those that grew there: certain impingements on foreign affairs are excluded because national uniformity is required; infringements are barred if they discriminate against or unduly burden our foreign relations; the courts will balance the state's interest in a regulation against the impact on U.S. foreign relations.

The *Zschernig* doctrine does not, of course, substitute the judgment of the federal courts for that of the federal political branches; it asserts only the authority of the courts to strike down state acts when the political branches have not acted. In the Commerce Clause cases, we saw, the Court recognized the right of Congress to permit burdens on commerce that would have been invalid had Congress not spoken. In *Zschernig*, the Court seemed to hold that a communication expressing State Department toleration of the Oregon law was not enough to validate it, but it was perhaps resisting *ad hoc* direction to the courts in par-

---

* It would presumably condemn also 'sense resolutions' on foreign policy by state legislatures though such resolutions are not law and could not be invalidated, and state legislatures presumably cannot be prevented or enjoined from adopting them. Some argue that such resolutions, e.g. those 'urging nuclear arms control and respect for human rights seem intended primarily to raise public consciousness, stimulate public discussion, and persuade or influence the federal government to consider or reexamine particular policies'. See Bilder, n. 65 to this chapter.

Some old state resolutions on foreign affairs are cited in WRIGHT (n. 3 to Ch. I) 264–5 n. 5. The practice continues.

ticular cases. It is difficult to believe that the Court would find constitutionally intolerable state intrusions on the conduct of foreign relations that the political branches formally approved or tolerated.* Domestic considerations apart, there might be foreign relations reasons why the political branches might deem it desirable to leave some matters to the states rather than deal with them by formal federal action.[68]

Zschernig was a judicial reaction to a state's contributions to the Cold War. Even while the Cold War endured, there were few such state incursions, few challenges to such state intrusions in the courts, and none (after *Zschernig*) that reached the Supreme Court. Other areas of international tension also invited state involvement; notably, during the latter years of apartheid in South Africa, state and municipal governments anticipated (and some supplemented) federal sanctions, and some of these sanctions by the states were challenged in court.[69] The Supreme Court, however, has not had occasion to return to *Zschernig* and the case remains a unique statement and a sole application of constitutional doctrine.**

STATES RIGHTS LIMITATIONS ON NATIONAL POLICY

If the states have been effectively excluded from foreign affairs, federalism has suggested some reciprocal limitations, deriving from states' rights, on federal powers to conduct foreign relations. In general, the Tenth Amendment ('The powers not delegated to the United States by the Constitution . . . are reserved to the States . . .') has been dismissed†️ as stating 'but a truism that all is retained which has not been surrendered'.[70] Yet it has remained the symbol of states' rights and of the doctrine of limited, enumerated, federal powers, a guide to interpreting constitutional grants of power to the federal government and an influence for limiting them.[71] In regard to foreign affairs, however, the Supreme Court has repeatedly rejected limitations based on 'invisible radiations' from that Amendment.[72] The Amendment was circumvented in principle when the Court accepted that the federal government has

---

* Compare the unwillingness of Justices to follow *ad hoc* Executive directions in Act of State cases. See Ch. V, p. 138.

** One would be bold to predict that it has a future life; might it remain on the Supreme Court's pages, a relic of the Cold War?

† But see *New York* v. *United States*, discussed this chapter, p. 166 and n. 76 to this chapter.

foreign affairs powers not expressly enumerated in the Constitution; little was left of it in fact when the courts recognized vast powers in Congress,[73] and federal powers to make treaties and executive agreements, to do other executive acts, and to make law through judicial power, without regard to reserved states' rights.

Whatever the states retain in regard to foreign affairs as a matter of constitutional right must be found in other doctrines. There are dicta by Justices and by writers asserting hypothetical limitations on federal power, including its foreign affairs powers, in specific constitutional guarantees to the states and in implied state sovereignty and inviolability. Justices have said that a treaty cannot cede a state's territory without its consent; presumably, the United States could not, by treaty or by statute for international purposes, modify the republican character of state governments or, perhaps, abolish all state militia.* Under the Eleventh Amendment,** foreign governments and foreign nationals cannot sue a state in the courts of the United States without its consent.[74] There is also something left, too—how much cannot be said with confidence—of the sovereign immunity of the states, which would presumably limit federal regulation under foreign affairs powers as well. State immunities have shrunk radically and state activities are generally subject to federal regulation,[75] but Justice Frankfurter said:[76]

There are, of course, State activities and State-owned property that partake of uniqueness from the point of view of intergovernmental relations. These inherently constitute a class by themselves. Only a State can own a Statehouse; only a State can get income by taxing. These could not be included for the purposes of federal taxation in any abstract category of taxpayers without taxing the State as a State.

State immunity to federal taxes might be particularly plausible since they are least restrictive of federal authority—the federal government can get revenue other than by taxing the states—but an early dictum had it generally that the federal government cannot 'destroy the [State] nor curtail in any substantial manner the exercise of its powers'.[77] Beginning in 1976, in *National League of Cities*, the Court struggled with the claim that the Tenth Amendment precludes Congressional regulation of governmental activities of a state that partakes of traditional governmental functions. A sharply divided Court abandoned that notion in 1985, with dissenting Justices threatening to reopen the issue. In 1992, an again-divided Court settled on a narrow immunity: Congress cannot command

---

  * See Ch. VII, pp. 193–4.
  ** In 1996 the Supreme Court gave the Eleventh Amendment renewed vitality of yet unknown significance. *See Seminole Tribe of Florida* v. *Florida*, 116 S. Ct. 1114.

state legislatures to enact or not to enact legislation, and in dicta a majority of the Justices declared that Congress cannot 'co-opt' state officials to do federal bidding.[78]

These issues may not be definitively resolved for a long time. However they are resolved, it remains to be seen whether a measure of state immunity would apply in foreign affairs as well, and which federal foreign affairs regulations (in what circumstances) might be held to invade such state immunity.

POLITICAL INFLUENCE OF THE STATES

If the constitutional limitations in favor of the states in foreign affairs are few and largely hypothetical, the federal system gives the states opportunities to affect foreign relations, not necessarily in fortunate, constructive ways. State actions (or inactions) can violate the obligations of the United States under international law, as when they 'deny justice' to foreign nationals or infringe on the human rights of their inhabitants in violation of conventions to which the United States is party.[79] States and state officials sometimes fail to carry out U.S. obligations to foreign countries or to their citizens, or deny aliens treaty rights, or fail to prevent private persons from violating them. And federal remedies against such state failures—principally through the federal courts—may not be available or effective, or may take inordinately long.[80] If the states will often heed informal State Department intercession in support of U.S. international obligations, the Department will usually have less influence to prevent embarrassing 'sense resolutions' by state legislatures on foreign issues.

The principal influence of the states in foreign relations derives from the constitutional, decentralized, federal framework of government and the political forces that animate it. Much of our foreign relations does not affect the states or local interests directly, and state governors and legislatures are often indifferent to and even ignorant of major national foreign policies. But where foreign affairs begin to touch the states, whether in their particular economic interest (as in issues of free trade versus protectionism), or even in small matters of pride or prejudice or principle, the plenary powers of the national government take on all the colors of federalism.* The President has a national constituency and is chief of a national party, but both are built of local blocks and he

* Consider also the extraordinary influence of particular states in particular matters, e.g. that of Florida in 1996 in achieving the enactment of the Helms-Burton Act on Cuba, Ch. V, n. 36.

cannot be impervious to their qualities and interests. His diplomatic representatives are, or are made, acutely aware of our federal character—as when they hesitate to negotiate about 'local matters', or insist on adding to treaties 'federal–state' clauses that are constitutionally unnecessary but politically attractive.* The Senate still substantially represents the states and has often protected their interests and adopted their views, as when it refused consent to treaties that would allow aliens to practice the professions regardless of state requirements, or entered reservations to human rights conventions so as not to override state laws permitting capital punishment for crimes committed by juveniles.[81] The House of Representatives represents 'the people', but it is the people of the states,[82] and is often even more 'parochial' than the Senate, sometimes obstructing 'enlightened', 'internationalist' federal regulation on behalf of interests that are even less than statewide. And, for their part, states assert their 'international' interests, sometimes in far-reaching forms.[83]

The political influence of the states in national policy rises and falls, but what has been said in the past about federalism generally still has ample relevance, even in regard to foreign relations:

The continuous existence of the states as governmental entities and their strategic role in the selection of the Congress and the President are so immutable a feature of the system that their importance tends to be ignored . . . The actual extent of central intervention in the governance of our affairs is determined far less by the formal power distribution than by the sheer existence of the states and their political power to influence the action of the national authority. . .

Far from a national authority that is expansionist by nature, the inherent tendency in our system is precisely the reverse, necessitating the widest support before intrusive measures of importance can receive significant consideration, reacting readily to opposition grounded in resistance within the states.[84]

Recent international issues of importance underscore both the weakness of state constitutional claims and their strong political relevance. During the Uruguay Round trade negotiations of the 1990s, for example, various federalism (and states' rights) issues were raised (principally by some who opposed the agreements generally). Some objected that provisions in the Agreements impinged on matters that had been, and are generally, governed by state law, such as product-safety regulation, banking and insurance, and local 'tax breaks' and other subsidy practices. Some objected because the Uruguay Round Agreements declared the responsibility of the national government for compliance with the

---

* See nn. 5, 81 to this chapter.

agreements, including compliance by state and local authorities. Some argued that such agreements were beyond the power of the federal government and violated the Tenth Amendment, or at least required the consent of the states.*

The appeals to constitutional argument are not persuasive. Federal regulation of foreign commerce commonly addresses matters that would otherwise be governed by state law. Federal regulation of foreign commerce can be effected by treaty, by Congressional–Executive agreement, or by ordinary Congressional legislation; and regulation by any of these methods are equally binding on the states. The United States is fully responsible for the observance of international agreements by state or local governments, whether or not the agreement expressly so provides.** To the extent that there is constitutional immunity for the states from federal action that purports to command or co-opt the state legislatures or state officials,† that immunity presumably applies to regulation by treaty as well as by statute or Congressional–Executive agreement; in fact, no international agreement to which the United States is party includes provisions that raise such issues.

In the Uruguay Round negotiations, constitutional arguments did not prevail but political sensitivity to state sensibilities were reflected in several ways. The Uruguay Round Agreements Act provides that the agreement shall not itself invalidate state law, but requires an act of Congress to achieve that end. The Act also provides that the courts may invalidate state law on the ground that it is inconsistent with the Agreement only in an action brought by the federal government for that purpose. Congress also provided a role for the states in the dispute settlement process.[85]

Political change during the 1990s is not likely to lead to a larger constitutional role for the states in U.S. foreign affairs, but it promises to continue to enhance their political relevance and influence, even in foreign affairs.

* Some argued that such provisions required that the agreements be concluded as treaties (with the consent of two-thirds of the Senate) rather than by Congressional–Executive agreement. See Ch. VII, footnote on p. 218.

** Except where the international agreement prescribes particular remedies and particular means of enforcement, the United States is free to decide how it will carry out its obligations and may leave much implementation to the states, but the United States remains internationally responsible for compliance. Of course, if the other parties agree, the United States may limit its obligations to supersede state law or to guaranty state compliance, but other parties resist such limitations. See the discussion of 'federal–state clauses' in Ch. VII, footnote on p. 192.

† See n. 78 to this chapter.

III

COOPERATION WITH OTHER NATIONS UNDER THE CONSTITUTION

The Constitution distributes the authority of the United States among the three branches of the federal government, identified and characterized according to 'classical' theory: the legislative power to Congress, the Executive power to the President; the Judicial power to a federal judiciary headed by the Supreme Court. But as regards the conduct of foreign affairs, the Framers were not wholly agreed as to how certain activities should be characterized and where responsibility for them should be allocated; surely, they were reluctant to entrust authority over them along the lines followed in domestic governance. We have seen an irregular distribution of authority between President and Congress in regard to war and lesser hostilities. Apparently, the Framers could not agree, or did not wish, to follow the traditional lines in allocating authority and responsibility in respect of international law, treaties and other international agreements. The Framers were firmly committed to the rule of international law ('The Law of Nations'), but except to declare that Congress had power to define offenses against the law of nations, the Constitution says nothing more about international law, about its relation to the Constitution, to U.S. law, and to state law, about the respective responsibilities of the branches of the federal government, and the obligations of the states, to respect and give effect to that law.

The Constitution has more say about treaties: the Framers did not wish to entrust authority to make them to one or another of the political branches, and they determined rather to mix and 'check and balance' their making. The Framers were concerned to assure the supremacy of treaties to state law, but they did not make explicit and clear the place of treaties in the hierarchy of U.S. law, in relation to the Constitution, and to acts of Congress. And they did not make clear and explicit the authority and responsibility of the various branches in assuring respect for treaty obligations, or in any decision to terminate those obligations.*

In the twentieth century, nations began to establish, by treaty or other international agreements, a multiplicity and variety of international arrangements and organziations which the Framers of the U.S. Constitution could not have anticipated. The government of the United States, the courts, students of the Constitution, have had to fit and squeeze these institutions into our constitutional framework, not always easily, or comfortably, or with confidence.

I address constitutional issues relating to treaties and other international agreements in Chapter VII, the constitutional issues of

---

* As twentieth century constitutions have learned to do.

international law and those—still largely hypothetical—of international organizations, in Chapter VIII.

Chapter VII

TREATIES, THE TREATY POWER, AND EXECUTIVE AGREEMENTS

TREATIES

For the Constitutional Fathers, the foreign relations of the new Republic depended heavily on treaties to be concluded (or not concluded) with other countries; therefore, who should have the power to make treaties, and the status of treaties when made, were questions of special concern to them.[1] The Framers were eager to abandon treaty-making by Congress, which, under the Articles of Confederation, determined whether to negotiate and with whom, appointed negotiators, wrote their instructions, followed their progress, approved, modified or rejected their product. Because they took treaties and international obligations seriously, the Framers were not eager for the United States to conclude treaties lightly or widely, and were disposed to render it difficult to make them.[2] They were concerned to end the anarchy that prevailed under the Articles of Confederation and to assure that treaties made by the United States would be honored by the individual states.[3]

And so, after dispute and compromise, the Framers gave the power to make treaties to the President, but only with the advice and consent of the Senate, and provided two-thirds of the Senators present concur (Article II, section 2); they provided that, like the Constitution itself and the laws of the United States, treaties shall be the supreme law of the land and binding on the states (Article VI, clause 2); they expressly forbade treaty-making to the states (Article I, section 10). The Framers did not stop to distinguish treaties from other international agreements or commitments.* They did not prescribe what purposes treaties might serve, or suggest limitations upon them. They did not anticipate and consider how to resolve potential conflict between treaties and the

---

* A distinction between treaties and 'Agreements or Compacts' with foreign states is implied in the limitations imposed on the states, Art. 1, sec. 10. See Ch. VI p. 151.

Constitution, or between treaties and laws, or competition for power between the treaty-makers and the lawmakers.

THE TREATY-MAKING PROCESS

Article II, section 2 of the Constitution provides that the President 'shall have Power, by and with the Advice and Consent of the Senate, to make Treaties, provided two thirds of the Senators present concur'.[4]

It is the President, then, who makes treaties, and the power to make them is listed in the Article dealing with the Executive power. Treaty-making has often been characterized as an executive function (in that special sense in which the conduct of foreign relations is executive),[5] but writers on the Constitution have considered the making of treaties to be different from other exercises of Presidential power, principally because of the Senate's role in the process;* perhaps too because treaties have particular legal and political qualities and consequences.

In the second half of the twentieth century, nations have increasingly turned to multilateral treaties for various forms of international governance as well as to codify customary international law. The process required by the Constitution applies equally to multilateral as to bilateral treaties: the President makes a treaty for the United States when he adheres to a multilateral treaty, whether or not U.S. representatives participated in its preparation, whether or not the United States signed it,**

---

* Contemporary writings sometimes refer to 'the treaty-makers.'

** Modern international practice commonly provides for signature subject to later ratification, but—especially in regard to multilateral treaties—it does not preclude accession to a treaty without prior signature. For the United States, the President, under his Foreign Affairs Power and by implication in his power to make treaties, has constitutional authority to sign a treaty for the United States, subject to ratification after he receives consent of the Senate.

Under international law, a treaty is not without some legal significance after signature and pending ratification. See RESTATEMENT (n. 2 to Preface) § 312(3). In the United States, the international legal significance of a treaty signed by the President but not yet consented to by the Senate (and therefore not yet ratified by the United States) must depend on the President's own constitutional authority. Some treaties provide for their provisional application pending ratification, for example the Convention on the Law of the Sea (1982) as modified by the 1994 agreement; such provisional application depends on the constitutional authority of the President, Ch. II, or on authorization, express or implied, by Congress, p. 215 this chapter. See, e.g., Charney, 'U.S. Provisional Application of the 1994 Deep Seabed Agreement', in *Law of the Sea Forum*, 88 AM. J. INT'L L. 687, 705 (1994). On whether or not it is already in force for other countries. Senate consent is required for U.S. adherence to a multilateral treaty as to a bilateral treaty.

The President's part in treaty-making seems clear.[6] He decides whether to negotiate with a particular country (or countries) on a particular subject. He appoints and instructs the negotiators and follows their progress in negotiation. If he approves what they have negotiated, he seeks the consent of the Senate, and if he obtains it he can 'make' the treaty.*

The President and the Senate

It is the Senate's part in treaty-making that has raised questions and generated issues. As originally conceived, no doubt, the Senate was to be a kind of Presidential council, affording him advice throughout the treaty-making process and on all aspects of it—whether to enter negotiations, who shall represent the United States, what should be the scope of negotiations, the positions to be taken, the responses to be made, the terms to be accepted.[7] Almost from the beginning, however, Presidents found that conception of the Senate's function uncongenial, perhaps unworkable; the Senate, for its part, also rejected it, seeking to deliberate and pass judgment later and independently, rather than to advise.[8] Once, President Washington talked to the Senate as a body about a forthcoming treaty,[9] but since then no President has done so, nor has advice often been sought or given by exchange of messages.[10] As the Senate grew, surely, the President could not readily seek its advice before he began to negotiate and at every new development in some distant, complex negotiation.

In a word, 'advice and consent' has effectively been reduced to 'consent'. The Senate does not formally advise on treaties before or during negotiations. (Failure to seek or obtain such advice no doubt has

provisional application generally, see RESTATEMENT (n. 2 to Preface) § 312, Comment *l*, Reporters' Note 7.

If the President wishes to have the United States adhere to a multilateral treaty (even one concluded by others without U.S. participation), he seeks the advice and consent of the Senate, and if the Senate consents, the President can 'make' the treaty, i.e., adhere to it for the United States.

* The Senate gives consent to making the treaty, the President makes it. If it had been previously signed for the United States (by authority of the President), the President later ratifies it for the United States (after he obtains Senate consent). See n. 6 to this chapter.

sometimes led to failure of later consent). Presidents have developed informal substitutes, consulting Senate leaders or members of its Foreign Relations Committee.* In our day, Presidents have appointed Senators to delegations negotiating treaties so that they will contribute their sense of what the Senate will accept (and later deter and disarm Senate opposition).[11] In the past there was controversy about this practice, in part because of the 'incompatibility clause' of the Constitution.** Some argued that the participation of Senators in the negotiation of a treaty derogated from independent consideration by the Senate; the practice is now common and no longer challenged.

The requirement of Senate consent is an important 'check' on Presidential power to make foreign policy by treaty; inevitably, it has bred controversy. A case has been made that often in our history the Senate denied consent not because it thought the proposed treaty was not in the national interest, but from considerations of partisan politics: a Senate controlled by the opposition party might withhold its consent from a significant treaty in order to deny a President political advantage, especially in an election year.[12] Once, Secretary of State John Hay, bloody from encounters with the Senate, said that he 'did not believe another important treaty would ever pass the Senate'.[13] President Wilson's searing experience with the Treaty of Versailles† gave further support for the Senate's appellation as the 'grave-yard of treaties'. There have been proposals to eliminate at least the need for concurrence by two-thirds of the Senators present, with its implicit assumption that a

* In a well-known instance after the Second World War, Senator Vandenberg was encouraged to promote a resolution in which the President was 'advised of the sense of the Senate' that the United States should conclude a North Atlantic treaty. See n. 11 to this chapter. Of course, the Senate can give advice on its own initiative, or upon informal suggestions.

** Art. I, sec. 6, cl. 2 provides: 'No Senator or Representative shall, during the Time for which he was elected, be appointed to any civil Office under the Authority of the United States, which shall have been created, or the Emoluments whereof shall have been increased during such time; and no Person holding any Office under the United States, shall be a Member of either House during his Continuance in Office.'

When President Madison appointed a Senator and a Representative to serve on the commission to negotiate peace with Great Britain in 1814, they resigned from Congress. There was recurrent controversy over the constitutionality of the practice of appointing members of Congress to delegations, again during the McKinley Administration, and the practice was abandoned, to be revived after the Treaty of Versailles fiasco.

† In an attempt to avoid the onus of patently rejecting the Treaty of Versailles, the Senate purported to consent, but with numerous and radical reservations.

Senator voting 'no' is *'ipso facto* twice as well informed and weighty as one of his colleagues who votes "yes" '.[14] After the Second World War, and especially during the decades of the Cold War, Presidents and the Senate often declared that partisan politics should 'stop at the water's edge', and U.S. treaty-making also profited.

In recent years, in part as a result of the efforts of Senators and of more effective coordination and informal consultations by the Executive branch, few treaties have been rejected by the Senate.[15] But a box-score of consents and rejections tells less than the whole story of the Senate's importance in treaty-making. Treaties are not fungible: one rejection of a Treaty of Versailles is not balanced by consent to ten routine extradition treaties. And if the Senate has become more sensitive to the onus of explicitly rejecting what the United States and other nations have labored to conclude, it has not hesitated to let treaties gather dust on Senate shelves.[16] Presidents, moreover, have avoided sending treaties (notably multilateral treaties) to the Senate, or have refrained from pressing for Senate action,* when its consent seemed improbable or might require a struggle which the President was not prepared to undertake. Negotiators have always kept clearly in mind that the treaties they produce will have to be acceptable to the Senate and meet its objections, political or constitutional, partisan or substantive, real or pretended.

The requirement of Senate consent introduces 'slippage' but also provides opportunity for second thoughts. Presidents have refused to send to the Senate treaties already negotiated, or have refrained from pressing for Senate consent to treaties submitted by their predecessors; they have withdrawn treaties from the Senate before it acted; they have refused to ratify treaties to which the Senate consented.[17] President Carter did not press for a Senate vote on SALT II with the Soviet Union when there appeared to be a significant likelihood of its defeat; later President Reagan withdrew the treaty from Senate consideration. For years, subsequent Presidents did not press the Senate to act on human rights covenants and conventions which had been transmitted by President Carter.[18] For its part, the Senate has sometimes given or denied consent and then reconsidered its action.[19] There is no authoritative decision or precedent on the question, but the Senate can probably withdraw, modify, or impose conditions on consent it had given, before the President concludes the treaty.[20]

---

* Sometimes Senate inaction reflects a lack of enthusiasm by the Executive branch, especially by a new Administration, for a treaty transmitted earlier. See, for example, the history of international human rights agreements, nn. 16 and 18 to this chapter.

Reservations and Other Conditions

In many cases the Senate has given its consent subject to conditions.[21] Whether the Senate insists on a modification in the terms of a treaty, or on a particular interpretation of it, or on some limitation of its consequences, Senate conditions may require renegotiation,* to the dismay of Presidents and the impatience of other governments. But all have long recognized this additional obstacle in the United States treaty process.[22]

In the latter part of the twentieth century, Senate conditions on its consent to a treaty have commonly taken the form of 'reservations', 'understandings', or 'declarations',** but the terms are not always used with care and with attention to the differences among them.†

A reservation is a condition imposed by a state upon its adherence to a treaty, usually to a multilateral treaty, modifying or limiting its obligation under the treaty or under some particular provision. Strictly, the Senate cannot itself enter a 'reservation'; it is the President who might enter a reservation on behalf of the United States, upon U.S. adherence to a treaty. But as a condition of its consent to U.S. adherence, the Senate can insist on change in the treaty. In the case of a bilateral treaty already negotiated by the President, the Senate might give its consent on condition that the President (and the other party) renegotiate and amend the treaty in some specific respect.‡ In the case of a multilateral

---

* Renegotiation is ordinarily not feasible in the case of multilateral treaties already concluded and in effect for other states. But ingenuity in response to special circumstances can produce even that result. Compare, for example, the conclusion of the 1994 Agreement effectively modifying the 1982 Convention on the Law of the Sea. See p. 176 note, this chapter.

** Or even 'provisos'. See, e.g., Senate consent to ratification of the International Covenant on Civil and Political Rights, n. 49 to this chapter.

† See n. 25 to this chapter. In the last decades of the twentieth century, a 'package' of reservations, understandings, and declarations, ('R.U.D.s') became a common attachment to major treaties, e.g. when the Senate consented to the Panama Canal treaty, to arms control agreements with the USSR, or to multilateral human rights conventions.

‡ If the Senate requires changes in a bilateral treaty, the United States would not ordinarily adhere to the treaty with the reservation asked by the Senate, but would negotiate a changed text.

Some speak of Senate 'amendments' to describe reservations that seek a change in the treaty obligations, as distinguished from other conditions the Senate might impose. Strictly, the Senate cannot 'amend' a treaty; it can refuse consent unless the parties amend it. For what is described as an effort by a Senate committee to negotiate directly with a foreign government, see W. HOLT, TREATIES DEFEATED BY THE SENATE (1933) 107, 180-1.

treaty, already negotiated by a number of states and often already in force for other states, the Senate might consent to U.S. adherence on condition that the President enter one or more reservations on behalf of the United States. (Unless later withdrawn, the U.S. reservation remains a 'permanent' attachment to its adherence to the treaty.)

The constitutional authority of the Senate to insist on reservations has not been seriously questioned.[23] If the Senate can give or withhold consent it can also give its consent on condition that changes be made. Or, one might say, the Senate withholds consent from the treaty presented to it but indicates how the treaty might be revised so as to earn its consent, and gives consent in advance to a treaty as so revised. (Of course, the President might decide not to 'make' the treaty in the terms that are satisfactory to the Senate.)[24]

Sometimes the Senate will express a particular interpretation of the treaty as a condition of its consent. Sometimes the Senate can be persuaded to achieve clarification or even some modest modification of a treaty provision without insisting on a reservation, by expressing instead its 'understanding' of the provision.[25] That understanding is ordinarily communicated to the other party (or parties) and, if accepted or acquiesced in, there is no issue, and the treaty need not be reopened nor a reservation entered.[26] There is danger, however, of failure of communication that may later engender doubt and controversy as to whether the parties had agreed to the same terms.[27]

The Senate has sometimes imposed conditions that seek not modification of the international obligations of the United States under a treaty but some control of its effect in the United States. In an extended and unedifying controversy with several Presidents early in the twentieth century, the Senate consented to United States adherence to general arbitration conventions only on condition that any specific submission to arbitration thereafter also obtain the consent of the Senate.[28] The Senate has sometimes insisted that a treaty should not take effect, or that action under it shall not be taken by U.S. officials,* without prior approval of Congress.[29] There have been conditions requiring the President to perform some domestic act.[30] On several occasions the Senate declared that nothing in the treaty shall enhance the powers of the President, or that nothing in the treaty shall add to, or subtract from, the reach of the powers of Congress.[31] In 1988, the Senate, in consenting to the Intermediate Nuclear Forces Treaty (INF) with the

---

* See the discussion of non-self-executing treaties, p. 198 below.

USSR,* declared a 'constitutional principle' to guide the interpretation of the treaty by the United States.[32]

A different question is whether the Senate can impose conditions on its consent to a treaty that are unrelated to the treaty itself. The Senate has never attempted to do so, but one may ask, hypothetically, whether it can tell the President that it will consent to some treaty only if he dismisses his Secretary of State. Perhaps such conditions were not contemplated, perhaps the Senate that made them would be abusing its power, and indeed it seems incredible that a Senate would put such a condition, at least formally and publicly. But since the Senate can withhold its consent for no reason, perhaps it can withhold it for any reason, and a President may have to buy that consent at whatever price and in whatever form the Senate asks. It would be particularly difficult to conclude that when the Senate imposes a condition that is not 'proper', the President can disregard the condition, treat the Senate's consent as unconditional and proceed to ratify the treaty.**

Differences between the Senate and the Executive branch have continued to trouble the treaty-making process. In general, the Executive has sought to discourage the Senate from imposing conditions on its consent. The Executive has also attempted to maintain distinctions between 'reservations', 'understandings', and 'declarations', and to determine which of these Senate statements are intended as conditions on its consent, and which of these conditions affected U.S. obligations under the treaty and had to be communicated to and accepted by the other party (or parties) if there is to be a treaty binding on the United States.[33]

One implication of the constitutional requirement of Senate consent surfaced in (1985–87) in a tempest surrounding the interpretation of a provision in the Anti-Ballistic Missile Treaty (ABM) with the USSR.[34] At stake was a politically important difference between a 'narrow' and a 'broad' interpretation of that treaty, between a construction that

---

* The Senate took its part in treaties particularly seriously and sought to enhance its importance, during the series of arms control treaties with the USSR in the 1970s and 1980s. Dissatisfied with how the Executive treated the various conditions it imposed, it also indicated which had to be communicated and which required explicit agreement by the USSR. See nn. 31, 32, 33 to this chapter.

** Compare the discussion of the doctrine of unconstitutional conditions, Ch. IV, p. 119. Under that doctrine the condition is held invalid, whereas a Senate condition, no matter how untenable, if not met, may vitiate Senate consent to the treaty.

The Senate has also taken to attaching to its resolutions a variety of statements which the Senate does not intend to be conditions upon its consent. That seems to free the Senate to be promiscuous with its declarations and some of them are of dubious 'propriety', though they may qualify as 'advice'. See n. 33 to this chapter.

would permit and one that would forbid steps by the United States toward a radical Strategic Defense Initiative (SDI or 'Star Wars') program. At the time the Senate gave consent, it had apparently understood the treaty to be more rather than less restrictive, less rather than more permissive; the Executive branch apparently shared that interpretation. Several years later the Executive branch (under a later Administration) was disposed to read the treaty as less restrictive, but the Senate persisted in its earlier understanding of the treaty.

The ABM confrontation was unprecedented, but it was perhaps an inevitable consequence of our unique, complex treaty process, involving independent, powerful, constitutionally-based institutions. The particular treaty and its circumstances no doubt contributed to exacerbating the controversy. The controversy involved a major security treaty, concluded after long negotiations that were heavily shrouded; the general subject of the treaty—arms control—and the particulars of the treaty under negotiation, were esoteric, and as to the subject as well as the particulars both the Executive branch and the Senate were ambivalent (and both internally divided). Moreover, both the President and Senate had been uneasy about making a commitment, both were distrustful of the USSR, and the Senate and the Executive did not trust each other fully. As to the particular treaty, a later President, less than wholly sympathetic to the treaty and eager to relax its restraints on the United States, was tempted to revise an earlier President's undertakings to which the Senate had consented. But the majority of the Senate continued to favor the treaty and resisted a new interpretation. Above all, perhaps, the Senate was determined to vindicate its earlier consent and to preserve the integrity of its consent power.*

* The Senate later attached its principle of treaty interpretation as a 'condition' to its consent to the ratification of the Intermediate Nuclear Forces Treaty (INF). See p. 181 above and note 32 to this chapter.

The controversy surrounding the interpretation of the ABM Treaty highlights larger consequences of our treaty process and of the separation of powers for the international relations of the United States. In the United States, all branches of the government are bound by a treaty made by the President as the Senate understood it. Presumably, the United States (the President) must pursue that interpretation also for international purposes. But the international system—including international courts and arbitral tribunals—is not bound by the subtleties of the United States treaty procedure or by internal interpretations that are not expressed, adopted, and communicated to the other parties to the treaty. The international system, then, may come to an interpretation of a treaty different from the one the Senate tacitly assumed. If that happens and is established, the international interpretation of the treaty may later become the meaning within the United States as well.

For a time the Executive branch appeared to take the position that since the Senate's understanding of the treaty had not been formally declared, the President was free to interpret the treaty later as he saw fit. That view, I think, was mistaken: whether or not the Senate expressed an understanding, what the Senate in fact thought the treaty meant is the treaty to which it consented. The challenge to that view was untenable, and the Executive branch may itself have later abandoned it.*

Once the Senate has consented, the President is free to make (or not to make) the treaty and the Senate has no further authority in respect of it. Attempts by the Senate to withdraw, modify or interpret its consent after a treaty is ratified have no legal weight; nor has the Senate any authoritative voice in interpreting a treaty after it is in effect, or any part in terminating it.** Of course, in its legislative capacity as one of the two houses of Congress (as distinguished from its executive role as one of the treaty-makers) the Senate participates in whatever Congress can do as to the legal effect of treaties in the United States.†

WHAT IS A TREATY?

The Constitution speaks of 'treaties', without defining them. For the Framers, no definition was needed: treaties were long and well known in international law and practice.[35] Treaties need no definition today, but, in fact, the term has been authoritatively defined, without dissent. A treaty is 'an agreement between two or more states or international organizations that is intended to be legally binding and is governed by

---

* In that case, there appears to have been also an issue as to whether the Senate was entitled to rely on informal Executive communications. The Executive branch insisted, in effect, that the Senate must accept what the President formally communicates and not form any understandings on the basis of informal communications from individuals in the Executive branch. There is something to be said for the view that ordinarily the Senate should not rely on views or communications of individual officials, but—at bottom—the Senate gives its consent to the treaty as it understands it, no matter how or from whom it obtains that understanding.

** See pp. 211–14. A Senate resolution explaining its understanding of a treaty to which it had previously consented without reservation was without legal effect. *Fourteen Diamond Rings* v. *United States*, 183 U.S. 176 (1901). But if, as a condition of its consent to a treaty, the Senate should reserve special powers to interpret or terminate the treaty, a President might have to accord it that role or refuse to ratify the treaty because he cannot meet its conditions. Compare the reservation to the Versailles Treaty, nn. 29 and 30 to this chapter.

† See p. 209 below.

international law'.[36] That, we may assume, defines a treaty also for purposes of the U.S. Constitution. But—for constitutional law as for international law—there must be an agreement, a bona fide agreement, between states,* not a 'mock-marriage'. So, hypothetically, if in order to circumvent the House of Representatives and the states, the President wrote a uniform divorce law, applicable to the United States alone, into 'a treaty', and the Prime Minister of Canada cooperated in the scheme by signing his name to it, it would presumably not be a treaty under international law, and therefore not a treaty under the Constitution.[37] This is a hypothetical example of a hypothetical limitation: no 'agreement' made by the President and Senate has ever been challenged as a 'pseudo-treaty'.

LIMITATIONS ON TREATIES

The Constitution does not expressly impose prohibitions or prescribe limits on the Treaty Power, nor does it patently imply that there are any.[38] No provision in any treaty has been held unconstitutional by the Supreme Court and few have been seriously challenged there.[39] It is now settled, however, that treaties are subject to the constitutional limitations that apply to all exercises of federal power, principally the prohibitions of the Bill of Rights; numerous statements also assert some minor limitations on the reach and compass of the Treaty Power.

Once, indeed, there was extant a myth that treaties are equal in authority to the Constitution and not subject to its limitations. The doctrine, propagated even by eminent authority, found its origins, no doubt, in the language of the Supremacy Clause (Article VI, clause 2): 'This Constitution, and the Laws of the United States which shall be made in Pursuance thereof; and all Treaties made, or which shall be made, under the Authority of the United States, shall be the supreme Law of the Land. . .'

* That may be what Jefferson had in mind in the first clause of his suggested limitations on the Treaty Power. See the footnote on p. 189, this chapter: a treaty 'must concern the foreign nation party to the contract, or it would be a mere nullity, *res inter alios acta*'.

To be distinguished is a unilateral treaty, an agreement with obligations only by one state to another. Neither international law nor U.S. constitutional law requires that a treaty have reciprocal undertakings; there have been many bona fide, valid unilateral treaties in the past, where the undertakings are all by one party, such as a cession of territory or a claims settlement, or a peace treaty (following unconditional surrender).

Reading that language, Justice Holmes said:[40]

Acts of Congress are the supreme law of the land when made in pursuance of the Constitution, while treaties are declared to be so when made under the authority of the United States. It is open to question whether the authority of the United States means more than the formal acts prescribed to make the convention.

Holmes read 'in pursuance' of the Constitution to mean 'consistent with its substantive requirements', and that phrase has been commonly so interpreted;[41] if so, the language does indeed lend itself to Holmes's dictum. Long before he wrote, however, that anomalous language of the Supremacy Clause had been explained otherwise: to the Framers, 'in pursuance of' the Constitution meant—or meant also—'following its adoption'. But they wished to provide in the Supremacy Clause that treaties made before the adoption of the Constitution (principally the treaties with France and Great Britain that were being resisted in some states) should also be the law of the land and binding on the states.[42] Hence the different locution for treaties than for 'the laws of the United States'.

Perhaps Holmes did not know of that explanation; perhaps he did not accept it. Perhaps he thought that if the Framers were seeking only to maintain the supremacy of preexisting treaties they might readily have designed explicit language to that end; it can be argued that preexisting treaties were fully taken care of in the phrase 'treaties made or which shall be made',[43] and that there must have been another purpose in the failure to require that treaties be 'pursuant' to the Constitution. One can suggest reasons why the Framers might have intended not to subject treaties to any constitutional limitations.[44] They might have thought that in its international relations the United States should be equal and sovereign, not hampered by restraints that limit what the federal government can do within its own national family.* It might have appeared

---

* Compare, for example, the suggestion that the powers essential to the common defense 'ought to exist without limitation . . . The circumstances that endanger the safety of nations are infinite, and for this reason no constitutional shackles can wisely be imposed on the power to which the care of it is committed.' THE FEDERALIST No. 23 (Hamilton).

The Netherlands Constitution (Article 60) and other contemporary constitutions apparently contemplate that, for the courts, treaties might not be subject to constitutional limitations applicable to acts of parliament. See n. 134 to this chapter.

It is not obvious that the Framers saw in the Constitution any limitations applicable to treaties. Compare Rawle, n. 38 to this chapter. The limitations of the original Constitution were principally those implied in federalism and the separation of

particularly unacceptable that an individual be able to assert his particular grievance in order to have a treaty declared unconstitutional by the courts, frustrate important national interests, and invite perhaps grave international consequences.[45]

Such arguments have in fact been made but, long before the suggestion lightly dropped by Holmes, the Supreme Court pronounced (albeit in dictum) that the Treaty Power does not extend 'so far as to authorize what the Constitution forbids'.[46] Holmes himself stressed that the treaty he was considering 'does not contravene any prohibitory words to be found in the Constitution'.[47] Congress has always assumed that there were limits on the Treaty Power for, from the beginning, it gave the federal courts jurisdiction over suits 'where is drawn in question the validity of a treaty'.[48] The treaty-makers themselves have thought they were subject to limitations.[49] During the extensive and intensive debates on the Bricker Amendment (1951–55) no one claimed that treaties were free of constitutional limitations: those who objected to making that clear by constitutional amendment insisted that it was clear enough without amendment.[50]

In 1957, Justice Black laid the issue to rest:[51]

no agreement with a foreign nation can confer power on the Congress, or on any other branch of Government, which is free from the restraints of the Constitution. . . . The prohibitions of the Constitution were designed to apply to all branches of the National Government and they cannot be nullified by the Executive or by the Executive and the Senate combined.

The prohibitions set forth in Article 1, section 9, then, though contained in the article devoted principally to Congress and following immediately upon the catalogue of its powers, would doubtless be held to apply to treaties as well:[52] a treaty cannot grant a title of nobility, or lay a duty on articles exported from any state, or give preference to the ports of one state over those of another. Treaties, surely, are also subject to the Bill of Rights.*

---

powers and these are hardly relevant to the Treaty Power. Today, the limitations of Art. I, sec. 9, probably apply to treaties but it is not clear that the Framers contemplated that result. Even the original Amendments, which became the Bill of Rights, were not obviously relevant to treaties, and the only provision that might be, the First Amendment, is in terms addressed to Congress only.

* Even the First Amendment, though expressly addressed to Congress, and the prohibitions implied elsewhere, e.g., in the citizenship clause of the Fourteenth Amendment. See Ch. IX, pp. 285 *et seq.*

An argument might be made that these prohibitions do not limit the power to make treaties, but only forbid giving them effect as law of the United States; that

The Constitution does not provide that some matters cannot be dealt with by treaty, or that particular dispositions are beyond the authority of the treaty-makers.* From our constitutional beginnings, however, there have been assertions that the Treaty Power is limited by implications in the character of treaties, in other provisions of the Constitution, in the Constitution as a whole, in the philosophy that permeates it and the institutions it established—notably in the separation of powers among the branches of the federal government and the division of authority between that government and the states.[53] In the Supreme Court, the best known statement of implied limitations on the Treaty Power is probably that of Justice Field in *Geofroy* v. *Riggs*:[54]

The treaty power, as expressed in the Constitution, is in terms unlimited except by those restraints which are found in that instrument against the action of the government or of its departments, and those arising from the nature of the government itself and of that of the States. It would not be contended that it extends so far as to authorize what the Constitution forbids, or a change in the character of the government or in that of one of the States, or a cession of any portion of the territory of the latter, without its consent . . . But with these exceptions, it is not perceived that there is any limit to the questions which can be adjusted touching any matter which is properly the subject of negotiation with a foreign country.

These and similar dicta,[55] I stress, were expressed by the Court long ago, and in the course of upholding an exercise of the Treaty Power; each statement was asserting the fullness of that power rather than restrictions upon it. Only cautious phrases, such as '*properly* the subject

conceptual distinction will generally have no consequence in fact, since Presidents will not knowingly make treaties that would be unenforceable. Whether these prohibitions apply outside the United States, see Ch. IX.

It is a different question whether a treaty that exceeds any of these limitations is binding in international law, whether the other party to the treaty can be charged with knowledge of our constitutional limitations, whether the United States can defend against an international claim on the ground that the treaty made in violation of a nation's constitution is 'fundamental' and the other party knew or had reason to know the lack of authority to make it. See RESTATEMENT (n. 2 to Preface) § 311(3) and Comment *c*; Vienna Convention on the Law of Treaties, May 23, 1969, arts. 46, 47, reprinted in 63 AM. J. INT'L L. 875, 890 (1969).

* By contrast, the Articles of Confederation provided that no treaty should restrain state legislatures 'from imposing such imposts and duties on foreigners as their own people are subjected to, or from prohibiting the exportation or importation of any species of goods or commodities whatsoever'. Art. IX. Compare Rawle, n. 38 to this chapter. On the right to prohibit the importation of slaves by treaty, see n. 52 to this chapter.

of negotiation with a foreign country', suggest possible limitation, but with the exceptions Justice Field mentioned (changes in the character of government, cession of state territory) there is no indication that any of the Justices had in mind any particular limitation or any category or principle of limitation. But some limitations have been suggested by others, notably by Thomas Jefferson,* and deserve brief attention.[56]

Limitations Implied in Federalism

In the past, the principal attacks on the scope of the Treaty Power flew banners of federalism and 'States' rights'.

The Constitution denies the states the power to make treaties and gives them no part in the national treaty-making process.** But states

---

* Thomas Jefferson early 'codified' a series of limitations on the Treaty Power in his Manual of Parliamentary Practice. 'By the Constitution of the United States this department of legislation is confined to two branches only of the ordinary legislature—the President originating and the Senate having a negative. To what subjects this power extends has not been defined in detail by the Constitution; nor are we entirely agreed among ourselves. 1. It is admitted that it must concern the foreign-nation party to the contract, or it would be a mere nullity, *res inter alios acta*. 2. By the general power to make treaties, the Constitution must have intended to comprehend only those subjects which are usually regulated by treaty, and can not be otherwise regulated. 3. it must have meant to except out of these the rights reserved to the States, for surely the President and Senate can not do by treaty what the whole Government is interdicted from doing in any way. 4. And also to except those subjects of legislation in which it gave a participation to the House of Representatives. This last exception is denied by some on the ground that it would leave very little matter for the treaty power to work on. The less the better, say others. . .' Sec. LII. The manual is widely reprinted e.g., in SENATE MANUAL, S.DOC. No. 102–1, 101nd Cong., 1st Sess. 21 *et seq.* (1993). The quoted section is there at 516–18.

Jefferson was no friend of the Treaty Power. The limitations he enumerates would leave little room for treaties; they have long proved to be 'bad guesses', and notable evidence that ours has not become a Jeffersonian Constitution. But similar limitations have been suggested by others, some again recently. See nn. 54 and 57 to this chapter.

In many other respects Jefferson's manual (based on British parliamentary practice), prepared for his own use as presiding officer of the Senate, is still recognized as authoritative and underlies the current rules of both houses of Congress.

** Art. I, sec. 10, and see Ch. VI. The Constitution responds to concerns of federalism in that the President, the principal treaty-maker, is elected by a process reflecting our origins as a union of states, and, especially, in that the Senate, the other participant in the treaty process, historically has been particularly representative of the states and of state interests. See n. 4 to this chapter.

have sometimes seen an interest in asserting limitations on the Treaty Power as on other exertions of federal authority. At bottom, their argument was that treaties could not deal with matters reserved to the states, as contemplated by the constitutional scheme* and as expressly provided in the Tenth Amendment.[57] The claim was repeatedly made and repeatedly rejected by the Supreme Court, finally and definitively in *Missouri* v. *Holland,*[58] perhaps the most famous and most discussed case in the constitutional law of foreign affairs.

The background of the case is illuminating. In 1913, Congress enacted a statute to regulate the hunting of migratory birds.[59] Two lower federal courts[60] declared the statute invalid, finding that it was not within any enumerated power of Congress,** and the Department of Justice feared that the statute might meet the same fate in the Supreme Court. It was suggested, however, that migratory birds were a subject of concern to other nations as well, for example Canada; and if the United States and Canada agreed to cooperate to protect the birds, Congress could enact the legislation it had previously adopted under its power to do what is 'necessary and proper' to implement the treaty. The treaty was made,[61] the statute enacted, and the Supreme Court upheld it.

Missouri v. *Holland* involved the validity of the act of Congress, not the validity of the treaty itself, but if 'the treaty is valid there can be no dispute about the validity of the statute under Article I, § 8, as a necessary and proper means to execute the powers of the Government'.[62] Justice Holmes articulated the argument of the State of Missouri and disposed of it:

It is said that a treaty cannot be valid if it infringes the Constitution, that there are limits, therefore, to the treaty-making power, and that one such limit is that what an act of Congress could not do unaided, in derogation of the powers reserved to the States, a treaty cannot do. An earlier act of Congress that attempted by itself and not in pursuance of a treaty to regulate the killing of migratory birds within the States had been held bad in the District Court. . .

Whether the two cases cited were decided rightly or not they cannot be accepted as a test of the treaty power . . . It is obvious that there may be matters of the sharpest exigency for the national well being that an act of Congress could not deal with but that a treaty followed by such an act could, and it is not lightly to be assumed that, in matters requiring national action, 'a power which must belong to and somewhere reside in every civilized government' is

---

* That argument was made by Jefferson, above.

** At the time, the courts took a narrow view of the power of Congress 'To regulate Commerce with foreign Nations and among the several States' (Art. I, sec. 8). See n. 60 to this chapter and Ch. III, p. 65.

not to be found . . . With regard to that we may add that when we are dealing with words that also are a constituent act, like the Constitution of the United States, we must realize that they have called into life a being the development of which could not have been foreseen completely by the most gifted of its begetters. It was enough for them to realize or to hope that they had created an organism; it has taken a century and has cost their successors much sweat and blood to prove that they created a nation. The case before us must be considered in the light of our whole experience and not merely in that of what was said a hundred years ago. The treaty in question does not contravene any prohibitory words to be found in the Constitution. The only question is whether it is forbidden by some invisible radiation from the general terms of the Tenth Amendment. We must consider what this country has become in deciding what that Amendment has reserved.[63]

Holmes's eloquence needs no applause but it may have distracted attention from the core of his argument.[64] What he said, simply, was that the Constitution delegated powers to various branches of the federal government, not only to Congress; the Treaty Power was delegated to the federal treaty-makers, a delegation additional to and independent of the delegations to Congress.* Since the Treaty Power was delegated to the federal government, whatever is within its scope is not reserved to the states: the Tenth Amendment is not material. Many matters, then, may appear to be 'reserved to the States' as regards domestic legislation if Congress does not have power to regulate them; but they are not reserved to the states so as to exclude their regulation by international agreement.**

The argument is clear and indisputable and disposes of the arguments of Jefferson and others who have made Missouri's claim before and since.[65] Without asking whether Congress could regulate such matters in the absence of treaty, the Court has consistently upheld the validity and supremacy of treaty provisions dealing with matters as local as the right to inherit land or to engage in local trade.[66] And yet, the argument has recurred in various guises and, even after *Missouri* v. *Holland,* even official American negotiators continued to assert that the United States could not by treaty regulate, say, armaments manufacturing, because manufacturing was a local activity reserved for regulation by the

* Unlike the delegations to Congress which give it authority over enumerated substantive areas of national policy, the treaty power is authority to make national policy (regardless of substantive content) by international means and process for an international purpose.

** They are, one might say, left to the states subject to 'defeasance' if the United States should decide to make a treaty about them.

states.[67] Later, United States representatives sometimes favored 'federal–state clauses' that would set obligations for federal states different from those of unitary states,* sometimes supported with arguments reflecting mistaken constitutional, 'reserved rights' limitations on the treaty-making powers.[68]

Eventually, the implications of *Missouri* v. *Holland* were recognized and understood, but not everywhere welcomed. They were particularly objectionable to those who resisted U.S. adherence to treaties by which the United States might accept common international standards for governmental behavior towards its own citizens, for example international human rights covenants and conventions. Between 1952 and 1957, there was a concerted effort bearing the name of Senator Bricker of Ohio to amend the Constitution in order, in particular, to 'overrule' *Missouri* v. *Holland*.[69] The principal clause of the principal version of the Bricker Amendment would have provided that 'A treaty shall become effective as internal law in the United States only through legislation which would be valid in the absence of treaty.'** Congress, then, would have no power to enact pursuant to a treaty a law that it could not enact apart from treaty, thus foreclosing legislation such as that upheld in *Missouri* v. *Holland*, and effectively cutting the Treaty Power down to the size of Congressional power. The amendment's proponents did not recognize, however, that *Missouri* v. *Holland* had already lost its import-

---

* At one time, the United States sought to limit its obligations under particular treaties to those matters that were 'within the jurisdiction' of the federal government, and to exclude any international obligation as to matters subject to the jurisdiction of the states. In time, recognizing that virtually any matter governed by treaty was 'within the jurisdiction' of the United States, the Executive branch took to declaring that the convention shall be implemented by the federal government to the extent that it 'exercises jurisdiction' over matters covered by the treaty, leaving to the states implementation of matters over which they exercise jurisdiction. See n. 68 to this chapter. But the federal government exercises jurisdiction over virtually all matters covered in treaties if only by making the treaty. It exercises jurisdiction over such matters because Congress has the power to legislate in respect of them. International law requires the United States to carry out its treaty obligations but, in the absence of special provision, does not prescribe how, or through which agencies, that shall be carried out. As a matter of international law, then, the United States could leave the implementation of any treaty provision to the states. Of course, the United States remains internationally responsible for any failure of implementation. See p. 203, this chapter.

** The provision would, in effect, have made all treaties non-self-executing. See p. 198 below.

ance:* its principal point, that there were 'matters of the sharpest exigency for the national well being that an act of Congress could not deal with but that a treaty followed by such an act could', ceased to be true in fact, for with expanding Congressional power there were virtually no matters of any exigency—including human rights legislation—with which Congress could not deal even in the absence of treaty.[70] After the Bricker controversy faded, further extensions of the powers of Congress to enact 'human rights' legislation, by new readings of the Thirteenth and Fourteenth Amendments,[71] rendered it even clearer that the Bricker Amendment would not have effectively barred adherence to the treaties at which it aimed.** For our purposes, however, I note that the amendment was not adopted, and its failure only reaffirmed *Missouri* v. *Holland* as the law of the Constitution.

Missouri v. *Holland*, I stress, did not say that there were no limitations on the Treaty Power in favor of the states, only that there were none in any 'invisible radiation' from the Tenth Amendment. The Constitution probably protects some few states' rights, activities, and properties against any federal invasion, even by treaty.† Justice Field (and others) said that without a State's consent its territory could not be ceded by treaty to a foreign country.[72] Because 'The United States shall guarantee to every State in the Union a Republican Form of Government'‡, the treaty-makers presumably could not adhere to a treaty that would modify the republican form of government of the states (or of any state).[73] 'A well-regulated militia, being necessary to the security of a free state',§ and the right to train the militia and appoint its officers being expressly reserved to the states§§ (subject to Congressional regulation), could the United States agree to abolish all state militia, for example in a treaty for general and complete disarmament?[74] There are perhaps remnants of state sovereign immunity that

---

* One purpose of some supporters of the amendment—to prevent bringing an end to racial segregation by international agreement—was frustrated and rendered moot when the U.S. Supreme Court held segregation to be a violation of the Constitution. *Brown* v. *Board of Education*, 347 U.S. 483 (1954).

** Senator Bricker lost the constitutional battle but perhaps not his political war. In large part because of 'Brickerite' opposition, the United States long refused to adhere to human rights covenants and conventions. When, finally, the United States adhered to several of them, it did so subject to major reservations, understandings and declarations (including 'federal–state' clauses, n. 68 to this chapter) which, in the view of many, substantially vitiated U.S. adherence. See pp. 202–3 and nn. 68 and 101 to this chapter.

† See generally Ch. VI, p. 165 *et seq.*   ‡ Art. IV, sec. 4.
§ The Second Amendment.   §§ Art. I, sec. 8, cl. 16.

might stir questions about a hypothetical treaty—say, a disarmament agreement with inspection provisions that permits intrusion upon the statehouse, or a treaty that commands state legislatures to adopt laws or that coopts state officials.[75]

Limitations Deriving from the Separation of Powers

Because the President and the Congress compete for power in the conduct of foreign relations, because the treaty-makers are the President and one house of Congress but not the other, because treaties, we shall see, often have effect as law (as do acts of Congress), it was inevitable that questions should arise about the relations between the 'treaty-makers' and the Congress, and not surprising that these relations might suggest limitations on the scope of the Treaty Power. Early in our history, members of the House of Representatives argued that treaties could regulate only that which could not be otherwise regulated;[76] and they could not deal with matters that were in the domain of Congress since that would exclude the House from its rightful legislative role.* In one sense, no regulation accomplished by treaty can be achieved by act of Congress, since only a treaty can create a system of regulation entailing international obligations:** legislation conditioned on reciprocity might approximate such a treaty but it would bind neither the United States nor the other nation.[77] But if the limitations suggested mean more, if they would preclude treaties on matters as to which Congress could legislate domestically, it would virtually wipe out[78] the Treaty Power.† Under modern, established views of the powers of Congress, there is little—or nothing—that is dealt with by treaty that could not also be the subject of legislation by Congress.

This limitation was hardly accepted by all even in our earliest days; it has now been long dead. That objection was rejected again in 1978, when some objected to treaties said to be giving away U.S. property,

---

* The first argument echoes Jefferson's second clause, the second argument his first clause. See p. 189 note, this chapter. Any such limitations in favor of the House (or of the Congress as a whole) might presumably be satisfied by associating the House (or the Congress as a whole) in the treaty-making process. Compare an analogous suggestion as regards the states, p. 189, and n. 76 to this chapter.

** Even a unilateral treaty, containing only undertakings by the United States, would create an irrevocable international obligation, which is not accomplished by an act of Congress to the same effect. Compare Calhoun, quoted in nn. 54, 78 to this chapter.

† As Jefferson recognized. See p. 189 and n. 76 to this chapter.

something, it was argued, that only Congress could do.[79] Treaties have dealt with many matters that were also subject to legislation, e.g., tariffs and other regulations of commerce with foreign nations; on many subjects, treaties and acts of Congress have been alternative means of regulation, one by agreement, the other unilaterally,* sometimes on condition of reciprocity.[80] The House of Representatives has frequently bristled, but its exclusion from the treaty process was the clear constitutional plan, and the House has not been able to command the cooperation of the Senate and the President to accept modification of their privileged prerogatives.[81] The House has had to find consolation in that it has some voice when, as often, the President must come to Congress for appropriation of funds or other implementation of a treaty, or when the treaty-makers voluntarily leave some subjects to regulation by Congress (e.g., international tariffs and trade). For political rather than constitutional reasons, Presidents and the Senate have also accepted that trade and tariff agreements** should generally be by executive agreement based on the authority of both houses of Congress rather than by treaty.[82] Presidents have also learned to take account of House sensibilities informally by consulting its leaders about major treaties.

The Treaty Power, then, is not limited by the powers of Congress,† but it is assumed to be subject to other radiations from the separation of powers. It has been stated that a treaty cannot increase, diminish, or redistribute the constitutional powers of the branches of the federal government or delegate them to others—say, the power of Congress to declare war, or the President's command of U.S. armed forces, or a court's exercise of judicial power, or indeed the power of the treaty-makers to make international agreements for the United States.[83] These

---

* Hence the occasional conflict between treaties and statutes, p. 209 this chapter. The converse argument, that some matters can be regulated only by treaty, not by Act of Congress, has also not survived.

A different question, discussed below, is whether the treaty-makers can make treaties on certain matters self-executing, or whether they require acts of Congress to give them effect as law of the land. See p. 203, this chapter.

** On other subjects, too, Presidents have sometimes preferred to seek approval of an international agreement by joint resolution of Congress. See p. 215 below.

† The judicial power, too, does not prevent treaties impinging on the U.S. judicial system. For example, it would not prevent a treaty whereby the United States and Great Britain would confer upon each other's courts jurisdiction over offenses committed on the other's vessels on the high seas. 19 OP. ATT'Y GEN. 644 (1890). For argument that the judicial power of the United States can devolve only on courts established by Congress (not by treaty), see Ch. VIII, pp. 266 *et seq* and nn. 81, 84 and 89 to Ch. VIII.

examples are almost wholly hypothetical, but such issues have been raised, particularly in regard to United States participation in international organizations; I consider them in that context. (Chapter VIII.)

Some have purported to find in the separation of powers a different limitation, that a treaty cannot 'bargain away' the powers of any of the branches—say, the power of Congress to impose a tariff or declare war. That argument is fallacious. Any treaty commitment by the United States 'bargains away' its earlier right to do the contrary, usually by act of Congress or the President: a treaty that grants free entry for goods makes it unlawful, under international law, for Congress to exercise its constitutional powers to impose duties or imposts; a treaty that gives immunity from judicial process to member representatives to the United Nations has 'bargained away' some authority of the Executive, the Congress, the federal courts, and their counterparts in every state and city. But such self-limitations are what many treaties are about, presumably in exchange for some advantage to the United States. A treaty, moreover, does not dispose of constitutional power: internationally the United States retains the power (not the right) to violate its treaty obligations; constitutionally, the President and Congress can exercise powers even in violation of a treaty undertaking.* Congress, for example, could authorize aggressive war in violation of the United Nations Charter or raise and support an army in violation of a disarmament agreement.

Domestic Matters, Not of 'International Concern'

In their doctrine, at least, those who saw limitations on the treaty power in principles of the separation of powers did not seek to restrict federal power, only the authority of the President-and-Senate alone to adhere to treaties on certain matters. Alleged limitations on the treaty power based on federalism would deny federal power, but ostensibly their object, too, was not to avoid international undertakings of the United States but to prevent federal aggrandizement and diminution of state authority.[84] (In theory, all agreed that the United States could adhere to those treaties with the consent of all the states.) Arguments from both separation of powers and federalism, however, probably carried strands of deeper objection, of resistance to 'foreign governance', to foreign influence and scrutiny. And so, when it proved that neither federalism nor separation of powers provided any significant limitation on the Treaty Power, a different limitation was conceived: under the

---

* I deal further with this question in relation to U.S. participation in international organizations, Ch. VIII.

Constitution, it was argued, only matters of 'international concern' are permissible subjects for treaties.[85] That limitation, of uncertain constitutional origins, was once widely accepted, and some invoked it to oppose adherence by the United States to modern international undertakings, e.g., human rights covenants and conventions.[86]

Authority for such a limitation was found in an address[87] by Charles Evans Hughes.* It may be that Hughes was merely echoing Jefferson's requirement** that a treaty be a bona fide agreement between the United States and another country: by hypothesis, a bona fide treaty deals with a foreign nation about matters 'which pertain to our external relations', that are of mutual 'international concern'. But Hughes was interpreted to mean that some matters are not appropriate subjects for agreement with another country because they are our own affair and not the legitimate 'concern' of any other country.[88] I know no basis for reading into the Constitution such a limitation on the subject matter of treaties.† (Nor would I know any formula for determining which matters are and which are not our 'business' or the proper 'business' of other countries.)

That 'Hughes doctrine' has now been authoritatively abandoned.[89] If there are reasons in foreign policy why the United States seeks an agreement with a foreign country, it does not matter that the subject is otherwise 'internal', that the treaty 'makes laws for the people of the United States in their internal concerns', or that—apart from treaty—the matter is 'normally and appropriately . . . within the local jurisdictions of the States'. Any treaty that has any effect within the United States, including the traditional treaties of friendship and commerce, are specifically designed to change the law of the United States that might otherwise apply, e.g., the rights of aliens here.[90] As other policies and laws of the United States become of interest to other countries, they are equally subject to modification by treaty if the United States has foreign policy reasons for negotiating about them.

If there were any basis for the Hughes doctrine, and if it barred some hypothetical agreement on some hypothetical subject, surely it is not relevant where some would have invoked it—to prevent adherence by the United States to international human rights covenants and

---

* He had been Governor of New York, Associate Justice of the Supreme Court, unsuccessful candidate for the Presidency, and Secretary of State; later he was appointed Chief Justice of the United States.

** See p. 189 note, this chapter.

† Such a constitutional doctrine would have made Senator Bricker's struggle to amend the Constitution largely unnecessary, legally as well as politically.

conventions.[91] Human rights had long been of international concern and the subject of international agreements when Hughes spoke—in the treaties of hundreds of years ago guaranteeing religious freedom, in agreements to abolish the slave trade, in the minority treaties of the nineteenth century and of Post-First World War. Since Hughes spoke, after the Second World War and the Holocaust, we entered 'the age of rights', and human rights became a focus of international concern, as reflected in peace treaties, in the Nuremberg Charter and in the United Nations Charter, in numerous international covenants and conventions[92] to which the states of the world have adhered.* For the United States, reciprocal or parallel human rights undertakings have obvious foreign relations purposes,[93] as Presidents and Senators have recognized.**

TREATIES AS LAW OF THE LAND

I have been discussing the constitutional requirements for making treaties, as well as once-argued constitutional limitations on the international obligations which the United States can assume by treaty. The Constitution also prescribes the place and the effect of treaties in the law of the United States.

Self-executing and Non-self-executing Treaties

In some constitutional systems, treaties are only international obligations, without effect as domestic law; it is for the parliament to translate them into law, and to enact any domestic legislation necessary to carry out their obligations. The U.S. Constitution established a different regime. The Supremacy Clause (Article VI, clause 2) provides:

---

* Towards the end of the twentieth century, all the states of the world have recognized that human rights are of international concern, for example, by joining to bring an end to apartheid in South Africa. Virtually every one of more than 180 states is party to one or more covenants or conventions.

** The United States has in fact adhered to a number of such agreements, including the Genocide Convention, the Convention Against Torture, the International Covenant on Civil and Political Rights, the Convention on the Elimination of All Forms of Racial Discrimination, and Presidents have requested Senate consent to ratification of the Convention on the Elimination of All Forms of Discrimination Against Women, the Convention on the Rights of the Child, and others. See n. 101 to this chapter.

This Constitution, and the Laws of the United States which shall be made in Pursuance thereof; and all Treaties made, or which shall be made, under the Authority of the United States, shall be the supreme Law of the Land; and the Judges in every State shall be bound thereby, any Thing in the Constitution or Laws of any State to the Contrary notwithstanding.

That clause, designed principally to assure the supremacy of treaties to state law, was interpreted early to mean also that treaties are law of the land of their own accord and do not require an act of Congress to translate them into law.* Chief Justice Marshall said:

A treaty is in its nature a contract between two nations, not a legislative act. It does not generally effect, of itself, the object to be accomplished, especially so far as its operation is infra-territorial; but is carried into execution by the sovereign power of the respective parties to the instrument.

In the United States a different principle is established. Our constitution declares a treaty to be the law of the land. It is, consequently, to be regarded in courts of justice as equivalent to an act of the legislature, whenever it operates of itself without the aid of any legislative provision.

Not all treaties, however, are in fact law of the land of their own accord. Marshall continued:

But when the terms of the stipulation import a contract, when either of the parties engages to perform a particular act, the treaty addresses itself to the political, not the judicial department; and the legislature must execute the contract before it can become a rule for the Court.[94]

Marshall distinguished between a treaty that 'operates of itself'—the normal treaty provision—and the exceptional treaty (or treaty provision) that promises 'to perform a particular act'. Both kinds of treaty contain 'promises', undertakings by the United States, binding under international law. But in a treaty that operates of itself, the undertaking by the United States automatically has the quality of law: the Executive and the courts are to give effect to the treaty undertaking without awaiting any act by Congress.[95] We denominate such a treaty 'self-executing'.[96] Marshall, however, felt obliged to read an exception into the Supremacy Clause. A treaty by which the United States promises 'to

* As an original matter, one might have asked whether the purpose of achieving the supremacy of federal treaties required that they become law automatically, and whether indeed that was the purpose and purport of the Supremacy Clause: the supremacy of treaties would have been achieved even if they required Congressional legislation to give them domestic effect as law. But Marshall's interpretation of the Supremacy Clause has been established law from our national beginnings.

perform a particular act', creates an obligation which the United States must carry out through the political branch that has the constitutional authority to perform the act promised.* Thus, if the United States has undertaken to enact a law, say to make genocide a crime, Congress has the obligation to enact such law; the courts cannot carry out the United States' promise to enact a law; they cannot treat the treaty in which the United States promised to enact a law as itself the law promised. Similarly, if the United States undertakes to do a particular act that in the United States can only be done by a law—say, to appropriate and pay money—that undertaking has to be carried out by Congress, the political branch that has constitutional authority to appropriate money.** The courts cannot consider the treaty itself as the equivalent of the act of Congress required by the Constitution.

By the Constitution, as Marshall recognized, treaty undertakings are generally, in principle, self-executing. Marshall, it appears, felt compelled to infer an exception for a treaty promise that by its character could not be self-executing. Whether a treaty promise is of that special character that cannot be self-executing often depends on how the treaty undertaking is couched. And sometimes the terms of the treaty are ambiguous so that it is not clear whether the undertaking by the United States was such that it could 'operate of itself' (and be enforced by the courts), or whether the United States promised only 'to perform a particular act' which, under the Constitution, only Congress can do, not the treaty itself.

What the treaty promised may have to be determined in the first instance by the Executive who must decide whether to proceed to 'take care' that the treaty itself be faithfully executed as law, or whether the Executive is required to seek implementation by Congress. Or, the courts, asked to give effect to the treaty as law, may have to decide whether the treaty should be read as promising only that the United States would 'perform a particular act', that the political branches (usually Congress) would enact a law that would provide the benefits promised. The courts have considered that to be a matter of interpreta-

---

* Sometimes federal legislation adopted prior to the treaty (and even for other purposes) may be available to implement a treaty obligation; sometimes the President may have authority to carry out those obligations without Congressional authorization. State law may also serve to implement non-self-executing obligations. Strictly, if a treaty is not self-executing it is not the treaty but the implementing legislation that is effectively 'law of the land'. Sometimes the implementing legislation gives the treaty itself legal effect or incorporates it by reference. See p. 203.

** Art. I, sec. 9. See p. 203 below.

tion of the agreement,* but agreements have often been drafted without attention to that question so that it may be difficult to determine what was contemplated.** In particular instances, United States negotiators have been careful to make clear that the treaty will require Congressional implementation: in the North Atlantic Treaty, for example, it was accepted by all parties that no events would put the United States automatically at war; if war were called for, Congress would have to declare it.[97]

The question whether a treaty is itself law or is promising to enact law becomes more difficult when the United States adheres to a multilateral treaty in the drafting of which it was only one participant, or did not participate at all. Such a treaty, intended for adherence by states having different constitutional jurisprudence as to treaties, might be drafted so as to make it self-executing for states whose jursiprudence contemplates such effect for treaties, and obligating others to execute the obligation promptly, but often the drafters do not have that problem in mind.

What seems clear, from the language of the Constitution and of John Marshall, is that in the United States the strong presumption should be that a treaty or a treaty provision is self-executing, and that a non-self-executing promise is highly exceptional. A tendency in the Executive branch and in the courts to interpret treaties and treaty provisions as non-self-executing runs counter to the language, and spirit, and history of Article VI of the Constitution.[98]

In recent years, the President, on his own initiative or at the behest of the U.S. Senate by declaration attached to its consent, has sometimes purported to declare non-self-executing treaties that by their terms and

* They will, therefore, give Executive views on the question 'great weight'.

It is sometimes said that whether a treaty is to be self-executing or not depends on the intent of the United States at the time the treaty is made. But the intent of the United States may not be the intent of the other party or parties. It is more accurate to say that the question is what the parties intended and what the United States promised and the other party (or parties) accepted. In the case of a multilateral treaty, in particular, what a party promised is determined by interpreting the provision, not by the intent of the party (unless communicated by reservation or understanding).

** Other parties to a treaty, of course, prefer that a treaty be self-executing in the United States in order that they may enjoy rights under it immediately upon proclamation of the treaty (see n. 95 to this chapter), without awaiting legislative implementation. Whether a treaty is self-executing or not, the obligation of the United States becomes effective with exchange of ratifications, and if the treaty is not self-executing the President is obliged to seek any required legislative implementation promptly.

by their character are (or could well be) self-executing, could 'operate of themselves' and be given effect as law of the land.* The Executive branch and the Senate have pursued that practice in particular in relation to U.S. adherence to human rights covenants and conventions.[99]

In my view, that recent practice, accepted without significant discussion,[100] is 'anti-Constitutional' in spirit and highly problematic as a matter of law.** In the Supremacy Clause, the Constitution declared treaties—generally, presumably all treaties—to be the law of the land. John Marshall read an exception into that Article in respect of treaties that by their character could not be self-executing; nothing in the Constitution, or in Chief Justice John Marshall's opinion, suggested that treaties which the Constitution declares to be law of the land need not be 'faithfully executed' by the President, or enforced by the courts, because the President or the Senate (or both) so decided. If the treaty-makers thought it was necessary or desirable to include a role for Congress in special cases, such as in taking the United States into war

---

* Congress has also declared non-self-executing some trade agreements concluded as Congressional–Executive agreements. See n. 183 to this chapter. There, however, the Supremacy Clause is not directly implicated and the role of the Senate not prejudiced; and requiring implementation does not complicate the process: Congress can authorize or approve the agreement and implement it simultaneously.

** To be distinguished, in my view, is a declaration by the Senate in regard to a particular treaty because of special circumstances, as in the *Niagara Power* case, nn. 29, 100 to this chapter.

The Senate might insist that declaring a treaty to be non-self-executing is a condition of its consent to the treaty, but that condition would seem to be against the spirit of Art. VI. However, the Senate might insist that the President not deposit the instrument of U.S. ratification until Congress adopted necessary implementing legislation, as the Senate did in consenting to the Genocide Convention and the Convention against Torture. See n. 101.

It has been argued that non-self-executing treaties are more 'democratic' because they leave law-making in the hands of Congress (not in the Senate alone) by majority (not two-thirds vote). That, however, is not what the Constitution provides or what the Framers intended. A role for the House of Representatives in making treaties was rejected and recurrent attempts to amend the Constitution to that effect have had little support. Leaving the Treaty Power where it lies, but making treaties non-self-executing, is particularly questionable since it requires the consent of two-thirds of the Senate and later the approval of the Senate again (by majority vote) to implement the treaty. Compare the discussion of Congressional–Executive agreements as an alternative to treaties, p. 217 below.

Of course, every self-executing treaty might have been written as a promise to execute, but that requires the agreement of other parties, which might prove to be particularly difficult in multilateral negotiations, and impossible when the United States joins a treaty already concluded.

pursuant to the North Atlantic Treaty, there was no suggestion—until the human rights conventions of recent date[101]—that there was a general power for one or both of the treaty-makers to do so for any treaty,[102] at will.*

Some obligations, it is accepted, cannot be executed by the treaty itself.[103] A treaty cannot appropriate funds: the Constitution expressly provides that 'No Money shall be drawn from the Treasury, but in Consequence of Appropriations made by Law', and a treaty is apparently not law for this purpose;[104] any financial undertaking by the United States, then, requires implementation by appropriation from Congress. A treaty, it is accepted, cannot itself enact criminal law: enforcement of a treaty obligation to criminalize certain acts—say genocide or torture—or the enforcement of other treaty obligations by penal sanction can be effected only by Congress.[105] It has often been said, too,** that the United States cannot declare war by treaty, only by resolution of Congress.[106]

The difference between self-executing and non-self-executing treaties is commonly misunderstood. Whether a treaty is self-executing or not, it is legally binding on the United States. Whether it is self-executing or not, it is supreme law of the land. If it is not self-executing, Marshall said, it is not 'a rule for the Court'; he did not suggest that it is not law for the President or for Congress. It is their obligation to see to it that it is faithfully implemented; it is their obligation to do what is necessary to make it a rule for the courts if the treaty requires that it be a rule for

---

* The practice has particular ironies in relation to human rights treaties, where it has formed part of a package of reservations, understandings, and declarations attached to U.S. ratification of major international covenants and conventions. See n. 101 to this chapter. The policy reflected by such adherence to those treaties has been criticized as a matter of the international law of treaties as well as of national policy. See the general comment by the Human Rights Committee under the Covenant, and n. 102 to this chapter. The human rights agreements have not come to the courts, and the courts have not judged the propriety of U.S. policy and practice.

** It has been argued, however, that pursuant to United States undertakings in the U.N. Charter, the President has authority to send troops to fight in Korea (in 1950) or in the Persian Gulf (1990), when called upon to do so by resolution of the Security Council. See Ch. VIII, pp. 255 *et seq.*

It is not clear why that power is denied to the treaty-makers while other enumerated powers of Congress do not preclude treaties on the same matters. That question is, and is likely to remain, academic: no treaty of the United States has ever been designed to put the United States into a state of war without a declaration or other authorization by Congress.

the courts, or if making it a rule for the courts is a necessary or a proper means for the United States to carry out its obligation.*

The status of a treaty as law of the land derives from, and depends on, its status as a valid, living treaty of the United States. It is not law of the land for either the President or for the courts to enforce if it is not made in accordance with constitutional requirements, or if it is beyond the power of the President and Senate to make, or if it violates constitutional prohibitions. It is not law of the land if it is not an effective treaty of the United States internationally because it is not binding[107] or is invalid under international law, or because it has expired, or has been terminated or destroyed by breach (whether by the United States or by the other party or parties).[108]

Legal effect has been given, however, to incidental provisions in a treaty (or in Senate conditions upon consenting to it) which themselves contain no international obligations,[109] for example, a provision that territory acquired under the treaty shall not be automatically 'incorporated' into the United States, but shall await the disposition of Congress.[110] Perhaps such provisions are considered penumbral to the treaty, sharing in its character as law of the land; perhaps the Treaty Power implies ancillary authority to regulate the incidental concomitants and consequences of a treaty, and such regulations, whether in the original treaty or if imposed by the Senate, may also have some effect as law.

Congressional Implementation

When a treaty requires domestic legislation or an appropriation of funds to carry out United States obligations, only the Congress can supply them. As *Missouri* v. *Holland* confirmed, Congress has the power to do what is 'necessary and proper' to implement a treaty even if its action might not have been within other Congressional powers.[111] But as early as the Jay Treaty, debate flared as to whether Congress is constitutionally and morally obligated to implement treaties.[112] In a draft for Washington's message to the House of Representatives, Hamilton wrote:

---

* Whether a treaty is or is not self-executing is not to be confused with other questions: Did the United States assume a legal obligation, and what obligation did it assume? If the United States assumed a legal obligation, does the treaty provide or contemplate rights and remedies for private beneficiaries of the obligation? See Ch. V. And might the treaty provision reflect or codify customary law? See Ch. VIII.

the House of Representatives have no moral power to refuse the execution of a treaty which is not contrary to the Constitution, because it pledges the public faith; and have no legal power to refuse its execution because it is a law—until at least it ceases to be a law by a regular act of revocation of the competent authority.[113]

In the House, on the other hand, Representatives, including James Madison, saw in this division of power an element of checks and balances and insisted on the right (if not the duty) of Congress to determine independently the desirability of appropriations or legislation.[114] The House resolved:

when a Treaty stipulates regulations on any of the subjects submitted by the Constitution to the power of Congress, it must depend, for its execution, as to such stipulations, on a law or laws to be passed by Congress. And it is the Constitutional right and duty of the House of Representatives, in all such cases, to deliberate on the expediency or inexpediency of carrying such Treaty into effect, and to determine and act thereon, as, in their judgment, may be most conducive to the public good.[115]

Like some other constitutional debates, this one, too, has not been authoritatively resolved in principle.[116] Hamilton's position would obviously make for a more efficient system, since otherwise treaty-makers might find that they had negotiated treaties but could not assure that the United States would carry them out; effectively, Presidents would have to consult the House of Representatives (as well as the Senate) and perhaps obtain its formal consent before making the treaty. Separation and checks and balances, on the other hand, were dear to the Constitutional Fathers, and many of them were still on the scene when implementation of the Jay Treaty passed the House only barely and after bitter debate.

Since then, members of Congress have sometimes asserted the power—and the right—not to carry out international obligations, but Congresses have in fact not failed to do so though sometimes they are slow to do so (as, for example, in the 1990s, the treaty obligations to pay U.S. dues to the United Nations). In general, Congress has responded to a sense of duty to carry out what the treaty-makers promised, to a reluctance to defy and confront the President (especially after he can no longer retreat), to an unwillingness to make the U.S. system appear undependable, even ludicrous. But the independence of the legislative process (subject only to the Presidential veto as provided in the Constitution) has given Congress opportunities to interpret the need for implementation and to shape and limit it in important details;

Congress has not always given the President exactly the laws he asked for or as much money as he said a treaty required.*

Interpretation

The obligation and authority to implement a treaty imply also the obligation and authority to interpret it and to determine what the treaty requires. For international purposes the President determines the U.S. view as to the meaning of a treaty.** Domestically, too, since the President has usually the principal, often the sole, responsibility for executing a treaty, the treaty means what he says it means. Congress, too, has occasion to interpret a treaty when it considers enacting implementing legislation, or other legislation to which the treaty might be relevant.[117] The courts also interpret treaties in cases before them. Both Congress and the courts have claimed the right to interpret a treaty independently, even while admitting that the Executive's interpretation is entitled to 'great weight'.[118] It could happen, then, that Congress and the courts would in effect apply treaty provisions that are effectively different from those that bind the United States internationally—another cost of the separation of powers.†

Enforcement of Treaty Obligations

Responsibility for carrying out treaty obligations falls on the President under his foreign affairs powers, and it is upon him that foreign governments will call when there is failure in compliance by the United States. If a treaty entails domestic regulation and legal consequence in the United States, and is not self-executing, or if it requires appropria-

---

* It has been argued that since Congress has the power to 'repeal' a treaty as domestic law, p. 209 below, it should have the power to refuse to implement it. The issues are not the same. The power of Congress to enact domestic legislation inconsistent with an earlier treaty is deemed an exercise of its independent power to make domestic laws; and usually such enactments come from a later Congress. To say that Congress can refuse to implement a treaty in the first instance would destroy the independence of the Treaty Power and give the House of Representatives a voice in treaty-making not intended for it; it would also put an unusual premium on avoiding non-self-executing treaties, p. 198 above.

** Subject to any 'understanding' imposed by the Senate in its consent to ratification, p. 181 above.

† The President is not free to give the treaty a meaning other than the Senate's interpretation when it consented to the treaty, though it be given a different meaning by other states or by an international tribunal. See p. 183 and n. 118 to this chapter.

tion of funds, the President has to seek Congressional action. Self-executing treaties, and other treaties after they are implemented by Congress, are subject to the President's duty to 'take care' that the laws be faithfully executed.*

Responsibility is also a source of authority, for a treaty gives the President powers he might not otherwise have: for example, if without a treaty a President cannot extradite an accused U.S. citizen to a foreign land, the treaty gives the President authority to do so.[119] Without Senate concurrence, the President can make additional agreements contemplated by the treaty, and probably others which he considers necessary and proper for giving effect to it. Presidents—President Truman in 1950, President Bush in 1990—claimed authority, deriving from the U.N. Charter, a treaty of the United States, to go to war pursuant to resolution of the United Nations Security Council.**

In principle, treaty obligations are carried out by the Executive branch. Undertakings that are, or are translated by Congress into, domestic law are executed by the President in the same way as other laws of the United States, sometimes, if necessary, by the use of federal marshals and the armed forces,[120] and by resort to the courts. When a treaty is relevant to a case before a court in the United States, the Executive can intervene, if only as *amicus curiae*, to call the obligations of the United States to the court's attention. The Executive branch has also communicated with state governors and legislatures to prevent or undo actions that might violate international obligations of the United States.

Where private rights are at stake, the courts have often enforced U.S. treaty obligations.[121] Federal violations of a treaty that is law of the land are infrequent, but in principle the courts will require compliance and enjoin violations by the Executive branch. Consider *Alvarez-Machain*, decided in 1992.[122] U.S. officials had abducted a Mexican citizen from Mexico and brought him to the United States for trial for violation of U.S. laws. The accused challenged the jurisdiction of the federal courts to try him because he had been brought to the United States in violation of international law and of the Extradition Treaty with Mexico. The Supreme Court concluded that the abduction did not violate the Extradition Treaty, but the Court's opinion clearly implied that if the abduction had been in violation of the treaty, the U.S. courts could not have proceeded with the trial.†

* U.S. CONST., Art. II, sec. 2. See Ch. II.　　　** See Ch. VIII, pp. 255 *et seq.*
† The Court did not consider the fact that the abduction was in violation of principles of customary law. See Ch. VIII. As to the applicability of the U.S. Constitution, see Ch. IX.

The courts have often acted to prevent or remedy treaty violations by the states. In general, an aggrieved person can seek relief from a violation of a treaty by state officials by declaratory judgment or injunction from an approprate state or federal court; or, when prosecuted or sued under a state statute, he (she) can assert in defense that the statute is inconsistent with a U.S. treaty. If necessary, the individual can usually carry the case to the Supreme Court for a final decision, as in the early case of *Ware* v. *Hylton*, where the Court allowed a British creditor to collect from a Virginia debtor, holding that the Virginia statute discharging the debt fell before the U.S. treaty that promised that such debts would be paid.[123] On several occasions the Supreme Court struck down state provisions denying or taxing inheritance to an alien as inconsistent with treaty obligations.[124]

Or take the case of Mr. Asakura. Officials of the City of Seattle prosecuted Asakura, a Japanese national, for operating a pawnshop in violation of an ordinance making it illegal for an alien to do so. Asakura defended on the ground that the ordinance was invalid as to him, since a treaty between the United States and Japan provided that the citizens of each country shall have the right to carry on trade in the territory of the other country on the same terms as citizens of the host country. His claim was rejected by the state courts, but the Supreme Court upheld it on appeal. The Court said:

The rule of equality established by it [the treaty] cannot be rendered nugatory in any part of the United States by municipal ordinances or state laws. It stands on the same footing of supremacy as do the provisions of the Constitution and the laws of the United States. It operates of itself without the aid of any legislation, state or national; and it will be applied and given authoritative effect by the courts.[125]

Consider, however, a later, less happy instance, also involving a treaty with Japan. In order to promote local products to the disadvantage of foreign competition, South Carolina required merchants selling Japanese textiles to advertise that they were doing so, a requirement that was probably in violation of a provision in the Treaty of Commerce, Friendship and Navigation between the United States and Japan. Like Asakura, a merchant wishing to sell Japanese textiles without posting the offending advertisement might have obtained a judgment nullifying the state statute; or he (she) could have disregarded the state's requirement, and the treaty would have effectively prevented his conviction for violating it. But no merchant appeared willing to challenge the requirement, political persuasion was not effective for some time, and the State

Department helplessly expressed regret to the Japanese Government.[126] The federal Government did not seek the assistance of the courts but there is support for the view that, even without specific authorization from Congress,[127] federal courts, under general jurisdictional statutes, could entertain a suit by the Attorney General or by the Secretary of State to enjoin treaty violations by state officials, or private interference with treaty rights.[128] The Executive branch may do better another time.

Treaties and Acts of Congress

Since treaties are law of the land, and since treaties often deal with matters that are also the subject of Congressional legislation, it can happen (and has happened) that, purposely or carelessly, a treaty and an act of Congress might enact inconsistent law.* The legal consequence has been long ago declared by the Supreme Court:

By the Constitution a treaty is placed on the same footing, and made of like obligation, with an act of legislation. Both are declared by that instrument to be the supreme law of the land, and no supreme efficacy is given to either over the other. When the two relate to the same subject, the courts will always endeavor to construe them so as to give effect to both, if that can be done without violating the language of either; but if the two are inconsistent, the one last in date will control the other, provided always the stipulation of the treaty on the subject is self-executing.[129]

Acts of Congress inconsistent with earlier treaty obligations have been given effect by the courts.[130] That is not to say, as is often said, that Congress can 'repeal' a treaty:[131] Congress is not acting upon the treaty but, exercising one of its legislative powers, it legislates without regard to the international obligations of the United States.** Such legislation does not affect the validity of the treaty and its continuing international

---

* The issue arises only for self-executing treaties. Since a non-self-executing treaty is not law for the courts of its own accord, any inconsistency between such a treaty and an Act of Congress is, as regards domestic law, an inconsistency between the two statutes, between the statute implementing the treaty and another Act of Congress. Since both are the work of Congress, there is less doctrinal difficulty in insisting that the later repeals the earlier, even if one of the statutes is pursuant to a treaty (giving rise to international obligations) and may even be constitutionally required of Congress.

** It is accepted that the Constitution does not deprive the federal government of the power to breach a treaty. See p. 212 below; the question here is whether it is Congress that has that power, and can act under its enumerated powers as though no treaty had been made.

obligations for the United States, but it compels the United States to be in default.

As an original matter, the equality in U.S. law of treaties and federal statutes seems hardly inevitable; surely, the Supremacy Clause which the Supreme Court invoked does not establish it. That clause says only that treaties and statutes are both law of the land, and both supreme over state laws and binding on state courts; it does not follow that they are equal to each other.* Indeed, the Supremacy Clause obviously did not intend to assert the equality of all supreme federal law, for it lists the Constitution as well as U.S. laws and treaties as supreme law of the land, and surely laws and treaties are not equal as law to the Constitution.

The language of the Supremacy Clause apart, the principle of the equality of statutes and treaties in U.S. law is not universally acclaimed. Some have argued that Congress is the paramount legislator and its statutes should prevail as law in the United States in the face of a treaty (even if the treaty came later).[132] (The treaty-makers then would have to seek new legislation to repeal the old, and—as in some parliamentary systems—might have to do so before the treaty is ratified so that they could assure U.S. compliance.) Supporters of this view note also that there is only one case in which the Supreme Court held that a treaty provision repealed an earlier statute, and that was a 'liquor prohibition' statute which had notoriously low estate, was widely disregarded, and was about to be repealed.[133]

On the other hand, one might well argue to the contrary, that a treaty should prevail as law even in the face of a subsequent statute.[134] The international obligations of the United States are the responsibility of the treaty-makers. The Senate was given a part in the process, but the House, and Congress as a whole, were purposely denied any voice in it. Congress, we have seen, has a constitutional obligation to implement the treaties which the President and the Senate make; it is anomalous** to accord it power to disregard a treaty obligation, compel its violation, and put the United States in default.[135] Particularly as regards multilateral treaties of general applicability† which establish universal standards—on human rights, international trade or finance, the law of the sea, protection of intellectual property (trademarks, copyrights,

---

  * 3 and 2 are both 'supreme' to 1 but they are not equal.
  ** Laws bow to treaties in some other constitutional systems. See n. 134 to this chapter.
  † It has been suggested that the *Whitney* doctrine should not be applied to multilateral treaties. See n. 129 to this chapter.

patents)—inconsistent legislation by Congress not only violates international obligations but ruptures international consensus which the President-and-Senate helped achieve. Perhaps, we shall see, the President can exercise authority on the international plane to derogate from U.S. obligation; should Congress be able to do so by domestic legislation?

At the end of the twentieth century, the power of Congress to enact laws that are inconsistent with U.S. treaty obligations, and the equality of treaties and statutes in domestic U.S. law, appear to be firmly established.*

BREACH AND TERMINATION OF TREATIES

The United States sometimes has the right to terminate a treaty by its own terms, at will or at some prescribed time after giving notice of intention to do so. The international law of treaties[136] permits termination for fraud or coercion in making the treaty or for important breach by the other party; a party may lawfully refuse to carry out its obligation because of a fundamental change in circumstances.** International law also recognizes the power—though not the right—of a state party to break a treaty and pay damages or abide other international consequences.†

No doubt, the federal government has the constitutional power to terminate treaties on behalf of the United States in all these ways and circumstances: neither the declaration in the Supremacy Clause that treaties are law of the land, nor anything else in the Constitution, denies the United States these powers which countries generally have under international law. But the Constitution tells us only who can make treaties for the United States; it does not say who can unmake them.

At various times, the power to terminate treaties has been claimed for the President, for the President-and-Senate, for President-and-Congress, for Congress.[137] Presidents have claimed authority, presumably under their foreign affairs power, to act for the United States to terminate

---

* See RESTATEMENT (n. 2 to Preface) § 115 and Reporters' Note 1. It has been argued, however, that the doctrine should not apply to inconsistencies between a statute and a general multilateral treaty establishing general international law. *Ibid.*

** The principle of *rebus sic stantibus.* See n. 136 to this chapter.

† International law does not commonly require 'specific performance' of an obligation, and permits the violator to pay damages instead. See RESTATEMENT (n. 2 to Preface) § 901.

treaties, whether in accordance with their terms, or in accordance with, or even in violation of, international law. Franklin Roosevelt, for example, denounced an extradition treaty with Greece in 1933 because Greece had refused to extradite the celebrated Mr. Insull; in 1939 he denounced the Treaty of Commerce, Friendship and Navigation with Japan.[138] In 1979, President Carter exercised the right which the United States had reserved to terminate the Defense Treaty with the Republic of China after a period of notice.*

In principle, one might argue, if the Framers required the President to obtain the Senate's consent for making a treaty, its consent ought to be required also for terminating it; and there is eminent (if aging) dictum to support that view.[139] But perhaps the Framers were concerned only to check the President in 'entangling' the United States; 'disentangling' is less risky and may have to be done quickly, and is often done piecemeal, or *ad hoc,* by various means and acts. In any event, since the President acts for the United States internationally he can effectively terminate a treaty; the Senate has not established its authority to join or veto him; it has, however, claimed the right to reserve a voice in the termination of a particular treaty as a condition of its consent.[140]

Congress, we have seen, has some power effectively to breach a treaty. Congress is probably required (morally, constitutionally) to pass legislation necessary and proper to implement treaty obligations, but it could refuse to do so, put the United States in default, perhaps compel the President to terminate the treaty or induce the other party to do so; often Congress can achieve these ends too at a later time, by enacting legislation inconsistent with treaty obligations.** Congress can also declare war and terminate or suspend treaty relations with the other belligerent.[141]

In earlier times, Congress purported also to denounce or abrogate treaties for the United States or to direct the President to do so. Those instances, no doubt, reflected the early but recurrent claims of Congress

---

* The President has the duty to see that the laws, including treaty-law, are faithfully executed, but that duty presumably ceases to exist when the treaty ceases to exist (RESTATEMENT (n. 2 to preface) § 111, Comment *b,* and § 339, Reporters' Note 1) even if its existence terminated because the President acted under his constitutional authority in another capacity to destroy it. Consider the asserted constitutional authority of the political branches to act without regard to international law, Chapter VIII, p. 241, and the power of Congress to legislate contrary to treaty, p. 209 above.

** If a treaty is not self-executing, Congress need only repeal its implementing legislation leaving the treaty obligation thereafter unfulfilled.

that it has general powers to make foreign policy, supported by arguments that the maintenance or termination of treaties is intimately related to war or peace for which Congress has primary responsibility.[142] But Congressional resolutions have no effect internationally unless the President adopts and communicates them; some Presidents have chosen to comply with Congressional wishes, but others have disregarded them.[143]

Controversy as to who has authority to terminate treaties has been infrequent, if only because the United States has not often been disposed to terminate treaties. Since our early years, the character of U.S. treaties has changed and their part in U.S. foreign relations has changed. In this century, many agreements, including some related to the Second World War, were not formal treaties and were not terminated; they lapsed or disintegrated. The number and subjects and dispositions of treaties during the Cold War proliferated and varied, but 'political' treaties by the United States have been few, and these were largely the product of United States initiative (e.g., NATO, SEATO); neither Presidents nor Congresses wished to terminate them before their agreed term. Tensions between the United States and other countries (e.g., Cuba) did not impel the United States to terminate treaties with them. In general, surely, President and Congress have not differed as to the desirability of maintaining existing treaties.

Important controversy as to who has constitutional authority to terminate a treaty arose in 1979. President Carter announced U.S. recognition of the People's Republic of China and withdrew recognition from the government of the Republic of China (on Taiwan). The State Department informed Taiwan that the 1955 Mutual Defense Treaty—which permitted termination by either party on one year's notice—would be terminated effective January 1, 1980. A number of Senators, led by Barry Goldwater, brought suit to challenge the President's termination of the treaty without the agreement of the Senate or of Congress. The Court of Appeals sustained the President's power to terminate the treaty, 'insofar as it rests upon the President's well-established authority to recognize, and withdraw recognition from, foreign governments'.[144] On appeal, the Supreme Court dismissed the suit, four of the Justices declaring the issue to be a non-justiciable political question 'because it involves the authority of the President in the conduct of our national foreign relations'.[145] Only Justice Brennan reached the merits and would have affirmed the decision of the Court of Appeals upholding the President's authority to terminate the treaty.

If issues as to who has power to terminate treaties arise again, it seems unlikely that Congress will succeed in establishing a right to terminate a treaty (or to share in the decision to terminate).* At the end of the twentieth century, it is apparently accepted that the President has authority under the Constitution to denounce or otherwise terminate a treaty, whether such action on behalf of the United States is permissible under international law or would put the United States in violation.** With termination by the President, the treaty no longer exists in international law and ceases to be law in the United States.†

The power to terminate a treaty is a political power: courts do not terminate treaties, but they may interpret political acts or even political silences to determine whether they implied or intended termination.[146] Courts do not sit in judgment on the political branches to prevent them from terminating or breaching a treaty.[147] Where fairly possible, the courts will interpret actions of the President or of Congress to render them consistent with the international obligations of the United States, but both President and Congress can exercise their respective constitutional powers regardless of treaty obligations, and the courts will give effect to the acts of the political branches within their constitutional powers even if they violate treaty obligations or other international law.‡ If there is a breach of a treaty by the other party, it is the President, not the courts, who will decide whether the United States will denounce the treaty, consider itself liberated from its obligations, or seek other relief, or none at all.[148]

---

* Especially with the changed character of war and its place in international relations, Congress will probably be unable to claim plausibly that the maintenance or termination of treaties is intimately related to war or peace; a President who wishes to maintain a treaty will doubtless treat a Congressional denunciation or directive to terminate it as only a hortatory 'sense resolution'. (Politically, of course, the President could not lightly disregard the sense of Congress, especially if both houses joined, asserted constitutional power, and publicly proclaimed a call for radical action.)

** The RESTATEMENT (n. 2 to Preface) has concluded that the President has authority to terminate a treaty on his own authority. See § 339.

† See p. 204, this chapter.

‡ The President can terminate a treaty or may decide to breach it. The Executive branch is bound by the treaty and obligated to take care that it be faithfully executed, and the courts will enjoin violations committed by lower-level officials at the behest of an aggrieved person unless the President terminates or breaches the treaty. For that reason, among others, attempts to enjoin Executive action in Vietnam on the ground that it violated U.S. obligations under the United Nations Charter did not succeed. See Chapter VIII, p. 255; compare generally Ch. IV, pp. 103 *et seq.*

EXECUTIVE AGREEMENTS

Since our national beginnings Presidents have made some 1600 treaties with the consent of the Senate; they have made many thousands of other international agreements without seeking Senate consent.[149] Some were 'Congressional–Executive agreements', made by the President as authorized in advance or approved afterwards by joint resolution of Congress. Many were made by the President on his own constitutional authority ('sole executive agreements').

The Constitution does not expressly confer authority to make international agreements other than treaties, but such agreements, varying widely in formality and in importance, have been common from our early history. The authority to make such agreements and their permissible scope, and their status as law, continue to be debated. Where do the President and Congress find constitutional authority to join to make international agreements? Can the President, by authority of Congress (acting by majority vote of both houses), conclude as a Congressional–Executive agreement any international agreement he might have made by treaty with the consent of two-thirds of the Senate? Where does the President find constitutional power to make any agreements on his own authority? How does one distinguish an agreement which can be made by the President alone from one requiring Senate consent or the approval of both houses of Congress? Are executive agreements subject to the same constitutional limitations as treaties, or to others? Do they have the same quality as law of the land, the same supremacy to state law, the same equality with acts of Congress?

CONGRESSIONAL–EXECUTIVE AGREEMENTS

Agreements made by joint authority of the President and Congress have come about in different ways. Congress has authorized the President to negotiate and conclude international agreements on particular subjects—on postal relations; foreign trade; 'lend-lease' (to allies during the Second World War); foreign assistance; nuclear reactors.[150] During the years following the Second World War, Congress authorized the President to conclude particular agreements already negotiated, for example the Headquarters Agreement with the United Nations, and various multilateral agreements establishing international organizations, e.g., the International Bank for Reconstruction and Development ('the World Bank'), and the International Monetary Fund.[151] In some instances Congress has approved Presidential agreements already made, by adopting implementing legislation or by appropriating funds to carry out the obligations assumed by the United States.[152]

Constitutional doctrine to justify Congressional–Executive agreements is not clear or agreed. The Constitution expressly prescribes the treaty procedure, and nowhere suggests that another method of making international agreements is available, and that it would do as well.[153] Congress itself has no authority to negotiate with foreign governments; it cannot, then, delegate any such authority to the President.[154] One might say that Congress can join its power to legislate in regard to the subject matter of an agreement to the President's authority to negotiate with foreign governments,[155] but international agreements are primarily international acts and make domestic law only incidentally, or secondarily. Many international agreements, moreover, make no domestic law at all, and some of the agreements authorized or approved by Congress, e.g., for participation in some international organizations, deal with matters that are not obviously within any enumerated power of Congress and perhaps not even within its unenumerated power (deriving from U.S. sovereignty) to legislate in matters relating to foreign affairs. Some commentators, therefore, have denied any power in President-and-Congress to make international agreements; surely, it is said, they cannot do so on matters not within any legislative powers of Congress.* Others have urged that even if neither the President nor Congress alone has authority to support a particular international agreement, together they embody the sovereignty of the United States in international relations and can exercise all the powers inherent in such sovereignty, which includes the power to make international agreements.[156]

---

* In *Missouri* v. *Holland,* Justice Holmes said that there may be matters of the sharpest exigency for the national well being that an act of Congress could not deal with. Ch. III, p. 72. In such cases, Congress could legislate only in support of a treaty, and presumably also in support of an executive agreement based on the President's constitutional authority, but it had no legislative power that would supply any deficiency in the President's constitutional authority to make such agreements. A broad power for Congress to legislate domestically on foreign affairs is now accepted but it, too, would not supply any lack in Presidential authority as regards matters which have no domestic legal import.

There have been suggestions that Congressional–Executive agreements satisfy the Constitution because the Senate can be deemed to give consent to the agreement by implication when it votes for a joint resolution to approve it. But formal and conceptual objections apart, approval by joint resolution does not require a two-thirds vote.

Neither Congresses, nor Presidents, nor courts, have been seriously troubled by these conceptual difficulties and differences. Whatever their theoretical merits, it is now widely accepted that the Congressional–Executive agreement is available for wide use, even general use,* and is a complete alternative to a treaty:[157] the President can seek approval of any agreement by joint resolution of both houses of Congress rather than by two-thirds of the Senate.[158] Like a treaty, such an agreement is the law of the land, superseding inconsistent state laws, as well as inconsistent provisions in earlier treaties, in other international agreements, or in acts of Congress.[159]

The Congressional–Executive agreement has had strong appeal. By permitting approval of an agreement by simple majority of both houses, it eliminates the 'veto' by one-third-plus-one of the Senators present which in the past had effectively buried important treaties.[160] It gives an equal role to the House of Representatives which has long resented the 'undemocratic' anachronism that excludes it from the treaty-making process.[161] Especially since so many treaties require legislative implementation (if only by appropriation of funds), the Congressional– Executive agreement assures cooperation by both houses, virtually eliminating the danger that the House of Representatives might later resist enacting the implementing legislation or appropriating funds. The Congressional–Executive agreement also simplifies the parliamentary process: a treaty goes to the Senate for consent and, often, to the Senate again and to the House for implementation; a Congressional–Executive agreement goes to both Houses in the first instance, and 'consent' and implementation can be achieved in a single action. The Congressional– Executive agreement also eliminates issues about self-executing and non-self-executing agreements, and about the consequences of inconsistency between international agreements and statutes: all such agreements are 'executed' by Congress, every agreement has Congressional sanction, and clearly the joint resolution approving it can repeal any inconsistent statutes.**

* The constitutionality of the Congressional–Executive agreement is established, see n. 157 to this chapter, but doubts might spark if it were used for an agreement traditionally dealt with by treaty and that seems to ask for the additional 'dignity' of a treaty, for example, a major alliance or disarmament arrangement. Constitutional objections might arise particularly if the agreement favored by the majority of the Senate were opposed by more than one-third of that body. Compare n. 14 to this chapter.

** In approving a Congressional–Executive agreement, Congress can limit its effect as law of the land. In the Uruguay Round Agreements Act, Congress provided that 'No provision of any of the Uruguay Round Agreements, nor the

Despite these advantages, despite arguments from 'democracy' and more authentic representative government, the Congressional–Executive agreement has not effectively replaced the treaty. No doubt, the Senate has been jealous for its special prerogatives; and perhaps the Framers' reasons for excluding the House have remained persuasive to the Senate and the President, sometimes even to some members of the House itself.[162] Perhaps the Executive has not pressed this alternative method of making international agreements because the Senate has proved sufficiently responsible and 'internationalist' (often more so than the House has been in related contexts); and there have appeared no important agreements which could command a majority but not two-thirds of the Senate and which the President was willing to fight for through both houses.* But the constitutionality of the Congressional–Executive agreement seems established, it is used regularly at least for trade and postal agreements, and remains available to Presidents for wide, even general use should the treaty process again prove difficult.**

application of any such provision to any person or circumstances, that is inconsistent with any law of the United States shall have effect.' Sect. 102 of the Uruguay Round Agreements Act. (This language is nearly identical to that in the Trade Agreements Act of 1979.) Congress also provided that no person other than the United States 'shall have any cause of action or defense under any of the Uruguay Round Agreements' or challenge 'any action or inaction of . . . the United States, any State, or any political subdivision of a state on the ground that such action or inaction is inconsistent' with one of those agreements. Sect. 102(c)(1). (This language is substantially broader than the corresponding provisions in the 1979 Trade Agreement Act, although it is not clear that the effect was any different.)

* Perhaps enthusiasm for an alternative to the treaty method fell victim to the Bricker Amendment controversy (1950–55) in which 'internationalists' who had earlier scorned the treaty process now found themselves resisting efforts to cripple it. The Bricker Amendment also sought to curtail or regulate executive agreements. See n. 40 to this chapter.

** Provided a majority of the Senate were willing.

When the United States decided to conclude the Uruguay Round Agreements in 1994, it was assumed that it would do so by Congressional–Executive Agreement. However, there was a flurry in the academy and in the halls of Congress, with some denying that the Congressional–Executive agreement was the full equivalent of a treaty, and insisting in particular that the United States could properly, constitutionally, adhere to the new World Trade Organization only by treaty, with the consent of two-thirds of the Senate. Opponents of U.S. adherence in particular argued that approval by treaty was constitutionally required because the agreement would impinge on states' rights. The Uruguay Round Agreements would seem to have been a particularly strange occasion for reopening the question since trade agreements had long been a principal use for Congressional–Executive Agreements. In the end,

SOLE EXECUTIVE AGREEMENTS

Without the consent of the Senate (or authorization or approval by both houses of Congress), Presidents from Washington to Clinton have made many thousands of agreements, differing in formality and importance, on matters running the gamut of U.S. foreign relations.[163] In 1817, the Rush–Bagot Agreement disarmed the Great Lakes. *Root–Takahira* (1908) and *Lansing–Ishii* (1917) defined U.S. policy in the Far East. A Gentlemen's Agreement with Japan (1907) limited Japanese immigration into the United States. Theodore Roosevelt put the bankrupt customs houses of Santo Domingo under U.S. control to prevent European creditors from seizing them. McKinley agreed to contribute troops to protect Western legations during the Boxer Rebellion and later accepted the Boxer Indemnity Protocol for the United States. Franklin Roosevelt exchanged over-age destroyers for British bases early during the Second World War. Potsdam and Yalta shaped the political face of the world after the Second World War. Since the Second World War there have been numerous sole agreements for the establishment of U.S. military bases in foreign countries.

Periodically, members of the Senate—the body denied a constitutional role when the President makes a sole agreement instead of a treaty— have objected to a particular agreement as beyond the President's constitutional authority.[164] On several occasions, the Senate[165] has sought to define and limit the President's authority to make sole agreements.[166] The power to make such agreements remains vast and undefined, and its constitutional foundations remain uncertain.*

No one has doubted that the President has the power to make some 'sole' executive agreements. His power to execute treaties** may include

the United States adhered by approval of both houses, but the controversy and the debate may have revived a debate that had long appeared resolved. See n. 157 to this chapter; compare n. 153 to this chapter.

* In a sense—and in principle—the sole executive agreement has been less controversial than the Congressional–Executive agreement. No one denies that the President has power to make some agreements on his own authority; an issue may arise only as to whether a particular agreement is within the President's sole authority or requires Senate consent. But if an agreement is not within the President's sole authority, it is argued, he requires two-thirds of the Senate's consent; the Constitution, it is argued, does not permit him to substitute the consent of a majority of both houses. See p. 218, above.

** Presidents have made many agreements pursuant to, and as contemplated by, treaties, or which they considered appropriate for implementing the treaty. In such cases it is assumed that the Senate's consent to the treaty implies consent to

authority to do so by supplemental executive agreement.[167] As Commander in Chief, for example, he can make armistice agreements, and, viewed broadly, that power might support many other agreements as well, including war-time commitments on territorial and political issues for the post-war, as at Yalta and Potsdam.* But the Supreme Court has found Presidential authority to make international agreements that would reach much farther. In *United States* v. *Belmont*, speaking of the 'Litvinov Assignment' on the occasion of U.S. recognition of the Soviet Union, Justice Sutherland said:[168]

The recognition, establishment of diplomatic relations, the assignment, and agreements with respect thereto, were all parts of one transaction, resulting in an international compact between the two governments. That the negotiations, acceptance of the assignment and agreements and understandings in respect thereof were within the competence of the President may not be doubted. Governmental power over internal affairs is distributed between the national government and the several states. Governmental power over external affairs is not distributed, but is vested exclusively in the national government. And in respect of what was done here, the Executive had authority to speak as the sole organ of that government. The assignment and the agreements in connection therewith did not, as in the case of treaties, as that term is used in the treaty making clause of the Constitution (Article II, § 2), require the advice and consent of the Senate.

A treaty signifies 'a compact made between two or more independent nations with a view to the public welfare' . . . But an international compact, as this was, is not always a treaty which requires the participation of the Senate. There are many such compacts, of which a protocol, a modus vivendi, a postal convention, and agreements like that now under consideration are illustrations.

Belmont involved an agreement incidental to recognition of the Soviet Union, and Sutherland's opinion gave some emphasis to that fact. Recognition of a foreign government is indisputably the President's sole responsibility, and for many it is an 'enumerated' power implied in the President's express authority to appoint and receive ambassadors.** *Belmont*, then, might hold only that the President's specific and exclusive powers (principally his power to recognize governments and his authority as Commander in Chief) support agreements on his sole authority.

supplementary agreements. Perhaps the President can claim also that by making such agreements he is taking care that the treaty be faithfully executed. See nn. 162, 165, 167 to this chapter.

* See Ch. II. Agreements as to post-war dispositions were obviously relevant to the tasks and commitments of the various allies in the conduct of war; for the United States, the President's authority in such matters is unquestioned.

** See Ch. II.

Belmont may also be seen as representing an additional category of agreements that the Supreme Court later established as within the President's power to make on his own authority. That case involved an agreement to settle claims by the United States and by U.S. citizens against the Soviet Union. Before and after that settlement, many Presidents have concluded numerous agreements settling international claims.[169] In 1981, in *Dames & Moore* v. *Regan*,[170] the Supreme Court upheld Presidential authority to make such agreements and gave effect to the President's agreement* to resolve the Iran Hostage crisis. By that settlement—among other provisions—the United States and Iran agreed to cancel certain claims between them and to establish a special tribunal to resolve other claims, including large numbers of outstanding claims by U.S. nationals against Iran. The United States also agreed to close its courts to those claims, as well as to suits by U.S. citizens against the Government of Iran for damages arising out of the Hostage crisis. The Supreme Court upheld the settlement as within the President's extensive powers in foreign affairs, noting that Presidents had settled international claims by sole executive agreement throughout our history, and that Congress had acquiesced in that practice** and had implemented many such agreements.

Agreements related to recognition of a foreign government or establishing or resuming diplomatic relations, and agreements to settle claims, we now know, can clearly be concluded as sole executive agreements. But *Belmont* suggested a much larger power. The whole conduct of our foreign relations, we have seen, is the President's, and that authority, too, has been claimed to be expressly 'enumerated' in the clause vesting the 'Executive power'. Sutherland, in fact, seemed to find authority for the Litvinov Agreement not in the President's exclusive control of recognition policy but in his authority as 'sole organ', in his 'foreign affairs power' which supports not only recognition but much if not most other foreign policy.[171]

There have indeed been suggestions, claiming support in *Belmont*, that the President is constitutionally free to make any agreement on any matter involving our relations with another country, but that, for

---

* The Algiers Accord was negotiated and concluded by President Carter; it was confirmed by President Reagan.

** The Supreme Court did not suggest that Congress's acquiescence rendered all particular claims settlements effectively Congressional–Executive agreements. Rather, the Court, I think, treated Congressional acquiescence over time as Congressional acceptance of the President's claim that he has constitutional authority to make such agreements on his own authority.

prudential reasons—especially if he will later require Congressional implementation—he will often seek Senate consent (or approval by both houses).[172] As a matter of constitutional construction, however, that view is unacceptable, for it would wholly remove the 'check' of Senate consent which the Framers struggled and compromised to write into the Constitution.[173] One is compelled to conclude that there are agreements which the President can make on his sole authority and others which he can make only with the consent of the Senate (or of both houses),[174] but neither Justice Sutherland nor any one else has told us which are which.[175]

The President's power to make sole executive agreements is not without limits, but its limits are difficult to determine and to state.* One might suggest that the President must go to the Senate with 'important' agreements,[176] but even that 'definition' must have at least one major qualification: executive agreements have been used for some very important agreements when either or both parties desired that the agreement remain confidential.[177]

Periodically, the Senate has attempted to assert its authority and call Presidents to order, but these efforts, too, have foundered on difficulties of definition and on Presidential insistence on primacy in foreign affairs. Consider the fate of Senator Fulbright's 'National Commitments Resolution' of 1969 which grew out of the unhappy involvement of the United States in Vietnam. As introduced, it would have:

Resolved, that it is the sense of the Senate that a national commitment by the United States to a foreign power necessarily and exclusively results from affirmative action taken by the executive and legislative branches of the U.S. Government through means of a treaty, convention, or other legislative instrumentality specifically intended to give effect to such a commitment.[178]

The proposed resolution was to be only a 'sense resolution', but it had little likelihood of being adopted, and no likelihood that any President would heed it, for it purported to deny all sole executive agreements whatsoever. Emergencies apart, and the need for private if not secret diplomacy apart, daily foreign relations and daily foreign policy inevitably involve 'commitments', if only in informal, sometimes urgent, *ad hoc* 'agreements'. No President could avoid them if he wished; the constitutional system would not last a month if he sought Senate (or Congressional) consent for every one of them.

* The Supreme Court has not held any sole executive agreement to be *ultra vires* the President and, as indicated, has upheld several agreements of particular character, but it has not laid down principles or given general guidance to define the President's power to act alone.

The 'Commitments Resolution' also suffered deeper difficulties. For what troubled the Senators particularly were not legally binding executive agreements, but political commitments such as those at Potsdam and Yalta which had become a focus of unhappiness, of regret and partisan recrimination during the Cold War, which were not and could not be legally binding at all, but which effectively pledged the faith and 'credit' of the United States nonetheless.

In the end, the resolution was sharply limited by defining 'national commitment' as:

the use of the armed forces of the United States on foreign territory, or a promise to assist a foreign country, government, or people by the use of the armed forces or financial resources of the United States, either immediately or upon the happening of certain events.[179]

Even as so limited, the Commitments Resolution remains only a 'sense resolution'. The political importance of the resolution is difficult to appraise. It is not invoked often, and a quarter century after its adoption many may be unaware of its existence. But it continues to reflect constitutional and political truth. No President has ever 'committed' the United States to go to war, and no responsible President is likely to do so. Congressional reassertion of its authority in the War Powers Resolution, and later in the resolution on the Persian Gulf War, and on Haiti,[180] inevitably discourages Presidents from making such commitments (and other countries from relying on them). If Presidents have authority to deploy forces for purposes short of war, it is difficult to deny them the power to undertake to do so by executive agreement or 'commitment', but such commitments would have to take account of the War Powers Resolution.*

Presidents as well as foreign government 'promisees' have always been aware that agreements 'to commit the financial resources' of the United States depend directly and immediately on appropriations by Congress.** The Commitments Resolution was obviously intended as a warning to Presidents, and as a reminder to foreign governments, that

---

* See Ch. IV, pp. 105 *et seq.* President Reagan committed the United States to use the U.S. Navy to protect shipping of some states during the Iraq–Iran War, and President Bush apparently promised similar assistance during the early days of the Gulf Crisis of 1990.

** Congress has usually felt obliged to appropriate funds required by treaty but it might not sense the same obligation if it considered the President's agreement to do so *ultra vires* because he acted on his own authority. Still, since the United States would be 'committed', Congress would be pressed to carry out the undertaking.

the Senate for its part reserves its right not to implement Presidential commitments; and the Resolution may effectively serve that end. But though Presidents as well as foreign governments know the difference between political commitments and legal obligations, and are well aware of the braking powers of Congress, they know, too, that in the end, Senates and Congresses, theoretically free to disown such commitments, cannot do so lightly.

The reaches of the President's power to make executive agreements remain highly uncertain as a matter of constitutional law, which might tempt activist Presidents into far-reaching undertakings. But constitutional tradition as well as other political forces are powerful deterrents. The Commitments Resolution purported to define the President's constitutional authority, but it was also an assertion by the Senate of its own constitutional authority, and in competition for constitutional power the Senate is not timid and not without important weapons.

The President has to get along with Congress, and with the Senate in particular, and he will not lightly risk antagonizing it by disregarding what it believes to be its constitutional prerogatives. Often the President will be careful to conclude an agreement by treaty, so as not to risk subsequent challenge to the authority of the agreement, especially if it is to have effect as domestic law so that its validity might be questioned in the courts. Often the treaty process will be used at the insistence of other parties to an agreement because they believe that a treaty has greater 'dignity' than an executive agreement, because its constitutional effectiveness is beyond doubt, because a treaty will 'commit' the Senate and the people of the United States and make its subsequent abrogation or violation less likely.

Unable to define the President's authority to make sole executive agreements, Congress sought to discourage Presidential abuse by assuring that Congress is informed of all sole agreements concluded. By the Case Act of 1972,[181] Congress has required the Executive branch to transmit to Congress every executive agreement (if necessary, under injunction of secrecy), thus rendering them subject to scrutiny.

If an agreement is within the President's power, there seem to be no formal requirements as to how it shall be made. It can be signed by the President or on his behalf; it can be made by Secretaries of State, by ambassadors, or by authorized lesser officials; and there is no reason why an executive agreement must be formal or even that it has to be in writing.[182]

LIMITATIONS ON EXECUTIVE AGREEMENTS

Whatever limitations the Constitution imposes on the subject matter of treaties* would apply, surely, to executive agreements as well.** But one of the limitations we considered—and discarded—in regard to the Treaty Power was declared to apply to executive agreements. In the *Capps* case,[183] a solitary case, decided in 1953, a United States Court of Appeals refused to give effect to an executive agreement regulating the export of potatoes by Canada to the United States.† Chief Judge Parker said:[184]

The answer is that while the President has certain inherent powers under the Constitution such as the power pertaining to his position as Commander in Chief of the Army and Navy and the power necessary to see that the laws are faithfully executed, the power to regulate interstate and foreign commerce is not among the powers incident to the Presidential office, but is expressly vested by the Constitution in the Congress.

Judge Parker's suggestion,‡ it should be clear, would not only deny to many executive agreements effect as domestic law in the United States; it denied the President's power to make them at all. His argument is unpersuasive. It takes the narrowest view of the President's power, not even mentioning his foreign affairs powers. Judge Parker found that the President did not have power to conclude an agreement regulating commerce because Congress had the power to regulate commerce. If the President cannot make agreements on any matter on which Congress could legislate, there could be no executive agreements with

* See Ch. V, pp. 111 *et seq.*

** I deal here with suggested limitations on the power to make executive agreements; related limitations on the status of executive agreements in domestic law are considered below, pp. 177, 226–8.

† The Supreme Court, expressly declining to consider the questions that concern us, affirmed on other grounds. See n. 183 to this chapter.

‡ Judge Parker might have limited himself to holding that the executive agreement could not prevail in the face of an earlier inconsistent act of Congress, but his statement announces a limitation that reaches much farther. However, Judge Parker himself reduced his suggestion to dictum by leaving open 'whatever the power of the executive with respect to making executive trade agreements regulating foreign commerce in the absence of action by Congress'.

Judge Parker decided the case at the height of the Bricker Amendment controversy, and, as one who opposed the amendment, he was perhaps eager to disarm supporters of the Amendment by reducing the 'threat' of a broad Presidential power to make executive agreements.

domestic legal consequences, since, we have seen, the legislative power of Congress has few and far limits. If Judge Parker denied the President the power to make executive agreements only as to matters on which Congress has 'express' powers to legislate, he was drawing a line between express and implied powers of Congress that makes little sense for any purpose. In either event, it is difficult to see why the powers of Congress to legislate are relevant to determine the scope of Presidential power to commit the United States when he does so by executive agreement, any more than when he does so by treaty.*

Judge Parker's dictum does not accord with the practice either before or since he wrote: Presidents have made executive agreements on matters as to which Congress could legislate, notably international trade.[185] Others have suggested other limitations: a sole executive agreement can be only 'temporary' or of short duration; or, some argued, it can be effective only for the term of the President who makes it.[186] These (and similar) suggestions, too, have no support in practice or in principle; they do not reflect the scope and the bounds of Presidential power generally or of the Treaty Power, where any limitations on the power to make executive agreements should lie.

EXECUTIVE AGREEMENTS AS LAW OF THE LAND

One suggestion has had it that, granting that the President can make many sole executive agreements, and that such agreements, like treaties,** are internationally binding, unlike treaties they are never self-executing and cannot be effective as domestic law[187] unless implemented by Congress.† If they are not law of the land they cannot be given effect by the courts and they do not supersede inconsistent state law.

If there was ever any basis for that view, the *Belmont* case and *Dames & Moore* surely reject it as general doctrine. By the Litvinov Agreement (involved in *Belmont*), the Soviet Union had assigned to the United States all claims by the Soviet Union against U.S. nationals, among them claims against New York banks, based on accounts of Russian

---

* See pp. 177, 225 above.

** And unlike Congressional–Executive agreements which find their constitutional support in the joint powers of Congress and the President, and there is no basis for doubting that such agreements are supreme law of the land.

† Congress is presumably obligated to implement them. But Congress might disclaim obligation to implement some agreements on the ground that they were *ultra vires* for lack of Senate consent.

nationals which the Soviet Government had nationalized.[188] The federal Government sought to recover these bank accounts for itself, but the state courts held that the United States stood no better than the Soviet Union (its assignor) and that the public policy of New York barred recovery. The Supreme Court reversed, Justice Sutherland saying:[189]

Plainly, the external powers of the United States are to be exercised without regard to state laws or policies . . . And while this rule in respect of treaties is established by the express language of cl. 2, Art. VI, of the Constitution, the same rule would result in the case of all international compacts and agreements from the very fact that complete power over international affairs is in the national government and is not and cannot be subject to any curtailment or interference on the part of the several states. [Citing *Curtiss-Wright*.] In respect of all international negotiations and compacts, and in respect of our foreign relations generally, state lines disappear. As to such purposes the State of New York does not exist.

Again, it has been suggested that the doctrine of the *Belmont* case gives supremacy over state law only to executive agreements intimately related to the President's power of recognition, and that even such agreements will supersede only state public policy not formal state laws. Neither of these limitations was expressed—or implied—in *Belmont*, or in the *Pink* case decided 5 years later by a reconstituted Supreme Court,[190] and the language and the reasoning of both cases would apply as well to any executive agreement and to any state law. *Dames & Moore*, the most recent Supreme Court essay on executive agreements, is less sweeping than *Belmont* in its rhetoric but no less broad in what it holds. *Dames & Moore*, too, gave a sole executive agreement effect as law. That agreement, too, affected private interests, denying them access to U.S. courts,[191] relegating their claims to the mercies of an unknown international tribunal.*

To be sure, the *Belmont* case is more than half a century old and may reflect doctrine of an earlier Supreme Court age when 'the Government' could do no or little wrong, particularly in foreign affairs. The Court is not likely to reconsider the holding that state law must bow before a valid executive agreement, but it might look again at some of the enthusiastic language of the earlier Justices. It will doubtless look again and harder at any executive agreement that impinges on private rights in the United States. Even at about the time of *Belmont*, sole executive actions were not sacred if they threatened personal freedoms. Except on that

* The agreement would bar suits in state courts as well. See n. 191 to this chapter.

ground it is difficult to understand why only a year before *Belmont* the Supreme Court held that the President did not have the power to extradite Mr. Neidecker to France when there was no treaty or act of Congress requiring it.[192] The Court did not deal with the case as involving an executive agreement but, surely, at least an informal agreement was inevitably involved.[193] Was the Court rejecting an *ad hoc* agreement making law for a particular case?* Would it have refused effect also to a formal sole executive extradition agreement of general applicability?

At least some sole executive agreements, then, can be self-executing and have some status as law of the land.[194] As with treaties, of course, a self-executing executive agreement would surely lose its effect as domestic law in the face of an inconsistent subsequent act of Congress. On the other hand, in the *Capps* case, an intermediate federal court held that an executive agreement—unlike a treaty—could not prevail even against an earlier act of Congress.[195] Yet many of the arguments why a treaty supersedes an earlier statute apply as well to executive agreements.[196] The Supreme Court built its doctrine that treaties are equal to and can supersede acts of Congress on the Supremacy Clause of the Constitution which declares both to be supreme law of the land; executive agreements, too, are supreme law of the land. If one sees the Treaty Power as basically a Presidential power (albeit subject to check by the Senate) there is no compelling reason for giving less effect to agreements that he has authority to make without the Senate.[197] If one accepts Presidential primacy in foreign affairs in relation to Congress, one might allow his agreements to prevail even in the face of earlier Congressional legislation.** If one grants the President some legislative authority in foreign affairs—as in regard to sovereign immunity†—one might grant it to him in this respect too.[198] The issue remains unresolved.

---

* The Litvinov Agreement in *Belmont* and *Pink* and the Iran Hostage settlement upheld in *Dames & Moore* also made law *ad hoc* for known, defined claims, but in issue was only property, not 'preferred freedoms'. See Ch. IX.

** In most instances, it might be argued, the statute would be of a general character and might be of an earlier time. As with treaties, moreover, Congress could prevail by reenacting its statute. The issue, then, would come down to a choice of 'presumption' or 'burden of going forward': the rule of the *Capps* case would bar effect to an executive agreement until Congress modified its earlier statute; a contrary rule would allow the President to prevail until Congress reasserted its earlier policy. Of course, in theory a President and a Congress might engage in a continuing round of overruling each other, but that is not likely to happen.

† See Ch. II, p. 54.

I sum up:

Inevitably, inherently, U.S. foreign affairs consist of, depend on, agreements with other states—bilateral or multilateral, formal or informal. The Constitution entrusted making such agreements to the President, but for agreements that qualify as 'treaties' he needs the consent of the Senate; history has accepted a joint resolution of Congress as an alternative to Senate consent, giving constitutional status to the 'Congressional–Executive agreement'. The President can also make many agreements on his own authority, including, surely, those related to establishing and maintaining diplomatic relations, agreements settling international claims, and military agreements within the Presidential authority as Commander in Chief. There are doubtless many other 'sole' agreements within the President's foreign affairs powers, but which they are is hardly agreed. On the other hand, the President—probably—may not on his own authority, commit the United States to go to war, or to provide money or other national resources.

Treaties and other international agreements often create obligations to be carried out within the United States, and many of them are 'self-executing' and have the effect of law to be carried out by the President and enforced by the courts; they are binding on the states. But in their capacity as international law, treaties and international agreements are subject to the U.S. Constitution, and they may be superseded by later acts of Congress. Other issues as to the place of treaties and other international agreements in U.S. law remain unresolved.

Treaties and other international agreements are international instruments, and their constitutional character and status derive from their character and status in international law. But the international legal system includes also a comprehensive customary law, most of it traditional and ancient, some resulting contemporarily by a subtle process from the practice of the states. The development and the determination of customary international law are the responsibility of the President, and he shall take care that it be faithfully observed, but Congress and the courts also attend to U.S. obligations under customary law, and customary international law is binding on the states.

Traditionally, customary international law and international agreements created obligations for nation states to be carried out by them through national institutions in their own ways and by their own means. In the twentieth century, and especially since the Second World War, the international political system has used treaties and other international agreements to establish durable international organizations with their own legal personality and character, their own institutions and bureaucracy, to perform tasks of international governance. For the United States, membership in international organizations and the authority they exercise and the activities they engage in have raised novel constitutional issues and suggested others that might arise.

I address constitutional issues of international law and international organization in the following chapter.

Chapter VIII

INTERNATIONAL LAW AND INTERNATIONAL ORGANIZATIONS: CONSTITUTIONAL ISSUES

As a member of the international political system of nation-states,* the United States is subject to international law—an international legal regime consisting principally of customary international law and treaties and other international agreements.[1] By international agreements the United States participates in a variety of international (intergovernmental) organizations. Like treaties, explicitly cited in the Constitution,** customary international law and the actions and activities of organizations impinge on U.S. domestic law and on the political institutions of the United States, and provide an additional, definable, component of the constitutional law of foreign affairs. Issues of separation and checks and balances, conflict and cooperation, interference and delegation, appear here too, but differently. U.S. responsibilities under customary international law and towards international organizations have raised issues about the relation of U.S. institutions to international institutions, and of constitutional rights and duties to rights and duties under international law.

In principle, the international obligations of the United States are no different whether they derive from customary law or were assumed by treaty.† Treaties earned several references in the Constitution‡ and its

* The entities of the political systems are formally, legally, 'states', though relations and law are denominated 'international' (not 'interstate'); the U.S. Constitution too, refers to 'the law of nations' (not 'the law of states').

** See generally Ch. VII.

† The obligation to carry out treaty undertakings is itself an obligation under customary law.

‡ The Constitution addresses treaties to determine their place in relation to the separation of powers and to federalism: which branch of the federal government makes them (Art. II); their inclusion in the jurisdiction of the federal courts (Art. III); their supremacy to state law (Art. VI). The Framers apparently saw no need to address customary international law from those perspectives.

place in constitutional jurisprudence has been addressed and developed by the Supreme Court. International law, essentially customary, was prominent in our early constitutional history, but has hardly been mentioned by the Supreme Court in the last hundred years, and its place in contemporary jurisprudence is less clear and is controversial in important degree. U.S. obligations in, or to, international organizations depend on the treaty establishing the organization, but some such treaties, e.g., the United Nations Charter, impinge on U.S. laws and institutions in unprecedented ways and may engender new constitutional doctrine.

INTERNATIONAL LAW IN THE CONSTITUTIONAL FRAMEWORK

Even now, in our third century under the Constitution and after a century of radical change in the international legal system, most of the international rights and obligations of the United States lie in unwritten, customary, international law. These include the many rights and obligations that for the United States (as for other states) derive from the axioms and fundamentals of the political system: the status of states in the system; the concept of 'state sovereignty' and its implications—independence, territorial integrity and inviolability; the fundamentals of property, contract, and tort in relations between nations; the law of treaties, including the principle *pacta sunt servanda*, that international agreements create obligations and must be observed; the concept of nationality, and a state's responsibility to treat foreign nationals in accordance with international principles of justice; the freedom of the seas; and many others.[2]

International Law as Law for *the United States*

'The United States', the first Chief Justice of the United States, John Jay, said, 'by taking a place among the nations of the earth [became] amenable to the law of nations'.[3]

At its birth as a nation,* the United States found international law—the 'law of nations'—in place, and we have contributed to its development in the intervening centuries.[4] The United States supplemented and modified customary law by thousands of treaties and other international

---

* For the United States at its birth, of course, the law of nations was wholly customary law, until the new nation began to conclude treaties.

agreements. International law—customary law and treaty law—has governed, shaped, and influenced U.S. national behavior since the beginning.[5]

International law is law for the United States. As such, it is obligatory upon all whose actions are attributable to the United States under international law: it is binding on Congress, and on the President and the Executive branch: on the states—on state legislatures and state officials, down to the lowest official of city, town or village; on the courts—on the federal courts, from the Supreme Court down to the federal magistrate or administrative judge, and on state courts, from the highest court of appeals to the village magistrate or police court judge. Traditional international law did not ordinarily address the acts of private citizens, but increasingly the law attends to private acts, as in the law against genocide and other gross violations of human rights, on war crimes, on piracy, hijacking and other acts of terrorism, or counterfeiting, even though the law continues to lodge international responsibility for such violations by persons subject to U.S. jurisdiction in the government of the United States. Increasingly, international law requires nation-states to enforce international norms and to punish their violations in national courts.*

It is principally the President, as 'sole organ' of the United States in its international relations, who is responsible for the behavior of the United States in respect of international law. The President makes legal claims for the United States and reacts to the claims of others. He reflects the views of the United States on legal questions and he justifies U.S. actions under the law—in diplomatic exchange, in judicial or arbitral proceedings, in organs of international organizations, or in the public forum. He participates on behalf of the United States in the inchoate, somewhat mysterious process by which customary international law is made, unmade, remade. Congress, state legislatures, federal and state officials also contribute to 'practice by the United States' which helps

---

* In 1993, the United Nations Security Council established tribunals for the trial of war crimes, crimes against humanity, and other gross violations of human rights committed in the former Yugoslavia and in Rwanda. Under the resolutions establishing the tribunals, the United States is legally bound to cooperate with the tribunal, e.g., by arresting and extraditing accused persons for trial by the tribunal. In 1994 the International Law Commission presented a report on a multilateral treaty to establish a permanent international criminal court. See nn. 86, 87 to this chapter.

Under the Genocide Convention and the Convention against Torture the United States is required to make any violation a crime under U.S. law. See n. 85 to this chapter.

make international law,* for example when they determine and give effect to the rights of foreign states, foreign diplomats, or foreign nationals in the United States, or of foreign vessels off our coasts. Federal and state courts also help make international law when they determine what that law requires in order to decide cases before them.** Congress and state legislatures, federal and state officials, even federal and state courts, can also derogate from international law when they commit acts that put the United States in violation of its obligations. But, in general, these other actors play on the domestic scene only; the President represents what they do to the rest of the world and seeks to justify them under international law; sometimes he confesses violation.

The Framers were strongly committed to the law of nations and assumed that the United States would share that commitment.[6] By, or pursuant to, international agreement, the United States has recognized the authority of international bodies that monitor compliance with particular legal obligations and has accepted the jurisdiction of international tribunals and other bodies for the settlement of many legal disputes.[7] Towards the end of the twentieth century, states—including the United States—have assumed obligations to cooperate with international criminal tribunals.[8] And, contrary to common impression, the United States—generally, ordinarily—carries out its international obligations, as it has for 200 years.†

International law and the political branches

The Framers assumed that the new federal government would carry out the obligations of the United States under international law. The Constitution expressly gives Congress the power to enact laws necessary and proper to carry out the powers vested in the government of the United States, including, surely, the power to do what international law requires of the United States. The Constitution expressly gives Congress the power to define offenses against the law of nations.‡ The President is given the Executive power generally, and he is to take care that the laws be faithfully executed.§ But the Constitution does not explicitly

* Customary international law results from the practice of states *opinio juris* (with a sense of legal obligation). See RESTATEMENT (n. 2 to Preface) § 102, Comment *c*.
** See Ch. V, pp. 136 *et seq.*
† 'It is probably the case that *almost all nations observe almost all principles of international law and almost all of their obligations almost all of the time*' (emphasis in the original). Henkin, HOW NATIONS BEHAVE (2d edn. 1979) 47.
‡ Art I, sec. 8; see Ch. III.   § Art. II. See Ch. II.

impose a duty on Congress and the President to carry out international obligations. Is failure to do so a dereliction of duty under the Constitution? Is an act by Congress or the President (otherwise within their powers) unconstitutional because it puts the United States in violation of international law or treaty?

In principle, every nation-state has the power*—*I do not say the right*—to violate international law and obligation and to suffer the consequences.[9] That power, it appears, is not denied to any nation-state or national government by its own constitution.[10] The U.S. Constitution does not address that question explicitly. The Supreme Court has not addressed it directly. But the Supreme Court, we have seen, has read the Constitution as giving acts of Congress a status in the hierarchy of U.S. law equal to that of a treaty,[11] and as requiring the courts to apply an act of Congress even if inconsistent with an earlier treaty undertaking. By that reading, we must assume that the Constitution does not forbid Congress to enact law that causes the United States to violate its treaty obligations, and that an act that does so, however deplorable, is not a violation of the Constitution.

The Constitution—and the Supreme Court—have had less to say as regards the obligation to respect customary international law. The Constitution took account of the law of nations, and, I believe, assumed that the United States would respect it.[12] Although, we shall see, international law is law of the United States, the Constitution does not say so explicitly and does not guide us as to the place of international law in the hierarchy of U.S. law. But an opaque, confused, and confusing dictum by the Supreme Court in 1900, in *The Paquete Habana*[13] (discussed below), has been interpreted to mean that the courts will give effect to an act of Congress inconsistent with a principle of customary law. If so, it has been assumed, the Constitution is being interpreted as not prohibiting Congress from enacting such laws and thereby putting the United States in violation, and such a law may also be deplorable but is not unconstitutional.

The President is situated differently. He is the direct and the principal repository of the international obligations of the United States. Under the Constitution, the President, as the national Executive and under his Foreign Affairs authority, has the power and the duty to carry out U.S. obligations under international law. In respect of international law as the law of the land, the President is bound to take care that 'the laws be faithfully executed'.

---

* That, some would say, is a power inherent in 'sovereignty'.

But, we have seen,* the United States has the 'sovereign' power—not the right—to denounce or breach a treaty, and it is presumably the President, under his Foreign Affairs power, who has the power to do so on behalf of the United States. And if the United States has the 'sovereign' power—not the right—to act in violation of other principles of international law, presumably the President can exercise that power for the United States, acting under one of his explicit powers or under authority he derives from the powers of the United States inherent in its sovereignty. If so, the fact that an action of the President puts the United States in violation of international law, however deplorable that be, does not, *ipso facto,* render that action a violation of the Constitution.[14]

Thus, under our Constitutional jurisprudence as we understand it today, an action by the President or by Congress that is within their constitutional authority does not become a violation of the Constitution because the Act places the United States in violation of a treaty provision or of a U.S. obligation under customary law. But treaties and principles of customary law are also law of the United States and therefore law for the courts; I consider below the consequences and implications of their character as law for the powers and duties of Congress and of the President, and particularly of the Executive branch, and for courts in deciding cases or controversies before them.

International Law as Law of the United States

International law, we have seen, is law *for* the United States in its relations with other nations. International law is also law *of* the United States, U.S. law for domestic governance. 'The Court', John Marshall said, 'is bound by the law of nations which is a part of the law of the land'; 'international law', the Court declared in 1900, in *The Paquete Habana,* 'is part of our law'.[15] International law is 'self-executing' and ordinarily does not require implementation by Congress.** It is there-

* See Chs. II and VII.
** Compare the law as to treaties, Ch. VII.

Some constitutional safeguards are interpreted to take account of the principles of international law that antedate the Constitution. See, for example, the right of an accused to have compulsory process for obtaining witnesses in his favor, the Sixth Amendment, into which right was read an exception where the witnesses enjoyed diplomatic immunity from process under international law. See n. 73 to Ch. IX.

Like some provisions in treaties or executive agreements, some principles of international law may require implementation in the United States. For example, war crimes and violations of the international law against genocide or torture, or other

fore part of the constitutional responsibility of the President to 'take care that the laws be faithfully executed'. It is part of our law for the courts to apply. Like treaties and executive agreements, customary international law bows before constitutional prohibitions, notably those of the Bill of Rights.*

International law as supreme federal law

International law, it is established, is law of the land and is supreme, but how it achieved that character and status is not wholly clear or agreed. The Constitution recognizes the 'law of nations' and gives Congress power to define offenses against that law; it says nothing more about international law. The Supremacy Clause of the U.S. Constitution provides that 'the Laws of the United States which shall be made in pursuance [of the Constitution], and all Treaties . . . made under the authority of the United States shall be the supreme Law of the Land', and binding on the states. That clause cites treaties and declares their supremacy; it does not mention customary international law. The Supremacy Clause establishes also the supremacy of 'the Laws of the United States', but it is not obvious that the term was intended to include principles of customary international law as U.S. law. Yet, there is nothing to suggest that the Framers intended higher constitutional status for treaties than for customary law, and much to suggest that they expected the United States to honor both scrupulously. Their commitment was to 'the law of nations' which for them was essentially customary law, including, notably, a state's obligation under customary law to carry out treaties. Their reticence about customary international law in contrast to the several references to treaties did not bespeak a judgment as to their comparative constitutional significances, but had other explanation. The Constitution had to determine who could make treaties for the United States; it sought to deny any treaty power to the states. The Framers wrote treaties explicitly into the Supremacy Clause because the supremacy of treaties to state law was a major issue that had to be resolved, and accepted by the states. Cases arising under treaties were declared to be within the judicial power of the United States because such cases were to be expected; the Framers probably did not anticipate cases or controversies arising under international law until Congress defined offenses under that law or enacted other legislation to

gross human rights violations could not be punished in the United States unless Congress enacted legislation to make them crimes.

* See Ch. IX.

implement international law, and cases arising under international law would then be cases arising under the laws of the United States.

Perhaps the Supremacy Clause cannot readily be read as declaring international law to be the law of the land;[16] if so, international law has become law of the United States by some other route, perhaps automatically, tacitly. Prior to union, international law had been part of the common law of England and of the American Colonies, then of the states. With union, the United States became a single nation-state with rights and obligations under international law, and perhaps, with union and as a concomitant of union, 'we the people', in ordaining the Constitution, tacitly recognized and accepted international law as U.S. law of extra-constitutional origin.*

For long, indeed, the history of international law as part of the common law of the states was a source of confusion and controversy. For many years under the Constitution, states appeared to continue to apply international law as part of their common law.**[17] But if for the states customary international law had only the status of their common law, it was presumably subject to modification or repeal by the state legislature. If so, too, state courts could decide for themselves what international law requires, and issues of customary international law, unlike questions arising under treaties, would not raise federal questions and could not be appealed to the Supreme Court for final adjudication.[18] Fifty states could have fifty different views on some issue of international law and the federal courts might have still another view. Indeed, not only would the states be free to disregard the views of the federal courts, but in cases where a federal court is required to apply the law of the state in which it sits, the court would have to apply the state's view on disputed questions of international law.[19]

Banco Nacional de Cuba v. *Sabbatino*,[20] decided in 1964, supports a better, more orderly view. The determination and application of international law are integral to the conduct of foreign relations and are the responsibility of the federal government. International law is determined, 'made', by the federal courts as though it were federal law, and their views bind the state courts.

Whatever the theory and the history, then, at the end of the twentieth century it is established that international law is law of the United States. Like 'the laws of the United States' cited in the Supremacy

* Compare *Curtiss-Wright*, Ch. I, pp. 25 *et seq.*

** In this regard, it is accepted, the hierarchy of law in the United States differs from that in some other countries where international law may be supreme to domestic legislation, and in some cases even to the constitution. See n. 10 to this Chapter.

Clause, customary law is supreme to state law. International law is considered to be included in the constitutional phrases extending the judicial power of the United States 'to cases arising under [the] Constitution, the laws of the United States, and treaties. . .' and in the Congressional statutes giving federal courts jurisdiction over cases arising under the laws of the United States. Questions of international law are federal questions; issues of international law that arise in the state courts, then, can be appealed to the Supreme Court. The Supreme Court can determine and establish a single, uniform rule of customary international law for the country, for the states as well as for the national government, for state courts as well as federal courts.[21]

International law in the courts

Courts in the United States determine and apply customary international law as they interpret and apply U.S. statutes, treaties, and executive agreements. In the oft-quoted language of Justice Gray in *The Paquete Habana*: 'International law is part of our law, and must be ascertained and administered by the courts of justice of appropriate jurisdiction, as often as questions of right depending upon it are duly presented for their determination.'[22]

In that case, the Supreme Court held that, under international prize law in time of war, fishing vessels belonging to enemy nationals were exempt from capture by armed vessels of the United States and could not be condemned and sold as prize of war. Before and since then, state and federal courts have applied international law in innumerable cases, notably, for example, when they dismiss proceedings against foreign governments, their diplomats, vessels or other public property, because international law gives them immunity from judicial process.[23]

International law and acts of Congress. International law is law of the land and will be enforced by the courts, but will they enforce it in the face of other, inconsistent law? Will the courts give effect to international law if the political branches determine to violate it?

International law, we have seen, is binding on the United States, therefore on Congress, and Congress has generally recognized its responsibility to implement and not to frustrate U.S. compliance. On a number of occasions, however, Congress has knowingly refused to carry out U.S. treaty obligations, for example, in the 1990s, the legal obligation of the United States to pay its dues to the United Nations. On a number of occasions, Congress enacted laws that would place the United States in violation of international law—for example, in 1971, laws that resulted in violation of the United Nations embargo of Rhodesian chrome.*

U.S. courts do not issue orders to Congress. They cannot direct Congress to appropriate funds, even when failure to do so results in a violation by the United States of an international obligation. In an appropriate case or controversy, a court can declare an act of Congress unconstitutional, but an act of Congress that is inconsistent with international law, I have suggested, is not *ipso facto* unconstitutional.

Here we are concerned not with the constitutionality of an act of Congress but with its relation to customary law as law of the United States and how the courts should treat them when they are in conflict. The Supreme Court has not addressed these questions directly. *The Paquete Habana* (1900) remains the Court's latest pronouncement on the place of international law in the law of the United States.** In restating the principle that 'international law is part of our law', Justice Gray saw fit to interject uncertain qualifications that have troubled our jurisprudence for a hundred years. He said: 'For this purpose, *where there is no treaty, and no controlling Executive or legislative act or judicial decision,*† resort must be had to the customs and usages of civilized nations'.[24]

Later in that opinion he wrote: 'This rule of international law is one which prize courts, administering the law of nations, are bound to take judicial notice of, and to give effect to, *in the absence of any treaty or other public act of their own government* in relation to the matter.'[25]

Justice Gray's qualifications are dictum: the case before him did not involve any treaty, or act of Congress (or of the President). They are not supported by explanation or authority. As regards acts of Congress, one may read Justice Gray in light of the fact that he wrote a dozen years after the Supreme Court had held‡ that an act of Congress is equal in law to a treaty, and that therefore a later statute will supersede an earlier treaty obligation for purposes of U.S. law. By that decision, in effect, the Court interpreted the Constitution as not prohibiting Congress to legislate contrary to U.S. treaty obligations and not warranting the courts in holding such legislation unconstitutional. It is perhaps plausible to read Justice Gray's reference to a 'controlling legislative act' as extending the same principle to customary international law. The Constitution, then, does not prevent Congress from enacting law inconsistent with U.S. obligations under customary international law, and the

---

* See n. 50 to this chapter.   ** But see *Sabbatino*, Ch. V., pp. 137–41.
† Emphasis added.   ‡ *Whitney* v. *Robertson*, n. 11 to this chapter.

courts are obliged to give effect to the later act of Congress (though that places the United States in violation of its international legal obligations).

In the case of treaties, the Supreme Court has read the Constitution as giving treaties and acts of Congress equal authority as law, and has decided that in case of conflict the later in time prevails. Justice Gray's passing dictum apart, the Court has not considered whether principles of customary international law—also the law of the land—are equal in law with treaties and with acts of Congress. For international law, treaty obligations and principles of customary international law are of equal rank, so that the later in time prevails.* Presumably, since their place in U.S. law derives from their character and status in international law, treaties and principles of customary law have equal status in U.S. jurisprudence too, and the courts would give effect to the later in time. An act of Congress, we saw, inconsistent with a preexisting U.S. treaty obligation, will be given effect by the courts. Without any support in constitutional text, the same principle, presumably, would require the courts to give effect to an act of Congress inconsistent with U.S. obligation under customary law.[26] Like a treaty, too, a supervening principle of international law should not be denied domestic effect because of some provision in an earlier act of Congress.[27]

The President, international law, and the courts. Justice Gray's passing dictum in the *Paquete Habana* has proven to be particularly confusing and troubling in respect of the authority of the President and the Executive branch. Gray seemed to declare that the courts must give effect to a principle of international law as U.S. law 'in the absence of a controlling Executive act', or 'a public act of our own Government'.[28] Some have assumed that by these qualifications the Court implied that when such executive (or other public) act contradicted a principle of customary law, the courts would give effect to the executive or other public act and not to the principle of international law.** Assuming that

* Subject to the doctrine of *jus cogens*: a treaty that is inconsistent with a customary norm that is 'peremptory', of superior, compelling character, is void. See the Vienna Convention on the Law of Treaties, Arts. 53, 64; RESTATEMENT (n. 2 to Preface) § 102, Comment *k* and Reporters' Note 6. And see Art. 103 of the United Nations Charter which provides that the Charter shall prevail over other treaty obligations.

** In fact, it is not clear that the Court's incidental qualification was addressing the significance of a public act that was inconsistent with the international principle. In context, the Court was telling the courts how they should determine whether a particular rule has become a principle of international law. The Court said that one has to explore the practice of states and distill a principle from that practice, unless

to be a correct interpretation of a passing and opaque dictum, it leaves much unexplained. If international law is part of our law, why should a 'controlling executive act' permit—or require—the courts not to give effect to this part of our law? And what kind of act would be 'controlling' for this purpose?

As regards an act of Congress, we have seen, the authority of the act is equal to that of a treaty and presumably also of a principle of customary international law. Congress does not claim authority to violate international obligations of the United States; it insists only that nothing in the Constitution suggests that the legislative powers of Congress are limited by a requirement that its acts be consistent with international law. The authority of the President in respect of international law, however, is more complicated, a complexity deriving from the fact that the President wears two different, distinct hats. His 'Executive power' includes the duty to take care that the laws, including treaties and customary international law insofar as they are part of U.S. law, be faithfully executed. But the President, we know, also has independent constitutional authority in foreign affairs as Executive, as treaty-maker, as 'sole organ', and as Commander in Chief. Under these powers, the President can act in ways that make or affect law in the United States, and it may be that as far as the Constitution is concerned he can exercise these powers even in ways that are inconsistent with U.S. international obligations. Thus, we have seen, the President can denounce   or otherwise terminate a treaty even when that puts the United States in violation of international law.* Similarly, the President may take other measures that are within his constitutional authority under his foreign affairs power even if they violate international law. For example, the President has acquired constitutional authority to deploy U.S. forces for purposes short of war. If, say, President Reagan had constitutional authority to bomb Libya (in 1986) because of its alleged responsibility for terrorist activities, his constitutional authority to do so was not diminished by the fact that the bombing may have violated U.S. obligations under the United Nations Charter. Surely, the courts would not enjoin the bombing.**

The confusion deriving from the President's dual constitutional character is aggravated when the President acts on matters within the United

---

a public act by some branch of the U.S. government has already determined and codified the principle on behalf of the United States. By this reading, the Court's statement did not address at all whether the Executive (or Congress) is free to act contrary to international law. And see n. 35 to this chapter.

* See Ch. VII.   ** See Ch. II and Ch. V, p. 146, n. 66 to Ch. V.

States and which, therefore, are subject to domestic U.S. law. A treaty may address matters that have effect on rights and interests within the United States; in respect of those matters a treaty is domestic law and it is the President's duty to execute the treaty. The courts will enjoin any violation of the treaty or any failure by Executive officials to give it effect.* But if the President, in the exercise of his foreign affairs powers, should denounce or otherwise terminate the treaty, the treaty no longer exists; it is no longer law of the land; the Executive branch will not execute it; the courts will not enforce it. Without terminating a treaty, the President, acting under his foreign affairs powers, may decide that one or more treaty provisions should not be carried out. Such a decision would create tension between the President's authority under his foreign affairs power to act without regard to U.S. international obligations, and the President's duty to take care that the treaty, as law of the United States, be faithfully executed. Perhaps because a decision to act in disregard of a treaty is rarely a decision of the President but a failure by lesser Executive officials, the courts have regularly called on the Executive branch to abide by U.S. treaty undertakings.

Unlike treaties, however, principles of customary international law cannot be denounced or terminated by the President and cannot be eliminated from the law of the United States by any Presidential act. If the President acts in violation of international law in a matter that does not affect rights and interests in the United States, the status of international law as law of the United States is ordinarily not implicated (and the President's act is not likely to come within the jurisdiction of U.S. courts). But where a principle of customary international law applies to rights and interests within the United States, a Presidential decision under his Foreign Affairs power to act in violation of that principle would conflict with the President's constitutional duty to take care that the principle of international law, as law of the United States, be faithfully executed.

In that case, too, it may be that the President's Foreign Affairs power, as a source of constitutional authority of some legislative import, may be exercised without regard to international legal restraints. But it should require an act of the President, not of some lower Executive official, and it should be an act that claims justification as an exercise of Presidential Foreign Affairs power. The courts ought not tolerate, and should give relief, when members of the Executive bureaucracy simply refuse or fail to give effect to principles of customary law as law of the

* See Ch. VII, p. 207. Compare *United States* v. *Alvarez-Machain*, 504 U.S. 655 (1992), discussed in Ch. IX, p. 306.

United States, as the courts do when the Executive fails to honor a treaty.

In recent decades, particularly with the growth of a customary international law of human rights, a number of persons have asked the courts to order the Executive branch to give effect to principles of customary law as law of the United States. And courts have floundered in trying to resolve the tension between Presidential authority to act, even in disregard of international law, and his duty to execute the law, including international law. The Supreme Court has not been helpful.*

One intermediate federal court struggled with the question in *Garcia-Mir* (1986).[29] In that case, the Attorney General of the United States had continued in detention for many months many Cubans who had come to the United States, whom the United States did not wish to admit but whom it could not deport because no other country would accept them. The persons detained claimed that their prolonged detention was arbitrary and therefore a violation of a principle of customary international law. The Court of Appeals accepted the argument that the detention violated international law but concluded that the detention, authorized by the Attorney General, is a 'controlling executive act' (in the words of *The Paquete Habana*) and therefore overrides the principle of international law prohibiting the detention.

In my view, *Garcia-Mir* misinterpreted and misapplied *The Paquete Habana*. The court of appeals apparently considered *any* act of the President to be 'controlling', and extended that to include an act by the Attorney General. The court took the view that the President—and the Attorney General—had power to 'disregard international law in the service of domestic needs';[30] I know nothing to support that conclusion. I do not believe the Attorney General (or the President) can disregard international law that is part of our law any more than he (or she) can disregard any other law. The court did not find that, as a result of some action within the President's constitutional power, the principle of inter-

---

* The President need not, may not, execute a treaty if it has been terminated, or has otherwise ceased to be binding under international law. He may not execute the treaty as law of the United States if Congress has enacted legislation superseding it. The President cannot terminate a principle of international law and such principles ordinarily continue in existence indefinitely; the President's obligation to take care that the principle be faithfully executed also remains. The President may not execute a principle of international law as U.S. law, if Congress has superseded it by subsequent legislation. I suggest here that the President's obligation to execute a principle of international law may bow before a Presidential act within his constitutional Foreign Affairs power. In the absence of such a Presidential act, the Executive branch is bound to take care that it be faithfully executed.

national law against arbitrary detention had ceased to be a legal obligation of the United States. There was no suggestion that the President,
acting under his constitutional power, had by executive agreement or
executive order, made law that superseded the rule of international law
forbidding arbitrary detention as domestic law. There was no suggestion
that the President ordered the detention in the valid exercise of some
independent constitutional authority as 'sole organ' or as Commander
in Chief that might have effect as law in the United States.

Only such Presidential acts, I believe, might constitute 'controlling
executive acts' permitting the courts to give them legal effect in disregard of international law as the law of this land. In the absence of such
controlling acts, the court in *Garcia-Mir* should have required the
Attorney General to take care that international law be faithfully executed and to terminate the detention.[31]

Violations of international law by foreign states. That international law
is the law of the United States means that, as in the case of treaties,
courts in the United States will give effect to the obligations of the
United States under customary international law: at the behest of
affected private parties,* courts will prevent violations of international
law by the states or by federal officials. That doctrine itself gives no one
rights, remedies, or defenses against a foreign government for its violation of international law.

That has not always been understood. Thus, when Castro's Cuba
expropriated U.S. properties, probably in violation of international law,
it was urged that the courts of the United States had to refuse to give
effect to these expropriations, must reject claims by the Cuban government of title to the property, and even afford the victim a remedy
against Cuba.[32] The argument overlooked that, though international
law is part of the law of the United States, the law of the United States
has no application to what Castro did in Cuba. Moreover, except as otherwise provided by treaty or by special doctrine (as in human rights
law), international law establishes rights, duties, and remedies for states
against states; Castro's violations, then, might be an 'international tort'
against the United States giving rights and remedies to the United
States, but not to any private victims. International law itself, finally,
does not require any particular reaction to violations of law; it does not
require nations and national courts to refuse legal effect to violations by
other nations. Whether and how the United States should react to such
violations are domestic, political questions: the courts will not assume

* Or, as regards violations by a state, perhaps at the behest of federal officials.
See Ch. VII, pp. 207–8 and corresponding notes.

any particular reaction, remedy, or consequence.[33] Of course, Congress could legislate that the courts should refuse to recognize Castro's title or should give private persons a remedy* against Cuba (and might incorporate by reference the norm of international law to guide the courts) but it would be not international law but the federal statute that gave the courts their mandate.[34]

In one recent series of cases, the federal courts have found authority in an old act of Congress to give remedies for certain violations of international law by foreign states or officials. Beginning in 1789, Congress has given the lower federal courts jurisdiction of cases 'where an alien sues for a tort only [committed] in violation of the law of nations'.[35] In 1980, in *Filartiga*, a court of appeals interpreted the statute as authorizing a remedy in tort to an alien against a foreign official who had committed torture, a gross violation of human rights which the court determined to be a violation of customary international law;** other courts have followed suit.[36]

At the end of the twentieth century, customary international law, together with treaties which depend on customary law, remains the core of international governance and a pillar of U.S. foreign relations. Like treaties, customary international law is law for the United States in relations with other nations, as well as law of the United States for its political institutions, its courts, and its citizens. Like treaties, customary international law must fit into the U.S. constitutional framework and must find and keep its place in constitutional jurisprudence. Unlike treaties which have developed their part in the constitutional life of the United States, customary international law remains full of constitutional uncertainties. The Supreme Court has barely glanced at customary law in the twentieth century, and what the Court said in 1900, in opaque dictum and in outdated context, has only sown and harvested confusion. Surely, it is for the Court 'to say what the law is', beginning by revisiting the reverence of the Framers for the Law of Nations, and establish its clear and honorable place in our constitutional life.

---

* Compare the Helms-Burton Act, 'Cuban Liberty and Democratic Solidarity (Libertad) Act of 1996'. P.L. 102–14, 1996, Ch. V, n. 36.

** The court did not feel obliged to decide whether the act of Congress merely provided a federal forum for acts that were torts under international law or at common law, or an applicable state law, or whether Congress implicitly defined a new federal tort law for the federal courts to apply in the circumstances indicated (as it might define criminal offenses against the law of nations). See U.S. Constitution, Art. I, sec. 8.

INTERNATIONAL ORGANIZATIONS IN THE U.S. CONSTITUTIONAL FRAMEWORK

The constitutional powers to make treaties and other international agreements saw new uses after the Second World War in the spectacular development of multilateral diplomacy and the mushrooming of international organizations. Since 1945, the United States has been a member of over a hundred international organizations differing widely in scope and function, from the United Nations to, say, the Cape Spartel Lighthouse.[37] These organizations have differed, too, in their structures and procedures, in the obligations they imposed on the United States, in the degree to which they impinge on its government, its officials and its citizens. New international institutions raised or suggested new constitutional questions and framed old questions in new contexts.

Constitutional limitations on U.S. participation even worth discussing arise only if an international organization begins to acquire attributes of government and to impinge directly on the lives and activities of the inhabitants of the United States, or on governmental activities of the states. In such cases one might have to consider whether a treaty or agreement has improperly delegated powers or functions of the federal government to supranational, international, or foreign bodies; has violated the separation of powers by redistributing functions among the branches of the United States government, or has imposed inappropriate functions upon them; has infringed upon any abiding sovereignty of the states; or has denied rights to individuals by subjecting them to foreign authority, or to regulations which the United States itself could not impose.

In fact, until the last decades of the twentieth century, international organizations and arrangements in being, and those which the United States had seriously considered, did not raise significant constitutional difficulties. The United States adhered to them by constitutionally appropriate process, by treaty or by executive agreement approved by Congress. The charters of such organizations dealt with matters clearly of 'foreign policy concern'* and, generally, contained undertakings by the United States that did not differ in kind from those in its traditional bilateral treaties. Membership in international organizations raised no issues under the Bill of Rights because, in general, the organizations impinged only on the United States government itself (not on individual citizens), and neither 'the United States', nor any branch of its

* Compare Ch. VII, p. 196.

government, nor any federal official in his or her official capacity, in relation to international organizations, has constitutional rights—to freedom of speech or of silence, to security from unreasonable searches or seizures, to equal protection of the law, to protections for liberty or property, to due process of law.*

During the Cold War, international organizations were modest in their aspirations, and powerful states—e.g., the United States—were particularly resistant to strong international institutions and to limitatons on their own autonomy. The end of the Cold War, however, promised more ambitious and more 'intrusive' international governance, and programs that might raise constitutional issues that earlier had been disparaged as hypothetical, academic. The United Nations Security Council was resurrected and undertook actions to maintain international peace and security. Some had large plans to pursue international peace and security and to prevent nuclear proliferation more actively, to govern the seas beyond national jurisdiction, and to address the needs of the global environment and the new promises of science and technology, by powerful international institutions. There were grand plans to divert massive national expenditures on armaments towards international organizations for international development.

In fact, however, the 'New World Order' did not materialize as anticipated. Within less than a decade, international organizations had to curb ambitions, especially as developed states—e.g., the United States—began to retreat into 'isolationist', less 'internationalist' moods and to press for organizational austerity. Only in international trade have states been moved to attempt novel and far-reaching institutional arrangements.** Towards the end of the century one cannot foresee with confidence the shape and character of international organization, and whether the constitutional problems they suggest for the United States are realistic or imaginary.

* See Ch. IX.

** See, e.g., the Uruguay Round Agreements, characterized as 'one of the most ambitious efforts at international lawmaking and institution building since the establishment of the United Nations'. D. Leebron, *Implementation of the Uruguay Round Results in the United States*, in J. JACKSON and A. SYKES, (eds.), IMPLEMENTING THE URUGUAY ROUND (1996).

On the law of the sea, the ambitious 1982 Convention was scaled back to some extent in the 1994 Agreement. See generally, RESTATEMENT (n. 2 to Preface) Part V; *Law of the Sea Forum: The 1994 Agreement on Implementation of the Seabed Provisions of the Convention on the Law of the Sea*, 88 AM. J. INT'L L. 687–96 (1994).

I do not address developments in the European Community, to which the United States is not party.

Hypothetical or real, the foreseeable institutions and programs for international governance need not be constitutionally troublesome.

U.S. Adherence to International Organizations

The United States has joined many organizations by treaty, and some by Congressional–Executive agreement. Even when the President joins an organization by sole executive agreement, he must seek Congressional approval at least in the form of an appropriation to pay the United States contribution to the organization (or use 'general purpose' funds authorized and appropriated by Congress and therefore subject to Congressional control).

U.S. Participation in International Organizations

The United States participates in an international organization pursuant to the treaty or agreement by which it adhered to the organization. That treaty or agreement gives the President the responsibility as well as the constitutional authority to participate in the organization, but only Congress can authorize and appropriate funds to pay U.S. dues and other financial obligations or any voluntary contributions to the organization's activities, and to defray the expenses of U.S. participation. As regards some organizations (notably the United Nations), Congress has enacted comprehensive legislation regulating U.S. participation.*

The Executive as U.S. representative

Subject to the terms of the international agreement and of Congressional legislation regulating U.S. participation, the President represents the United States to and in the organization through representatives he appoints (usually with the consent of the Senate). Like other diplomatic representatives, those representing the United States in international organizations are instructed by the President. Attempts by Congress to instruct U.S. representatives are highly questionable as a matter of constitutional separation of powers, and are usually only hortatory or are likely to be treated as such by the President. Of course, financial assessments by and contributions to the organization will depend on Congressional appropriations, and its advice as to how to vote on such matters cannot go wholly unheeded.

* The United Nations Participation Act of 1945, n. 38 to this chapter.

The United Nations

By almost any measure, the most important international organization of which the United States is a member is the United Nations. Participation in the United Nations has also raised the most significant constitutional issues for the United States.

By treaty implemented by acts of Congress,[38] the United States adhered to the United Nations Charter, is a member of the United Nations Organization, and a 'Permanent Member' having special rights and responsibilities in the Security Council.[39] The Charter forbids all members—therefore also the United States—to use or threaten force[40] against the territorial integrity or political independence of other states* and requires members to cooperate with the Organization in maintaining international peace and security and in promoting social and economic ends.[41]

The prohibition on the use of force is the principal norm of modern international law. It was designed to abolish war and to prohibit other uses of force between states, however they might be characterized or denominated. By adhering to the Charter, the United States has given up the right to go to war at will.[42] Some have asked whether these undertakings are consistent with the Constitution, which clearly contemplated that the United States might go to war and gave Congress the power to decide to do so. The Charter, in effect, also prohibits the President to exercise his constitutional powers to send troops abroad for purposes short of war, where to do so would violate the law of nations.**

Such objections misconceive the character of treaties and their place in the constitutional pattern. By any treaty undertaking, the United States limits its right to do what it could do freely in the absence of treaty (if it is within the constitutional power of some branch of the federal government to do). The powers of Congress and the President to wage war or to use force for other purposes have no greater constitutional sanctity than have their other powers, and no greater immunity from being limited by treaty, whether by a bilateral treaty of alliance, friendship or non-aggression, or by the United Nations Charter estab-

---

* Article 2(4) of the U.N. Charter provides: 'All Members shall refrain in their international relations from the threat or use of force against the territorial integrity or political independence of any state, or in any other manner inconsistent with the Purposes of the United Nations.' Article 51 provides, in effect, an exception permitting the use of force in self-defense against armed attack.

** See Ch. IV.

lishing general international law. Moreover, we have seen, the United
Nations Charter does not deprive the Congress or the President of constitutional power: both the Congress and the President continue to have
their *power*—though not the *right* under international law—to declare
war, use force, or otherwise act in violation of the United Nations
Charter, as they have the power (though not the right) to disregard other
international obligations.

A different question is whether, by adhering to the United Nations
Charter and accepting the authority of the United Nations Security
Council, the treaty-makers have improperly delegated powers of
Congress or of the President to an international body.[43] The United
Nations Charter established the Security Council as the principal organ
of the United Nations with primary responsibility to maintain international peace and security. The members of the United Nations have
agreed that the Council acts on their behalf, and they are legally committed to carry out its decisions.* Under Chapter VII of the Charter, the
Security Council can determine the existence of a threat to peace, a
breach of the peace, or an act of aggression, and the Council may make
recommendations or decide what measures shall be taken (Article 39).**

* Articles 24(1), 25.
** In the language of the Charter, 'decisions' by the Council are mandatory. The
Council may also 'authorize' action or 'recommend' action by willing states.
Sometimes the Council 'calls upon' states, a term that is ambiguous, so that com-
pliance may or may not be wholly voluntary.

In the United Nations, in addition to the comprehensive authority of the Security
Council to 'legislate'—to determine policy and issue mandatory directives to member states—in maintaining peace, the Council and the General Assembly make law
when they interpret their own authority or the obligations of members under the
Charter, and members have sometimes found themselves effectively bound in ways
they had not intended and do not desire. The Assembly has asserted the right to
assess members for various purposes including its peace-keeping efforts and economic and social programs; it has interpreted the Charter as establishing human
rights standards that at least some members deny and resist.

General Assembly resolutions have also purported to declare international law for
members, and the United States has rejected some of these assertions. For the
United States, the Senate, of course, never consented to such unanticipated interpretations, but it can be deemed to have consented to the system that produces them.
(There is no Senate consent to later interpretations of any treaty by the President,
or by the courts or by international tribunals.) Compare, for example, the resolution declaring the use of nuclear weapons illegal, G.A.Res. 1653, U.N. GAOR Supp.
17 at 4–5, U.N. Doc. A/5100 (1962), or the Moratorium Resolution on the right to
mine in the deep seabed, G.A Res. 2574, U.N. GAOR Supp. 30 at 11, U.N. Doc
A/7630 (1969).

It may decide on mandatory non-military measures (Article 41) or on military measures (Article 42). The Charter requires member states to conclude special agreements to make armed forces available to the Security Council (Article 43).

Under the Charter, then, the United States is legally bound—a consequence of its treaty undertaking—to carry out 'decisions', mandatory orders, by the Security Council, such as those imposing non-military sanctions to help maintain international peace and security (Article 41), or to take military actions under Article 42. The United States is bound to conclude 'Article 43' agreements to provide armed forces for the Security Council.

Under the U.S. Constitution, the Charter, as a treaty of the United States, is the law of the land, and law for the United States. The President has the duty to take care that the laws be faithfully executed.[44] That includes, also, a duty to take care that treaties be faithfully carried out. Duty to act brings with it authority (power) to act. Some U.S. obligations under the Charter may be carried out by the President under his authority to execute the treaty; some obligations under the Charter may require implementation by Congress. Congress is internationally obligated, and has the power under the Constitution, to enact laws necessary and proper to carry out the obligations and responsibilities of the United States under the Charter. The President has the responsibility of seeking such Congressional action; he has the duty to see that such Congressional legislation is faithfully executed.

The President is also bound (and has power) to negotiate 'Article 43 agreements' to make armed forces available to the Security Council. The United States obligation to make such agreements might have served to authorize the President to conclude them on his own authority, had Article 43 not expressly provided* that the obligation to conclude the agreement is 'subject to ratification by the signatory states in accordance with their constitutional processes'.[45] Congress explicitly limited the President's authority: the United Nations Participation Act authorized the President to conclude Article 43 agreements but explicitly provided that they should be subject to the consent of Congress.[46]

It has been argued that pursuant to these provisions the Security Council can direct the United States to take action not determined by Congress or the President and which they may be unwilling to take.**

* The provision was probably written into the Charter to make it acceptable to the United States Senate.

** Under Chapter VII of the Charter, the Security Council has authority to direct the United States to impose and respect an embargo and other economic

And, it might be said, if the United States should conclude an 'Article 43 agreement' to place troops at the disposal of the Security Council,[47] the Council (rather than the President or Congress) could send U.S. troops to war,* and some 'U.N. Command', not the President of the United States, might be their Commander in Chief.

These objections are not substantial. The United Nations Charter does not take power from U.S. political institutions. The Security Council cannot order the United States (or any state) to take military action; the Security Council can send U.S. forces into military actions only after the United States has entered into an Article 43 agreement, and such an agreement can be made only with the approval of Congress. In the absence of an Article 43 agreement, the Security Council can only recommend or authorize the use of force, and authority to send forces pursuant to such a recommendation or authorization lies in Congress (or is subject to its control).** The Security Council can order economic sanctions if the President does not object, but Congress itself gave approval in advance to U.S. participation in such sanctions if the President supports them.

In fact, the Constitution and our constitutional institutions have proved wholly adequate to U.N. needs. During the long years of the Cold War, the underlying constitutional issues raised by international governance remained hypothetical and theoretical. The principal purpose of the United Nations—maintaining international peace—was largely frustrated, and its principal organ, the United Nations Security Council, largely quiescent. Except in Korea,† the United Nations developed peace-keeping (instead of peace-making) procedures, and U.S. participation in such activities was essentially voluntary. The United States participated by Presidential authority; Congress appropriated funds for

---

sanctions. Article 41. The Council can take actions using U.S. military contingents provided pursuant to agreements which the United States is obligated to conclude (but which have not yet been concluded). Articles 42, 43. In my view, in the absence of Article 43 agreements, the Council can only recommend (not mandate) that member states take military action.

* A related objection is that the Charter commits the United States to go to war in certain circumstances, and that under the Constitution such a commitment can be made only by act of Congress, not by treaty. In fact, the Constitution does not forbid a treaty that commits the country to war, although it may preclude a provision that would automatically put the country into war in certain circumstances. See Ch. VII, p. 184. In any event, the U.N. Charter does not commit the United States to go to war unless the Security Council orders it, and the United States could prevent such an order by its veto.

** See p. 252 above. † See p. 255 below.

both the obligatory dues to the United Nations and for voluntary contributions; the United States recognized its legal obligation to pay mandatory assessments, even when Congress frequently kept the United States in arrears.

During the Cold War, the United Nations Security Council adopted only two mandatory resolutions (both with U.S. concurrence) imposing legal obligations on the United States. It imposed an embargo on trade with the 'unlawful government' of Rhodesia*; it ordered an embargo on the sale of arms to South Africa. After the Cold War, the Security Council increased its activity. It imposed mandatory embargoes against Libya when it failed to extradite two suspected terrorists; against Iraq (following the invasion of Kuwait, discussed below); against Haiti; against the former Yugoslavia. The Security Council also established an International Tribunal for the former Yugoslavia and directed members to cooperate with it.[48] The United States—the President with Congressional support or acquiescence—led the Council in every instance.

There is an answer of another kind, probably a complete answer,** to constitutional objections: the United States has a veto in the Security Council.[49] Every mandatory action by the Security Council is taken with the consent or the acquiescence of the United States; every such action by the Council, then, has the concurrence of the President acting under his own vast powers in foreign relations and pursuant to a treaty of the United States consented to by the Senate and implemented by Congress.[50] But that 'safeguard', too, may not be the whole, or the essential, response. At bottom, constitutional support for U.S. participation in international organizations must lie in a vision of the Constitution and in its character. The Framers may not have anticipated, or even conceived of, international organizations and 'international governance'. But even as conceived, surely as it has developed, the Constitution, I believe, lodges faith in the wisdom of the people and their representatives. The Constitution need not be interpreted to be a straitjacket making it impossible for the United States to participate in the affairs of its times and to respond to new needs by new means and new remedies.†

---

  * Later Zimbabwe. The United States honored the Rhodesian embargo until Congress legislated against it. See n. 50 to this chapter.

  ** Another complete answer to constitutional objections to delegation is that, as with any international obligation, the United States has the ultimate decision as to whether it will comply. See pp. 232 *et seq.*

  † See p. 262. Early in the twentieth century, Congress concluded that it can exercise its powers effectively only through administrative agencies, and U.S.

President, Congress and the United Nations

Constitutional issues of a different order have been engendered by U.S. responses to United Nations actions.

The President represents the United States in the United Nations and participates in its deliberations and decisions. Then it is the President's responsibility to respond to United Nations resolutions and actions, and it is his duty to carry out any that the United States is legally bound to honor.* But some United Nations decisions stir the interest of Congress, and some of them impinge on its constitutional concerns and may invite tension between Congress and the President.

The principal issues between President and Congress have arisen out of the few military actions sponsored by the United Nations. Since its creation, the United Nations Security Council has sponsored two collective military actions to defend a state victim of an armed attack and to restore and maintain international peace and security. In 1950, the Council recommended that member states place troops under a Unified Command to come to the defense of South Korea against aggression from North Korea.[51] In 1990, the Council authorized willing states to come to the defense of Kuwait against aggression by Iraq.[52]

In both Korea and the Gulf War, the United States led the Security Council into action. In Korea, the United States headed the unified command the Council had recommended. In the Gulf War, the United States again led the states authorized by the Council and willing to act on behalf of the United Nations and in collective self-defense with Kuwait. United States involvement in both U.N. military actions raised—or should have raised—constitutional issues. President Truman sent hundreds of thousands of troops into war (though denominated a 'police action') without seeking Congressional authorization. He claimed authority to act from the United Nations Security Council resolutions. Criticism from a few Senators (from the opposition, minority party) was muted. The war—a 'hot eruption' during the Cold War—had strong national support. An accommodating Congress acquiesced in the action and supported it by appropriation of funds and military service legislation.[53]

constitutional jurisprudence accommodated to that 'fourth branch' of government. At the end of the twentieth century, the political branches have found that they can achieve effective governance only through international agencies. Is there any reason why the Constitution cannot accommodate to that development?

* Congress has confirmed and regulated the President's responsibilities in the United Nations Participation Act of 1945. See pp. 250, 252, 257.

In the Gulf Crisis, the United States took two related but legally discrete sets of action. After Iraq's invasion of Kuwait, the United States moved to defend Saudi Arabia against possible attack; it also pressed Iraq to evacuate Kuwait. To defend Saudi Arabia, the United States deployed armed forces to Saudi territory (with the consent of the Saudi Government). That deployment raised no significant issues under international law but it raised questions of Presidential authority under the Constitution. President Bush acted without Congressional authorization or approval. No doubt he claimed authority from the precedents established during 200 years by Presidential deployment of armed forces in support of foreign policy purposes short of war.* In the Gulf, forces were deployed in the first instance not to engage in war but as a shield for Saudi Arabia, for deterrent purposes.**

The constitutional authority of the President came into question also as regards the subsequent actions taken by the United States for the liberation of Kuwait. The United States took the lead in developing the United Nations action, in obtaining the adoption of successive Security Council resolutions, and in implementing and enforcing them. In accordance with a mandatory Security Council resolution, the United States imposed an embargo and other sanctions against Iraq. It also deployed maritime forces to the area, and used forcible measures to enforce the embargo. Later, the United States led the use of force to liberate Kuwait as authorized by the Security Council.

As to most of these measures by the United States, the President might have acted on his own authority.† In my view, the President might plausibly claim that he had the duty, therefore the authority, to carry out any mandatory, self-executing provisions of the Charter, a treaty of the United States, as well as mandatory resolutions of the Security Council, since the Charter obligated the United States to heed such resolutions. Thus, for example, the President could carry out mandatory decisions by the Security Council under Article 41 calling upon member states to apply measures not involving the use of armed force, e.g., economic sanctions, interruption of communications, rupture of diplomatic relations.[54]

On the other hand, in my view, there is no basis for deriving from the Charter any authority for the President to do on behalf of the United

* See Ch. IV.

** The President might have argued also that, since the United States deterrent was highly likely to be effective, such deployment was not inconsistent with the War Powers Resolution, since the forces of the United States were not in fact put into a situation 'where imminent involvement in hostilities is clearly indicated by the circumstances'. See Ch. IV, pp. 105, 106.

† In fact, Congress had expressly given him authority. See n. 54 to this chapter.

States what the Security Council did not mandate, but only authorized or recommended.* There was, then, no international legal obligation on the United States to carry out the resolution of the Security Council 'authorizing' it to use force to assure compliance with the sanctions resolution, or the resolution authorizing the United States to use force to liberate Kuwait.[55] There was, then, no duty on the President to take care that such Security Council resolutions be executed. The President, then, derived no authority from them, or from the Charter, to use force for such purposes.**

The President's power to use force on his own authority would be no greater if the military action by the United States were seen as action in collective self-defense with Kuwait. Article 51 of the United Nations Charter *permits* action by states in collective self-defense with a victim of an armed attack; it does not even recommend such action; surely it does not mandate it. There is no legal obligation on the United States to come to the assistance of a victim of an armed attack; there is, then, no international obligation from which the President might derive authority to do so.

Congress apparently so interpreted the Charter shortly after it was adopted. The United Nations Participation Act authorized the President to carry out Security Council resolutions under Article 41 which impose economic sanctions and other measures not involving the use of force.[56] The Participation Act also authorized the President to negotiate Article 43 agreements but to conclude them only subject to Congressional consent. Congress expressly denied the President any authority to make forces available to the Security Council other than pursuant to Article 43 agreements.[57] Clearly, Congress did not think the President had any constitutional authority of his own, or derived any authority from the United Nations Charter, to make forces available for war, whether for a Security Council action under Article 42 or for collective self-defense with a state victim of an armed attack under Article 51.

President Truman's action in Korea, I conclude, was without constitutional support until ratified by Congress. President Bush's action would have been unconstitutional had Congress not authorized it.[58]

---

* It is not clear that the Security Council has authority under the Charter to *order* states to use the force necessary to make sanctions effective. In the case of Iraq, the Security Council did not do so: it 'called upon' states to enforce the embargo and 'authorized' states to use the necessary force to that end. S.C. Res. 678.

** Congressional legislation authorizing sanctions, n. 54 to this chapter, did not say whether the President could use force to enforce the sanctions. But compare n. 57 to this chapter. The President might have claimed authority to use force as a measure 'short of war', under his foreign affairs powers. See Ch. IV.

President Clinton faced a similar issue in 1993–94 when the Security Council imposed an embargo and authorized the use of force in Haiti to help restore the democratically elected government overturned by a military coup. President Clinton claimed that such action was within his authority and could be taken without Congressional authorization, invoking, *inter alia,* the authorization by the Security Council. In the end, however, the President, though claiming he was not constitutionally obliged to do so, sought[59] Congressional authorization to invade Haiti.*

I have been discussing constitutional authority to carry out the obligations of the United States under the United Nations Charter or under mandatory Security Council resolutions. Having the power, however, Congress nonetheless might fail to enact the necessary laws (or to appropriate funds), thereby putting the United States in violation of those obligations. Or, Congress might adopt measures inconsistent with the obligations of the United States; for example, it might make war in violation of the United Nations Charter, or enact law contrary to a mandatory Security Council resolution.** The President will fight such wars or enforce such laws, and the courts will give them effect, though doing so would put the United States in violation of its international obligations.[60]

The United Nations Charter (and other organizational charters to which the United States is party) are the law of the land; the Constitution requires that the President take care that the laws be faithfully executed. But Presidents have sometimes failed to carry out U.S. obligations or have even acted in violation of such obligations. Lower courts have refused to enjoin such Presidential violations where the President has constitutional power or statutory authorization to take the action challenged,[61] for example military action that might have violated Article 2(4) of the United Nations Charter.†

The end of the Cold War brought major disorder in the former Soviet Union and in the former Yugoslavia, as well as in Africa (Somalia,

* Invasion became unnecessary when the military authorities in Haiti agreed to give up power and the democratically elected president was restored. U.S. forces entered Haiti peacefully, by invitation, to help maintain his authority and to restore law and order.

** In 1995, both houses of Congress passed resolutions lifting the arms embargo against the Bosnian government, in violation of the mandatory Security Council resolution. President Clinton vetoed it. See 31 WEEKLY COMPILATION OF PRESIDENTIAL DOCUMENTS 1433, Aug. 11, 1995.

† Some lower courts, erroneously in my view, treated such challenges to Presidential actions as raising non-justiciable, 'political questions'. See Ch. V, p. 144 and nn. 66, 67.

Rwanda), and increased demands for United Nations peacemaking and peacekeeping and for greater United States participation in such efforts. But in the 1990s, a changed political climate in the United States led to some resistance and encouraged moves in Congress to impose obstacles to United States participation, such as bills to prohibit the President from placing U.S. forces deployed for peacekeeping under a foreign command.[62] In my view, the authority of Congress to prohibit such command arrangements is highly questionable. Under its war powers, I believe, Congress has constitutional authority to regulate Presidential deployments of U.S. forces, even for peacekeeping; but command arrangements would seem to be the President's prerogative, under his authority as Commander in Chief, even under the narrowest construction of the scope of that authority and the broadest view of Congressional war powers.*

Most of the constitutional issues raised in relation to United States participation in the United Nations have swirled about the war-making powers, but the obligation of the United States to pay dues and other assessments to the United Nations has also evoked some controversy. The governing constitutional principles seem clear. Article 17(2) of the Charter provides: 'The expenses of the organization shall be borne by the Members as apportioned by the General Assembly.' That has been construed as imposing a legal obligation on members to pay what the Assembly assesses them for the regular budget of the organization. An advisory opinion by the International Court of Justice concluded that United Nations expenditures for peacekeeping may also be assessed by the General Assembly under Article 17(2), and are also mandatory.[63] The United States therefore has an international legal obligation to pay such assessments and Congress is constitutionally obligated to appropriate money to pay them. In the 1990s, Congress failed to appropriate funds to pay outstanding obligations to the United Nations, including assessments for the costs of peacekeeping, but no one doubted that Congress was being less than responsible, and was compelling the United States to default on its legal obligations.

NATO

During more than 40 years, United States participation in NATO[64] has raised similar as well as different questions. Has the United States delegated the power to declare war to other nations or to multilateral

* See Ch. IV.

bodies? Do the treaty and the organization it created impinge in other ways on the powers of the President or of Congress?

Again, during the Cold War, these questions did not appear serious. The North Atlantic Treaty does not purport automatically to put the United States into war in given circumstances. Rather, it provides that if an armed attack occurs against one party, every other party shall take forthwith 'such action as it deems necessary, including the use of armed force'; and that provision shall be 'carried out by the Parties in accordance with their respective constitutional processes'.[65] No doubt the Treaty imposes the obligation to go to war in some circumstances, but that is no different from other treaty undertakings that are to be carried out by the President or Congress.

Nor are there unconstitutional delegations in international command arrangements or deployments of troops. The principal NATO commander, who has always been a U.S. national, is under orders not of the President of the United States but of the NATO Council; in the Council, however, the United States has had a veto in principle (in the requirement of unanimity), and the dominant voice in fact.[66] Even if United States troops served under foreign command, it could hardly stir constitutional difficulties for the President, temporarily and revocably, to put troops under an allied command in a common cause, as was done in both World Wars. The arrangements would have the approval of the President and would be subject to his continuing control, and he could terminate them at any time (even if that should involve breach of an international agreement).

The changing role of NATO after the Cold War, however, has brought calls for a reexamination of United States participation in it. During 1991, hostilities within the former Yugoslavia brought proposals for NATO intervention with different possible roles for the United States, including various command arrangements. Those that have been suggested (and are likely to be adopted) seem to be well within the constitutional authority of the President and Congress.*

Regulation of U.S. Activities by International Agencies

Every international organization 'legislates', if only its annual budget and rules for the governance of the organization. Many also have

---

* Proposals to impose limitations on placing U.S. forces under a foreign command have not been adopted; some of them would raise constitutional questions as interfering with the President's authority as Commander in Chief. See p. 259 and n. 62 to this chapter.

broader legislative or regulatory authority.[67] The United Nations General Assembly was given authority to make rules for the administration of trust territories, and the Security Council for strategic trust territories (of which there has been only one, administered by the United States).[68] The International Monetary Fund has authority to limit the extent to which a government can modify the rate of exchange of its currency.[69] The International Civil Aviation Organization (ICAO) promulgates 'international standards and commended practices'.[70] Some organizations fix prices, as under the Commodity Agreements—wheat, sugar, coffee.[71] In 1948, the General Agreement on Tariffs and Trade (GATT) established an international trade regime; in 1995, the United States adhered to the World Trade Organization which succeeded GATT.[72] New areas of human activity—trade, environment, recombinant DNA research—are being regulated by international agencies and others seem likely subjects for international regulation before long. The United States adheres to these and similar arrangements by constitutionally-approved processes, by treaty or Congressional–Executive agreement. International rules and regulations pursuant to such arrangements bear the constitutional authority of Congress or of the treaty-makers who concluded the arrangements. As such, they are the law of the land, subject to the U.S. Constitution, equal to acts of Congress, and supreme to state law. Some may be law of the land of their own force; some may become law in the United States when implemented by Congress or in some instances by the President.

United States participation in such organizations and arrangements have suggested issues of derogation from United States 'sovereignty', of improper delegation of U. S. governmental authority, or violation of the principles of separation of powers; some applications, it might be claimed, deprive affected persons of their liberty or property without due process of law.*

Such issues have not come to court and few who would raise them are likely to have standing and to overcome other obstacles to adjudication. As hypothetical questions, they are difficult to evaluate. Some might insist that the Constitution is not implicated or relevant, since it governs only the government of the United States, not foreign or international entities. But a hypothetical court in a hypothetical case is likely to rule that the political branches cannot escape constitutional limits and

---

* Congress has effectively exempted such agencies from the operation of general statutes, such as the Administrative Procedure Act, applicable to domestic activities, which has an explicit exception for foreign affairs. Administrative Procedure Act of 1946, 60 Stat 237 (codified as amended in scattered sections of 5 U.S.C.).

constitutional responsibility by delegating 'governmental' authority to others.

Assuming that constitutional restraints apply, some of the issues are readily disposed of. Arguments that adherence to such arrangements derogate from United States 'sovereignty' are not persuasive. 'Sovereignty' is not a constitutional concept or an apparent constitutional concern. Any international undertaking by the United States can be said to derogate from United States 'sovereignty' in that it limits United States freedom to act lawfully, but the Constitution recognizes that the United States was and would be subject to the law of nations, and explicitly contemplates that the United States would make treaties and thereby assume international obligations.

Treaties are subject to constitutional restraints, however, and there is no reason to except those that establish international institutions and arrangements. But it is difficult to accommodate contemporary arrangements to a constitutional system that did not contemplate them and to judge them by constitutional standards designed for internal applications. Needless to say, the Framers did not anticipate contemporary international organizations or arrangements, but there is nothing to suggest that the Framers had a limited conception of what treaties might or should be used for, or that they intended to limit the ability of the United States to cooperate to meet needs of international governance which the future might bring.

United States participation in international regulatory agencies suggests issues of 'separation of powers' in novel contexts. Domestic regulatory agencies have been accepted into the U.S. constitutional system though they do not fall comfortably into the original framework of three branches of government. Can international regulatory agencies be similarly accommodated, or should they be considered, treated—as they indeed are—as outside the constitutional framework because they are not agencies of the U.S. government?

Delegation by Congress (and presumably by the treaty-makers) of authority otherwise vested in Congress is presumably subject to the limitations governing Congressional delegation generally. Congress can delegate its authority within defined limits and subject to clear guidelines. Perhaps United States participation in deliberations, determinations, and operations of the international agency, under Executive authority (as 'sole organ'), reduces the element of delegation. Perhaps the fact that the United States retains the power to terminate its participation saves any otherwise questionable delegations.*

* See Ch. IV, pp. 123 *et seq.*

Perhaps a complete answer to objections on grounds of delegation of constitutional power, or other issues of separation of powers, is that generally they are irrelevant. One can make a case that international organizations have substantial legislative power, and something of a case that they sometimes create law for the United States; there is little case for finding in any of these instances an unconstitutional delegation by the United States of the legislative power of Congress. In most existing instances 'legislation' by an international organization is only a recommendation or exhortation which the United States is not legally bound to accept.* In the few organizations that formally have power to make binding regulations, the United States has either a veto, the benefits of 'weighted voting', or other special voting arrangements that render it difficult for any regulation to be established without U.S. concurrence.** These 'legislative' or 'regulatory' bodies, then, are essentially forums for negotiating agreements; and it could hardly make a constitutional difference that U.S. representatives reach international agreement within some organ of an international organization rather than by negotiating a formal agreement in a plenipotentiary conference. For constitutional purposes, the 'agreements' produced in these organizations are effectively Presidential agreements; or they are properly seen as implementations of the original treaty establishing the organization and giving it 'regulatory powers', and, in consenting to that agreement, the Senate may be said to have consented in advance to any regulations authorized by the agreement.[73]

Even if an organization were able to assess contributions or impose law upon the United States against its will, it is not exercising powers that belong to Congress, for it is not exercising legislative powers of the United States, not the 'legislative Powers herein granted'.† It is creating

---

* World Health Organization (WHO) 'regulations', for example, are voluntary and are adopted by the United States only if the appropriate federal officials so decide. International Labor Organization (ILO) conventions on labor standards, and human rights covenants and conventions promulgated by the United Nations General Assembly, also are only recommended to the United States and would be binding only if formally adhered to by the United States.

** As in the International Monetary Fund, the International Bank for Reconstruction and Development, the Wheat Agreement and the Fishery conventions, nn. 69 and 71 to this chapter. Binding decisions of the United Nations Security Council, for example, to impose an embargo on an aggressor nation, are subject to United States veto. See p. 253 above.

† U.S. Const. Art. I, sec. 1, prescribing the legislative power of *the United States.* Compare the parallel reference to the 'judicial Power of the United States' in Art. III, sec. 1.

law *for* the United States not *of* the United States,* international law for
the United States as a nation and for its government, not domestic U.S.
law for the governance of the inhabitants of the United States. Like law
made by treaty, law made by international organizations creates international obligations that the United States might be required to implement in this country; again, the United States can refuse to enact that
law and incur a violation.

International agreements might raise issues of separation of powers,
or of abdication of constitutional responsibility, if they purported to delegate the powers of the Federal government (or of any of its branches)
to an international agency or other external authority, but that is a
strictly hypothetical question. In fact, the United States has not entered
into any agreement that gives to any outside body authority to legislate
law in the United States, or to supersede or nullify U.S. law. An international regulation might impose obligations on the United States that
might require changes in U.S. law, but it is the United States that will
have to legislate to that end, whether it does so by giving legal effect
directly to a self-executing treaty, or by act of Congress to implement
the agreement.**

For similar reasons, other arrangements and organizations that have
been the subject of more or less serious negotiation would not create
constitutional difficulties for the United States, though particular forms
and details might be troublesome. Under fantastic proposals for
'General and Complete Disarmament' during an earlier era, for example,
or—more recently—by successive arms control agreements, the United
States could agree to abolish or limit existing armies and armaments,
and to refrain from the manufacture,† possession, testing or research
and development of particular weapons in the future.[74] It could agree to
create a complex international arrangement to carry on comprehensive
inspection that would penetrate secrecy of governmental operations,
require reporting, and subject government installations, activities, and

---

* Compare Ch. VII, pp. 198–206 above.
** Perhaps, like law made by treaties, some law made by international organizations cannot be self-executing but would require implementation by Congress. See
Ch. VII.
† In December 1995, it was reported that in negotiations between the United
States and the Russian Federation on monitoring a High-Enriched Uranium (HEU)
agreement, the Russian Federation had insisted that its inspectors be allowed into
the American nuclear fuel fabrication plants. Owners of the plants objected, insist-
ing that their techniques were proprietary. See W. Pizard, III, *Rifts Surface in U.S.-
Russian Talks over Monitoring the HEU Agreement*, 20 Nuclear Fuel 3 (Dec. 1995).

files to unlimited surveillance, and its officials to international interrogation. Within large limits, it could subject the activities of its citizens also to relevant, reasonable limitations and surveillance like those imposed by Congress through domestic regulatory programs. Issues of delegation could be wholly avoided if international authority, regulation and administration were brought to bear only on the government of the United States rather than directly on individuals in the United States, with the U.S. government responsible for the regulation of the activities of its citizens, their property, and their interests.

Consider, even, the original Acheson–Lilienthal plan of 1947 for the international development and control of atomic energy.[75] That proposal might have given to an international authority power to regulate the activities not only of the government of the United States but of mining companies, manufacturers, scientists, laborers, and citizens generally. A body with such powers and functions, it would have been argued, would be exercising governmental authority within the United States, assuming functions of the President and Congress. Again, constitutional objections would have been eliminated if the United States government stood between the international authority and the individual, if the requirements of the Authority were imposed upon the government of the United States and implemented and enforced by the government in the same ways as other treaty obligations or the regulations of its own administrative agencies. (Of course, some regulations might have been challenged as violating individual rights and liberties)* but often these too might have bowed to compelling public interests.

Expanding international regulation of trade has also produced complex arrangements blending national and international institutions, but those that have been put in place appear not to raise important constitutional difficulties. NAFTA and the Uruguay Round Trade Agreements include rules relating to investment and trade in services, but the rules they establish in matters such as banking, insurance, and acquisition of real property by foreign nationals, could, as they apply to the United States, be superseded by Congress under its Commerce Power, and its legislation would prevail in U.S. domestic law when any treaty obligation conflicts with a 'subsequent act of Congress'.**

Some procedures and proceedings of international bodies may raise claims that they deny affected parties 'due process of law', but many analogous procedures afforded by U.S. domestic agencies pursuant to U.S. law are not constitutionally required and presumably would not be

---

* See p. 266 below and Ch. IX.   ** See Ch. VII.

required of international agencies. These are, by definition, not U.S. agencies, not agencies of Congress or of the Executive; their procedures may follow those of other national legal systems. It would be difficult—and probably unnecessary—to squeeze them into traditional U.S. molds.

I have been discussing constitutional issues of delegation of authority and separation of powers. A different order of issues would arise if international regulations impinged directly on individual rights and interests within the United States. Here international intrusions would probably have to satisfy the standards applicable to official U.S. actions. Arms control inspections of public premises, or interrogation of public officials, raise no warning flags, since the United States government has no rights under the Bill of Rights. But inspection of private properties would bring the Fourth Amendment into play, and whether inspections were by U.S. officials, or by international officials, would presumably have to satisfy the court that they are not 'unreasonable' searches and seizures. Much might be found reasonable if necessary to maintain a major U.S. commitment to an international program important to international peace and security. Interrogations of private persons, whether conducted by U.S. or international officials, would have to respect the privilege against self-incrimination (and in some circumstances might have to be accompanied by a grant of immunity from prosecution).[76]

International Judicial Tribunals

United States participation in international judicial tribunals would raise similar as well as additional issues. The United States was a party to the Nuremberg Charter.[77] It is a party to the Statute of the International Court of Justice.[78] There are international courts, commissions, and committees that consider charges of violation of human rights,[79] some of which the United States might be eligible to join. There have been proposals for international criminal tribunals to which the United States might subscribe.[80]

Article III, section 1, of the Constitution provides:

The judicial Power of the United States, shall be vested in one supreme Court, and in such inferior Courts as the Congress may from time to time ordain and establish. The Judges, both of the supreme and inferior Courts, shall hold their Offices during good Behavior, and shall, at stated Times, receive for their Services, a Compensation, which shall not be diminished during their Continuance in Office.

That article defines and allocates 'the judicial Power of the United States', the power to administer law and justice under the authority of the United States for persons subject to its jurisdiction and laws. When the United States accepts the jurisdiction of the International Court of Justice,* or of other judicial or arbitral bodies that decide cases or controversies between nation states, it is not delegating to those tribunals any of the judicial power of the United States.[81] Nor would United States participation in such tribunals raise other issues under Article III, or under provisions in the Bill of Rights requiring due process of law and particular safeguards in criminal proceedings. The Bill of Rights, like the rest of the Constitution, safeguards individuals; it accords no rights to the government of the United States. International tribunals with jurisdiction over controversies between states do not apply criminal law, and their proceedings are not 'criminal proceedings'.** The prohibitions and safeguards of the Constitution govern only the actions of the United States government,† not those of an international body exercising international functions, even if the United States is party to it.[82]

The United States, then, could accept the jurisdiction of a tribunal such as the Inter-American Court of Human Rights, with jurisdiction over complaints of human rights violations brought by other states or by an international body. It could even, I have little doubt, adhere to an international court or tribunal that could hear complaints against the United States by individuals, including its own citizens or residents.[83] Nothing in the Constitution, we have seen, prevents the United States from undertaking international obligations in regard to its own citizens and residents;‡ nothing prevents the United States from submitting its compliance with such obligations to scrutiny and judgment by an international tribunal. There would seem to be no compelling constitutional reasons why the relations between the United States and its citizens could not be subject to both the laws and courts of the United States and to international law administered by international tribunals exercising international judicial power.[84]

* The United States is party to some 70 treaties that include provisions authorizing any party to bring another party to the Court to resolve a dispute arising out of the interpretation or application of the treaty. The United States had also accepted the compulsory jurisdiction of the Court by declaration under Article 36(2) of its statute, but President Reagan terminated that declaration, and efforts to seek Senate consent to a new declaration have not matured. See n. 78 to this chapter.

** Development in international law that would recognize state crimes, as distinguished from violations that were only 'delicts', have not included bringing states or governments to trial before a criminal court. The Nuremburg Charter provided for criminal proceedings to bring to trial Nazi leaders, not the German State.

† And of the states of the United States. Ch. IX, p. 284.

‡ See Ch. VII, pp. 185 *et seq.*

International Criminal Courts

Periodically there have been proposals for international courts to enforce international criminal law against individuals,[85] in past times for piracy, slave-running, arms smuggling, more recently, for waging aggressive war, genocide, and other gross violations of human rights, hijacking airplanes, other terrorist activities, or drug smuggling. In the past, the United States did not seriously consider adhering to any such court, but the difficulties of controlling terrorism and of regulating international drug smuggling by national police and criminal process alone have revived proposals for international criminal courts, and lawyers have had to ponder the constitutional implications of the various proposals. In the 1990s, the United Nations Security Council established a tribunal to prosecute war crimes, genocide, and other gross violations of human rights in the former Yugoslavia and in Rwanda.[86] In 1994, the International Law Commission completed a draft statute for a permanent International Criminal Court to be established by treaty.[87]

Adherence by the United States to the proposed Criminal Court would raise constitutional questions, but not insuperable obstacles. If an international criminal court sat outside the United States and imposed punishment outside the United States, it would not be exercising judicial power or other governmental authority of the United States. The United States, I believe, could adhere to such a tribunal, agree that U.S. nationals might be tried by it, and even extradite persons for such trials, as it can agree to extradite persons, including U.S. nationals, to a foreign country for trial in its courts for violation of its laws.[88] Constitutional issues would appear, however, if an international court were to sit in the United States, apply international law to acts committed in the United States by citizens or residents of the United States, and execute punishment in the United States. It would be argued that only U.S. law can apply in the United States, and criminal laws only if enacted by Congress (or by the states); and that only U.S. courts may try persons for violations of law in the United States, and such courts must be established by Congress (or by the states).[89] If, perhaps, a criminal court could also be created by treaty, it must still be a U.S. court, its judges must be appointed by the President with the consent of the Senate and assured of life tenure and undiminished compensation,[90] and its proceedings must include trial by jury and the other safeguards of the Bill of Rights.[91]

The crux of that argument—that under the Constitution only the law of the United States can apply to acts committed in the United States, and that only courts of the United States can sit here in judgment on such acts—is not, however, always and necessarily so. Foreign consuls have long enforced the criminal laws of their countries in the United States, applying them to acts performed in the United States, for example by visiting seamen, even when their acts are also subject to U.S. law and the jurisdiction of U.S. courts.[92] Under the NATO Status of Forces Agreement, allied soldiers and their civilian dependents, and allied defense employees, in the United States, can be tried by allied military courts for acts committed here, even when these are also violations of U.S. law and triable in our courts.[93] Similarly, during the Second World War, Congress permitted allied forces in the United States to try their troops by military tribunal, authorized U.S. courts to order witnesses (presumably even U.S. citizens) to appear before these tribunals, and made contempt of such tribunals or perjury before them federal crimes.[94] The constitutionality of such hospitality to foreign criminal law has never been considered by the Supreme Court, but there is no reason to believe that the Court would forbid it. Those tribunals do not apply the law of the United States or exercise judicial power of the United States, but act under authority granted them by their own law.* To allow the foreign government to exercise its jurisdiction on U.S. territory instead of taking the accused home or elsewhere for trial would not seem constitutionally impermissible.[95]

Similarly, there is nothing in the Constitution that would seem to forbid the United States to agree to an international tribunal, whether sitting in the United States or elsewhere, that would apply international law to acts committed by individuals in the United States, including U.S. citizens and residents.[96] It would be international law that governed their acts and that was being applied by the international tribunal; international judicial power which the tribunal was exercising; international punishment that was imposed and executed by international authority. The tribunal would not be exercising governmental authority of the United States but the authority of the international community, of a group of nations of which the United States was but one, and acting in the same capacity as other states, not as the territorial sovereign.[97]

The Yugoslav International War Crimes Tribunal established in 1993 by the United Nations Security Council raises no significant constitutional issues for the United States. The statute of the tribunal obligates member states—including the United States—to cooperate with the prosecution to apprehend and bring to justice persons charged with the

* In such circumstances, the United States in effect agrees not to apply its laws or to exercise its jurisdiction.

designated crimes.[98] The United States may participate in making an alleged war criminal available for trial by the tribunal, as it does in traditional extradition procedures pursuant to treaty with a foreign state. As in extradition to another state, the United States would not have to ensure a constitutionally fair trial; the United States does not commonly conclude treaties with repressive countries, and though the United States may decide not to extradite in a particular case, it has never been authoritatively established[99] that it would be unconstitutional for the United States to extradite in circumstances in which the accused is not likely to receive all the safeguards of a fair trial in the United States.*

If the proposed permanent International Criminal Court came into existence and the United States adhered to it, United States participation would not be constitutionally troublesome. The Court would probably have jurisdiction to try only for violation of selected common criminal offenses, not for acts that in the United States are protected as 'liberty' and not punishable without satisfying the requirements of 'substantive due process' of law.** And the procedures for rendition, apprehension, trial, and punishment are not likely to raise issues more troubling than those that are constitutionally accepted in interstate extradition.

Unlike extradition for trial and punishment in another country, statutes for international tribunals have to provide specially for punishment, presumably by or in some country. Since it would be international not U.S punishment, the United States might not be constitutionally responsible even if some punishment might not satisfy U.S. constitutional standards, but an international statute is likely to provide safeguards no less favorable to the accused than those contemplated by international human rights covenants and conventions which generally are at least as protective as the U.S. Bill of Rights. (Probably, I would argue, the United States could not itself administer punishment that would be cruel or unusual by U.S. constitutional standards.) By analogy to the pattern of agreements by which the United States has agreed to incarcerate—in the United States—U.S. citizens convicted and sentenced to prison in another country,[100] the United States could presumably agree to administer sentences of imprisonment imposed by an international criminal court.

* See Ch. IX, p. 289 and n. 91.

** But the obligations assumed by the United States under international law, in particular under the Covenant of Civil and Political Rights, require the United States 'to respect and ensure' a fair trial for all persons subject to its jurisdiction. (ICCPR, Arts. 2, 9, 14) which may be interpreted as prohibiting extradition in some circumstances. Compare the *Soering* case, n. 22 to Ch. IX.

Dispute Resolution pursuant to International Agreements

The United States is party to several international agreements which provide for mandatory dispute settlement, in some instances by arrangements that are complex and far-reaching—such as those in the Uruguay Round Agreements of 1994.* Insofar as such arrangements apply to and involve only the United States government (not individuals or companies), they do not raise issues under the Bill of Rights. Under the 1994 Uruguay Round Agreements, if the dispute settlement panel of the World Trade Organization concludes that a U.S. statute violates U.S. obligations under the agreements, the panel's decision does not invalidate the law,** but it creates an obligation for Congress to effect any change in U.S. law necessary to achieve compliance.[101] In some instances, an unusual arrangement modifies established procedures under U.S. law, raising issues of displacement of constitutionally-established institutions and processes. In 1987, when a free-trade agreement was being negotiated between Canada and the United States, Canada expressed the view that U.S. anti-dumping and countervailing duty laws were being unfairly applied by courts in the United States. To meet the Canadian objection, the United States–Canada Free Trade Agreement created a binational panel to review final determinations by domestic agencies, and established an 'Extraordinary Challenge Committee' to review the decisions of the binational panel.† No private resort to the courts is available, except for constitutional claims.[102]

Some argued that this arrangement violates Article III establishing the Judicial power of the United States in the federal courts, and that the procedure for appointing members of the binational panel and the Challenge Committee do not satisfy the appointments clause in Article II. I do not think so. The relevant provisions are properly seen as an agreement by the United States to have some of its laws and executive actions reviewed by an international tribunal. As such, the agreement violates no provision of the Constitution or any constitutional

---

* The 1982 Convention on the Law of the Sea also has a complex of dispute settlement arrangements but none that would involve private individuals or companies, and U.S. adherence to that Convention would not raise significant constitutional issues. See RESTATEMENT (n. 2 to Preface) Part V.

** Neither the Uruguay Round Agreements nor the North American Free Trade Agreement (NAFTA) create private rights of action against a federal, state, or local government entity on grounds of inconsistency with the Uruguay Round Agreements.

† A similar procedure was carried over into the North American Free Trade Agreement.

principle. Such arrangements do not entail any delegation to an international body of legislative or judicial power of the United States. Panel members would not be acting as officers of the United States, and their appointment, therefore, does not implicate the power to appoint officers of the United States. The Constitution does not require that determinations of import duties be subject to review at all, and review by an international body (rather than a U.S. court, or no review at all), therefore, raises no constitutional issues. The arrangement seems fair and reasonable and does not deprive affected persons of due process of law.

Even if the Panel were considered a U.S. body exercising review in place of U.S. courts, the arrangement is not constitutionally defective. The Constitution does not require that, if review is provided, it be by 'an Article III' court* or by any court. Congress can provide for review by a non-official body, so long as the review is according to standards set by Congress and the means for selecting the body and its procedures are reasonable and fair.

Some of the constitutional objections I have considered, and the constitutional justification they have invoked, may appear artificial, almost grotesque.** It is difficult to accept that United States participation in contemporary forms of multinational cooperation should depend on 'technicalities' about 'delegation', 'judicial power', and 'case or controversy', and on forms and devices to satisfy them. The Framers did not presume to anticipate what the interests of the United States require today, and surely they did not presume to prevent it. They did insist—and we must insist today—on a few basic safeguards: respect for the political process, the integrity of national institutions, the rights of individuals.

International organizations, in sum, raise no constitutional difficulties when they impose international obligations for the United States to carry out in accordance with its normal constitutional procedures. Novel arrangements might raise significant issues if they distorted domestic institutions or impinged substantially and directly on individuals in the United States, particularly if they deprived persons of civil rights or liberties; but no existing international institutions in fact entailed such intrusions in the past, none is now in prospect, and the

* See Ch. V.
** From the point of view of constitutional law, there are other ways of looking at international tribunals applying criminal law to U.S. citizens in the United States, and other, more technical arguments both for and against full participation by the United States. Some of them are suggested in HENKIN, ARMS CONTROL, (n. 3 to Ch. VI) Ch. VIII.

national mood pervading Congress after the Cold War makes such 'intrusive' entangling arrangements unforeseeable. If such an institution appeared, if the United States should decide that participation in such an organization were in the national interest, the constitutional issues would have to be decided without precedent and on the basis of very general principles that hardly compel the answer. Like many constitutional questions, those cannot be decided with confidence, surely not hypothetically, divorced from a particular proposal and context. Political as well as legal doubts could, of course, be eliminated by constitutional amendment, but often, even without that slow, uncongenial process, creative legal imagination can find ways and suggest means to bring such arrangements largely within a dynamic, flexible, hospitable Constitution.*

* See p. 254 above.

IV

CONSTITUTIONAL LIMITATIONS: INDIVIDUAL RIGHTS AND FOREIGN AFFAIRS

The foreign affairs of the United States are governed and shaped—of course—by the constitutional system of government I have described. Constitutionalism implies limitations on governmental authority, and the U.S. Constitution effectively imposes some limitations by dividing authority between the federal government and the states and by separating powers within the federal government. U.S. constitutionalism implies also another, explicit, fundamental principle of limitations on government—the obligation to respect individual rights. The idea of constitutionalism, the commitment to constitutional legitimacy, and the limitations implied in federalism and in separation of powers, all inure to individual benefit; the idea of rights, the specific rights recognized, the requirement that government respect and secure rights, and the protection of rights by an independent judiciary, favor the individual directly.[1]

The commitment to individual rights derives from our theory of government, which sees man (men and women) as endowed with inherent rights, rights which are not gifts from government but which, rather, underlie and support society and government. The theory is famously articulated in the Declaration of Independence of the American Colonies of 1776.* That theory is not explicit in the U.S. Constitution**

---

* 'We hold these truths to be self-evident, that all men are created equal, that they are endowed by their creator with certain unalienable rights, that among these are life, liberty and the pursuit of happiness.'

** The theory of rights has not become prominent in U.S. constitutional jurisprudence, but it helps explain the language of the Bill of Rights and some of its doctrines.

Ours is an eighteenth century constitution reflecting the prevailing 'Enlightened' views. The Constitution did not give the people their rights, for these antedate and are independent of the Constitution; the Constitution recognizes and takes account of these rights and denies to government the authority to infringe them. Thus, for example, the Bill of Rights confers no freedom of speech; instead, it forbids Congress to make law abridging 'the freedom of speech', an antecedent freedom. The Second Amendment confers no right to bear arms but '*the right* of the people to keep and bear Arms, shall not be infringed'. Or the Fourth Amendment: '*The right* of the people to be secure in their persons . . . shall not be violated. . .' And the Ninth Amendment encapsulates U.S. constitutional rights theory: 'The enumeration in the Constitution, of certain rights, shall not be construed to deny or disparage others retained by the people.'

The inherent character of most individual rights has not been important to their constitutional protection. And the Ninth Amendment, preserving other rights not mentioned in the Constitution, has not in fact proved to be a source of protection for additional unenumerated rights. Instead, unenumerated rights later found protection as 'liberty' secured by the requirement of due process of law. See Ch. IX, p. 290. Certain rights might be said to be conferred by the Constitution and its Amendments, e.g., those to be enjoyed by persons accused of crime (the Fifth and

but is implied in its conception, its character and structure, and in many of its provisions. Early, the commitment to individual rights was made explicit in the Bill of Rights, appended to the Constitution by amendment in 1791, and in subsequent amendments, notably the Civil War Amendments, in particular the Fourteenth Amendment.

The Framers were deeply committed to individual rights, but in the original conception the Constitution was to safeguard individual rights principally by assuring republican government, by separating powers within the central government, and by dividing authority between it and the states.* And in some circumstances, at least, an aggrieved individual could invoke the aid of the courts to maintain that constitutional system of government.** But in the original Constitution there were few guarantees of individual rights or liberties.[2] And although the Bill of Rights was added immediately, it did not quickly convert the Constitution into a bulwark for individual rights, or transform the content of constitutional jurisprudence.[3] Having established their authority to monitor respect for the Constitution, the courts early decided various issues of federalism and resolved some uncertainties in the separation of powers;[4] but there was hardly a case during more than a hundred years in which the Supreme Court considered a claim that an Act of Congress or some other action of the federal government violated an individual's constitutional rights.†

All that, we know, has changed.[5] Today, the courts monitor the separation of federal powers only extraordinarily and infrequently, and there are few states' rights left to be protected against federal invasion.‡

Sixth Amendments), but these too may be seen as elaborations on the inherent liberty of the individual. The right to vote, presumably, is not an inherent right, but a distillation from popular sovereignty implied in 'We the People'.

* See n. 3 to Intro. to Pt II. It was assumed also that the federal government would have little power or opportunity to impinge on individual rights, that the individual would be governed essentially by his (her) state government and protected by the state constitution, the state Bill of Rights, and the state courts.

** Where there is a 'case or controversy', the individual is deemed to have 'standing', and the issue is otherwise justiciable. See Ch. V, p. 142.

† The only decision by the Supreme Court applying the Bill of Rights before the Civil War was *Dred Scott* which invalidated the Missouri Compromise on the ground that it denied a slave owner his property without due process of law. *Scott v. Sandford*, 60 U.S. (19 How.) 393 (1857). The Alien and Sedition Laws at the turn of the eighteenth century did not reach the Supreme Court and were allowed to expire.

‡ In the last decades of the twentieth century, the Court upset several extraordinary arrangements legislated by Congress as violations of the Separation of

Increasingly, on the other hand, the courts have invoked, extended, and intensified the protections of the Bill of Rights and of later constitutional amendments, and for the courts, at least, the Constitution has long been primarily a bulwark for the individual against excesses by either federal or state authorities.*

The Bill of Rights originally applied only to the federal government, but the Court has held that the Fourteenth Amendment incorporated almost all its provisions and thereby made them applicable to the states. The Fourteenth Amendment was intended to apply primarily to the states, but its principal provisions have in fact been held applicable to the federal government as well. The all-important safeguard of 'due process of law' is required of the federal government by the Fifth Amendment and of the states by the Fourteenth Amendment. Equal protection of the laws, required of the states by the Fourteenth Amendment, has been held to be implicit in due process of law and therefore required also of the federal government.**

Powers (see, e.g., n. 121 to Ch. IV). In monitoring federalism, the Court in 1992 struck down an act of Congress because it sought to 'co-opt' state legislatures, and in 1995 the Court looked hard at, and invalidated, an act of Congress, enacted presumably under the Commerce Power, because a majority of the Justices could not find a significant link between the activity regulated and interstate commerce. See n. 8 to Ch. III. It remains to be seen whether these cases portend that challenges to the reach of Congressional power will again become common judicial fare. Only the 'dormant Commerce Clause', which the courts apply to invalidate state burdens on interstate or foreign commerce, continues to be a busy source of federalism jurisprudence. See Ch. V.

* The large part of constitutional rights law addresses violations by the states, which do not commonly impinge on foreign affairs, see Ch. IX, p. 309. But Congress, and especially the Executive branch, also continue to throw up individual rights issues, some of them affecting foreign affairs.

** The Fourteenth Amendment protects the privileges and immunities of U.S. citizens against infringement by the states, but, since these are declared to be rights of U.S. citizenship, they may not be denied by the federal government either. These privileges and immunities are not defined in the Constitution, but the Supreme Court enumerated some of them in the *Slaughter House Cases*, Ch. IX p. 309.

Art. IV, sect. 2 of the Constitution provides that 'The Citizens of each State shall be entitled to all Privileges and Immunities of Citizens in the several States.' That provision has been interpreted as prohibiting discrimination by any state against citizens of other states in respect of their fundamental rights. It does not seem to offer such protection to non-citizens, and would therefore not prohibit distinctions in these respects between citizens and foreign nationals or stateless persons. That section also seems to be addressed only to the states, not to the federal government, but such fundamental rights might be protected for all persons, against both state

In principle, constitutional rights are not absolute. Rights to life, liberty and property are subject to some limitations to secure the rights of others and the general welfare. Some of the protections of the Bill of Rights are qualified by their terms, for example, they provide protection only 'against *unreasonable* searches and seizures', and 'cruel and unusual' punishment. Even safeguards expressed in absolute terms, for example, 'Congress shall *make no law* abridging the freedom of speech, or of the press . . .' do not necessarily invalidate all regulations of expression.* Ordinarily, rights 'trump' and prevail over other values, but rights sometimes bow to the public interest, and governmental actions carry a presumption of constitutionality. The Supreme Court has identified some rights, notably those enumerated in the First Amendment, as fundamental, or 'preferred', so that governmental actions impinging on such rights will be subject to stricter judicial scrutiny[6] and will be upheld only if they serve an important or even a compelling public interest.

Individual rights are limitations on the conduct of government** in foreign relations as elsewhere. In foreign relations, too, rights have to be respected and will ordinarily 'trump', but here too they are not absolute and one may expect that the national interest in war and peace, and even lesser concerns of Foreign relations, would weigh importantly in the balance. Inevitably, of course, these constitutional rights constrain foreign policy, preventing what the United States government might wish to do, precluding some forms of international cooperation. How the United States behaves towards its inhabitants, citizens as well as foreign nationals, is increasingly of legitimate interest to other nations, and the constitutional rights of individuals have become a condition of U.S. foreign

---

and federal governments, by virtue of the due process and the equal protection clauses. See n. 38 to Ch. IX.

A constitutional right to travel freely within the United States has long been accepted, but the Justices were not agreed as to whence it derives. See Ch. IX, p. 291.

* See Ch. IX, at pp. 286 *et seq.*

** By the theory of government enunciated in the Declaration of Independence (see p. 277), the people institute government to secure their inherent rights, presumably against violation by one's neighbors. Of course, government itself must also respect those rights. But the Bill of Rights and later Amendments have been interpreted as applying only to 'state action', to violations by state or federal authority, not by private persons. Only the Thirteenth Amendment governs private action as well. Other rights may be secured against private violation by state legislation or common law, or by civil rights acts and other federal legislation enacted by Congress under its enumerated powers, principally the Commerce Power.

policy. Constitutional guarantees for individual rights also help assure compliance by the United States with its international obligations, in its treatment of foreign nationals, and increasingly also under the growing international law of human rights.[7]

Chapter IX

INDIVIDUAL RIGHTS AND FOREIGN AFFAIRS

The Constitution was ordained and established by 'We the People of the United States', but the people are not the subject of the Constitution: the individual, even *qua* citizen, is mentioned infrequently, and he (she) appears in constitutional law not laden with duties, responsibilities, opportunities, or even 'inherent rights', but principally as the beneficiary of limitations imposed on government. In this chapter, too, I am concerned with the individual not as an actor in the nation's foreign relations, or even as a member of the chorus, but as a source of constitutional limitation on foreign policy and process.*

Nothing in the Constitution suggests that the rights of individuals in respect of foreign affairs are different from what they are in relation to other exercises of governmental power. But special constitutional theories, and peculiarities of constitutional language, about foreign relations, their high place in national policy and interest, the asserted needs for extraordinary freedom of action for those who conduct them, the different constitutional issues they raise and the different contexts in which these arise, have engendered views that individual rights are fewer and narrower than elsewhere. These views have not prevailed in principle, but constitutional protections for individuals sometimes do have a different look.

APPLICABILITY OF CONSTITUTIONAL SAFEGUARDS

That, under *Curtiss-Wright,* foreign relations powers inhere in U.S. sovereignty and are perhaps extra-constitutional, might suggest that they are not subject to constitutional limitations, even to safeguards for

---

* I present here only a brief summary of the rich and comprehensive jurisprudence of constitutional rights, with emphasis on what is intimately related to U.S. foreign relations.

individual rights.[1] That conclusion is hardly compelled, since the
Framers of the Bill of Rights might well have sought to protect the people even against excesses in the exercise of sovereign, extra-
constitutional powers. In any event, that view has no support. *Curtiss-
Wright* itself exempted foreign relations only from limitations on delegation inherent in the separation of powers; it did not suggest that other
constitutional limitations were also inapplicable. And the Court's opinion expressly said that the President's plenary power in foreign affairs,
'of course, like every other governmental power, must be exercised in
subordination to the applicable provisions of the Constitution'.[2] In a
later case,* even while upholding an act of Congress, the Court said:

Broad as the power in the National Government to regulate foreign affairs must
be, it is not without limitation. The restrictions confining Congress in the exercise of any of the powers expressly delegated to it in the Constitution apply with
equal vigor when that body seeks to regulate our relations with other nations.[3]

Nor is any particular exercise of foreign affairs power exempt from
limitations in favor of individual rights. Arguments, based on the language of the Supremacy Clause, that treaties are not subject to constitutional prohibitions, are now well at rest.** The First Amendment
provides that 'Congress shall make no law' abridging freedom of speech,
press, religion, assembly or petition, but these freedoms are protected
also from infringement by treaty, by Executive agreement or action, or
by court order.[4]

The Constitution safeguards rights of all persons in the United
States,† including some whose rights may have particular relevance for
U.S. foreign relations. The rights provisions in the original Constitution,
in the Bill of Rights and in later Amendments, protect not only U.S. cit-

---

* The Court's decision in that case, *Perez* v. *Brownell*, upholding the power of
Congress to deprive a person of his (her) citizenship, was later overruled. See n. 5
to this chapter.

Though generally prepared to give full sway to the plenary foreign affairs powers
of President and Congress, see Ch. V, the Court has tended to be less expansive
about them when they are exercised in ways that impinge on individual rights.
Compare the narrow reading of the 'necessary and proper' clause in the court-
martial cases, n. 44 to Ch.III, and stricter limitations on Congressional delegation
of authority in the passport cases, nn. 112, 113 to Ch. IV. Also the limitation on
Executive extradition, Ch. IV, p. 90.

** See Ch. VII, p. 185.

† As to the applicability of constitutional safeguards outside United States territory, see p. 305 below.

izens but all 'persons', including foreign nationals* and stateless persons, not only permanent residents but also tourists and other visitors and persons in transit, even undocumented aliens.

In foreign affairs as elsewhere, the principal safeguards for individual rights are in the Bill of Rights. But the conduct of foreign relations must take account also of guarantees added by amendment later. In the citizenship clause of the Fourteenth Amendment, the Supreme Court found a prohibition on involuntary expatriation of a U.S. citizen; and that clause governs the acquisition or loss of U.S. citizenship generally, and largely defines U.S. nationality for purposes of U.S. international relations.[5] The privileges and immunities of national citizenship guaranteed by that Amendment include the right to be protected by the federal government when they are in foreign territory or on the high seas.[6]

THE BILL OF RIGHTS

In principle, the Bill of Rights limits governmental authority in the conduct of foreign relations as in other federal activity.** None of the provisions in the Bill of Rights has particular relevance for U.S. foreign relations; all of its provisions might impinge on foreign relations in some contexts. As regards foreign affairs, too, the safeguards of the Bill of Rights are not absolute. The protections that are expressly qualified, e.g., those against *unreasonable* searches and seizures, or against *cruel* and *unusual* punishments, are qualified as well when applied to the conduct of foreign relations, though here the qualifications may have different application and significance. The safeguards that are cast in

* Including foreign diplomats. Under international law, diplomatic personnel accredited to the United States (or who are in transit in the United States) enjoy immunity from police action and from the jurisdiction of the courts, but if their immunity were waived and they were brought to trial they would enjoy the safeguards of the Bill of Rights in any criminal proceedings. In principle, the Constitution would seem to guarantee them also other freedoms, for example, those of the First Amendment, but it would not prevent the United States from declaring a diplomat *persona non grata*, or terminating his (her) stay in the United States for abuse of the privilege of residence under the U.N. Headquarters Agreement. See n. 73 to this chapter. Foreign governments, and foreign diplomats in their official capacity, have no constitutional rights. See Damnosch, *Foreign States and the Constitution*, 71 Va. L. Rev. 483 (1987). And see pp. 288–9, and n. 20 to this chapter.

** See n. 44. Aliens are entitled also to equal protection of the laws; as to permissible distinctions between citizens and aliens, see p. 293.

I deal with limitations on the states at p. 309.

absolute terms, as in the First Amendment, are surely no more absolute
as regards the conduct of foreign relations, and though those guarantees
are accorded extraordinary protection, they will sometimes be outweighed
by the perceived needs of U.S. foreign policy. Indeed, foreign policy interests are commonly—perhaps too readily—identified with 'national security', and often—perhaps too readily—declared a compelling national
interest brooking no limitations for the sake of private interests.*
Sometimes, however, the courts have moved beyond simplistic balancing
of abstract values and have scrutinized more rigorously, asking how deep
the invasion of rights, how serious the limitation on national policy.**

Freedom of Speech and Press

The freedom of speech has been described as the 'matrix, the indispensable condition', of nearly every other freedom,[7] and the freedom of the
press ranks at least as high in our constitutional values.[8] Both are fundamental rights and, though they are not absolute and must be balanced
against public interests, will generally 'trump' any but compelling interests.[9] But one may expect that the national interest in war and peace,
and even lesser concerns of foreign relations, would have important
weight in any balance. Hypothetically,† it is far from obvious that the
courts would invalidate, say, a statute or treaty that forbids publication

* The Court has even ventured the opinion that 'Matters intimately related to
foreign policy and national security are rarely proper subjects for judicial intervention'. *Haig* v. *Agee*, see n. 35 to this chapter. It is not clear whether the Court was
implying that such issues are non-justiciable ('political questions'); that such matters
need not trouble the courts since they are clearly within the power of the federal
authorities; or that, because of the importance of the public interest, the Court need
apply only minimal, most perfunctory scrutiny.

** I do not address individual rights in time of war. In principle, the Constitution
(and the Amendments) apply in war as in peace. There is no provision for suspension of the Constitution, or of any rights: only 'the privilege of the writ of habeas
corpus may be suspended', and only in cases of rebellion or invasion, and only by
Congress (not by the President; see Ch. IV, n. 52). And that provision permits
suspension only of the remedy of habeas corpus; it does not permit suspension of
any rights. Nevertheless, it is accepted that, under its war power, Congress can
impose military service, with all its limitations on individual freedom, and can
regulate liberty and property in respects necessary to wage war successfully. During
the Second World War, the Court upheld the power of the President, without
specific authorization from Congress, to intern alien enemies and to relocate U.S.
citizens on the basis of their ethnicity. See n. 36 to this chapter.

† Hypothetically, other safeguards in the First Amendment might also be threatened by foreign policy actions. The provisions precluding the establishment of

of matter inciting to war or seriously exacerbating international relations,[10] or private research related to nuclear or biological weapons.[11]

The courts have read into the First Amendment a basic distinction between limitation on expression on the basis of its content, and regulations of time, place, or manner of expression.[12] Regulation of the basis of content is highly suspect, and rights will prevail except in rare circumstances and only to serve the strongest public interest. Regulation of time, place, or manner of expression is also to be scrutinized, but such regulation will stand more readily since it does not deny freedom of expression in other places, at other times, or by other manner. Here too, however, the courts will balance, and will give important weight to the foreign policy needs of the United States, largely as determined by the political branches.

For historic as well as technological reasons, beginning when radio stations and television channels were limited in number and had to be allocated and regulated,* the Constitution has been read to permit regulation of the electronic media that would not stand if applied to the print-press.[13] Regulation of these media for foreign policy purposes, by legislation or by international agreements or through international organizations, is also less likely to court constitutional difficulties, but such regulation too does not totally escape constitutional restraints, in foreign as in domestic context.

Supreme Court cases addressing the balance between freedom of expression and national foreign policy interests are not many.** In

religion or abridging the free exercise thereof might be challenged by some U.S. treaty arrangement with a 'fundamentalist' government. The people might assert their right to assemble or to petition the government on matters relating to foreign policy. Hypothetical cases suggest hypothetical issues under other Amendments: an agreement for general and complete disarmament forbids the bearing of arms even by state militia, in the face of the Second Amendment (see HENKIN, ARMS CONTROL (n. 3 to Ch. VI) at 34–6); an allied command on peace-time maneuvers is quartered in private homes without the owner's consent (the Third Amendment).

* Regulation of electronic media found support also in a felt need to defend home and family against 'electronic' invasion. See n. 13 to this chapter.

** The First Amendment was surely implicated in other laws that are (or were) part of our foreign relations landscape, but their validity has not been determined by the Supreme Court. The Alien and Sedition Laws of our early years were widely challenged but expired before their constitutionality could be authoritatively adjudicated. See n. 18 to Ch. III. The Logan Act, which prohibits any U.S. citizen from corresponding with a foreign government with intent to influence it in relation to a dispute with the United States, has been law since 1799, but, though sometimes threatened, no prosecution has in fact been brought, and serious challenges to the constitutionality of the Act have never been adjudicated. See n. 16 to this chapter.

general, foreign policy interests have prevailed. In *Haig* v. *Agee*, the Court upheld the Secretary of State's authority to revoke Agee's passport, rejecting, virtually out of hand, his claim that his freedom of speech included the right to travel abroad and identify and 'uncover' agents of the Central Intelligence Agency.[14] In *Kleindienst* v. *Mandel*, the Court upheld the authority of the Attorney General to refuse a visa to an invited lecturer, denying not only his First Amendment claims but also those of U.S. citizens in the United States who wished to hear him.[15] Challenges that the Foreign Agents Registration Act, at least in some of its applications, interfered with freedom of expression and association did not persuade the Supreme Court.[16] Only once—in *The Pentagon Papers* case—did the First Amendment clearly prevail; the Supreme Court* refused to grant the Executive branch an injunction against press publication of 'classified' (confidential) papers, concluding that the Government had not met its heavy burden of justifying 'prior restraint' of publication.[17] On the other hand, overturning a jurisprudence of decades during which it was assumed that the government (in the District of Columbia) could prohibit picketing of foreign embassies, the Court drew lines, upholding a 'place' distinction barring picketing within some distance from an embassy, but invalidating a 'content' limitation that would have barred signs bringing a foreign government into 'public disrepute'.[18]

Unreasonable Searches and Seizures

The Fourth Amendment protects only against *unreasonable* searches and seizures. The national interest in maintaining an international disarmament system, or environmental safeguards, or labor standards, might render it reasonable for the United States to accept reciprocal inspection arrangements, and might render not 'unreasonable' some intrusive inspections of private establishments and records in the United States, even by international or foreign inspectors.[19] But foreign governments, and presumably foreign diplomats in their official capacity, have no con-

---

* The denial of the injunction was not unanimous, and the opinions of the Justices scattered widely. Some Justices refused to enjoin publication on their own authority but implied that they would have issued the injunction if it had been authorized by Congress in such circumstances. Some Justices who agreed that an injunction should not issue because it constituted a 'prior restraint', intimated that they would have upheld a criminal conviction after publication. In subsequent 'national security' cases, however, lower courts authorized even some prior restraint. See n. 17 to this chapter.

stitutional rights, and there are no constitutional obstacles, say, to 'tapping' wires of foreign embassies.[20] Safeguards against unreasonable search and seizure also limit the freedom of government to monitor espionage and smuggling.[21]

Safeguards in the Criminal Process

The provisions in the Fifth, Sixth, and Eighth Amendments that guarantee fair criminal procedure and punishment* apply also to persons charged with violating laws that regulate foreign commerce or define offenses against the law of nations, or in trials by the United States of foreign nationals (whether for ordinary crimes or, say, for espionage).[22] The United States could not adhere to a treaty establishing an international criminal court without considering the applicability of the rights assured to persons charged with crime by the Fourth, Fifth, Sixth and Eighth Amendments.**

Due Process of Law

The Fifth Amendment includes the provision that 'No person shall be . . . deprived of life, liberty, or property without due process of law'. In addition to the specific guarantees provided in the criminal process, 'due process of law' requires, in regard to foreign relations as to other matters, fair procedures—for aliens† as for citizens, for corporations as for individuals, in civil as in criminal proceedings, before administrative bodies and in courts.[23]

'Procedural due process' requires fair judicial and administrative procedures, but it has not been held to require that a legislature afford hearings to those who might be affected by contemplated legislation, or that,

---

* The Fifth Amendment requires indictment by grand jury, provides a privilege against self-incrimination, and forbids double jeopardy. The Sixth Amendment guarantees a speedy public trial by jury, the right to be confronted with the witnesses against him (her) and to have compulsory process and the right to counsel. The Eighth Amendment protects against excessive bail, excessive fines, and 'cruel and unusual punishments'. See n. 22 to this chapter.

The prohibition on double jeopardy does not bar trial under the authority of two different jurisdictions, e.g., the United States and one of the states. *Abbate* v. *United States*, 359 U.S. 187 (1959); *Bartkus* v. *Illinois*, 359 U.S. 121 (1959). The double jeopardy clause was held not to be violated when a person is tried by the United States and by a foreign state. *United States* v. *McRary*, 616 F.2d 181, 184 (5th Cir. 1980).

** See Ch. VIII, p. 268.

† On due process in immigration, see pp. 303–4 below.

before they promulgate rules or regulations, administrative agencies grant hearings to those who might be affected.[24] Due process does not require opportunity to be heard in respect of the 'legislative' acts of the Executive in matters affecting foreign relations, whether under its own constitutional authority or by delegation from Congress: thus, whether the Executive acts by general order or in a particular case, an interested person cannot demand a hearing by the Executive branch as of constitutional right—before the Executive branch suggests that a foreign state or accredited diplomat is entitled to immunity;* that an arms embargo or a tariff authorized by statute** should be imposed in particular circumstances or in regard to particular goods; or that the Act of State doctrine should not apply to a foreign state's confiscation of one's property.[25]

It is long established that 'due process' also imposes substantive limitations on what government can do.† The day is gone when the Supreme Court used the due process clause to strike down economic regulations on the ground that deviations from *laissez faire* deprived individuals (or corporations) of property or of the 'liberty' to contract as they will.[26] But there remains in 'substantive due process' a requirement, however vague and variable with reference to time and circumstance, that a law—and presumably also any official act, including an international agreement—'shall not be unreasonable, arbitrary or capricious, and that the means selected shall have real and substantial relation to the object sought to be attained'.[27] No economic regulation has been held by the Supreme Court to run afoul of that standard since it was formulated in 1934 and established in 1937,‡ and strong presumptions giving the legislature the benefit of every doubt make it unlikely that many will.[28] Foreign relations legislation or regulations, or international agreements, are surely no more vulnerable to such objections than domestic prohibitions or regulations that adversely affect the eco-

---

* See Ch. II, p. 54.

** As in the legislation involved in *Curtiss-Wright*, discussed in Ch. I.

† It is the Due Process Clause that is sometimes invoked also when a party challenges acts of either political branch as beyond its constitutional powers, whether because they usurp powers reserved to the states, or invade the domain of another branch of the federal government, or purport to exercise power to regulate or tax persons or interests in another state or in a foreign country.

‡ Does the Supreme Court's step in 1995, in *Lopez*, to begin to scrutinize Congressional legislation for significant links to interstate commerce (n. 8 to Ch. III) promise also stronger scrutiny of state and federal law for 'rationality' under the due process clause? Compare also signs of additional recognition for states' rights, pp. 166, 167, notes.

nomic rights of one or of many. No court would hold that restrictions on trade with Cuba or Communist China, or—earlier—with Rhodesia or the Republic of South Africa—denied due process because they inflicted financial losses on those who wished to trade with those countries. No court would heed the claim of an arms manufacturer that an arms control agreement deprived him of the liberty to carry on his trade, or of his property interest in his business or his patents.[29]

'Substantive due process' protects also a person's 'liberty', and here the constitutional safeguard is greater and judicial deference to the political branches less.[30] The courts give heightened protection not only to the important liberties of the First Amendment* but also to other important personal liberties, scrutinizing infringements of such liberties more carefully and upholding them only for important public interests. Substantive due process requires heightened scrutiny of invasions of a right of 'privacy', of autonomy in personal matters, some of which have implications for foreign affairs.[31] In 1958, the Court held[32] that the right to travel abroad is 'a part of the liberty of which the citizen cannot be deprived without due process of law', and avoided a constitutional decision only because, as a matter of statutory interpretation, it was reluctant to 'infer that Congress gave the Secretary of State unbridled discretion to grant or withhold it'. Six years later, the Court invalidated a statutory provision making it a crime for members of certain Communist organizations to obtain or use passports, because that prohibition 'too broadly and indiscriminately restricts the right to travel and thereby abridges the liberty guaranteed by the Fifth Amendment'.[33]

Later, however, the Court defined the right to due process more narrowly and increased judicial deference to the Executive branch. In 1965, in upholding an Executive decision not to validate passports for travel to Cuba, the Court said that 'the fact that a liberty cannot be inhibited without due process of law does not mean that it can under no circumstances be inhibited'.[34] More striking was *Haig* v. *Agee*,[35] which held that despite the due process clause, the Secretary of State could, in the interest of national security, revoke a passport of one who claimed a right to travel and to speak abroad even to uncover and disclose the identity of C.I.A. agents. In time of war, the Court upheld unprecedented invasions of liberty and property, as in the sad chapter of the relocation of American citizens of Japanese ancestry.[36] And to date the Court has not reconsidered its holding that an alien who has long been resident here can be deported for whatever reasons seem proper to Congress.**

* See p. 286 above.   ** See p. 304, and n. 75 below.

Equal Protection of the Laws

The Bill of Rights contains no explicit guarantee of the equal protection of the laws. The provision in the Fourteenth Amendment requiring such equal protection was addressed only to the states. But the Supreme Court has held that substantive due process effectively requires equal protection by the federal government* as the Fourteenth Amendment explicitly requires it of the states.[37]

Simply (perhaps too simply) put, equal protection requires the law to treat all persons alike. Obviously, that prohibits invidious discrimination against individuals or groups on grounds such as race, religion, gender. Similarly, equal protection does not permit other distinctions between persons or groups that have no reasonable ground. But equal protection permits distinctions and classifications resulting in treatment that is different for different persons or groups because they are different or differently situated in relevant respects, provided the difference in treatment corresponds to the difference in circumstances.** Government, however, does not deny equal protection if it fails to regulate all that may require regulation, or fails to do so at the same time or in the same manner. Similarly, government—federal or state—can tax some activities or goods or interests, and not others.

Justice Holmes once depreciated claims to equal protection as 'the usual last resort of constitutional arguments',[38] and, as in regard to substantive due process, the Supreme Court has long given to government the benefit of every presumption and every doubt.[39] In the late 1960s, seeking constitutional support for claims that had great social appeal, but reluctant to revive the 'disreputable' substantive due process in economic and social matters,† the Court began to give new vitality instead to equal protection. In the result, although equal protection remained largely unavailable to challenge common distinctions in social and economic regulation (or non-regulation), some distinctions became more or less suspect, and other distinctions were more sharply scrutinized when they applied to particular interests. Thus, the Court found the Constitution to be particularly sensitive to distinctions that, though pur-

---

* It has become safe to say that the equal protection doctrine is the same for the federal government as for the states. See n. 38 to this chapter.

** The equal protection clause *permits* but does not *require* unequal, 'offsetting' treatment for unequals. For Aristotle, it appears, justice *required* that unequals be treated unequally.

† Sometimes described as *Lochnerism*, after the discredited *Lochner* v. *New York*, n. 26 to this chapter.

porting to have some rational public purpose, were redolent ᴠ
ethnic or religious prejudice, or reflected other unexamined assuɪ.
or stereotypes. Racial classifications in particular were declareᴅ
pect', were to be 'strictly scrutinized', and were constitutionally to.
ble only if they served a 'compelling public interest'.[40]

Distinctions based on gender were not branded as 'suspect' but are
also to be questioned for possible prejudice or stereotype, will be carefully (if not 'strictly') scrutinized, and will stand only if they serve an
important (if less than 'compelling') public interest.[41] Other distinctions—between citizen and alien, between children born in or out of
wedlock, and distinctions based on age—also earned differing degrees of
skepticism and scrutiny.[42] In a corresponding development,[43] other distinctions were rigorously scrutinized and held to require stronger
justification if applied in respect to 'fundamental rights or interests' such
as the rights enumerated in the Bill of Rights.*

The constitutional requirement of equal protection applies in matters
relating to or affecting foreign relations as elsewhere. In principle and in
general, the requirement to provide equal protection does not impinge
on U.S. foreign relations in any special ways. Distinctions between foreign and domestic matters permeate the law, and the courts tend to
uphold them as rational and reasonable. But foreign relations often
involve unusual distinctions, such as different treatment for different
foreign nations; and some distinctions in law or national policy between
different individuals, for example between U.S. citizens and aliens, have
particular relevance for U.S. foreign affairs. Also, though equal protection of the laws is required of both states and federal governments, constitutional doctrine looks differently at some distinctions in foreign
affairs when made by the federal government or by the states.

Aliens and citizens

The equal protection of the laws has nothing to say to differences in
U.S. foreign relations or policy towards different countries: foreign
nations have no constitutional rights in the United States.** But equal
protection issues begin to surface when U.S. foreign policy, or federal

---

* The Court has accepted as fundamental the rights protected by the Bill of
Rights as well as the right to vote or to travel freely in the United States, and distinctions in the enjoyment of these rights are strictly scrutinized. It has not recognized as fundamental (for these purposes) the right to a public education, housing,
or welfare benefits. The state, therefore, may establish systems reflecting
classifications or distinctions that have some rational basis even if they result in
gross inequalities, e.g., between rich and poor. See n. 44 to this chapter.

** See Damnosch, p. 285 n.

or state law, distinguishes among individuals—between U.S. citizens and non-citizens, between aliens in different status (residents, tourists, 'undocumented'),* between nationals of one foreign country and those of another, between foreign nationals and stateless persons.

The Constitution guarantees the rights of all 'persons', aliens as well as citizens. The Constitution requires equal protection too for all 'persons' (not only for citizens).[44] All the distinctions I have listed, then, *prima facie* raise issues of 'unequal protection' and have to be justified.

Aliens in the United States are subject to multiple sources of governance. Like all inhabitants, they are governed by federal and state law of general applicability (including the federal and state constitutions). Federal as well as state laws often distinguish between citizens and aliens; Congress has also enacted laws applying to aliens in particular. Historically, traditionally, many aliens have been subject also to law made by treaty, notably treaties of friendship, commerce, and navigation (FCN) between the United States and their country of nationality.[45] Such treaties are law of the United States and have guaranteed to their beneficiaries in the United States rights of residence, property, occupation, and trade, sometimes 'national' treatment (i.e., treatment equal to that of U.S. citizens), sometimes 'most favored nation' treatment (i.e., treatment, in various respects, that is no less favorable than that accorded to nationals of any other foreign nation). Sometimes, nationals of particular foreign states have been the beneficiaries (or the victims) of special agreements or policies, resulting in different legal treatment for their nationals in the United States, as when the United States makes different extradition agreements with some countries than with others, or different commercial, financial, or travel arrangements; or when, because of relations with particular countries (the Soviet Union, Cuba, Iran, South Africa, at various times), the United States imposed disadvantages on their nationals, sometimes, for example, freezing their assets in the United States.

Treaties and other agreements or arrangements are generally the law of the land; they are also subject to the Constitution.** Yet no one has

---

* Under its power to regulate immigration (see Ch. III), Congress may admit aliens to the United States for different purposes, in different status, and under different conditions. Any alien in the United States, in whatever status, and even an 'undocumented' alien (a person not lawfully in the United States), enjoys the protections of the Bill of Rights, including the right to the equal protection of the laws. See nn. 44, 99, 100, 101 to this chapter. But the equal protection of the laws does not preclude reasonable distinctions between aliens admitted in different status, or between documented and undocumented aliens. See n. 44 to this chapter.
** See Ch. VII.

seriously suggested that different treatment for different aliens in the United States, under different FCN treaties, different extradition treaties, or different trade arrangements, had to be justified under the principles of the equal protection of the laws. Perhaps it was assumed that such distinctions among states and among their nationals, staples of international relations for all countries, were governed by international law only, not by the U.S. constitutional principles. Perhaps differences resulting from variations in such traditional, universal arrangements seemed obviously 'reasonable' and 'rational', therefore wholly within equal protection principles.*

Equal protection principles have not served aliens significantly in respect of federal regulations of aliens, federal discriminations against aliens, or other distinctions in U.S. law between aliens and citizens. In earlier times, it was apparently assumed that every alien in the United States, even if long resident here, was an extension and an embodiment of the state of his (her) nationality. Therefore, the treatment of aliens in U.S. law was seen as an aspect of U.S. foreign relations, intimately related to U.S. foreign policy interests, to national security, to war and peace, to sacred 'sovereignty'. The status and rights of aliens in the United States were thought to be governed by international law and by treaties with the states of their nationality, rather than by the U.S. Constitution. If an issue as to the treatment of an alien came to court, and even if it were admitted that the U.S. Constitution was somehow implicated, federal policy and particular federal actions were favored by every presumption. As regards federal law, moreover, the requirement of equal protection of the laws generally came late,[46] and its applicability to the treatment of aliens was not obvious (or not recognized). When it became clear that equal protection was required of the federal government, rethinking (and justifying) long-established distinctions between citizens and aliens did not come readily and (at the end of the twentieth century) may not have come or been fully recognized yet. No act of Congress regulating aliens, no distinction between citizen and alien mandated or authorized by Congress, has been disapproved by the courts.

The Supreme Court, we shall see, has long held that the states may not deny aliens the equal protection of the laws. Indeed, during the heyday of the 'new equal protection', the Court ruled that distinctions

* Special arrangements with particular countries were reasonable from an additional aspect, since they often served to bring about better treatment for U.S. citizens in the other country. U.S. legislation that is based on reciprocity, p. 72 above and n. 48 to Ch. III, has never been thought to raise equal protection difficulties.

between citizens and aliens in state law were a 'suspect classification', and the Court invalidated such distinctions for various purposes.* During the same judicial era, we have seen, the Court moved steadily to 'homogenize', equalize, the protection of rights against the states and against the federal government, and applied the same standards of equal protection to the federal government as to the states. Yet even while the Court was striking down state discriminations against aliens it continued to uphold comparable distinctions maintained by the federal government—such as the exclusion of aliens from the U.S. Civil Service.[47]

Aliens enjoy the right to equal protection of the law in respect of state law, and of federal laws of general applicability. Might they not also be entitled to freedom from the discrimination implied in laws directed against them? Indeed, might all distinctions between alien and citizens in U.S. law be *prima facie* suspect, requiring authentic justification?

It remains to be seen whether federal treatment of aliens will remain impervious to meaningful judicial scrutiny, whether the links of federal treatment of aliens to national foreign policy (and national security) will continue to be taken as granted, whether the national interest in maintaining particular distinctions between citizens and aliens will be assumed to be compelling (or important). Surely, the treatment of aliens who have renounced their foreign nationality or who are otherwise stateless is ordinarily remote from U.S. foreign policy. And it is not unthinkable that some discriminations between citizen and alien—for example, those barring aliens from various public employment—long accepted as 'reasonable', and the requirement of citizenship for other entitlements, privileges or opportunities, might be reexamined, at least

---

* See p. 309 below.

Federal laws governing aliens have sometimes been considered within the plenary powers of Congress and not subject to constitutional restraint. As regards admission to the United States, discriminations based on national origin were the foundation of our immigration laws for many years until 1965. The Supreme Court never considered their constitutionality; it is not clear that any one had standing to challenge them, and it is unlikely that during that era the Court would have invalidated them. See p. 303–4 below.

Denying aliens the right to vote can find some support in the Fifteenth Amendment which provides that the right of citizens to vote shall not be abridged on account of race, color, or previous condition of servitude. On limiting voting to citizens, see n. 47 to this chapter. For the exclusion of aliens from other benefits, see nn. 44, 99, 100, 101 to this chapter.

where the distinction between citizen and alien appears to have little significance for U.S. foreign relations.*

'Taking' and 'Just Compensation'

There is also some protection, and perhaps great promise, in the final clause in the Fifth Amendment, the provision that private property shall not 'be taken for public use, without just compensation'. That clause has obvious significance for foreign relations when the property of a foreign national is taken by eminent domain,[48] or when any private property is taken to build an embassy or for some other foreign relations use. The 'taking' clause may also be acquiring larger relevance, for the Court has been moving the line between what is and what is not a 'taking', and what is and what is not a public 'use'.

Every governmental regulation that prohibits, limits, or regulates the use of property or a person's ability to earn income—for example, fire and health regulations, zoning restrictions, limitations on wages or prices**—can be said to be 'taking' someone's property for a public use. No one, however, would claim that such regulations require that those adversely affected be compensated; for compensation, there must be a 'taking' for 'use'.[49] But even as confined to their more literal sense, those terms are not self-defining. In 1946,[50] a majority of the Court held that in peacetime, when U.S. military aircraft regularly flew low over a farmer's property, frightening his chickens and ruining his egg business, the United States had partially 'taken' the farmer's airspace and owed him compensation under the Fifth Amendment. In 1952, a majority of the Supreme Court held[51] that the United States had to pay for oil and gas, belonging to a U.S. company in the Philippines, which had been taken by U.S. armed forces for their use during the Second World War, but that the United States did not have to pay for oil and gas that U.S. forces destroyed to keep it from falling into enemy hands. The difference between those cases (and between majority and dissent in each case) may be a difference between more or less literal and more or less 'sophisticated' interpretations of 'taking' and of 'public use', between taking by eminent domain and the economic losses that are sometimes inflicted by governmental regulation. Later cases continued to try to

---

* That the United States is now party to the International Covenant on Civil and Political Rights and other Human Rights conventions which apply equally to all persons subject to its jurisdiction may influence U.S. constitutional jurisprudence. See n. 7 to Intro. to Pt IV.
** And indeed all public taxation!!

draw those lines, not always to everyone's satisfaction.[52] But beginning in the 1980s, the Supreme Court has been increasingly sympathetic to claims that some regulations constituted a taking.[53] At bottom, of course, the lines drawn represent differences as to whether economic loss resulting from a public policy shall be suffered wholly by those directly affected, or shall be borne by the community, the taxpayer, as an element in the cost of that policy.*

The question for the future is whether expanding concepts of 'taking' and 'use', and judicial disposition to widen the constitutional policy of distributing the cost of public endeavor, might extend to include some 'incidental' costs of foreign relations and foreign policy. Here, too, history offers lessons. Consider a famous old case, *Ware* v. *Hylton*, decided in 1796.[54] During the War of American Independence, a Virginia statute provided that any monies owing by Virginia citizens to British creditors might be paid instead to the State of Virginia; and the Virginia statute declared that the debts shall thereby be discharged. Later, however, the peace treaty with Great Britain reaffirmed all debts to British creditors and required that they be paid.** The Supreme Court held that although Hylton had paid his debt into the Virginia Treasury, he had to pay his British creditor as required by the treaty.

To us, to make Hylton pay twice would seem to be unfair, an obvious deprivation of property without substantive due process of law, but for the Supreme Court of 1796 that did not invalidate the treaty. Perhaps, in those early days, the Court did not yet consider that the due process clause imposed substantive limitations.† Probably, the Court assumed that the citizen would be relieved of the dual burden: Justice Cushing suggested that Virginia was bound 'in justice and honor, to indemnify the debtor, for what it in fact received'.[55] But Justice Chase had a different idea:

That Congress had the power to sacrifice the *rights* and *interests* of *private* citizens to secure the safety and prosperity of the public, I have no doubt; but the immutable principles of justice; the public faith of the states, that confiscated

---

* *Caltex* (n. 51 above), the war-time case, perhaps reflects also a special reluctance to compensate a particular, corporate victim of war when 'the strange arithmetic of chance' left so many others without recourse for their various losses in life, liberty, and property.

** The Framers apparently had that provision in particular in mind when they established the supremacy of preexisting treaties over state laws. Ch. VII, p. 198.

† The first and only application of substantive due process before the Civil War was in the *Dred Scott* case in 1857, which invalidated an act of Congress, in fact a statute claiming authority from a treaty. See Intro. to Pt IV, p. 278.

and received *British* debts, pledged to the debtors; and the rights of the debtors violated by the treaty; all combine to prove, that ample compensation ought to be made to all the debtors who have been injured by the treaty for the benefit of the *public*. This principle is recognized by the Constitution, which declares, 'that *private* property shall not be taken for *public* use without just *compensation*'.[56]

There is no evidence that Hylton sought or obtained compensation from the United States, and there appears to be no later case awarding compensation for any 'taking' by treaty.[57] In 1952, however, in a foreign affairs case involving an act of Congress (not a treaty), the Supreme Court gave some support to the old suggestion by Justice Chase.[58] In that case, the Court upheld the power of Congress to authorize the Alien Property Custodian to 'seize' certain obligations owned by an enemy alien and collect them from the obligor, where the latter was in the United States but the negotiable debenture was not, and therefore could not be physically taken. The Court said that if the obligor should in the future be compelled by a foreign court to make payment on the debenture to a holder in due course, the obligor would be entitled to compensation from the United States under the Fifth Amendment to the extent of any double liability. '[O]nly with this assurance against double liability can it fairly be said that the present seizure is not itself an unconstitutional taking of petitioners' property.'[59]

The Supreme Court opinions quoted here lend support to the view that making someone pay twice in order to achieve some overriding foreign relations purpose may not be constitutionally impermissible, but that it constitutes a taking for a public use that requires just compensation; and, perhaps, if no compensation is forthcoming the original taking becomes unlawful as an arbitrary deprivation of property without (substantive) due process of law. But double payment, surely, is not the only form of deprivation of property, and *Ware* v. *Hylton*, in particular, involved a treaty provision unique in our history. What of the common international agreements that affect private property rights not by reinstating claims against U.S. citizens that have been paid, but by nullifying claims by U.S. citizens that have not been paid?

International agreements settling claims by nationals of one state against nationals of another state (or against the government of another state) are established in international practice reflecting traditional international law. A private claimant may be able to recover under the laws of his (her) country or that of the debtor (or even of some third country), but in international law the individual and his debt have had no independent existence: the claim is only a right of the claimant's government against that of the alleged debtor. For international law and diplomacy, then, what begins life as a debt between an individual and a foreign government, or between individuals of different nationalities, is, or becomes, automatically a debt between governments. And governments have dealt with such private claims as their own, treating them as national assets, and as counters, 'chips', in international bargaining. Settlement agreements have lumped, or linked, claims deriving from private debts with others that were intergovernmental in origin, and concessions in regard to one category of claims might be set off against concessions in the other, or against larger political considerations unrelated to debts. In result, except as an agreement might provide otherwise, international claims settlements generally wipe out the underlying private debt, terminating any recourse under domestic law as well.

The United States has been party to many such settlements, terminating claims of its citizens against other states or against their citizens, usually in exchange for a lump sum payment to the United States.[60] Some settlement agreements established machinery for hearing individual claims and awarding individual recovery against the lump sum payment; other agreements have said nothing about payment to individuals, and payment by the foreign government was made into the Treasury of the United States.* In the past, the United States has sometimes disposed of the claims of its citizens without their consent, or even without consultation with them, usually without exclusive regard for their interests, as distinguished from those of the nation as a whole.[61] Often there was no assurance that the lump sum settlement was the best 'deal' that could have been obtained, that it was a fair deal, that private claims of citizens were not sacrificed to some other national interest; often, surely, one could not be certain that the private party recovered the full 'value' of his (her) claim.

Particularly instructive is another old story, the story of the 'French Spoliation Claims'. By treaty in 1800, the United States renounced claims of U.S. shipowners against France, arising out of alleged spoliations; France, in exchange, effectively forgave the United States and abandoned any claims against it for alleged breach of a treaty undertaking to support France in war against Great Britain.[62] Here there was no cash payment to the United States in liquidation of the claims of the shipowners, but, clearly, the United States had 'taken' and 'used' those claims to offset claims against the United States. Yet for 85 years

---

* As an act of grace, Congress sometimes provided that private claims 'settled' by an agreement should be examined and paid, in full or on a *pro rata* basis. See nn. 61, 67 to this chapter.

Congress failed to appropriate funds to compensate the U.S. claimants.[63]

No one has successfully argued in the Supreme Court that in purporting to dispose of private claims, in the details of a particular settlement, in the procedures established for making awards to private claimants, in Congressional legislation providing (or failing to provide) for award and payment to them, the United States deprived claimants of property without due process of law; or that it impaired the obligation of their contracts;[64] or that it appropriated their claims for a public purpose and was obligated to pay them just compensation for any loss.[65] In the past, at least, the Court refused to scrutinize any settlement, and affirmed that Congress has discretion to decide whether and how and to what extent to compensate the original creditors.[66] Perhaps the Court refused to see these settlements as involving any 'taking' of property. Perhaps it took the international theory at face value: claims between nationals of different countries are not private claims, but are only claims between governments. Perhaps the Court concluded that since usually the claimant had no assured recovery against a foreign national, even less so against a foreign government, the United States did not deprive him (her) of anything of real value. Perhaps the Court thought that what was involved was the political judgment of the negotiators that the settlement was in the national interest, usually too in the best interest of the claimants, and that no court could effectively review that judgment or analyze and weigh its components.[67] But once, in a famous proceeding arising out of the French Spoliation Claims, the Court of Claims in effect gave Congress an advisory opinion, saying:

But in the negotiation of 1800 we used 'individual' claims against 'national' claims, and the set-off was of French national claims against American individual claims. That any Government has the right to do this, as it has the right to refuse war in protection of a wronged citizen, or to take other action, which, at the expense of the individual, is most beneficial to the whole people, is too clear for discussion. Nevertheless, the citizen whose property is thus sacrificed for the safety and welfare of his country has his claim against that country; he has a right to compensation, which exists even if no remedy in the courts or elsewhere be given him. A right often exists where there is no remedy, and a most frequent illustration of this is found in the relation of the subject to his sovereign, the citizen to his Government.

It seems to us that this 'bargain' (again using Madison's word), by which the present peace and quiet of the United States, as well as their future prosperity and greatness were largely secured, and which was brought about by the sacrifice of the interests of individual citizens, falls within the intent and meaning of the Constitution, which prohibits the taking of private property for public use without just compensation.[68]

A hundred years ago, the Court of Claims could give no relief since Congress had not provided any.* Now Congress has given the Court of Claims jurisdiction of all claims for just compensation under the Fifth Amendment, and has been automatically appropriating funds to pay that court's judgments.[69] Now, too, we have seen, the Supreme Court has shown an increasing willingness to read 'take' and 'use' in the Fifth Amendment more 'realistically'. Will the Court begin also to see such takings behind the legal and diplomatic fictions of international claims settlements and, at least in some cases, allow the Court of Claims to assess the claim and award a judgment for any difference between its value and what the claimant eventually receives?[70]

The Court had an opportunity to address that issue in a contemporary case, arising out of the searing national crisis resulting from the seizure of U.S. hostages in Iran in 1979–80. President Carter concluded an agreement that included provisions for settling claims, among them private claims of U.S. nationals against Iran. In upholding the Iran Hostage Settlement, the Court found no constitutional infirmity in the provisions that would close the U.S. courts to claims against Iran and relegate claimants to an Iran–U.S. Arbitration Tribunal. Claims that the United States had 'taken' private claims for a public use and should pay just compensation were premature, pending the outcome of the international arbitrations.[71]

The line between regulation and taking remains fluid.** Changing notions of fairness and reasonableness may yet engender constitutional rights to a remedy where none had existed, in regard to other foreign affairs regulations as well. One who sues a sovereign or a diplomat will have his (her) suit dismissed because international law gives the defend-

---

* The United States cannot be sued without its consent and when Congress grants consent it is in effect bounded by the remedies that Congress provides. See nn. 61, 67 to this chapter.

** And the Court might yet ask whether regulation for foreign affairs is governed by considerations different from those that govern domestic regulation, and whether regulation by statute differs from regulation by treaty. Might the Court move the line between 'regulation' and 'taking' in other foreign affairs contexts, too, and hold, for example, that a treaty that requires the United States to terminate an arms business, confiscate drugs or plow-under poppy fields, or give up 'rights' acquired by mining companies in the sea-bed beyond national jurisdiction, entails some taking of property for a public use, and is a loss that should be borne by the community as part of the cost of the nation's foreign policy?

ant immunity,* leaving the plaintiff without a day in court, ai
without a remedy. This has been the rule of international law
law of the land in the United States since before the Constituti
until international law and practice change, it seems unlikely that the
Constitution will provide the plaintiff a remedy (though Congress might
do so voluntarily). But where history and established international law
do not bar the plaintiff, for example, when immunities are accorded to
certain public international organizations, their officials and member
representatives, by treaty or by act of Congress;[72] or where the plaintiff
can claim that international law does not require it but immunity was
nonetheless 'suggested' by the United States because it is required by
U.S. foreign policy interests**—might the Constitution yet be read to
require that the plaintiff be afforded another remedy or be compensated
by the United States?[73]

IMMIGRATION, EXCLUSION, DEPORTATION

The conduct of foreign affairs generally, then, is subject to limitations
for individual rights. Aliens in the United States, whose treatment often
implicates foreign relations, enjoy all the protections of the Bill of
Rights.† It is less clear that (or when, or to what extent) such limitations
apply to laws and policies governing immigration into the United States
or the deportation of aliens from the United States—laws and policies
that have their own, special mix of foreign and domestic affairs.

More than a hundred years ago, in the *Chinese Exclusion Case*,‡ the
Supreme Court declared that Congressional control over entry and
immigration into the United States is 'plenary' because jurisdiction over
its own territory was part of United States independence and inherent
in its sovereignty. Nothing in that doctrine, or in its subsequent elaboration in *Curtiss-Wright*, necessarily implied that such powers of
Congress were not subject to the Bill of Rights or to other constitutional
limitations. But beginning in *Chinese Exclusion* the Court has ruled that

---

* The Foreign Sovereign Immunities Act of 1976 has defined (and restricted) the
immunity of foreign states. See p. 56 n., above.
** See Ch. II, p. 59. Might such a claim be made also when the plaintiff has his
day in court but the law applies some special doctrine, such as Act of State, which
results in a judgment different from what might have issued if the sensibilities of a
foreign government were not at stake? Compare p. 290 above, and n. 25 this chapter.
† See n. 44 to this chapter.   ‡ Also discussed in Ch. I, p. 16.

U.S. laws and policies in respect of immigration were not subject to the Bill of Rights,* including its requirements of due process of law and the equal protection of the laws.[74] And no immigration laws, not even provisions reflecting policies of blatant racial discrimination, have in fact been invalidated.

Congress has repealed the patently 'racist' immigration laws of the 1920s,** but the immigration laws retain other provisions that might not pass muster as 'due process of law' in other contexts.[75] The Court has held that a would-be entrant is entitled to a fair hearing on the claim that he (she) is a U.S. citizen, but an alien seeking admission to the United States has been due no process beyond consideration and decision by the designated administrative officer in the light of applicable laws of Congress.[76] Courts have ruled that laws of Congress are properly interpreted to permit indefinite detention of persons physically present in the United States pending their exclusion or deportation,† and that such detention does not violate the Constitution.[77]

The Supreme Court has also upheld U.S. laws that provided for the deportation of aliens, even those long resident in the United States, for any reason.[78] The resident alien, then, enjoys all constitutional rights equally with citizens,‡ but all those rights—and more—evaporate if Congress should decide to deport him (her). More than forty years ago, Justice Frankfurter, writing for the majority of the Supreme Court, suggested that, if the Court 'were writing on a clean slate', it might well conclude that deportation deprived a person of his liberty and, if grounds for deportation were arbitrary, might deny him due process of law.[79] But neither then nor since has the Court risen to clean the constitutional slate.

It is difficult to believe that racist immigration laws would survive constitutional challenge at the end of the twentieth century. It is difficult to believe that the Constitution permits indefinite detention of persons declared inadmissible under prevailing law whom the United States can-

---

* A person seeking admission to the United States to deliver lectures challenged his exclusion as violating his freedom of expression as well as the First Amendment rights of those in the United States who wished to hear him. The Court did not say that the First Amendment was inapplicable, but it rejected the argument. See p. 387–8 above and n. 15 to this chapter.

** Known as the National Origins Act of 1924, its invidious purpose was famous though less blatant than those of the *Chinese Exclusion Acts* of 1882, 1884, 1888, 1892 and 1894.

† As to what international law says about indefinite detention, see Ch. VIII, pp. 244–5.

‡ See p. 293 above.

not deport because no other country will accept them. It is difficult to believe that at the end of the twentieth century the Court would uphold a law that provides for deportation of a law-abiding resident alien. The Court has in fact refrained from reaffirming the plenary, non-reviewable power of Congress over immigration, and some see signs of some erosion of the doctrine,[80] but not of any disposition to reexamine it. The *Chinese Exclusion Case*—its very title, an abiding embarrassment—cries for reconsideration and rejection.

THE CONSTITUTION ABROAD

In 1891, the Supreme Court upheld the conviction of a seaman, John Ross, for killing a ship's officer on a U.S. vessel in Japanese waters. He had been tried by a U.S. consul authorized by Congress to prosecute and try U.S. citizens for violations of designated U.S. laws. Ross challenged the validity of his trial because it had not provided him the safeguards in the criminal process required by the Bill of Rights. The Court did not attempt to construe and apply the relevant clauses of the Constitution; it concluded, rather, that 'the Constitution can have no operation in another country'.[81] Ross was entitled to a fair trial but not to the specific protections of the Constitution.

Why the Justices thought the Constitution was 'territorial', like a deity of old, is not clear.* Perhaps they assumed that to have been the intention of the Framers. Perhaps they thought that some, or all, of the Constitution's provisions were not appropriate or could not be effective elsewhere.

Whatever its original rationale, that doctrine appeared to have died in 1957. In *Reid* v. *Covert*,[82] the Supreme Court held that Congress could not provide trial by court-martial abroad for the wife of a member of the armed forces because Congress had no power to deprive a U.S. civilian of constitutional rights to a jury trial and other procedural safeguards. The plurality opinion by Justice Black dismissed *Ross* as 'a relic from a different era';[83] Justice Black wrote that wherever it acts the

---

* Perhaps the Justices considered that applying the Constitution in another country would somehow violate that country's sovereignty. (The act of Congress authorizing consular prosecution and trial, and the conduct of the trial, were not a violation since the host country consented by treaty.) But it has not been considered a violation of territorial sovereignty for a state to apply its laws to its own nationals in the territory of another state even without the latter's consent. Compare Ch. III, p. 71.

United States 'can only act in accordance with all the limitations imposed by the Constitution'.[84] Following *Reid*, several lower courts held that the Constitution protects even the rights of aliens from actions by the United States abroad—e.g., a right to be free of unreasonable searches and seizures at sea by U.S. officers,[85] a right to fair criminal procedure when tried in a court established in a foreign country under U.S. authority.[86]

In 1990, it appeared that *In re Ross* was not as dead as had been thought. In *Verdugo*,[87] the Court held that a national of Mexico could not invoke the protections of the Fourth Amendment against unreasonable search and seizure conducted by U.S. officials at his home in Mexico. *Verdugo* was no doubt the result of a changed composition of the Supreme Court with an ideology different from that represented by *Reid* v. *Covert*, but how far the Court will take its new doctrine is not yet clear. It seems unlikely that a majority of the Court would have held the Fourth Amendment inapplicable had the accused been a U.S. citizen. We do not know with certainty whether in rejecting the claim of a foreign national to the protections of the Fourth Amendment, the Court was speaking to that Amendment in particular, in view of its reference to the rights of 'the people' to be secure, or whether it promised also to reaffirm the statement in In re *Ross* that the Constitution can have 'no operations in another country'* and to reject claims under other provisions of the Bill of Rights by aliens abroad (and perhaps even by U.S. citizens). But those who took seriously Justice Black's flat declaration that wherever the United States acts, it acts subject to constitutional limitations; those who were inclined to read the Constitution not as a social contract for themselves only, but as establishing a 'community of conscience' requiring their representatives and officials to behave decently wherever and against whomsoever they act;[88] those who thought that we had left behind us the jurisprudence of a particularly xenophobic era of the late 1880s[89]—are bound to be disappointed by *Verdugo* and fearful of more to come.

The spirit of *Verdugo* may promise also to reaffirm other old cases that some hoped the Court would abandon. In 1886, in *Ker* v. *Illinois*,[90] the Court held that a person arrested by U.S. officials in a foreign country in violation of international law could nonetheless be tried in the United States. In 1992, in *Alvarez-Machain*, the Court held that a national of Mexico abducted from Mexico by U.S. officials and brought to the United States could be tried here since his abduction did not

---

* Might the Constitution have 'operation' where no other country is sovereign, e.g., the high seas? Compare *Sale*, n. 91 this chapter.

violate the extradition treaty with Mexico.* The Court did not consider it relevant that the abduction was a violation of customary international law. It did not deem it relevant to consider whether the abduction deprived the victim of his (her) liberty without due process of law. Without further consideration, the Court declared: 'if we conclude that the Treaty does not prohibit the abduction, the rule in *Ker* applies' and the trial may proceed.[91]

In sum, there are differences in the extent to which individual rights may limit the foreign policy of the United States at home or abroad. In the United States, virtually all the safeguards of the Constitution apply to all who are here—citizens, alien residents, even those sojourning temporarily or in transit. Outside the United States, constitutional protection for the individual against governmental action is enjoyed, we may continue to assume, by U.S. citizens, perhaps also by alien residents of the United States who are temporarily abroad. On the other hand, after *Verdugo*, foreign nationals abroad may not succeed[92] even with some constitutional claims that lower courts had previously recognized.**

A related but different issue was involved in the famous controversy at the turn of the last century, whether 'the Constitution follows the Flag'. There the question was not whether the Constitution applies abroad but whether newly acquired territories were still 'abroad' for constitutional purposes, or had become part of the United States. In *The Insular Cases*, a majority of the Supreme Court held that the

* Also see the case upholding the interdiction and return of Haitian refugees in 1993, n. 91 to this chapter. At the time of the events, the United States was not yet party to the International Covenant on Civil and Political Rights. See n. 7 to Intro. to Pt IV.

** A foreign national living in a foreign country presumably could not invoke the Constitution when he (she) was aggrieved, say, by discrimination in U.S. trade or immigration policy, when a U.S. consul capriciously denied him (her) a visa, or when a military purchasing agent refused to buy from him (her) on account of his (her) race. Surely, someone in Vietnam, in Panama, or in the Persian Gulf could not object that the President of the United States had no constitutional authority to wage war there. See n. 92 to this chapter.

After the Second World War, the United States commonly acted abroad in capacities to which the usual constitutional safeguards do not apply: for example, when the United States exercised authority as an occupying power, the President, as Commander in Chief, could establish courts for the trial of crimes committed there, and even U.S. citizens, it was held, could be tried in such courts without jury trial or other safeguards provided in the Bill of Rights. See *Madsen* v. *Kinsella*, 343 U.S. 341 (1952). The continuing validity of those cases is, fortunately, hypothetical, since the United States is no longer an occupying power anywhere. Analogous issues might arise, however, in unincorporated territories, p. 308 below.

Constitution did not apply fully in territories acquired by conquest and consequent cession from Spain, unless, until, Congress 'incorporated' them into the United States.[93] In 'unincorporated' territories, only 'fundamental' constitutional rights applied, so that, for example, U.S. authorities did not have to provide indictment by grand jury or trial by jury.*

The likelihood that the United States will acquire new territories in the years ahead seems remote, and it is not out of the question that some territories now still 'unincorporated' will achieve independence, or be incorporated, or perhaps even be accorded statehood. Today, despite the aspersions cast on them, *The Insular Cases* continue to govern the United States in unincorporated territories such as Guam.[94]

It remains to be seen, however, whether the content of the 'fundamental rights' that obtain in unincorporated territory might expand. The term 'fundamental rights' has found its way into U.S. constitutional jurisprudence with different meanings in different contexts. Once, for example, it had been established doctrine that the Constitution, by the due process clause of the Fourteenth Amendment, required of the states (of the United States) only that they respect fundamental rights;[95] later, the Court held that almost all the provisions of the Bill of Rights are indeed 'fundamental', and applicable to the states (see below).** Might an individual now claim these rights also in an unincorporated territory? Or will the Court continue to apply there the concept it has since rejected for the states, concluding that what is fundamental for the people of unincorporated territories, who have 'wholly dissimilar traditions and constitutions',† are only those rights that are 'basic to a free society', that are 'implied in the concept of ordered liberty', the denial of which would 'shock the conscience'?

* Later, in his plurality opinion in *Reid* v. *Covert*, n. 82 to this chapter, Justice Black distinguished these cases 'in that they involved the power of Congress to provide rules and regulations to govern temporarily territories with wholly dissimilar traditions and institutions . . ', but in any event 'neither the cases nor their reasoning should be given any further expansion'.

** See nn. 93, 94 to this chapter. In deciding which provisions of the Bill of Rights are to be incorporated the Court has characterized the rights in various terms, sometimes as 'fundamental' or some equivalent. See n. 97 to this chapter.

† And how long do their dissimilar traditions and institutions remain dissimilar, after decades of U.S. authority and influence?

THE STATES AND INDIVIDUAL RIGHTS

I have been discussing individual rights that limit the freedom of the federal government to conduct foreign relations. The states do not conduct foreign relations, but they do influence them,* and the extent to which they can do so is also limited by constitutional safeguards for individual rights.**

In general, the rights of the individual against infringement by the states have become virtually identical with those protected against the federal government. The original Constitution forbade the states to pass any bill of attainder, *ex post facto* laws, or law impairing the obligation of contracts (Art. I, sec. 10). And though originally the Bill of Rights did not apply to the states,[96] virtually all of its provisions now do, having been 'incorporated' in the Fourteenth Amendment.[97] The due process clause of that Amendment, in particular, affords procedural and substantive protections identical to those that by the same clause in the Fifth Amendment govern the federal government. States must provide due process of law to aliens as to citizens. The Fourteenth Amendment forbids the states to enforce any law which shall abridge the privileges and immunities of U.S. citizenship, and these include several related to U.S. foreign affairs, for example, 'the care and protection of the federal government when on the high seas or within the jurisdiction of a foreign government' and 'all rights secured to our citizens by treaties with foreign nations', rights which are 'dependent upon citizenship of the United States, and not citizenship of a State'.[98]

The Fourteenth Amendment forbids the states to deny the equal protection of the laws to any person, including aliens;[99] and in respect of aliens, equal protection makes far greater demands of the states than of the federal government. Alienage, we have seen, has been identified with foreign nationality and with U.S. foreign relations, and the United States may regulate their condition and treat them differently from citizens. But the status, treatment and rights of aliens in the United States are a national concern, not for the states to interfere in. Discriminations and distinctions between citizens and aliens that might be reasonable if made by the federal government in the conduct of its international

---

* See Ch. VI.

** Aliens and other individuals have also found protection against state regulation in constitutional principle not directly designed to promote individual rights, for example in the limitations of the Commerce Clause, in federal supremacy and preemption, in the doctrine forbidding state intrusion into foreign relations.

relations might yet constitute denials of equal protection if practiced by a state.*

Thus, from the early days of the Fourteenth Amendment, the Equal Protection Clause has protected aliens against state discriminations denying them equal right to common employment. A hundred years later, new doctrine giving new vitality to equal protection principles rendered state distinctions between citizens and aliens a 'suspect classification', requiring a 'compelling state interest' to support a discrimination against aliens. The Supreme Court has held that a state may not deny an alien equal treatment as regards welfare assistance,[100] and, despite earlier cases suggesting the contrary,[101] the Constitution (or the unspoken will of Congress) has been read to require the states to allow aliens to practice law or medicine and even hold public employment.[102] A state can exclude aliens only from 'matters firmly within a state's constitutional prerogatives', in the exercise of its 'historical power to exclude aliens from participation in its democratic institutions' and 'to preserve the basic conception of a political community'.[103] That exception extends to membership in the state police force, teaching in public schools, serving as deputy probation officers, serving on state and federal juries, but not to serving as notaries public.[104]

Respect for individual rights ranks high—perhaps highest—among the elements of U.S. constitutionalism, and despite occasional careless rhetoric, the federal government must respect those rights in its conduct of foreign affairs as in domestic governance. Foreign affairs are important national interests, but not all actions in foreign affairs are compelling. Foreign affairs may implicate national security, but ordinarily only remotely. Invasion of individual rights may be essential to serve a compelling public interest, but only rarely. The sovereignty of the United States, the powers of the political branches in foreign affairs, are 'plenary'—subject to individual rights.

---

* State discriminations against aliens may also conflict with the policy of Congress implied in the immigration laws pursuant to which a person was admitted to residence. See *Takahashi*, n. 99 to this chapter. And some state denials of rights to aliens are prohibited by federal Civil Rights legislation. See n. 99 to this chapter.

CONCLUSION

Chapter X

AN EIGHTEENTH CENTURY CONSTITUTION FOR THE TWENTY-FIRST CENTURY

At the end of the twentieth century, after two World Wars and decades of Cold War, there is 'one world'* and the United States is its dominant power. The end of the century finds us also deep into the 'age of constitutionalism', and the United States is a model—one model—of a constitutionalist polity. Inevitably, then, how the United States runs its public affairs, not least how it conducts foreign relations under its Constitution, is of deep interest, within and beyond the United States.

This study of Foreign Affairs and the U.S. Constitution has set forth the relevant provisions of the Constitution, expounded how they have been construed, and identified abiding issues and uncertainties in their interpretation. Students of government and politics, U.S. citizens, and friends (or critics) elsewhere, might ask also whether 'it works': does the Constitution promote an effective system for the governance of U.S. foreign relations at the turn of a new century? Some might look at the constitutional law of foreign affairs, as they might at U.S. constitutional law generally, under the aspect of 'constitutionalism': to what extent and in what measure does our foreign affairs system meet the demands of the rule of law, popular sovereignty and democratic government, separation of powers and limited government, respect for individual rights?

The United States Constitution has not escaped criticism. Nearly 150 years ago Thomas Babington Macaulay wrote: 'Your Constitution, sir, is all sail and no anchor.'[1]

Lord Macaulay's *mot* appears to be not quite *juste* today as regards the Constitution as a whole, but it remains not wholly inapt or unjust as applied to constitutional prescriptions for the conduct of foreign relations. The Constitution, we know, is not what it was: indeed,

* Persistent colloquial references to 'the Third World' fail to take account of the fact that, with the demise of the USSR and its empire, there is no longer a 'Second World'. More accurate are references to 'the developing world', an economic rather than a political classification, though one not without political significance.

constitutional history might suggest that one cannot look twice into the same Constitution; but the constitutional law of foreign affairs has not changed wildly. The United States is changed, the world is changed, and relations between them are changed, in ways that 'could not have been foreseen by the most gifted of its begetters'.[2] Yet the early issues are the same, and answers remain uncertain and elusive. The principal difficulty has been that, from the beginning, the compromises, irresolutions, oversights, and intentional silences of the Constitution left it unclear—to pursue Macaulay's metaphor—who had sail and who had rudder, and, most important, where is command. In the twentieth century—before, between and after World Wars, during and after the Cold War—the uncertainties have been particularly troubling, because the stuff of foreign relations has rendered ambiguity of authority and responsibility particularly troubling, and sometimes dangerous.

Uncertainty in the constitutional law of foreign relations should not be exaggerated. Much is clear, and the relations of the United States are conducted every minute of every day with respectable efficiency within the framework of the Constitution. The President conducts foreign relations, and no one challenges his authority and responsibility even when Congresses resolve and members of Congress travel and televise. The President largely makes foreign policy, even if Congresses and members of Congress do not refrain from telling him what it ought to be. (There is generally little disposition even to challenge his uses of the armed forces for foreign relations purposes where they are not likely to become involved in hostilities.) At the other end of the constitutional axis, Congress alone clearly adopts domestic legislation, regulates foreign commerce, authorizes spending and appropriates money, and—happily not often—makes war.

Of the uncertainties I have exposed in this volume many are lawyer's uncertainties, not uninteresting, not unimportant to individuals affected by them, but they do not bring tension to the conduct of government or disturbance to relations with other nations. Whether the courts may make law, in what circumstances, within what limits; where exactly do and should the courts place international law in the hierarchy of U.S. law; what respect do judges owe to Executive declarations and 'suggestions'; what intrusions by the states should the courts tolerate when the political branches have not spoken; what issues should the courts characterize as 'political questions' and refuse to adjudicate—none of these is beyond clarification, or beyond effective control if the political branches desire it. Even false, exasperating 'issues', e.g., whether, under the Constitution, the United States may adhere to human rights treaties, did not raise serious differences within the political branches or with other countries, and have stopped being the important obstacles to new forms of international cooperation.*

The Constitution remains what the courts say it is, and some of the uncertainties might yet be resolved by the Justices of the Supreme Court some later day. Failure to resolve them to date may be due in part to judicial diffidence in relation to foreign affairs, the product of conceptualisms about sacrosanct 'sovereignty', of unexamined assumptions reflected in incantations about 'war and peace', of set habits of thought about international relations, about how they are conducted, about the 'proper' role of courts in regard to them. But intellectual and judicial fashions change, and activist courts will strain at restraints imposed by their predecessors. At the end of the twentieth century, after the Cold War, in a nation turning inward to face deep domestic problems, the old constitutional assumptions that foreign affairs are different and special may not survive unexamined. But, I believe, they will survive essentially. Courts will not begin to intervene lightly in the foreign policy process. They will continue to protect the nation and extend the remedies available to the federal government against frolics by the states. But the courts are not likely to keep their doors closed for long to claims of individual rights and freedoms threatened by the conduct of foreign relations. In such cases the courts may erode requirements of standing, attenuate the doctrine of political questions, enlarge the protections of the Bill of Rights. Even when 'it is only money', courts are likely to extend rights to compensation for losses resulting from foreign policy so that its costs will be borne not by the fortuitous 'victim' alone but by the general taxpayer.

The abiding constitutional uncertainties lie principally—some might say wholly—in the separation, distribution, fragmentation of powers between the President and Congress (or between President and Senate). Despite cycles in national political mood—of 'isolationism' and 'interventionism', collective international action or unilateralism; despite waves of activism and self-restraint by Presidents and Congresses, the division of powers in the conduct of foreign relations is not, has not been, and cannot be what it is in domestic affairs. If it were possible to distinguish and divide 'making foreign policy' from 'conducting foreign relations', it is not the distinction and division we have lived by for more

* Even some of the issues of 'separation of powers', e.g., executive privilege, or Presidential impounding of funds, or Presidential 'war-making', or 'dirty tricks' by intelligence agencies (Ch. IV), have not themselves seriously disturbed the process for conducting foreign relations, though they often reflect turbulence in that process.

than 200 years. Separation of powers, particularly the divisions of power in foreign relations, has always carried invitation to cooperation as well as to conflict. The division of power to determine U.S. foreign policy between two branches sometimes pulling in different directions, and, in particular, the separation of the power to decide for war or peace from the power to make other foreign policy, have bred failures of cooperation, interference, inefficiency, duplication and frustration, conflict and confusion.

Some of these uncertainties and conflicts, no doubt, arise out of different constitutional interpretations, which in theory might yet be resolved: I do not think that they will be resolved soon. The difficult issues come in clusters and during crises, in the context of a Cuba (1898), or Vietnam (mid-1960s), or the Gulf War (1991), or Haiti (1994), and those conditions are not conducive to deliberate constitutional deliberation. For their parts, Congresses and Presidents are not more likely to resolve the issues than they have been, and each branch will no doubt continue to claim prerogatives in principle even when yielding some of them in practice. The courts, despite sometimes misguided efforts to compel them to do so[3] are not likely to step into intense confrontations between President and Congress, or to inhibit either branch when the other does not object. Whether from the sense that the boundary between Congress and President (and between Senate and President, between executive agreement and treaty, between political commitment and binding agreement) cannot be defined by law, whether from realization of the inherent limitations of judicial power or from prudence, whether under a doctrine of 'political questions' or by other judicial devices and formulae for abstention, courts will not rush to make certain what was left uncertain, to curtail the power of the political branches, to arbitrate their differences. Then, in time, the issues may recede, stirring neither controversy nor case. If the courts do speak to Separation occasionally,* they will speak only delphically; hard cases will make as little law as possible,[4] as the Justices reach for the narrowest grounds; and struggle and uncertainty will continue. The few old Separation cases will remain, unreviewed. The Justices will not build and refine steadily case by case, will not develop clear philosophies, expertise or experts, only that confident sense that the deepest ills of the constitutional system are not theirs to cure.

---

* As in the *Steel Seizure Case,* Ch. IV, not strictly a foreign affairs case, and not one where Congress was deeply committed. The Court's opinions deal with the President's powers as a legal question not as an inter-branch constitutional political controversy.

Much of the disturbance in the conduct of foreign affairs, however, is not due to constitutional uncertainty and issue: it is what the Constitution intended. And many differences between Congress and the President are not of constitutional dimension even when the Constitution is invoked by one or the other in ritual incantation. If Congress refuses to authorize a weapons program requested by the President, or the President vetoes a tariff adopted by Congress, or the Senate refuses or delays consent to a human rights convention or an arms control treaty negotiated by the President, the controversy may be bitter but it does not involve competition for constitutional power—only the kind of conflict prescribed by the Constitution when it separated powers and checked and balanced functions. When the President exercises power which he holds concurrently with and subject to the power of Congress, there may be controversy when Congress repudiates his initiative, but it is not constitutional controversy. Neither are there constitutional issues, for our purposes, when the complaint is not that the Constitution has been violated but that it is not working very well.*

The constitutional system for the conduct of foreign relations has chronic ailments. Some have asked whether, despite political adaptations, the constitutional framework, designed for a small new nation and reflecting eighteenth century political compromises and eighteenth century concern to prevent too-strong government,[5] is sufficient to the United States today.** There have been suggestions for amending the Constitution, many only cosmetic, some radical;† none seems clearly

* That, I believe, was the lesson of the national *crise* over Vietnam which assumed the appearance of a constitutional crisis, evoked soul-searching examination of the adequacy of the Constitution, and engendered proposals for its amendment. In my view, Vietnam showed that, in important cases, 'usurpation' of authority, as between the President and Congress, may not be the real issue. The real complaint about Vietnam was not that the President usurped constitutional power but that, acting within his powers, he virtually compelled Congress to go along. That was a complaint against the Constitution. It is not the only respect in which, in our constitutional system, one of the Branches has been able to compel cooperation by another, or to use its dominance in one area to exact concessions in others. And that may even be what the Framers contemplated.

** More than three-quarters of a century ago, Henry Adams said: 'The fathers had intended to neutralize the energy of government and had succeeded, but their machine was never meant to do the work of a twenty-million horse-power society in the twentieth century, where much work needed to be quickly and efficiently done . . . bad machinery merely added to friction.' THE EDUCATION OF HENRY ADAMS 375 (1918).

† The recurrent proposal to give the House an equal voice with the Senate in treaty-making has much to commend it in principle but is not directed at any

necessary or desirable, none seems clearly worth the effort, few are likely to materialize in our amendment-resisting Constitution.* The conflict, confusion, uncertainty, frustration, inefficiency, and occasional national detriment which comes from the 'irregular' division of powers in the conduct of foreign relations will not be cured by tinkering or even by major surgery on some organ. If those who can amend the Constitution were all willing, if they could all agree on changes to be made, I do not believe they would succeed: the boundaries between President and Congress are fluid and cannot be defined or redefined; foreign affairs are not in fact separable, and the machinery for running them cannot be isolated from the rest of government; nor could one transplant a new organ for the conduct of foreign affairs leaving the rest of the body politic as is.

I do not suggest that our system is the best of all possible systems or that it is working well, only that it cannot be effectively improved by constitutional amendment. Perhaps that reflects an impression that without constitutional amendment we muddle through, and a perhaps tired conclusion that that is the best one can hope for in our kind of

problem that matters today, and is not likely to be adopted. The Senate has sometimes 'graciously' granted the House equality, particularly in respect of international trade agreements (such as the World Trade Organization agreement), but it will not forego its privileged status 'as of right' and irrevocably. Presidents too are not eager to erect additional obstacles to treaty-making. More important, the amendment is unnecessary. The Senate has not in recent years been a graveyard of treaties; there have been few instances where a treaty that could not get the consent of two-thirds of the Senate would obtain a majority of both houses; and, above all, the Constitution already effectively permits approval of international agreements by resolution of Congress. See Ch. VII.

* In more than 200 years there have been 27 amendments to the Constitution. The first ten were part of the original 'package', the price of ratification of the Constitution; the Thirteenth, Fourteenth and Fifteenth constituted the peace treaty of the Civil War; the Eighteenth ('Prohibition') and the Twenty-First largely canceled each other. Some of the rest are 'patching' or picayune, surely reflecting no major modification of the system, e.g., the Twenty-Fourth, outlawing the poll tax after it was virtually defunct and about to be invalidated even without amendment. (Compare *Harper* v. *Virginia Board of Elections*, 383 U.S. 663 (1966).) The latest, the Twenty-Seventh Amendment, finally brought into effect in 1992 more than 200 years after it was approved by Congress, limits the power of Congress to vary its own salaries; it is hardly a major contribution to political reform.

Apart from the difficult process involved, one reason why the Constitution has hardly been amended is, no doubt, that without amendment the Supreme Court has read it differently as great need arose. E.g., *NLRB* v. *Jones & Laughlin Steel Corp.*, 301 U.S. 1 (1937), n. 6 to Ch. III; *Brown* v. *Board of Education*, 347 U.S. 483 (1954).

human government. Conflict never quite becomes all-out war, confusion is not quite chaos, frustration does not grind government to a standstill. Like the proverbial 'love-hate' marriage, that of Congress and President goes on: that the tensions continue and recur, that the arguments, constitutional and political, repeat and reecho, may only suggest that it will go on. There are—and will be—strong Presidents and weak ones, assertive Congresses and acquiescent ones, responsible and less responsible Presidents and Congresses. The President wields power with few limits when Congress does not resist or protest;* Congress sometimes asserts power even when the President does resist or protest. At bottom, between as well as during controversies, each needs the other, and each knows how to convert the other's need into power.

The complexities of government have increased mutual dependence, making it virtually impossible for one branch long to pursue a course to which the other objects strongly. Surely, Presidents cannot use troops for any extended time and purpose, whether in war or far short of war, without Congressional acquiescence. But Congress cannot 'sit it out', for whether it wishes or not, it shares responsibility if only because it has authority. If reality, including the two-party system, has modified the theoretical 'separation of powers', if Congress has not been as successful in maintaining its prerogatives, if it cannot readily prevent, repeal, contradict or derogate from Presidential policy, occasional road blocks and threats of more serious ones, coupled with periodic reclamations of Congressional power, remind Presidents and other governments that ours is a unique, home-built contraption.

That under a less than certain and less than happy constitutional arrangement, the conduct of foreign relations continues to function is due in substantial part to infra- or extra-constitutional arrangements and accommodations. Congress has made its part more effective by various devices: standing committees and subcommittees, special committees, even joint committees of both houses, are now permanent elements in the foreign policy machinery, and consultation between them and officials of the Executive branch are integral to the foreign policy process. Committee staffs in particular observe, consult, negotiate with members of the Executive branch daily and help shape executive decisions as well as legislation and other Congressional assertions of policy. Collaboration and coordination have become at least slogans, although

* President Truman is quoted as having said that the President's powers would have made Caesar or Genghis Khan or Napoleon bite his nails with envy. See C. ROSSITER, THE AMERICAN PRESIDENCY 30 (1960); see also U.S. PUBLIC PAPERS OF THE PRESIDENTS OF THE UNITED STATES: HARRY S. TRUMAN, 1952–53 1061 (1966).

the two branches are not always agreed on their import and the obligations they imply. There has been continuing calibration and imaginative adaptations and new procedures—'fast track', special dispute settlement arrangements, even a limited 'line-item' veto for the President though not yet an effective substitute for the 'legislative veto' for Congress.

The War Powers Act of 1973 demonstrates the difficulty of resolving basic constitutional uncertainties by confrontational legislation of dos and don'ts. There, and elsewhere, the quest must be for more and better cooperation, consultation, accommodation, by better legislative-executive *modi vivendi et operandi*. Vietnam, in particular, persuaded many that separating the authority to go to war from the authority to use other means of foreign policy has proven, or has become, unworkable, and that there is need to develop and improve institutions and procedures to mitigate the deficiencies of that constitutional conception.[6] Here 'checks'—as by giving one branch a veto on the other—do not work very well. The need, I believe, is for built-in 'balances', for arrangements and procedures that will assure appropriate roles for both in the making of foreign policy. The Executive must learn to conduct foreign relations with less secrecy and greater responsibility. Congress must have a timely, honest, meaningful role, and the flow of information to fulfill it. Congress's part cannot be equal to the President's, but the constitutional conception (as well as the impulsions of a democratic foreign policy) suggest that the degree and kind of Congressional participation should increase as the means of foreign policy begin to include uses of force and to approach a national commitment to war, and as the cost of policy begins to loom large in the competition for national resources. But Congress will have to assert and demand a role.* 'Only Congress itself can prevent power from slipping through its fingers'.[7]

---

* Once, in 1973, Congress bestirred and mobilized itself, and adopted major foreign affairs legislation—the War Powers Resolution—designed to assert the powers of Congress as it saw them, and to limit authority claimed by the President. During the quarter century since the Resolution was enacted, all Presidents have challenged its constitutionality, none of them has paid it careful heed. There have been recurrent proposals to repeal or amend it.

The War Powers Act, in its principal provisions not unconstitutional, clearly has not had the effect desired and hoped for, but it is not obvious that is has not served to deter or restrain Presidential adventures, given Presidents pause, induced caution, encouraged consultation. Presidents have claimed that they did not need to attend to it, but they have—in the Gulf War (1991), even in Haiti (1994). The Act needs to be fixed by clarification or amendment, or by interpretation and changed implementation; in my view, it would be foolish to repeal it without satisfactory replacement.

Of course, cooperation is a good thing, surely better than conflict. In the history of our foreign affairs, periods of competition and cooperation have alternated, but since the Second World War, developing institutions, political forces, and the growing complexity of foreign relations, have intensified the need for cooperation. But cooperation does not require abdication. The Framers thought they had good reasons for prescribing limits to cooperation, separation, tension, even some conflict. If effective government, in foreign relations as elsewhere, requires cooperation, democratic government, in foreign relations as elsewhere, abhors Congressional abdication and often enjoins it to provide loyal opposition.[8] The President provides initiative and efficiency, and these are not to be depreciated. But the Congress is in several senses the more representative branch and brings to bear the influences of public opinion, diversity, concern for local and individual rights. At its best, of course, there is a counterpoint of Presidential expertise and some inexpert Congressional wisdom, producing foreign policy and foreign relations not always efficient but supporting larger, deeper national interests.

The quest must be for improved operation and cooperation, not for limitations on national responsibility or national power. One tragedy of Vietnam, I believe, was the impulse it gave to an impatient tendency to deal with political mistakes not by improving procedures and selecting better officials but by denying power to offices and institutions so they can be safely entrusted to mediocrity. We have not yet escaped the 'republican tendency of reducing executive power'.[9] 'We fear to grant power and are unwilling to recognize it when it exists.'[10] Decades ago, in a related context, I wrote: [11]

Many will have deep sympathy for those who dream of old days thought good, or better; who yearn for decentralization even in foreign affairs and matters of international concern, for limitations on federal power, for increase in the importance of the states; who thrill to a wild, poignant, romantic wish to turn back all the clocks, to unlearn the learnings, until the atom is unsplit, weapons unforged, oceans unnarrowed, the Civil War unfought. The wish remains idle, and the effort to diminish power in this area for fear that it may not be used wisely is quixotic, if not suicidal. It is not the moment to attempt it when all ability, flexibility, wisdom are needed for cooperation for survival by a frightened race, on a diminishing earth, reaching for the moon.

Since that was written, we have reached the moon, but the lesson is yet to be learned.

If the courts are not likely to bring certainty to the law of separation of powers, one may hope, and expect, that they will bring greater clarity and contemporary sensitivity to the jurisprudence of individual rights in the conduct of foreign relations. The Justices ought not perpetuate the myth that in foreign affairs, the powers of Congress are 'plenary', if that means that they are not subject to the Bill of Rights. The Justices ought not perpetuate the myth that individual rights always and inevitably bow to the alleged needs of foreign policy.* One may expect, in particular, that the Supreme Court will shed the uncritical rhetoric of 'sovereignty' and declare new doctrine in respect of immigration and the exclusion, detention, or deportation of aliens. They might well abandon the fiction that persons physically under U.S. control may not be within its jurisdiction for constitutional purposes, and see any detention by U.S. authorities as a deprivation of liberty that must satisfy the requirements of due process of law, procedural due process as well as substantive due process. Taking the clear hint by Justice Frankfurter, they would clean the constitutional slate, and hold that deporting a law-abiding resident alien is a deprivation of liberty—of fundamental liberties—and must satisfy substantive as well as procedural due process of law. Many continue to hope that the Court will reexamine and reject doctrine born during xenophobic days in the latter days of the nineteenth century—*Chinese Exclusion, Ross, Ker*—and embrace what Justices declared half a century ago—that the Constitution governs any exercise of U.S. authority, within or outside the United States. Recognizing that the United States has promoted and embraced international human rights standards deriving from ours, Justices might yet conclude that a decent respect to the opinions of mankind requires that we look to international standards to illuminate our constitutional values of liberty, equality, property.

The Constitution remains a remarkable instrument. For all its warts, defects, and deficiencies, it remains the reflection and representation of our constitutional culture, of our commitment to 'constitutionalism'— to governance only in accordance with the Constitution** and by rule of law, to popular sovereignty and improving democracy, to limited government, to checks and balances, to respect for individual rights— all subject to judicial review by a final 'infallible' judiciary.

* For contemporary examples, in the *Pentagon Papers* case (see n. 17 to Ch. IX), and in addressing limitations on picketing embassies, the Justices have ruled that the public interest does not always 'trump' important individual rights.

** We have reason to be proud of the fact that the Constitution cannot be suspended, and that we have not had extra-constitutional government, no man on horseback. In 1974, Richard Nixon, Commander in Chief of the mightiest armed forces in history, bowed to the mandate of nine old men, and then had to resign his office.

There is a better known and more flattering judgment on the United States Constitution than Macaulay's. Gladstone said: [12]

But, as the British Constitution is the most subtle organism which has proceeded from the womb and the long gestation of progressive history, so the American Constitution is, so far as I can see, the most wonderful work ever struck off at a given time by the brain and purpose of man.

There is no reason to believe that he excluded from his judgment the mechanism which the Framers struck off for the conduct of foreign relations. Today, after more than another hundred years of 'progressive history', we can still accept his flattery, but soberly, and with a wry smile.

ENDNOTES

NOTES, PREFACE TO THE FIRST EDITION, pp. xi to xiii

1. Q. WRIGHT, THE CONTROL OF AMERICAN FOREIGN RELATIONS (1922).
2. In particular, from my own writings, *The Treaty Makers and the Law Makers: the Niagara Reservation*, 56 COLUM.L.REV. 1151 (1956); *The Treaty Makers and the Law Makers: the Law of the Land and Foreign Relations*, 107 U.PA.L.REV. 903 (1959); *The Foreign Affairs Powers of the Federal Courts: Sabbatino*, 64 COLUM.L.REV. 805 (1964); *The Constitution, Treaties, and International Human Rights*, 116 U.PA.L.REV. 1012 (1968); *'International Concern' and the Treaty Power of the United States*, 63 AM.J.INT'L L. 272 (1969); *Vietnam in the Courts of the United States: 'Political Questions'*, 23 J.INT'L AFF. 210 (1969). Also, *Treaty-Making Powers and their Implementation under a Federal Constitution: The American Experience*, unpublished.
3. E. CORWIN, THE PRESIDENT, OFFICE AND POWERS (1787–1957) (4th edn. 1957) . . . See also his THE PRESIDENT'S CONTROL OF FOREIGN RELATIONS (1917), and THE CONSTITUTION AND WORLD ORGANIZATION (1944). Corwin also edited THE CONSTITUTION OF THE UNITED STATES OF AMERICA: ANALYSIS AND INTERPRETATION, S. DOC. No. 170, 82d Cong., 2d Sess. (1953) [In updating this work, references to Corwin are to the 5th edition (n. 5 to Intro. to Pt. II).]

NOTES, PREFACE TO THE SECOND EDITION, pp. xv to xvii

1. See e.g., L. TRIBE, AMERICAN CONSTITUTIONAL LAW (2d edn. 1987).
2. RESTATEMENT OF THE LAW, THIRD, THE FOREIGN RELATIONS LAW OF THE UNITED STATES, 1987. Constitutional issues are considered throughout the Restatement, but in particular in § 1 and its Reporters' Notes, and in §§ 111–15, 302–3, 311, 339, 721–2.
3. See, e.g., FOREIGN AFFAIRS AND THE U.S. CONSTITUTION (HENKIN, GLENNON, AND ROGERS, EDS. 1990); GLENNON, CONSTITUTIONAL DIPLOMACY (1990). See also works listed in n. 5 to the Intro. to Pt II.

   Since the previous edition, I have also added to my own knowledge and understanding and have published some of what I have learned. See, *inter alia,* CONSTITUTIONALISM, DEMOCRACY AND FOREIGN AFFAIRS (1990); THE AGE OF RIGHTS (1990); also, *Constitutionalism, Democracy and Foreign Affairs,* 67 IND. L.J. 879 (1992); *Human Dignity and Constitutional Rights,* in HUMAN DIGNITY, THE BILL OF RIGHTS AND CONSTITUTIONAL VALUES (Meyer and Parent, eds. 1991); *U.S. Nuclear Defense Policy: The Constitutional Framework,* 26 ATLANTIC COMMUNITY QUARTERLY 62 (1988); *Foreign Affairs and the Constitution,* in FOREIGN AFFAIRS, Winter 1987/1988, p. 284; *The Constitution and United States Sovereignty,* 100 HARV. L. REV. 853 (1987); *The Constitution as Compact and as Conscience,* 27 WM. & MARY L. REV. 11 (1985); *The Constitution at Sea,* 31 MAINE L. REV. 201 (1984); *International Law as Law in the United States,* 82 MICH. L. REV. 1555 (1984); *Litigating the President's Power to Terminate Treaties,* 73 AM. J. INT'L L. 647 (1979); *The Constitution and Foreign Affairs,* in ESSAYS ON THE CONSTITUTION OF THE UNITED STATES (M.J. Harmon, ed. 1978); *Is There a 'Political Question' Doctrine?,* 85 YALE L. J. 597 (1976).
4. My gratitude to those who helped me in the first edition is not exhausted, and should not be forgotten. Before writing the first edition, I had studied the questions here discussed for 15 years, as I taught them to classes and seminars at the University of Pennsylvania and Columbia University. At the University of Pennsylvania the seminars were a joint effort with my colleague and friend Professor Covey Oliver, and no doubt much that appears here was learned with him and from him. Much was learned too from generations of students. I single out for mention and appreciation some who assisted me directly and extensively: Stuart Licht, J.D. Columbia 1973, as well as Joel Goldberg, J.D. Columbia 1970, Alan Garfunkel and Michael Stolzer, J.D. Columbia 1972, and Barbara Black, J.D. Columbia 1973. Linda Threlkeld was invaluable in various ways. Not least, I remain grateful to my friend and colleague Professor Albert J. Rosenthal who read the manuscript of the previous edition and made many valuable suggestions.

NOTES, INTRODUCTION, pp. 1 to 9

1. See Justice Jackson concurring in *Youngstown Sheet & Tube Co.* v. *Sawyer*, 343 U.S. 579, 653 (1952): 'That instrument must be understood as an Eighteenth-Century sketch of a government hoped for, not as a blueprint of the Government that is.' I have suggested that the Constitution reflected a commitment to 'constitutionalism'. See CONSTITUTIONALISM, DEMOCRACY AND FOREIGN AFFAIRS (1990), Introduction.

2. As, for example, in the literature churned up by the Vietnam controversy, n. 26 to Ch. IV.

3. There was a small resurgence of limitation on federal power vis-à-vis the states when the Court held that the federal government could not hinder the state in its performance of traditional functions of government. See *National League of Cities* v. *Usery*, 426 U.S. 833 (1976), *overruled by Garcia* v. *San Antonio Metropolitan Transit Authority*, 469 U.S. 528 (1985). *Garcia* was modified in *New York* v. *United States*, when the Court held that Congress may not 'commandeer' the states' legislative processes by directing them to enact and enforce a federal regulatory program. 504 U.S. 144 (1992). Such federalism issues will doubtless continue to arise but they are not likely to be important to foreign affairs. In recent years, the Supreme Court has addressed a spate of separation of powers issues, see Ch. IV, but these, too, are not likely to affect the governance of foreign affairs.

4. Writing between his two terms of service on the Supreme Court, Charles Evans Hughes said: 'We are under a Constitution, but the Constitution is what the judges say it is, and the judiciary is the safeguard of our liberty and property under the Constitution.' See C.E. HUGHES, ADDRESSES 185 (2d edn. 1916).

5. In constitutional questions, 'when convinced of former error, this Court has never felt constrained to follow precedent'. *Smith* v. *Allwright*, 321 U.S. 649, 665 (1944). In recent years, the Court has been re-examining past decisions, but none directly relating to foreign affairs. See, e.g., *Garcia* v. *San Antonio Metropolitan Transit Authority*, 469 U.S. 528 (1985); *Adarand Constructions Inc.* v. *Pena*, 115 S.Ct. 2097 (1995). But cf. *Planned Parenthood of Southeastern Pennsylvania* v. *Casey*, 505 U.S. 833 (1992).

NOTES, CHAPTER I. THE CONSTITUTIONAL AUTHORITY OF THE
FEDERAL GOVERNMENT, pp. 13 to 22

1. The 'capacity to enter into relations with other States' is considered an essential
   qualification for statehood under international law. See, e.g., Article 1 of the
   Convention on Rights and Duties of States, Montevideo, 1933, 49 Stat. 3097;
   RESTATEMENT (n. 2 to the Preface) § 201.
2. J. RODGERS, WORLD POLICING AND THE CONSTITUTION 14 (1945).
3. See, e.g., Q. WRIGHT, THE CONTROL OF AMERICAN FOREIGN RELATIONS (1922),
   132–4. Compare: 'The Constitution confers absolutely on the government of the
   Union, the powers of making war, and of making treaties; consequently, that
   government possesses the power of acquiring territory, either by conquest or by
   treaty'. *American Ins. Co.* v. *Canter*, 26 U.S. (1 Pet.) 511, 516, 542 (1828). *Cf.*
   Cohens v. *Virginia*, 19 U.S. (6 Wheat.) 264, 415–16 (1821). Justice Story speaks
   of powers that result not merely from aggregating enumerated powers but 'from
   the aggregate powers of the national government'. As an example he cites jurisdiction over conquered territory. 'This would perhaps rather be a result from
   the whole mass of the powers of the national government, and from the nature
   of political society, than a consequence or incident of the powers specially enumerated.' 2 J. STORY, COMMENTARIES ON THE CONSTITUTION 148 (5th edn. 1891).
   See also Strong, J., in Legal Tender Cases, 79 U.S. (12 Wall.) 457, 534–5
   (1870). But *cf.* 1 W. WILLOUGHBY, PRINCIPLES OF CONSTITUTIONAL LAW OF THE
   UNITED STATES (2nd edn. 1929), § 54; compare n. 5 to this chapter. See Ch. V,
   pp. 77–78.

   It has been argued that all foreign affairs relate to war and peace and, except
   for what is expressly given the President, are therefore the responsibility of
   Congress implied in or resulting from its power to declare war. Compare
   Ch. III, p. 75.
4. With many, many variations on that theme, in particular Marshall's oft-
   repeated reminder that 'it is *a constitution* we are expounding'. *McCulloch* v.
   Maryland, 17 U.S. (4 Wheat.) 316, 407 (1819).
5. 130 U.S. 581, 603–4 (1889). A year later the Court found that the United
   States, because it is a nation, had authority under international law to acquire territory by discovery and occupation and to exercise jurisdiction over it. *Jones* v.
   United States, 137 U.S. 202, 212 (1890). Compare STORY, (n. 3 to this chapter).
6. 299 U.S. 304 (1936). Sutherland had special interest and expertise in foreign
   relations. He had been United States Senator from the State of Utah and a
   member of the Senate Foreign Relations Committee, and had delivered lectures
   published as CONSTITUTIONAL POWERS AND WORLD AFFAIRS (1919). In 1909 he
   had written an article anticipating the distinction he later propounded: THE
   INTERNAL AND EXTERNAL POWERS OF THE NATIONAL GOVERNMENT, S.DOC.NO.
   417, 288, 61st Cong., 2d Sess. (1910). According to one writer, 'a careful check
   indicates that the whole theory [of *Curtiss-Wright*] and a great amount of its
   phraseology had become engraved on Mr. Sutherland's mind before he joined
   the Court, waiting for the opportunity to be made the law of the land. The

circumstances show that he had preformed opinions on the subject and that when he spoke in the *Curtiss-Wright* decision, he did little to reexamine his long cherished ideas.' Levitan, *The Foreign Relations Power: An Analysis of Mr. Justice Sutherland's Theory*, 55 YALE L.J. 467, 478 (1946). For Sutherland's sources, see n. 10 to this chapter.

7. 299 U.S. at 318.

8. In other cases it is not clear whether, according to my distinction, the Court is talking *Chinese Exclusion* or *Curtiss-Wright*: e.g.: 'As a nation with all the attributes of sovereignty, the United States is vested with all the powers of government necessary to maintain an effective control of international relations.' *Burnet* v. *Brooks*, 288 U.S. 378, 396 (1933). Or: 'But there may be powers implied, necessary or incidental to the expressed powers. As a government, the United States is invested with all the attributes of sovereignty. As it has the character of nationality it has the powers of nationality, especially those which concern its relations and intercourse with other countries.' *Mackenzie* v. *Hare*, 239 U.S. 299, 311 (1915). 'Federal authority to regulate aliens derives from various sources, including. . . its broad authority over foreign affairs.' *Toll* v. *Moreno*, 458 U.S. 1, 10 (1981). Compare *Legal Tender Cases*, 19 U.S. (12 Wall.) 457, 555 (1870) (concurring opinion, Bradley, J.), with *Perez* v. *Brownell*, 356 U.S. 44, 58 (1958), quoted in n. 16 to this chapter.

Sutherland's view need not depend on whether the Constitution was a compact among the states or among the people of the states. See *McCulloch* v. *Maryland*, 17 U.S. (4 Wheat.) 316, 403 (1819) (Marshall, C.J.). See also *Chisholm* v. *Georgia*, 2 U.S. (2 Dall.) 419, 471 (1793); *Martin* v. *Hunter's Lessee*, 14 U.S. (1 Wheat.) 304, 324–5 (1816).

9. See, e.g., Levitan, *The Foreign Relations Power: An Analysis of Mr. Justice Sutherland's Theory*, (n. 6 to this chapter); see also C. Lofgren, *The Foreign Relations Power: United States* v. *Curtiss-Wright Export Corporation: An Historical Reassessment*, in GOVERNMENT FROM REFLECTION AND CHOICE 167 (1986) (Sutherland's history is 'shockingly inaccurate'). And see n. 10 below.

10. For evidence and argument against Sutherland, see generally Van Tyne, *Sovereignty in the American Revolution: An Historical Study*, 12 AM. HIST. REV. 529 (1907). See also the array of views in C. BUTLER, THE TREATY-MAKING POWER OF THE UNITED STATES §§ 137–41 and §§ 142–3 (1902). Essentially, the case against Sutherland consists of Luther Martin's statement, FARRAND (n. 11 to this chapter) 323; also Justice Iredell in *Penhallow* v. *Doane*, 3 U.S. (3 Dall.) 54, 94 (1795), (n. 11 to this chapter), who might have granted that in war the Continental Congress 'stood, like Jove, amidst the deities of old, paramount, and supreme' (Paterson, J., *id.* at 81), but thought that Congress had power because the states had delegated it. Compare Justice Chase in *Ware* v. *Hylton*, 3 U.S. (3 Dall.) 199, 224, (1769) 231; also Marshall, C.J., in *Gibbons* v. *Ogden*, 22 U.S. (9 Wheat.) 1, 187 (1824); and the discussion of the nature of the Confederation in THE FEDERALIST No. 43 (Madison); also *Talbot* v. *The Commanders*, 1 U.S. (1 Dall.) 95, 99 (High Ct. of Err. and App., Pa. 1784); *People* v. *Gerke*, 5 Cal. 381, 385 (1855).

The language of the Declaration of Independence lends some support to the

330 Notes, Chapter I Constitutional Authority of the Federal Government

view that thirteen independent sovereign states were declared, and some states followed with individual declarations of their own independence. See also the assertions of sovereignty in early state constitutions, e.g., CONN. CONST. PREAMBLE (1776); MASS. CONST. part. I, art. IV (1780); N.H CONST. part I, art. VII (1784). The Articles of Confederation provided: 'each state retains its sovereignty, freedom and independence, and every Power, Jurisdiction and right, which is not by this confederation expressly delegated to the United States, in Congress assembled'. (Article II).

Some of the states appointed agents and negotiated with foreign countries for money and arms. See, e.g., Benjamin Franklin's complaint against their competition with his efforts, in a letter to the Congressional Committee of Foreign Affairs, dated May 26, 1779, quoted in 3 F. WHARTON, THE REVOLUTIONARY DIPLOMATIC CORRESPONDENCE OF THE UNITED STATES 192 (1889). (Apparently the practice did not stop with the adoption of the Articles of Confederation, though the Articles forbade the states, without the consent of Congress, to send or receive 'any embassy' (Art. VI).) Individual states did not, it seems, conclude treaties with foreign countries, but the treaties with France in 1778 were executed between 'The Most Christian King, and the thirteen United States of North America' (the word 'thirteen' is omitted from one of the treaties), each of them mentioned by name, and they were ratified by each of the states individually; in various respects the terms of the treaties seem to treat each of the thirteen as a separate sovereign. 1 W. MALLOY (ed.), TREATIES, CONVENTIONS, INTERNATIONAL ACTS, PROTOCOLS AND AGREEMENTS BETWEEN THE UNITED STATES OF AMERICA AND OTHER POWERS 1776–1909, S.DOC. NO. 357, 61st Cong., 2d Sess. at 468, 479 (1910). Later, the Continental Congress adopted a resolution to instruct its negotiators 'That these United States be considered in all such treaties, and in every case arising under them as one nation, upon the principles of the Federal constitution'. 3 SECRET JOURNALS OF CONGRESS 452, March 26, 1784. See J.G. Davis's notes to Samuel Miller's LECTURES ON THE CONSTITUTION OF THE UNITED STATES 53–4 (Davis ed. 1891); Davis's notes, at 36–58, were perhaps a source of Sutherland's theory; compare also 1 WILLOUGHBY (n. 3 to Ch. 1) 90, 514–16.

On the whole there is perhaps no disagreement that, under the Articles, the states retained no external sovereignty. It is not agreed whether the states had sovereignty before the Articles, whether after the Articles were concluded, the states could have gained (or regained) sovereignty at will, whether sovereignty passed directly from the United States under the Articles to the United States under the Constitution. On these questions, too, Sutherland may have the better of the argument, for from independence nationhood seems to have been the dominant pattern, and manifestations of state autonomy exceptional. Of course, the time at which the United States became one state in international society has had only historic interest after events and actions prior to 1789 ceased to raise issues, but in the recent past some states claimed that they had had sovereignty before the U.S. Constitution, as a basis for claiming title to sea-bed off their coasts. The Supreme Court rejected their claims in the *Maine* case, (n. 11 to this chapter). The early history may continue to be relevant for the resolution of claims to land or resources by Native Americans. See, e.g., *Oneida Indian Nation* v. *State of New York*, 860 F.2d 1145 (2d Cir. 1988), *cert. denied.*, 493 U.S. 871 (1989).

11. Farrand reports that at the Constitutional Convention James Wilson of Pennsylvania 'could not admit that when the colonies became independent of Great Britain they became independent also of each other'. He read the Declaration of Independence to mean that they became independent 'not *Individually* but *Unitedly*', and 'were confederated as they were independent'. 1 M. FARRAND, THE RECORDS OF THE CONVENTION OF 1787, at 324 (Rev. edn. 1966). Sutherland quotes King of Massachusetts: 'The States were not "sovereigns" in the sense contended for by some.' 299 U.S. at 317. See also Justice Paterson in *Penhallow* v. *Doane*, 3 U.S. (3 Dall.) 54, 81 (1795); *Chisholm* v. *Georgia*, 2 U.S. (2 Dall.) 419, 470 (1793). For other support for Sutherland's position, see Professor Richard Morris's testimony before a master in *United States* v. *Maine*, 420 U.S. 515 (1975). See also Morris, *The Forging of the Union Reconsidered: A Historical Refutation of State Sovereignty over Seabeds*, 74 COLUM. L. REV. 1056 (1974). Morris concludes that most of those who addressed the question at the Constitutional Convention, most of the early Justices of the Supreme Court, and the principal Founding Fathers, took the 'nationalist' view.

12. Compare Taney, C.J.: 'The states, by the adoption of the existing Constitution, have become divested of all their national attributes, except such as relate purely to their internal concerns.' *Holmes* v. *Jennison*, 39 U.S. (14 Pet.) 540, 550 (1840). Compare n. 16 to this chapter.

13. During the years between *The Chinese Exclusion Case* and *Curtiss-Wright*, the Court rejected claims of federal power inherent in sovereignty where foreign affairs were not at issue. See *Kansas* v. *Colorado*, 206 U.S. 46 (1907) (dismissing U.S. petition to intervene on ground it had inherent legislative authority to appropriate navigable waters). Compare *Ex parte Quirin*, 317 U.S. 1, 25 (1942) ('Congress and the President, like the courts, possess no power not derived from the Constitution.')

14. See, e.g., *Rodriguez-Fernandez* v. *Wilkinson*, 505 F. Supp. 787 (D. Kan. 1980), *aff'd*, 654 F.2d 1382, 1388 (10th Cir. 1981) (the appellate court affirmed, but on the basis of domestic law); note also the court's comments in *Jean* v. *Nelson*, 727 F.2d 957, 964 n. 4 (11th Cir. 1984), *aff'd*, 472 U.S. 846 (1985).

15. Earlier in our history, the people of the United States divided sharply on issues of national power, reflecting in part different views as to the sources of that power; certainly, the kind of opinion written, in some cases perhaps too the result, would have been different for different lawyers. Whether the United States could acquire the Philippines, for example, seemed to some at the time to depend on whether the powers of the United States derived exclusively from the Constitution and its enumerations or might be sought also in international law and practice. See, e.g., E. STAWOOD, A HISTORY OF THE PRESIDENCY: 1897–1916 (1916) n. 26.

16. Later restatements, however, tacitly avoid some of Sutherland's 'underpinnings'. In *Perez* v. *Brownell*, for example, the Court, by Justice Frankfurter,

said: 'The States that joined together to form a single Nation and to create, through the Constitution, a Federal Government to conduct the affairs of that Nation must be held to have granted that Government the powers indispensable to its functioning effectively in the company of sovereign nations.' 356 U.S. 44, 57 (1958), *overruled* in *Afroyim* v. *Rusk*, 387 U.S. 253 (1967). Neither the dissent in *Perez* nor the overruling majority in *Afroyim* questioned the *Curtiss-Wright* element in Frankfurter's opinion. Justice Jackson, concurring in *Youngstown Sheet & Tube Co.* v. *Sawyer,* referred to Sutherland's essay as 'dictum', 343 U.S. 579, 635–6 n.2 (1952). See n. 53 to Ch. III and pp. 70–72. In addition to citing *Curtiss-Wright* to support unenumerated federal powers in foreign affairs, the Court has cited, and others have quoted again and again, Sutherland's reference in that case to the President's 'very delicate, plenary and exclusive power. . . as the sole organ of the federal government in the field of international relations'. See Ch. II. The Court has also referred to a dictum in *Curtiss-Wright* that the Constitution has no force in a foreign country except in respect of U.S. citizens. See *Verdugo*, n. 87 to Ch. IX. In no case has the Supreme Court deemed it necessary to revisit Sutherland's theory; the theory has been recognized in appellate courts, perhaps grudgingly. See, e.g., *United States* v. *Glasser*, 750 F.2d 1197 (3rd Cir. 1984), *cert. denied*, 471 U.S. 1018 and 1068 (1985), and *Oneida Indian Nation*, 860 F.2d at 1160–1, n. 10 to this chapter. The principal uses of *Curtiss-Wright* are for some of its famous dicta or its rhetorical flourishes. See, e.g., *Perpich* v. *Dept. of Defense*, 496 U.S. 334, at n. 28 (1990); *Regan* v. *Wald*, 468 U.S. 222, 243 (1984); *Dames & Moore* v. *Regan*, 453 U.S. 654, 661 (1981).

17.   299 U.S. at 318, citing *Jones* v. *United States*, 137 U.S. 202, 212 (1890); *Fong Yue Ting* v. *United States*, 149 U.S. 698, 705 *et seq.* (1893); *B. Altman & Co.* v. *United States*, 224 U.S. 583, 600–1 (1912).

18.   *The Chinese Exclusion Case*, 130 U.S. 581 (1889); *United States* v. *Bowman*, 260 U.S. 94 (1922); compare *Burnet* v. *Brooks*, 288 U.S. 378 (1933).

19.   *Hines* v. *Davidowitz*, 312 U.S. 52 (1941); *Perez* v. *Brownell*, 356 U.S. 44 (1958), *overruled* in *Afroyim* v. *Rusk*, 387 U.S. 253 (1967); *Zemel* v. *Rusk*, 381 U.S. 1 (1965). See also *Haig* v. *Agee*, 453 U.S. 280 (1981).

20.   See nn. 6, 7 to Ch. III; nn. 42, 44 to Ch. VI.

21.   See *Banco Nacional de Cuba* v. *Sabbatino*, 376 U.S. 398 (1964), Chapter V, pp. 137–40.

   That the Court at one time thought executive power readily distinguishable from legislative power, see *Youngstown Sheet & Tube Co.* v. *Sawyer*, 343 U.S. 579 (1952), discussed in the Intro. to Pt II, and in Chapter IV. More recent cases illustrate the difficulty of arriving at agreed applications of the separation of powers among the branches. See n. 2 to Intro. to Part II.

NOTES, INTRODUCTION TO PART II, pp. 25 to 30

1. 299 U.S. 304, 316 (1936).
2. Separation of powers has been deeply imbedded in our constitutional culture, but during most of our constitutional life separation did not loom large in the jurisprudence of the Supreme Court. See Ch. IV. In the 1980s, the Supreme Court decided several major separation cases. *Bowsher* v. *Synar*, 478 U.S. 714 (1986) (Balanced Budget Act); *Morrison* v. *Olson*, 487 U.S. 654 (1988) (appointment of independent counsel); *Mistretta* v. *United States*, 488 U.S. 361 (1989) (sentencing guidelines); *Plaut* v. *Spendthrift Farms, Inc.*, 115 S.Ct. 1447 (1995); but only *INS* v. *Chadha*, 462 U.S. 919 (1983), invalidating the legislative veto, has had significant relevance to foreign affairs. The Supreme Court can often avoid questions as to respective powers of Congress and the President; by finding that President and Congress concurred, the Court had to consider only the powers of both together. See, e.g., *United States* v. *Curtiss-Wright Export Corp.*, 299 U.S. 304 (1936); *Ex parte Quirin*, 317 U.S. 1 (1942); *Hirabayashi* v. *United States*, 320 U.S. 81 (1943); *Chicago & Southern Air Lines* v. *Waterman S.S. Corp.*, 333 U.S. 103, 109–10, 112–14 (1948). See also *Dames & Moore* v. *Regan*, 453 U.S. 654 (1981); *Barclays Bank* v. *Franchise Tax Board of California*, 114 S.Ct. 2268, 2286 (1994). Some Justices would treat this subject as a nonjusticiable political question. See, e.g., Justice Rehnquist's opinion in *Goldwater* v. *Carter*, 444 U.S. 996 (1979). See Ch. V.
3. 'The doctrine of separation of powers was adopted by the Convention of 1787 not to promote efficiency but to preclude the exercise of arbitrary power. The purpose was not to avoid friction, but, by means of the inevitable friction incident to the distribution of the governmental powers among three departments, to save the people from autocracy.' Justice Brandeis dissenting in *Myers* v. *United States*, 272 U.S. 52, 293 (1926). See also Madison in THE FEDERALIST Nos. 47, 51. Compare Madison: '. . . if there is a principle in our constitution, indeed in any free Constitution, more sacred than another, it is that which separates the legislative, executive, and judicial powers'. 1 ANNALS OF CONG. 604 (1789); see also *id.*, at 516–17.

   Madison devoted one of the Federalist Papers to showing that 'unless these departments be so far connected and blended as to give each a constitutional control over the others, the degree of separation which the maxim requires, as essential to a free government, can never in practice be duly maintained'. THE FEDERALIST No. 48 at 308 (Madison). Compare: 'The actual art of governing under our Constitution does not and cannot conform to judicial definitions of the power of any of its branches based on isolated clauses or even single Articles torn from context. While the Constitution diffuses power the better to secure liberty, it also contemplates that practice will integrate the dispersed powers into a workable government. It enjoins upon its branches separateness but interdependence, autonomy but reciprocity.' Justice Jackson concurring in *Youngstown Sheet & Tube Co.* v. *Sawyer*, 343 U.S. 579, 635 (1952). Compare *Ex parte Grossman*, 267 U.S. 87, 119–20 (1925).

In THE FEDERALIST, Madison argued, *inter alia,* that the separation of powers provided better security for individual rights than would a Bill of Rights, and the Framers therefore did not think it necessary (or desirable) to include such a bill of rights in the Constitution. See THE FEDERALIST Nos. 47, 48, 51, 84. See Henkin, *The Idea of Rights in the U.S. Constitution,* in THE AGE OF RIGHTS (1990), ch. 7, pp. 109-14.

4. 'Congress and the President. . . possess no power not derived from the Constitution.' *Ex parte Quirin,* 317 U.S. 1, 25 (1942).

5. Works on the U.S. Constitution increasingly pay attention to the respective powers of Congress and President in foreign affairs. There seems to be more studies of the Presidency than of Congress, but views on the powers of Congress inevitably permeate writings on the Presidency, and vice-versa. For a survey of the President's powers in foreign affairs, with attention to selected issues, see E. CORWIN, THE PRESIDENT: OFFICE AND POWERS 1787–1984 (5th rev. edn. 1984), Ch. V; other chapters in that work are not irrelevant. Antecedents and early constitutional conceptions of the office are discussed in Corwin's Chapter I; see also CORWIN, THE PRESIDENT'S CONTROL OF FOREIGN RELATIONS (1917). Other works include L. FISHER, PRESIDENTIAL WAR POWER (1995); P. SHANE AND H. BRUFF, THE LAW OF PRESIDENTIAL POWER: CASES AND MATERIALS (1988); A. SOFAER, WAR, FOREIGN AFFAIRS AND CONSTITUTIONAL POWER: THE ORIGINS (1976) and successor volume by H.C. Cox (1984), covering 1829–1901. For works on Congress in foreign affairs, see J. SIBLEY, TO ADVISE AND CONSENT: THE UNITED STATES CONGRESS AND FOREIGN POLICY IN THE TWENTIETH CENTURY (1991); J. ROBINSON, CONGRESS AND FOREIGN POLICY-MAKING (Rev. edn. 1967); H. CARROLL, THE HOUSE OF REPRESENTATIVES AND FOREIGN AFFAIRS (1958); *Congress and Foreign Relations,* ANNALS OF THE AMERICAN ACADEMY OF POLITICAL AND SOCIAL SCIENCE (1953); R. DAHL, CONGRESS AND FOREIGN POLICY (1950). There are also specialized volumes, e.g., those on the Senate's part in treaty-making, cited in Ch. VII.

Scholarly writings on the conflicts and cooperation of the branches in foreign affairs include L. FISHER, CONSTITUTIONAL CONFLICTS BETWEEN CONGRESS AND THE PRESIDENT (1985); THE CONSTITUTION BETWEEN FRIENDS: CONGRESS, THE PRESIDENT AND THE LAW (1978); and PRESIDENT AND CONGRESS: POWER AND POLICY (1972); H. MANSFIELD, ED., CONGRESS AGAINST THE PRESIDENT (1975); PYLE AND PIOUS, THE PRESIDENT, CONGRESS AND THE CONSTITUTION (1984).

There are also writings on the respective powers of Congress and the President in respect of war powers and national security. See ELY, WAR AND RESPONSIBILITY (1993); H. KOH, THE NATIONAL SECURITY CONSTITUTION: SHARING POWER AFTER THE IRAN-CONTRA AFFAIR (1990); H. SHUMAN AND W. THOMAS, EDS., THE CONSTITUTION AND NATIONAL SECURITY (1990); F. WORMUTH AND E. FIRMAGE, TO CHAIN THE DOG OF WAR: THE WAR POWER OF CONGRESS IN HISTORY AND LAW (1986); E. KEYNES, UNDECLARED WAR: THE TWILIGHT ZONE OF CONSTITUTIONAL POWER (1982). Compare M. FOLEY, THE SILENCE OF CONSTITUTIONS (1989).

6. *Youngstown Sheet & Tube Co.* v. *Sawyer,* 343 U.S. 579 (1952). That, at least, was the view of Justice Black in an opinion for a majority of the Court, but

some of that majority seemed to go along on other grounds. Compare the concurring opinions of Frankfurter and Jackson, *id.* at 593, 634, discussed in n. 15 to Ch. IV.

That separation requires the branches to be 'forever separate and distinct' and forbids usurpation, see also *Springer* v. *Government of Philippine Islands,* 277 U.S. 189, 201–2 (1928); *cf. Kilbourn* v. *Thompson,* 103 U.S. 168, 182, 190–1 (1881). But compare Justice Holmes dissenting in *Springer,* at 209: 'The great ordinances of the Constitution do not establish and divide the fields of black and white. Even the more specific of them are found to terminate in a penumbra shading gradually from one extreme to the other.' See also the discussion in *Buckley* v. *Valeo,* 424 U.S. 1, 120–4 (1976). And see n. 3 to this introduction.

7. That acting together Congress and the President can exercise all federal powers, *cf. Hamilton* v. *Dillin,* 88 U.S. (21 Wall.) 73, 88 (1875); *Wilson* v. *Shaw,* 204 U.S. 24, 32 (1907). Acting together the President and Congress can do what neither can do alone—for example, make international agreements fully equivalent to a treaty. See Ch. VII, p. 215.

8. And that obtained even before the Articles. See, e.g., Justice Paterson in *Penhallow* v. *Doane,* 3 U.S. (3 Dall.) 54, 80 (1795).

9. ARTICLES OF CONFEDERATION, Arts. V, IX.

10. See Ch. I, n. 10. The 'retrograde from unity' and the inability of the Continental Congress to enforce its treaties are described in 1 BUTLER, THE TREATY POWER §§ 164, 165 (1902). Unhappiness with state disregard of treaties was repeatedly voiced at the Constitutional Convention (see 1 FARRAND (n. 11 to Ch. I) 164, 171, 316; 3 *id.* at 113, 548), and was a particular impetus to the explicit establishment of the supremacy of treaties. (Art. VI, sec. 2; see Ch. VII.)

11. See generally C. THACH, THE CREATION OF THE PRESIDENCY, 1775–1789 (1923).

NOTES, CHAPTER II. THE PRESIDENT, pp. 31 to 62

1. *United States* v. *Curtiss-Wright Export Corp.*, 299 U.S. 304, 320 (1936). Similar statements abound.
2. Writings on the power of the President are listed in n. 5 to the Intro. to Pt II.
3. For an early appeal to the President's conscience, compare *Marbury* v. *Madison*, 5 U.S. (1 Cranch) 137, 165–6 (1803).
4. On the Iran–Contra Affair, see SENATORS W. COHEN AND G. MITCHELL, MEN OF ZEAL (1988), and P. KORNBLUH AND M. BYRNE, THE IRAN-CONTRA SCANDAL (1993).
5. See Ch. VIII, p. 244. Compare the suggestion of Harlan, J., dissenting, in *The Pentagon Papers Case,* that the courts should give effect to classifications of documents if made by the Head of the Department. *New York Times Co.* v. *United States,* 403 U.S. 713, 757–8 (1971), n. 17 to Ch. IX.
6. T. ROOSEVELT, AN AUTOBIOGRAPHY 371–2 (Macmillan ed. 1913).
7. W. H. TAFT, OUR CHIEF MAGISTRATE AND HIS POWERS 143–7 (1916). See also 45 CONG.REC. 6067–9 (1910) (remarks of Senators Borah and Bacon), and 54 CONG.REC. 863–82 (1917) (remarks of Senator Work). But President Truman seemed to echo Theodore Roosevelt, in 2 MEMOIRS 472–3 (1956); he did not even suggest that he was limited by what Congress forbade him.

    An even more radical view of Presidential power, at least in time of war, was expressed by Franklin D. Roosevelt in his famous message demanding that Congress repeal a provision of the Emergency Price Control Act: 'I ask the Congress to take this action by the first of October. Inaction on your part by that date will leave me with an inescapable responsibility to the people of this country to see to it that the war effort is no longer imperiled by threat of economic chaos.

    In the event that the Congress should fail to act, and act adequately, I shall accept the responsibility, and I will act.

    The President has the powers, under the Constitution and under Congressional acts, to take measures necessary to avert a disaster which would interfere with the winning of the war.

    I have given the most thoughtful consideration to meeting this issue without further reference to the Congress. I have determined, however, on this vital matter to consult with Congress.

    The American people can be sure that I will use my powers with a full sense of my responsibility to the Constitution and to my country. The American people can also be sure that I shall not hesitate to use every power vested in me to accomplish the defeat of our enemies in any part of the world where our own safety demands such defeat.

    When the war is won, the powers under which I act automatically revert to the people—to whom they belong.' 88 CONG.REC. 7044 (1942), quoted and discussed in CORWIN, THE PRESIDENT (n. 5 to Intro. to Pt II) 285–7.
8. *Youngstown Sheet & Tube Co.* v. *Sawyer,* 343 U.S. 579 (1952). Justice Black's majority opinion held that seizing private property was an act of legislative

character and could not be done by the President on his own authority. But some of the Justices who constituted the majority, though they joined Justice Black's opinion, apparently considered that Congress had in fact tacitly forbidden the President to seize the steel mills. See n. 15 to Ch. IV.

9. Some of the arguments that follow are in WRIGHT (n. 3 to Ch. I) 146–50.

10. In his famous 'Pacificus' letter supporting Washington's power to proclaim neutrality. See 7 A. HAMILTON, WORKS 76, 81 (Hamilton ed. 1851).

The debate between 'Pacificus' and 'Helvidius' (Madison) is set forth and discussed in E. CORWIN, THE PRESIDENT'S CONTROL OF FOREIGN RELATIONS 8–27 (1917). He also reproduces there an early twentieth century replay, between Senator Spooner and Senator Bacon, *id.* at 169–204. See also 60 CONG.REC. 1417–21 (1906).

11. Montesquieu saw two different kinds of executive power: '*la puissance exécutrice des choses qui dépendent du droit des gens, et la puissance exécutrice de celles qui dépendent du droit civil*'. By the former, '*il fait la paix ou la guerre, envoit ou reçoit des ambassades, établit la sureté, prévient les invasions*'. MONTESQUIEU, DE L'ESPRIT DES LOIS, Livre XI, C. VI (Amable LeRoy, ed.) (Lyon, 1805). He, as well as Rousseau and Blackstone, saw foreign relations as properly the responsibility of the monarch. Compare W. BLACKSTONE, COMMENTARIES ON THE LAWS OF ENGLAND (1765) §§ 253–4. Locke spoke of the 'federative' power as distinct from the executive power but saw them as belonging in the same hands; THE SECOND TREATISE OF CIVIL GOVERNMENT, Chapter XII, §§ 143–8 (Gateway ed. 1968). Vattel, however, noted that some rulers are obliged to take the advice of a senate, or of the representatives of the nation. THE LAW OF NATIONS, Book II, Chapter XII; Book III, Chapter I; Book IV, Chapter II (Ingraham ed. 1883). Blackstone, Locke and Montesquieu are quoted in CORWIN, THE PRESIDENT 462–4. In THE FEDERALIST No. 75, at 450, Hamilton said that the power to make treaties seems 'to form a distinct department, and to belong, properly, neither to the legislative nor to the executive'.

Jefferson, too—hardly an exponent of expansive constitutional construction or of large Presidential power—wrote: 'The transaction of business with foreign nations is *Executive altogether.* It belongs, then, to the head of that department except as to such portions of it as are specially submitted to the Senate. *Exceptions are to be construed strictly.*' 5 T. JEFFERSON, WRITINGS 162 (Ford ed. 1852) (emphasis in original).

12. Hamilton continued:

'The enumeration ought therefore to be considered, as intended merely to specify the principal articles implied in the definition of executive power; leaving the rest to flow from the general grant of that power, interpreted in conformity with other parts of the Constitution, and with the principles of free government.

The general doctrine of our Constitution then is, that the *executive power* of the nation is vested in the President; subject only to the *exceptions* and *qualifications,* which are expressed in the instrument.' (Emphasis in original). 7 HAMILTON, WORKS 76, 81. See also J. Q. Adams in THE JUBILEE OF THE CONSTITUTION 70–1, 76 (1839).

Abraham Sofaer has suggested that the difference in language between Art. I and Art. II might be attributable to Gouveneur Morris's last-minute stylistic changes in the draft of the Constitution, some of which he made in order to try to attain objectives he favored without appearing to violate the Convention's agreements; Morris had unsuccessfully supported a broad grant of power to the President. See A. SOFAER, WAR, FOREIGN AFFAIRS AND CONSTITUTIONAL POWER: THE ORIGINS 37 (1976).

13. 6 J. MADISON, WRITINGS 138, 147–50 (Hunt ed. 1910). Madison insisted that under the Constitution foreign relations are legislative in character, pointing to the powers of Congress to regulate foreign commerce and declare war; even the treaty power, he said, is more legislative than executive. Compare Chapter III, p. 77 and Chapter VII, p. 176. Earlier, however, in 1789, in the House of Representatives, Madison had argued that the power to remove officials was 'in its nature' an 'executive power' belonging to the President. See I ANNALS OF CONG. 378–80, 461–4 (1789). Compare Chief Justice Taft in the *Myers* case below.

Madison's reply to Hamilton was apparently instigated by Jefferson. See 6 JEFFERSON, WRITINGS 38 (Ford ed. 1892.) Perhaps Jefferson was rejecting not Hamilton's reading of the 'executive Power' clause, which Jefferson also seemed to accept, but Hamilton's attempt to put so much power into it. Or perhaps Jefferson, like Madison (and indeed like Hamilton, in reverse) had changed his views. See generally CORWIN, THE PRESIDENT (n. 5 to Intro. to Pt II) 207–12.

For others opposing Hamilton's reading of the 'Executive Power' clause see the Senate debate, n. 10 to this chapter; and compare the statements of Webster and Calhoun quoted in CORWIN, THE PRESIDENT (n. 5 to Intro. to Pt. III) 367–8. Taft, who later, as Chief Justice, invoked 'Executive power' in *Myers,* had rejected it as a blanket grant of foreign affairs powers. See Taft, n. 7 to this chapter, at 73, 140, 144.

14. But compare the Court's finding that there is an inherent executive power to exclude aliens, n. 32 to this chapter. And see the discussion of Presidential power in *New York Times Co.* v. *United States,* 403 U.S. 713 (1971), for example in the opinion of Marshall J., concurring, *id.* at 740.

15. *Myers* v. *United States,* 272 U.S. 52, 128 (1926). But *cf.* Holmes, J., dissenting, *id.* at 177, and McReynolds, J., dissenting, *id.* at 178, 183. And see n. 21 to this chapter.

Compare *Kansas* v. *Colorado,* 206 U.S. 46, 81–2 (1907), where Justice Brewer based an argument similar to Hamilton's on the absence of the words 'herein granted' in Art. III, to support a broad judicial power.

16. *Youngstown Sheet & Tube Co.* v. *Sawyer,* 343 U.S. 579 (1952). Only Chief Justice Vinson dissenting says: 'The whole of the "executive power" is vested in the President', and speaks of '[t]his comprehensive grant of the executive power', *id.* at 681–2.

17. 343 U.S. at 641. See also Justice Douglas concurring, *id.* at 632. Compare Daniel Webster: 'It is true, that the Constitution declares that the executive power shall be vested in the President; but the first question which then arises is, *What is executive power?. . .* executive power is not a thing so well known, and so accurately defined, as that the written constitution of a limited government can be

supposed to have conferred it in the lump.' (emphasis in original). 7 WRITINGS AND SPEECHES 186 (Nat'l ed. 1903).

18. In the *Steel Seizure Case,* 343 U.S. at 634–5, Justice Jackson also said: 'A judge, like an executive adviser, may be surprised at the poverty of really useful and unambiguous authority applicable to concrete problems of executive power as they actually present themselves. Just what our forefathers did envision, or would have envisioned had they foreseen modern conditions, must be divined from materials almost as enigmatic as the dreams Joseph was called upon to interpret for Pharaoh. A century and a half of partisan debate and scholarly speculation yields no net result but only supplies more or less apt quotations from respected sources on each side of any question. They largely cancel each other. And the court decisions are indecisive because of the judicial practice of dealing with the largest questions in the most narrow way.' (Footnote omitted.)

Those who insist that foreign relations are primarily the responsibility of Congress (Ch. III, p. 76) might argue that when Congress has not acted to prohibit the President, the President acts by tacit delegation from Congress. Compare, for instance, the Supreme Court's opinion in *Dames & Moore* v. *Regan,* 453 U.S. 654 (1981): 'Crucial to our decision today is the conclusion that Congress has implicitly approved the practice of claim settlement by executive agreement.' *Id.,* at 680. Compare the argument that in some cases Congress silently authorizes the States to regulate commerce. See, e.g., *Southern Pacific Co.* v. *Arizona,* 325 U.S. 761, 768 (1945), citing Dowling, *Interstate Commerce and State Power,* 27 VA.L.REV. 1 (1940). But the latter argument developed because the Constitution gave Congress the power to regulate commerce, and tacit delegation by Congress could explain why States can do some things that are admittedly regulations of commerce. There may be instances where tacit delegation by Congress to the President is also a reasonable inference from circumstances (*cf. United States* v. *Midwest Oil Co.,* 236 U.S. 459 (1915)), but in general the President purports to act in foreign affairs on his own authority (not pursuant to delegated Congressional authority). In some cases, admittedly, his power is secondary to that of Congress and bows to it when conflict occurs. See Ch. IV, p. 96.

19. Marshall's statement in the House of Representatives, 10 ANNALS OF CONG. 613 (1800), has been repeatedly cited and invoked by the Supreme Court, e.g., in *United States* v. *Curtiss-Wright Export Corp.,* 299 U.S. 304, 319 (1936). Marshall was justifying an extradition to Great Britain of Jonathan Robbins, assumed to be a U.S. citizen; since a request for extradition involved 'a national demand made upon the nation' it could be made only on the President since he was the sole channel of communication. See generally, Wedgwood, *The Revolutionary Martyrdom of Jonathan Robbins,* 100 YALE L.J. 229 (1990).

Compare Jefferson's letter to the French Minister Genêt: '[The President] being the only channel of communication between this country and foreign nations, it is from him alone that foreign nations or their agents are to learn what is or has been the will of the nation; and whatever he communicates as such, they have a right, and are bound to consider as the expression of the nation, and no foreign agent can be allowed to question it.' 6 T. JEFFERSON, WRITINGS 51 (Ford ed. 1895).

Literally, at least, and in context, both Marshall and Jefferson spoke of the President only as the sole organ of communication and did not imply any power to make foreign policy. Substantive power was later read into the phrase, e.g., by Sutherland in *Curtiss-Wright*, 299 U.S. at 319–21. Earlier, in justifying the President's treaty-making role, Hamilton had referred to 'the constitutional agency of the President in the conduct of foreign negotiations'. THE FEDERALIST No. 75, at 451.

20. Even from Congress, see Ch. IV. On the right to withhold from the public, see *The Pentagon Papers Case*, n. 17 to Ch. IX. The authority of the President over his department of foreign affairs was recognized by the first Congress: 'That there shall be an Executive department, to be denominated the Department of Foreign Affairs, and that there shall be a principal officer therein, to be called the Secretary for the Department of Foreign Affairs, who shall perform and execute such duties as shall from time to time be enjoined on or intrusted to him by the President of the United States, agreeable to the Constitution, relative to correspondences, commissions or instructions to or with public ministers or consuls, from the United States, or to negotiations with public ministers from foreign states or princes, or to memorials or other applications from foreign public ministers or other foreigners, or to such other matters respecting foreign affairs, as the President of the United States shall assign to the said department; and furthermore, that the said principal officer shall conduct the business of the said department in such manner as the President of the United States shall from time to time order or instruct.' Act of July 27, 1789, 1 Stat. 28–9.

    Congress also supported the President's monopoly on communications by the early 'Logan Act'. See n. 16 to Ch. IX. See Warren, *Memorandum on the History and Scope of the Laws Prohibiting Correspondence with a Foreign Government*, S.Doc.No. 696, 64th Cong., 2d Sess. (1917), and CORWIN, THE PRESIDENT (n. 5 to Intro. to Pt. II) 213–14 and notes.

21. And Congress could not constitutionally ordain otherwise, *Myers* v. *United States*, 272 U.S. 52 (1926). 'There are some "purely executive" officials who must be removable by the President at will if he is to be able to accomplish his constitutional role.' *Morrison* v. *Olson*, 487 U.S. 654, 690 (1988). Andrew Johnson invited impeachment and was nearly convicted when he removed his Secretary of War Stanton in the face of the Tenure of Office Act of 1867. See CORWIN, THE PRESIDENT (n. 5 to Intro. to Pt. II) 70–2 and notes. The Supreme Court in *Myers* expressly upheld President Johnson, 272 U.S. at 164–76. *Myers* has not been followed as to an appointee to an office that is not 'purely executive', 'who occupies no place in the executive department and who exercises no part of the executive power vested by the Constitution in the President'. *Humphrey's Executor* v. *United States*, 295 U.S. 602, 627–8 (1935); *Wiener* v. *United States*, 357 U.S. 349 (1958). See Ch. IV, p. 122.

22. Attorneys General early upheld the President's power to appoint special agents without Senate confirmation. See, e.g., 1 OP. ATT'Y GEN. 65, 186, 204–6, 212–13 (1855). During the first century of the nation's existence more than 400 Presidential agents were appointed. S.Doc.No. 231, 56th Cong., 2d Sess., part

8, at 337–62 (1901); H.R.Doc.No. 387, 66th Cong., 1st Sess., part 2, at 5 (1919). The Senate has sometimes denied the President's power to appoint persons to negotiate agreements or carry on diplomatic negotiations without having them confirmed by the Senate. See n. 30 to Ch. VII. Presidential agents are often paid out of the President's 'contingency fund' for which he does not have to account—see 31 U.S.C. §§ 716, 3526 (1983 and Supp. 1995). See, generally, Wriston, *The Special Envoy,* 38 FOREIGN AFFAIRS 219 (1960); H. WRISTON, EXECUTIVE AGENTS IN AMERICAN FOREIGN RELATIONS (1929).

23. U.S.CONST. Art. II, sec. 3. That includes 'all possible diplomatic agents which any foreign power may accredit to the United States'. 7 OP.ATT'Y GEN. 209 (1871). Compare *In re Baiz,* 135 U.S. 403, 431–2 (1890).

24. That was Madison's view in his 'Helvidius' letter, n. 10 to this chapter. See Ch. III, p. 77. But President Truman is reported to have said, 'I make American Foreign Policy'. L. KOENIG, THE CHIEF EXECUTIVE 211 (1964). Richard Nixon is quoted as referring to the President as 'The Sovereign'; see the footnote on p. 34, this chapter.

25. On several occasions in the past, Congress pretended to share in the power of recognition, to force the President's hand, even to exercise it independently; but it was claiming a concurrent power, not denying it to the President. Today Congress recognizes the President's sole and exclusive authority in these matters. See Ch. IV, p. 88.

26. Traditional international law required neutrality of those who sought the benefits of that status, but a nation could lawfully decide to become a belligerent.

    That the President had authority to recognize belligerency, see, e.g., Secretary of State John Quincy Adams quoted in Wright, *The Power to Declare Neutrality Under American Law,* 34 AM.J.INT'L L. 302, 308 (1940). See *The Prize Cases,* 67 U.S. (2 Black) 635, 670 (1862) (President can impose a status of belligerency on those who attack the United States); *cf. United States v. Palmer,* 16 U.S. (3 Wheat.) 610, 643 (1818). Members of Congress differed on the President's authority, some denying it because such recognition had commercial and other domestic consequences. See, e.g., 28 CONG.REC. 2121; for the opposite view, see *id.* at 2164. Some thought that the power to recognize belligerency or the independence of foreign nations is a 'joint power'. *Id.* at 3078. See also Hale, *Power to Recognize the Independence of a New Foreign State,* S.Doc.No. 56, 54th Cong., 2d Sess. 28 (1897).

    The laws of neutrality and belligerency have been modified, if not superseded, by the UN Charter outlawing war. See Ch. VIII.

27. Washington ordered prosecutions for transgressions of neutrality as violations of international law. 11 Stat. 753 (App.1859), 1 MESSAGES AND PAPERS OF THE PRESIDENTS 148–9 (Richardson ed. 1897). The word 'neutrality' was ultimately omitted from Washington's proclamation as a concession to Jefferson. See Letter to James Madison, June 23, 1793, 6 T. JEFFERSON, WRITINGS 315–16 (Ford ed. 1895). The Act of 1794 can be seen as domestic legislation implementing and effectively ratifying Washington's neutrality proclamation, but later Presidents eschewed declaring neutrality on their own authority and

Congress has since both declared and implemented neutrality. See Ch. III, p. 76.

That F. D. Roosevelt deviated from Congressional neutrality policy, see CORWIN, THE PRESIDENT (n. 5 to Intro. to Pt. II) 232–4, 273–4. Compare his decision to send troops to Greenland and Iceland, apparently in the face of legislation forbidding it. See Chapter IV, p. 100.

Some might find in the *Curtiss-Wright* case an implication that the President might have imposed an arms embargo on his own authority, but he could not have imposed criminal penalties for its violation. See Ch. IV, p. 89.

28. For the Truman Proclamation, see Presidential Proclamation No. 2667, Sept. 28, 1945, 10 FED. REG. 12303 (1945); for the Reagan Proclamation on the Exclusive Economic Zone, see 19 WEEKLY COMPILATION OF PRESIDENTIAL DOCUMENTS 383 (1983), 22 I.L.M. 464 (1983). The President can act to acquire territory for the United States under international law, but he probably cannot, on his own authority, incorporate such territory into the United States. See n. 35 to Ch. III; Ch. IV, p. 104.

29. 'That the President's control of foreign relations includes the settlement of claims is indisputable.' Frankfurter, J., concurring in *United States* v. *Pink*, 315 U.S. 203, 240 (1942). Compare the majority opinion, *id.* at 229. See also the agreement settling the Iran Hostages controversy, upheld in *Dames & Moore* v. *Regan*, 453 U.S. 654 (1981). The President, however, probably cannot dispose of United States property without authority from Congress. See Chapter IV, p. 89, and compare Chapter VII, p. 219.

The President accounts to other nations for the treatment of their nationals in the United States, but the protection of aliens in fact depends largely on the judiciary and on the states. See 1 OP. ATT'Y GEN. 25 (1792); 3 OP. ATT'Y GEN. 253 (1837).

30. But the Supreme Court has denied the President power to extradite on his own authority, Ch. IV, p. 90. An Attorney General rendered the opinion that in the absence of treaty the President could extend to the German Government the privilege of taking the testimony of prisoners in federal prisons but not in state prisons. 17 OP.ATT'Y GEN. 565 (1883).

Presidential responses to foreign overtures often can be seen as involving informal executive agreements. Compare Ch. VII, p. 228.

31. Compare *Tucker* v. *Alexandroff*, 183 U.S. 424, 435 (1902): 'While no act of Congress authorizes the executive department to permit the introduction of foreign troops, the power to give such permission without legislative assent was probably assumed to exist from the authority of the President as Commander-in-Chief of the military and armed forces of the United States.'

An Attorney General ruled that the President could admit British flying students and authorize their instruction at United States Army Air Corps training centers. 40 OP.ATT'Y GEN. 58 (1941).

32. In upholding a broad delegation to the President of power to exclude aliens, the Supreme Court said: 'The exclusion of aliens is a fundamental act of sovereignty. The right to do so stems not alone from legislative power but is inherent in the executive power to control the foreign affairs of the nation. When

Congress prescribes a procedure concerning the admissibility of aliens, it is not dealing alone with a legislative power. It is implementing an inherent executive power.' *United States ex rel. Knauff* v. *Shaughnessy*, 338 U.S. 537, 542 (1950). Later the Court reiterated that 'the power of exclusion of aliens is also inherent in the executive department of the sovereign'. *Id.* at 543. The Court seemed to say not merely that the Executive can bar aliens whose entry is unauthorized by law, but that the policy, the 'law' to exclude aliens, can be made by the President alone, at least when Congress has not legislated otherwise. Admission, especially for extended sojourn, might be a legislative responsibility, but President Carter admitted many thousand Cuban refugees as part of the Mariel boatlift in 1980, citing his responsibility as President to administer the law of the United States fairly and humanely. 16 WEEKLY COMPILATION OF PRESIDENTIAL DOCUMENTS 834, May 5, 1980. Presumably he saw his authority in conjunction with Congressional law on refugees. See also *Sale* v. *Haitian Centers Council*, 113 S.Ct. 3028 (1993), Chapter IX, note 91.

33. See 22 OP.ATT'Y GEN. 13 (1898); 30 OP.ATT'Y GEN. 217, 221 (1913). See also CORWIN, THE PRESIDENT (n. 5 to Intro. to Pt. II) 226–7 and notes. Congress later gave the President authority to license and regulate cables, ch. 12, 42 Stat. 8 (1921), *as amended,* 47 U.S.C. §§ 34–9 (1994).

Congress has enacted comprehensive legislation giving the President large authority as regards the certification of carriers for foreign air transportation. The Supreme Court said: 'Congress may of course delegate very large grants of its power over foreign commerce to the President. The President also possesses in his own right certain powers conferred by the Constitution on him as Commander-in-Chief and as the Nation's organ in foreign affairs. For present purposes the [President's] order draws vitality from either *or both sources.* Legislative and Executive powers are pooled obviously to the end that commercial strategic and diplomatic interests of the country may be coordinated and advanced without collision or deadlock between agencies.' *Chicago & Southern Air Lines, Inc.* v. *Waterman S.S. Corp.*, 333 U.S. 103, 109–10 (1948); also *id.* at 111.

34. Writing in 1908, Professor Woodrow Wilson, generally a supporter of Congressional power, said: 'One of the President's powers is his control, which is very absolute, of the foreign relations of the nation.' W. WILSON, CONSTITUTIONAL GOVERNMENT IN THE UNITED STATES 77–8 (1908).

35. THE FEDERALIST NO. 69 at 418 (Hamilton). Later, however, Hamilton castigated President Jefferson for insisting that he 'was unauthorized by the Constitution, without the sanction of Congress, to go beyond the line of *Defense* against the Barbary States'. Compare Jefferson in 1 RICHARDSON (n. 27 to Ch. II) 326, with 7 A. HAMILTON, WORKS 745–8 (Hamilton ed. 1851). In *The Prize Cases,* 67 U.S. (2 Black) 635, 668 (1862), the Supreme Court supported Hamilton. See WRIGHT 2 (n. 3 to Ch. I) 286–9.

36. In 1863, Lincoln promulgated the rules of the Lieber Commission, in General Orders No. 100, reprinted in 3 THE WAR OF THE REBELLION: A COMPILATION OF THE OFFICIAL RECORDS OF THE UNION AND CONFEDERATE ARMIES, Ser. III (Scott ed. 1901).

'The power of the executive to establish rules and regulations for the government of the army is undoubted.' *United States* v. *Eliason*, 41 U.S. (16 Pet.) 291, 301 (1842). In that case, however, the President had established regulations pursuant to an act of Congress. *Cf. Smith* v. *Whitney*, 116 U.S. 167, 180–1 (1886). But see *Kurtz* v. *Moffitt*, 115 U.S. 487, 503 (1885), where the Court gave effect to regulations providing rewards for apprehension of deserters, promulgated on the President's own authority.

37. Lincoln, then, could also plausibly rely on his authority to take care that the Constitution and the laws of the United States be faithfully executed. He acted also in warranted expectation that Congress would ratify what he did. Some of Lincoln's acts might afford a precedent for Presidential authority in foreign wars as well, e.g., closing the post offices to treasonable mail, taking money from the treasury, enlarging the Army. See Corwin, The President (n. 5 to Intro. to Pt. II) 266 and notes. For important initiatives by F.D.R. during the Second World War, see *id.*, at 277 *et seq.* See generally, L. Fisher, Presidential War Power (1995).

38. See *Fleming* v. *Page*, 50 U.S. (9 How.) 603, 615 (1850). See also *Mitchell* v. *Harmony*, 54 U.S. (13 How.) 115 (1851); *United States* v. *Russell*, 80 U.S. (13 Wall.) 623 (1871); *Totten* v. *United States*, 92 U.S. 105 (1875); *In re Yamashita*, 327 U.S. 1 (1946). See Wright (n. 3 to Ch. I) 196. But *cf. Brown* v. *United States*, 12 U.S. (8 Cranch) 110 (1814). During the Second World War the Supreme Court avoided examining the reach of the President's powers as Commander in Chief in time of war, finding in each case that there had been Congressional authorization or approval. See, e.g., *Hirabayashi* v. *United States*, 320 U.S. 81, 92 (1943); *Ex parte Quirin*, 317 U.S. 1, 29 (1942).

39. Without according them the constitutional protections enjoyed by the accused in criminal proceedings in the United States, and even where Congress provided an alternative means of trial by court-martial. *Madsen* v. *Kinsella*, 343 U.S. 341 (1952). See also *Cross* v. *Harrison*, 57 U.S. (16 How.) 164 (1853); *Dooley* v. *United States*, 182 U.S. 222 (1901); *Santiago* v. *Nogueras*, 214 U.S. 260 (1909). But compare the later cases limiting court-martials in time of peace, n. 44 to Ch. III.

40. That was clearly contemplated by the Framers (see n. 64 to Ch. III), and has been repeatedly done by Presidents since the beginning. 'If a war be made by invasion of a foreign nation, the President is not only authorized but bound to resist force by force.' *The Prize Cases*, 67 U.S. (2 Black) 635, 668 (1862). The Supreme Court has held that 'the authority to decide whether the exigency has arisen belongs exclusively to the President, and . . . his decision is conclusive upon all other persons'. *Martin* v. *Mott*, 25 U.S. (12 Wheat.) 19, 30 (1827). See also *The Prize Cases*, above at 670. No doubt the consent of Congress to go to war in the event of invasion or attack could be assumed. In 1795, Congress expressly authorized the President to call forth the militia whenever 'the United States shall be invaded, or be in imminent danger of invasion'. 1 Stat. 424.

It has been suggested that the President can go to war also in the case of an attack on an ally, but that would not appear to be within this exception to Congressional power as originally conceived. Congress did not recognize such power in its restatement of the President's authority in the War Powers Resolution, 50 U.S.C.A. § 1541(c) (1988). See Ch. IV. In such a case the President might claim to be acting pursuant to the treaty of alliance, but such treaties have usually provided for United States action in accordance with constitutional procedures, apparently contemplating recourse to Congress for a declaration of war. See Ch. VII, p. 201, and Ch. VIII, p. 260.

41. See *The Prize Cases*, 67 U.S. (2 Black) 635, 668 (1862). President Wilson even claimed the right to strike deep in Mexico. See CORWIN, THE PRESIDENT (n. 5 to Intro. to Pt. II) 450.

42. See n. 198 to Ch. VII and n. 26 to Ch. IV; Ch. IV, p. 100.

43. See 30 OP.ATT'Y GEN. 291 (1914), justifying the closing of the Marconi station under both the foreign affairs and Commander in Chief powers, to implement U.S. neutrality under international law. Corwin suggests that there was authority for Wilson's act in a Congressional statute, Pub.L.No.264, ch. 287, 37 Stat. 302 (1912), but Attorney General Gregory did not rely on it. See CORWIN, THE PRESIDENT (n. 5 to Intro. to Pt. II) 227. Today the action would raise serious questions under the First Amendment. See Ch. IX.

44. Wilson said he had the power to arm U.S. merchant vessels in defense against German submarines but wished to have Congressional support. When a proposed Congressional resolution died in a Senate filibuster, Wilson proceeded on his own authority. See E. CORWIN, THE PRESIDENT'S CONTROL OF FOREIGN RELATIONS 152–6 (1917); WRIGHT (n. 3 to Ch. I) 294–6. Wright thought Wilson had authority also under existing legislation.

45. The numbers vary widely depending on the principle of inclusion. See 137 CONG. REC. 130–5, daily edn. Jan. 10, 1991.

46. In numerous instances Presidents sought and obtained Congressional approval; in some there was later ratification. See *Background Information on the Use of United States Armed Forces in Foreign Countries,* 1970 Revision by the Foreign Affairs Division, Legislative Reference Service, Library of Congress, for the Subcommittee on National Security Policy and Scientific Development of the House Committee on Foreign Affairs, 91st Cong. 2nd Sess. 15 *et seq.* and Appendices I and II, at 32–7; CORWIN, THE PRESIDENT (n. 5 to Intro. to Pt. II) 253–4; WRIGHT (n. 3 to Ch. I) 293–9; and see Ch. IV, p. 97.

47. Jackson, J., concurring in the *Steel Seizure Case,* agreed that 'Commander in Chief' is 'something more than an empty title' but expressly rejected the suggestion that it vests the President with 'power to do anything, anywhere, that can be done with an army or navy'. 343 U.S. 579, 641–2 (1952). But compare W. H. TAFT, OUR CHIEF MAGISTRATE AND HIS POWERS 94–5 (1916): 'The President is the Commander-in-Chief of the army and navy, and the militia when called into the service of the United States. Under this, he can order the army and navy anywhere he will, if the appropriations furnish the means of transportation.'

That the power to wage war is given to Congress provides one limitation on the President's use of the armed forces, but some argue that that is the only limitation, and that the President can use the troops 'short of war'. See Ch. IV, p. 99.

There have been small constitutional issues about the President's use of the militia. Art. I, sec. 8, cl. 15, gives to Congress the power 'to provide for calling forth the Militia to execute the Laws of the Union, suppress Insurrections and repel Invasions', and Art. II, sec. 2 makes the President Commander in Chief of the militia 'when called into the actual Service of the United States'. Even after the militia was organized into the National Guard and was made available for service outside the United States, the Attorney General expressed the opinion that the President could send the state militia outside the United States only when necessary to repel invasion. 29 OP.ATT'Y GEN. 322 (1912). Later, Congress provided that the militia could be 'federalized' and automatically transformed from state militia into national forces; Presidents, then, could use them abroad for other purposes. *Cf.* Selective Draft Law Cases, 245 U.S. 366 (1918); *Cox* v. *Wood*, 247 U.S. 3 (1918). See Perpich, n. 16 to Ch. III. Compare the discussion as to whether the United States could agree to abolish the state militia by a disarmament treaty, Ch. VII, p. 193.

48. So long as he stays short of war, see Ch. IV, p. 99. Compare Secretary of State Acheson: 'Not only has the President the authority to use the armed forces in carrying out the broad foreign policy of the United States and implementing treaties, but it is equally clear that this authority may not be interfered with by the Congress in the exercise of powers which it has under the Constitution.' 'Assignment of Ground Forces of the United States to Duty in the European Area', *Hearings by Sen. Comm. on Foreign Relations and Armed Services*, 82d Cong., 1st Sess. 92–3 (1951). But see SEN. COMM. ON FOREIGN RELATIONS, WAR POWERS, S.REP.NO.606, 92d Cong. 2d Sess. (1972).

49. The power to use force to protect citizens abroad was recognized in *Durand* v. *Hollins*, 8 F.Cas. 111, No. 4186 (C.C.S.D.N.Y. 1869); see also *In re Neagle*, 135 U.S. 1 (1890), n. 54 to this chapter. See CORWIN, THE PRESIDENT (n. 5 to Intro. to Pt. II) 224–34 and notes. The right to protection abroad has been said to be one of the privileges and immunities of citizens of the United States. *Slaughter-House Cases*, 83 U.S. (16 Wall.) 36, 79 (1872). In 1975, President Ford asserted authority to deploy U.S. forces to rescue U.S. nationals from Saigon immediately before its fall.

In early days, the United States Navy was often used for *ad hoc* foreign policy purposes including the ferrying of American diplomats, as in nineteenth century China.

50. Doubts about Presidential authority to extradite pursuant to treaty without Congressional authorization (see, e.g., Catron J., in *In re* Kaine, 55 U.S. (14 How.) 103, 112 (1852)), have long been resolved: see *Valentine* v. *United States ex rel. Neidecker*, 299 U.S. 5 (1936); *Fong Yue Ting* v. *United States*, 149 U.S. 698, 714 (1893); *cf. United States* v. *Robbins*, 27 F.Cas. 825, No. 16,175 (D.C.S.C. 1799), and John Marshall's statement in the House of Representatives, n. 19 to this chapter. The President probably had authority pursuant to treaty (even without Congressional authorization) to return deserting seaman, but not, it has been said, in the absence of treaty. See n. 13 to Ch. IV. Treaties on that subject were terminated and are no longer made. Ch. 153, 38 Stat. 1164, 1184 (1915). See WRIGHT (n. 3 to Ch. I) 195.

Story is reported to have said that the President did not have authority to carry out awards of foreign consuls based on treaty in the absence of Congressional legislation. See 2 J. B. MOORE, DIGEST OF INTERNATIONAL LAW 298; 5 *id.* 223. It is unlikely that this view would be followed today, but the question is academic since Congress has enacted legislation giving the courts authority to enforce such awards. See 22 U.S.C. § 258a (1994). Compare n. 32 to Ch. VIII.

51. See WRIGHT (n. 3 to Ch. I) 192–4, 296.
52. See, e.g., 1 OP.ATT'Y GEN. 560, 566, 570–1 (1822); S.EXEC.DOC.NO. 123, 26th Cong., 2d Sess. 379, 384, 853, 1288, cited in CORWIN, THE PRESIDENT (n. 5 to Intro. to Pt. II) 483.
53. See *Ex parte Toscano*, 208 F. 938 (D.Cal.1913). As to neutrality, see also n. 27 to this chapter, and WRIGHT (n. 3 to Ch. I) 196.
54. Compare State Department Solicitor J. R. CLARK, RIGHT TO PROTECT CITIZENS IN FOREIGN COUNTRIES BY LANDING FORCES 44–8 (3d rev. edn. 1934); Wright, *Constitutional Procedure in the United States for Carrying Out Obligations for Military Sanctions,* 38 AM.J.INT'L L. 678, 680, 684 (1944); Mathews, *The Constitutional Power of the President to Conclude International Agreements,* 64 YALE L.J. 345, 360 n. 88, 365 n. 107, 367 and nn. 115, 118–20 (1955). Writers have not distinguished between (a) authority to carry out the obligations of the United States under treaty or customary law (which can plausibly be found in the 'take care' clause); (b) authority to exercise rights reserved to the United States by international law or given it by treaty; and (c) authority to compel other states to carry out their international obligations to the United States.

Sometimes cited is Mr. Justice Miller in *In re Neagle*, 135 U.S. 1 (1890). Neagle, a United States deputy marshall detailed to act as bodyguard for Justice Field, was charged with killing an assailant. He sought habeas corpus under a statute authorizing the writ for persons detained 'for an act done or committed in pursuance of a law of the United States'. The Court held that although he was appointed on the authority of the Executive without statutory authorization, Neagle's act was committed 'in pursuance of a law of the United States'. Speaking of the 'take care' clause, Mr. Justice Miller asked, rhetorically (at 64): 'Is this duty limited to the enforcement of acts of Congress or of treaties of the United States according to their *express* terms, or does it include the rights, duties and obligations growing out of the Constitution itself, our international relations, and all the protection implied by the nature of the government under the Constitution?' (Emphasis in original.)

The suggestion that the President's power to execute the laws embraces also 'the rights. . . growing out of. . . our international relations' was of course dictum. Miller did proceed to narrate how the Secretary of State intervened to obtain the release from foreign internment of Martin Koszta who had declared his intention to become a U.S. citizen, and the Justice's opinion seems to imply that diplomatic protection as in that case was in exercise of the 'take care' clause. But Miller did not say that in such crises the President 'executes' international law; more likely he had in mind that diplomatic protection was one of the privileges of U.S. citizenship and it is that 'law' which the President was executing. See n. 49 to this chapter. And Congress had expressly authorized the use of any means 'not amounting to acts of war' to obtain the release of U.S. citizens unjustly detained. Expatriation Act of July 27, 1868, ch. 249, 15 Stat. 223, 224. Surely nothing in Miller's opinion implies that the 'take care' clause would support the use of force against other kinds of violations of international law abroad by foreign states. (Compare Lamar, J., dissenting, 135 U.S. at 85, who seemed to derive the power to intervene by threat of force on behalf of Martin Koszta in that 'the Constitution. . . expressly commits all matters pertaining to our diplomatic negotiations to the treaty-making power'.)

55. Jefferson's use of force against the Barbary Pirates is often cited as an exercise of the President's power to see that international law is faithfully executed. International law gave the United States the right to act against pirates, a right which the President could exercise; but it seems strained to say that the President was exercising authority to see that the pirates complied with international law. Compare nn. 21, 25 to Ch. III. Apart from authority under his foreign affairs powers and as Commander in Chief, he apparently had authority from Congress and was therefore executing U.S. law. See 2 Stat. 129 (1802).

56. Compare 29 OP.ATT'Y GEN. 322 (1912). Madison wrote about the President's power of 'executing the *national* laws' (emphasis added). 1 J. MADISON, THE CONSTITUTIONAL CONVENTION OF 1787, at 52–3 (Hunt ed. 1908). The President has no constitutional authority to execute the laws of the States or of any foreign government.

57. See, e.g., *The Paquete Habana*, 175 U.S. 677 (1900); *Berizzi Bros. Co. v. The Pesaro*, 271 U.S. 562 (1926). Under international law the United States can prescribe law also for persons abroad who are not U.S. nationals but only under the 'protective principle', i.e., in special circumstances to protect state interests, e.g., to punish espionage or counterfeiting of U.S. currency, and perhaps also in selected cases subject to 'universal jurisdiction', e.g., piracy or 'war crimes'. See generally 1 L. OPPENHEIM, INTERNATIONAL LAW § 139 (Jennings and Watts, 9th edn. 1992); RESTATEMENT (n. 2 to Preface) §§ 402(3), 404.

Lincoln indeed built his war powers during the Civil War on the 'take care' clause combined with his authority as Commander in Chief, but, since no right to secede was recognized, he was seeking to enforce not international law but the Constitution and laws of the United States, within the United States, against inhabitants of the United States.

58. William Howard Taft, when Secretary of War to President Theodore Roosevelt, urged that the 'take care' clause authorized the President to intervene to maintain order in Cuba, because in the Platt Amendment to the treaty with Cuba the Cuban government had consented to such intervention. See W. H. TAFT, OUR CHIEF MAGISTRATE AND HIS POWERS 85–8 (1938). Compare his view that the President had authority to govern in the Panama Canal Zone pursuant to treaty when Congress failed to provide for such government. *Id.* at 83–5. In that instance, Congress having authorized the building of the Canal, and government in the Zone being necessary to that end, the President's authority to govern can be said to derive from his responsibility to execute the act of Congress. Congress, moreover, knew and acquiesced and later ratified.

The rights of the United States under international law include all that is not forbidden to it by customary law or treaty, (*cf. The S.S. 'Lotus'*, [1927] P.C.I.J., ser. A, No. 9, in 2 M. HUDSON, WORLD COURT REPORTS 20 (1935)), constituting, then, the mass of actions and policies of the United States that make up or impinge on its foreign relations. These indeed are largely within the President's foreign affairs authority, but they hardly seem to be within his responsibility to see that the law, even international law, is faithfully executed. Rights granted the United States by treaty are also perhaps in the President's discretion to exercise under his foreign affairs power but these too do not seem to be law that he is to see 'faithfully executed'. The President probably has authority also to further national policy established in treaties of the United States, but, again, it does not seem plausible to say that in such cases he is 'faithfully executing' the law of the United States, though there, as when he is given discretion (not directive) by Congress, he may be said to be exercising 'executive' power.

59. Omnibus Crime Control and Safe Streets Act of 1968, codified at 18 U.S.C. §2511(3), repealed by Pub.L.No. 95–511, § 201(c) (1978), discussed in *United States v. United States District Court*, 407 U.S. 297, 313 (1972). The quoted statement may be read to imply some delegation of authority to the President by Congress, but it was couched as a constitutional judgment, not a legislative grant.

60. *Home Building & Loan Assn.* v. *Blaisdell*, 290 U.S. 398, 425 (1934).

61. See, e.g., *United States* v. *United States District Court*, n. 59 above. The Court held that the President cannot authorize electronic surveillance of private persons for 'national security' in the face of the Fourth Amendment. The Court refrained from deciding whether the President could exercise surveillance over foreign governments and their agents without a judicial warrant, but no one seemed to doubt that the President had authority to conduct such surveillance subject to warrant. Congress has delegated but also restricted and regulated Presidential power in the International Emergency Economic Powers Act of 1977. 50 U.S.C. §§ 1701–06 (1988 & Supp. V 1993), and the Foreign Intelligence Surveillance Act of 1978, 50 U.S.C. §§ 1801 *et seq.* (1988). And see Ch. IX.

62. The United States maintains no diplomatic relations with unrecognized governments, and their representatives enjoy no privileges or immunities in the United States. Unrecognized governments cannot bring suit in the courts of the United States. See RESTATEMENT (n. 2 to Preface) §205; *Guaranty Trust Co. of New York* v. *United States*, 304 U.S. 126 (1938); *Banco Nacional de Cuba* v. *Sabbatino*, 376 U.S. 398, 408–12 (1964); *Republic of Vietnam* v. *Pfizer, Inc.*, 556 F.2d 892 (8th Cir. 1977); *Russian Socialist Federated Soviet Republic* v. *Cibrario*, 235 N.Y. 255, 139 N.E. 259 (1923). But compare *National Petrochemical Company of Iran* v. *M/T Stolt Sheaf*, 860 F.2d 551, 554 (2d Cir. 1988).

As to the legal effect given by the United States to the acts of an unrecognized government, compare *Salimoff & Co.* v. *Standard Oil of N.Y.*, 262 N.Y. 220, 186 N.E. 679 (1933), and *Upright* v. *Mercury Business Machines Co.*, 13 A.D.2d 36, 213 N.Y.S.2d 417 (1961), with *Bank of China* v. *Wells Fargo Bank*, 104 F.Supp 59 (N.D.Cal. 1952), *rev'd on other grounds*, 209 F.2d 467 (9th Cir.

1953), and *Petrogradsky Mejdunarodny Kommerchesky Bank* v. *National City Bank*, 253 N.Y. 23 (1930).

As to the application of the Act of State doctrine to unrecognized governments, see RESTATEMENT (n. 2 to Preface) §443, Comment *b*.

63. *The Paquete Habana*, 175 U.S. 677, 700 (1900). See Ch. VIII.

64. After the First World War, noting that increased 'state trading' by other governments claimed the benefits of immunity while U.S. private enterprise could not, the State Department urged that the United States refuse to grant immunity to vessels of foreign governments used for commercial purposes, or to the governments themselves as regards claims arising out of commercial transactions. The Attorney General of the United States rejected the proposal, asserting in effect that sovereign immunity was a question of international law and that international law knew no such distinction; the sovereign was immune regardless of the nature of the claim against him, and his vessels and other property were immune regardless of the public purpose for which they were used. See 2 G. HACKWORTH, DIGEST OF INTERNATIONAL LAW 429–30 (1941). Later, the view of the State Department was, in effect, adopted by Judge Mack in the lower court in *The Pesaro*, 277 F. 473 (S.D.N.Y.1921). When Judge Mack's decree was vacated for other reasons, the issue came anew before Judge Augustus N. Hand who took a contrary position, 13 F.2d 468 (S.D.N.Y. 1926); he was affirmed by the Supreme Court which found that international law accorded immunity to such vessels as well. *Berizzi Bros. Co.* v. *S.S. Pesaro*, 271 U.S. 562 (1926). A quarter of a century later, in the 'Tate Letter', the State Department announced that henceforth it would follow the 'restrictive' theory of immunity. 26 DEP'T STATE BULL. 984 (1952). It refused, however, to extend that doctrine to permit attachment and seizure or execution on the property of a foreign government, even when it was used for commercial purposes. See letter of Secretary of State to Attorney General, referred to in *New York & Cuba Mail S.S. Co.* v. *Republic of Korea*, 132 F. Supp. 684, 685 (S.D.N.Y.1955).

In 1976, Congress enacted the Foreign Sovereign Immunities Act, 28 U.S.C. §1330, 1391, 1602–11 (1988 & Supp. V 1993), adopting and defining the restrictive theory of immunity. See Ch. V.

65. 318 U.S. 578, 589 (1943).

66. 324 U.S. 30, 36, 38 (1945).

67. Compare *Ex parte Muir*, 254 U.S. 522 (1921); *Berizzi Bros. Co.* v. *The Pesaro*, 271 U.S. 562 (1926). Compare also *Victory Transport, Inc.* v. *Comisaria General de Abastecimientos y Transportes*, 336 F.2d 354 (2d Cir. 1964), *cert. denied*, 381 U.S. 934 (1965). Upon request of the Executive branch, Congress enacted the restrictive theory. See n. 64 above.

68. It is possible, but difficult, to read Justice Stone's opinions in these cases as announcing only that the Executive had determined what international law required of the United States and that his views of international law are binding on the courts. The courts have often said that, when necessary to the decision of the case before them, they interpret what international law, or a particular treaty, requires, though they will give 'great weight' to Executive views. See RESTATEMENT (n. 2 to Preface) § 444. See Ch. VIII, p. 241, Ch. VII,

p. 206. Nothing in the sovereign immunity cases rejects or modifies that doctrine. Stone was apparently giving effect not to Executive views of international law but to 'national policy' on immunity even if it was contrary to, or not based on or related to, international law. The Court's doctrine has been criticized particularly by those who were reluctant to see what had been a question of international law converted into a question of national policy. See, e.g., Jessup, *Has the Supreme Court Abdicated One of its Functions?*, 40 AM.J.INT'L L. 168 (1946).

69. *United States* v. *Belmont*, 301 U.S. 324 (1937); *United States* v. *Pink*, 315 U.S. 203 (1942). The opinion in *Belmont* was written by Justice Sutherland; Justice Stone concurred but thought it was not necessary to consider the effect of the agreement. He took that position also in *Pink* where he dissented because, he said, the agreement did not purport to give the United States better rights than the Soviet Union would have had.

70. 315 U.S. at 229–30.

71. *Bernstein* v. *Van Heyghen Frères Société Anonyme*, 163 F.2d 246, 249 (2d Cir. 1947), *cert. denied*, 332 U.S. 772 (1947). In that case the plaintiff sought to recover damages for the loss of his shipping company, which the Nazis had compelled him to transfer (when he was still a German national) pursuant to the anti-Jewish Nuremberg laws, and which was later sold to the defendant, a Belgian corporation. Judge Hand found that under the Act of State doctrine the courts of the United States could not sit in judgment on the Nazi laws applied in German territory, and had to give them effect. In the course of deciding, however, Judge Hand found it relevant to inquire 'whether since the cessation of hostilities with Germany our own Executive, which is the authority to which we must look for the final word in such matters, has declared that the commonly accepted [Act of State] doctrine . . . does not apply.' 163 F.2d at 249. After examination he concluded that the Executive had not lifted the restraints of Act of State. The Circuit Court ruled to the same effect in a later case involving similar facts, *Bernstein* v. *N. V. Nederlandsche-Amerikaansche Stoomvaart-Maatschappij*, 173 F.2d 71 (2d Cir. 1949).

Seizing Judge Hand's hint, Bernstein addressed an inquiry to the Department of State. The Department responded in a letter saying: 'The policy of the Executive, with respect to claims asserted in the United States for the restitution of identifiable property (or compensation in lieu thereof) lost through force, coercion, or duress as a result of Nazi persecution in Germany, is to relieve American courts from any restraint upon the exercise of their jurisdiction to pass upon the validity of the acts of Nazi officials.' Letter of Acting Legal Adviser Tate, April 13, 1949, 20 DEP'T STATE BULL. 592, quoted in *Banco Nacional de Cuba* v. *Sabbatino*, 376 U.S. 398, 419 (1964).

Thereupon, the Court of Appeals, quoting the Department's letter, decided that the Act of State doctrine would not apply '[I]n view of this supervening expression of the Executive Policy', and revised its mandate. *Bernstein* v. *N.V. Nederlandsche-Amerikaansche Stoomvaart-Maatschappij*, 210 F.2d 375, 376 (2d Cir. 1954). (The case was later settled and did not reach the Supreme Court.)

But compare the views of Judge Irving Lehman of the New York Court of

Appeals in *Anderson* v. *N. V. Transandine Handelmaatschappij*, 289 N.Y. 9, 20, 43 N.E.2d 502, 507 (1942). For a discussion of Act of State in other contexts see Ch. V.

72. *Cf.* THE FEDERALIST No. 64 at 394, cited with approval in *United States* v. *Pink*, 315 U.S. 203, 230 (1942): 'All constitutional acts of power, whether in the executive or in the judicial department, have as much legal validity and obligation as if they proceeded from the legislature.' (Jay was speaking of the treaty power.)

There may be an additional issue in that the Court was giving legislative effect not to a formal act of the President but to the views of the State Department asserted in a particular case. Does the State Department in effect have power to make law *ad hoc* for specific cases, although Congress probably cannot constitutionally pass special legislation for a particular case? As to whether the State Department is granting 'due process' to the plaintiffs who are effectively being denied a day in court, see Ch. IX, p. 289.

73. Some distinctions might be attempted. Perhaps executive agreements, involving international obligations like those in treaties, have more claim to domestic legal status than unilateral acts of the President. See Ch. VII, p. 177, 226. In the immunity cases, perhaps the State Department should be followed because immunity is a sensitive issue applicable to all countries and involves the reciprocal rights of the United States abroad. Act of State also involves delicate issues of sitting in judgment on the acts of friendly foreign governments. In both kinds of cases the Department is in effect deciding United States positions on doctrines of international law or comity. Compare n. 85 below. Would the same judicial deference be required if the State Department urged that failure to dismiss a suit against a foreign tourist, say the son of a foreign Chief of State, would seriously impair our foreign relations, or that failure to dismiss a particular proceeding might prevent an important international agreement to establish peace, say in the former Yugoslavia? Compare *Kadic* v. *Karadzic*, 70 F.3d 232 (2d dir. 1995), *rev'g* 866 F.Supp. 734 (S.D.N.Y. 1994). The immunity cases, moreover, require dismissing a suit; Act of State, too, is a special doctrine for judicial guidance in choosing the appropriate law in a transnational transaction. Neither attempts to regulate the activities of private persons or establish rules of substantive law to determine their rights.

74. *Banco Nacional de Cuba* v. *Sabbatino*, 376 U.S. 398 (1964), discussed in Ch. V, p. 137.

75. In the Supreme Court, the Executive branch appeared *amicus curiae* to urge that the lower courts be overruled and the Act of State doctrine applied. It warned that judicial interference might adversely affect the foreign relations of the United States and, in particular, that it would jeopardize diplomatic efforts to vindicate broader American interests including the rights of other Americans who had suffered Cuban expropriation. See Brief pp. 12, 22, and Argument of Deputy Attorney General Katzenbach, 32 U.S.L.W. 3158 (Oct. 29. 1963). That Act of State was executive policy might reasonably have been inferred also from long executive acquiescence in the doctrine and from the very limited and guarded waiver of it in the *Bernstein* case, n. 71 above. See Henkin, *The*

Foreign Affairs Power of the Federal Courts: Sabbatino, 64 COLUM.L.REV. 805, 821–3 (1964).

76. 389 U.S. 429 (1968). See Ch. VI, pp. 163, 164–5.
77. 389 U.S. at 432.
78. Memorandum for the United States at 5. The Solicitor General continued: 'Appellant's apprehension of a deterioration of international relations, unsubstantiated by experience, does not constitute the kind of "changed circumstances" which might call for a re-examination of *Clark* v. *Allen* [an earlier case in which the Court had upheld a California reciprocal inheritance statute].'

Later, in a brief *amicus curiae,* the Solicitor General said that the Government 'does not . . . contend that the operation of the Oregon escheat statute in the circumstances of this case unduly interferes with the United States' conduct of foreign relations'. Brief for the United States as *amicus curiae* at 6, n. 5.

Of these statements by the Executive branch, the opinion of the majority of the Court said simply: 'The Government's acquiescence in the ruling of *Clark* v. *Allen* certainly does not justify extending the principle of that case, as we would be required to do here to uphold the Oregon statute as applied; for it has more than 'some incidental or indirect effect in foreign countries', and its great potential for disruption or embarrassment makes us hesitate to place it in the category of a diplomatic bagatelle.' 389 U.S. at 434–5.

79. 389 U.S. at 443 (concurring opinion).
80. At its first consideration, the Court of Appeals had applied the Act of State doctrine to dismiss a counterclaim by First National for the value of properties confiscated by the Cuban Government. *Banco Nacional de Cuba* v. *First National City Bank,* 431 F.2d 394 (2d Cir. 1970). While the case was before the Supreme Court on petition for certiorari, the Legal Adviser of the State Department addressed his letter to the Supreme Court. (The full text of the letter appears in the subsequent opinion of the Court of Appeals, 442 F.2d at 536–8.) The Supreme Court vacated the judgment and remanded the case to the Court of Appeals for reconsideration in light of that letter. 400 U.S. 1019 (1971). The Court of Appeals reaffirmed its earlier decision saying that *Bernstein* should be narrowly construed and confined to its facts—the act of state of a defunct Nazi government. Virtually without considering whether it was free to do so, the court simply disregarded the State Department letter and applied its own views (and those of the Supreme Court in *Sabbatino*) as to what the Act of State doctrine should be. 442 F.2d 530 (1971). Judge Hays dissented sharply, following *Bernstein. Id.* at 538.
81. *First National City Bank* v. *Banco Nacional de Cuba,* 406 U.S. 759 (1972).
82. Justice Rehnquist (joined by Chief Justice Burger and Justice White) said: 'We conclude that where the Executive Branch, charged as it is with primary responsibility for the conduct of foreign affairs, expressly represents to the Court that application of the act of state doctrine would not advance the interests of American foreign policy, that doctrine should not be applied by the courts . . . The only reason for not deciding the case by use of otherwise applicable legal principles would be the fear that legal interpretation by the

judiciary of the act of a foreign sovereign within its own territory might frustrate the conduct of this country's foreign relations. But the branch of the government responsible for the conduct of those foreign relations has advised us that such a consequence need not be feared in this case. The judiciary is therefore free to decide the case without the limitations that would otherwise be imposed upon it by the judicially created act of state doctrine.' 406 U.S. at 768.

I note that even these three Justices said that the 'judiciary is therefore free'; the implication seems to be not that the courts must adopt the Executive view on the act of state doctrine but that since the Executive says that the doctrine is unnecessary in the circumstances the courts are free not to apply it if *they* think it unnecessary or undesirable. The dissenting justices rejected the *Bernstein* doctrine explicitly and would have followed *Sabbatino*. Douglas and Powell, JJ., concurring, refused to apply it, Douglas saying it should not 'govern here', and Powell that he would be 'uncomfortable' with it. (Douglas, J., would establish a special rule for counterclaims; Powell concurred because he basically disagreed with *Sabbatino*.)

83. But *cf.* Justice Brennan, dissenting, 406 U.S. 789 n. 13 (1972).
84. *New York Times Co.* v. *United States*, 403 U.S. 713 (1971), discussed in Chapter IX, note 17.
85. When in the 'Tate Letter', 26 DEP'T STATE BULL. 984 (1952), n. 64 to this chapter, the State Department adopted the restrictive theory of immunity, it said: 'It is realized that a shift in policy by the executive cannot control the courts, but it is felt that the courts are less likely to allow a plea of sovereign immunity where the executive has declined to do so.' *Id.* at 985. The statement seems inconsistent with Justice Stone's opinions. Was the Department saying that it did not intend to lay down binding policy, only to assert a view of international law which it would follow but as to which the courts were free to make their own determination? Was the Department being coy, or reluctant to accept the responsibility? Was it uncertain about the continuing validity of what the Supreme Court had said? The Supreme Court has never had occasion to consider the effect of that letter but lower courts have applied the doctrine it espoused. The Tate Letter was superseded by the Foreign Sovereign Immunities Act, n. 64 above.
86. Under the Second Hickenlooper Amendment, 78 Stat. 1009, 1013 (1964), as amended, 22 U.S.C. § 2370(e) (2) (1994), n. 36 to Ch. V, the President can insist that the courts apply Act of State even where the Amendment would otherwise bar it. The Executive has not yet exercised that right in any case. Of course, if the President should do so he would not be acting on his own authority but by authority of Congress.

NOTES, CHAPTER III. THE CONGRESS, pp. 63 to 82

1. Writings on the powers of Congress in foreign affairs are listed in n. 5 to the Intro. to Pt II.
2. Legislative powers are also conferred on Congress in other articles, e.g., the power to regulate the time, place, and manner of holding elections for Representatives and effectively of Senators (Art. I, sec. 4; *cf.* the Seventeenth Amendment); to consent to various state acts (Art. I, sec. 10); to create federal offices (Art. II, sec. 2); to establish lower federal courts (Art. III, sec. 1) and regulate the appellate jurisdiction of the Supreme Court (Art. III, sec. 2); to implement the Full Faith and Credit Clause (Art. IV, sec. 1); to admit new states (Art. IV, sec. 3); to propose constitutional amendments (Art. V). See also the enforcement clauses of various amendments to the Constitution, e.g., the Thirteenth, Fourteenth, Fifteenth, Nineteenth, Twentieth, Twenty-Third, Twenty-Fourth, Twenty-Sixth Amendments, some of which have proved to be rich sources of new power. See p. 72, this chapter.
3. This is generally considered a dead power. No letters of marque or reprisal have been issued by the United States since before the Civil War. The European powers agreed to end privateering in the Declaration of Paris (1856). See F. PIGGOTT, THE DECLARATION OF PARIS, 1856 (1919). For the suggestion that CIA covert paramilitary operations in Nicaragua under the Reagan Administration were a variation on letters of marque and reprisal, and as such illegal since this power is explicitly reserved to Congress, see J. Lobel, *Covert War and Congressional Authority: Hidden War and Forgotten Power*, 134 U.PA.L.REV. 1035 (1986).
4. There have been infrequent use and little judicial examination, for example, of the power of Congress to consent to state compacts with foreign nations, or to other state acts addressed in Art. I, sec. 10, cl. 3.
5. *Gibbons* v. *Ogden*, 22 U.S. (9 Wheat.) 1, 189 (1824).
6. *McDermott* v. *Wisconsin*, 228 U.S. 115 (1913); *The Shreveport Rate Case*, 234 U.S. 342 (1914); *N.L.R.B.* v. *Jones & Laughlin Steel Corp.*, 301 U.S. 1 (1937); *United States* v. *Darby*, 312 U.S. 100 (1941); *Wickard* v. *Filburn*, 317 U.S. 111 (1942); *United States* v. *Sullivan*, 332 U.S. 689 (1948); and see nn. 7, 8 to this chapter.
7. Congress can regulate the transportation of people and things across state lines for economic ends or for 'police power' reasons of health, safety, morals, and other public welfare; the wages of a maintenance man in a building that houses small manufacturers whose goods cross state lines, or the compensation of a clerk hurt at her desk in the office of an interstate railroad company; the amount of wheat a farmer grows for his own consumption; the labeling by a local pharmacist of drugs that had once come from another state; racial discrimination by 'local' hotels and restaurants; loan-sharking even by one not engaged in interstate commerce but who was seen as part of a class of loan sharks. See *United States* v. *Darby*, 312 U.S. 100 (1941); *A.B. Kirschbaum Co.* v. *Walling*, 316 U.S. 517 (1942); *Wickard* v. *Filburn*, 317 U.S. 111 (1942); *United States* v. *Sullivan*, 332 U.S. 689 (1948); *Reed* v. *Pennsylvania R.R.*, 351 U.S. 502 (1956); *Heart of*

Atlanta Motel v. *United States*, 379 U.S. 241 (1964); *Katzenbach* v. *McClung*, 379 U.S. 294 (1964); *Perez* v. *United States*, 402 U.S. 146 (1971). See also *Gooch* v. *United States*, 297 U.S. 124 (1936) (statute forbidding transportation in interstate or foreign commerce of kidnaped persons); *Kentucky Whip & Collar Co.* v. *Illinois Central R.R.*, 299 U.S. 334 (1937) (upholding statute prohibiting transportation of convict-made goods into a state in violation of its law); *Electric Bond & Share Co.* v. *SEC*, 303 U.S. 419 (1938) (upholding statute forbidding the use of instrumentalities of interstate commerce and of mails by unregistered companies). But see *United States* v. *Lopez*, n. 8 to this chapter. Congress can even regulate the activities of state governments themselves. *Garcia* v. *San Antonio M.T.A.*, 469 U.S. 528 (1985), overruling *National League of Cities* v. *Usery*, 426 U.S. 833 (1976). But it cannot mandate or coopt the state legislature or state agencies. *New York* v. *United States*, 505 U.S. 144 (1992). It can, however, condition federal grants on action by the state legislature or a state agency.

8. Before 1995, the last Supreme Court decision invalidating an act of Congress as beyond the Commerce Power was *Carter* v. *Carter Coal Co.*, 298 U.S. 238 (1936). The revolution came with *N.L.R.B.* v. *Jones & Laughlin Steel Corp.*, 301 U.S. 1 (1937). See generally Stern, *The Commerce Clause and the National Economy 1933–46*, 59 HARV.L.REV. 645 (1946). In 1995, in *United States* v. *Lopez*, 115 S.Ct. 1624 (1995), the Court invalidated a provision in an act of Congress making it a crime to bring a gun into or near a school. The majority ruled that Congress had not demonstrated a significant link between its regulation and interstate commerce. It expressed the fear that if this legislation were upheld, all aspects of education could be regulated by Congress and taken from the states.

9. It has been argued that the powers given to Congress in regard to foreign commerce exceed those for interstate commerce, since the latter were at the expense of the reserved powers of the states, whereas control of foreign commerce is an aspect of federal power over foreign relations which the states never had. See, e.g., the dissenting opinion in *Lottery Case*, 188 U.S. 321, 373–4 (1903); *Brolan* v. *United States*, 236 U.S. 216, 222 (1915). It is generally accepted, however, that the power of Congress is the same as regards both interstate and foreign commerce. See *The License Cases*, 46 U.S. (5 How.) 504, 578 (1847); *Pittsburgh & Southern Coal Co.* v. *Bates*, 156 U.S. 577, 587 (1895). Some of the cases defining the Commerce Power involved foreign commerce, e.g., *Buttfield* v. *Stranahan*, 192 U.S. 470 (1904); *The Abby Dodge*, 223 U.S. 166 (1912); *Weber* v. *Freed*, 239 U.S. 325 (1915); *Brolan* v. *United States*, above; *Trustees of University of Illinois* v. *United States*, 289 U.S. 48 (1933). Compare *Armement Deppe, S. A.* v. *United States*, 399 F.2d 794 (5th Cir. 1968), *cert. denied*, 393 U.S. 1094 (1969), where the Court of Appeals found Congressional power to regulate shipping contracts among foreign companies that affected U.S. commerce.

10. Chief Justice Marshall in *Gibbons* v. *Ogden*, n. 5 to this chapter, at 193, said that the power of Congress comprehends 'every species of commercial intercourse between the United States and foreign nations'.

11. Art. I, sec. 8, cl. 2 and cl. 5. These Congressional powers supply authority for international agreements on these matters; even United States adherence to international organizations such as the International Bank for Reconstruction and Development and the International Monetary Fund was authorized by Congress rather than effected by treaty. See the Bretton Woods Agreements Act, ch. 339, 59 Stat. 512 (1945), *now codified at* 22 U.S.C. §§ 286a–286k (1994). On the power of Congress to authorize international agreements generally, see Ch. VII, p. 215.

12. See *The Lottawanna*, 88 U.S. (21 Wall.) 558, 577 (1875). But compare *The Belfast*, 74 U.S. (7 Wall.) 624, 640 (1869), and *In re Garnett*, 141 U.S. 1, 12 (1891).

13. See *Nishimura Ekiu* v. *United States*, 142 U.S. 651, 659 (1892); *Head Money Cases*, 112 U.S. 580, 591–6 (1884). That Congress had power to regulate immigration seems to be assumed by Art. 1, sec. 9: 'The Migration or Importation of such Persons as any of the States now existing shall think proper to admit, shall not be prohibited by the Congress prior to the Year one thousand eight hundred and eight. . .' But that clause referred to the importation of slaves, a form of property clearly within the power to regulate foreign commerce; the immigration of free persons is not as obviously 'foreign commerce', and later cases preferred to find Congressional authority over immigration in the powers inherent in sovereignty. See this chapter, p. 70, and Ch. IX.

14. See *Hirabayashi* v. *United States*, 320 U.S. 81, 93 (1943); *Home Building & Loan Assoc.* v. *Blaisdell*, 290 U.S. 398, 426 (1934); *United States* v. *Macintosh*, 283 U.S. 605, 622 (1931) ('the plenary power to wage war with all the force necessary to make it effective') *overruled on other grounds, Girouard* v. *U.S.*, 328 U.S. 61, 64 (1946) ('the oath required of aliens does not in terms require that they promise to bear arms'). See also Chase, J., in *Ex parte Milligan*, 71 U.S. (4 Wall.) 2, 139 (1866) ('all legislation essential to the prosecution of war with vigor and success'). Chief Justice Marshall listed the power 'to declare and conduct a war' as one of the enumerated powers of Congress. *McCulloch* v. *Maryland*, 17 U.S. (4 Wheat.) 316, 407 (1819). On Sutherland's view that the power to wage war was inherent in sovereignty, see Ch. I, p. 18, Congress might claim legislative power in that source also. See Justice Paterson in *Penhallow* v. *Doane*, 3 U.S. (3 Dall.) 54, 80–1 (1795), on the war power of the Continental Congress, n. 11 to Ch. I.

15. Young men were drafted into military service and sent to distant battles; property was taken for the war (subject to compensation) and property of alien enemies was sequestered (without compensation); the economy of the nation was regulated, with production, prices, wages, and rents controlled, and the most local of businesses subjected to scrutiny to assure compliance with the war program. Special restrictions were imposed on basic freedoms of speech and press, of domestic and international travel. Alien enemies were interned. The Supreme Court even acquiesced in a less than glorious page in our history when military officials imposed special restrictions on U.S. citizens of Japanese ancestry, interned them, and relocated them far from their homes. *Korematsu*

v. *United States,* 323 U.S. 214 (1944). See Ch. IX, p. 292. Compare the vast legislative powers exercised by the states during the Revolutionary War. CORWIN, THE PRESIDENT (n. 5 to Intro. to Pt. II) 499–501.

In effect the war power also gives Congress the power to acquire territory by conquest, see *American Ins. Co.* v. *Canter,* 26 U.S. (1 Pet.) 516, 542 (1828), n. 53 to this chapter, and to incorporate conquered territory into the United States, see Ch. IX.

16. The Supreme Court has not considered the validity of some of these programs but I have little doubt they would be upheld. Compare *Ashwander* v. *TVA,* 297 U.S. 288, 327–8 (1936); *Silesian-American Corp.* v. *Clark,* 332 U.S. 469, 476 (1947); see 2 STORY, COMMENTARIES (n. 3 to Ch. I) § 1185, at 104. In *Martin* v. *Mott,* 25 U.S. (12 Wheat.) 19, 29 (1827), Story said that 'the power to provide for repelling invasions includes the power to provide against the attempt and danger of invasion, as the necessary and proper means to effectuate the object'.

Compulsory military service was upheld during the First World War in *Selective Draft Law Cases,* 245 U.S. 366 (1918). The courts have given short shrift to more recent challenges to the power of Congress to require such service, even when the country was not at war. See *United States* v. *O'Brien,* 391 U.S. 367, 377 (1968) ('The constitutional power of Congress to raise and support armies and to make all laws necessary and proper to that end is broad and sweeping'); *Perpich* v. *Dept. of Defense,* 496 U.S. 334 (1990) (Congress can authorize assigning the National Guard to active duty without either consent of state governors or declaration of a national emergency). The validity of federal security programs in principle has been assumed. Compare *Greene* v. *McElroy,* 360 U.S. 474 (1959). Some of these programs no doubt find support in other powers of Congress as well, e.g., the power to 'raise and support Armies', and to 'provide and maintain a Navy', Art. I, sec. 8, cl. 12 and cl. 13. 'Security checks' for federal employees can be supported also by the power of Congress to establish executive offices, Art. II, sec. 2. Compare Ch. IV, p. 121.

17. *Woods* v. *Miller Co.,* 333 U.S. 138 (1948); *Lichter* v. *United States,* 334 U.S. 742, 755, 757–8 (1948); *cf. Hamilton* v. *Kentucky Distilleries & Warehouse Co.,* 251 U.S. 146 (1919). Alien enemies could be kept in internment even after the fighting stopped. *Ludecke* v. *Watkins,* 335 U.S. 160 (1948). But see Justice Jackson concurring in *Woods* v. *Miller,* above, at 146–7, stressing the dangers of this 'open-ended' view of the war powers.

18. Even in ways that violate international law, since the Constitution has been held not to forbid Congress to act in disregard of international law. See Ch. VIII, p. 240. The power to deal with aliens and alien enemies was asserted as early as the Alien Enemies Act of 1798, ch. 58, 1 Stat. 570, ch. 66, 1 Stat. 577, and even its opponents did not doubt that the power to enact it was implied in the power to declare war. See generally *Ludecke,* n. 17 to this chapter.

19. Compare *The Chinese Exclusion Case,* 130 U.S. 581, 606 (1889), discussed in Ch. IX.

20. Art. I, sec. 8, cl. 10. The Articles of Confederation gave Congress exclusive power to appoint courts for the trial of piracies and felonies committed on the high seas. Article IX. At the Constitutional Convention, it was decided that

'felonies' and 'offences against the law of nations' were too vague and should require definition by Congress. 1 J. ELLIOT, DEBATES IN THE SEVERAL STATE CONVENTIONS ON THE ADOPTION OF THE FEDERAL CONSTITUTION 46 (1866).

By legislation enacted in 1789, Congress conferred jurisdiction upon the lower federal courts over civil actions by aliens 'for a tort only, committed in violation of the law of nations'. See, as amended, 28 U.S.C. § 1350 (1988 & Supp. V 1993). Some courts have exercised jurisdiction under that clause of suits in tort for torture committed by a foreign official in a foreign country on the ground that official torture was a violation of the law of nations. See, e.g., *Filartiga* v. *Pena-Irala*, 630 F.2d 876 (2d Cir. 1980). (For cases following *Filartiga*, see n. 36 to Ch. VIII.) It has been suggested that Congress enacted that statute under its power to define offenses against the law of nations but did so by making a violation a tort (rather than a criminal offense). The 1789 provision can find support in other powers of Congress, e.g., in Art. III giving Congress power to confer jurisdiction on the federal courts in cases arising under 'the laws of the United States' (including thereby international law) and U.S. treaties (see Chs. V, VIII), or in the Foreign Affairs Power of Congress.

21. Piracy as defined by the law of nations is punishable under 18 U.S.C. § 1651 (1994). See also Pub. L. No. 103–272, 108 Stat. 1241 (1994), as amended, Pub. L. No. 103–429, 108 Stat. 4385 (1994). A statute punishing 'piracy, as defined by the law of nations' was held sufficiently explicit. *United States* v. *Smith*, 18 U.S. (5 Wheat.) 153 (1820).

22. For the view that the 'law of nations' comprised more than is encompassed in contemporary public international law, and included also, at least, private international law, see, e.g., Rheinstein, *The Constitutional Bases of Jurisdiction*, 22 U.CHI.L.REV. 775, 802–17 (1955).

23. That was argued by Judge Edwards in *Tel-Oren* v. *Libyan Arab Republic*, 726 F.2d 774, 794 (D.C. Cir. 1984), *cert. denied*, 470 U.S. 1003 (1985). But see *Kadic* v. *Karadzic*, 70 F.3d 232 (2d Cir. 1995), reversing the District Court's decision, 866 F. Supp. 734 (S.D.N.Y. 1994) finding no subject matter jurisdiction. See Ch. VIII, n. 36.

24. Including state officials. Compare the statutes that punish acts under color of state law that violate constitutional rights, e.g., 18 U.S.C. §§ 242, 245 (1994). As regards some applications of that legislation, Congressional power derives from the enforcement clauses of the Fourteenth Amendment. Compare, e.g., *United States* v. *Guest*, 383 U.S. 745 (1966).

25. Congress was held to have defined such offenses by reference, in the Articles of War. *Ex parte Quirin*, 317 U.S. 1, 27–8 (1942). Compare *In re Yamashita*, 327 U.S. 1, 26 (1946) (dissenting opinion).

Violations of fishing regulations of international administrative agencies are violations of federal law in some circumstances. See, e.g., The Whaling Convention Act of 1949, ch. 653, 64 Stat. 421 (1950), 16 U.S.C. §§ 916 *et seq.* (1994), implementing the Convention for the Regulation of Whaling, Dec. 2, 1946, 62 Stat. 1716 (1948), T.I.A.S. No. 1849, 161 U.N.T.S. 72. Perhaps these are also offenses against the laws of nations; they are surely punishable under the 'necessary and proper' clause, p. 73 above.

There is an old conceptual dispute as to whether piracy is an international crime, an offense against the law of nations, or whether international law merely permits nations to apply national laws against piracy even though it ordinarily permits them to apply their laws only to acts committed in their territory or by their own nationals. See HENKIN, PUGH, SCHACHTER & SMIT, INTERNATIONAL LAW, CASES AND MATERIALS (3d edn. 1993). See also n. 57 to Ch. II.

26. Convention on the Prevention and Punishment of the Crime of Genocide, adopted December 9, 1948, 78 U.N.T.S. 277; Convention against Torture and other Cruel and Inhuman and Degrading Treatment or Punishment, adopted 10 December 1984, U.N. Doc. G. A. Res. 39/46 (1984) reprinted in 23 I.L.M. 1027 (1984); for other conventions to which the United States is (or may soon be) party, see n. 7 to Intro. to Pt IV. The Nuremberg principles have not been incorporated in any multilateral treaty, but they were unanimously approved by the General Assembly, G.A.Res. 161, U.N.Doc. A/236 at 1144 (1946), and are accepted as customary international law.

Article VI of the Genocide Convention provides: 'Persons charged with genocide or any of the other acts enumerated in Article III shall be tried by a competent tribunal of the State in the territory of which the act was committed, or by such international penal tribunals as may have jurisdiction with respect to those Contracting Parties which shall have accepted its jurisdiction.'

No such international tribunals have been established. But in 1993, the U.N. Security Council established an international tribunal for the trial of war crimes and other gross violations in the former Yugoslavia, and in 1994, the International Law Commission completed a statute for an International Criminal Court with general jurisdiction to be determined mostly by treaty. See Ch. VIII, p. 266.

The United States adhered to the Genocide Convention in 1988; the Convention is implemented in 18 U.S.C. § 1091 (1994). In 1990, the Senate consented to U.S. ratification of the U.N. Convention against Torture, and the United States ratified the Convention in 1994, after implementing legislation had been passed. See 18 U.S.C. § 2340 (1994).

27. *United States* v. *Arjona*, 120 U.S. 479, 487–88 (1887). Earlier, Story seemed to read the clause to the same effect: 'It is obvious, that this power has an intimate connection and relation with the power to regulate commerce and intercourse with foreign nations, and the rights and duties of the national government in peace and war, arising out of the law of nations. As the United States are responsible to foreign governments for all violations of the law of nations, and as the welfare of the Union is essentially connected with the conduct of our citizens, in regard to foreign nations, Congress ought to possess the power to define and punish all such offences, which may interrupt our intercourse and harmony with and our duties to them'. 2 STORY, COMMENTARIES (n. 3 to Ch. I) § 1165, at 95.

See generally Fredman, Comment, *The Offenses Clause: Congress' International Penal Power*, 8 COLUM.J.TRANSNAT'L L. 279 (1969).

Statutes such as that in *Arjona* can also be supported today under the Commerce Power, the Foreign Affairs Power, perhaps even the War Power.

28. It is an offense to assault a foreign diplomat, 18 U.S.C. § 112 (1994). See also 18 U.S.C. § 915 (impersonation of foreign diplomats, consuls or officers); 18 U.S.C. § 962 (arming a vessel against a friendly nation); 18 U.S.C. § 956 (conspiracy to injure property of foreign government). In the past, anyone swearing out a writ or executing process against a foreign diplomat under United States law was deemed a 'violator of the laws of nations and a disturber of the public repose'. 1 Stat. 117 (1790), 22 U.S.C. § 253, *repealed*, Pub.L. No. 95–393, § 9, Dec. 30, 1978. The United Nations has promoted the Convention on the Prevention and Punishment of Crimes Against Internationally Protected Persons, Including Diplomatic Agents, 28 U.S.T. 1975, T.I.A.S. 8532, 1035 U.N.T.S. 167 (1977), implemented in the United States by 18 U.S.C. §§ 11, 112, 970, 1116 and 1201. See RESTATEMENT (n. 2 to Preface) § 464, Reporters' Note 6. The implementation legislation is readily supported by the 'define offences' clause, the power to enact legislation necessary and proper to carry out treaty obligations (see Ch. VII, p. 190), as well as the general foreign affairs power of Congress. Compare 22 U.S.C. §§ 461–5 (1994) (offenses against the declared neutrality of the United States). See also *Frend* v. *United States*, 100 F.2d 691 (D.C.Cir.1938) (upholding prohibition on picketing of embassies), and *Greenberg* v. *Murphy*, 329 F.Supp. 37 (S.D.N.Y.1971) (barring picketing of UN). In *Boos* v. *Barry*, 485 U.S. 312 (1988), the Court invalidated an ordinance prohibiting picketing within 500 feet of a foreign embassy with signs that tend to bring that foreign government into 'public odium' or 'public disrepute', but the Court upheld limitations not based on the content of the message, intimating that a narrower statute, such as 18 U.S.C. § 112 (b)(2), prohibiting intimidation, coercion, threatening or harassment of a foreign official, was valid. See Ch. IX.

29. See Ch. I. But *cf.* Brennan, J., concurring in *Kennedy* v. *Mendoza-Martinez*, 372 U.S. 144, 195–6 (1963): 'under our Constitution, only a delimited portion of sovereignty has been assigned to the Government of which Congress is the legislative arm. To say that there inheres in United States sovereignty the power to sever the tie of citizenship does not answer the inquiry into whether that power has been granted to Congress.' The Court, he said, can assume that Congress has this power only on 'some sense of the inevitable fitness of things'. *Id.* at 196.

The Court has not considered how the powers inherent in national sovereignty are divided among the three branches of government. But in upholding an act of Congress requiring a U.S. citizen to return to give testimony in a federal court, the Supreme Court said: 'What in England was the prerogative of the sovereign in this respect, pertains under our constitutional system to the national authority which may be exercised by the Congress by virtue of the legislative power to prescribe the duties of the citizens of the United States. It is also beyond controversy that one of the duties which the citizen owes to his government is to support the administration of justice by attending its courts and giving his testimony whenever he is properly summoned. . . And the

Congress may provide for the performance of this duty and prescribe penalties for disobedience.' (Citations omitted). *Blackmer* v. *United States,* 284 U.S. 421, 437–8 (1932). See also *Mackenzie* v. *Hare,* 239 U.S. 299, 311 (1915), discussed this chapter, p. 71 and n. 40 to this chapter.

A power fully equivalent to the 'sovereignty' or 'foreign relations' power of Congress might be built from several powers of Congress, or as 'necessary and proper' to carry out the foreign affairs powers of the President. See this chapter, p. 73. See generally Henkin, *The Treaty Makers and the Law Makers: The Law of the Land and Foreign Relations,* 107 U.PA.L.REV. 903, 913 *et seq.,* especially 915 n.26 (1959).

30. *Perez* v. *Brownell,* 356 U.S. 44, 59 (1958), discussed in n. 41 to this chapter.

31. Compare the legislation, supportable also by other powers, n. 28 to this chapter. And see the Logan Act, n. 16 to Ch. IX, imposing criminal penalties for U.S. citizens who carry on 'correspondence or intercourse with any foreign government . . . with intent to influence the measures or conduct of any foreign government . . . in relation to any disputes or controversies with the United States, or to defeat the measures of the United States'.

32. 22 U.S.C. §§ 256–8a (1994). See n. 50 to Ch. VIII.

33. See, e.g., Johnson Debt Default Act of April 13, 1934, ch. 112, 48 Stat. 574. Such legislation is presumably also within the Commerce Power.

34. See the Foreign Sovereign Immunities Act, n. 64 to Ch. II, the Second Hickenlooper Amendment, now in 22 U.S.C. § 2370(e)(2) (1994). In *Banco Nacional de Cuba* v. *Farr,* 383 F.2d 166, 182 (2d Cir. 1967), *cert. denied,* 390 U.S. 956 (1968), *rehearing denied,* 390 U.S. 1037 (1968), the Court of Appeals found ample Congressional power for such legislation in the Commerce Clause, supported by the necessary and proper clause, and additional authority in the power to define and punish offenses against the law of nations. See n. 86 to Ch. II.

35. Congress legislated to establish an exclusive fishing zone and a Fishery Conservation Zone in the seas outside the U.S. territorial seas. See 16 U.S.C. §§ 1091, 1801 (1994). Before President Truman proclaimed exclusive rights in the Continential Shelf, n. 28 to Ch. II, Congress had considered legislation to that end. The legislation died in committee, but not from any doubts about the constitutional authority of Congress to enact such a law.

Congress has asserted U.S. sovereignty in its airspace, 49 U.S.C. §§ 1508, 1521–3 (1988) *repealed,* Pub. L. No. 103–272, 108 Stat. 1379 (1994), and continues to do so. Pub. L. No. 103–272, § 1(e), 108 Stat. 1379 (1994). Congessional legislation on aviation can find support also in its Commerce power and its War power and its power to implement treaties to which the U.S. is a party.

36. See Ch. VII, p. 215. That this authority of Congress is presumably based on its Foreign Affairs Power, see my article *The Treaty Makers and the Law Makers: The Law of the Land and Foreign Relations,* 107 U.PA.L.REV. 903, 926–9 (1959).

37. See the discussion of immigration in Ch. IX.

38. In *Hines* v. *Davidowitz,* 312 U.S. 52 (1941), the Supreme Court held that since Congress had provided for the registration of aliens, Pennsylvania could not.

Congress repealed the law requiring the registration of aliens in the Act of June 27, 1952. For the current law on alien registration, see 8 U.S.C. §§1302 *et seq.* (1994).

39. See, e.g., in times past, exemptions from military service. But see now 50 U.S.C. § 456(a)(1) (1990). And see p. 71 this chapter.

In *Hines* v. *Davidowitz*, 312 U.S. 52, 62–3 (1941), Justice Black said: 'When the national government by treaty or Statute established rules and regulations touching the rights, privileges, obligations or burdens of aliens as such, the treaty or statute is the supreme law of the land.' He added that 'the regulation of aliens is . . . intimately blended and intertwined with responsibilities of the national government'. *Id.* at 66. But *cf.* Stone's dissent, *id.* at 76, denying a general power in Congress to regulate aliens. The law now seems clear that for many if not all purposes the power to regulate aliens flows from the power to admit them, and both depend on the Foreign Affairs Power. *Cf. Takahashi* v. *Fish & Game Com.*, 334 U.S. 410 (1948), and *Graham* v. *Richardson*, 403 U.S. 365 (1971).

See also the act authorizing war-time allies to exercise court-martial jurisdiction over their troops in the United States, Service Courts of Friendly Foreign Forces Act, ch. 326, 58 Stat. 643 (1944), 22 U.S.C. §§ 701–6 (1994); *cf.* North Atlantic Treaty Status of Forces Agreement, June 19, 1951, [1953] 4 U.S.T. 1792; T.I.A.S. No. 2846. See Ch. VIII.

40. Ch. 2534, § 3, 34 Stat. 1228 (1907). *Mackenzie* v. *Hare*, 239 U.S. 299 (1915). As applied to naturalized citizens, such regulations might be seen also as conditions of naturalization under Congress' power to 'establish an Uniform Rule of Naturalization', Art. 1, sec. 8. But see the following note.

41. *Perez* v. *Brownell*, 356 U.S. 44 (1958). That case was later overruled, *Afroyim* v. *Rusk*, 387 U.S. 253 (1967), on the ground that Congress cannot take away a person's citizenship against his or her will. In *Rogers* v. *Bellei*, 401 U.S. 815 (1971), the Court held that Congress can withdraw derivative citizenship conferred by statute. See n. 5 to Ch. IX. In none of these cases did any one doubt that the subject was within the powers granted to Congress. Compare n. 16 to Ch. I.

There are loose suggestions that the power to expatriate is implied in the power of Congress to establish a 'uniform Rule of Naturalization' but while expatriation in given circumstances might be imposed as a condition of naturalization (see *Bellei,* above), it is difficult to find in that clause the power to cancel the citizenship of one who has it by birth. See n. 3 to Ch. IX.

42. See *Grin* v. *Shine*, 187 U.S. 181, 191 (1902); *Valentine* v. *United States ex rel. Neidecker*, 299 U.S. 5, 8–9 (1936). The power of Congress to deport aliens would seem to support also their extradition (even in the absence of a treaty obligation), but extradition of a citizen of the United States would have to be justified in a broad Foreign Affairs Power.

43. *United States* v. *Bowman*, 260 U.S. 94 (1922); *Blackmer* v. *United States*, 284 U.S. 421 (1932). *Cf. Kawakita* v. *United States*, 343 U. S. 717 (1952); *Steele* v. *Bulova Watch Co.*, 344 U.S. 280 (1952). But in *Blackmer* the Court seemed to draw on U.S. sovereignty for authority to compel the citizen to return to the United States. See n. 29 to this chapter.

Ordinarily laws of Congress are construed to apply only in the United States. See *American Banana Co.* v. *United Fruit Co.*, 213 U.S. 347, 357 (1909); *Robertson* v. *R.R. Labor Board*, 268 U.S. 619, 622 (1925); *Foley Bros., Inc.* v. *Filardo*, 336 U.S. 281, 285 (1949); and see *E.E.O.C.* v. *Arabian American Oil Company*, 499 U.S. 244 (1991), *Sale* v. *Haitian Centers Council, Inc.*, 113 S.Ct. 2549, 2560 (1993); but *cf. Blackmer*, above; *Vermilya-Brown Co.* v. *Connell*, 335 U.S. 377 (1948). For other statutes that apply to U.S. citizens abroad, see, e.g., 18 U.S.C. §2381 (treason); 18 U.S.C. §§793–4 (espionage); 18 U.S.C. §1621 (perjury); 18 U.S.C. §953 (the Logan Act, forbidding private diplomacy, n. 16 to Ch. IX); see also 26 U.S.C. §7201 (tax evasion).

44. *Reid* v. *Covert*, 354 U.S. 1 (1957). For a discussion of the protection abroad of individual rights guaranteed by the Constitution, see Ch. IX. Also, compare *O'Callahan* v. *Parker*, 395 U.S. 258 (1969), *overruled by Solorio* v. *U.S.*, 483 U.S. 435 (1987), with *Relford* v. *Commandant, U.S. Disciplinary Barracks*, 401 U.S. 355 (1971) *overruled by Solorio* as stated in *U.S.* v. *Avila*, 27 M.J. 62, 63 (1988); *cf. United States ex rel. Fleming* v. *Chafee*, 330 F.Supp. 193 (E.D.N.Y. 1971), *aff'd*, 458 F.2d 544 (2d Cir. 1972), *rev'd, Warner* v. *Fleming*, 413 U.S. 665 (1973).

The 'Offences clause' expressly authorizes Congress to define and punish felonies on the high seas. Congress can also legislate maritime law, regulate navigable streams, and govern territory belonging to the United States. Since 1790, for example, Congress has made it a crime to commit murder and other felonies 'upon the high seas, or in any river, haven, basin, or bay, out of the jurisdiction of any particular state. . .' Act of April 30, 1790, ch. 9, § 8, 1 Stat. 112, 113–14; *cf.* 18 U.S.C. § 1652 (1994).

45. Compare *Kinsella* v. *United States ex rel. Singleton*, 361 U.S. 234, 246 (1960); *United States ex rel. Toth* v. *Quarles*, 350 U.S. 11, 21 (1955).

46. International law recognizes the right of a state to apply its laws to its nationals anywhere but, with exceptions, forbids the exercise of legislative authority over others outside its territory. See RESTATEMENT (n. 2 to Preface) §§ 402–4.

It has been suggested that where a treaty permits the United States to try and punish certain offenses committed in a foreign country, Congress can legislate against such offenses under its power to do what is necessary and proper to implement the treaty. See Ch. VII, p. 190. But generally such treaties merely permit the United States to apply its laws to these persons, and it is not obvious that the penal statutes are 'necessary and proper' to implement such permissive treaties and give Congress legislative powers it would not otherwise have. Compare the North Atlantic Treaty Status of Forces Agreement, June 19, 1951, [1953] 4 U.S.T. 1792, T.I.A.S. No. 2846, and the cases rejecting courtmartial authority, n. 44 to this chapter. Compare also the suggestion that Congress can prescribe the 'duties of citizens' in *Blackmer* v. *United States*, quoted in n. 29 to this chapter.

47. Henkin, *The Treaty Makers and the Law Makers: The Law of the Land and Foreign Relations*, 107 U.Pa.L.Rev. 903, 920–30 (1959). On that view, surely, this power renders redundant other powers of Congress, e.g., the power to define offenses against the law of nations, perhaps even the Foreign Commerce

Power and the War Power. That of course is the implication of Sutherland's statement in *Curtiss-Wright* that if these powers had not been mentioned in the Constitution they would nonetheless belong to the United States as inherent in its sovereignty. See Ch. I, p. 18.

48. It is now established, too, that any matter, including the human rights of its own citizens, is a valid subject for a treaty if the United States concludes it for foreign relations purposes. See Ch. VII, p. 197. The argument that any matter appropriate for a treaty is *ipso facto* within the Foreign Affairs Power of Congress would also support the common view that Congress can repeal as domestic law even a treaty dealing with matters not within the enumerated powers of Congress. See my article, n. 47 above, at pp. 929–30; see Ch. VII, n. 130.

As regards reciprocal legislation, see, for example, the Nolan Act, ch. 26, 415 Stat. 1313 (1921); *Robertson* v. *General Electric Co.*, 32 F.2d 495 (4th Cir. 1929), *cert. denied*, 280 U.S. 571 (1929). As the opinion in *Robertson* states, Congress used reciprocal legislation as a substitute for a treaty with Germany to which the Senate failed to consent. (Germany, in its turn, also adopted legislation.) For an early collection of reciprocal statutes by Congress, see my article, n. 47 above, at p. 921 n. 41.

49. 252 U.S. 416, 433 (1920), discussed in Ch. VII, p. 189.

50. See, e.g., *United States* v. *Doremus*, 249 U.S. 86 (1919); *United States* v. *Kahriger*, 345 U.S. 22 (1953), overruled on other grounds, *Marchetti* v. *United States*, 390 U.S. 39 (1968).

51. As long ago as 1806, Congress appropriated $50,000 for the 'wretched sufferers' of an earthquake in Venezuela. See 31 ANNALS OF CONG. 58 (1817). (Lend-lease during the Second World War, perhaps foreign aid, too, could be supported also by the War Power.)

'[T]he power to spend [is] subject to limitations', *United States* v. *Butler*, 297 U.S. 1, 66 (1936). In that case, the Supreme Court struck down legislation authorizing contracts under which the United States would make payments to farmers who agreed to curtail production, as an attempt to 'purchase' acquiescence to a regulation that was not within the enumerated powers of Congress. But the Court affirmed Hamilton's view that the Spending Power is an independent power with independent purposes: Congress can spend for purposes beyond those included in its enumerated legislative powers.

No spending program or appropriation has been successfully challenged as not for 'the common Defence or general Welfare', and clearly 'general Welfare' has been interpreted with the widest latitude. Of course, spending programs are particularly difficult to challenge since a federal taxpayer, *qua* taxpayer, has standing to challenge expenditures only on the ground that they contravene 'specific constitutional limitations imposed upon the . . . taxing and spending power', and to date that has been found only in the Establishment of Religion clause. *Flast* v. *Cohen*, 392 U.S. 83, 102–3 (1968); compare *Massachusetts* v. *Mellon*, 262 U.S. 447 (1923); *Valley Forge Christian College* v. *Americans United for Separation of Church and State, Inc.*, 454 U.S. 464 (1982).

The Spending Power is to be distinguished from the 'Appropriations Power', the power of Congress to appropriate funds necessary and proper to carry out any of its substantive powers and those of other branches of government, see Art. I, sec. 9. See this chapter, p. 74.

The power to spend also includes the power to impose conditions on spending, for example, provisions denying aid to countries that violate human rights. See, e.g., the Foreign Assistance Act of 1961, as amended, §§116, 502B and 22 U.S.C. §2151n, §2304 (1994); International Financial Institutions Act of 1977, §§701, 703, 22 U.S.C. §262d, and note (1994); the Jackson–Vanik Amendment, Trade Act of 1974, 19 U.S.C. §§2192, 2193, 2432, 2437 and 2439 (1994). See generally, INT'L HUMAN RIGHTS LAW GROUP and R.LILLICH, U.S. LEGISLATION RELATING HUMAN RIGHTS TO U.S. FOREIGN POLICY (2d edn. 1980); D. Weissbrodt, *Human Rights Legislation and U.S. Foreign Policy,* 7 GA. J. INT'L & COMP. L. 231 (1977). Also, HENKIN, THE AGE OF RIGHTS (1990) Chapter 5.

52. See, e.g., 39 U.S.C. §407 (1988) (authorization for international postal agreements). For legislation dealing with international patent regulation see, e.g., 35 U.S.C. §§102, 119, 184 (1994); see also 15 U.S.C. §1126 (1994) (trademark regulation); 17 U.S.C. §107 (1994) (copyright regulations).

The power of Congress to issue and protect patents and copyrights is enumerated in Art. 1, sec. 8, cl. 8; trademarks are regulated under the Commerce Power. Compare the *Trade-Mark Cases,* 100 U.S. 82 (1879), with the Lanham Act of 1946, ch. 540, 60 Stat. 428, as amended, 15 U.S.C. §§1051 *et seq.* (1994).

53. President Jefferson and others seemed to have doubts about the constitutionality of the Louisiana Purchase, but their concern was not the absence of authority in the federal government to acquire territory by treaty but doubt as to whether the United States could acquire additional territory at all. That doubt has long been laid to rest. See, e.g., Justice Jackson concurring in *Youngstown Sheet & Tube Co.* v. *Sawyer,* 343 U.S. 579, 638 n. 5 (1952).

The United States has the power to acquire territory by conquest or treaty. See *American Ins. Co.* v. *Canter,* 26 U.S. (1 Pet.) 516, 542 (1828); *Mormon Church* v. *United States,* 136 U.S. 1, 42 (1890). The Supreme Court in *Canter* suggested that Congress can acquire and govern such territories by virtue of the powers inherent in the sovereignty of the United States, 26 U.S. at 542–3, 546. But Congress also has the express power 'to make all needful Rules and Regulations respecting the Territory, or other Property belonging to the United States'. Art. IV, sec. 3, cl. 2. That power, and the power to admit new states *(id.,* cl. 1), might be held to imply for Congress authority to acquire territory by any necessary and proper means; but some argued that the territory clause referred only to territory then already belonging to the United States.

In the *Insular Cases* the Supreme Court upheld and applied provisions in a peace treaty leaving to Congress the future status of territories ceded to the United States. *Downes* v. *Bidwell,* 182 U.S. 244 (1901). That Congress can decide whether territory should be 'incorporated' into the United States or remain 'unincorporated', see also *Dorr* v. *United States,* 195 U.S. 138 (1904); *Balzac* v. *Puerto Rico,* 258 U.S. 298 (1922). For the protections for individual rights in such territories, see Ch. IX, p. 308.

Although of relatively small importance today, the power of the United States to acquire territory through discovery was recognized in *Jones* v. *United States*, 137 U.S. 202 (1890). The power may become important once again if the United States should claim territorial rights in space or additional rights in or under the seas. Compare the Truman Proclamation on the Continental Shelf, n. 28 to Ch. II, and the Congressional declaration of national sovereignty in air space (see n. 35 to this chapter), 49 U.S.C. § 40103 (1995); *cf. Braniff Airways* v. *Nebraska State Board*, 347 U.S. 590, 596 (1954). Resolutions of the United Nations have declared that neither of these environments is subject to national appropriation. Declaration of Legal Principles Governing the Activities of States in the Exploration and Use of Outer Space, G.A.Res.1962, 18 U.N. GAOR Supp. 15, at 15, U.N.Doc. A/5515 (1963); Declaration of Principles Governing the Sea-Bed and the Ocean Floor, and the Subsoil Thereof, Beyond the Limits of National Jurisdiction, G.A.Res. 2749, 25 U.N. GAOR Supp. 28, at 24, U.N. Doc. A/8097 (1970). See also the 1982 Convention on the Law of the Sea, article 89. The United States has accepted that principle as to outer space by treaty. See Treaty on Principles Governing the Activities of States in the Exploration and Use of Outer Space, Including the Moon and Other Celestial Bodies, Jan. 27, 1967, Art. 2, [1967] 18 U.S.T. 2410, T.I.A.S.No.6347. The limits of national jurisdiction in the seas were redefined during the period 1970–82, and President Reagan accepted these new limits without adhering to the 1982 Convention on the Law of the Sea. President Clinton has pressed for Senate consent to the 1982 Convention, as modified by a 1994 agreement, but as of 1996 it has not yet been forthcoming.

54. The power to dispose of property is explicit in Art. IV, sec. 3, cl. 2. *Ashwander* v. *TVA*, 297 U.S. 288 (1936), might be read to imply that Congress can acquire property only for purposes that come within its other powers, but that would include its Foreign Affairs Power as well. In *United States* v. *Gratiot*, 39 U.S. (14 Pet.) 526, 537 (1840), the Court said that the power of Congress to deal with or dispose of U.S. property 'is . . . without limitation'. See also *Alabama* v. *Texas*, 347 U.S. 272, 273–4 (1954); *Kleppe* v. *New Mexico*, 426 U.S. 519, 539 (1976).

The power of eminent domain—an aspect of the property power, supported by the 'necessary and proper clause', and implied in the requirement of 'just compensation' in Amendment V—can be used for foreign affairs purposes as for others. See, e.g., *United States ex rel. TVA* v. *Welch*, 327 U.S. 546 (1946); *Berman* v. *Parker*, 348 U.S. 26 (1954).

55. See *United States* v. *Bevans*, 16 U.S. (3 Wheat.) 336 (1818); *The Propeller Genesee Chief* v. *Fitzhugh*, 53 U.S. (12 How.) 443 (1851); *Southern Pacific Co.* v. *Jensen*, 244 U.S. 205, 215 (1917); Note, *From Judicial Grant to Legislative Power: The Admiralty Clause in the Nineteenth Century*, 67 HARV.L.REV. 1214 (1954). The property power, nn. 53, 54 to this chapter, would support Congressional authority to deal with the territorial sea, its bed, and resources, to assert fishing zones and an Exclusive Economic Zone for the United States. See *United States* v. *California*, 332 U.S. 19 (1947); *Alabama* v. *Texas*, 347 U.S. 272 (1954). Congress has also legislated for the continental shelf of the United

States in the Outer Continental Shelf Lands Act, ch. 345, 67 Stat. 462 (1953), 43 U.S.C. §§1331 *et seq.* (1988 & Supp. V 1993). Congress has adopted the Fishery Conservation and Management Act of 1976, 16 U.S.C. §1801 (1994), amended by the Fisheries Act of 1995, Pub. L. No. 104–43, 109 Stat. 366. If the United States ratifies the 1982 Convention on the Law of the Sea, n. 53 above, U.S. rights on the Continental Shelf and in the Exclusive Economic Zone would be confirmed by treaty.

56. See n. 7 to the Intro. to Pt IV. Congress can also regulate the rights of aliens under its Foreign Affairs Power, p. 70 above. The rights to equal protection and due process apply to aliens as well. See RESTATEMENT (n. 2 to Preface) § 722 and Ch. IX. After the Civil War Congress enacted basic civil rights legislation applicable to 'all persons', including aliens. Act of April 9, 1866, ch. 31, 14 Stat. 27, re-enacted in the Enforcement Act of 1870, ch. 114, 16 Stat. 140, codified in REV.STAT. §§ 1977–91 (1874), now 42 U.S.C. §§ 1981 *et seq.* (1988 & Supp. V 1993). See generally MUTHARIKA, THE ALIEN UNDER AMERICAN LAW (1980).

The power of Congress under the Fourteenth Amendment was extended to new reaches in *Katzenbach* v. *Morgan*, 384 U.S. 641 (1966); *United States* v. *Guest*, 383 U.S. 745 (1966); but *cf. Oregon* v. *Mitchell*, 400 U.S. 112 (1970). Compare also *Rome* v. *United States*, 446 U.S. 156 (1980). The Thirteenth Amendment has been interpreted to give Congress authority to remove whatever it deems to be a badge of slavery, for example, private discrimination in housing against blacks; *Jones* v. *Alfred H. Mayer Co.*, 392 U.S. 409 (1968); also *Runyon* v. *McCrary*, 427 U.S. 160 (1976); *cf. Patterson* v. *McLean Credit Union*, 491 U.S. 164 (1989). Both the Thirteenth and Fourteenth Amendments, then, now support wide civil rights legislation. The vast powers of Congress under the Fifteenth Amendment to eliminate racial discrimination in voting (*South Carolina* v. *Katzenbach*, 383 U.S. 301 (1966)) are also not without significance for U.S. foreign relations in view of contemporary international interest in racial discrimination and in democracy.

57. *McCulloch* v. *Maryland*, 17 U.S. (4 Wheat.) 316, 421 (1819). But compare Justice Clark in *Kinsella* v. *United States ex rel. Singleton*, 361 U.S. 234, 247 (1960): 'The latter clause is not itself a grant of power, but a *caveat* that the Congress possesses all the means necessary to carry out the specifically granted "foregoing" powers of §8 and all other powers vested by this Constitution. . .'. 'As James Madison explained, the "necessary and proper" clause is "but merely a declaration, for the removal of all uncertainty, that the means of carrying into execution those [powers] otherwise granted are included in the grant".' But compare the opinion of Justice Whittaker, *id.* at 259; Justice Harlan, *id.* at 253–5. It is fair to assume that the Court took a limited view of the necessary and proper clause in those cases only in order to safeguard the right to a jury trial for persons not themselves in the armed services. See n. 44 to this chapter. After those cases, the Court again reverted to Marshall's broad view of the clause, e.g., in *United States* v. *Oregon*, 366 U.S. 643 (1961); and *cf. Relford* v. *Commandant*, n. 44 to this chapter.

58. See, e.g., *Legal Tender Cases*, 79 U.S. (12 Wall.) 457, 556 (1870) (Justice

Bradley concurring); *United States* v. *Arjona,* 120 U.S. 479, 487 (1887) p. 69 this chapter. Although literally the clause confers the power to implement only 'the foregoing Powers, and all other Powers vested by this Constitution', Congress can doubtless implement also the powers of the United States inherent in sovereignty. Compare: 'Congress has broad power under the Necessary and Proper Clause to enact legislation for the regulation of foreign affairs.' *Kennedy* v. *Mendoza-Martinez,* 372 U.S. 144, 160 (1963).

59.   252 U.S. 416, 432 (1920). See Ch. VII, p. 189. Holmes himself would probably not have held the statute regulating migratory birds beyond the powers of Congress even in the absence of treaty, but he had to carry his brethren who did not share his view of the Commerce Power. See his dissent in *Hammer* v. *Dagenhart,* 247 U.S. 251, 277 (1918). Today the Commerce Power alone reaches beyond what even Holmes, I guess, would have then accepted. See nn. 7, 8 to this chapter.

60.   The non-legislative character of a declaration of war has been cited to deny the President power to veto such a declaration. See Intro. to Pt II, p. 27.

61.   For the view that traditional war between states is no longer 'done' and has lost its prime place in the conduct of foreign policy, see L. HENKIN, HOW NATIONS BEHAVE (2d edn. 1979), Chapter 7. Compare n. 26 to Ch. II.

62.   See generally, 2 L. OPPENHEIM, INTERNATIONAL LAW, Part II, Chapter 2 (II) at 301–35, and Part III (Lauterpacht 7th edn. 1952). See *Techt* v. *Hughes,* 229 N.Y. 222, 128 N.E. 185, *cert. denied,* 254 U.S. 643 (1920); compare Ch. VII, n. 141. For the argument that the UN Charter has changed all that, see n. 26 to Ch. II, and Ch. VIII.

63.   The Third Amendment provides, by implication, that in time of war soldiers may be quartered in private homes without the consent of the owner, if prescribed by law.

     The Fifth Amendment provides that in time of war persons in the militia may be tried for crime without grand jury indictment, and the same exception has been read into the jury trial requirement in the Sixth Amendment. The power to try military personnel generally by court-martial is different in time of war from what it is in time of peace. Compare the cases in n. 44 to this chapter; compare *Ex parte Quirin,* 317 U.S. 1 (1942).

64.   See, e.g., *Talbot* v. *Seeman,* in which Chief Justice Marshall stated: 'The whole powers of war [were] by the constitution . . . vested in congress'. 5 U.S. (1 Cranch) 1, 28 (1801). See also Marshall in *McCulloch* v. *Maryland,* quoted in n. 14 to this chapter. See generally Ch. IV and the materials on the Vietnam War.

     It was originally proposed that Congress be given the power 'to make war'. 2 FARRAND (n. 11 to Ch. I) 168. The language was changed, it appears, so as not to deny the President power to make war when necessary to repel invasion. *Id.* at 318. See the discussion of the War Powers Resolution in Ch. IV. Today, war, except in self defense against armed attack, is forbidden by the UN Charter, but Congress presumably remains constitutionally free to declare war in violation of the UN Charter or other international law. See Ch. VII, p. 196; Ch. VIII, p. 250.

65. It has been suggested that a formal declaration of war is constitutionally required because the Framers wished to make going to war difficult and to assure public awareness and support for the war. I know no basis for this suggestion, and it does not reflect eighteenth century attitudes. Compare CORWIN, THE PRESIDENT (n. 5 to Intro to Pt II) 230–1.

Even after Vietnam had become, undeniably, a war, and national controversy about it had begun, the Senate Committee holding hearings on the National Commitments Resolution affirmed: 'The committee does not believe that formal declarations of war are the only available means by which Congress can authorize the President to initiate limited or general hostilities. Joint resolutions such as those pertaining to Formosa, the Middle East, and the Gulf of Tonkin are a proper method of granting authority.' S.REP.NO.797, 90th Cong., 1st Sess. 25 (1967).

Increasingly, in our day, wars are being fought without declaration, perhaps because wars are illegal under the UN Charter, perhaps because nations seek to avoid the traditional consequences of declared war on relations with third nations or even with some of the belligerents. Compare the Nixon statement, n. 33 to Ch. IV. For early Congressional authorization of hostilities other than by declaration of war, see, e.g.: ch. 48, 1 Stat. 561 (1798), ch. 60, *id.* at 572 (France); ch. 4, 2 Stat. 129 (1802) (Tripoli); ch. 90, 3 Stat. 230 (1815) (Algiers). For more recent authorizations see, e.g.: ch. 4, 69 Stat. 7 (1955) (Formosa); Pub.L.No.85–7, 71 Stat. 5 (1957) (Middle East); Pub.L.No.87–733, 76 Stat. 697 (1962) (Cuban quarantine); H.Con.Res. 570, 76 Stat. 1429 (1962) (Berlin). And see the Tonkin Gulf Resolution, n. 38 to Ch. IV. For a comparison of these resolutions see 110 CONG.REC. 18428–29 (1964). For an earlier authorization, see J.Res.No.10, 38 Stat. 770 (1914), quoted in CORWIN, THE PRESIDENT (n. 5 to Intro to Pt. II) 485 n. 96. That Congress intended undeclared limited war against France in 1798–1800, see *Bas* v. *Tingy*, 4 U.S. (4 Dall.) 37, 39, 40–1, 43, 45 (1800); *Talbot* v. *Seeman*, 5 U.S. (1 Cranch) 1 (1801).

Congress ratified Presidential wars in the Civil War, in Korea, perhaps also in the Mexican War, where the Congressional declaration in terms recognized that war existed. See n. 33 to Ch. IV. The Supreme Court upheld subsequent Congressional ratification as fully effective in *The Prize Cases*, 67 U.S. (2 Black) 635, 670–1 (1862). And see the discussion of Vietnam in Ch. IV. Subsequent ratification has been given the effect of prior authorization in other contexts, e.g., *Mitchell* v. *Clark*, 110 U.S. 633, 640 (1884); *United States* v. *Heinszen & Co.*, 206 U.S. 370 (1907). Subsequent ratification is constitutionally effective even if it is done merely by appropriation of funds. *Wilson* v. *Shaw*, 204 U.S. 24 (1907); *Isbrandtsen-Moller Co.* v. *United States*, 300 U.S. 139, 147 (1937); *Brooks* v. *Dewar*, 313 U.S. 354, 360–1 (1941); *Hirabayashi* v. *United States*, 320 U.S. 81, 91 (1943); *Fleming* v. *Mohawk Wrecking & Lumber Co.*, 331 U.S. 111, 116 (1947). But *cf. Ex parte Endo*, 323 U.S. 283, 303 n. 24 (1944).

66. Ch. 40, 42 Stat. 105 (1921); ch. 519, 65 Stat. 451 (1951). Under Article IX of the Articles of Confederation, Congress had 'the sole and exclusive right and power of determining on peace and war' but there Congress had the treaty

power as well. A motion to give Congress the power to make peace was voted down in the Constitutional Convention, 2 FARRAND (n. 11 to Ch. I) 319, 540–1; Story says that it was assumed that peace would be made by Treaty. STORY, COMMENTARIES (n. 3 to Ch. I) § 1173, at 98. WRIGHT (n. 3 to Ch. I), at 292, questioned the propriety of ending the First World War by Congressional resolution repealing the Declaration of War, but the power to end the state of war by resolution is now well established. See *Commercial Trust Co.* v. *Miller*, 262 U.S. 51, 57 (1923): '[T]he power which declared the necessity, is the power to declare its cessation and what the cessation requires. The power is legislative.' See also *Ludecke* v. *Watkins*, 335 U.S. 160, 168–9 (1948); see Mathews, *The Termination of War*, 19 MICH.L.REV. 819, 833–4 (1921). Compare the discussion of the repeal of the Tonkin Gulf Resolution, Ch. IV, p. 103.

67. The phrase is Hamilton's in The Pacificus letters, but he considered that it was the President who could determine the condition of the nation. See Ch. II, p. 39.

68. See Chapter XLI, 1 Stat. 372 (1794); also *id.* at 400; the last neutrality act was that of 1939, ch. 2, 54 Stat. 4; principal provisions of the 1939 Act were repealed in 1941, ch. 473, 55 Stat. 764.

69. J.Res.No.24, 30 Stat. 738 (1898). In 1882 Congress adopted 'An Act to establish diplomatic relations with Persia'. Ch. 399, 22 Stat. 301. For Congressional statements asserting Congressional control of recognition, see 1 G. HACKWORTH, DIGEST OF INTERNATIONAL LAW 162–3 (1940). See generally Bakker, *Congress and the Power to Recognize*, in 3 COLUMBIA ESSAYS IN INTERNATIONAL AFFAIRS, THE DEAN'S PAPERS, 1967, at 403 (1968). And see n. 71 below.

70. 5 Stat. 797 (1845) (Texas); 30 Stat. 750 (1898) (Hawaiian Islands). The treaty with Texas had been rejected by the Senate, principally to avoid war with Mexico. The Senate did not vote consent to the treaty with the Hawaiian Republic but it supported a Joint Resolution to approve the annexation. See S. CRANDALL, TREATIES THEIR MAKING AND ENFORCEMENT (2nd edn. 1916) 135–8.

71. CONG.GLOBE, 38th Cong., 2d Sess. 65–7 (1864). The resolution—in response to Seward's statement to France that Congress does not speak for the United States, this chapter, p. 81—is also set forth in the course of Hale's memorandum on the power of Congress to recognize the independence of a new foreign state; the memorandum recites various efforts by Congress to act in foreign affairs during the nineteenth century. S.Doc.No.56, 54th Cong., 2d Sess. 47 (1897).

72. See n. 13 to Ch. II.

73. Compare *Blackmer* v. *United States*, quoted in n. 29 to this chapter. In a famous debate in 1906 with Senator Spooner (see n. 10 to Ch. II), Senator Bacon said: 'Congress and not the President is supreme under the Constitution in the control of our foreign affairs.' And 'the Constitution has invested Congress with almost all the prerogatives of sovereignty'. 40 CONG.REC. 2132, 2134 (1906).

74. For a later replay of Madison and Senator Bacon, see Fulbright, in *Hearings on Separation of Powers before the Subcomm. on Separation of Powers of the*

Senate Comm. on the Judiciary, 90th Cong., 1st Sess. 43–4 (1967). Senator
Fulbright recognized that the conduct of foreign relations was the responsibility of the President but believed that Congress had the power to make foreign
policy, and he was concerned about the erosion of its authority and responsibility. While recognizing some overlap between shaping foreign policy and conducting foreign relations, e.g., in foreign aid, Fulbright said: 'The criteria of
responsible and constructive debate are restraint in matters of detail and the
day-to-day conduct of foreign policy, combined with diligence and energy in
discussing the values, direction, and purpose of American foreign policy. Just
as it is an excess of democracy when Congress is overly aggressive in attempting to supervise the conduct of policy, it is a failure of democracy when it fails
to participate actively in determining policy objectives and in the making of
significant decisions.' *Id.* at 52.

See also Senator Fulbright's statements in 'U.S. Commitments to Foreign
Powers', *Hearings on S.Res. 151 Before the Senate Comm. on Foreign Relations*,
90th Cong., 1st Sess. 79–80, 183–4 (1967); Senator E. McCarthy, *id.* at 33. See
also an earlier statement by Senator Morse: 'under our Constitution foreign
policy does not belong to the President of the United States and the Secretary
of State. They are but the administrators of the people's foreign policy.' 107
CONG.REC. 6575 (1961). See generally HENKIN, CONSTITUTIONALISM, DEMO-
CRACY AND FOREIGN AFFAIRS (1990).

75. In denying the sovereignty of the States, King (of Massachusetts) said:
'Considering them as political Beings, they were dumb, for they could not
speak to any forign (sic) Sovereign whatever. They were deaf, for they could
not hear any propositions from such Sovereign.' 1 FARRAND (n. 11 to Ch. I)
323.

76. The abrogation of the treaty with France in 1798 has been characterized as, in
the circumstances, a partial declaration of war. Compare *Bas* v. *Tingy*, 4 U.S.
(4 Dall.) 37 (1800); CORWIN, THE PRESIDENT (n. 5 to Intro. to Pt. II) 481 n. 75.
See Chapter VII, n. 137. Congressional recognition of Cuban independence in
1898 (n. 69 to this chapter) followed President McKinley's reference of the
Cuban question to Congress and formed a 'package' with the declaration of
war against Spain. See 30 Stat. 364, 738 (1898).

77. The power of Congress to join with the President to conclude international
agreements, as an alternative to a treaty by President-and-Senate, also remains
well established (see Ch. VII, p. 215); but that authority is not challenged by
Presidents and is indeed invoked, at least by the President who joins in such
agreements. Compare the suggestions that when President and Congress join
in an international act they represent the full sovereignty of the United States
(n. 7 to the Intro. to Pt II) or that in the Treaty Power the Constitution
accepted Senate consent as a lesser safeguard, but that approval of an agreement by the whole Congress is effective *a fortiori*, n. 156 to Ch. VII.

78. Art. I, sec. 9, cls. 5 and 6. For the suggestion that the 'export clause' should
be interpreted as forbidding also more sophisticated controls designed for
domestic economic purposes, see Note, *Constitutionality of Export Controls*, 76
YALE L.J. 200 (1966). Compare *Fairbank* v. *United States*, 181 U.S. 283 (1901)

(stamp tax on export bill of lading); *United States* v. *Hvoslef*, 237 U.S. 1 (1915) (tax on marine charter parties); *Thames & Mersey Marine Ins. Co.* v. *United States*, 237 U.S. 19 (1915) (tax on marine insurance policy on exports), reaffirmed, *United States* v. *International Business Machines Corp.*, 116 S.Ct. 1793 (1996). The Constitutional Convention apparently assumed that the 'export clause' limited only commercial regulation and would not prohibit an embargo under the war power. 2 FARRAND (n. 11 to Ch. I) 61–2. The provision prohibiting port preferences was designed to prevent preferences between ports based on their location in different states; it does not forbid discriminations between individual ports generally. *Louisiana Public Service Common* v. *Texas & N.O.R.R.*, 284 U.S. 125, 131 (1931).

Clause 1 of section 9 was designed to deny Congress the power to prohibit the importation of slaves before 1808, or to impose a tax or duty of more than ten dollars per slave. See n. 13 to this chapter. Clause 7 contains the provision that 'No money shall be drawn from the Treasury, but in Consequence of Appropriations made by Law; and a regular Statement and Account of the Receipts and Expenditures of all public Money shall be published from time to time.'

There are hypothetical foreign policy consequences also in the provision forbidding the grant of titles of nobility, or requiring the consent of Congress for any U.S. official to accept 'any present, Emolument, Office, or Title, of any kind whatever, from any King, Prince, or foreign State'. (Clause 8).

As regards matters as to which Congressional power derives from the sovereignty of the United States, it has been argued that such powers cannot be exercised in violation of international law; the argument is not persuasive since sovereignty includes the power (not the right) to act in violation of international law. See Ch. VII, p. 196, Ch. VIII, pp. 250–1.

79. 9 RICHARDSON (n. 27 to Ch. II) 438–86, quoted in CORWIN, THE PRESIDENT (n. 5 to Intro. to Pt. II) 476–7 n. 46. See also WRIGHT (n. 3 to Ch. I) 278–83. But *cf.* 24 DEP'T STATE BULL. 556–7 (1951) (reaction of Secretary of State Acheson to Senate resolution expressing friendship for the Soviet people during the Berlin crisis of 1951). For some references to early Congressional expressions of policy, and different reactions of different Presidents, see WRIGHT, above; CORWIN, above at 213–14, 222–3 and n. 66. Increasingly, of course, foreign governments monitor Congressional proceedings and are fully aware of Congressional views and sentiments.

In the past, at least, attempts by foreign governments to talk directly to Congress or members of Congress or to the people of the United States were sorely resented. Compare the reaction to the communication by the German Embassy published in American newspapers, Telegram from Mr. Bryan, Secretary of State, to Mr. Gerard, Ambassador in Germany, May 13, 1915, [1915 Supp.] FOREIGN REL.U.S. 393, 395 (1928). Foreign governments still tend to be discreet but Congress has invited formal addresses by foreign statesmen (usually at Executive instigation) and members of Congress have been known to invite discussion with foreign diplomats, sometimes to the helpless dismay of the Executive branch.

80. Congressional resolutions whether or not expressed as 'sense resolutions' have sometimes effectively become national policy: for example, the Lodge Resolution in 1912 barring the Western Hemisphere to foreign powers for military and naval purposes, even when done through quasi-public corporations. S.Res. 371, 62d Cong., 2d Sess., 48 CONG.REC. 10046–7 (1912). (It was directed against a reported attempt by a Japanese company to establish a coaling station in Mexico.)

    Sometimes Congress has resolved to condemn Executive actions: e.g., on Feb. 7, 1894, the House adopted a resolution condemning 'the action of the United States minister in employing United States naval forces and illegally aiding in overthrowing the constitutional Government of the Hawaiian Islands'. 26 CONG.REC. 2001–2002 (1894). Compare the resolution of the House condemning 'Polk's war' cited n. 33 to Ch. IV.

    Contrary to common assumption, the President is not always more 'internationalist' than Congress. In 1927 Coolidge failed to heed a Senate Resolution favoring arbitration of the oil dispute with Mexico. See S.Res. 327, 69th Cong., 2d Sess., 68 CONG.REC. 2233 (1927). For a report on the propriety of the House of Representatives expressing itself on foreign affairs, see H.R.REP. No. 1569, 68th Cong., 2d Sess. 10 (1925).

81. WRIGHT (n. 3 to Ch. I) 279–81; 6 MOORE, DIGEST (n. 50 to Ch. II) 497–8.

82. 37 DEP'T STATE BULL. 142 (1957), in response to French objections to Senator John F. Kennedy's statements, 103 CONG.REC. 10780 *et seq.* especially at 10788 col. 1 (1957).

83. Compare *Watkins* v. *United States*, 354 U.S. 178 (1957); *Barenblatt* v. *United States*, 360 U.S. 109 (1959); *Eastland* v. *United States Serviceman's Fund*, 421 U.S. 491 (1975).

84. It is reported, for example, that in July 1949, Secretary of State Marshall promised the Senate Foreign Relations Committee that there would be no recognition of Communist China without consultation with the Committee. See D. CHEEVER & H. HAVILAND, AMERICAN FOREIGN POLICY AND THE SEPARATION OF POWERS 11 (1952). Compare n. 158 to Ch. VII.

NOTES, CHAPTER IV. SEPARATION OF POWERS:
COMPETITION, CONFLICT, AND COOPERATION, pp. 83 to 130

1. See n. 2 to the Intro. to Pt II. For an earlier attempt to define the distribution of authority between President and Congress in foreign affairs, see WRIGHT (n. 3 to Ch. I) 335–6.
2. See the Appendix in 'War Powers: Origins and Purposes', *Hearing before the Subcommittee on Arms Control, International Security and Science of the Committee on Foreign Affairs*, H.R., 100th Cong. 2d Sess. (1988).
3. See Appendices to 'H.R. 1013, H.R. 1371 and other proposals', *Hearings before the Subcommittee on Legislation of the Permanent Select Committee on Intelligence*, H.R., 100th Cong. 1st Sess. (1987), pp. 211 *et seq.*
4. See HENKIN, THE AGE OF RIGHTS, Ch. 5, pp. 68–73 (1990). For the legislation, see n. 51 to Ch. III.
5. 'Legislative and Executive powers are pooled obviously to the end that commercial, strategic, and diplomatic interests of the country may be coordinated and advanced without collision or deadlock between agencies.' *Chicago & Southern Air Lines, Inc.* v. *Waterman S.S. Corp.*, 333 U.S. 103, 110 (1948), quoted more fully, n. 33 to Ch. II.
6. Presidents sometimes claim authority for a particular act 'under the Constitution and Laws'. See Ch. II, p. 52. In such cases, a challenge to the President's action requires showing that the Executive act is not within the President's constitutional authority and was not authorized by any act of Congress. For example, a President sought by Executive Order to limit the transfer of capital abroad. See Executive Order 11387, January 3, 1968, 33 Fed. Reg. 47. A Senate subcommittee declared that the President's order was not authorized by Congress and usurped Congressional authority. See Senate Comm. on the Judiciary, Separation of Powers, S.Rep. No. 549, 91st Cong., 1st Sess. 16 (1969). In another instance, a Presidential proclamation imposing a duty on imported goods was held invalid by the Customs Court as not within the President's constitutional authority, and not authorized by a 1917 statute. *United States* v. *Yoshida International, Inc.*, 378 F.Supp 1155 (Customs Court 1974). On appeal, the Customs Court of Patent Appeals reversed, holding the President's order to be within authority conferred upon him by Congress. 66 C.C.P.A. 15 (1975). See also *Alcon Sales Div.* v. *United States*, 534 F.2d 920 (C.C.PA. 1976), *cert. denied*, 429 U.S. 986 (1976). See RESTATEMENT (n. 2 to Preface) § 812, Comment *c* and Reporters' Note 2. To avoid deciding the constitutional question the Supreme Court has sometimes found authorization from Congress where it was less than clear. See, e.g., *Regan* v. *Wald*, 468 U.S. 222 (1984) (upholding Executive limitations on travel to Cuba). In 1995, President Clinton drew on the Treasury's Exchange Stabilization Fund to lend money to Mexico to 'bail-out' its economy. There was criticism in Congress and steps taken to limit the power of the President to make future loans to Mexico. See Pub.L.No. 104–6, 109 Stat. 73, § 403 (1995), and 53 CONG.Q.WKLY.REP. 1035 No. 14, April 8, 1995.

7. As the Supreme Court held in invalidating President Truman's seizure of the steel mills in *Youngstown Sheet and Tube Co.* v. *Sawyer*, 343 U.S. 579 (1952), n. 15 below. Justice Black's majority opinion made much—some think too much—of an obvious and inherent difference between legislative and executive power. See also *Kent* v. *Dulles*, quoted p. 91, this chapter; and Justice Black dissenting in *Zemel* v. *Rusk*, 381 U.S. 1, 20–1 (1965).

   Congress, in turn, cannot invade the Executive's power of appointing officials, Art. II, sec. 2, cl. 1 (see p. 88, this chapter), or his power to remove some officials, p. 122, this chapter. See *Buckley* v. *Valeo*, 424 U.S. 1 (1976); *Bowsher* v. *Synar*, 478 U.S. 714 (1986). Neither can Congress usurp his power to pardon criminal offenders. Art. II, sec. 2, cl. 2. *Ex parte Garland*, 71 U.S. (4 Wall.) 333 (1866); see *United States* v. *Klein*, 80 U.S. (13 Wall.) 128 (1871); *Ex parte Grossman*, 267 U.S. 87 (1925). But Congress has power to grant a general amnesty. *Brown* v. *Walker*, 161 U.S. 591, 601 (1896).

8. See Ch. III, pp. 79–80. But Congress has participated in interparliamentary bodies See, e.g., Interparliamentary Union Act, 22 U.S.C. §§276–276k (1994).

9. Compare the Executive Order limiting transfers of capital, n. 6 to this chapter.

   The Supreme Court held that the President had power as Commander in Chief to impose tariffs on goods coming into Puerto Rico and the Philippine Islands from the United States while the islands were under occupation, but that such authority terminated when the treaty with Spain came into effect ceding these territories to the United States. *Dooley* v. *United States*, 182 U.S. 222 (1901); *Lincoln* v. *United States*, 197 U.S. 419 (1905), *reaffirmed*, 202 U.S. 484 (1906). (Congress, however, could ratify his acts and give them retroactive effect. *United States* v. *Heinszen & Co.*, 206 U.S. 370 (1907).) In those cases, of course, when the island became United States territory, any duties on goods passing between them and other parts of the United States would not be within any foreign affairs authority of the President.

10. That the President may be acting beyond his constitutional authority does not ordinarily render his actions invalid under international law. Ordinarily, other nations are entitled, and indeed required, to treat the President as 'sole organ' and his acts as those of the United States. Ordinarily, the United States is internationally bound by what the President does in its behalf even if he had acted *ultra vires*. See n. 174 to Ch. VII.

11. Especially since the 'necessary and proper' clause (Art. I, sec. 8, cl. 18) gives Congress the power to implement the powers of the President. See Ch. III, p. 73; compare, generally, J. HART, THE ORDINANCE MAKING POWERS OF THE PRESIDENT OF THE UNITED STATES (1925) Chapter IX. Compare also the dissenting opinion in the *Steel Seizure Case*, n. 15 to this chapter, which argued that the President had power to seize the steel mills as a means of executing various laws and other federal authority.

    The *Curtiss-Wright* case, Ch. I, might be read to imply that the President might have imposed an arms embargo on his own authority; but he could not have prosecuted violators unless an act of Congress rendered it a crime and prescribed penalties for such violation. See p. 90, this chapter; n. 105 to Ch. VII.

12. President Lincoln apparently incurred obligations of two million dollars without Congressional authorization or appropriation. Few believe he had constitutional authority to do so, but his acts were later ratified by Congress. For that and other instances of Presidential expenditure without authorization, or Presidential 'overdraft' or diversion of funds to other purposes, see L. WILMERDING, THE SPENDING POWER (1943), cited in CORWIN, THE PRESIDENT (n. 5 to Intro. to Pt. II) 445–50. In the 1970s, Congress asserted authority to oversee Presidential spending. See *id.* at 196–7.

13. *Valentine* v. *United States ex rel. Neidecker*, 299 U.S. 5 (1936). In that case, the extradition treaty with France provided that neither party 'shall be bound' to extradite its own nationals. The Court said that there being no treaty obligation to do so, the President had no authority to extradite a U.S. citizen.

   In 1825, President J. Q. Adams took the position that he had no authority to extradite a fugitive because the applicable extradition treaty was no longer in force. See the letter quoted by Justice Thompson in *Holmes* v. *Jennison*, 39 U.S. (14 Pet.) 540, 582–3 (1840); see also Taney's opinion, *id.* at 574, discussed in Chapter VI, p. 153. But Lincoln extradited Arguelles to Spain on his own authority. See n. 164 to Ch. VII.

   Attorney General Cushing was of the opinion that the President could not return deserting seamen in the absence of a treaty. 6 OP. ATT'Y GEN. 148, 209 (1871). But compare the Supreme Court's statement that the Executive has the power to exclude aliens from the United States, n. 32 to Ch. II.

   In 1995, a lower federal court held that Congress could not give the Secretary of State authority to refuse to extradite a person whom a judge declared to be extraditable under a treaty. The decision was stayed by the D.C. Circuit Court of Appeals in September 1995. *Lobue* v. *Christopher* 893 F.Supp. 65 (D.D.C. 1995).

14. See Chapter II, p. 54; Chapter VII, p. 227. But the executive agreements given effect in those cases involved only money, not the liberty of a citizen accused of crime.

   Any extradition might be seen as involving an *ad hoc* agreement with the foreign country, and might seem readily within the President's powers to conclude executive agreements. See Ch. VII, p. 228. It might be argued, however, that the Act of Congress which provides procedures for implementation '[w]henever there is a treaty or convention for extradition . . .' ch. 645, § 3184, 62 Stat. 822 (1948), as amended 18 U.S.C. § 3184 (1994), implies that there shall be no extradition in the absence of treaty. As to whether an executive agreement can prevail in the face of an inconsistent statute, see Ch. VII, p. 228.

15. 343 U.S. 579 (1952). In 1952, while American troops were fighting in Korea, a labor dispute in the steel industry led the union to give notice of a nation-wide strike. A few hours before the strike was scheduled to take effect, President Truman issued an Executive Order reciting that steel was indispensable to the production of weapons, and that the President believed that work stoppage would jeopardize the national defense; he directed the Secretary of Commerce to take possession of most of the steel mills and keep them running. The President reported the action to Congress, but Congress took no action.

Affirming a lower court decision, the Supreme Court declared the seizure to be beyond the President's power because it was an exercise of 'legislative' power. See also Douglas, J., concurring, *id.* at 630. But three Justices dissented, and some of the six Justices in the majority relied heavily, if not exclusively, on the fact that the President's action was inconsistent with Congressional policy, Congress having provided a different procedure for handling such strikes and indeed having refused to adopt a provision authorizing plant seizures. It is not unfair to assume that the majority of the Justices in the case might have upheld the President's power had Congress not acted at all. Doubtless with that in mind, Justice Jackson, concurring, wrote explicitly of 'a zone of twilight in which he and Congress may have concurrent authority, or in which its distribution is uncertain'. *Id.* at 647, quoted this chapter, p. 94.

Compare *United States* v. *Midwest Oil Co.*, 236 U.S. 459 (1915); *La Abra Silver Mining Co.* v. *United States*, 175 U.S. 423, 459–61 (1899); *Myers* v. *United States*, 272 U.S. 52, 161 (1926) ; also *Little* v. *Barreme*, 6 U.S. (2 Cranch) 170, 177 (1804). But the much-cited Hale memorandum, S.Doc.No.56, 54th Cong.2d Sess. 4 (1897), echoing Madison, argued that the Constitution did not intend 'to place any given power in two or all three branches of the Government concurrently'. See this chapter, p. 86 footnote.

16. 357 U.S. 116, 129 (1958). The four dissenting Justices did not consider the President's independent authority, having found that Congress had authorized denying passports in such cases. 357 U.S. at 130. Compare *Zemel* v. *Rusk*, 381 U.S. 1 (1965), with *United States* v. *Laub*, 385 U.S. 475 (1967); see n. 113 to this chapter, and Ch. IX.

17. *Haig* v. *Agee*, 453 U.S. 280 (1981); *Regan* v. *Wald*, 468 U.S. 222 (1984).

18. See n. 35 to Ch. III.

19. Members of Congress challenged the authority of President Carter to cancel the Defense Treaty with the National Republic of China (Taiwan), but the Supreme Court refused to decide the constitutional issue. See *Goldwater* v. *Carter*, 444 U.S. 996 (1979), discussed in Ch. VII, p. 213.

20. See, e.g., Taney's effort in *Ex parte Milligan*, 71 U.S. (4 Wall.) 2, 139–40 (1866).

21. Surely by treaty, with the consent of the Senate; see n. 48 to this chapter.

22. *Madsen* v. *Kinsella*, 343 U.S. 341 (1952). The Court apparently concluded that Congress did not intend to preclude the alternative means, trial by an occupation court. But *cf. United States ex rel. Hirshberg* v. *Cooke*, 336 U.S. 210 (1949) (since Congress did not authorize it, the Navy could not court-martial someone for an offense committed during a prior enlistment).

23. *Youngstown Sheet & Tube Co.* v. *Sawyer*, 343 U.S. 579, 635–7 (1952) (Jackson, J., concurring).

24. See the various opinions in *Youngstown Sheet & Tube Co.* v. *Sawyer*, n. 15 to this chapter. *Youngstown* has not been considered a 'foreign affairs case'. The President claimed to be acting within 'the aggregate of his constitutional powers', but the majority of the Supreme Court did not treat the case as involving the reach of his foreign affairs power, and even the dissenting justices invoked only incidentally that power or the fact that the steel strike threatened important U.S. foreign policy interests and its prosecution of the war in Korea.

25. This would unquestionably be true if the act of Congress followed. Compare the power of Congress to supersede even treaty provisions as domestic law, Ch. VII, p. 209.

General statements cast doubt on the President's authority to supersede an Act of Congress, e.g.: 'No power was ever vested in the President to repeal an Act of Congress', *United States* v. *Clarke*, 87 U.S. (20 Wall.) 92, 112–13 (1874). And see cases in the following note. Compare the discussion of sole executive agreements, Chapter VII, p. 228.

In the *Steel Seizure Case* the concurring Justices held, in effect, that the President could not act inconsistently with an earlier Act of Congress. See n. 15 to this chapter.

26. In 1898, the Acting Attorney General thought that the President had concurrent power to control the landing of foreign submarine cables, subject to Congressional supremacy. 22 OP.ATT'Y GEN. 13. In *United States* v. *Western Union Telegraph Co.*, 272 F. 311 (S.D. N.Y.1921), *dismissed*, 260 U.S. 754 (1922), the President was denied the power to exclude an Atlantic cable by a company claiming a license under an act of Congress. In 1941, Attorney General Jackson held that the President was barred by statute from transferring certain 'mosquito boats' to a foreign power even by executive agreement. 39 OP.ATT'Y GEN. 484 (1941); see also Justice Jackson's concurring opinion in *Youngstown Sheet & Tube Co.* v. *Sawyer*, 343 U.S. 579, 634 n. 14 (1952) and n. 31 to Ch. II. See n. 198 to Ch. VII. See also *Gelston* v. *Hoyt*, 16 U.S. (3 Wheat.) 246, 330–3 (1818), which held that the President could not authorize revenue officers to seize a vessel for violating neutrality when the statute authorized seizure only by the military. Compare *Little* v. *Barreme*, 6 U.S. (2 Cranch) 170, 177–8 (1804). See also *The Orono*, 18 F.Cas. 830 (No. 10,585) (C.C.Mass. 1812), and President's Proclamation Declared Illegal, 19 F.Cas. 1289 (No. 11,391) (C.C.N.C.1812).

27. 28 U.S.C. §1602 *et seq.* (1994), discussed in Ch. VIII, p. 239 and Ch. II, p. 54.

28. It has been argued that the power of Congress to declare war is not a legislative power and can be exercised without the concurrence of the President. See, e.g., Senator Morgan of Alabama, 28 CONG. REC. 2107 (1896); *contra,* C. BERDAHL, WAR POWERS OF THE EXECUTIVE IN THE UNITED STATES 95 (1921); see generally Baldwin, *The Share of the President of the United States in a Declaration of War*, 12 AM.J.INT'L L. 1 (1918). The issue has remained hypothetical since all declarations of war in U.S. history to date were made in response to Presidential request. But President Cleveland is reported to have said in 1897 that if Congress declared war on Spain on account of Cuba he would refuse to order the Army and Navy to fight. See 2 R. MCELROY, GROVER CLEVELAND 249–50 (1923), cited in CORWIN, THE PRESIDENT (n. 5 to Intro. to Pt. II) 484–5, n. 95.

29. Congress had provided that members of the forces inducted under the Selective Service Act might be sent only to U.S. territories or in the Western Hemisphere. Ch. 720, § 3(e), 54 Stat. 886 (1940). Roosevelt acted by executive agreement; see the discussion, n. 198 to Ch. VII, as to whether executive

agreements stand better than unilateral executive acts and might prevail in the face of an earlier act of Congress.

Compare the statute authorizing detail of small numbers of forces to China subject to the proviso that 'United States naval or Marine Corps personnel shall not accompany Chinese troops, aircraft, or ships on other than training maneuvers or cruises'. Ch. 580, 60 Stat. 539 (1946). Once Congress also purported to limit the President's use of the armed forces for law enforcement in the United States, Ch. 263, § 15, 20 Stat. 152 (1878). For Congressional efforts to control the use of troops by withholding appropriations see n. 67 to this chapter.

Other conflicts between the President's powers as Commander in Chief and Congressional powers have not been frequent, but in 1867 Congress purported to take away some of President Andrew Johnson's powers as Commander in Chief and vest them in General Grant. See debate, CONG.GLOBE, 39th Cong., 2d Sess. 1851–5 (1867); ch. 170, §§ 2, 6, 14 Stat. 486, 487 (1867); see generally A. MCLAUGHLIN, A CONSTITUTIONAL HISTORY OF THE UNITED STATES 662 (student's edn. 1935); and compare the *Hirshberg* case in n. 22 to this chapter.

30. Instead, the Senate adopted what was largely a 'sense' resolution, approving the dispatch of four divisions, calling on the President to consult with both foreign affairs committees before sending troops abroad under the North Atlantic Treaty, requiring Congressional approval for any policy involving the assignment of troops abroad and for sending any additional troops, and requesting Presidential reports on the implementation of the North Atlantic Treaty. S.Res. 99, 82nd Cong., 1st Sess., 97 CONG.REC. 3282–3 (1951). President Truman said that he did not need Congressional approval but he would consult with members of the Senate Foreign Relations Committee and the Armed Services Committee before sending troops to the North Atlantic Treaty area. See N.Y. Times, Jan. 12, 1951. Compare the 'Commitments Resolution', Ch. VII, p. 222.

A Senate Report quoted at length (and seemed to accept) an Executive memorandum supporting Presidential authority to send troops abroad. S.REP.NO. 175, 82d Cong., 1st Sess. (1951). See also 'Assignment of Ground Forces of the United States to Duty in the European Area', *Hearings on S.Res. 99 and S.Con.Res. 18 Before the Sen. Comm. on Foreign Relations and the Comm. on Armed Services*, 82d Cong., 1st Sess. (1951).

For an earlier debate on the constitutionality of Congressional efforts to control the President's use of the armed forces see, e.g., the extended debates on the Lend-Lease Bill, recounted in Jones, *The President, Congress, and Foreign Relations*, 29 CALIF.L.REV. 565, 582–94 (1941); CORWIN, THE PRESIDENT (n. 5 to Intro. to Pt. II) 152–61.

31. The 'Byrd Amendment' prohibited the expenditure of Department of Defense funds in Somalia after March 31, 1994, thereby requiring the withdrawal of U.S. forces from Somalia by that date. Pub.L.No. 103–39, Title VIII § 8151, 107 Stat. 1475 (1993). The Nunn–Mitchell Amendment required U.S. forces to begin to lift the enforcement of the U.N. arms embargo against Bosnia after a certain date in given circumstances. Pub.L.No. 103–60, Div. A Title XV § 1512, 107 Stat. 1839 (1993). See 50 U.S.C. §1541 (1988).

32. Under the Hamilton Plan at the Constitutional Convention the Executive was to have 'the direction of war when authorized or begun'. 1 FARRAND (n. 11 to Ch. I) 292.

For a collection of statements by Presidents, especially early Presidents, asserting that only Congress can commit the nation to war, see Wormuth, *The Vietnam War: The President versus the Constitution*, in 2 FALK, VIETNAM 711; and Lawyers Memorandum, *Indochina: The Constitutional Crisis*, 116 CONG.REC. 15,410–16 (1970). Also, SENATE COMM. ON FOREIGN RELATIONS, NATIONAL COMMITMENTS, S.REP. No.797, 90th Cong., 1st Sess. 9–12 (1967). See generally WORMUTH & FIRMAGE, TO CHAIN THE DOG OF WAR: THE WAR POWERS OF CONGRESS IN HISTORY AND LAW (1986); A. SOFAER, WAR, FOREIGN AFFAIRS AND CONSTITUTIONAL POWER, THE ORIGINS (1976).

President Truman seemed to consider Korea different because he acted pursuant to a U.N. resolution. See Note, *Congress, The President, the Power to Commit Forces to Combat*, 81 HARV.L.REV. 1771, 1791–2 (1968), reprinted in 2 FALK, VIETNAM (n. 36 below) at 616, 636–7; see remarks of Truman and Acheson in 23 DEP'T STATE BULL. 3, 5–6 (1950); see *Authority of the President to Repel the Attack in Korea*, 23 DEP'T STATE BULL. 173. But see n. 37 to this chapter, and Ch. VIII.

33. Hamilton anticipated that the President exercising his powers might 'affect the exercise of the power of the legislature to declare war. Nevertheless, the executive cannot thereby control the exercise of that power. The legislature is still free to perform its duties, according to its own sense of them; though the executive, in the exercise of its constitutional powers, may establish an antecedent state of things which ought to weigh in the legislative decisions. . . . While, therefore, the legislature can alone declare war, can alone actually transfer the nation from a state of peace to a state of hostility, it belongs to the 'executive power' to do whatever else the law of nations, cooperating with the treaties of the country, enjoin in the intercourse of the United States with foreign powers.' Letters of Pacificus No. 1, 7 A. HAMILTON, WORKS 83–4 (Hamilton, ed. 1851), n. 10 to Ch. II.

Compare the House Resolution of 1848 referring to the Mexican war 'unnecessarily and unconstitutionally begun by the President of the United States'. CONG.GLOBE, 30th Cong., 1st Sess. 95 (1848). There have been somewhat similar accusations against F. D. Roosevelt as regards the Second World War. For the view that Franklin Roosevelt exceeded his powers in 1940–41 see SENATE COMM. ON FOREIGN RELATIONS, 91st Cong., 2d Sess., *Documents Relating to the War Power of Congress, the President's Authority as Commander-in-Chief and the War in Inodochina* 15 (Comm. Print 1970). And compare CORWIN, THE PRESIDENT (n. 5 to Intro. to Pt. II) 232–4. Corwin concludes (at 234): 'A summary history of the wars in which the United States has engaged since the adoption of the Constitution will concede to Congress that policies and views advanced within its walls were primarily responsible for two of these wars, the War of 1812 and the war with Spain. But our four great wars . . . were the outcome of presidential policies in the making of which Congress played a distinctly secondary role'.

Earlier WRIGHT (n. 3 to Ch. I) (at 286–9) pointed out that even Congressional declarations of war have been, in terms, recognitions of war; compare also Ch. 4, 2 Stat. 129 (1802). But perhaps Congress was merely seeking to put the onus for starting the war on the enemy. Apparently only the Declaration of War in 1812 followed substantial debate in Congress (24 ANNALS OF CONG. 1631–83 (1812)). For an accusation that Theodore Roosevelt was trying to force Congress to declare war, see Senator Morgan's speech, 38 CONG.REC. 426, 434–41 (1904), some of it quoted in CORWIN, THE PRESIDENT (n. 5 to Intro. to Pt. II) 484.

President Nixon, while a private citizen, said that 'there will never be another declaration of war . . . that time is gone'. Interview, WETA-TV Channel 26, Nov. 27, 1967, quoted in Wallace, *The President's Exclusive Foreign Affairs Powers over Foreign Aid,* 1970 DUKE L.J. 293, 309. But perhaps he meant only that even wars authorized by Congress would be fought without formal declaration.

34. Compare President Bush's request for Congressional approval for the actions in the Persian Gulf, and President Clinton's views on action in Haiti, n. 60 to this chapter.

35. Andrew Jackson said that the President should seek Congressional approval for policy that would probably lead to War. 4 RICHARDSON (n. 27 to Ch. II) 1484. Compare C. BERDAHL, THE WAR POWERS OF THE EXECUTIVE IN THE UNITED STATES 27–30 (1921).

36. The Vietnam War produced a spate of articles and memoranda dealing with the constitutional authority of the President to fight in Vietnam. Most of them are reprinted in THE VIETNAM WAR AND INTERNATIONAL LAW (1969), edited for the American Society of International Law by Professor Richard Falk; constitutional issues are dealt with especially in volumes 2 and 3. See, in particular, Note, *Congress, the President, and the Power to Commit Forces to Combat,* 81 HARV.L.REV. 1771, 1791–2 (1968), reprinted in 2 FALK, VIETNAM at 616, 636–7. See also *Symposium on United States Action in Cambodia,* 65 AM.J.INT'L L. 1 (1971); *Hammarskjöld Forum: Expansion of the Vietnam War into Cambodia— the Legal Issues,* 45 N.Y.U.L.REV. 625 (1970); *Legality of United States Participation in the Vietnam Conflict: a Symposium,* 75 YALE L.J. 1084 (1966); *Legal Memorandum on the Amendment to End the War,* 116 CONG.REC. 16,120 (1970); *Symposium of Lawyers on Indochina,* May 20, 1970, *id.* at 17,387; *Lawyer's Memorandum, Indochina: The Constitutional Crisis,* Part I, *id.* at 15,410 and Part II, *id.* at 16,478; E. Rostow *et al., Letter on Constitutional Authority of President in Using American Troops, id.* at 18,338.

37. In Korea, President Truman acted without advance authorization from Congress. Presumably, he claimed authority to act in the first instance to protect U.S. lives and property; then, pursuant to the U.N. Security Council resolution, in implementation of the U.N. Charter (a treaty of the United States), and the U.N. Participation Act adopted by Congress. Some question whether the Charter and the Act authorized the President ever after to go to war at the behest of the U.N. especially when, as in that case, U.N. action was only a recommendation and was taken at the request of the United States, effectively of the Executive branch. See Ch. VIII, p. 255. President Truman acted in

urgency, and there was early consultation with Congressional leaders; the circumstances perhaps gave him the right to expect Congressional ratification; and Congress did approve and ratify, implicitly, by appropriation of funds and renewal of the Selective Service Laws with full knowledge and the intent to approve what the President was doing.

The Korean War also produced debate, but only a few members of Congress expressly challenged the President's authority. See, e.g., POWERS OF THE PRESIDENT TO SEND THE ARMED FORCES OUTSIDE THE UNITED STATES, (n. 30 above); 96 CONG.REC. 9228–31, 9232–3, 9268–9, 9320, 9322–3, 9327–9, 9538–9, 9647–9 (1950). See generally G. PAIGE, THE KOREAN DECISION (1968).

On U.S. participation in the Persian Gulf War, see Ch. VIII, p. 255.

38. Pub.L.No.90–5, Title IV § 401, 81 Stat. 5 (1967).

In the Tonkin Gulf Resolution, Pub.L.No.88–408, 78 Stat. 384 (1964), 'the Congress approves and supports the determination of the President, as Commander in Chief, to take all necessary measures to repel any armed attack against the forces of the United States and to prevent further aggression'. Section 2 of the Resolution provides: 'The United States regards as vital to its national interest and to world peace the maintenance of international peace and security in southeast Asia. Consonant with the Constitution of the United States and the Charter of the United Nations and in accordance with its obligations under the Southeast Asia Collective Defense Treaty, the United States is, therefore, prepared, as the President determines, to take all necessary steps, including the use of armed force, to assist any member or protocol state of the Southeast Asia Collective Defense Treaty requesting assistance in defense of its freedom.' Compare the testimony of Undersecretary of State Nicholas Katzenbach, 113 CONG.REC. 23390–2 (1967), also in 'U.S. Commitments to Foreign Powers', *Hearings on S.Res. 151 before the Senate Comm. on Foreign Relations,* 90th Cong. 1st Sess. 77 *et seq.* (1967). See generally J. GALLOWAY, THE GULF OF TONKIN RESOLUTION (1970).

For appropriations to support the Vietnam War, see, e.g., The Supplemental Defense Appropriation Act of May 7, 1965, Pub.L.No.89–18, 79 Stat. 109; Defense Appropriations Act of 1970, Pub.L.No.91–171, § 638, 83 Stat. 486.

That Congress had authorized the Vietnam War was held in *Orlando* v. *Laird,* 443 F.2d 1039 (2d Cir. 1971), *cert. denied,* 404 U.S. 869 (1971).

39. See n. 33 to this chapter.

40. Both supporters and opponents of the Resolution seemed to recognize that the President was being authorized to go to war if he thought it necessary. Compare, e.g., Senator Fulbright, 110 CONG.REC. 18409 (1964), with Senator Morse, *id.* at 18430.

Senator Fulbright who piloted the Resolution through the Senate later said: 'Figuratively speaking, we did not deal with the resolution in terms of what it said and in terms of the power it would vest in the Presidency; we dealt with it in terms of how we thought it would be used by the man who occupied the Presidency. Our judgment turned out to be wrong, but even if it had been right, even if the administration had applied the resolution in the way we then thought it would, the abridgment of the legislative process and our consent to so sweeping a grant of power was not only a mistake but a failure of responsibility on the part of the Congress.' Fulbright appeared to be of the view that the Resolution constituted an unconstitutional delegation by Congress to the President of the war power. See 'Separation of Powers', *Hearings Before the Subcomm. on Separation of Powers of the Sen. Comm. on the Judiciary,* 90th Cong., 1st Sess. 47 (1967). Some would characterize it an authorization to carry hostilities as far as the President deemed necessary, including full-scale war.

For extended debates as to what the Tonkin Resolution authorized, see the exchanges between Undersecretary of State Katzenbach and several Senators, in *Hearings, National Commitments,* (n. 38 above) 82 *et seq.*

41. Section 3 of the Resolution, n. 38 to this chapter, provides: 'This resolution shall expire when the President shall determine that the peace and security of the area is reasonably assured by international conditions created by action of the United Nations or otherwise, except that it may be terminated earlier by concurrent resolution of the Congress.'

42. See, e.g., the tabling on March 1, 1966, of amendments offered by Senators Morse and Gruening, which would have repealed the Tonkin Resolution and barred the use of draftees in Southeast Asia without Congressional consent. The vote was 92–5 against the Morse Amendment and 94–2 against the Gruening Amendment. 112 CONG.REC. 4404, 4406 (1966). See also various attempts to have Congress limit U.S. involvement in Cambodia and set a date for withdrawal of U. S. troops, n. 45 to this chapter. On the effect of the later repeal of the Tonkin Resolution, see this chapter, p. 103 and n. 47 below.

43. Compare the reference by John Quincy Adams to 'that error in our Constitution which confers upon the legislative assemblies the power of declaring war, which, in the theory of government, according to Montesquieu and Rousseau, is strictly an Executive Act'. Later he referred to the 'absurdity' of 'having given to Congress, instead of the Executive, the power of declaring war'. 4 MEMOIRS OF JOHN QUINCY ADAMS 32 (C. F. Adams ed. 1875). It appears, however, that he thought that practice had effectively corrected this error.

That 'short of war' is not an effective constitutional standard see Jones, *The President, Congress and Foreign Relations,* 29 CALIF.L.REV. 565, 579 (1941).

44. See Rehnquist, *The Constitutional Issues—Administration Position* 45 N.Y.U.L.REV. 628 (1970) *(Hammarskjöld Forum: Expansion of the Viet Nam War into Cambodia—The Legal Issues),* reprinted in 3 FALK, VIETNAM (n. 36 to this chapter) 175. See the text of the Tonkin Gulf Resolution, n. 38 to this chapter.

45. See the McGovern-Hatfield Amendment 'to end the war' (S. Amend. 862), rejected by the Senate, 116 CONG.REC. 30683 (1970), and the Cooper-Church Amendment (S. Amend. 620) to limit U.S. involvement in Cambodia, adopted by the Senate, *id.* at 22251, but failed in conference. See CONGRESSIONAL QUARTERLY, WEEKLY REPORT 3008–12 (Dec. 18, 1970). In 1971, however, the supplemental foreign aid authorization which the President signed into law included a provision that the funds authorized shall not be used to finance the

introduction of U.S. combat troops or any U.S. military advisers into Cambodia. Special Foreign Assistance Act of 1971, Pub.L.No.91–652, §§ 7, 84 Stat. 1943 (1971).

Several attempts were made in the first session of the 92d Congress to add a troop withdrawal amendment to the bill extending the draft. The Senate adopted Senator Mansfield's amendment (S. Amend. 214) which urged the President to set a final date for withdrawal contingent upon the release of all prisoners of war. 117 CONG.REC. S9718. The amendment, a non-binding expression of policy, was rejected by the House, 117 CONG.REC. H5943, and was dropped in conference. See CONGRESSIONAL QUARTERLY, WEEKLY REPORT 2665 (Dec. 25, 1971).

46. See nn. 16, 64, 65 to Ch. III.

47. Its repeal (Pub.L.No.91–672, § 12, 84 Stat. 2055 (1971)) could properly be interpreted only as withdrawing authority for new military actions in the area in the future. That Congress repealed the resolution while appropriating funds for continuance of the war and rejecting resolutions for its termination left no doubt that repeal was not intended as the equivalent of a resolution to terminate the war. Compare *Da Costa* v. *Laird*, 448 F.2d 1368 (2d Cir. 1971), *cert. denied*, 405 U.S. 979 (1972).

48. Compare Madison's Helvidius Letter no. 1, Chapter II, n. 10: 'Those who are to *conduct a war* cannot in the nature of things, be proper or safe judges, whether *a war ought* to be *commenced, continued*, or *concluded*.'

No one doubts the power of the President (and Senate) to end war by treaty. The Supreme Court has said that ' "the State of War" may be terminated by treaty or legislation or Presidential proclamation'. *Ludecke* v. *Watkins*, 335 U.S. 160, 168 (1948). It is not clear whether the Court meant that the President might do so by proclamation on his own authority. Wilson denied the President's power to end war by proclamation. See C. ROSSITER, THE SUPREME COURT AND THE COMMANDER IN CHIEF 79 and n. 23 (1951). So did Madison in the first Helvidius Letter, 6 J. MADISON, WRITINGS 148 (Hunt ed. 1910), Chapter II, n. 13. Blackstone thought that the power to decide for war and the power to make peace should be in the same hands, but for him they would both be lodged in the Executive, the Monarch. 1 BLACKSTONE, COMMENTARIES (n. 11 to Ch. II) §§ 257–8. Compare: 'It should therefore be difficult in a republic to declare war; but not to make peace.' 2 STORY, COMMENTARIES (n. 3 to Ch. I) §1171, at 97.

Perhaps, since Congress has the power to decide that the United States should go to war, the President ought not be able to say that it should not go to war, or should not remain at war, in effect repealing the declaration of war. Compare the proposal at the Constitutional Convention that would have denied the President a role in making peace treaties, n. 65 to Ch. VII. Perhaps it is not the power to end war that is denied the President alone, but authority to conclude the political and territorial arrangements that sometimes go with peace, especially any involving the territory of the United States. Compare *Fleming* v. *Page*, this chapter, p. 104. Presidents can perhaps effectively end a state of war merely by resuming diplomatic relations with the former enemy.

49. Congress decided to fight a limited war against France at the end of the eighteenth century, and the Supreme Court recognized that it could do so. *Bas* v.
Tingy, 4 U.S. (4 Dall.) 37 (1800); *Talbot* v. *Seeman*, 1 U.S. (1 Cranch) 1 (1801),
n. 65 to Ch. III. See A. SOFAER, WAR, FOREIGN AFFAIRS AND CONSTITUTIONAL
POWER, THE ORIGINS (1976), at 161–3.

Compare: 'The sovereignty, as to declaring war and limiting its effects, rests
with the legislature. The sovereignty, as to its execution, rests with the president. If the legislature do not limit the nature of the war, all the regulations and
rights of general war attach upon it.' Story, J., dissenting in *Brown* v. *United
States*, 12 U.S. (8 Cranch) 110, 153–4 (1814). See also *id.* at 145: 'congress (for
with them rests the sovereignty of the nation as to the right of making war,
and declaring its limits and effects) . . .' At 147: 'If, indeed, there be a limit
imposed as to the extent to which hostilities may be carried by the executive,
I admit that the executive cannot lawfully transcend that limit . . .' And at
149: 'If any of such acts are disapproved by the legislature, it is in their power
to narrow and limit the extent to which the rights of war shall be exercised
. . .' And see Marshall, C. J., quoted nn. 14, 64 to Ch. III.

But *cf. Ex parte Milligan*, 71 U.S. (4 Wall.) 2, 139 (1866): 'This power [of
Congress] necessarily extends to all legislation essential to the prosecution of
war with vigor and success except such as interferes with the command of the
forces and the conduct of campaigns. That power and duty belong to the
President as Commander-in-Chief.' I assume that the Court's dictum of exception applies to detailed, tactical decisions on the conduct of the war. But *cf.* C.
BERDAHL, THE WAR POWERS OF THE EXECUTIVE OF THE UNITED STATES 116–17
(1921).

During the War of 1812, soon after the declaration of war, the House passed
a bill authorizing the President to 'occupy and hold, the whole or any part of
East Florida, including Amelia Island, and also those parts of West Florida
which are now in possession and under the jurisdiction of the United States'.
24 ANNALS OF CONG. 1684–5 (1812); 23 ANNALS OF CONG. 323–4 (1812)
[1811–1812]. A Senate amendment proposed authorization to occupy Canada
also. *Id.* at 325. The whole bill died in the Senate, *Id.* at 326.

During the Mexican War, a House resolution demanding the withdrawal of
American troops to the east bank of the Rio Grande was defeated 137–41.
CONG.GLOBE, 30th Cong., 1st Sess. 93 (1847). A similar resolution calling for
the withdrawal of American forces from Mexico to 'defensive positions' was
tabled. *Id.* at 179.

Congress early asserted its authority to investigate the conduct of war, as in
the famous case of General St. Clair. During the Civil War Congress established a committee to investigate the conduct of the war, which asserted substantial authority. See Pierson, *The Committee on the Conduct of the Civil War*,
23 AM. HISTORICAL REV. 550 (1918). The committee was the subject of controversy but no one at the time seemed to challenge Congressional authority to
scrutinize the conduct of the war, on constitutional grounds. There were
numerous efforts to get Congress to direct the ending of hostilities in Vietnam
(see n. 45 above), but none were successful until 1973. Pub.L.No. 93–559, § 34,

88 Stat. 1805 (1974), *repealed* Pub.L.No. 94–329, Title IV, § 413(a), 90 Stat. 761 (1976).

It has even been suggested that the President could not veto Congressional restrictions or termination of hostilities. Ratner, *The Coordinated War Making Power,* 44 S.CALIF.L.REV. 461, 478 (1971). For the President's power to end war, see n. 48 to this chapter.

50. It has been argued that nuclear war is *sui generis* and that even a declaration of war by Congress should not be deemed to authorize nuclear war, or to authorize the President to convert a conventional one into nuclear war, without express Congressional authorization. J. Stone, *Presidential First Use is Unlawful,* 56 FOREIGN POLICY 94 (1984).

51. *Brown* v. *United States,* 12 U.S. (8 Cranch) 110 (1814). Story had ruled to the contrary when deciding the case as a circuit judge, and later, sitting on the Supreme Court, he adhered to his view that the President had the power unless Congress denied it. *Id.* at 129, 145, 149 *et seq.* It is not clear whether Story's view was that during wars declared by Congress the President had authority flowing automatically from his constitutional power as Commander in Chief, or that Congress had conferred it upon him implicitly by its declaration of war. Story admitted that Congress could have denied or limited the President's powers. Compare this chapter, pp. 102–4 and n. 49 above.

52. *The Prize Cases,* 67 U.S. (2 Black) 635 (1862). Even before the Civil War, the Court recognized the power of military authorities to seize or destroy private property—including the property of citizens—in case of military necessity, subject to compensation. *Cf. Mitchell* v. *Harmony,* 54 U.S. (13 How.) 115, 134 (1851). For later cases, compare *United States* v. *Russell,* 81 U.S. (13 Wall.) 623 (1871) ; *Totten* v. *United States,* 92 U.S. 105 (1875) ; see 40 OP. ATT'Y GEN. 250, 253 (1942). And compare Ch. IX, p. 297. President Lincoln's Emancipation Proclamation may be seen as asserting even larger Executive authority but that was later ratified by the Thirteenth Amendment.

I do not consider here limitations on Presidential war-power in favor of U.S. citizens within the United States. See, e.g., *Ex parte Milligan,* 71 U.S. (4 Wall.) 2 (1866), which held, after the war, that a loyal citizen could not be tried by court-martial where civilian courts were functioning. *Cf.* also *Ex parte Merryman,* 17 Fed. Cas. 144 (C.C.D. MI. 1861).

53. See 12 U.S. (8 Cranch) at 124–9.

54. See Trading With the Enemy Act of 1917, ch. 106, 40 Stat. 411, as amended by the First War Powers Act, 1941, ch. 593, § 301, 55 Stat. 839. *Cf. Silesian-American Corp.* v. *Clark,* 332 U.S. 469 (1947); *Uebersee Finanz-Korp.* v. *McGrath,* 343 U.S. 205 (1952). See also the International Emergency Economic Powers Act, 50 U.S.C. §§ 1701–06 (1988 & Supp. V 1993).

55. *Fleming* v. *Page,* 50 U.S. (9 How.) 603 (1850). See Ch. IX.

56. Compare the Truman Proclamation claiming for the United States the natural resources of its Continental Shelf, Ch. II, p. 44. Previous attempts to deal with the matter by legislation died in committee. S.J.Res. 208, 75th Cong., 1st Sess., 81 CONG. REC. 8882, 9236, 9548 (1937)(Senator Nye); S.J.Res. 24, 76th Cong., 1st Sess., 84 CONG. REC. 70 (1939) (Senator Nye); S.J.Res. 83, *id.* at 1976 (Senator Walsh); H.R.J.Res. 176, *id.* at 1646, 6235 (Rep. Hobbs); H.R.J.Res.

181, *id.* at 1850 (Rep. O'Connor). In 1983, President Reagan claimed for the United States the Exclusive Economic Zone; Congress was not asked to confirm it. 19 WEEKLY COMPILATION OF PRESIDENTIAL DOCUMENTS 383 (1983), 83 DEP'T STATE BULL. No. 2075 at 70–1 (1983), 22 I.L.M. 464 (1983). See n. 28 to Ch. II.

57. Pub.L.No. 93–148, 87 Stat. 555 (1973), 50 U.S.C. §§ 1541 *et seq.* (1988).

58. Section 2(c), 50 U.S.C. § 1541(c). Compare section 3 of the Senate version of the War Powers Resolution, S.440, 93rd Cong., 1st Sess., July 23, 1973, and see the Conference Report on the War Powers Resolution, H.R.Rep. No. 547, 93d Cong., 1st Sess., October 4, 1973. For interpretation and application of the Resolution (up to 1981), see 3 UNITED STATES FOREIGN RELATIONS LAW: DOCUMENTS AND SOURCES 137 (Glennon & Franck, eds. 1981).

59. 'Message from President Nixon Vetoing the War Powers Resolution', PUBLIC PAPERS OF THE PRESIDENTS OF THE UNITED STATES, RICHARD NIXON, Oct. 24, 1974, reprinted in 3 UNITED STATES FOREIGN RELATIONS LAW: DOCUMENTS AND SOURCES (Glennon and Franck, eds. 1981) 123.

60. S.J.Res. 20, 102d Cong., 1st Sess (1991). On the military action in Haiti in 1994, see Damrosch, *Agora: The 1994 U.S. Action in Haiti* in 89 AM. J. INT'L L. 58 (1995). Compare Trimble, *id.* at 84; also the views of the Executive Department, *id.* at 122; and see *id.* at 127.

61. In 1995, Senator Dole introduced a bill 'To clarify the war powers of Congress and the President in the post-Cold War period', which would repeal the War Powers Resolution but continue to require the President to consult Congress 'in every possible instance . . . before introducing United States Armed Forces into hostilities'; the Bill would also prohibit the President from putting U.S. armed forces under foreign command without Congressional approval. 'Peace Powers Act of 1995', S.5, 104th Cong., 1st Sess. (1995) introduced Jan. 4, 1995. Compare Senator Biden's bill which '[c]onfers and confirms Presidential authority to use force abroad', S. 564, 104th Cong., 1st Sess. (1995).

  For some of many writings on the War Powers Resolution, see ELY, WAR AND RESPONSIBILITY: CONSTITUTIONAL LESSONS OF VIETNAM AND ITS AFTERMATH (1993) and *War and Responsibility: A Symposium on Congress, the President, and the Authority to Initiate Hostilities*, 50 MIAMI L.REV. 1 (1995).

62. Congress purposely did not include covert actions in the War Powers Resolution. Damrosch, *Covert Operations*, 83 AM.J. INT'LL.795, 797 (1989). See also, Bentley, *Keeping Secrets: The Church Committee, Covert Action, and Nicaragua*, 25 COLUM.J. TRANSNAT'L L. 601 (1987). See generally, KOH, THE NATIONAL SECURITY CONSTITUTION: SHARING POWER AFTER THE IRAN-CONTRA AFFAIR (1990), W.M. REISMAN AND J. BAKER, REGULATING COVERT ACTION: PRACTICES, CONTEXTS, AND POLICIES OF COVERT COERCION ABROAD IN INTERNATIONAL AND AMERICAN LAW (1992).

  For major elements of intelligence legislation, see, e.g., Foreign Intelligence Surveillance Act of 1978, Pub.L.No. 95–511, 92 Stat. 1783 (1978), codified and amended at 50 U.S.C. §§ 1801 *et seq.* (1988) (as amended by Pub. L.No. 103-359, 108 Stat. 3443 (1994); Intelligence Oversight Act, 50 U.S.C. § 413 (1988 & Supp. IV 1992); the Boland Amendments (restricting U.S. aid to the Contras in Nicaragua), see n. 63 below; 22 U.S.C. §2414 (1994) (President must report on military sales and foreign assistance). Compare the Hughes–Ryan Amendment, formerly 22 U.S.C. § 2422, *repealed*, Pub.L.No. 102–88, § 601, 105 Stat. 441 (1991), and the unsuccessful Cooper–Church amendment which sought to limit U.S. military involvement in Cambodia, n. 45 to this chapter. See also, 'Compilation of Intelligence Laws and Related Laws and Executive Orders of Interest to the National Intelligence Community (as amended through June 8, 1993)', *Permanent Select Committee on Intelligence*, H.R., 103rd Cong., 1st Sess., (1993).

Even without explicit legislation requiring prior notice of intelligence activities, there is evidence that both branches recognize an Executive obligation to inform Congress. 'It was always understood that new initiatives in any aspect of intelligence activities, if they had important or vital—and there are arguments on those phrases—implications for policy, cost or risk would be reported [to Congress] before they were carried out.' Testimony of William Miller, former staff director of the Senate Intelligence Committee, in 'H.R. 1013, H.R. 1371 and other proposals', n. 3 to this chapter.

63. The Boland Amendments. For a history of these amendments, see Note, *The Boland Amendments and Foreign Affairs Deference*, 88 COLUM. L.REV. 1534, 1566–9 (1988).

64. See n. 62 above. 'Timely notice' of the 'Iran–Contra' activities came 11 months after the fact, and only after the story had been 'leaked' to the press. See 'H.R. 1013, H.R. 1371 and other proposals', n. 3 to this chapter.

65. Presidential authority, perhaps obligation, to propose legislation can be found in Art. II, sec. 3: 'He shall from time to time give the Congress Information of the State of the Union, and recommend to their Consideration such Measures as he shall judge necessary and expedient. . .' On the potentialities of 'the legislative leadership of the President' in foreign affairs, see Jones, *The President, Congress, and Foreign Relations*, 29 CALIF.L.REV. 565, 567–75 (1941).

Presidents have sought Congressional authorization even when they might perhaps have acted on their own authority. Justice Jackson suggested that this was sound and prudent policy especially if their action might face judicial review. *Youngstown Sheet & Tube Co.* v. *Sawyer*, 343 U.S. 579, 647 n. 16 (1952). Presidents have also sought Congressional endorsement of policy, sometimes in vain for many years, as for the Monroe Doctrine. *Cf.* D. PERKINS, THE MONROE DOCTRINE 1826–1867, at 217–23 (1933). Compare the Persian Gulf Resolution, n. 60 above.

66. On the obligation of Congress to implement treaties, see Ch. VII, p. 205. For an assertion of autonomy for the power of the purse generally, made in 1967, see the Statement of Senator Morse (erstwhile professor of law), *Hearings, Separation of Powers* (n. 40 above) 57, 63–4.

67. An effort in 1842 to delete funds for a Minister to Mexico was defeated. CONG.GLOBE, 27th Cong., 1st Sess., Appendix, 513–14 (1842). For a more recent effort, in 1940, to compel the severance of diplomatic relations with the Soviet Union, see 86 CONG.REC. 1172–1192 (1940). See generally Nobleman, *Financial Aspects of Congressional Participation in Foreign Relations*, 289 ANNALS OF THE AMERICAN ACADEMY OF POLITICAL AND SOCIAL SCIENCE 145

(1953). Compare the discussion of conditions on appropriations, p. 119, this chapter.

It is accepted that Theodore Roosevelt sent the fleet around the world and compelled Congress to appropriate funds to bring it back. See CORWIN, THE PRESIDENT (n. 5 to Intro. to Pt. II) 159. In 1912, after Senator Root objected to such an amendment as unconstitutional, the Senate defeated an amendment to an appropriation bill that would have forbidden the use of the funds for supporting troops outside the United States or sending or returning them. 48 CONG.REC. 10921–30 (1912). A Congressional rider to a 1969 statute provided that none of the funds appropriated by the Act 'shall be used to finance the introduction of American ground combat troops into Laos or Thailand'. Pub.L.No.91–171, § 643, Stat. 487 (1969). And Congress eventually voted to terminate funding for all combat activities in Southeast Asia, although this enactment came 3 months after the withdrawal of the last U.S. troop unit. See the Eagleton 'End the War' Amendment, Pub.L.No. 93–52, 87 Stat. 130 (1973). Compare nn. 29, 49 to this chapter. For other instances See CORWIN, THE PRESIDENT (n. 5 to Intro. to Pt. II) 158–9, 401–4. See generally E. CARPER, THE DEFENSE APPROPRIATION RIDER (1960).

In 1983, Congress authorized the introduction of forces into Lebanon, but provided that this authorization would terminate in 18 months. Pub.L.No.98–119, §§ 1–8, 97 Stat. 805. And see the legislation cited in n. 31 to this chapter.

68. See generally, e.g., Wallace, *The President's Exclusive Foreign Affairs Powers over Foreign Aid,* 1970 DUKE L.J. 293, 453.

69. See, e.g., Henkin, 'U.S. Nuclear Defense Policy: the Constitutional Framework', 26 ATLANTIC COMMUNITY Q. 63 (Spring 1988) (reprinted in THE CONSTITUTION AND NATIONAL SECURITY (Shuman & Thomas, eds. 1990).

70. Nevertheless, a Senate subcommittee has concluded: 'To a large extent, it appears that much of the "power of the purse" has shifted from Congress to the President.' SENATE COMM. OF THE JUDICIARY, SEPARATION OF POWERS, REP. No.549, 91 Cong., 1st Sess. 12 (1969). See n. 83 to this chapter.

71. The President is expressly required to give Congress 'from time to time' 'Information of the State of the Union', (Art II, sec. 3), and State of the Union messages have included major declarations of policy, e.g., the Monroe Doctrine. Congress also requests reports from the President on numerous subjects, including many relating to foreign affairs, e.g., the annual report on the United Nations and country reports on the condition of human rights around the world. See generally REPORTS TO BE MADE TO CONGRESS, H.R.DOC.No.23, 87th Cong., 1st Sess. (1961); Human Rights Country Reports are required by the Foreign Assistance Act of 1961, codified and amended as 22 U.S.C. § 2151n (1994).

The Continental Congress established a Department of Foreign Affairs and provided that 'any member of Congress' shall have access to all its papers 'provided that no copy shall be taken of matters of a secret nature without the special leave of Congress'. See Wolkinson, *Demands of Congressional Committees*

for Executive Papers, 10 FED. BAR J. 103, 328 (1949). That department, however, was a department of Congress, there being no executive branch.
For opinions strongly upholding executive privilege, see 40 OP. ATT'Y GEN. 45 (1941); 41 *id.* at 507, 525–31 (1960). An early article on 'executive privilege' is Warren, *Presidential Declarations of Independence,* 10 B.U.L.REV. 1 (1930). See also CORWIN, THE PRESIDENT (n. 5 to Intro. to Pt. II) 125–33, 212–13, 473–6. For more recent writings, see, e.g., Berger, *Executive Privilege* v. *Congressional Inquiry,* 12 U.C.L.A.L.REV. 1044, 1288 (1965); Bishop, *The Executive's Right of Privacy: An Unresolved Constitutional Question,* 66 YALE L.J. 477 (1957); Collins, *The Power of Congressional Committees of Investigation to Obtain Information from the Executive Branch: the Argument for the Legislative Branch,* 39 GEO.L.J. 563 (1951); Hruska, *Executive Records in Congressional Investigations—Duty to Disclose—Duty to Withhold,* 35 NEB.L.REV. 310 (1955); Kramer and Marcuse, *Executive Privilege—A Study of the Period 1953–1960,* 29 GEO.WASH.L.REV. 623, 827 (1961). Compare Henkin, *The Right to Know and the Duty to Withhold: The Case of the Pentagon Papers,* 120 U.PA.L.REV. 271 (1971).

72. 1 RICHARDSON (n. 27 to Ch. II) 186–8.
73. The President has even refused to disclose information about a treaty to the Senate. See CORWIN, THE PRESIDENT (n. 5 to Intro. to Pt. II) 212–13 and n.41. Many instances of Presidential refusal are collected in 40 OP. ATT'Y GEN. 45 (1954); see also Kramer and Marcuse, n. 71 to this chapter.
  Congress apart, the Supreme Court has recognized the need for executive secrecy in foreign relations, see, e.g., *United States* v. *Curtiss-Wright Export Corp.,* 299 U.S. 304, 320 (1936); *Chicago & Southern Air Lines, Inc.* v. *Waterman S. S. Corp.,* 333 U.S. 103, 111 (1948); *Zemel* v. *Rusk,* 381 U.S. 1, 17 (1963). Compare *Totten* v. *United States,* 92 U.S. 105, 107 (1875). In *Jencks* v. *United States,* the Supreme Court required the Government to make witnesses' reports available to the accused or drop the prosecution. 353 U.S. 657 (1957). In *United States* v. *Reynolds,* a suit against the United States, the court found a governmental privilege in the circumstances but suggested that if it appeared necessary the trial judge would inspect the documents to determine whether they were privileged. 345 U.S. 1 (1953). And compare the various opinions in *New York Times Co.* v. *United States,* 403 U.S. 713 (1971), n. 17 to Ch. IX; also Mr. Justice Douglas dissenting in *Gravel* v. *United States,* 408 U.S. 606, 637–46 (1972).
  In *Marbury* v. *Madison* the Attorney General claimed the right to refuse to divulge to the courts anything relating to his official transactions while he was acting as Secretary of State. Chief Justice Marshall said that the Attorney General was required to communicate what was being asked, but Marshall accepted the privilege in principle. He said: 'There was nothing confidential required to be disclosed. If there had been he was not obliged to answer it; and if he thought that anything was communicated to him in confidence he was not bound to disclose it.' 5 U.S. (1 Cranch) 137, 143–45 (1803).
74. For a Congressional view, see HOUSE COMM. ON GOVERNMENT OPERATIONS, EXECUTIVE BRANCH PRACTICES IN WITHHOLDING INFORMATION FROM CONGRESSIONAL

COMMITTEES, H.R.REP.No.2207, 86th Cong., 2d Sess. (1960); and compare Collins, n. 71 to this chapter. An executive view is in SUBCOMM. ON CONSTITUTIONAL RIGHTS OF THE SENATE COMM. ON THE JUDICIARY, THE POWERS OF THE PRESIDENT TO WITHHOLD INFORMATION FROM THE CONGRESS— MEMORANDUM OF THE ATTORNEY GENERAL, 85th Cong., 2d Sess., Parts I and II. (Comm.Prints 1958 and 1959).

Even Congressional Committees have sometimes recognized that the Executive has the legal right to refuse information under the 'doctrine of executive privilege'. See, e.g., S.REP.No.1761, 86th Cong., 2d Sess. 22 (1960); compare also the Senate Report quoted in *Curtiss-Wright,* 299 U.S. at 319, quoted in n. 8 to Ch. VII.

In 1948 the House passed a joint resolution purporting to require the Executive to furnish any information required by Congressional Committees, H.R.J.Res. 342, 80th Cong., 2d Sess., 94 CONG.REC. 5821 (1948). In the Senate, the resolution died in Committee. Although a House Resolution 'directed' the Secretary of State to transmit 'full and complete information' with respect to any agreements or commitments between President Truman and the British Prime Minister, at least some Representatives agreed that it was within the President's province to refuse to divulge the information if he considered it would be incompatible with the national interest. See, e.g., 98 CONG.REC. 1205, 1215 (1952).

75. The Foreign Assistance Act of 1961, Pub.L.No. 87–195, § 634(c), 75 Stat. 455, as amended, 22 U.S.C. § 2394(c), (d) (1994), requiring that certain documents and information be given to Congress, or disbursements of aid should cease. Congress usually does not press this device to a showdown, and waives noncompliance if the President certifies that he has forbidden disclosure and gives his reasons for so doing. *Ibid.* See also Mutual Security Appropriations Act of 1960, Pub.L.No.86–383, § 111(d), 73 Stat. 720; Mutual Security and Related Agencies Appropriation Act of 1961, Pub.L.No.86–704, § 101(d), 74 Stat. 778 (1960). But compare Mutual Security Act of 1959, Pub.L.No.86–108, § 404(h) with § 401(i), (j), and (m), 73 Stat. 254. On the constitutionality of such provisions, see 41 OP.ATT'Y GEN. 507 (1960). Compare HOUSE COMM. ON GOVERNMENT OPERATIONS, AVAILABILITY OF INFORMATION FROM FEDERAL DEPARTMENTS AND AGENCIES, H.R.REP.No.818, 87th Cong., 1st Sess. (1961).

76. The President himself is not subject to subpoena, mandamus or injunction by the courts. See *Mississippi* v. *Johnson,* 71 U.S. (4 Wall.) 475 (1867). He could not be held in contempt by Congress but it could, of course, impeach him. And see n. 79.

Congress might be able to cite a federal official for contempt. Compare *Jurney* v. *MacCracken,* 294 U.S. 125 (1935); *Anderson* v. *Dunn,* 19 U.S. (6 Wheat.) 204 (1821); compare also *Groppi* v. *Leslie,* 404 U.S. 496 (1972). But if he acted on Presidential orders the President would doubtless protect him: even after a change of administration an Attorney General is not likely to prosecute for the crime of contempt of Congress (2 U.S.C. § 192 (1994)) an executive official who had acted under Presidential orders.

It is believed that failure of one official to give information to Congress led to his rejection by the Senate when he was later nominated to a cabinet post.

See Exec.Rep.No.4, 86th Cong., 1st Sess., 105 CONG.REC. 9982–7 (1959); also *id.* 10271, 10907–28; Zinn, *Extent of the Control of the Executive by the Congress of the United States,* HOUSE COMM. ON GOVERNMENT OPERATIONS, 87th Cong., 2d Sess., 19 n.7 (Comm.Print, 1962).

77. Cited in *United States* v. *Curtiss-Wright Export Corp.,* 299 U.S. 304, 321 (1936). See the famous remarks of Senator Spooner, 40 CONG.REC. 1420 (1906):
    'It is a Department which from the beginning the Senate has never assumed the right to direct or control, except as to clearly defined matters relating to duty imposed by statute and not connected with the conduct of our foreign relations.

    We *direct* all the other heads of departments to transmit to the Senate designated papers or information. We do not address directions to the Secretary of State, nor do we direct requests even, to the Secretary of State. We direct requests to the real head of that Department, the President of the United States, and, as a matter of courtesy, we add the qualifying words, "if in his judgment not incompatible with the public interest".'

78. It was reported that Presidents Kennedy and Johnson directed that the Executive branch cooperate with Congress and avoid denying information to its committees except where absolutely necessary.

    One writer has said: '. . . on the whole, a good case can be made out for the proposition that the present imprecise situation is, in fact, reasonably satisfactory. Neither the executive nor the Congress is very sure of its rights, and both usually evince a tactful disposition not to push the assertion of their rights to abusive extremes. Of such is the system of checks and balances'. Bishop, 66 YALE L.J. at 491 (1957), n. 71 to this chapter.

    It has been suggested that only the President himself should be able to assert Executive privilege, and only the House (or Senate) itself, by formal resolution, ask for information which the Executive branch would withhold. Maass, *Hearings, Separation of Powers* (n. 40 to Ch. IV) 197.

    Compare the suggestion of Justice Harlan in *The Pentagon Papers Case, New York Times Co.* v. *United States,* 403 U.S. 713, 757 (1971), that the courts should examine only whether the subject is within the Executive's competence and whether the head of the Executive Department himself has certified to the need for secrecy.

79. See *United States* v. *Nixon,* 418 U.S. 683 (1974). Lower courts held the papers of the President not immune to subpoena for the judicial process. *In re Subpoena to Richard M. Nixon,* 360 F. Supp. 1 (D.D.C. 1973), *aff'd, Nixon* v. *Sirica,* 487 F.2d 700 (D.C. Cir. 1973). The Supreme Court also upheld an act of Congress authorizing the Administration of General Services to take custody of Nixon papers and tapes to preserve them for public access. *Nixon* v. *Administration of General Services,* 433 U.S. 425 (1977).

80. *United States* v. *North,* 708 F.Supp. 380, 383 (D.D.C. 1988), *rev'd in part on other grounds,* 920 F.2d 940 (D.C. Cir. 1990).

81. See, e.g., Jefferson, Letter to Mrs. John Adams, Sept. 11, 1804, in THE WRITINGS OF THOMAS JEFFERSON 310–11 (Ford ed. 1897). Compare Jackson, 3 RICHARDSON (n. 27 to Ch. II) 1144–5; Lincoln, First Inaugural Address, 7

RICHARDSON (n. 27 to Ch. II) 3206, 3207, 3210–11. See also Curtis's argument on behalf of President Johnson in his impeachment proceedings, CONG.GLOBE 40th Cong., 2d Sess. (Supp.) 26–7 (1868).

82. See, e.g., Vinson, C. J., dissenting in *Youngstown Sheet & Tube Co.* v. *Sawyer*, 343 U.S. 579, 700 (1952). Compare *United States* v. *Midwest Oil Co.*, 236 U.S. 459 (1915) and cases, n. 15 to this chapter.

83. 'This term describes a variety of actions which may be taken by the executive branch with respect to the expenditure of funds appropriated by Congress. "Impounding" may result from directions by the President to the head of an agency to refuse to spend or to delay the expenditure of appropriated funds, from the issuance of such an order by the agency head himself, or from a decision by the Bureau of the Budget "apportioning" a part or all of the appropriations as reserves.

The effect of such actions is to restrict the use of funds below the level authorized and appropriated by Congress and thereby to affect adversely the implementation of a public activity or program established by Congress. In its most extreme form, "impounding" affords the President the equivalent of an "item veto" which may be exercised to restrict or to halt programs of which he disapproves. In effect, impounding grants to the President his own "power of the purse" which may effectively frustrate congressional decisions and enacted law. The impounding power was first asserted by President Roosevelt in 1941, in an effort to defer public works projects he considered nonessential in view of the war emergency. Congress continued to appropriate funds for these projects and the President did not wish to veto entire appropriations bills. Accordingly, he directed the Bureau of the Budget to place the funds for these projects in reserves unavailable for expenditure by the agencies.

In more recent years, impoundment has been used primarily in the national defense area. Among the most well-known examples are B-70 bomber program and the nuclear frigate construction. In the domestic field, highway construction and aid to impacted schools have been subject to executive impounding.' SENATE COMMITTEE ON THE JUDICIARY, SEPARATION OF POWERS (S.Rep No. 91–549, 91st Cong., 1st Sess. (1969) 12–13.

In 1948, Truman refused to spend about $800 million to expand the Air Force. Eisenhower refused to expend funds to maintain the full strength of the Marine Corps. See M. RAMSEY, IMPOUNDMENT BY THE EXECUTIVE DEPARTMENT OF FUNDS WHICH CONGRESS AUTHORIZED IT TO SPEND OR OBLIGATE 4 (Library of Congress Legislative Reference Service, 1968). For the controversy involving the effort to direct the President to build the 'RS 70' airplane see H.R. REP.NO.1406, 87th Cong. 2d. Sess. 3–9 (1961); compare 108 CONG. REC. 4714 (1962). See *Hearings, Separation of Powers* (n. 40 to this chapter) 28–9, 40. See generally 'Executive Impoundment of Appropriated Funds', *Hearings Before the Subcomm. on Separation of Powers of the Senate Comm. on the Judiciary*, 92d Cong., 1st Sess. (1971).

84. Pub.L.No. 93–344, 88 Stat. 297 (1974), 2 U.S.C. §§ 621 *et seq.* (1994).

85. Compare *Kendall* v. *United States ex rel. Stokes*, 37 U.S. (12 Pet.) 612–13 (1838):

'It was urged at the bar, that the postmaster general was alone subject to the direction and control of the president, with respect to execution of the duty imposed upon him by this law; and this right of the president is claimed, as growing out of the obligation imposed upon him by the constitution, to take care that the laws be faithfully executed. This is a doctrine that cannot receive the sanction of this court. It would be vesting in the president a dispensing power, which has no countenance for its support, in any part of the constitution; and is asserting a principle, which if carried out in its results, to all cases falling within it, would be clothing the president with a power entirely to control the legislation of congress, and paralyze the administration of justice.

To contend that the obligation imposed on the president to see the laws faithfully executed, implies a power to forbid their execution, is a novel construction of the constitution and entirely inadmissible.'

In another context (in his famous Proclamation on Nullification) President Jackson said: 'the laws of the United States must be executed. I have no discretionary power on the subject; my duty is emphatically pronounced in the Constitution'. 3 RICHARDSON (n. 27 to Ch. II) 1217.

86. Section 3(d) of the Mutual Security Act of 1952, ch. 449, 66 Stat. 141, included: 'Not less than $25,000,000 of the funds made available [under specified sections] shall be used for economic, technical, and military assistance to Spain in accordance with the provisions of the Act.' President Truman said, *inter alia:* 'I do not regard this provision as a directive, which would be unconstitutional, but instead as an authorization, in addition to the authority already in existence under which loans to Spain may be made. . . Money will be loaned to Spain whenever mutually advantageous arrangements can be made . . . and whenever such loans will serve the interest of the United States in the conduct of foreign relations'. 23 DEP'T STATE BULL. 517 (1950). Compare the appropriation for aid to China despite Presidential objection, China Aid Act of 1948, ch. 169, Title IV, 62 Stat. 158–59 (authorization); ch. 685, *id.* at 1056 (appropriation); see Nobleman, ANNALS (n. 67 above) 160.

87. Grant objected and persuaded Congress to withdraw. See 9 RICHARDSON (n. 27 to Ch. II) 4331–2.

88. Ch. 149, 37 Stat. 913 (1913), 22 U.S.C. § 262 (1994). Congress is free, of course, to request or 'call upon' the President or to express its sense that something be done or not done, Ch. III, p. 79. But even such resolutions are often controversial; a sense resolution introduced by Senator Joseph McCarthy in June, 1955, that before a 'Big Four summit meeting' is held there should be agreement to discuss the status of countries under communist control, was defeated by a vote of 77–4. S.Res. 116, 84th Cong., 1st Sess., 101 CONG.REC. 8723–5, 8933–60 (1955).

The Trade Expansion Act of 1962, Pub.L.No.87–794, § 243, 76 Stat. 878 (1962), *repealed* Pub.L.No.93–618, 88 Stat. 2072 (1975), see 19 U.S.C. § 1873, required the inclusion of members of Congress on delegations to negotiate trade agreements. Such a provision may claim justification in that the agreements are negotiated upon Congressional authority (Ch. VII, p. 215), but

Presidents might reject it in principle as interference with their appointive powers or negotiating authority.

Presidents have sometimes resented Congressional intrusion upon the 'unitary executive', by conferring duties and transferring responsibilities directly to Executive officials. For instances close to Foreign Affairs, see, e.g., legislation conferring responsibility upon the U.S. Trade Representative, in Omnibus Trade and Competitveness Act of 1988, § 1301(a), amending § 301 of the Trade Act of 1974, Pub.L.No. 93-618, 88 Stat. 1978 (1975), codified at 19 U.S.C. § 2411 (1994). See Leebron, cited in n. 85 to Ch. VI. See, generally, *Bowsher* v. *Synar*, 478 U.S. 714 (1986), and, for an early case, *Kendall* v. *United States ex rel. Stokes*, 37 U.S. (12 Pet.) 524 (1838). Compare Lessig and Sunstein, *The President and the Administration*, 94 Colum. L. Rev. 1 (1994), with Calabresi and Prakash, *The President's Power to Execute the Law*, 104 Yale L.J. 541 (1994). In foreign affairs, the President's objections may be stronger. See, e.g., Marshall, C.J., in *Marbury* v. *Madison*, 5 U.S. (1 Cranch) at 166.

89. Compare p. 113, this chapter. That Congress cannot impose 'unconstitutional conditions' on appropriations, see 41 Op.Att'y Gen. 230 (1955). *Cf. Butler* v. *United States*, 297 U.S. 1, 74 (1936); Frankfurter, J., concurring in *United States* v. *Lovett*, 328 U.S. 303, 329 (1946); *Lovett* v. *United States*, 104 Ct.Cl. 557, 593 (1945) (Madden, J. concurring); Corwin, The President (n. 5 to Intro. to Pt. II) 447–50 n. 64; Herblock Cartoon facing 41 Calif.L.Rev. 566 (1953). For a notable veto message by President Hayes objecting to House of Representatives conditions to an appropriation, see 9 Richardson (n. 27 to Ch. II) 4482–83, quoted in Corwin, The President (n. 5 to Intro. to Pt. II) 160. See generally, Rosenthal, *Conditional Federal Spending and the Constitution*, 39 Stan.L.Rev. 1103 (1987).

90. Representative Findlay proposed 'to shut off the salaries of any State Department personnel who might use their official time to advance' the nuclear nonproliferation treaty, but his amendment did not get very far. See *Hearings, National Commitments* (n. 38 to Ch. IV) 235–6. If Congress cannot remove an executive officer (note 106, to this chapter) it cannot do so by denying his salary. Compare *United States* v. *Lovett*, 328 U.S. 303, 329 (1946) (Frankfurter, J., concurring).

91. For example, Joint Resolution of May 15, 1924, ch. 155, 43 Stat. 119, 120, authorized an appropriation for a delegation to the International Opium Conference. Congress provided that: '[T]he representatives of the United States shall sign no agreement which does not fulfill the conditions necessary for the suppression of the habit-forming narcotic drug traffic as stated in the preamble.' (The conditions related to: (1) the designation of certain opium uses as 'illegitimate' and (2) the control of the production of raw opium.) The U.S. delegation heeded the Congressional conditions (perhaps because its chief was the chairman of the House Foreign Affairs Committee and had himself proposed the conditions); when these proved unacceptable to other governments the delegation withdrew from the Conference. But the delegates to a later Opium Conference in 1931 disregarded the conditions. See Nobleman, Annals (n. 67 to this chapter) 156 and authorities cited.

In 1826, an attempt to add a rider instructing the delegation to a Panama Conference was defeated. Daniel Webster opposed the rider arguing that while Congress was free to refuse to appropriate funds to implement foreign policy, it could not attach conditions to such appropriations. See Hale Memorandum, S.Doc.No.56, 54th Cong., 2d Sess. 37–40 (1897).

Compare the statement of Senator Borah in regard to the Commander in Chief power: 'Undoubtedly the Congress may refuse to appropriate and undoubtedly the Congress may say that an appropriation is for a specific purpose. In that respect the President would undoubtedly be bound by it. But the Congress could not, through the power of appropriation, in my judgment, infringe upon the right of the President to command whatever army he might find.' 69 CONG. REC. 6760 (1928), quoted in CORWIN, THE PRESIDENT (n. 5 to Intro. to Pt. II) 449–50.

92. See Mutual Security Act of 1954, ch. 937, §§ 105(b) (1), 121, 68 Stat. 835, 837. In 1950 the House passed an amendment to terminate assistance to the United Kingdom so long as Ireland remained partitioned, but the amendment died in conference. See 96 CONG.REC. 4344–8, 7221–5 (1950) (conference report on amendments to the Economic Cooperation Act of 1948).

93. Foreign Assistance Act of 1961, Pub.L.No.87–195, § 620, 75 Stat. 444–5, as amended, 22 U.S.C. § 2370(a), (f), (n) (*repealed*), (o), (p) (*repealed*), (s) (1994). See also the Mutual Defense Act of 1951 which suspended aid to any country permitting shipment of embargoed materials to the USSR unless the President found that 'unusual circumstances indicate that the cessation of aid would clearly be detrimental to the security of the United States'. Ch. 575, § 103(b), 65 Stat. 646; Foreign Assistance Act of 1948, ch. 169, § 103, 62 Stat. 138 (1948).

Congress also required that 50% of all our assistance be shipped in American vessels. See Act of August 26, 1954, ch. 936, 68 Stat. 832, as amended, 46 U.S.C. § 1241(b) (1) (1988).

There are other provisions that are not directives, for example that the President 'consider' terminating assistance to a country that permits or fails to prevent mob action against United States property. See Foreign Assistance Act of 1967, Pub.L.No.90–137, § 301(f) (1), 81 Stat. 459, 22 U.S.C. § 2370(j) (1994); see also several hortatory provisions in the human rights provisions of the Foreign Assistance Act of 1961, n. 71 above, and the Foreign Assistance and Related Program Appropriations Act of 1978, §507, 22 U.S.C. § 262d-1 (1994).

94. The First Hickenlooper Amendment is in sec. 301(e) of the Foreign Assistance Act of 1963, Pub.L.No.88–205, 77 Stat. 386, as amended, 22 U.S.C. § 2370(e) (1) (1994); compare related provisions in the Inter-American Development Bank Act, Pub.L.No.89–6, 79 Stat. 24 (1965), as amended 22 U.S.C. § 283*l*(c) (1994). (The Second Hickenlooper Amendment, Pub.L.No.88–633, § 301(d), 78 Stat. 1013 (1964), as amended, 22 U.S.C. § 2370(e) (2) (1994), contained in the Foreign Assistance Act of 1964, is a modification of the Act of State doctrine addressed to the courts (Ch. V, p. 137), not a condition on spending, and has no relation to foreign assistance.)

95. See 22 U.S.C. § 2304 (1994).

96. See Trade Act of 1974 (Jackson–Vanik amendment), 19 U.S.C. §§ 2192, 2193, 2432, 2437 and 2439 (1994).

97. Congress might be saying that it is for the general welfare of the United States to assist some governments and not others, or even the same government if it follows certain policies but not if it follows others. Where the conditions seek to induce some action (or inaction) by the recipient, the argument could be made that Congress cannot use the spending power to 'buy up' regulatory authority it does not otherwise have. Compare the disagreement between majority and dissent as to conditions on spending in *United States* v. *Butler*, 297 U.S. 1 (1936). But, though the *Butler* case was carefully distinguished, the broader power of Congress largely prevailed in the *Social Security Cases, Steward Machine Co.* v. *Davis*, 301 U.S. 548 (1937), and *Helvering* v. *Davis*, 301 U.S. 619 (1937). In the foreign aid cases moreover (unlike *Butler*), Congress is not trying to regulate domestic activities that are otherwise under the jurisdiction of the states; it is not 'buying' state power and distorting the federal system.

The argument against conditions designed to induce Presidential action would be much stronger if, say, Congress conditioned foreign assistance on the President's appointing X as foreign aid administrator. That condition is no doubt improper, but would it fall, and would the appropriation then stand unconditionally? The President is probably not free to disregard improper conditions on foreign assistance and proceed to make the contribution on behalf of the United States unless one can assume that Congress would have made the contribution unconditionally if it had known its conditions would fail. Compare the discussion of improper conditions on Senate consent to treaties, Ch. VII, p. 182. Of course, Congress can effectively impose even such conditions informally.

98. Congress once established 'ceilings' on the amounts that could be appropriated for the payment of annual contributions to various international organizations. Of course, if the international organization has authority to bind the United States and proceeds to assess the United States for more than the Congressional ceiling, the United States is, internationally, in default. Later, Congress legislated instead to forbid any U.S. representative to commit the U.S. to contribute more than 33.33% of the budget of any organization to which the legislation applied; this, of course, does not prevent an international organization from imposing a higher assessment. The power of Congress to instruct delegates to international organizations in this respect is as questionable as in respect of any other international act or negotiation. See H.REP.No. 1257, 81st Cong., 2d Sess. 7–8 (1950); ch. 651, 66 STAT. 550–1 (1952). See generally, Nobleman, ANNALS (n. 67 to this chapter) 160–3.

Compare also sec. 110, ch. 328, 67 Stat, 372 (1953), which prohibited the use of appropriated funds to pay any U.S. contribution 'to any international organization which engages in the direct or indirect promotion of the principle or doctrine of one world government or one world citizenship'; and S.REP.No.309, 83rd Cong., 1st Session, p. 7 (1953) in which a Senate Committee recommended legislation that would have cut off U.S. contributions to the United Nations if Communist China were admitted to membership.

In 1971 Congress placed the United States in default when it refused to appropriate funds to pay its obligations to the International Labor Organization. In the 1990s Congress has failed to pay its dues to the United Nations, amassing a debt that reached $1.4 billion in 1995. See 'Even Its Allies Castigate U.S. Over Failure to Pay U.N. Dues', *New York Times*, p.3, Oct. 3, 1995.

99. Compare the provision in sec. 107(b) of the Foreign Assistance Act of 1966 that the President 'shall seek to assure' that no U.S. contribution to the UN Development Program should go to the Castro regime. Pub.L.No.89–583, 80 Stat. 800 (1966), *as amended*, 22 U.S.C. § 2221(b), *repealed by* Act of Dec. 29, 1981. Compare sec. 107(c) which provides that contributions to the United Nations Relief and Works Agency for Palestine Refugees should be made only on condition that the Agency 'take all possible measures to assure that no part of the United States contribution' be used to assist any refugee receiving military training as a member of the 'so-called Palestine Liberation Army'. 22 U.S.C. § 2221(c) (1994).

100. Sometimes there are 'suggestions' by committees or members of Congress. Compare those to the United States Representative to the International Bank for Reconstruction and Development to vote against a loan to Greece. *Hearings on Proposed World Bank Loan to NIBID of Greece before the Subcommittee on International Finance of the House Comm. on Banking and Currency*, 90th Cong., 2d Sess. 17–18, 26 (1968).

In the 1950s, the Department of State, under pressure of Congressional committees, arranged for 'advisory screening' of U.S. citizens for employment in the United Nations and other international organizations. See e.g., *Report on the Activities of United States Citizens Employed by the United Nations*, SUBCOMMITTEE TO INVESTIGATE THE ADMINISTRATION OF THE INTERNAL SECURITY ACT AND OTHER INTERNAL SECURITY LAWS OF THE SENATE COMMITTEE ON THE JUDICIARY 82d Cong., 2d Sess. (Comm.Print 1953). See 31 DEP'T STATE BULL. 279, 354 (1954).

101. Compare n. 93 above and the 'loopholes' afforded the President in the legislation denying foreign assistance to countries guilty of gross violations of human rights, n. 71 to this chapter.

102. Compare 3 OP.ATT'Y GEN. 188 (1837); CORWIN, THE PRESIDENT (n. 5 to Intro. to Pt. II) 93, 412 n. 32; see Chapter VII, p. 180.

There have also been issues arising out of the President's power to make recess appointments. Attorneys General have expressed the view that under Art. II, sec. 2, cl. 3, permitting him to fill vacancies 'that may happen during the Recess of the Senate', he can make a recess appointment even when the vacancy occurred earlier, while the Senate was in session. See CORWIN, THE PRESIDENT (n. 5 to Intro. to Pt. II) 93–4, 412–13 n. 34.

103. Compare the discussion of consent to treaties in Ch. VII, p. 182. Presidents have insisted that the Senate cannot withdraw its consent once given, at least after the commission of office has been signed. On one occasion the Supreme Court avoided the issue by holding that the Senate had acted in violation of its own rules. *United States* v. *Smith*, 286 U.S. 6 (1932); see CORWIN, THE

PRESIDENT (n. 5 to Intro. to Pt. II) 91–2. Withdrawal of consent after an appointee has taken office would of course be in effect an attempt to remove him from office; see n. 106 to this chapter.

104. Until 1855, Congress merely appropriated lump sums 'for the support of such persons as he shall commission to serve the United States in foreign parts' (1 Stat. 128 (1790)), or later, for the 'expenses of the intercourse between the United States and foreign nations' (3 Stat. 422 (1818)). (But in those days appropriations for departments dealing with domestic affairs were also general and brief.) Even the early statutes, however, fixed maximum salaries for specified diplomatic ranks, e.g., 1 Stat. 128 (1790). Then (in ch. 133, 10 Stat. 619) Congress began to assign definite diplomatic ranks to representatives to named countries, with specified compensation and given qualification (including a requirement of U. S. citizenship). Attorney General Cushing gave the opinion that such legislation by Congress was beyond its authority and could only be recommendatory, 7 OP.ATT'Y GEN. 186, 217, 242 (1855); but Presidents have long ago conceded. Even the distinction among the ranks mentioned in the Constitution (Ambassadors, other public Ministers and Consuls), as to which the President claimed autonomy, and other personnel in offices created by Congress, has effectively disappeared. The first comprehensive regulation of the Foreign Service was the Rogers Act of 1924, ch. 182, 43 Stat. 140. It was overhauled in the Foreign Service Act of 1946, ch. 957, 60 Stat. 999, *repealed* Pub.L.No.96–465, Title II § 2205(1), 94 Stat. 2159 (1980). There was previously a small recognition of the President's 'inherent authority', in 22 U.S.C. § 811a, *repealed* Pub.L.No.103–236, § 162(a), 108 Stat. 405 (1994). Compare the President's acquired power to appoint special agents (without Senate consent), Chb. II, p. 41.

   For an essay on Congressional control of federal offices generally, see Justice Brandeis dissenting in *Myers* v. *United States*, 272 U.S. at 264–74 (1926).

105. In one famous instance Congress, in creating posts in the Judge Advocate's Department of the Army, provided that 'one such vacancy, not below the grade of major, shall be filled by the appointment of a person from civil life, not less than forty-five nor more than fifty years of age, who shall have been for ten years a judge of the Supreme Court of the Philippine Islands, shall have served for two years as a captain in the Regular or Volunteer Army, and shall be proficient in the Spanish language and laws'. Ch. 134, § 8, 39 Stat. 169 (1916). There was only one person in the world who met those 'qualifications', and he got the job. In 1884 Congress passed a bill which authorized the President 'to nominate, and by and with the consent of the Senate to appoint Fitz John Porter' to the position of Colonel in the Army. But President Arthur vetoed the bill on the ground that if it was mandatory it usurped the President's power of appointment, and if merely a recommendation it does not belong on the statute books. 10 RICHARDSON (n. 27 to Ch. II) 4808–10. See CORWIN, THE PRESIDENT (n. 5 to Intro. to Pt. II) 409–11.

   Compare the President's objection to a provision that no compensation for service in the Executive branch shall be paid to three named persons unless the President reappointed them with the consent of the Senate. H.R.Doc.No.264, 78th Cong., 1st Sess. (1943). The Supreme Court held the provision unconstitutional as a bill of attainder. See *United States* v. *Lovett*, 328 U.S. 303 (1946).

106. Compare *Myers* v. *United States*, 272 U.S. 52 (1926), with *Humphrey's Ex'r* v. *United States*, 295 U.S. 602 (1935), and *Wiener* v. *United States*, 357 U.S. 349 (1958), n. 21 to Ch. II. See also *Morgan* v. *TVA*, 28 F.Supp. 732 (E.D.Tenn.1939), *cert. denied*, 312 U.S. 701 (1941). Congress can limit the power to remove 'inferior officers'. *United States* v. *Perkins*, 116 U.S. 483 (1886).

107. *Kendall* v. *United States ex rel. Stokes*, 37 U.S. (12 Pet.) 524, 610 (1838). That case in effect upheld also the power of a court of appropriate jurisdiction to mandamus federal officials. Compare 28 U.S.C. § 1361 (1988).

108. See *United States ex rel. Ulrich* v. *Kellogg*, 30 F.2d 984 (D.C. Cir. 1929); *cf. Loza-Bedoya* v. *Immigration and Naturalization Service*, 410 F.2d 343 (9th Cir. 1969). But the President may have authority to exclude an alien even if he bears a visa given by a consular officer. Compare n. 32 to Ch. II.

109. This conclusion is apparently derived from 8 U.S.C. § 1104(a) (1994). See generally, Rosenfield, *Consular Non-reviewability: A Case Study in Administrative Absolutism*, 41 AMER. BAR ASSOC. J. 1109 (1955); Note, *Judicial Review of Visa Denials: Reexamining Consular Nonreviewability*, 52 N.Y.U.L.REV. 1137 (1977); Nafziger, *Review of Visa Denials by Consular Officers*, 66 WASH. L.REV. 1 (1991). Compare the role of consuls in applications for admission to the United States as refugees, 8 U.S.C. § 1157 (1994).

110. Justice Jackson, concurring in *Youngstown Sheet & Tubing Co.* v. *Sawyer*, 343 U.S. 579, 646, quoted p. 94, this chapter. In a special sense, the President in turn may be said to 'delegate' power to Congress when he seeks its consent for actions that he could probably take on his own constitutional authority. See, e.g., n. 44 to Ch. II, and n. 65 to this chapter.

111. The doctrine that power is not to be freely delegated is sometimes traced to John Locke. See THE SECOND TREATISE ON CIVIL GOVERNMENT Chapter XI, § 141, at 118 (Gateway ed. 1960). In the United States, limits on delegation have been deemed rooted not only in the separation of powers, but also in common law concepts that deny to an agent the power to delegate his authority, and in notions of due process of law. Compare *Hampton & Co.* v. *United States*, 276 U.S. 394, 405 (1928). See generally, Jaffe, *An Essay on Delegation of Legislative Power*, 47 COLUM.L.REV . 339, 561 (1947).

The Supreme Court has not struck down any domestic delegation since 1935. *Panama Refining Co.* v. *Ryan*, 293 U.S. 388 (1935) (delegation to the President); *Schechter Poultry Corp.* v. *United States*, 295 U.S. 495 (1935). Compare *Sunshine Anthracite Coal Co.* v. *Adkins*, 310 U.S. 381 (1940); *United States* v. *Rock Royal Cooperative, Inc.*, 307 U.S. 533 (1939); *Currin* v. *Wallace*, 306 U.S. 1 (1939); and particularly war-time delegations, *Bowles* v. *Willingham*, 321 U.S. 503 (1944); *Yakus* v. *United States*, 321 U.S. 414 (1944). The Supreme Court has said that delegation is permitted for 'interstitial' legislation if Congress determines the basic policy and lays down guide lines.

Compare Chief Justice Marshall in *Wayman* v. *Southard*, 23 U.S. (10 Wheat.) 1, 43 (1825). But the Court has accepted vague and general guidelines, e.g., 'public interest', 'public convenience and necessity'. *New York Central Securities Co.* v. *United States*, 287 U.S. 12, 24 (1932); *FCC* v. *Pottsville Broadcasting Co.*, 309 U.S. 134, 138 (1940). But see *Kent* v. *Dulles*, 357 U.S. 116, 129 (1958), n. 113 to this chapter; *cf.* L. JAFFE, JUDICIAL CONTROL OF ADMINISTRATIVE ACTION 71–2 (1965). The Court has moved far from the earlier cases, but they have not been overruled and the basic principle that the Constitution implies some limitations on delegation no doubt stands. See also Justice Scalia's dissent in *Mistretta* v. *United States*, 488 U.S. 361, 413 (1989).

112. 299 U.S. 304 at 320. Compare Justice Lamar's statement that in foreign relations 'even the internal adjustment of federal power, with its complex system of checks and balances, [is] unknown'. *In re Neagle*, 135 U.S. 1, 85 (1890). Without announcing any special doctrine about the scope of delegation in foreign affairs, the Court upheld extensive delegations long before *Curtiss-Wright*. E.g., *The Aurora* v. *United States*, 11 U.S. (7 Cranch) 382 (1813); *The Thomas Gibbons*, 12 U.S. (8 Cranch) 421, 429 (1814). Extensive delegations in regard to tariffs were upheld in *Field* v. *Clark*, 143 U.S. 649, 690 (1892), and *Hampton & Co.* v. *United States*, 276 U.S. 394 (1928). See also *United States ex rel. Knauff* v. *Shaughnessy*, 338 U.S. 537, 542 (1950). But compare *Zemel* v. *Rusk*, 381 U.S. 1, 17–18 (1964): '[Curtiss-Wright] does not mean that simply because a statute deals with foreign relations, it can grant the Executive totally unrestricted freedom of choice.' See Black, J., dissenting, *id.* at 20–3. And see n. 113 to this chapter.

113. In *Kent* v. *Dulles*, 357 U.S. 116 (1959), in considering Congressional delegation to the Secretary of State of authority to limit travel by citizens outside the United States, the Court said that 'if that power is to be delegated, the standards must be adequate to pass scrutiny by the accepted tests'. It cited *Panama Refining*, n. 111 above, and did not mention *Curtiss-Wright*. Perhaps the Court's opinion alluded to that case and the tariff cases when it said: 'If we were dealing with political questions entrusted to the Chief Executive by the Constitution we would have a different case. But there is more involved here.' 357 U.S. at 129. The implication may be that as regards the delegation of power to regulate important individual rights, *Panama Refining* is applicable again, and in foreign as in domestic affairs. And compare *Zemel*, quoted in n. 112 above.

Subdelegation to other officials by the President, whether of his constitutional authority or of powers delegated to him by Congress, has not been seriously challenged. As regards his powers in foreign affairs, at least, there is little that the President must do in person. Compare, e.g., *Wilcox* v. *McConnell*, 38 U.S. (13 Pet.) 498, 513 (1839); *Williams* v. *United States*, 42 U.S. (1 How.) 290, 296 (1843); *McElrath* v. *United States*, 102 U.S. 426, 436 (1880); *United States ex rel. Knauff* v. *Shaughnessy*, 338 U.S. 537, 543 (1950); also 7 OP.ATT'Y GEN. 453 (1871). See Marshall, quoted in n. 61 to Ch. V. But compare the suggestion that the President's power to terminate a treaty or to exercise constitutional power in violation of international law should be exercised by the President, not by a low official. See Ch. VIII. See generally, Ch. II, p. 34 footnote.

114. Ch. 583, § 6, 59 Stat. 621 (1945), 22 U.S.C. § 287(d) (1994).
115. Ch. 141, § 10, 65 Stat. 75 (1951). The provision was repeated in later acts, e.g., 69 Stat. 162, 163 (1955), 19 U.S.C. § 1351(a) (1) (A) (1994).
116. Section 8(d)(2). 50 U.S.C. § 1547(d)(2) (1988).
117. This was done with the Federal Rules of Civil Procedure. See *Sibbach* v. *Wilson & Co.*, 312 U.S. 1, 14–16 (1941). See 37 OP.ATT'Y GEN. 56, 63 (1933); 100 CONG.REC. 4879 (1954).

Section 123(c) of the Atomic Energy Act of 1954 provided that proposed bilateral agreements for cooperation with other nations shall not go into effect until 'the proposed agreement for cooperation, together with the approval and the determination of the President, has been submitted to the Joint Committee [of Congress on Atomic Energy] and a period of thirty days has elapsed while Congress is in session . . .'. Ch. 1073, 68 Stat. 940, as amended, 42 U.S.C. § 2153 (c) (1988). A later amendment provided that the Joint Committee may by resolution waive all or part of the 30-day waiting period. Pub.L.No. 85-681, § 4, 72 Stat. 632 (1958). (Another 1958 Amendment added that certain agreements had to lie before the Joint Committee for 60 days while Congress is in session and could not become effective if both houses disapproved the agreement by concurrent resolution. Pub.L.No. 85-479, § 4, 72 Stat. 277, 42 U.S.C. § 2153 (d) (1988) (as amended by Pub.L.No. 103-337, 108 Stat. 3092 (1994). Compare the following notes to this chapter.)

118. 'The actual form of the veto can vary greatly depending on the way in which three sets of variables are combined. First, the wielder of the device can vary. The veto can be—and has been—vested in the whole Congress, in one House of Congress, in the committees, and even in a committee chairman. Second, the manner in which the veto is expressed can vary. It can be expressed in a negative, affirmative, or deliberative manner and, in addition, it may be tied on to the appropriations process rather than defined as a condition on which the authorization of a proposal is made contingent. In the first instance, a proposal of the executive goes into effect unless negated within a specified period. In the second instance, a proposal of the executive does not go into effect unless it is affirmed. In the third instance, a proposal of the executive does not go into effect until it has lain before Congress or some agent of Congress for a specified period. Here, in contrast to the above instances where neither two-House action nor submission to the President is required, theoretically the actual disallowance of the proposal must take the form of regular legislation. However, in reality many of the committees of Congress are so strong that the mere hint of their disapproval often is sufficient to convince the executive not to take the proposed step. When the veto is attached to the appropriations process, the provision restricts the use of appropriated funds or the appropriation of funds until some further form of legislative assent has been secured. Finally, the nature of the majority necessary to put the veto into effect can vary. Thus far, simple, absolute, and constitutional, i.e., two-thirds, majorities have been required.' Cooper & Cooper, *The*

Legislative Veto and the Constitution, 30 Geo.Wash.L.Rev. 467, 468–9 (1962) (footnotes omitted).

For another example of the use of the legislative veto in matters related to foreign affairs, see Pub.L.No.85–686, § 6, 72 Stat. 676 (1958), *repealed,* Pub.L.No.87–794, § 257(e) (1), 76 Stat. 882 (1962) (reciprocal trade; concurrent resolution to require two-thirds vote of each house).

A principal use of such a veto of Presidential action was in the Reorganization Acts. The 1939 Act provided that any plan for reorganization of an executive agency shall lie on the table for 60 days and shall then become effective unless disapproved by concurrent resolution. See Ch. 36, § 5(a), 53 Stat. 562–3 (1939). The 1949 Act provided for 'veto' of a reorganization plan by resolution of either house. Ch. 226, § 6(a), 63 Stat. 205 (1949).

General legislative 'oversight' of the execution of the laws was provided in 2 U.S.C. §§ 190b, 190d, *repealed,* S.Res. 4 § 301(b) (1977).

119. Art. I, sec. 7. Corwin noted that the literal requirements of that provision have been long ago, and inevitably, disregarded. Corwin, The President (n. 5 to Intro. to Pt. II) 149–52.

That the concurrence of the President is not necessary to resolutions for amending the Constitution (Art. V) has been upheld from our early history, *Hollingsworth* v. *Virginia,* 3 U.S. (3 Dall.) 378 (1798); the constitutional language lends itself to that interpretation. See the view that declarations of war do not require Presidential concurrence. n. 60 to Ch. III, and n. 28 to this chapter.

120. Before the Court decided the issue, Presidents had challenged the validity of various forms of Committee veto provisions. See *Hearings, Separation of Powers* (n. 40 above) 215–28 and especially 2 Public Papers of the Presidents: Lyndon B. Johnson 1963–64, at 1249, 1250 (1965), reprinted in *Hearings* at 224; Wilson's veto message reprinted *id.* at 203; see also Maass, *id.* at 187–8; Wozencraft, *id.* at 201; Bickel, *id.* at 245. See generally, Cooper and Cooper, n. 118 to this chapter; Ginnane, *The Control of Federal Administration by Congressional Resolutions and Committees,* 66 Harv.L.Rev. 569 (1953), and an interesting footnote, Mr. Justice Jackson's *A Presidential Legal Opinion, id.* at 1353; Newman & Keeton, *Congress and the Faithful Execution of the Laws—Should Legislators Supervise Administrators?,* 41 Calif.L.Rev. 568 (1953). And see 37 Op.Att'y Gen. 56 (1933).

121. 462 U.S. 919 (1983). For arguments that *Chadha* may not apply to any foreign affairs legislation, or to some foreign affairs legislation, see M. Pomerance, *United States Foreign Relations Law after* Chadha, 15 Cal. W. Int'l L.J. 201 (1985).

122. In Kendall, n. 107 to this chapter. See generally Symposium, *Separation of Powers and the Executive branch,* 57 Geo. Wash. L. Rev. 401–703 (1989).

'The independent agency is a constitutional sport, an anomalous institution created without regard to the basic principle of separation of powers upon which our government was founded.' G. Miller, *Independent Agencies,* 1988 Sup. Ct. Rev. 41, 96–7. See also J. Freedman, Crisis and Legitimacy: The Administrative Process and American Government (1978); Strauss, *The*

Place of Agencies in Government: Separation of Powers and the Fourth Branch, 84 COLUM. L. REV. 573 (1984); Shane, *Independent Policymaking and Presidential Power: A Constitutional Analysis*, 57 GEO. WASH. L. REV. 596, 608 (1989).

123. Congress and the Supreme Court have recognized the special authority of the President in relation to the administrative agencies that regulate foreign air travel. See *Chicago & Southern Air Lines, Inc.* v. *Waterman S.S. Corp.*, 303 U.S. 103, 109 (1948). A few rarely cited cases support the view that the President should maintain some control over the conduct of foreign policy by independent agencies. See *British Airways* v. *Civil Aeronautics Board*, 563 F.2d 3 (2d Cir. 1977); *Zoelsch* v. *Arthur Andersen & Co.*, 824 F.2d 27 (1987); *N.R.D.C.* v. *N.R.C.*, 647 F.2d 1345 (D.C. Cir. 1991). See also G. Miller, *The Unitary Executive in a Unified Theory of Constitutional Law: The Problem of Interpretation*, 15 CARDOZO L. REV. 201 (1993).

NOTES, CHAPTER V: THE COURTS IN FOREIGN AFFAIRS,
pp. 131 to 148

1. *Marbury* v. *Madison*, 1 Cranch (5 U.S.) 137 (1803); *Cooper* v. *Aaron*, 358 U.S. 1, 17–20 (1958). See n. 4 to Introduction.

    It has been disputed whether the grant of jurisdiction over 'cases arising under the Constitution', and the declaration in the Supremacy Clause that the Constitution and the laws 'in pursuance thereof' are law of the land, were intended to grant to the courts the power to declare acts of Congress unconstitutional, or whether the courts developed that power on their own. Compare, e.g., Wechsler, *Toward Neutral Principles of Constitutional Law*, 73 HARV.L.REV. 1 (1959), and R. BERGER, CONGRESS v. THE SUPREME COURT cc. 7, 8 (1960), with L. HAND, THE BILL OF RIGHTS (1958), and 2 W. CROSSKEY, POLITICS AND THE CONSTITUTION IN THE HISTORY OF THE UNITED STATES c. XXVIII (1953). The former view has apparently prevailed.

2. Since *Erie R.R.* v. *Tompkins*, 304 U.S. 64 (1938), a federal court in a diversity of citizenship case applies the common law as 'found' by the courts of the state in which the federal court sits.

3. See, e.g., maritime law: 'the Congress has largely left to this Court the responsibility for fashioning the controlling rules of admiralty law', *Fitzgerald* v. *U.S. Lines Co.*, 374 U.S. 16, 20 (1963); '[a]dmiralty law is judge-made law to a great extent', *Edmonds* v. *Compagnie Generale Transatlantique*, 443 U.S. 256, 259 (1979). These are quoted in *Northwest Airlines Inc.* v. *Transport Workers Union*, 451 U.S. 77, 96 (1981). See n. 16 below.

4. See Holmes, J., dissenting in *Southern Pacific Co.* v. *Jensen*, 244 U.S. 205, 218, 221 (1917): 'Judges do and must legislate, but they can do so only interstitially; they are confined from molar to molecular motions.' Compare: 'Congress acts . . . against the background of the total *corpus juris* of the states in much the same way that a state legislature acts against the background of the common law, assumed to govern unless changed by legislation'. H. HART and H. WECHSLER'S, THE FEDERAL COURTS AND THE FEDERAL SYSTEM 533 (Bator, Meltzer, Mishkin, Shapiro, 3d edn., 1988). See generally, Hart, *The Relations Between State and Federal Law*, 54 COLUM.L.REV. 489 (1954). Federal courts, then, make law in the interstices of the interstices which federal law generally occupies in the U.S. legal system.

5. See, e.g., Henkin, *Some Reflections on Current Constitutional Controversy*, 109 U.PA.L.REV. 637, 650 *et seq.* (1961); HENKIN, CONSTITUTIONALISM, DEMOCRACY, AND FOREIGN AFFAIRS (1990), Ch. 3.

6. *Cf.* L. BOUDIN, GOVERNMENT BY JUDICIARY (1932).

7. Alexander Hamilton's phrase in THE FEDERALIST No.78, made popular by Professor Alexander Bickel in his book, THE LEAST DANGEROUS BRANCH (1962).

8. Issues related to foreign affairs often come before state courts, which also interpret and apply federal statutes and review their constitutionality. State courts derive their jurisdiction from their own constitutions and laws and are not subject to the case or controversy requirement (see p. 142) of the Federal Constitution,

but must, of course, provide due process of law and other constitutional requirements applicable to the states. But a state proceeding that did not involve a case or controversy cannot be reviewed by the Supreme Court. See, e.g., *Doremus* v. *Board of Education*, 342 U.S. 429 (1952). Federal questions in state cases are subject to federal law and to review by the Supreme Court. 28 U.S.C. § 1257 (1988).

The jurisdiction of state courts is governed by state law, but Congress has also provided for the use of state courts to enforce federal regulatory acts. In earlier days, states sometimes claimed the right to refuse, e.g., *United States* v. *Lathrop*, 17 Johns. 4, 8 (N.Y. 1819). But the Supreme Court has since held that state courts of appropriate jurisdiction could not properly refuse a Congressional assignment. *Testa* v. *Katt*, 330 U.S. 386 (1947). It remains to be seen whether the Court's mood at the end of the twentieth century, to protect state institutions from being 'coopted' by the federal government, will extend to state courts. See Ch. VI, p. 167. Especially when federal courts were few and their jurisdiction not fully extended by Congress, Congress relied on states and state courts to punish offenses against the law of nations. See n. 6 to Ch. VIII. For the role of state courts in federal matters, see generally H. HART AND H. WECHSLER'S, THE FEDERAL COURTS AND THE FEDERAL SYSTEM (Bator, Meltzer, Mishkin, Shapiro, 3d edn., 1988), especially at 495–500.

9. The judicial power extends to cases arising under the Constitution, laws, and treaties, no matter who the parties. Cases affecting foreign diplomats, and diversity cases to which a foreign state or a foreign national is party, can come to the federal courts regardless of the subject matter of the case. See *Cohens* v. *Virginia*, 19 U.S. (6 Wheat.) 264, 378 (1821).

10. Since the Judiciary Act of 1789, ch. 20, § 13, 1 Stat. 73, 80–1, now, as amended, 28 U.S.C. § 1251 (1994). Generally, suits against an accredited diplomat are consistent with the law of nations only when his (her) government waives immunity.

The lower federal courts can exercise only the jurisdiction that Congress grants them. *Cary* v. *Curtis*, 44 U.S. (3 How.) 236, 245 (1845); *Sheldon* v. *Sill*, 49 U.S. (8 How.) 441 (1850); also, *Kline* v. *Burke Construction Co.*, 260 U.S. 226, 233–4 (1922). There is an old controversy as to whether Congress was constitutionally obligated to confer on federal courts all the judicial power vested by Art. III. Story's view that Congress was so obligated has not prevailed. Compare *Martin* v. *Hunter's Lessee*, 14 U.S. (1 Wheat.) 304, 328–32 (1816) (Story, J.), with *Turner* v. *Bank of North-America*, 4 U.S. (4 Dall.) 8, 10n. (1799) (Chase, J.).

Congress cannot add to the original jurisdiction of the Supreme Court (*Marbury* v. *Madison*, 5 U.S. (1 Cranch) 137 (1803)), or take any of it away, but it can give to other federal courts concurrent jurisdiction of matters that are within the Supreme Court's original jurisdiction. *Börs* v. *Preston*, 111 U.S. 252 (1884); *Ames* v. *Kansas*, 111 U.S. 449, 469 (1884). Congress left exclusively to the Supreme Court only suits against ambassadors, ministers, and their servants, but gave lower federal courts jurisdiction of suits by them, and others that affect them. See Judiciary Act of 1789, above. The Court will commonly decline to exercise original jurisdiction in cases in which lower federal courts are available. Compare, for example, *Illinois* v. *City of Milwaukee*, 406 U.S. 91 (1972); *Washington* v. *General Motors Corp.*, 406 U.S. 109 (1972). Compare *Massachusetts* v. *Missouri*, 308 U.S. 1, 19 (1939), and *Ohio* v. *Wyandotte Chemicals Corp.*, 401 U.S. 493 (1971), where the Court declined jurisdiction although no other federal tribunal was clearly available. The constitutional grant of original jurisdiction to the Supreme Court does not preclude suits against consuls in state courts. *Popovici* v. *Agler*, 280 U.S. 379, 383–4 (1930).

Congress can regulate the appellate jurisdiction of the Supreme Court and, in effect, the Court has appellate jurisdiction only to the extent that Congress grants it. See *Sheldon* v. *Sill*, above; *Ex parte McCardle*, 74 U.S. 506 (1868).

11. *Harisiades* v. *Shaughnessy*, 342 U.S. 580, 589 (1952), quoted in, *inter alia*, *Regan* v. *Wald*, 468 U.S. 222, 242 (1984).

12. See, e.g., the travel and passport cases Ch. IX, p. 291. That courts will construe a statute—where fairly possible—to avoid declaring it unconstitutional, even to avoid a serious constitutional question, see *Crowell* v. *Benson*, 285 U.S. 22, 62 (1932). For a list of 'canons' developed by the Supreme Court to avoid invalidating acts of Congress, see Justice Brandeis concurring in *Ashwander* v. *Tennessee Valley Authority*, 297 U.S. 288, 346–8 (1936). A more 'activist' Supreme Court during the 1960s seemed far less loath, and indeed some Justices seemed to consider it their duty, to reach and decide constitutional issues. *Cf.* Douglas, J., concurring in *Flast* v. *Cohen*, 392 U.S. 83, 107 (1968); Fortas, J., *id.* at 115–16; and Brennan, J., concurring in *School Dist.* v. *Schempp*, 374 U.S. 203, 230, 266–7 n. 30 (1963). And compare the dissenting Justices in the Vietnam cases, n. 67 to this chapter.

13. *United States* v. *Belmont*, 301 U.S. 324, 331 (1937). See also Ch. VI, p. 157.

14. I owe the adjective to Professor Louis Lusky. See Lusky, By What Right (1975), pp. 47–9.

On the dormant commerce clause, see Tushnet, *Rethinking the Dormant Commerce Clause*, 1979 Wis. L.Rev. 125; Eule, *Laying the Dormant Commerce Clause to Rest*, 91 Yale L.J. 425 (1982).

15. *Zschernig* v. *Miller*, 389 U.S. 429, 432 (1968), held that the Constitution bars the states from intruding on foreign relations even when the political branches have not acted. See Ch. VI, pp. 162–5.

16. In several instances the Supreme Court found that in establishing a federal regulatory system Congress had in effect directed the courts to supply federal common law for the interstices, as in regard to bankruptcy; or even to develop a new body of law, e.g., to govern labor relations within the framework of federal labor laws; or to protect uniquely federal interests that should not be subject to the vagaries and diversities of the different laws of the different states. *Textile Workers Union of America* v. *Lincoln Mills*, 353 U.S. 448 (1957); *United States* v. *Standard Oil Co.*, 332 U.S. 301, 308 (1947); *Clearfield Trust Co.* v. *United States*, 318 U.S. 363 (1943); *D'Oench, Duhme & Co.* v. *F.D.I.C.*, 315 U.S. 447, 469 (1942); see *Illinois* v. *City of Milwaukee*, 406 U.S. 91 (1972). It seems unlikely that the Court would find constitutional obstacles to such delegations. But *cf.* Hill, *The Law-Making Power of the Federal*

Courts: Constitutional Preemption, 67 COLUM.L.REV. 1024, 1030 n. 33 (1967).

The Supreme Court has also found that the Constitution itself implies power for the federal courts to make law—to maintain and develop the judge-made maritime law inherited from England; or to govern relationships between states in regard to boundary disputes, respective water rights, or other quasi-'international' issues of the kind that come for original adjudication before the Supreme Court; or to create a constitutional remedy. See, e.g., *Southern Pac. Co.* v. *Jensen,* 244 U.S. 205 (1917); *Connecticut* v. *Massachusetts,* 282 U.S. 660 (1931); *Hinderlider* v. *La Plata River Co.,* 304 U.S. 92 (1938); *Texas* v. *New Jersey,* 379 U.S. 674 (1965). *Bivens* v. *Six Unknown Named Agents of the Federal Bureau of Narcotics,* 403 U.S. 388 (1971). *Cf. West Virginia ex rel. Dyer* v. *Sims,* 341 U.S. 22, 28 (1951) (construction of interstate compact). And see the *Sabbatino* case discussed in this chapter, p. 137. In developing law for cases between states, the Court has sometimes looked to the common law; see, e.g., *Missouri* v. *Illinois,* 180 U.S. 208, 243–8 (1901). See Note, *What Rules of Decision Should Control in Interstate Controversies?,* 21 HARV.L.REV. 132 (1907).

Ultimately, of course, all that federal courts do derives authority from the Constitution which conceived them and ordained their power, and from the Congress which created them and fixed their jurisdiction (within constitutional limits). One might argue, then, that the federal courts have some law-making authority inherent in their judicial character, that the laws so made are supported by the Constitution and Congress, perhaps, too, that they are supreme to state law. But which explicit law-making authority is inherent in the judicial function is hardly agreed. Surely, it does not include the power to make law on every subject within their jurisdiction. Compare *Erie R.R.* v. *Tompkins,* 304 U.S. 64 (1938), denying that power for cases of diversity jurisdiction, n. 2 to this chapter. And compare the cases that held that there is no common-law criminal jurisdiction in the federal courts. *United States* v. *Hudson & Goodwin,* 11 U.S. (7 Cranch) 32 (1812).

See generally, Friendly, *In Praise of* Erie—*and of the New Federal Common Law,* 39 N.Y.U. L.REV. 383 (1964), reprinted in BENCHMARKS (1967), Chapter 9, and Hill, above. But *cf.* Note, *The Federal Common Law,* 82 HARV.L.REV. 1512 (1969). Hill took a broad view of the law-making power of the federal courts, but he might have taken an even broader view after the Supreme Court decided *Zschernig* v. *Miller,* 389 U.S. 429 (1968), n. 15 to this chapter, and Ch. VI, pp. 162–5. Compare Hill at 1056–7.

17. Except insofar as Congress expressly left to the courts the determination and application of 'the law of nations'. See, e.g., *United States* v. *Smith,* 18 U.S. (5 Wheat.) 153, 160–2 (1820); *Ex parte Quirin,* 317 U.S. 1, 27–8 (1942), n. 21 to Ch. III.

18. See n. 3 to this chapter. Indeed, the power of Congress to legislate on maritime matters has been inferred from the constitutional grant of judicial power to the courts. See Chapter III, p. 73. Other law made by the courts on authority inferred from constitutional grants of jurisdiction might also have relevance for foreign

affairs, for example the law to be applied in original suits in the Supreme Court and the law for construing compacts with foreign states. See nn. 10, 16 to this chapter.

19. The exact meaning and constitutional status of international comity are uncertain. The Supreme Court has said that comity is 'neither a matter of absolute obligation, on the one hand, nor of mere courtesy and good will, upon the other'. *Hilton* v. *Guyot*, 159 U.S. 113, 163–4 (1895), quoted in *Banco Nacional de Cuba* v. *Sabbatino*, 376 U.S. 398, 409 (1964). For the constitutional status of comity in the past, compare *Hilton* v. *Guyot* with *Cowans* v. *Ticonderoga Pulp & Paper Co.*, 219 A.D. 120, 219 N.Y.S. 284, *aff'd*, 246 N.Y. 603, 159 N.E. 669 (1927); *cf. Vladikavkazsky Ry.* v. *New York Trust Co.*, 263 N.Y. 369, 378, 189 N.E. 456, 460 (1934); also *Johnston* v. *Compagnie Générale Transatlantique*, 242 N.Y. 381, 152 N.E. 121 (1926). See n. 20 below. See Henkin, *The Foreign Affairs Power of the Federal Courts*: Sabbatino, 64 COLUM.L.REV. 805, 820 n. 49 (1964); RESTATEMENT (n. 2 to Preface) § 101, Comment *e*, § 403, Comment *a*, § 443, Comment *a*.

20. See, e.g., *Johnston* v. *Compagnie Générale Transatlantique*, 242 N.Y. 381, 152 N.E. 121 (1926), which chose not to follow the rule laid down by the Supreme Court in *Hilton* v. *Guyot*, 159 U.S. 113 (1895), that, with some exceptions, foreign judgments should be executed only on the basis of reciprocity. But see n. 29 to this chapter.

21. For a hundred years, federal courts applied the common law, as they saw and developed it, in suits between citizens of different states, which can come to the federal courts even if they involve no federal question. Art. III, sec. 2; *Swift* v. *Tyson*, 41 U.S. (16 Pet.) 1 (1842). That case was overruled in *Erie R.R.* v. *Tompkins*, 304 U.S. 64 (1938), which held that in diversity-of-citizenship cases a federal court must apply the common law as determined by the courts of the state in which it sits. On the early application of the *Erie* doctrine to customary international law, see n. 19 to Ch. VIII, p. 238; in *Bergman* v. *De Sieyes*, 170 F.2d 360 (2d Cir. 1948), in an opinion often cited as one of his rare mistakes, Judge Learned Hand said that since international law was part of the common law, in a 'diversity of citizenship' case the state court's interpretation of international law is binding on federal courts. As regards its application to issues of the conflict of laws and the effect to be given to foreign judgments, see n. 29 to this chapter.

22. *Banco Nacional de Cuba* v. *Sabbatino*, 376 U.S. 398 (1964), discussed also in Ch. II, p. 57.

23. The District Court granted summary judgment for the defendant principally because the Cuban Government had not granted prompt, adequate and effective compensation. 193 F.Supp. 375 (S.D.N.Y. 1961) (alternative holding). The Court of Appeals affirmed, finding a violation of international law in particular in that the nationalization was not for a proper public purpose and was designed to retaliate and discriminate against the United States and its citizens. 307 F.2d 845 (2d Cir. 1962).

24. 376 U.S. at 421, 423–5.

25. See n. 75 to Ch. II.

26. Justice Harlan seemed to find the federal courts' power in the fact that foreign
     relations are 'intrinsically federal' and that the Judiciary is a separate, inde-
     pendent branch. Neither of these facts nor both combined, however, necessar-
     ily require or support an independent legislative power in the courts. Harlan's
     reference to the intrinsically federal character of foreign relations perhaps
     echoes *Curtiss-Wright*, but that case did not tell us how the inherent sovereign
     powers of the United States are distributed among the branches; if it be deemed
     to imply a 'judicial foreign affairs power' it hardly suggests that the courts must
     have a legislative power in regard to foreign affairs. See Henkin, *The Foreign
     Affair Power of the Federal Courts*: Sabbatino, 64 COLUM.L.REV. at 814–19
     (1964); compare Hill, (n. 16 to this chapter), at 1062–7. But the law-making
     power of the courts recognized by the Supreme Court has not been challenged
     and appears to be established, though not frequently exercised.
27. 376 U.S. at 426. The Supreme Court has continued to determine the scope of
     Act of State doctrine on its own authority. See e.g. *W.S. Kirkpatrick* v.
     Environmental Tectonics Corporation, 493 U.S. 400 (1990), in which the Court
     distinguished between cases that require a court to 'declare invalid the official
     act of a foreign sovereign' and those that require only imputing an 'unlawful
     motivation' to foreign officials.
        Despite superficial similarities, Act of State (under *Sabbatino*) differs funda-
     mentally from the sovereign immunity cases, Ch. II, p. 54. Here the Court
     declared national policy to apply a doctrine not required by international law;
     in the immunity cases, the Court recognized the authority of the Executive to
     make national policy regardless of international law. The consequences are also
     different: immunity results in dismissing the proceeding and preventing judicial
     determination; Act of State is a rule of law applied to reach a substantive deci-
     sion in the case. These distinctions were blurred by both Justice Rehnquist and
     Justice Brennan in *First National City Bank* v. *Banco Nacional de Cuba*, 406
     U.S. 759, 760, 776 (1972), Ch. II, p. 59. In *Alfred Dunhill of London* v. *Republic
     of Cuba*, 425 U.S. 682 (1976), several Justices suggested that the courts should
     not apply the Act of State doctrine to acts of a commercial character. Compare
     a similar distinction applied in sovereign immunity, Ch. II, p. 54 above. Lower
     courts have also suggested that the Act of State doctrine should not apply
     where the act of state violates a provision in a treaty with the United States.
     See *Kalamazoo Spice Extraction Co.* v. *Government of Socialist Ethiopia*, 729
     F.2d 422 (6th Cir. 1984); RESTATEMENT (n. 2 to Preface) § 443, Comment *b*,
     Reporters' Note 5.
28. 376 U.S. at 426. Justice Harlan went out of his way to establish this power in
     the federal courts, and Act of State as supreme federal law; as he recognized,
     New York law apparently also accepted the doctrine, and the result in the case
     could have been reached as well under state law. See 376 U.S. at 424–5.
        Sabbatino did not purport to deny the states the power to make similar law
     where there was no federal law, or where the state law was not inconsistent
     with federal law, or where the federal law did not reveal a purpose to exclude
     the states. (Compare the preemption doctrine, Ch. VI.) Justice Harlan said
     expressly that the Constitution does not require the Act of State doctrine,

apparently even of the states. But compare *Zschernig*, n. 15 to this chapter; see Friendly, n. 16 to this chapter.

29. See generally RESTATEMENT (n. 2 to Preface) Part IV, Chapter 8; G. BORN, INTERNATIONAL CIVIL LITIGATION IN UNITED STATES COURTS (2d edn., 1992); R. BRAND, ENFORCING FOREIGN JUDGMENTS IN THE UNITED STATES AND U.S. JUDGMENTS ABROAD (1992). Strong argument for broad federal judicial power and supremacy, particularly on matters such as respect for foreign judgments, is made by Moore, *Federalism and Foreign Relations*, 1965 DUKE L.J. 248, 262–3; see Hill, (n. 16 to this chapter), at 1044–6. In my view, Congress can legislate on these matters under its foreign affairs power (Ch. III, p. 70) and the President can make treaties about them (n. 87 to Ch. VII); in the absence of political action, the federal courts, under *Sabbatino*, can also make law and make it binding on the states as well. See Henkin, *The Foreign Affairs Power of the Federal Courts: Sabbatino*, 64 COLUM.L.REV. 805, 820–1, n. 51 (1964). See generally Friendly, n. 16 to this chapter.

The federal courts could presumably also promote other forms of judicial cooperation with foreign courts; and perhaps, like Congress, they can even impose new duties on the state courts consistent with their jurisdiction. *Cf. Testa* v. *Katt*, 330 U.S. 386 (1947), n. 8 above.

Sabbatino suggests that the standing of foreign governments to sue in U.S. courts, even in state courts, is a question of national policy, implying, I believe, that the states must follow rules made by the federal courts, perhaps also by the Executive. 376 U.S. at 408. See Hill, above, at 1068. See Ch. II.

30. The Supreme Court has appellate jurisdiction only if Congress has conferred it. See n. 10 to this chapter.

Federal common law is supreme if one reads 'the Laws of the United States' in the Supremacy Clause (Art. VI, cl. 2) as including federal judge-made law. For the federal courts to have jurisdiction of cases raising such issues one would have to find also that they are cases 'arising under this Constitution' or under 'the Laws of the United States'. Art. III, sec. 2. The Supreme Court would have jurisdiction to review state cases refusing to honor federal judge-made law if in these cases the validity of a state statute can be said to be drawn into question on the ground of its being 'repugnant to the Constitution' (i.e., the Supremacy Clause) or repugnant to 'laws of the United States'. 28 U.S.C. § 1257(2), (3) (1994). There is authority to support such jurisdiction. Compare *Hinderlider* v. *La Plata River Co.*, 304 U.S. 92, 110 (1938); *Illinois* v. *City of Milwaukee*, 406 U.S. 91 (1972) (interpreting similar language in 28 U.S.C. § 1331(a), for purposes of district court jurisdiction). Compare Justice Thomas: 'In our federal system, a state trial court's interpretation of federal law is no less authoritative than that of the federal court of appeals in whose circuit the trial court is located.' *Lockhart* v. *Fretwell*, 113 S.Ct. 838, 846 (1993) (Thomas, J., concurring). See generally, Hart, *The Relations between State and Federal Law*, 54 COLUM.L.REV. 489, 500 (1954); Bator, *The State Courts and Federal Constitutional Litigation*, 22 WM. & MARY L.REV. 605 (1981); Hoke, *Transcending Conventional Supremacy: A Reconstruction of the Supremacy Clause*, 24 CONN. L.REV. 829 (1992).

31. 376 U.S. at 423.

32. *Ibid.* Act of State itself has uncertainties which courts might feel less than

confident to resolve in the light of foreign policy needs. Compare Henkin, *Sabbatino*, n. 26 to this chapter, at 826–30; see n. 23 above.

33. Act of State itself is essentially a special rule of conflicts denying the state of the forum its usual freedom to assert its own public policy and to refuse to apply the law of the state where a transaction 'occurred'. See Henkin, n. 26 to this chapter at 808–10. Compare Justice Rehnquist in *First National City Bank* v. *Banco Nacional de Cuba*, 406 U.S. 759, 768 (1972); see generally RESTATEMENT (n. 2 to Preface) §§ 443, 444.

34. A broad judicial foreign affairs power is supported by Hill, n. 16 to this chapter, and an even broader one, apparently, by Moore, *Federalism and Foreign Relations*, 1965 DUKE L.J. 248, but how broad is not clear.

35. See n. 75 to Ch. II.

36. See the Second Hickenlooper Amendment, 22 U.S.C. § 2370(e)(2) (1994), upheld and applied in the aftermath of *Sabbatino* itself: *Banco Nacional de Cuba* v. *Farr*, 243 F.Supp. 957, 966, 972 (S.D.N.Y. 1965), aff'd, 383 F.2d 166 (2d Cir. 1967), *cert. denied*, 390 U.S. 956 (1968), *rehearing denied*, 390 U.S. 1037 (1968). In 1996 Congress effectively abolished the doctrine in respect of Cuba for purposes of the Cuban Liberty and Democratic (Libertad) Act of 1996, Pub.L. No. 104–14, Mar. 12, 1996.

   I have never seen much substance in the arguments that Congress could not modify the judicial doctrine. See Henkin, *Act of State Today: Recollections in Tranquility*, 6 COLUM.J.TRANSNATIONAL L. 175, 177–8 (1967). It is suggested, even, that the law-making authority of the courts exists only to the extent of federal political power, and that the authority of political branches to supersede the courts follows. Hill, n. 16 to this chapter, at 1046–56. But *cf.* Cardozo, *Congress Versus Sabbatino: Constitutional Considerations*, 4 COLUM.J. TRANSNAT'L L. 297 (1966); R. FALK, THE AFTERMATH OF SABBATINO (1965).

   The Hickenlooper Amendment apparently directs the courts not to apply the Act of State doctrine to expropriations for which prompt, adequate, and effective compensation is not provided, unless the President certifies that the doctrine is nonetheless required by the foreign relations of the United States. By this statute, Congress seems to have, incidentally, given legislative approval to the Act of State doctrine generally, rendering it no longer dependent on judicial legislation alone. Compare the effort of the State Department to go beyond the Hickenlooper Amendment and assert additional exceptions, Ch. II, p. 58.

37. See Henkin, *Sabbatino*, n. 26 to this chapter, at 826–8.

38. 406 U.S. 759 (1972), Ch. II, p. 59.

39. In several cases after *Sabbatino* and *First National City Bank*, the Executive suggested to the Court that the foreign relations interests of the United States did not require the courts to respect the act of state in the particular case. See, e.g., *Kalamazoo Spice*, n. 27 above; RESTATEMENT (n. 2 to Preface) § 443, Comment *h*, Reporters' Note 8. The courts indicated that they were not compelled to follow the Executive suggestion but in fact did so. The Executive Branch suggested to Congress that it modify the Act of State doctrine by statute, but except for the Second Hickenlooper Amendment, and the Helms-Burton Act relating to Cuba, n. 36 above, Congress has not acted. See RESTATEMENT (n. 2 to Preface) § 444, Comment *a*.

40. Generally known as the McNabb-Mallory Rule, after *McNabb* v. *United States*, 318 U.S. 332 (1943), and *Mallory* v. *United States*, 354 U.S. 449 (1957). Congress has since laid down guidelines for federal judges in criminal cases. 18 U.S.C. § 3501 (1994). For a discussion of supervisory powers, see Beale, *Reconsidering Supervisory Power in Criminal Cases: Constitutional and Statutory Limits on the Authority of the Federal Courts*, 84 COLUM.L.REV. 1433 (1984). Compare *United States* v. *Alvarez-Sanchez*, 114 S.Ct. 1599 (1994).

41. *In* Alvarez-Machqin, Ch. VII, p. 207 and n. 122, the Court was in effect refusing to assert its supervisory power.

42. *Muskrat* v. *United States*, 219 U.S. 346 (1911); *Massachusetts* v. *Mellon*, 262 U.S. 447 (1923); *Tileston* v. *Ullman*, 318 U.S. 44 (1943). See also *Lampasas* v. *Bell*, 180 U.S. 276 (1901); *Braxton County Court* v. *West Virginia ex rel. Dillon*, 208 U.S. 192 (1908). The vitality of some of these cases is now open to question. *Cf. Griswold* v. *Connecticut*, 381 U.S. 479 (1965). See also the limitations on taxpayer suits, n. 46 below.

43. Neither the United States nor a state can be sued without its consent. See the Eleventh Amendment to the Constitution; *cf. Chisholm* v. *Georgia*, 2 U.S. (2 Dall.) 419, 478 (1793); *Cohens* v. *Virginia*, 19 U.S. (6 Wheat.) 264, 412 (1821); also *United States* v. *Lee*, 106 U.S. 196 (1882). And see *Seminole Tribe of Florida* v. *Florida*, 116 S.Ct. 1114 (1996). A suit will lie to enjoin a federal or state official on the ground that he (she) is acting under an unconstitutional statute; such a suit is deemed not a suit against the United States or against the state, but rather against the official. See *Ex parte Young*, 209 U.S. 123 (1908).

    The President is not personally amenable to judicial jurisdiction. *Mississippi* v. *Johnson*, 71 U.S. (4 Wall.) 475 (1867), but he is subject to judicial subpoena to produce tapes or documents. See *United States* v. *Nixon*, 418 U.S. 683 (1974); also *Nixon* v. *Sirica*, 487 F.2d 700 (D.C.Cir. 1973). The President is immune from civil suit or claims arising out of his official acts. See *Nixon* v. *Fitzgerald*, 457 U.S. 731 (1982). The President enjoys executive privilege to protect confidentiality within the Executive branch, but that privilege may bow to the needs of administration of justice; the Supreme Court perhaps implied that Executive privilege based on the needs of diplomatic or military secrecy might be absolute. *United States* v. *Nixon*, above. See n. 71 to Ch. IV.

44. The Justices refused to construe treaties and advise on other questions of international law arising out of the French wars. See 3 THE CORRESPONDENCE AND PUBLIC PAPERS OF JOHN JAY 486–9 (Johnston ed. 1890); 1 C. WARREN, THE SUPREME COURT IN UNITED STATES HISTORY 110–11 (1922).

45. *Massachusetts* v. *Mellon*, 262 U.S. 447 (1923); *cf. Massachusetts* v. *Laird*, 400 U.S. 886 (1970), n. 3 to Ch. X; also *Lee* v. *Humphrey*, 352 U.S. 904 (1956) (denying motion of Governor of Utah for leave to file original proceeding to prevent expenditures for defense and foreign affairs). A state can sometimes test federal 'usurpation' in upholding its own authority against private challenge. When Maryland convicted McCulloch of failing to pay a tax, he challenged the Maryland tax as inconsistent with an act of Congress, and Maryland defended its tax on the ground that the federal act was beyond the power of Congress. *McCulloch* v. *Maryland*, 17 U.S. (4 Wheat.) 316 (1819). Compare the

cases in which the states resisted the asserted supremacy of a treaty, e.g., *Asakura* v. *Seattle*, 265 U.S. 332 (1924), Ch. VII, p. 208.

On the other hand, the Court regularly monitors state encroachment on the federal domain, as in the dormant commerce clause cases, p. 135, this chapter, and Ch. VI, p. 158, in suits against state agencies or officials.

46. Citizen suits have been rejected even when it appeared that alleged constitutional violations would not otherwise be adjudicated. *Ex parte Levitt*, 302 U.S. 633 (1937); *United States* v. *Richardson*, 418 U.S. 166 (1974); *Schlesinger* v. *Reservists Committee to Stop the War*, 418 U.S. 208 (1974). Taxpayer suits are also generally barred. *Massachusetts* v. *Mellon*, 262 U.S. 447 (1923), largely reaffirmed in *Flast* v. *Cohen*, 392 U.S. 83 (1968), which, with small exception, bars taxpayer suits to challenge spending even on the ground that it is unconstitutional. See *Sierra Club* v. *Morton*, 405 U.S. 727 (1972); *Valley Forge Christian College* v. *Americans United for Separation of Church and State*, 454 U.S. 464 (1982). On suits by state taxpayers, see *Doremus* v. *Board of Education*, 342 U.S. 429 (1952).

47. The private plaintiff will usually allege that because the action is unconstitutional he (she) is deprived of liberty or property without due process of law in violation of the Fifth or the Fourteenth Amendment. See, e.g., *Carter* v. *Carter Coal Co.*, 298 U.S. 238 (1936); *Youngstown Sheet & Tube Co.* v. *Sawyer*, 343 U.S. 579 (1952).

48. For Vietnam War cases see n. 67 to this chapter. For a case during the Persian Gulf War, see *Ange* v. *Bush*, 752 F.Supp 509 (D.D.C. 1990).

49. See Ch. I, p. 21. Between 1936 and 1995, the Court invalidated only one act of Congress as beyond its powers, *Oregon* v. *Mitchell*, 400 U.S. 112 (1970) (voting for 18-year-olds in state elections); and only a few as infringing the Bill of Rights or other safeguards for individual rights, e.g., *Tot* v. *United States*, 319 U.S. 463 (1943); *United States* v. *Lovett*, 328 U.S. 303 (1946); *Afroyim* v. *Rusk*, 387 U.S. 253 (1967). Also, *Reid* v. *Covert*, 354 U.S. 1 (1957), and related cases held that Congress cannot prescribe trial by court-martial for those not in the military, n. 44 to Ch. III. These cases speak in terms of the limits of the necessary and proper clause, but the Court was really protecting the right to a jury trial. See n. 57 to Ch. III.

In 1995, the Court invalidated an act of Congress making it a crime to bring a gun into a school zone, on the ground that Congress had not demonstrated that such guns had a significant link to interstate commerce. *United States* v. *Lopez*, 115 S.Ct. 1624 (1995). It remains to be seen how significant the ruling will be to limit the power of Congress in matters affecting interstate or foreign commerce. See Ch. III, p. 65.

50. See, e.g., *Missouri* v. *Holland*, 252 U.S. 416 (1920), discussed in Ch. VII. Persons accused of violating federal statutes have sometimes challenged federal authority, usually without success, e.g., *United States* v. *Arjona*, 120 U.S. 479 (1887) (conviction for counterfeiting foreign currency), Ch. III, p. 69. And see the Commerce Power cases, Ch. III.

51. See 28 U.S.C. §§ 1254, 1257 (1988). See the Vietnam War cases, n. 67 to this chapter. The Court also exercises discretion as to whether to entertain original suits. See n. 10 to this chapter. Since 1988 the Supreme Court's appellate

jurisdiction is almost wholly discretionary, with hardly any appeal to the Court as of right. Before that date, a significant part of the Court's jurisdiction was mandatory, but even as to cases that in principle were entitled to review as of right, the Supreme Court had developed doctrines and procedures for giving many of them short shrift, as by dismissing for want of a substantial federal question. *Zucht* v. *King*, 260 U.S. 174 (1922); previous U.S. Sup.Ct. Rule 15(e). Unlike denials of certiorari, however, such dismissals decided the federal issue. But *cf. Poe* v. *Ullman*, 367 U.S. 497 (1961).

The appellate jurisdiction of the Supreme Court is subject to comprehensive Congressional control. At least that seems to be the import of *Ex parte McCardle*, 74 U.S. (7 Wall.) 506 (1869); but *cf. United States* v. *Klein*, 80 U.S. (13 Wall.) 128 (1871). *McCardle* is cited in *Glidden Co.* v. *Zdanok*, 370 U.S. 530, 567, 605 (1962), but at least Justice Douglas, dissenting, suggested that the case would not be followed today and that the power of Congress to make exceptions and regulations for appellate jurisdiction of the Supreme Court (Art. III, sec. 2, cl. 2) might yet be limited. For the view that the clause was intended to give Congress only very limited authority, see R. BERGER, CONGRESS v. THE SUPREME COURT 285–96 (1969); Ratner, *Congressional Power Over the Appellate Jurisdiction of the Supreme Court*, 109 U.PA.L.REV. 157 (1960). Compare Hart, *The Power of Congress to Limit the Jurisdiction of Federal Courts: An Exercise in Dialectic*, 66 HARV.L.REV. 1362 (1953), with Wechsler, *The Courts and the Constitution*, 65 COLUM.L.REV. 1001 (1965). Also see Gunther, *Congressional Power to Curtail Federal Court Jurisdiction: An Opinionated Guide to the Ongoing Debate*, 36 STAN. L.REV. 201 (1984).

52. I draw here on my comment, *Vietnam in the Courts of the United States: 'Political Questions'*, 63 AM.J.INT'L L. 284 (1969) and my article, *Is There a 'Political Question' Doctrine?* 85 YALE L.J. 597 (1976). See also HENKIN, CONSTITUTIONALISM, DEMOCRACY AND FOREIGN AFFAIRS (1990), Ch. 3. For a general discussion see Scharpf, *Judicial Review and the Political Question: A Functional Analysis*, 75 YALE L.J. 517 (1966). See also Nathanson, *The Supreme Court as a Unit of the National Government: Herein of Separation of Powers and Political Questions*, 6 J.PUBLIC L. 331 (1957). For earlier discussions, see Finkelstein, *Judicial Self-Limitation*, 37 HARV.L.REV. 338 (1924); C.POST, THE SUPREME COURT AND POLITICAL QUESTIONS (1936).

53. But see my article in 85 YALE L.J., n. 52 above.

54. Compare, e.g., Wechsler, *Toward Neutral Principles of Constitutional Law*, 73 HARV.L.REV. 1, 9 (1959), with Bickel, *The Supreme Court, 1960 Term—Foreword: The Passive Virtues*, 75 HARV.L.REV. 40, 46 (1961). Later (at p.75) Bickel says: 'Such is the basis of the political-question doctrine: the court's sense of lack of capacity, compounded in unequal parts of the strangeness of the issue and the suspicion that it will have to yield more often and more substantially to expediency than to principle; the sheer momentousness of it, which unbalances judgment and prevents one from subsuming the normal calculations of probabilities; the anxiety not so much that judicial judgment will be ignored, as that perhaps it should be, but won't; finally and in sum ('in a

mature democracy'), the inner vulnerability of an institution which is elect-
orally irresponsible and has no earth to draw strength from.'

55. See his dissent in *Baker* v. *Carr*, 369 U.S. 186, 266, 267 (1962); compare his opinion in *Colegrove* v. *Green*, 328 U.S. 549 (1946).

56. 369 U.S. 186 (1962).

57. 369 U.S. at 210.

58. 369 U.S. at 217.

59. Compare Wechsler, n. 54 to this chapter. So, for example, the Court will not hear that there has been a failure to carry out the constitutional obligation that 'the United States shall guarantee to every State in this Union a Republican Form of Government' (Art. IV, sec. 4). *Luther* v. *Borden*, 48 U.S. (7 How.) 1 (1849); the discussion in *Baker* v. *Carr* seems to reaffirm that case. But *cf. Roudebush* v. *Hartke*, 405 U.S. 15 (1972). The Supreme Court has stated that the Senate's 'sole Power to try all Impeachments' (Art. 1, sec. 3) is independent of the courts, and the courts cannot review Senate procedures alleged to be contrary to the Constitution and the Bill of Rights. See *Nixon* v. *United States*, 506 U.S. 224 (1993). Compare also *Powell* v. *McCormack*, 395 U.S. 486 (1969), on the reviewability of determinations by a house of Congress of the qualifications of its members. See U.S. Constitution, Art. I, sec. 5.

60. In *Goldwater* v. *Carter*, 444 U.S. 996 (1979), four Justices expressed the view that the courts should not decide whether the President has authority to ter-
minate a treaty without the consent of Congress, or other issues of authority between the President and Congress, at least where the issue was not raised by a private party. Justice Powell, as well as Justice Brennan, the author of the modern restatement of the political question doctrine in *Baker* v. *Carr*, rejected that view. See *Nixon* and *Powell*, n. 59 to this chapter.

Lower courts have dismissed cases on 'political question' grounds (though they do not always invoke the political question doctrine explicitly). See *Crockett* v. *Reagan*, 558 F.Supp. 893 (D.D.C. 1982), *aff'd*, 720 F.2d 1355 (D.C.Cir. 1983), *cert. denied*, 467 U.S. 1251 (1984); *Greenham Women Against Cruise Missiles* v. *Reagan*, 591 F.Supp. 1332 (S.D.N.Y. 1984), *aff'd*, 755 F.2d 34 (2d Cir. 1985); *Sanchez-Espinoza* v. *Reagan*, 770 F.2d 202 (D.C. Cir. 1985). In a number of cases dismissed by lower courts on 'political question' grounds, the court of appeals held the political question doctrine inapplicable (though sometimes dismissing the case on other grounds). See, e.g., *Planned Parenthood Federation, Inc.* v. *Agency for Int'l Dev.*, 670 F.Supp. 538 (S.D.N.Y. 1987), *aff'd in part and rev'd in part*, 838 F.2d 649 (2d Cir. 1988); *Comm. of U.S. Citizens Living in Nicaragua* v. *Reagan*, 859 F.2d 929 (D.C.Cir. 1988); *Linder* v. *Portocarrero*, 747 F.Supp. 1452 (S.D.Fl. 1990), *aff'd in part and rev'd in part*, 963 F.2d 332 (11th Cir. 1992). However, in *Occidental* v. *A Certain Cargo*, 577 F.2d 1196 (5th Cir. 1978), the Court of Appeals invoked the political question doctrine after the district court had decided the case on the basis of the Act of State doctrine.

61. The courts have often used the words 'political question' in this very different sense and context, in all kinds of cases. They have said, for example, that their concern is only whether the political branches of government, federal or state,

have exceeded constitutional limitations; as long as they act within their constitutional powers, the desirability or wisdom of what they do is a 'political question' which is not for the courts to consider. Such statements imply no special doctrine of judicial abstention; in that sense there are political questions in virtually every case, whenever a court reads and applies the Constitution or an act of Congress.

Marshall was speaking of such political questions in *Marbury* v. *Madison*, 5 U.S. (1 Cranch) 137, 165–6 (1803): 'By the constitution of the United States, the president is invested with certain important political powers, in the exercise of which he is to use his own discretion, and is accountable only to his country in his political character, and to his own conscience. To aid him in the performance of these duties, he is authorized to appoint certain officers, who act by his authority, and in conformity with his orders. In such cases, their acts are his acts; and whatever opinion may be entertained of the manner in which executive discretion may used, still there exists, and can exist, no power to control that discretion. The subjects are political: they respect the nation, not individual rights, and being entrusted to the executive, the decision of the executive is conclusive. The application of this remark will be perceived, by adverting to the act of congress for establishing the department of foreign affairs. This officer, as his duties were prescribed by that act, is to conform precisely to the will of the president: he is the mere organ by whom that will is communicated. The acts of such an officer, as an officer, can never be examinable by the court. . .

The conclusion from this reasoning is, that where the heads of departments are the political or confidential agents of the executive, merely to execute the will of the president, or rather to act in cases in which the executive possesses a constitutional or legal discretion, nothing can be more perfectly clear, than that their acts are only politically examinable. . .'

Baker v. *Carr* does not seem to recognize the distinction I stress. See, e.g., 369 U.S. at 211 n. 31, where the Court cites an example of 'sweeping statements to the effect that all questions touching foreign relations are political questions'. The example reads: 'The conduct of the foreign relations of our Government is committed by the Constitution to the Executive and Legislative—'the political'—Departments of the Government, and the propriety of what may be done in the exercise of this political power is not subject to judicial inquiry or decision.' *Oetjen* v. *Central Leather Co.*, 246 U.S. 297, 302 (1918). But if, as is probable, 'propriety' there did not mean constitutionality, the statement is unexceptional and commonplace: so long as the political branches are acting within their constitutional powers, 'wisdom', 'desirability', 'propriety', are not for the courts to review.

62. See, e.g., *Williams* v. *Suffolk Ins. Co.*, 38 U.S. (13 Pet.) 415, 420 (1839): 'And can there be any doubt, that when the executive branch of government, which is charged with our foreign relations, shall, in its correspondence with a foreign nation, assume a fact in regard to the sovereignty of any island or country, it is conclusive on the judicial department? And in this view it is not material to inquire, nor is it the province of the court to determine, whether

the executive be right or wrong. It is enough to know, that in the exercise of his constitutional functions, he had decided the question. Having done this, under the responsibilities which belong to him, it is obligatory on the people and government of the Union.'

See also *Jones* v. *United States*, 137 U.S. 202, 212 (1890): 'Who is the sovereign, *de jure* or *de facto*, of a territory is not a judicial, but a political question, the determination of which by the legislative and executive departments of any government conclusively binds the judges. . .' *Cf. Cordova* v. *Grant*, 248 U.S. 413 (1919); *Foster & Elam* v. *Neilson*, 27 U.S. (2 Pet.) 253, 306, 309 (1829); *Garcia* v. *Lee*, 37 U.S. (12 Pet.) 511 (1838); *Kennett* v. *Chambers*, 55 U.S. (14 How.) 38, 50–1 (1852).

63. *Rose* v. *Himely*, 8 U.S. (4 Cranch) 241, 272 (1808), overrruled on other grounds, *Hudson* v. *Guestier*, 10 U.S. (6 Cranch) 281 (1810); *Gelston* v. *Hoyt*, 16 U.S. (3 Wheat.) 246, 322 (1818); *United States* v. *Palmer*, 16 U.S. (3 Wheat.) 610, 634–5 (1818); *Guaranty Trust Co.* v. *United States*, 304 U.S. 126, 137–8 (1938); *cf. Terlinden* v. *Ames*, 184 U.S. 270 (1902); *Oetjen* v. *Central Leather Co.*, 246 U.S. 297 (1918). See RESTATEMENT (n. 2 to Preface) § 111, Reporters' Note 1; 7 Op.Att'y Gen. 186, 217 (1855). In the Federal Reserve Act of 1941, 48 Stat. 184, 12 U.S.C. § 632 (1994), Congress provided that a certificate of the Secretary of State that a foreign government is recognized is binding on the bank. On the status of unrecognized governments in U.S. courts, see n. 62 to Ch. II.

Similarly, it is a political question in this sense only when the courts say that how the United States shall respond to a breach of international law or treaty by another state is not for the courts to decide. See Chapter VII, p. 214 and n. 33 to Ch. VIII. In the sovereign immunity and Act of State cases, too, Ch. II, p. 54, the courts are not abstaining but are giving effect to 'legislation' by the President or Congress. See n. 27 to this chapter.

64. The Court was not saying anything different in cases such as *Chicago & Southern Air Lines, Inc.* v. *Waterman S.S. Corp.*, 333 U.S. 103, 111–14 (1948): 'But even if courts could require full disclosure, the very nature of executive decisions as to foreign policy is political, not judicial. Such decisions are wholly confided by our Constitution to the political departments of the government, Executive and Legislative. They are delicate, complex, and involve large elements of prophecy. They are and should be undertaken only by those directly responsible to the people whose welfare they advance or imperil. They are decisions of a kind for which the Judiciary has neither aptitude, facilities nor responsibility and which has long been held to belong in the domain of political power not subject to judicial intrusion or inquiry.'

Compare also: 'It is pertinent to observe that any policy toward aliens is vitally and intricately interwoven with contemporaneous policies in regard to the conduct of foreign relations, the war power, and the maintenance of a republican form of government. Such matters are so exclusively entrusted to the political branches of government as to be largely immune from judicial inquiry or interference.' Justice Jackson in *Harisiades* v. *Shaughnessy*, 342 U.S. 580, 588–9 (1952).

See also *United States* v. *Curtiss-Wright Export Corp.*, 299 U.S. 304, 319–21 (1936). In that case, the Court held that an action by the President pursuant to delegation by Congress was amply within their powers; it did not say that the constitutional validity of the action could not be examined.

Whether the Court would hear claims that in reaching such foreign affairs decisions the President violated some general prohibition in the Constitution— e.g., that he denied due process of law—is a different question and one which the Court has not addressed. Refusal to do so would require something closer to what I call a strict 'political question' doctrine. The doctrine might contemplate abstention as to some constitutional claims, not others. Compare *Gomillion* v. *Lightfoot*, 364 U.S. 339 (1960). In my view, the Court should not apply the political question doctrine in such cases.

65. International Treaty Providing For the Renunciation of War, 46 Stat. 2343 [1929–1931]; U.N. Charter, article 2(4), n. 40 to Ch. VIII and p. 250.

66. See Ch. VII, p. 214. This issue, then, raises a political question only in the second sense—a question within the constitutional powers of the political branches to decide.

In *United States* v. *Mitchell*, 369 F.2d 323 (2d Cir. 1966), *cert. denied*, 386 U.S. 972 (1967), the petitioner apparently argued that the Vietnam War was a violation of international law, and that he would be guilty of an offense because the Nuremberg Charter imposed individual responsibility for waging a war of aggression and denied the defense of 'superior orders'. In dissenting from the denial of certiorari, Justice Douglas urged that the Court should decide, *inter alia*, whether the question as to waging aggressive war is justiciable and whether the Nuremberg Charter was a defense.

67. See e.g., *Luftig* v. *McNamara*, 373 F.2d 664 (D.C.Cir.), *cert. denied*, 387 U.S. 945 (1967); *Mora* v. *McNamara*, 387 F.2d 862 (D.C.Cir.), *cert. denied*, 389 U.S. 934 (1967). (Stewart and Douglas, JJ., dissented in opinions urging that the justiciability of the constitutional issues, and other questions, be decided). Compare *Orlando* v. *Laird*, 443 F.2d 1039 (2d Cir. 1971), *cert. denied*, 404 U.S. 869 (1971), Douglas and Brennan, JJ., dissenting; also *Da Costa* v. *Laird*, 448 F.2d 1368 (2d Cir. 1971), *cert. denied*, 405 U.S. 979 (1972), and *Atlee* v. *Laird*, 347 F.Supp. 689 (E.D. Pa. 1972), *aff'd without opinion sub nom.*, *Atlee* v. *Richardson*, 411 U.S. 911 (1973); *Holtzman* v. *Schlesinger*, 484 F.2d 1307 (2d Cir. 1973), *cert. denied*, 416 U.S. 936 (1974). See Sugarman, *Judicial Decisions Concerning the Constitutionality of United States Military Activity in Indo-China: A Bibliography of Court Decisions*, 13 COLUM.J.TRANSNAT'L L. 470 (1974).

68. Without apparent hesitation, the Court decided that President Truman exceeded his constitutional powers (and invaded those of Congress) when he seized the steel mills. *Youngstown Sheet & Tube Co.* v. *Sawyer*, 343 U.S. 579 (1952). The Court also decided that the President usurped Congressional powers in other cases, Ch. IV, p. 104. For other cases where the Court considered Separation of Powers issues, see *Plaut* v. *Spendthrift Farm, Inc.*, 115 S.Ct. 1447 (1995); *Myers* v. *United States*, 272 U.S. 52 (1926); *United States* v. *Klein*, 80 U.S. (13 Wall.) 128 (1871). See also the opinion of four Justices in *Goldwater* v. *Carter*, n. 60 above.

69. The Supreme Court has not invoked the political question doctrine to dismiss an individual's claim that a foreign relations action deprived him or her of constitutional rights. Compare, e.g., *Japan Whaling Association* v. *American Cetacean Society*, 478 U.S. 221 (1986).

I have argued that judicial abstention from review in such cases is an abdication of an essential function of the courts in our constitutional democracy-subject-to-rights. Constitutionalism, Democracy and Foreign Affairs (1990), Ch. 3.

NOTES, CHAPTER VI. THE ABIDING SIGNIFICANCE OF
FEDERALISM: THE STATES AND FOREIGN AFFAIRS, pp. 149 to 169

1. *Gibbons* v. *Ogden*, 22 U.S. (9 Wheat.) 1 228 (Johnson, J., concurring); *Holmes* v. *Jennison*, 39 U.S. (14 Pet.) 540, 575–6 (1840) (Taney, C.J.); *United States* v. *Belmont*, 301 U.S. 324, 331 (1937) (Sutherland, J.). Taney's opinion in *Holmes* v. *Jennison* includes an extensive denigration of the authority of the states in foreign affairs.

2. For a few other examples: 'For local interests the several States of the Union exist; but for national purposes, embracing our relations with foreign nations, we are but one people, one nation, one power.' *The Chinese Exclusion Case*, 130 U.S. 581, 606 (1889). And *United States* v. *Pink*: 'Power over external affairs is not shared by the States; it is vested in the national government exclusively.' 315 U.S. 203, 233 (1942). Compare Marshall, C.J., in *Cohens* v. *Virginia*, 19 U.S. (6 Wheat.) 264, 413–14 (1821). See also Calhoun: 'In our relation to the rest of the world . . . the States disappear', quoted in n. 54 to Ch. VII.

    The need for national control and the dangers of state interference in foreign affairs are emphasized in several of the Federalist Papers, notably Nos. 3, 4, 5, 42, and 80. In No. 42 Madison said, 'If we are to be one nation in any respect, it clearly ought to be in respect to other nations.'

    Even the Constitution of the Confederate States continued virtually the same limitations on the states in regard to foreign relations as are in the United States Constitution. See the Constitution of the Confederate States, March 11, 1861, Art. 1, sec. 10, quoted 1 BUTLER, THE TREATY POWER (n. 10 to Ch. I) 229–31.

3. Under the Articles of Confederation Congress urged the states to provide for the punishment of offenses against the law of nations. See n. 6 to Ch. VII. And compare the *De Longchamps* case, see n. 105 to Ch. VII. Under the U.S. Constitution, Congress enacted laws to punish some offenses against the law of nations and gave the federal courts exclusive jurisdiction of them (e.g., Judicial Code of 1911, § 256, 36 Stat. 1087, 1160–1) but the states remained free to pass additional laws enforceable in their courts. See *Fox* v. *Ohio*, 46 U.S. (5 How.) 410, 416 (1847). And some offenses against the law of nations, not having been defined and legislated by Congress, remain for the states to enforce. See WRIGHT (n. 3 to Ch. I) 178–9. The general protection of foreign nationals, for which the United States is responsible to the state of nationality under international law, is still left largely to state law, state officials and state courts. See p. 163, this chapter.

    That treaties would sometimes be relevant to decisions in state courts was, of course, the reason for the express reference to them in the Supremacy Clause, Art. VI, sec. 2. Long ago, some treaties were left largely to enforcement by the states, e.g., those relating to migratory bird conservation. See Koenig, *Federal and State Cooperation under the Constitution*, 36 MICH.L.REV. 752, 775–6 (1934). See the recent practice of the United States in ratifying human rights treaties to declare that it will leave much implementation to the states. See n. 82 to this chapter.

In general, Congress has from the beginning left enforcement of many national policies to state officials and state courts. Early federal regulatory acts provided for enforcement proceedings in state courts. See, e.g., Carriage Tax Act § 10, 1 Stat. 373 (1794); Alien Enemies Act, § 2, 1 Stat. 577 (1798). And, in 1815, Congress conferred upon the state courts jurisdiction over federal tax claims, including prosecutions for fines, penalties, forfeitures, and regulated state judicial proceedings in such cases. 3 Stat. 244 (1815). The states have been generally willing to exercise this function and it is now accepted that Congress could require it of them. Compare *Testa* v. *Katt*, 330 U.S. 386 (1947); *Claflin* v. *Houseman*, 93 U.S. 130, 136–7 (1876); *McKnett* v. *St. Louis & S. F. Ry.*, 292 U.S. 230 (1934). But Congress cannot impose duties on state legislatures. See *New York* v. *United States*, n. 71 to this chapter. On state and local cooperation in national policy, see generally L. HENKIN, ARMS CONTROL AND INSPECTION IN AMERICAN LAW (1958), Ch. VI and notes. See the discussion of 'federal state' clauses this chapter, pp. 167–8.

4. The federal courts have exclusive jurisdiction of actions brought against ambassadors, public ministers, consuls and vice consuls of foreign states, 28 U.S.C. §§ 1251, 1351 (1994), but where exclusive federal jurisdiction is not expressly reserved, it is retained by the states, as in suits brought by ambassadors or consuls, or in suits brought against foreign governments not denied immunity by the Foreign Sovereign Immunities Act, Ch. II, p. 54, (if they waive immunity). Compare *Popovici* v. *Agler*, 280 U.S. 379, 383–4 (1930). State courts also have substantial concurrent jurisdiction in regard to maritime matters. See *Madruga* v. *Superior Court of California*, 346 U.S. 556, 560–1 (1954).

5. See, e.g., the U.S. instruments of ratification of the International Covenant on Civil and Political Rights, 31 I.L.M. 645 (1992), and of the Convention on the Elimination of all Forms of Racial Discrimination.

6. Uruguay Round Agreements Act, Pub. L. No. 103–465, 108 Stat. 4809 (1994).

7. *United States* v. *Curtiss-Wright Export Corp.*, 299 U.S. 304 (1936), quoted in Ch. I, p. 18.

8. *Brown* v. *Maryland*, 25 U.S. (12 Wheat.) 419 (1827); *Hooven & Allison Co.* v. *Evatt*, 324 U.S. 652 (1945); *cf. Youngstown Sheet & Tube Co.* v. *Bowers*, 358 U.S. 534 (1959); *Dept. of Revenue* v. *James Beam Distilling Co.*, 377 U.S. 341 (1964). See Note, *State Taxation of Imports—When Does an Import Cease to be an Import?*, 58 HARV.L.REV. 858 (1945).

9. *Empresa Siderurgica* v. *Merced County*, 337 U.S. 154, 157 (1949); *Joy Oil Co.* v. *State Tax Commission*, 337 U.S. 286 (1949); *cf. Richfield Oil Corp.* v. *State Board*, 329 U.S. 69 (1946); *Michelin Tire Corp.* v. *Wages*, 423 U.S. 276 (1976). See also *United States* v. *International Business Machines Corp.*, 116 S.Ct. 1793 (1996), Chapter III, n. 78 above.

10. Consent to state agreements can probably be given by treaty as well as by Congress. Compare Art. IX of the 1899 Treaty with Mexico under which some states would extradite directly to Mexico. 31 Stat. 1818, 1824–25 (1899), T.S. 242. (That extradition inevitably involves 'agreement', see pp. 153, 154, 155, this chapter).

Congressional consent to state agreements has sometimes been found to be implied. See *Virginia* v. *Tennessee*, 148 U.S. 503 (1893) and *Russell* v. *American Ass'n.*, 139 Tenn. 124, 201 S.W. 151 (1918).

In 1839, the Secretary of State agreed with the British minister to leave the regulation of issues in disputed territory to the State of Maine and the Province of New Brunswick, pending the final settlement of the boundary dispute. See CRANDALL, TREATIES (n. 70 to Ch. III) 113.

11. But compare the State Department's communication, n. 30 to this chapter.

12. Taney insisted on the distinction between treaties and agreements but appears to suggest that the difference is formal: 'For when we speak of "a treaty", we mean an instrument written and executed with the formalities customary among nations. . . .' *Holmes* v. *Jennison*, 39 U.S. (14 Pet.) 540, 571 (1840). That a treaty entails formality might indeed be a sufficient reason for prohibiting it to the states since formality may imply international 'sovereignty', and involves the states in diplomatic intercourse and negotiation. Taney further suggests, quoting Vattel, that a principal difference between treaties and compacts is that the former are 'for perpetuity, or for a considerable time'. *Id.* at 572.

13. See 2 STORY COMMENTARIES (n. 3 to Ch. I) § 1402. He adds: 'Perhaps the language of the former clause may be more plausibly interpreted from the terms used, "treaty, alliance, or confederation" and upon the ground, that the sense of each is best known by its association (*noscitur a sociis*) to apply to treaties of a political character; such as treaties of alliance for purposes of peace and war; and treaties of confederation, in which the parties are leagued for mutual government, political cooperation, and the exercise of political sovereignty; and treaties of cession of sovereignty, or conferring internal political jurisdiction, or external political dependence, or general commercial privileges. The latter clause, "compacts and agreements", might then very properly apply to such as regarded what might be deemed mere private rights of sovereignty; such as questions of boundary; interests in land situated in the territory of each other; and other internal regulations for the mutual comfort and convenience of States bordering on each other . . . In such cases, the consent of Congress may be properly required, in order to check any infringement of the rights of the national government; and, at the same time, a total prohibition to enter into any compact or agreement might be attended with permanent inconvenience or public mischief.' *Id.* at § 1403.

Frankfurter and Landis expressed a different view: 'There is no self-executing test differentiating "compact" from "treaty". Story and other writers have attempted an analytical classification . . . The attempt is bound to go shipwreck for we are in a field in which political judgment is, to say the least, one of the important factors.' They conclude that it must be left to Congress 'to circumscribe the area of agreement open to the States'. Frankfurter and Landis, *The Compact Clause of the Constitution—A Study In Interstate Adjustments*, 34 YALE L.J. 685, 695 n. 37 (1925). Compare Naujoks, *Compacts and Agreements Between States and Between States and a Foreign Power*, 36 MARQUETTE L.REV. 219, 231–3 (1952). K. Heron, *The Interstate Compact in Transition: From Cooperative State Action to Congressionally Coerced Agreements*, 60 ST. JOHN's L. REV. 1 (1985); J. Girardot, *Toward a Rational*

Scheme of Interstate Water Compact Adjudication, 23 UNIV. MICH. J. OF L. REFORM 151 (1989).

14. Especially since Congress has acquired the equivalent of a treaty-making authority through Congressional–Executive agreements, Ch. VII, pp. 215–18. Compare F. ZIMMERMAN & M. WENDELL, THE INTERSTATE COMPACT SINCE 1925 74–5 (1951).

15. See ch. 758, 70 Stat. 701 (1956), repealed, Pub.L.No. 85–145, 71 Stat. 367 (1957); but the repealing statute gave consent to an agreement providing for the continued existence of the Buffalo and Fort Erie Public Bridge Authority. These and similar grants of consent contain clauses expressly reserving the right of Congress to amend, alter or repeal the authorization.

16. Pub. L. 85–76, § 1, 72 Stat. 1701 (1958), *codified in* 30 U.S.C. § 28-1 (1994).

17. Ch. 246, 63 Stat. 271 (1949), ch. 267, 66 Stat. 71 (1952), repealed by Act of June 30, 1978, Pub.L.No. 95–307, § 8(a), 92 Stat 356. But 16 U.S.C. § 1647(b) (1994) provides that 'contracts and cooperative agreements [formed under the repealed law] shall remain in effect until revoked or amended by their own terms or under other provisions of the law'.

18. Federal Civil Defense Act of 1950, ch. 1228, § 203, 64 Stat. 1251 (1951), repealed by Act of Oct. 5, 1994, Pub.L.No. 103–337, Div. C., Title 34, § 3412(a), 108 Stat. 311, which shifted the emphasis of the Federal Emergency Management Act from nuclear attack-related activities to a risk-based strategy to improve preparedness for all hazards.

19. Ch. 201, 68 Stat. 92 (1954), codified as amended, 33 U.S.C. §§ 981 *et seq.* (1994).

20. 'We do not perceive any difference in the meaning, except that the word "compact" is generally used with reference to more formal and serious engagements than is usually implied in the term "agreement". . .' Justice Field in *Virginia* v. *Tennessee*, 148 U.S. 503, 520 (1893). But compacts are presumably less formal than treaties. See n. 12 above.

The law of compacts is meager and virtually all of it has been developed in respect of interstate compacts; the law of foreign compacts would probably be the same in many respects but the foreign element and the relevance to U.S. foreign relations might sometimes suggest a difference. In regard to interstate compacts, the court held that the consent of Congress need not be given in advance or in any particular form, and can even be implied. See *Virginia* v. *Tennessee*, 148 U.S. at 517, 521; *Green* v. *Biddle*, 21 U.S. (8 Wheat.) 1, (1823); *Poole* v. *Fleeger*, 36 U.S. (11 Pet.) 185, 209 (1837); *Virginia* v. *West Virginia*, 78 U.S. (11 Wall.) 39 (1871); *Wharton* v. *Wise*, 153 U.S. 155, 172–3 (1894). And the consent of Congress may be conditional. *Cf. James* v. *Dravo Contracting Co.*, 302 U.S. 134 (1937). Congress has authority to compel compliance with such compacts. *Virginia* v. *West Virginia*, 246 U.S. 565, 601 (1918).

The classic discussion of the compact clause (again, principally, in regard to interstate compacts) is Frankfurter and Landis, n. 13 to this chapter. See also ZIMMERMAN & WENDELL, n. 14 to this chapter; Dunbar, *Interstate Compacts and Congressional Consent*, 36 VA.L.REV. 753 (1950); Weinfield, *What Did the*

Framers of the Federal Constitution Mean by 'Agreements or Compacts?', 3
U.Chi.L.Rev. 453 (1936).
'The compact . . . adapts to our Union of sovereign States the age-old treaty-
making power of independent sovereign nations'. *Hinderlider* v. *La Plata River
Co.*, 304 U.S. 92, 104 (1938). In colonial days, boundary disputes were usually
settled by negotiation, their agreement subject to approval of the Crown. See
Frankfurter and Landis, above at 692. Under the Articles of Confederation
boundary disputes between states were to be appealed to the Congress. Article
IX.
   In *Cuyler* v. *Adams*, 449 U.S. 433. (1981), the Court elaborated *Virginia* v.
Tennessee: 'where Congress has authorized the States to enter into a cooperative agreement, and where the subject matter of that agreement is an appropriate subject for Congressional legislation, the consent of Congress transforms
the States' agreement into federal law under the Compact Clause'. See generally, Note, *Cuyler* v. *Adams and the Characterization of Compact Law*, 77 Va.
L. Rev. 1387 (1991).

21. 39 U.S. (14 Pet.) 540 (1840).
22. After the writ of error was dismissed, the Supreme Court of Judicature of the
    State of Vermont discharged Holmes. 'The judges of that court were satisfied,
    on an examination of the opinions delivered by the justices of the supreme
    court, that by a majority of the court it was held, that the power claimed to
    deliver up George Holmes did not exist.' Reporter's Note, 39 U.S. (14 Pet.) at
    598.
23. 39 U.S. (14 Pet.) at 572–4. Taney's conclusion that Governor Jennison had
    entered into an agreement that was invalid for want of Congressional consent
    was an alternative ground of decision, probably in an effort to base it on an
    express constitutional prohibition. He went on to find also that because the
    power to extradite was granted to the federal government it was denied to the
    states. See n. 57 to this chapter.
       Justice Thompson seemed to admit that the Governor had no authority to
    act as he did, but found that the Supreme Court had no jurisdiction of the case.
    Id. at 579–81. The Taney position that a state may not extradite to a foreign
    country was later adopted in dictum in *United States* v. *Rauscher*, 119 U.S. 407,
    414 (1886). See also Restatement (n. 2 to Preface) § 478, Reporters' note 8.
24. Taney found indeed that it was apparently the policy of the United States not
    to extradite persons to foreign governments and state extradition would be
    inconsistent with that policy. *Id.* at 574.
25. *Virginia* v. *Tennessee*, 148 U.S. 503, 519 (1893). The Court held that prelimin-
    ary arrangements to ascertain and adjust the boundary between the two states
    did not constitute an agreement requiring Congressional consent. Subsequent
    agreement to establish the boundary probably required consent if it effected
    important change since it increased the political power of the enlarged state,
    but the Court found such consent in that Congress had acted on the new
    boundaries. *Id.* at 521–2.
26. A number of unpublished agreements are reported in Rodgers, *The Capacity
    of States of The Union to Conclude International Agreements: The Background*

and Some Recent Developments, 61 AM.J.INT'L L. 1021, 1025–27 (1967). He describes, *inter alia*, proposals for a Mexican–Gulf South Association, to include Mexico and six States of the United States, to promote education, commerce and tourism, and a proposed cultural agreement between Louisiana and Quebec. (That agreement later came to fruition in 1970. See Rodgers, *Conclusion of Quebec–Louisiana Agreement on Cultural Cooperation*, 64 AM.J.INT'L L. 380 (1970)).

McHenry County v. *Brady*, 37 N.D. 59, 163 N.W. 540 (1917), upheld an arrangement whereby a county in North Dakota constructed a drainage ditch in cooperation with a Canadian town. The state court held that it did not require the consent of Congress since it did not increase the 'political power' of the state.

In recent decades, more than 830 cities and other municipal governments have established official 'sister city' relationships with over 1,270 cities and communities in 90 other countries. Almost every state has established trade or investment offices in foreign countries. Over 28 cities have declared themselves 'sanctuaries' for Central American refugees. See Bilder, n. 67, below.

27. Perhaps authority for these arrangements is deemed to be implied in the U.N. Headquarters Agreement, June 26, 1947, 61 Stat. 3416, T.I.A.S. No. 1676; that agreement was authorized by Congress, ch. 482, 61 Stat. 756 (1947). See n. 27 to Ch. VII.

28. See 14, MAINE REV.STAT.ANN. §§ 6352–403 (1994); N.J.CODE Title 2A:41A-1 (1994); 42 PA.S.C.A. § 7522 (1994); N.Y. UNCONSOLIDATED LAW ch. 108 § 1 (Consol. 1994).

29. States have enacted reciprocal legislation especially in the area of child support after negotiations with foreign governments. The first such arrangement was made in 1960 between Michigan and Ontario. Subsequent reciprocal statutes were made between the various U.S. states and Canada and the United Kingdom. See Dehart, *Comity, Conventions, and the Constitution: State and Federal Initiatives in International Support Enforcement*, 28 FAM. L. Q. 89 (1994). See also, Cavers, *International Enforcement of Family Support*, 81 COLUM. L. REV. 994, (1981). For discussion of reciprocal legislation, see *Robertson* v. *General Electric Co.*, n. 48 to Ch. III.

30. In some instances state authorities have sought the advice of the State Department. In 1936, the Legal Adviser of the State Department informed the Director of the Department of Motor Vehicles of California that an arrangement with its counterpart across the Mexican border for reciprocal exemption of motor vehicles from registration and fees would require the consent of Congress and might infringe the Treaty Power. In regard to a proposed compact for the promotion of trade between Florida and Cuba, the State Department wrote in 1937 that the 'Department's policy in regard to promotion of commerce with foreign countries and the negotiation of commercial treaties does not contemplate the conclusion of special agreements or pacts between separate states and foreign governments even if the consent of Congress to such special agreements could be obtained'. 5 HACKWORTH, DIGEST OF INTERNATIONAL LAW 25 (1943).

31. Congress has given its consent in advance to an interstate compact, and has placed conditions on that consent—even to the point of designing and developing every detail of a 'regional agency'. See Heron, *The Interstate Compact in Transition: From Cooperative State Action to Congressionally Coerced Agreements*, 60 St. John's l. Rev. 1, (1985).

32. See *Cuyler* v. *Adams*, 449 U.S. 433 (1981), n. 20, above.

33. Surely, constitutional provisions that give Congress power to legislate in regard to U.S. courts, national armed forces, the national capital, deny such power to the states. Other grants of power to Congress have also been held to exclude the states. A state cannot naturalize or denaturalize persons. See *Chirac* v. *Chirac*, 15 U.S. (2 Wheat.) 259, 269 (1817). But a state court held that a state may grant the right to vote to resident aliens who have declared their intention to become citizens. See *Spragins* v. *Houghton*, 3 Ill. 377 (1840). See generally Neuman, *'We are the People': Alien Suffrage in German and American Perspective*, 13 Mich. J. Int'l L. 259 (1992). The states are not forbidden to define and punish piracies and offenses against the law of nations, especially if international law be deemed part of the common law of the state. Congress, in fact, left many offenses to be punished by the state. See n. 70 to this chapter. The states can have bankruptcy laws if Congress does not act. *Sturges* v. *Crowninshield*, 17 U.S. (4 Wheat) 122, 195–7 (1819); *Ogden* v. *Saunders*, 25 U.S. (12 Wheat) 213, 368–9 (1827). A state may also punish the issuance of counterfeit coins. *Fox* v. *Ohio*, 46 U.S. (5 How.) 410 (1847). And in the absence of federal legislation a state might regulate patent rights. *Cf. Allen* v. *Riley*, 203 U.S. 347 (1906). But Congress has in fact regulated in these matters and generally preempted the state.

34. *Takahashi* v. *Fish & Game Commission*, 334 U.S. 410 (1948).

35. *Missouri* v. *Holland*, 252 U.S. 416 (1920); *Ware* v. *Hylton*, 3 U.S. (3 Dall.) 199 (1769); *Hauenstein* v. *Lynham*, 100 U.S. 483 (1880); *Asakura* v. *Seattle*, 265 U.S. 332 (1924). See Ch. VII.

    U.S. adherence to human rights conventions, even if declared to be non-self-executing, declares national policy and might supersede state laws. See Ch. VII, p. 209. Provisions in the instruments of ratification declaring that implementations may be left to the states do not affect the supremacy of such agreements to state law. But compare the older 'federal–state' clauses which effectively entered a reservation excluding U.S. obligations on matters over which states had jurisdiction, n. 68 to Ch. VII.

36. In one respect, at one time, the Constitution itself may have prevented federal preemption. Compare sec. 2 of the Eighteenth Amendment to the Constitution: 'The Congress and the several States shall have concurrent power to enforce this article by appropriate legislation.' That Amendment was repealed by Amendment XXI.

37. *Rice* v. *Santa Fe Elevator Corp.*, 331 U.S. 218, 230 (1947). See also *Hines* v. *Davidowitz*, n. 57 below; *Campbell* v. *Hussey*, 368 U.S. 297 (1961); *Arkansas Electric Co-op Corp.* v. *Arkansas Public Service Commission*, 461 U.S. 375 (1983); *Morales* v. *T.W.A.*, 504 U.S. 374 (1992). Cases finding no preemption include *Pacific Gas & Electric Co.* v. *State Energy Commission*, 461 U.S. 190 (1983); *Wisconsin Public Intervenor* v. *Montier*, 501 U.S. 597 (1991).

38. For example, under 'long-arm statutes', states have asserted jurisdiction to adjudicate claims against aliens and alien corporations that do business in the state or have 'minimum contacts', with it. Compare *Velandra* v. *Regie Nationale des Usines Renault*, 336 F.2d 292 (6th Cir. 1964), with *Duple Motor Bodies, Ltd.* v. *Hollingsworth*, 417 F.2d 231 (9th Cir. 1969). *Cf. TACA International Airlines, S.A.* v. *Rolls-Royce of England, Ltd.*, 15 N.Y.2d 97, 204 N.E.2d 329 (1965); *Aquascutum of London, Inc.* v. *SS American Champion*, 426 F.2d 205 (2d Cir. 1970). See also *Asahi Metal Industry Co.* v. *Superior Court of California*, 480 U.S. 102 (1987), and *Helicopteros Nacionales de Colombia* v. *Hall*, 466 U.S. 408 (1984).

39. Some Justices insisted that the Commerce Clause implies no limitation on the states and that they can regulate commerce unless Congress says that they shall not, either directly or by enacting its own regulations which supersede inconsistent state laws. See Chief Justice Taney in the *License Cases*, 46 U.S. (5 How.) 504, 573 (1847); Justice Black dissenting in *Southern Pacific Co.* v. *Arizona*, 325 U.S. 761, 784 (1945). Justice Douglas urged that the Commerce Clause itself forbids only state discrimination against interstate or foreign commerce, *id.* at 795; *McCarroll* v. *Dixie Greyhound Lines, Inc.*, 309 U.S. 176, 183–89 (1940). The Court, however, has never accepted these views, perhaps because it considered that the inertia of government made it unlikely that Congress could consider and overcome all the obstructions to interstate commerce. 'The practical result is that in default of action by us [the States] will go on suffocating and retarding and Balkanizing American commerce, trade and industry.' Justice Jackson concurring in *Duckworth* v. *Arkansas*, 314 U.S. 390, 400 (1941).

    It has been suggested that it was not the Constitution itself that denied the states power to regulate interstate or foreign commerce, but Congress, whether by action or inaction. On this view, when the Supreme Court concluded that a state burden on commerce was forbidden, it was deciding that Congressional silence in that instance implied a prohibition, whereas in other cases Congressional silence implied that the states were free to act. Doctrines such as *Cooley* and the others, then, were guides to interpreting Congressional silence. The suggestion was inspired, no doubt, by a desire to find a basis for a prohibition on the states in what is textually an affirmative grant to Congress, and even more, to justify holding the grant to Congress 'concurrent' with state power in some cases, exclusive in others; it would also help explain how Congress could authorize the states to do what they could not do if Congress were silent (this chapter, pp. 156 *et seq.*). See Dowling, *Interstate Commerce and State Power*, 27 VA.L.REV. 1 (1940), cited in *Southern Pacific Co.* v. *Arizona*, above, at 769. See also Dowling, *Interstate Commerce and State Power—Revised Version*, 47 COLUM.L.REV. 547 (1947). *Cf.* Field, J., concurring in *Bowman* v. *Chicago and Northwestern Ry. Co.*, 125 U.S. 465, 507–8 (1888). The difficulties with the suggestion are obvious. See T. R. POWELL, VAGARIES AND VARIETY IN CONSTITUTIONAL INTERPRETATION 161–4 (1956). The courts have found prohibitions on the states implied in other affirmative grants to Congress. See n. 33 to this chapter.

The Twenty-first Amendment substantially relieved the states of the prohibitions of the Commerce Clause (and of other provisions of the Constitution)
as regards intoxicating liquors. *State Board* v. *Young's Market Co.*, 299 U.S.
59 (1936); *Mahoney* v. *Triner Corp.*, 304 U.S. 401 (1938); *Indianapolis Brewing
Co.* v. *Liquor Control Commission*, 305 U.S. 391 (1939). But *cf. Collins* v.
Yosemite Park & Curry Co., 304 U.S. 518 (1938). The Amendment did not,
however, repeal the Export-Import Clause and the 'original package' doctrine
as regards liquor. *Dept. of Revenue* v. *James Beam Distilling Co.*, 377 U.S. 341
(1964); *cf. Hostetter* v. *Idlewild Bon Voyage Liquor Corp.*, 377 U.S. 324 (1964).
See also *California Retail Liquor Dealers Ass'n.* v. *Midcal Aluminium, Inc.*, 445
U.S. 97 (1980); *Bacchus Imports, Ltd.* v. *Dias*, 468 U.S. 263 (1984); *Liquor
Corp.* v. *Duff*, 479 U.S. 335 (1987) (holding that a New York law requiring
liquor retails to charge at least 112% of wholesaler's posted bottle price violated the Sherman Act and was not saved by the Twenty-First Amendment);
and *Healy* v. *Beer Inst.*, 491 U.S. 324 (1989).

40. Even Justice Douglas joined in striking down a state regulation inconsistent
with that of other states and thus creating burdens on interstate traffic. *Bibb* v.
Navajo Freight Lines, Inc., 359 U.S. 520 (1959).

41. The judicial applications of the Commerce Clause against the states were no
doubt prominent in the mind of Justice Holmes when he said: 'I do not think
the United States would come to an end if we lost our power to declare an act
of Congress void. I do think the Union would be imperiled if we could not
make that declaration as to the law of the several States.' O. W. HOLMES, *Law
and the Court*, in COLLECTED LEGAL PAPERS, 291, 295–6 (1920).

42. See, e.g., *Wilson* v. *Black Bird Creek Marsh Co.*, 27 U.S. (2 Pet.) 245 (1829).
But for many years the Supreme Court sometimes seemed to decide what the
states could not do by asking what Congress could; and it denied power to
Congress to do what it could not bring itself to forbid to the states. It sowed
confusion in deciding cases exploring the reach of Congressional power by citing cases on the limits of state power, and vice versa. Strange distinctions were
drawn between what is 'commerce' and what is not, what is a regulation of commerce and what merely an exercise of 'police power' affecting commerce, which
led to other strange distinctions, e.g., between direct and indirect burdens on
commerce. Most of this, happily, is history. See, e.g., *United States* v. *Darby*,
312 U.S. 100 (1941): *Wickard* v. *Filburn*, 317 U.S. 11 (1942) and other cases
cited in n. 44 to this chapter. See Stern, *The Commerce Clause and the National
Economy, 1933–1946*, 59 HARV.L.REV. 645, 883 (1946). But see *Lopez*, p. 65.

43. *Cooley* v. *Board of Wardens of the Port of Philadelphia*, 53 U.S. (12 How.) 299,
319 (1851). The Court held that pilotage laws did not 'admit only of one uniform system' and upheld the local law. In that case Congress had in fact
adopted the pilotage laws of the states, but the Court assumed that if these
were forbidden by the Constitution, Congress could not 'validate' them. *Id.* at
318. Now, we know, Congress can permit what would be forbidden if it were
silent.

44. The Court distinguished between direct and indirect effects on interstate commerce to determine whether local activities could be regulated by Congress.

Compare *Carter* v. *Carter Coal Co.*, 298 U.S. 238, 307–8 (1936); *Schechter Poultry Corp.* v. *United States*, 295 U.S. 495, 54647 (1935); also *Heisler* v. *Thomas Colliery Co.*, 260 U.S. 245, 259–60 (1922); *Kidd* v. *Pearson*, 128 U.S. 1, 20–1 (1888). The Court abandoned that distinction in *Darby* and other cases cited in n. 42. It is not the distinction now made in judging whether the state burdens on interstate or foreign commerce are acceptable. See n. 51 below.

45. *Southern Pacific Co.* v. *Arizona*, 325 U.S. 761, 768 (1945).
46. In commerce cases there is little presumption of constitutionality, and the 'balancing' done in the first instance by state legislatures is given little weight. But compare Black, J., dissenting in *Southern Pacific Co.* v. *Arizona*, 325 U.S. 761, 784 (1945). See *Kassel* v. *Consolidated Freightways Corporation of Delaware*, 450 U.S. 662 (1986) (although the Supreme Court has been reluctant to invalidate state regulations that touch upon safety, especially highway safety, constitutionality of such regulations depends on importance of state regulatory concern in light of burden on interstate commerce).

   No doubt the Court has not been above including unarticulated factors in the balance, as when it found regulations that discriminated on account of race more burdensome to interstate or foreign commerce than those that forbade such discrimination. Compare *Morgan* v. *Virginia*, 328 U.S. 373 (1946), with *Bob-Lo Excursion Co.* v. *Michigan*, 333 U.S. 29 (1948).

47. Compare, for example, *Southern Railway Co.* v. *King*, 217 U.S. 524 (1910), with *Seaboard Airline R.R. Co.* v. *Blackwell*, 244 U.S. 310 (1917); the Court's opinion in *H.P. Hood & Sons* v. *Du Mond*, 336 U.S. 525 (1949), with Frankfurter's dissenting opinion there, at 564.
48. See, e.g., *H.P. Hood & Sons, and Baldwin* v. *G.A.F. Seelig*, n. 49 to this chapter; also *Philadelphia* v. *New Jersey*, 437 U.S. 617 (1978); for an early case see *Welton* v. *Missouri*, 91 U.S. (1 Ott.) 275 (1876). But even that principle has an occasional exception. See, e.g., *Maine* v. *Taylor*, 477 U.S. 131 (1986) (upholding a law banning importation of out-of-state baitfish because its environmental purpose could not be achieved in non-discriminatory ways).
49. See Justice Cardozo in *Baldwin* v. *G.A.F. Seelig, Inc.*, 294 U.S. 511, 523 (1935): 'Economic welfare is always related to health. . . Let such an exception be admitted, and all that a state will have to do in times of stress and strain is to say that its farmers and merchants and workmen must be protected against competition from without, lest they go upon the poor relief lists or perish altogether. . . The Constitution was framed under the dominion of a political philosophy less parochial in range. It was framed upon the theory that the peoples of the several states must sink or swim together, and that in the long run prosperity and salvation are in union and not division.'

   Compare Justice Brandeis in *Buck* v. *Kuykendall*, 267 U.S. 307 (1925). Also, *H. P. Hood & Sons* v. *Du Mond*, 336 U.S. 525 (1949); *Philadelphia* v. *New Jersey*, 437 U.S. 617 (1978); *Hunt* v. *Washington State Apple Advertising Comm'n*, 432 U.S. 333 (1977). But see *Maine* v. *Taylor*, n. 48 above.

   The States may, however, exclude foreign corporations and require them to incorporate in the state. See *Lafayette Ins. Co.* v. *French*, 59 U.S. (18 How.)

404, 407 (1937); *Hemphill* v. *Orloff*, 277 U.S. 537, 548 (1928); *Atlantic Refining Co.* v. *Virginia*, 302 U.S. 22, 26 (1937); *Asbury Hospital* v. *Cass County*, 326 U.S. 207, 211–12 (1945). But *cf. Western Union Tel. Co.* v. *Kansas*, 216 U.S. 1 (1910); *Terral* v. *Burke Construction Co.*, 257 U.S. 529, 532–3 (1922). States have also imposed citizenship requirements on directors of corporations. See Ala. Stat. § 5-6A-1 (1994); Ariz. Stat. § 10-958 (1995); and Ill. Stat. ch. 215 § 5/10 (1995).

50. The Court struck down a city ordinance of Madison, Wisconsin, which forbade the sale of milk unless pasteurized within 5 miles of the city, because it considered that reasonable alternatives were available which would protect local health without discriminating against out-of-state milk or out-of-state pasteurization. *Dean Milk Co.* v. *City of Madison*, 340 U.S. 349 (1951). In *Bibb* v. *Navajo Freight Lines, Inc.*, 359 U.S. 520 (1959), the Court invalidated an Illinois regulation requiring that trucks using its highways employ a particular mudguard different from one required by other states, because it was not shown that its safety advantages warranted the heavy burden on companies whose trucks traveled in many states.

51. *Pike* v. *Bruce Church, Inc.*, 397 U.S. 137 (1970). The Court has held, however, that the restrictions of the Commerce Clause do not apply (or perhaps do not apply in the same way) when the state is not regulating private commercial activity but is itself a participant in the commercial market. *Hughes* v. *Alexander Scrap Corp.*, 426 U.S. 794 (1976). Even when acting as an entrepreneur, however, the state is subject to Art. IV, sec. 3, of the Constitution which forbids denying the privileges and immunities of citizenship to citizens of other states; the Court held that denying ordinary employment to citizens of other states violates that provision. *Exxon Corp.* v. *Governor of Maryland*, 437 U.S. 177 (1978); *United Building and Construction Trades* v. *Camden*, 465 U.S. 208 (1984). That provision does not apply to citizens of foreign nations, but the latter enjoy other constitutional protections. See Ch. IX.

52. Perhaps *a fortiori*, and perhaps the limitations on the states should be more stringent in regard to foreign commerce. Compare n. 9 to Ch. III; see p. 161n., and the additional limitations on the states in regard to foreign commerce, e.g., the 'original package' doctrine, this chapter, p. 152; and *Zschernig* v. *Miller*, this chapter, p. 163.

    Some of the cases that defined what the Commerce Clause required of the states in fact involved foreign commerce. e.g., *City of New York* v. *Miln*, 36 U.S. (11 Pet.) 102 (1837), and *The Passenger Cases*, 48 U.S. (7 How.) 283 (1849), *distinguished* in *Henderson* v. *Mayor of New York*, 92 U.S. 259 (1876); *The License Cases*, 46 U.S. (5 How.) 504 (1847); *Chy Lung* v. *Freeman*, 92 U.S. 275 (1875); *New York ex rel. Silz* v. *Hesterberg*, 211 U.S. 31 (1908); *Sanitary District* v. *United States*, 266 U.S. 405 (1925); *Bayside Fish Flour Co.* v. *Gentry*, 297 U.S. 422 (1936); *Kelly* v. *Washington*, 302 U.S. 1 (1937); *Hale* v. *Bimco Trading, Inc.*, 306 U.S. 375 (1939); *Huron Portland Cement Co.* v. *City of Detroit*, 362 U.S. 440 (1960); *Askew* v. *America Waterways Operators*, 411 U.S. 325 (1973).

53. At one time the Court struck down taxes on 'the interstate transaction itself',

Freeman v. *Hewit*, 329 U.S. 249 (1946); taxes that obviously discriminate against interstate or foreign commerce; and even those that seem 'neutral' but weigh particularly on out-of-state commerce, for example a tax on 'drummers' as applied to companies that engage in no other local activity in the state. *Robbins* v. *Shelby County Taxing District*, 120 U.S. 489 (1887). But it has permitted states to select subjects for taxation in ways that might entail hidden discrimination against out-of-state goods, as when a dairy state decides to tax margarine. States have substantial leeway as to types and rates of taxation including formulae for apportioning the local part of a complex interstate or international enterprise; and, increasingly, the Court allows the state to identify and tax some local incident of an interstate or foreign transaction so that interstate or foreign commerce would 'pay its way'. See generally, Brown, *The Open Economy: Justice Frankfurter and the Position of the Judiciary*, 67 YALE L.J. 219 (1957), and P. HARTMAN, STATE TAXATION OF INTERSTATE COMMERCE (1953). Congress has commissioned studies of the field but good reports have not yet produced comprehensive overhauling. See SUBCOMM. OF THE HOUSE COMM. ON THE JUDICIARY, STATE TAXATION OF INTERSTATE COMMERCE, H.R.REP. No 565, 89th Cong., 1st Sess. (1965). See n. 55 to this chapter.

In *Complete Auto Transit* v. *Brady*, the court in effect overruled this long line of 'free trade' cases that had established interstate commerce as immune from most forms of state taxation, and instead adopted the four part test described in this chapter, p. 161. See generally D. Regan, *The Supreme Court and State Protectionism: Making Sense of Dormant Commerce*, 84 MICH. L. REV. 1091 (1986) and D. Shaviro, *An Economic and Political Look at Federalism in Taxation*, 90 MICH. L. REV. 895 (1992).

54. The Constitution is read to protect interstate and foreign commerce against multiple taxation by several states, but presumably it would not be held to bar state taxation merely because the object is also subject to tax by one or more foreign governments.

For taxes invalidated as burdens on foreign commerce, see e.g., *McGoldrick* v. *Gulf Oil Corp.*, 309 U.S. 414 (1939); *Joseph* v. *Carter & Weeks Co.*, 330 U.S. 422 (1947). Usually a state tax burdening foreign commerce is invalidated under the Import or Export Clauses, nn. 8 and 9 to this chapter.

55. See *Complete Auto Transit, Inc.* v. *Brady*, 430 U.S. 274 (1977); *Japan Line* v. *County of Los Angeles*, 441 U.S. 434 (1979). In *Container Corp of America* v. *Franchise Tax Board*, 463 U.S. 159 (1983), the Court found that the tests of *Japan Line* did not prevent California from applying the unitary business theory of taxation to a corporation with foreign subsidiaries.

In 1994 the Court upheld California's use of a 'worldwide combined reporting' method to determine the corporate franchise tax owed by members of a unitary multinational corporate group doing business in the state, as applied to a domestic corporation that had a foreign parent company, as well as to a foreign corporation with foreign parents or foreign subsidiaries. *Barclays Bank* v. *Franchise Tax Board of California*, 114 S.Ct. 2268 (1994). See also RESTATEMENT (n. 2 to Preface) § 412, Reporters' note 7.

56. See *Leisy* v. *Hardin*, 135 U.S. 100 (1890). Congress could also regulate in

support of state law, forbidding the transportation of some articles into states that bar them. *In re Rahrer*, 140 U.S. 545 (1891). The Supreme Court, however, held that Congress could not adopt state laws that would modify the maritime law. *Knickerbocker Ice Co.* v. *Stewart*, 253 U.S. 149 (1920); *Washington* v. *W. C. Dawson & Co.*, 264 U.S. 219 (1924). Although never overruled, it is unlikely that those cases still express constitutional limits on Congressional authority, since the Court later allowed Congress to adopt state laws in other areas. Compare *Davis* v. *Department of Labor and Industries*, 317 U.S. 249 (1942); *Prudential Insurance Co.* v. *Benjamin*, 328 U.S. 408 (1946).

57. In *Holmes* v. *Jennison*, this chapter, p. 153, Taney suggested that, even when the federal government had not acted, the states were excluded from one kind of incursion into foreign relations, extradition to foreign countries. For him the attempt by the Governor of Vermont to extradite Holmes was an 'agreement' with Canada prohibited to the states unless Congress consented, but he offered an alternative objection: extradition policy was entrusted to the federal government and concurrent jurisdiction in the states would be 'totally contradictory and repugnant to the power granted to the United States'. (*Id.* at 574). That conclusion apparently reflected the view that in regard to extradition federal silence was itself a policy, that from 'its nature', the power to extradite 'can never be dormant in the hands of the general government'. (*Id.* at 576). Extradition, moreover, inevitably involved communication with a foreign government and it 'was one of the main objects of the Constitution . . . to cut off all communications between foreign governments, and the several state authorities'. (*Id.* at 575–6). Whether there were other matters which were exclusively federal, as to which federal silence barred the states, he did not say; but he did not appear to be suggesting a general principle that even when the political branches had not acted the states could not adopt laws or perform other acts of local government that impinge on the foreign relations of the United States. Taney indeed denied that the Commerce Power, even, implied any prohibitions on the states if Congress had not acted. See his opinion in *The License Cases*, 46 U.S. (5 How.) 504, 573 (1847), n. 39 above.

In 1941, the Supreme Court said: 'And whether or not registration of aliens is of such a nature, that the Constitution permits only of one uniform national system, it cannot be denied that the Congress might validly conclude that such uniformity is desirable.' *Hines* v. *Davidowitz*, 312 U.S. 52, 73 (1941). That statement might be read to imply that there may be matters forbidden to the states even when Congress is silent, because a 'uniform national system' is required, echoing the Cooley Doctrine as to implied prohibitions on state regulation of commerce, p. 159, above. But in *Hines* Congress had acted, and the question was whether Pennsylvania's alien registration system could coexist with the federal system, not whether the state could register aliens if Congress did not register them. The Court expressly left open the contention that 'the federal power in this field, whether exercised or unexercised, is exclusive'. *Id.* at 62.

58. But *cf.* n. 8 to Ch. V. The federal Act of State doctrine has not been applied in the circumstances cited. Compare Henkin, *The Foreign Affairs Power of the Federal Courts: Sabbatino*, 64 Colum.L.Rev. 805, 826–30 (1964). There is the

possibility of state impingement on foreign relations also in that a state can regulate the conduct of its citizens on the high seas. See *Skiriotes* v. *Florida*, 313 U.S. 69 (1941); *cf. The Hamilton*, 207 U.S. 398 (1907). And a state has jurisdiction over its absent domiciliaries for purposes of a personal judgment. *Milliken* v. *Meyer*, 311 U.S. 457, 462 (1940). States may impinge on foreign relations also by applying their 'long arm' statutes to aliens and alien corporations. See n. 38 to this chapter.

59. See the debates that raged as to whether the United States could prevent New York courts from trying for murder a British soldier, Alexander McLeod, who allegedly killed someone in the course of *The Caroline* incident. McLeod was acquitted by the New York courts but the question of state–federal power was never decided. For the whole story see 1 WHARTON, DIGEST OF INTERNATIONAL LAW, 21, and 3 *id.* § 350 (1886).

The Department of State 'does not believe that the States should decline to enact statutes concerning recognition of foreign judgments on the ground that the United States may at some future date become a party to the Hague Convention on the Recognition and Enforcement of Foreign Judgments'. Letter from Ambassador Kearney to Professor Homburger, dated March 14, 1969, reprinted in 63 AM.J.INT'L L. 816–17 (1969).

One might suggest that when a state acts in a matter that affects foreign relations and could be regulated by the federal government, the state is making federal law, subject to later rejection or modification by federal authority. In a sense this is what happens when a state court decides issues of maritime law or international law (see Ch. VIII, p. 234) not previously decided by the federal courts, or newly interprets and applies a federal statute. Usually, however, it is assumed that the state merely presumes to apply state law and it can do so except to the extent that the Constitution bars it, as in some regulations of foreign commerce, or if what it does is an intrusion into foreign relations under the doctrine of *Zschernig* v. *Miller* discussed at pp. 163–5.

60. *Clark* v. *Allen*, 331 U.S. 503 (1947). In *Blythe* v. *Hinckley*, 180 U.S. 333 (1901), it was argued that a California provision permitting aliens to inherit real property invaded the Treaty Power. The Court said: 'If [the plaintiff] means that it has never heretofore been asserted, that in the absence of any treaty whatever upon the subject, the State had no right to pass a law in regard to the inheritance of property within its borders by an alien, counsel may be correct. The absence of such a claim is not so extraordinary as is the claim itself.' *Id.* at 340. Referring to *Blythe* v. *Hinckley*, the Court in *Allen* said: 'The Court rejected the argument as being an extraordinary one. The objection to the present statute is equally far-fetched. . . What California has done will have some incidental or indirect effect in foreign countries. But that is true of many state laws which none would claim cross the forbidden line.' 331 U.S. at 517.

Five years before *Zschernig* the Court dismissed a substantially similar claim for want of a substantial federal question. *Ioannou* v. *New York*, 371 U.S. 30 (1962), *reh'g denied*, 391 U.S. 604 (1968).

61. 389 U.S. 429 (1968).
62. *Id.* at 434.

63. *Id.* at 432.
64. The Court did not build sturdy underpinnings for its constitutional doctrine or face substantial arguments against it. Critics might insist that even if the federal foreign relations power is largely extra-constitutional, inherent in sovereignty (Ch. I, p. 27), international sovereignty implies nothing about the distribution of responsibility between nation and state in a federal system. What the Constitution says about foreign affairs also provides little basis for the Court's doctrine. Article I indeed forbids the states to make treaties or do other specified acts in foreign relations, but these, singly or together, do not support the general exclusion announced in *Zschernig*; and the prohibition to the states of some things might even imply that others are permitted. Nor is the *Zschernig* doctrine the natural inference from the expressed grants to the federal branches or from 'the Constitution as a whole', for in other matters even explicit grant of power to the federal government does not necessarily foreclose state action where federal power has not been exercised. Nor is there support for *Zschernig* in the history of the Constitution in practice.

    Perhaps the Court considered that sovereignty as it relates to foreign affairs implies exclusive, central control even in a federal system. Perhaps the majority thought that what the Constitution expressly forbade to the states in regard to foreign relations implied wider prohibitions as well. Perhaps it concluded that the power to conduct foreign relations (like the power to extradite for Taney, n. 57 to this chapter) 'can never be dormant in the hands of the general government' and that its concurrent exercise by the states would be 'totally contradictory and repugnant'.

    Perhaps, too, the Court was impressed by the Commerce Clause cases where in the absence of Congressional regulation the courts protect the national interest against what it considers undue invasion by the states. But in those cases, the Court has felt, and Congress has agreed, that the courts should intervene because it could not be left to Congress to anticipate or deal with all the possible state encroachments on the national interest; and federal administrative agencies could not effectively do so in all cases. In foreign affairs, one might argue, the President is 'always in session' and has full authority, and there are executive agencies, principally the State Department, expert and informed, which could consider whether a state action unduly interferes with foreign relations. Perhaps the Court was not prepared to reaffirm that the Department of State had constitutional authority to supersede state law. See Ch. II, pp. 39 *et seq.*
65. There are perhaps some intimations in that the Court expressly refused to overrule *Clark* v. *Allen*, 331 U.S. 503 (1947): 'At the time *Clark* v. *Allen* was decided, the case seemed to involve no more than a routine reading of foreign laws. . . The Government's acquiescence in the ruling of *Clark* v. *Allen* certainly does not justify extending the principle of that case, as we would be required to do here to uphold the Oregon statute as applied; for it has more than "some incidental or indirect effect in foreign countries", and its great potential for disruption or embarrassment makes us hesitate to place it in the category of a diplomatic bagatelle.

    As we read the decisions that followed in the wake of *Clark* v. *Allen*, we find that they radiate some of the attitudes of the "cold war", where the search is for the "democracy quotient" of a foreign regime as opposed to the Marxist theory. The Oregon statute introduces the concept of "confiscation", which is of course opposed to the Just Compensation Clause of the Fifth Amendment. And this has led into minute inquiries concerning the actual administration of foreign law, into the credibility of foreign diplomatic statements, and into speculation whether the fact that some received delivery of funds should "not preclude wonderment as to how many may have been denied 'the right to receive' . . ." That kind of state involvement in foreign affairs and international relations—matters which the Constitution entrusts solely to the Federal Government—is not sanctioned by *Clark* v. *Allen*.' 389 U.S. at 433–6.

66. In *Sabbatino*, the Court had said that the Constitution itself did not require the Act of State doctrine and did not therefore forbid courts (either state or federal, presumably) to sit in judgment on the acts of foreign governments in regard to property in their own territory. See Ch. V, p. 137. Perhaps a state's legitimate interest in refusing to give effect to a foreign act of state is greater than Oregon's in *Zschernig* for though a state's interest in regulating inheritance is long recognized, and its insistence on reciprocity may help some Oregon citizen obtain an inheritance, the other limitations in this case reflected a desire to attack Communism—an element in foreign policy that might well be left to the national government. But the only authority cited by the Court is language in *Hines* v. *Davidowitz*, n. 57 to this chapter, where the Court invalidated (because Congress had acted in the matter) Pennsylvania's alien registration statute which involved no judgments or reflections on any foreign government, did not directly 'intrude' on foreign relations, and had no apparent purpose to do so.

On the other hand, as Justice Harlan, concurring in the result in *Zschernig* on other grounds, points out, states have been allowed to 'sit in judgment' on foreign countries in other contexts. Under the Uniform Foreign Money-Judgments Recognition Act, for example, a foreign judgment is not to be recognized if it 'was rendered under a system which does not provide impartial tribunals or procedures compatible with the requirements of due process of law'. Under the rules of the conflict-of-laws generally, 'the tort law of a foreign country will not be applied if that country is shown to be "uncivilized" '. 389 U.S. at 461–2.

Compare the Florida Territorial Waters Act which required a license for aliens to fish in the state's territorial waters, but denied licenses to any vessels owned by a Communist state, to an alien Communist, or to other alien vessels 'on the basis of reciprocity or retorsion' unless the State Department transmitted a formal suggestion that the state of the vessel is a friendly ally or neutral. [1963] FLA. LAWS, ch. 63-202, at 457, as amended, FLA.STAT.ANN. § 370.21(3)(1994); see Moore, *Federalism and Foreign Relations*, (1965) DUKE L.J. 48, 311–19. A conviction under the statute was apparently affirmed. See *id.* at 312–13 and notes; 3 I.L.M. 317 (1964).

67. It has been suggested that all should turn on whether the purpose of the state regulation is to influence foreign relations. But though in some cases such a

purpose is obvious, often it is not. In other contexts the Court has been reluctant to probe legislative purpose. Compare, e.g., *United States* v. *Kahriger,* 345 U.S. 22 (1953), overruled on other grounds. *Marchetti* v. *United States,* 390 U.S. 39 (1968); *Kassel* v. *Consolidated Freightways,* 450 U.S. 662 (1986); and *Tayyari* v. *New Mex. State. Univ.,* 495 F. Supp. 1365 (D.N.M. 1980), in which the court struck down a university Regents' action to deny admission to students whose home governments held or permitted holding U.S. citizens as hostages.

Some believe that the Court may already have limited the promise of *Zschernig* when it affirmed *per curiam* in *Gorun* v. *Fall,* 393 U.S. 398 (1968), and dismissed for want of a substantial federal question in *Gorun* v. *Montana,* 399 U.S. 901 (1970). See also *De Canas* v. *Bica,* 424 U.S. 351 (1976). See generally, Maier, *The Bases and Range of Federal Common Law in Private International Matters,* 5 VAND.J.TRANSNAT'L L. 133 (1971), and Bilder, *The Role of States and Cities in Foreign Relations* 83 AM. J.INT'L L. 829 (1989).

State and municipal governments have passed statues and ordinances that impinge on foreign policy, such as 'Buy American' laws. In *R.S.B. Technical Sales Corp.* v. *North Jersey District Water Supply Commission of the State of New Jersey,* 381 A.2d 774 (1977), the New Jersey Supreme Court concluded that the New Jersey Buy-American statute was constitutional because a requirement that the state purchase American goods, when available, did not entail any criticism of foreign governments. In *Bethlehem Steel Corp.* v. *Board of Commissioners,* 276 Cal. App. 2d 221 (1969), however, a California court of appeals struck down a similar statute on the grounds that it offered 'great potential for disruption' with established trade policies of the federal government and thus exceeded state authority. See generally, Borchers and Dauer, *Taming the New Breed of Nuclear Free Zone Ordinances: Statutory and Constitutional Infirmities in Local Procurement Ordinances Blacklisting the Producers of Nuclear Weapons Components,* 40 HASTINGS L.J. 87 (1988). And see the anti-apartheid legislation, n. 69 below.

68. Compare the express right of states to make agreements with foreign countries with the consent of Congress, Art. 1, § 10, and the instance cited in n. 10 to this chapter.

69. A 1986 California state law prohibited the investment of state funds in South Africa, requiring California's Public Employees' Retirement System and State Teachers' Retirement System to divest itself of more than $4 billion invested in that country. In March 1994, the law was repealed and in July of that year $200,000 was appropriated for establishing a state office of trade and investment in sub-Saharan Africa.

Board of Trustees v. *Baltimore,* 317 Md. 72, 562 A.2d 720 (1989), upheld the constitutionality of a municipal ordinance requiring divestment by a city workers pension fund of investments in companies doing business in South Africa.

Twenty three states, 14 countries and 80 cities enacted divestment or procurement legislation or ordinances directed at South Africa's apartheid policies. See Bilder, *The Role of States and Cities in Foreign Affairs,* 83 AM. J. INT'L L. 821 (1989). Congress was aware of these divestment statutes, but it refrained from preempting them when it enacted the Comprehensive Anti-Apartheid Act of 1986. 22 U.S.C. §§5000–5116 (1994).

However, the New York Court of Appeals struck down a decision of the New York City Commission on Human Rights which found that the New York Times had aided and abetted invidious discrimination practices by publishing advertisements of employment opportunities in the Republic of South Africa. *New York Times Co.* v. *City of New York Commission on Human Rights*, 41 N.Y.2d 345 (1977). The court cited *Zschernig* and concluded that 'Each locality in each State may not adopt its own foreign policy. This would be disastrous, not only because of multiplicity and divergence of policies, but because local decisions are often influenced by pragmatic local considerations which are not necessarily controlling or even relevant as to national policy determined by the Federal Government at Washington.' *Id.* at 353.

70. *United States* v. *Darby*, 312 U.S. 100, 124 (1941). But see *New York* v. *United States*, n. 75 below.

71. The Tenth Amendment was invoked by Justice Douglas dissenting in *United States* v. *Oregon*, 366 U.S. 643, 654 (1961), and in *Maryland* v. *Wirtz*, 392 U.S. 183, 205 (1968). Compare *Oregon* v. *Mitchell*, 400 U.S. 112 (1970). See n. 78 below.

72. Expressly in *Missouri* v. *Holland*, 252 U.S. 416, 433–5 (1920), Ch. VII, p. 189 *et seq.*

73. The Hartford Convention in 1812 was perhaps the only occasion when states rights, were urged in protest against a declaration of war. See, T. DWIGHT, HISTORY OF THE HARTFORD CONVENTION 352–79 (1833), partially reprinted in DOCUMENTS OF AMERICAN HISTORY, Doc.No.115 at 209 (Commager, edn. 1968). See *Massachusetts* v. *Laird*, 400 U.S. 886 (1970).

74. *Monaco* v. *Mississippi*, 292 U.S. 313, 330 (1934): 'We perceive no ground upon which it can be said that any waiver of consent by a State of the Union has run in favor of a foreign State. As to suits brought by a foreign State, we think that the States of the Union retain the same immunity that they enjoy with respect to suits by individuals whether citizens of the United States or citizens or subjects of a foreign State. The foreign State enjoys a similar sovereign immunity and without her consent may not be sued by a State of the Union.'

75. State-owned liquor and mineral waters are subject to federal tax, *New York* v. *United States*, 326 U.S. 572 (1946); railroads and wharves owned by the state are subject to regulation under the Commerce Power, *California* v. *Taylor*, 353 U.S. 553 (1957); *United States* v. *California*, 297 U.S. 175 (1936); *California* v. *United States*, 320 U.S. 577 (1944); timber owned and sold by the state is subject to federal price regulation under the war powers, *Case* v. *Bowles*, 327 U.S. 92 (1946); state hospitals and schools are subject to federal fair labor standards, *Maryland* v. *Wirtz*, 392 U.S. 183 (1968); a state university must pay federal customs duties, *University of Illinois* v. *United States*, 289 U.S. 48 (1933); state property can be taken for federal use subject to compensation, *cf. St. Louis* v. *Western Union Tel. Co.*, 148 U.S. 92, 101 (1893); *Missouri ex rel. Camden County* v. *Union Electric Light & Power Co.*, 42 F.2d 692 (W.D.Mo.1930); the federal power to regulate commerce extends to control navigable waters within

United States jurisdiction, even if state water supplies may be adversely affected, *Sanitary District* v. *United States*, 266 U.S. 405 (1925).

76. An earlier case entitled *New York* v. *United States*, 326 U.S. 572, 582 (1946). Justice Frankfurter was not speaking for the Court but a majority expressed similar view (*id.* at 586) and the dissenting opinion of Douglas, J., asserted even greater immunity for the states (*id.* at 590, 598). See also Douglas, J., dissenting in *Maryland* v. *Wirtz*, 392 U.S. 183, 201 (1968). But compare *St. Louis* v. *Western Union Tel. Co.*, 148 U.S. 92, 101 (1893), implying that federal eminent domain might be available even against 'statehouse grounds'.

Some claims of state immunity to federal regulation might raise 'political questions' which the courts will not adjudicate. In the earlier *New York* v. *United States*, (above at 581–2), Justice Frankfurter suggested that 'the claim of implied immunity by States from federal taxation raises questions not wholly unlike provisions of the Constitution, such as that of Art. IV, § 4, guaranteeing States a republican form of government . . . which this Court has deemed not within its duty to adjudicate'. But Justice Frankfurter was a leading exponent of judicial abstention in political questions, and the Court has since refused to follow his lead. See *Baker* v. *Carr*, 369 U.S. 186 (1962), Ch. V, p. 144. The political question guidelines in *Baker* v. *Carr* would seem to exclude issues of federalism since they identify the doctrine as essentially a function of the separation of powers of the federal government.

77. *Metcalf & Eddy* v. *Mitchell*, 269 U.S. 514, 523–4 (1926).

78. *National League of Cities* v. *Usery*, 426 U.S. 833 (1976); *Garcia* v. *San Antonio Metropolitan Transit Authority*, 469 U.S. 528 (1985); *New York* v. *United States*, 505 U.S. 114 (1992). And see *F.E.R.C.* v. *Mississippi* 456 U.S. U.S. 742 (1982). We do not know whether the short-lived doctrine of *National League of Cities*, would have had any application to Congressional regulation in foreign affairs, or to regulation by treaty. We do not know whether *New York* v. *United States* would have such application.

79. See RESTATEMENT (n. 2 to Preface) § 711, Comment *a*. And see Ch. IX.

80. In one famous unfortunate instance the United States indemnified the Italian Government when a mob lynched Italian nationals in New Orleans. See 6 MOORE, DIGEST (n. 50 to Ch. II) 837–41. For other instances in which the United States was held internationally responsible for actions (or inactions) of states, see BUTLER, THE TREATY POWER (n. 10 to Ch. I) 142–59 (1902). See also WRIGHT (n. 3 to Ch. I) 30, 265; Hale Memorandum, S.Doc.No.56, 54th Cong., 2d Sess. 5 (1897). For more recent cases, see those before the claims commission with Mexico reported in W. BISHOP, INTERNATIONAL LAW, CASES AND MATERIALS c. 9 (3d edn. 1971).

A state cannot be sued by foreign countries or their nationals on its bonds or other obligations. In *Hauenstein* v. *Lynham*, 100 U.S. 483 (1880), for example, it was almost 20 years after Hauenstein died before the Supreme Court decided that, under the applicable treaty, Virginia could not escheat his property but had to permit his Swiss heirs to inherit. For a discussion of obstacles to the enforcement of treaties against violation by the states, see Ch. VII, p. 208 *et seq.*

81. See U.S. reservations to the International Covenant on Civil and Political Rights, n. 5, above. See generally, n. 101 to Ch. VII. For a different example, after the Supreme Court found that the territorial sea and the resources of its sea-bed are of great importance to the nation in its international relations and belong to the United States rather than the coastal state, *United States* v. *California*, 332 U.S. 19 (1947), Congress gave the resources of the sea and submerged land to the states. Submerged Lands Act of 1953, ch. 65, 67 Stat. 29 (1953), 43 U.S.C. §§ 1301–15 (1988 & Supp. V 1993).

82. Compare Marshall, C.J., in *Cohens* v. *Virginia*, 19 U.S. (6 Wheat.) 264, 413–14 (1821).

83. Florida has gone so far as to pass the 'Florida International Affairs Act', whose purpose is to 'articulate a clear policy for international economic development and policy formation in Florida by means of a strategic plan for the coordination and advancement of public and private trade promotion programs and related educational activities'. Fla. Stat. §288.801 (1991). The commission created by the act is called upon, among other things, to study and make recommendations on the 'state's policy concerns related to immigration, criminal justice, human rights, drugs, and other internationally related issues'. Fla. Stat. §288.804(13) (1991). Whether and how Florida will act on any of these recommendations remains to be seen.

84. Wechsler, *The Political Safeguards of Federalism: The Role of the States in the Composition and Selection of the National Government*, 54 COLUM.L.REV. 543, 544, 558 (1966). He also said: 'National action has thus always been regarded as exceptional in our polity, an intrusion to be justified by some necessity, the special rather than the ordinary case. . . National power may be quite unquestioned in a given situation; those who would advocate its exercise must none the less answer the preliminary question why the matter should not be left to the states. If I have drawn too much significance from the mere fact of the existence of the states, the error surely will be rectified by pointing also to their crucial role in the selection and the composition of national authority. More is involved here than that aspect of the compromise between the larger and the smaller states that yielded their equality of status in the Senate. Representatives no less than Senators are allotted by the Constitution to the states, although their number varies with state population as determined by the census. . . And with the President, as with Congress, the crucial instrument of the selection— whether through electors or, in the event of failure of majority, by the House voting as state units—is again the states. The consequence, of course, is that the states are the strategic yardsticks for the measurement of interest and opinion, the special centers of political activity, the separate geographical determinants of national as well as local politics.' *Id.* at 544–5, 546.

    Thirty years after Professor Wechsler wrote, the statement remains essentially accurate, and even increasingly cogent.

85. See generally, D. Leebron, *Implementation of the Uruguay Round Results in the United States*, in IMPLEMENTING THE URUGUAY ROUND (Jackson and Sykes, eds., 1996). In adhering to international human rights agreements, the federal government has also indicated it would leave a large area of implementation to the states. See n. 101 to Ch. VII.

NOTES, CHAPTER VII. TREATIES, THE TREATY POWER, AND
EXECUTIVE AGREEMENTS, pp. 175 to 230

1. 'On June 11, 1776, the date on which the committee to draft a declaration of
independence was chosen, the Congress resolved that committees to prepare a
form of confederation and a plan of treaties to be proposed to foreign powers
should be constituted. On the following day the two committees were chosen.
Closely associated then in origin are these three features of our national life—
independence, union, and treaty making.' S. CRANDALL, TREATIES THEIR MAKING
AND ENFORCEMENT 19 (2d edn. 1916) citing 2 JOURNALS OF CONGRESS (1800 ed.)
197, 198.

   Compare: 'The power of making treaties is an important one, especially as it
relates to war, peace, and commerce; and it should not be delegated but in such
a mode, and with such precautions, as will afford the highest security that it will
be exercised by men the best qualified for the purpose, and in the manner most
conducive to the public good.' THE FEDERALIST No. 64, (Jay) at 390.

2. Clearly the prevailing mood at the Convention was that it should not be too
easy to make treaties. Even the 'nationalists' among the Framers neither desired
nor expected many treaties. Compare, e.g., Morris and Madison, 2 FARRAND
(n. 11 to Ch. I) 393, 548. At the Pennsylvania Convention, Wilson said: 'Neither
the President nor the Senate, solely, can complete a treaty; they are checks upon
each other, and are so balanced as to produce security to the people.' 2 J. ELLIOT
(ed.) DEBATES IN THE SEVERAL STATE CONVENTIONS ON THE ADOPTION OF THE
FEDERAL CONSTITUTION (1896), 507. Later, Jefferson wrote: 'On the subject of
treaties, our system is to have none with any nation, as far as can be avoided.'
11 T. JEFFERSON, WRITINGS 38–9 (Bergh ed. 1907). Compare Washington's
Farewell Address, 1 RICHARDSON 205. Only six treaties were concluded under the
Articles, and the United States did not make many during the early years under
the Constitution. As of 1989 the United States was party to 890 treaties. See
Congressional Research Service, TREATIES AND OTHER INTERNATIONAL
AGREEMENTS, A STUDY PREPARED FOR THE COMMITTEE ON FOREIGN RELATIONS BY
THE CONGRESSIONAL RESEARCH SERVICE, S. Rpt. 103–5, (1993).

   U.S. treaties and other international agreements that entered into force up to
the end of 1949 were published in the United States Statutes-at-Large. (An index
to treaties and other international agreements printed in the Statutes may be
found at 64 Stat. B1107.) Treaties and international agreements since 1945 are
in the TREATIES AND OTHER INTERNATIONAL ACTS SERIES, (T.I.A.S.). Beginning in
1950, they have been published in a compilation by the Department of State,
U.S. TREATIES AND OTHER INTERNATIONAL AGREEMENTS, (U.S.T.).

   There are authoritative collections of international agreements of the United
States: MALLOY, TREATIES, CONVENTIONS, INTERNATIONAL ACTS, PROTOCOLS, AND
AGREEMENTS BETWEEN THE UNITED STATES AND OTHER POWERS (1910–1938),
covering the period 1776 to 1937; MILLER, TREATIES AND OTHER INTERNATIONAL
ACTS OF THE UNITED STATES OF AMERICA (1931–1948), covering the period 1776
to 1863; and BEVANS, TREATIES AND OTHER INTERNATIONAL ACTS OF THE UNITED

STATES OF AMERICA (1968–1974), covering the period 1776 to 1950; also HEIN's UNITED STATES TREATIES AND OTHER INTERNATIONAL AGREEMENTS (since 1982). Since 1962, many treaties and agreements are published by the American Society of International Law in INTERNATIONAL LEGAL MATERIALS. Agreements registered with the United Nations are published in the UNITED NATIONS TREATY SERIES (U.N.T.S.). (There was a comparable LEAGUE OF NATIONS TREATY SERIES (L.N.T.S.).) See RESTATEMENT (n. 2 to Preface) § 312, Comment *j*, and Reporters' Note 5.

3. Failure of states to observe the treaties made by the Continental Congress was one of the principal impulses leading to the Constitutional Convention. See T. BAILEY, A DIPLOMATIC HISTORY OF THE AMERICAN PEOPLE, Chapter V (8th edn. 1968). At the Convention, Madison said: 'Will it prevent those violations of the law of nations and of Treaties which if not prevented must involve us in the calamities of foreign wars? The tendency of the States to these violations has been manifested in sundry instances. The files of Congs. contain complaints already, from almost every nation with which treaties have been formed. Hitherto indulgence has been shewn to us. This cannot be the permanent disposition of foreign nations. A rupture with other powers is among the greatest of national calamities. It ought therefore to be effectually provided that no part of a nation shall have it in its power to bring them on the whole. The existing confederacy does (not) sufficiently provide against this evil. The proposed amendment to it does not supply the omission. It leaves the will of the States as uncontrouled as ever.' 1 FARRAND (n. 11 to Ch. I) 316; also *id.* at 426, 513. See also THE FEDERALIST No. 15 at 106 (Hamilton); No. 22 at 144–5 (Hamilton), No. 42 at 265 (Madison).

4. The treaty-making process—as distinguished from the constitutional status of treaties (notably their supremacy to state law)—received little consideration at the Convention. Early it was proposed that treaties be made by the Senate. Towards the end of the Convention the present version was proposed and accepted with little discussion. (Hamilton had suggested it earlier, in the plan he originally submitted to the Convention, but his proposal did not contain the two-thirds requirement.) It was obviously a compromise resulting from other compromises. 'It was evident that the convention was getting tired. The Committee had recommended that the power of appointment and the making of treaties be taken from the senate and vested in the President "by and with the advice and consent of the senate". With surprising unanimity and surprisingly little debate, these important changes were agreed to.' M. FARRAND, THE FRAMING OF THE CONSTITUTION OF THE UNITED STATES (1913). Many at the Convention apparently considered that the President would in effect be an agent of the Senate. THE FEDERALIST No. 64 (Jay). See Bestor, *Respective Roles of the Senate and President in Making and Abrogation of Treaties—The Original Intent of the Framers of the Constitution Historically Examined,* 55 WASH. L. REV. 1 (1979). Proposals to require the approval of the House of Representatives (as well as the Senate) were rejected because its fluctuating membership and the short-term of its members would preclude the development of expertise, and its numbers would render it incapable of quick action and of secrecy. Compare THE

FEDERALIST No. 64 (Jay), No. 75 (Hamilton), and the views of 'Marcos' (Iredell) and others, quoted in BUTLER, THE TREATY POWER (n. 10 to Ch. I) §§ 253–4. See also 2 J. MADISON, JOURNAL OF THE CONSTITUTIONAL CONVENTION OF 1787 at 327 (Hunt ed. 1908); 4 ELLIOT'S DEBATES (n. 2 above) 253–67.

The choice of the Senate for the treaty-making process reflected also its character as the particular representative of state interests. It may not have been irrelevant, too, that both President and Senate were only indirectly responsible to 'the people', to popular vote. Compare THE FEDERALIST No. 64 (Jay). Madison wished to give the Senate alone the power to make peace because the President 'would necessarily derive so much power and importance from a state of war that he might be tempted, if authorized, to impede a treaty of peace'. 2 FARRAND (n. 11 to Ch. I) 540. See Ch. IV. Compare HENKIN, CONSTITUTIONAL-ISM, DEMOCRACY AND FOREIGN AFFAIRS (1990), Ch. 2.

The two-thirds requirement, however, was the subject of some debate. Among other suggestions, Madison proposed excepting peace treaties from that requirement so that a minority could not insist on continuing a war. There were also suggestions to require two-thirds of the entire Senate (rather than of those present). A proposal for Senate approval by simple majority was defeated by one vote. See 2 FARRAND (n. 11 to Ch. I) 532–54.

The two-thirds vote requirement can be seen as intended to approximate and continue the situation in the Congress under the Articles of Confederation. In 1789 the consent of two-thirds of the Senate, then consisting of representatives of thirteen States, would be roughly the same as the assent of nine States required under the Articles (Art. IX) in the Congress of thirteen States. (Compare THE FEDERALIST No. 75 (Hamilton).) Under the Articles, however, each state had one vote; in the Senate, Senators from the same state might not vote alike. In the Senate, also, a treaty requires only the consent of two-thirds of the Senators. For the growth of the treaty-making provisions at the Convention, see 1 BUTLER, THE TREATY POWER (n. 10 to Ch. I) §§ 17 *et seq.* CRANDALL, TREATIES (n. 1 above) Ch. 4; W. HOLT, TREATIES DEFEATED BY THE SENATE, Ch. 1 (1933). For a European perspective on treaty-making, see L. WILDHABER, TREATY-MAKING POWER AND CONSTITUTION: AN INTERNATIONAL AND COMPARATIVE STUDY (1971); also, NATIONAL TREATY LAW AND PRACTICE (M. Leigh and M. Blakeslee, eds., 1995).

5. See Ch. II. See especially the views later expressed by Alexander Hamilton, cited in Ch. II, pp. 45–6. On the other hand, Madison in the first Helvidius letter said: '. . . there are sufficient indications that the power of treaties is regarded by the constitution as materially different from mere executive power, and as having more affinity to the legislative than to the executive character'. HUNT, 6 J.MADISON, WRITINGS 138 (1910), n. 10 to Ch. II. That under the Articles treaties were the responsibility of Congress is not revealing since Congress had both executive and legislative functions. Earlier in The Federalist Papers, Hamilton had written: 'The power in question seems therefore to form a distinct department, and to belong, properly, neither to the legislative nor to the executive. The qualities elsewhere detailed as indispensable in the management of foreign negotiations, point out the Executive as the most fit agent in those transactions; while

the vast importance of the trust, and the operation of treaties as laws, plead strongly for the participation of the whole or a portion of the legislative body in the office of making them.' THE FEDERALIST No. 75 (Hamilton) at 451. See also THE FEDERALIST No. 64 (Jay). Hamilton was probably drawing on Locke who had written of a 'federative branch' of government distinct from the executive, but Locke thought that the federative and executive power should lie in the same hands. See n. 10 to Ch. II.

6. Exchange of ratifications binds the United States internationally; in the past it was accepted that when ratified, a treaty became effective retroactively as of the time of signature (*Haver* v. *Yaker*, 76 U.S. (9 Wall.) 32 (1869)) but that is no longer the accepted understanding. For domestic purposes, the treaty becomes law only upon proclamation by the President. *Ibid.*

It is the President, not the Senate who 'ratifies' a treaty (on behalf of the United States), but even the Supreme Court has referred to the Senate's action as 'ratification'. See *B. Altman & Co.* v. *United States*, 224 U.S. 583, 600–1 (1912); *Wilson* v. *Girard*, 354 U.S. 524, 526 (1957); *Barclays Bank* v. *Franchise Tax Board of Cal.*, 114 S.Ct. 2268, 2284 (1994).

7. See THE FEDERALIST No. 64 (Jay); also CORWIN, THE PRESIDENT (n. 5 to Intro. to Pt. II) 237–40. See also n. 4 above. For a recent example of Senate advice that the President negotiate certain agreements, see n. 32 below. Compare the directions by Congress that the President negotiate certain agreements, n. 82 below.

8. 'The wording of the Constitution itself visualizes treaty-making as one continuous process to be performed by a single authority, the President acting throughout in consultation with the Senate. From the first, however, the Senate insisted upon asserting its independence of identity in the treaty-making business, thereby splitting the constitutional authority into two authorities, performing separate differentiated functions, a Presidential function of formulation and negotiation followed by a Senatorial function—completely legislative in character and motivation—of criticism and amendment, or of criticism and rejection'. (Original in italics). E. CORWIN, THE CONSTITUTION AND WORLD ORGANIZATION 36 (1944).

Compare: 'The President is the constitutional representative of the United States with regard to foreign nations. He manages our concerns with foreign nations and must necessarily be most competent to determine when, how, and upon what subjects negotiation may be urged with the greatest prospect of success. For his conduct he is responsible to the Constitution. The committee considers this responsibility the surest pledge for the faithful discharge of his duty. They think the interference of the Senate in the direction of foreign negotiations calculated to diminish that responsibility and thereby to impair the best security for the national safety. The nature of transactions with foreign nations, moreover, requires caution and unity of design, and their success frequently depends on secrecy and dispatch. U.S. Senate, Reports, Committee on Foreign Relations, vol. 8, p. 24.' Quoted in *Curtiss-Wright*, 299 U.S. at 319.

For the developing role of the Senate, see R. HAYDEN, THE SENATE AND TREATIES, 1789–1817 (1920). There are suggestions that the 'advice' intended by the Constitution was to be as to whether or not to ratify. *Id.* at 6, 35. See generally, Riesenfeld and Abbott, *The Scope of Senate Control over Conclusion and Operation of Treaties*, 67 CHI.-KENT L. REV. 571 (1991).

9. Washington had told a Senate committee that oral communication seemed indispensable. 11 G. WASHINGTON, WRITINGS 417 (Ford ed. 1893). The Senate thereupon adopted a rule as to the procedure to be followed when the President met with the Senate. Senate Rule XXXVI(1).

Once Washington apparently came to the Senate seeking immediate yes-or-no answers to several questions about an Indian Treaty; the Senate insisted on a few days to refer it to committee and deliberate about it, not in the President's presence. The story is widely told, e.g., in CORWIN, THE PRESIDENT (n. 5 to Intro. to Pt. II) 239–40.

The Jay Treaty was a particular source of difficulties between the President and the Senate. The Senate defeated a resolution asking Washington what Jay was off to negotiate about. In bitter public debate after the Jay Treaty was concluded, some urged the impeachment of Washington because, among other reasons, he had violated the Constitution in negotiating a treaty without the previous advice of the Senate. 5 J.MARSHALL, THE LIFE OF GEORGE WASHINGTON 229 (1926). See generally HAYDEN, TREATIES (n. 8 above) 58–94.

10. Early Presidents sought such advice by message on some eighteen occasions, most of them by President Washington during the negotiation of the Jay Treaty. CRANDALL, TREATIES (n. 1 above) 68–75. In 1846, President Polk asked the Senate's advice as to an agreement to divide Oregon at the 49th parallel before he began negotiating. President Harding asked the Senate to approve U.S. adherence to the World Court in advance of executive negotiation of an agreement. Later, Secretary Kellogg sent to the Senate Foreign Relations Committee a proposed Arbitration Agreement with France before it was negotiated. See D. BYRN-JONES, FRANK B. KELLOGG 248–9 (1937). Other instances of prior 'consultation' are cited in the Appendix to H.R.REP.No. 1569, 68th Cong., 2d Sess. 19–20 (1925). Until 1815, Presidents often submitted to the Senate for confirmation the names of commissioners designated to negotiate treaties and advised the Senate of the general purpose of the negotiations. CRANDALL, TREATIES (n. 1 above) 75.

In 1953, Secretary Dulles assured the Senate: 'It will be our effort to see that the Senate gets its opportunity to "advise and consent" in time so that it does not have to choose between adopting treaties it does not like or embarrassing our international position by rejecting what has already been negotiated out with foreign governments.' 28 DEP'T STATE BULL. 591–2 (1953). There is no evidence that he or other Secretaries in fact formally sought the advice of the Senate (as distinguished from consultation with committees or individual Senators).

Early 'leaks' by members or staff of the Senate contributed to the development of the practice to tell the Senate nothing until negotiation was concluded. There is nothing in the Constitution that precludes a secret treaty, but especially as the Senate grew in membership it was accepted that secret agreements could not go to the Senate for formal consent. For examples of Senate leaks despite self-imposed injunctions of secrecy, see HOLT (n. 4 above) at 16, 90 n. 32, 95, 138 n. 66, 139 n. 67, 167–8, 183, 193, 217. The Senate held secret hearings on treaties until the Versailles Treaty. *Id.* at 282. It now considers treaties generally in 'open executive session', i.e., in its executive capacity (as treaty-maker, rather than as legislator) but usually not in secret. Compare Senate Rules XXXVI(3), XXXVII(1). On the other hand, the Senate has often concealed treaties submitted to it, and what it was doing (or not doing) about them, by imposing an injunction of secrecy, which Presidents for their part did not feel free to violate. Compare Senate Rules XXXVI(3), XXXVII(1); Hudson, *The 'Injunction of Secrecy' with Respect to American Treaties*, 23 AM.INT'L L. 329 (1929).

11. See, for example, the role of Senator Vandenberg, p. 178, this chapter. For the text of the Vandenberg Resolution, see S.Res. 239, 80th Cong., 2d Sess., 94 CONG. REC. 7791 (1948). Congress (by resolution of both houses) has sometimes urged the President to make a treaty.

12. Holt's book (n. 4 above) is a brief for that thesis. He ends his volume as follows (at 307): 'The fate of the treaty of Versailles turned the attention of thoughtful people to the treaty-making power of the United States. They saw that the exercise of that power had produced such bitter conflicts between the President and the Senate and had so increased the opportunities for political warfare unconnected with the merits of the question that many treaties had been lost. They knew that the ratification of nearly every important treaty had been endangered by a constitutional system which, instead of permitting a decision solely on the merits of the question, produces impotence and friction. They realized that if no disaster had resulted it was due partly to good fortune and chiefly to the relative unimportance of foreign relations in the history of the United States so that few treaties had contained vital issues. They also realized that, if the United States was to play the part in world affairs demanded by its interests and its strength, a deadlock between the President and the Senate over a treaty involving a really critical foreign problem may end in ruin.'
    Compare also D. FLEMING, THE TREATY VETO OF THE AMERICAN SENATE (1930). But cf. R. DANGERFIELD, IN DEFENSE OF THE SENATE: A STUDY IN TREATY-MAKING (1933).

13. 2 W. THAYER, THE LIFE AND LETTERS OF JOHN HAY 170 (1915). Hay also said: 'A treaty entering the Senate is like a bull going into the arena: no one can say just how or when the final blow will fall—but one thing is certain—it will never leave the arena alive.' *Id.* at 393. He thought the Senate 'veto' on treaties to be the 'original mistake in the Constitution'. 3 J. HAY, LETTERS OF JOHN HAY AND EXTRACTS FROM DIARY (privately printed 1908).

14. John W. Davis, 48 A.B.A.REP. at 203 (1923). Compare: 'It is a painful and humiliating state of things, but I see no escape from it, since the Fathers in their wisdom chose to assume that one-third of the Senate in opposition would always be right, and the President and the majority generally wrong.' John Hay to President McKinley, Aug. 19, 1899, quoted in HOLT (n. 4 above) 192. Dangerfield, (n. 12 to this chapter), at 311–12, however, stresses that up to 1928 only seven treaties received a majority vote in the Senate but failed for lack of the required two-thirds.

There have been innumerable proposals to amend the Constitution to drop the two-thirds requirement and to give the House of Representatives a voice in treaty-making equal to that of the Senate. Others have sought escape from the two-thirds requirement without constitutional amendment by promoting the approval of international agreements by simple majority in both houses. See this chapter, p. 215.

Senate rules made it possible for a minority of one-third-plus-one during debate to strike particular treaty provisions, thereby making the treaty as a whole less acceptable and unlikely later to attract the two-thirds vote. See HOLT (n. 4 above) 36–7. In the Versailles debates, the opposition exploited a different rule requiring only a simple majority to vote amendments to a treaty, and perhaps render the treaty less likely to attract a two-thirds vote.

15. On June 15, 1934, the Senate approved twelve treaties in an hour. See 78 CONG. REC. 11561 *et seq.* For a graphic description of the Senate's record on treaties submitted for its consent between 1789 and 1967, see 62 AM.J.INT'L L.. 162–3 (1968). See also U.S. DEP'T OF STATE, PUB.NO.2311, TREATIES SUBMITTED TO THE SENATE, 1935–1944 (1945), and CONGRESSIONAL RESEARCH SERVICE REPORT, S. PRT. 103–5, TREATIES AND OTHER INTERNATIONAL AGREEMENTS (1993).

16. This is more likely to happen in the case of a multilateral treaty where no particular nation negotiated it with the United States and is waiting for the United States to ratify it, e.g., the Genocide Treaty which was before the Senate from 1949 to 1984, and was not ratified until 1987. See Senate Consent to Ratification of Genocide Convention, 132 CONG. REC. S 1362, Feb. 19, 1986, and Genocide Implementation Act of 1987, signed, 4 Nov. 1988, Pub.L.No. 100–606, 102 Stat. 3045.

    It has been suggested that the Senate should either consent or reject, and that withholding action is 'of questionable propriety'. WRIGHT (n. 3 to Ch. I) 253. The practice is well established, however, and makes it possible readily to pick a treaty from the Senate shelf years after it was put there.

17. See CRANDALL, TREATIES (n. 1 above) 94–9. President Cleveland withdrew the Hawaii Treaty from Senate consideration because he felt that it had been improperly negotiated by his predecessors. See 9 RICHARDSON, MESSAGES AND PAPERS OF THE PRESIDENTS 460 (1899). Successor Administrations did not press for Senate consent to the Genocide Convention, sent to the Senate by President Truman, until 1984. See n. 16 above.

    Presidents have also refused to proceed with treaties because of reservations imposed by the Senate. See CRANDALL, TREATIES (n. 1 above) 97–9.

18. See the history of the Genocide Convention, n. 16 above. Conventions and covenants signed by President Carter in 1977 and 1980 were not ratified until 1992–94, some not by then. See n. 101 to this chapter. SALT II with the USSR was sent to the Senate in 1979 and withdrawn by the President in 1980.

19. CRANDALL, TREATIES (n. 1 above) 82–4. A treaty with Mexico was rejected by the Senate twice. See HOLT (n. 4 above) 132–3.

20. Compare the efforts of the Senate to withdraw its consent to the appointment of an officer, n. 103 to Ch. IV.

21. The Senate entered a reservation to the Jay Treaty, the first treaty made by the

United States following the adoption of the Constitution. Senate Resolution of June 24, 1795, 1 S.Exec.J. 64, quoted in D. MILLER, RESERVATIONS TO TREATIES 4–5 (1919).

In the days when the Senate approved instructions to negotiators, it apparently felt obligated to consent to a treaty concluded in accordance with the instructions. CRANDALL, TREATIES (n. 1 above) 79.

22. President Monroe reported that Lord Harrowby, the British Foreign Minister, 'censured in strong terms the practise into which we had fallen of ratifying treaties, with exceptions to parts of them, a practise which he termed new, unauthorized and not to be sanctioned'. 3 AMERICAN STATE PAPERS, FOREIGN RELATIONS (Gales and Seaton eds. 1832–61) 93. See HAYDEN, TREATIES (n. 8 above) 150. See also Canning to Rush, Aug. 27, 1824, 5 AMERICAN STATE PAPERS, above at 364–5. The treaty of Ghent provided that it shall become binding when ratified by both sides 'without alteration by either of the contracting parties'. 8 Stat. 218, 223 (1814).

23. The Supreme Court has expressly recognized the power of the Senate to give consent with reservations. See *Haver* v. *Yaker*, 76 U.S. (9 Wall.) 32, 35 (1869); Brown, J., concurring in *Fourteen Diamond Rings* v. *United States*, 183 U.S. 176, 182 (1901). See generally, D. MILLER, RESERVATIONS TO TREATIES (1919).

But reservations must not be 'incompatible with the object and purpose of the treaty'. Vienna Convention on the Law of Treaties, article 19. See also, RESTATEMENT (n. 2 to Preface) § 313(c).

24. See n. 17 above. A reservation by another party, entered after the Senate had consented to the original treaty, presents the United States with a modified treaty and requires new consent. Such later reservations have in the past often (not always) been submitted for Senate consent. See, e.g., the Treaty with France 1800, 1 MALLOY, TREATIES (n. 10 to Ch. I) 496; HAYDEN, TREATIES (n. 8 above) 124. See generally, CRANDALL, TREATIES (n. 1 above) 86–9; 5 MOORE, DIGEST (n. 50 to Ch. II) 207. See MILLER, RESERVATIONS TO TREATIES 11–14 (1919). The principle was reaffirmed by the Department of State in 60 AM.J.INT'L L. 562 (1966), but in fact foreign reservations have apparently not been submitted for Senate consent in many years. Perhaps that is because reservations by others after ratification by the United States are likely to occur in respect of multilateral treaties, and have not affected U.S. rights or obligations in ways deemed of major importance; perhaps, in these cases, the Executive concluded that, the Senate, knowing the practice, had waived the need for its consent, or that he can accept these particular modifications on his own authority. See Ch. VIII.

25. The Senate has not always been careful in distinguishing between 'reservations', 'conditions', 'declarations', and 'understandings'. See for example, the amendments, conditions, reservations, and understandings to the Panama Canal Treaty, and the Treaty Concerning the Permanent Neutrality and Operation of the Panama Canal, Sept. 7, 1977, Panama–United States, T.I.A.S. Nos. 10,030 and 10,029.

The Senate has sometimes taken the occasion of consent to a treaty to express policy in the form of a reservation or understanding. e.g., Convention for the Pacific Settlement of International Disputes, July 29, 1899, 32 Stat. 1779, 1801 (1903), T.S. No. 392; General Act of the International Conference at Algeciras and An Additional Protocol, April 7, 1906, 34 Stat. 2905, 2946 (1907), T.S. No. 456. See MALLOY, TREATIES (n. 10 to Ch. I) 2032, 2047, 2183; WRIGHT (n. 3 to Ch. I) 282. And see the Senate declarations attached to its consent to ratification of the Intermediate Nuclear Forces Treaty with the Soviet Union, n. 32 below; see also n. 33 below.

26. The Senate has sometimes insisted that its understandings be mentioned in the ratification of the treaty 'as conveying the true meaning of the treaty, and will in effect form a part of the treaty'. Treaty with Mexico Respecting Utilization of Waters of the Colorado and Tijuana Rivers and the Rio Grande, 59 Stat. 1219, 1263–5 (1945), T.S. No. 994, at 53–5 (1946); *Hidalgo County Water Control & Improvement Dist.* v. *Hedrick,* 226 F.2d 1, 5, 8 (5th Cir. 1955), *cert. denied,* 350 U.S. 983 (1956). The Senate has sometimes given its consent 'subject to the following understandings and reservations' without indicating which was which.

   In some cases, the other party expressly consented to the Senate understandings. See, e.g., the 1911 Treaty with Japan, 37 Stat. 1508 (1913), T.S. No. 558.

27. Compare the experience under the Headquarters Agreement between the United States and the United Nations which was not sent to the Senate for its consent as to a treaty, but concluded by the President under authority of a joint resolution of Congress. See 61 Stat. 756 (1947), T.I.A.S. No.1676. Section 6 of the Joint Resolution contained a provision that: "Nothing in the agreement shall be construed as in any way diminishing, abridging, or weakening the right of the United States to safeguard its own security and completely to control the entrance of aliens into any territory of the United States other than the headquarters district and its immediate vicinity, as to be defined and fixed in a supplementary agreement between the Government of the United States and the United Nations in pursuance of section 13(3)(e) of the agreement, and such areas as it is reasonably necessary to traverse in transit between the same and foreign countries. Moreover, nothing in section 14 of the agreement with respect to facilitating entrance into the United States by persons who wish to visit the headquarters district and do not enjoy the right of entry provided in section 11 of the agreement shall be construed to amend or suspend in any way the immigration laws of the United States or to commit the United States in any way to effect any amendment or suspension of such laws.' 61 Stat. at 767–78.

   The text of the resolution was communicated to the United Nations, but neither the Secretary General nor the General Assembly reacted to it, and the character of the security clause (as a reservation, understanding, or something else) and its purport were not agreed or discussed when the agreement was concluded, perhaps because neither the U.S. Executive branch nor the United Nations wished to face its possible implications. In 1953, however, the United States invoked the security provision to justify its refusal to admit to the United States for travel to the U.N. Headquarters a representative of an approved non-governmental organization, whom the U.S. considered a threat to its security. The Secretary General claimed that the United Nations was not bound by that provision; the United States insisted that for its part under its Constitution there was no agreement except subject to that provision. The issue was not resolved in principle. See Annual Report of Secretary General, 8 U.N. GAOR Supp. 1 at 144 (1953); 9 *id.* Supp. 1 at 100 (1954) ; 14 U.N. BULL. 339 (1953), 15 *id.* 102; [1953] U.N. YEAR BOOK 501-3.

28. See 36 Stat. 2199, 2240 (1909), 35 Stat. 1960 (1908); MALLOY, TREATIES (n. 10 to Ch. I) 814, 2247. Presidents resisted these reservations. See CRANDALL, TREATIES (n. 1 above) 98-9. See HOLT (n. 4 above) 204 *et seq.*, 230 *et seq.;* WRIGHT (n. 3 to Ch. I) 109-10; 1 WILLOUGHBY (n. 3 to Ch. I) 541-3.

29. Particularly as to treaties that affect the revenue, e.g., Treaty with Great Britain concerning Canada, 10 Stat. 1089, 1092 (1854); Treaty with Hawaii, 19 Stat. 625, 627 (1875); Treaty with Mexico, 24 Stat. 987, 988 (1883); Commercial Convention with Cuba, 33 Stat. 2136, 2143 (1903). See A HINDS, PRECEDENTS OF THE HOUSE OF REPRESENTATIVES vol. 2 §§ 1531-3, at 994-1002 (1903); 1 WILLOUGHBY, (n. 3 to Ch. I) 558-60; S.Doc. No. 47, 57th Cong., 2d Sess. (1902), reprinted in 2 HINDS, above at 1001-2; see also *United States* v. *American Sugar Co.*, 202 U.S. 563 (1906), where the Supreme Court gave effect to the Senate's reservation that the Cuba Convention should not take effect until it had been approved by Congress. Compare 42 Stat. 1946, 1949 (1921). Compare the Senate condition that the President postpone ratification of the Genocide Convention and the Convention against Torture until Congress enacted implementing legislation. See n. 16 above.

The reservations to the Treaty of Versailles included several designed to ensure for Congress a major role in the implementation of the treaty. See Wright, *Validity of the Proposed Reservations to the Peace Treaty,* 20 COLUM.L.REV. 121, 125, 126, 138-42 (1920). One reservation would have authorized denunciation of the Treaty by concurrent resolution of Congress (without Presidential assent). Compare Ch. IV, p. 125.

The legal effect of such a 'reservation' has been seriously debated in only one instance, involving a treaty with Canada to divide the waters of the Niagara River. In the United States there were divisions of opinion and interest as to the regime that should govern the exploitation of the U.S. share of the waters. Had the treaty been ratified without more, these waters would have been subject to general federal legislation governing waters belonging to the United States for which no special provision was made. In consenting to ratification of the treaty, the Senate resolved that the United States reserves the right to provide for redevelopment of its share of the waters by act of Congress, and no such redevelopment should be undertaken until specifically authorized by Act of Congress. Both the United States and Canada treated this provision like other 'reservations'; the President asked Canada to accept it and Canada— though somewhat mystified—did. See Uses of the Waters of the Niagara River, Convention Between the United States of America and Canada, Feb. 27, 1950, [1950] 1 U.S.T. 694, T.I.A.S. No. 2130. See generally Henkin, *The Treaty Makers and the Law Makers: The Niagara Power Reservation,* 56 COLUM. L.

REV. 1151, 1154–8 (1956). The relevant portions of the treaty and the diplomatic exchanges are quoted there.

Some who wished to see the treaty come into effect without the Senate's limitation argued that the reservation had no legal effect: it was not a proper treaty provision since it contained no element of international obligation. See, e.g., the Memorandum of Law by Thomas F. Moore, Jr., counsel for the Power Authority of the State of New York, reproduced in N. Y. Times, Oct. 29, 1955, at 9, col. 1. That objection, of course, did not relate to the Senate's part in the treaty-making process; it would apply as well if the same provision had been inserted by the negotiators in the original treaty. See pp. 179 *et seq.*, this chapter. But the arguments failed to consider the Senate proviso as a condition to its consent. If the Senate gave its consent only on condition that the United States share of the waters should await disposition by Congress, the treaty could take effect only subject to that condition. If the Senate's condition did not operate to prevent the treaty from coming into effect, it is questionable whether the President had authority to ratify the treaty until Congress adopted the implementing legislation called for by the Senate, and whether his ratification in disregard of the Senate's condition would be constitutionally effective. See Henkin, *Niagara* (above) 1176–81. For this reason (and others), I believe that the Court of Appeals for the District of Columbia erred in refusing to give effect to the Senate 'reservation'. The court's judgment was vacated by the Supreme Court when the issue became moot because Congress adopted the legislation called for by the Senate. See *Power Authority* v. *Federal Power Comm'n*, 247 F.2d 538 (D.C.Cir. 1957), vacated and remanded with directions to dismiss as moot, *sub nom.*, *American Public Power Ass'n* v. *Power Authority*, 355 U.S. 64 (1957). But compare the practice of declaring human rights treaties to be non self-executing, criticized below pp. 201–3.

New York Indians v. *United States*, 170 U.S. 1 (1898), is different. There the Supreme Court refused to let the President's non-compliance with the Senate's requirements (which the Court said were perhaps only directory, not mandatory) defeat the claim of the Indians under the treaty. The Supreme Court has often been particularly solicitous for Native American interests. *Cf.* *Squire* v. *Capoeman*, 351 U.S. 1, 6, 7 (1956); *United States* v. *Shoshone Tribe*, 304 U.S. 111, 117 (1938).

Similarly, when the Senate gives consent to a treaty on condition that officers appointed by the President pursuant to the treaty shall require Senate approval, such declarations do not prevent the treaty to which they are attached from coming into effect, but the President who proceeds to ratify the treaty has been deemed obligated to conform to the condition.

A very different condition couched as an understanding was that appended by the Senate in consenting to the London Treaty, 73 CONG.REC. 378 (1930): *'Resolved further,* That in ratifying said treaty the Senate does so with the distinct and explicit understanding that there are no secret files, documents, letters, understandings, or agreements which in any way, directly or indirectly, modify, change, add to, or take away from any of the stipulations, agreements, or statements in said treaty; and that the Senate ratifies said treaty with the distinct and explicit understanding that, excepting the agreement brought about through the exchange of notes between the Governments of the United States, Great Britain, and Japan having reference to Article XIX, there is no agreement, secret or otherwise, expressed or implied between any of the parties to said treaty as to any construction that shall hereafter be given to any statement or provision contained therein.'

This 'understanding' does not amend or interpret the treaty, nor does it require any action. Presumably it serves to deny Senate consent to any secret agreed construction that might exist. Perhaps, even, the Senate's consent would not be effective if a secret understanding in fact existed, so that the President could not proceed to ratify.

30. The Senate Reservation to the Reciprocal Military Service Convention with Great Britain, June 3, 1918, 40 Stat. 1620, required the President, before ratifying the Convention, to issue a general certificate exempting from military service citizens of the United States in Great Britain who were outside the ages of military service specified in the laws of the United States. He complied in substance by an exchange of diplomatic notes. See S.EXEC.DOC. No. 5, presented as H.R.Doc. No. 1220, 65th Cong., 2d Sess. 2, 7 (1918).

In consenting to a treaty with Korea in 1883 the Senate resolved that it 'does not admit or acquiesce' in any assertion of a right 'to negotiate treaties or carry on diplomatic negotiations' other than by persons confirmed by the Senate. MALLOY, TREATIES (n. 10 to Ch. I) 340. The Senate has lost that one. See p. 177.

Some of the Senate reservations to the Treaty of Versailles would have enhanced the powers of some organs of the federal government and limited the authority of others. See Wright, *Validity of the Proposed Reservations to the Peace Treaty*, 20 COLUM.L.REV. 121, 123–4 (1920).

31. Compare a far-reaching expression by the Senate in consenting to ratification of the Convention on the Organization for Economic Cooperation and Development: 'with the interpretation and explanation of the intent of the Senate, that nothing in the convention, or the advice and consent of the Senate to the ratification thereof, confers any power on the Executive to bind the United States in substantive matters beyond what the Executive now has, or to bind the United States without compliance with applicable procedures imposed by domestic law, or confers any power on the Congress to take action in fields previously beyond the authority of Congress, or limits Congress in the exercise of any power it now has'. 107 CONG.REC. 4149 (1961); 12 U.S.T. 1728, 1751, T.I.A.S. No. 4891 (1961). Compare analogous Congressional 'reservations', Ch. IV, pp. 105 *et seq.*

32. In 1988, in consenting to the INF Treaty—following the controversy as to the interpretation of the ABM treaty, this chapter, p. 182,—the Senate declared a principle of treaty interpretation as a constitutional principle, in the guise of a condition. The Senate resolution provided:

'That the Senate advise and consent to ratification of the Treaty . . . subject to the following—

(a) Conditions:

(1) Provided, that the Senate's advice and consent to ratification of the INF

Treaty is subject to the condition, based on the Treaty Clause of the Constitution, that—

(A) the United States shall interpret the Treaty in accordance with the common understanding of the Treaty shared by the President and the Senate at the time the Senate gave its advice and consent to ratification.' 134 Cong.Rec. S6937 (daily edn. May 27, 1988).

In my view the constitutional principle declared by the Senate is sound, but its title as a 'condition' is dubious. The President, eager to make the treaty, accepted the Senate's consent subject to the Senate's 'condition', but issued a statement declaring the condition to be 'improper'.

The Senate resolution, in consenting to the INF Treaty, also declared that because the incentive for Soviet noncompliance and the difficulties of monitoring will be great, the United States should rely primarily on its own technical means of verification. The Senate took the occasion to advise the President as to the kinds of further agreements he should negotiate. It declared its strong belief that respect for human rights and fundamental freedoms is essential to the development of friendly relations and called upon the USSR to live up to international human rights agreements (some of which the United States itself had not ratified). For the text of the Senate Resolution, see Cong.Rec. S6937: 134, (daily edn., May 27, 1988), reprinted in 82 Am. J. Int'l L. 810–15 (1988). And compare the START II Treaty, to which the Senate consented subject to six conditions and seven declarations. 142 Cong.Rec. S461-3, daily ed. Jan. 26, 1996.

33. In 1979, the Senate Foreign Relations Committee, noting that '[in] recent years . . . the Senate has concerned itself directly with the United States "Instrument of Ratification" ', expressed dissatisfaction with the manner in which the Executive had communicated such Senate declarations to the other treaty party. The Committee therefore proposed in its report on SALT II an explicit categorization of three kinds of provisions in the Senate resolution on the treaty:

Category I: provisions that do not directly involve formal notice to or agreement by the Soviet Union.

Category II: provisions that would be formally communicated to the Soviet Union as official statements of the United States Government in ratifying the Treaty, but which do not require their agreement.

Category III: provisions that would require the explicit agreement of the Soviet Union for the Treaty to come into force. (S. Exec. Rep. No. 14, 96th Cong. 1st Sess. 72–8 (1979))

SALT II was not ratified, and was later withdrawn from the Senate, and the future of this categorization scheme in U.S. practice is uncertain. But Professor Glennon says, 'The new terminology appears to have stuck. During Senate consideration of the INF treaty and the CFE treaty, "condition" seemed to supplant entirely the labels of "reservation" and "understanding". So too, did the three categories of conditions.' S. Exec. Rep. No. 100–15, 100th Cong., 1st. Sess. (1988) (INF treaty). M. Glennon, *Constitutional Power of the United States Senate to Consent to Treaties*, 67 Chi.-Kent L. Rev. 533, 535 (1991).

34. See Anti Ballistic Missile Systems Treaty, May 26, 1972, 23 UST 3435, T.I.A.S.

No. 7503. And see n. 32 to this chapter. I draw here on my book, CONSTITUTIONALISM, DEMOCRACY AND FOREIGN AFFAIRS (1990), pp. 52–4. The Clinton Administration later adopted the 'narrow interpretation' of the Treaty, pp. 182–83 above.

35. I draw here on my articles *The Constitution, Treaties, and International Human Rights*, 116 U.PA. L.REV. 1012 (1968), and *'International Concern' and the Treaty Power of the United States*, 63 AM. J. INT'L L. 272 (1969).

36. RESTATEMENT (n. 2 to Preface) § 301, adapting Article 1 of the Vienna Convention on the Law of Treaties. In an earlier accepted definition, a treaty was 'a formal instrument of agreement by which two or more States establish or seek to establish a relation under international law between themselves.' Harvard Law School Research in International Law, Draft Convention on the Law of Treaties, 29 AM.J.INT'L L., Supp., Pt. 3, 653, 686 (1935). The Supreme Court once quoted a simpler definition: 'a compact made between two or more independent nations with a view to the public welfare'. *B. Altman & Co.* v. *United States*, 224 U.S. 583, 600 (1912).

37. In this hypothetical case, Canada might be estopped from questioning its character as a treaty; one could nonetheless argue that it is beyond the power of the treaty-makers. This 'limitation' on the Treaty Power should not be confused with a different alleged requirement, that a treaty deal with a matter that is of 'international concern'. For example, in the Niagara Treaty debates, n. 29 above, it was argued that the Senate Reservation did not have status as a treaty provision under the Constitution because it did not 'concern Canada'. But no one claimed that it was not bona fide or that Canada agreed to it from improper motives to help circumvent the separation of powers of the United States Government. The argument there seemed closer to that implied in the so called 'international concern' requirement and I consider it in that context. See p. 196.

38. William Rawle, one of the earliest expounders of the Constitution, and an ardent exponent of states' rights, noted that unlike the Articles of Confederation '[i]n our present Constitution no limitations [on the treaty power] were held necessary'. W. RAWLE, A VIEW OF THE CONSTITUTION OF THE UNITED STATES 65 (2d edn. 1829).

39. But *cf. Burdell* v. *Canadian Pacific Airlines, Ltd.*, Cir.Ct., Cook County, Ill., Nov. 7, 1968, noted in 63 AM.J.INT'L L. 339 (1969) (holding the venue and damage-limitation provisions of the Warsaw Convention unconstitutional). And *cf.* W. COWLES, TREATIES AND CONSTITUTIONAL LAW 294–5 (1941), whose thesis is that the Supreme Court has in fact declined to enforce treaty provisions where they infringed on private property rights. The case he makes is open to question.

In 1995 a district court in California held unconstitutional the application of a treaty under which Swiss authorities froze Swiss bank accounts of a U.S. citizen at the request of the Department of Justice, without satisfying the requirements of the Fourth Amendment. *Collello* v. *United States Securities and Exchange Commission*, 908 F. Supp. 738 (C.D.Cal. 1995).

40. *Missouri* v. *Holland*, 252 U.S. 416, 433 (1920), discussed in another regard at pp. 190–4.

Shortly after that case was decided Professor Thomas Reed Powell said of the opinion: 'Its hint that there may be no other test to be applied than whether the treaty has been duly concluded indicates that the court might hold that specific constitutional limitations in favor of individual liberty and property are not applicable to deprivations wrought by treaties.' Powell, *Constitutional Law in 1919–20*, 19 MICH.L.REV. 1, 13 (1920). The possibility of such an interpretation was recognized also in Stinson, *The Treaty-Making Power and the Restraint of the Common Law*, 1 B.U.L.REV. 111, 112 (1921), and in 6 CORNELL L.Q. 91, 92 (1920). See also *United States* v. *Reid*, 73 F.2d 153, 155 (9th Cir. 1934), *cert. denied for untimeliness*, 299 U.S. 544 (1936); that case was referred to unfavorably in *Perkins* v. *Elg*, 307 U.S. 325, 349 n. 31 (1939). For earlier views to this effect, compare PAMPHLETS ON THE CONSTITUTION OF THE UNITED STATES 279, 306 (Ford ed. 1888); H. DAVIS, THE JUDICIAL VETO 100 (1914).

That a treaty is not subject to constitutional limitations has been suggested on the additional ground that under international law a sovereign nation may enter into any treaty, and that this principle of international law, antedating the Constitution, was not modified by the adoption of the Constitution. It has even been argued that the Constitution could not effectively limit the treaty powers of the United States, a 'sovereign' nation. See Potter, *Inhibitions Upon the Treaty-Making Power of the United States*, 28 AM. J. INT'L L. 456 (1934).

A. Sutherland, *Restricting the Treaty Power*, 65 HARV.L.REV. 1305, 1319 (1952), notes that the President and the Senate evidently thought that they had the authority to contravene the Eighteenth Amendment of the Constitution by treaty when they ratified the Smuggling of Intoxicating Liquors Agreement, Jan. 23, 1924, 43 Stat. 1761, T.S. No. 685. There was, however, disagreement within the Executive branch as to whether the Eighteenth Amendment limited diplomatic exemptions from baggage inspection. See 1 C. HYDE, INTERNATIONAL LAW 759 (1922).

The Bricker Amendment, discussed at pp. 192–3, and n. 69 below, included a provision that would have explicitly declared treaties to be subject to the Constitution. The subject was much discussed in the various hearings on the proposed Amendment. *Hearings on S.J. Res. 130 Before a Subcomm.. of the Senate Comm. on the Judiciary*, 82d Cong., 2d Sess. 121, 132, 256, 313–16, 364, 413, 484, 486, 530 (1952); *Hearings on S.J. Res. 1 & 43 Before a Subcomm. of the Senate Comm. on the Judiciary*, 83d Cong., 1st Sess. 924, 959, 994, 999, 1010, 1070, 1123, 1130, 1136 (1953); *Hearings on S.J. Res. 1 Before a Subcomm. of the Senate Comm. on the Judiciary*, 84th Cong., 1st Sess. 185–6, 281–2, 297, 581–2 (1955). Some proponents of the Amendment argued that it was not clear that a treaty was invalid if it was inconsistent with the Constitution, but they cited little authority for the view they feared. See, e.g., statements of Frank Holman, *Bricker Hearings*, 1953, 142–9.

John Foster Dulles, shortly before he became Secretary of State, said: 'The treaty making power is an extraordinary power, liable to abuse. Treaties make international law and also they make domestic law. Under our Constitution, treaties become the supreme law of the land. They are, indeed, more supreme than ordinary laws for congressional laws are invalid if they do not conform to the Constitution, whereas treaty law can overrule the Constitution. Treaties, for example, can take powers away from the Congress and give them to the

President; they can take powers from the States and give them to the Federal Government or to some international body, and they can cut across the rights given the people by their constitutional Bill of Rights.' Address at the regional meeting of the ABA, April 11, 1952, reprinted *id.* at 862.

Later, when Secretary of State, Dulles explained that he did not believe the treaty power could be unlimited and that the only personal rights which could be limited by treaties would be 'property' rights through the exercise of eminent domain. *Bricker Hearings,* 1955, above at 177–9.

There are other ambiguous, misleading statements, e.g.: 'The treaty, then, as to the point in question, is of equal force with the Constitution itself and, certainly, with any law whatever.' Cushing, J., in *Ware* v. *Hylton,* 3 U.S. (3 Dall.) 199, 284 (1769). Also: treaties have 'the same effect as an act of Congress, and [are] of equal force with the Constitution'. *Pollard* v. *Kibbe,* 39 U.S. (14 Pet. 353,) 415 (1840). In context, however, such statements apparently meant only that treaties were equally supreme to state law, not that they could disregard constitutional limitations.

41. See, e.g., the opinion of the Court of Appeals of Virginia quoted in *Martin* v. *Hunter's Lessee,* 14 U.S. (1 Wheat.) 304, 323–4 (1816); also *Marbury* v. *Madison,* 5 U.S. (1 Cranch) 137, 180 (1803); *Gibbons* v. *Ogden,* 22 U.S. (9 Wheat.) 1, 210–11 (1824); *cf. Field* v. *Clark,* 143 U.S. 649, 669. 673 (1892); see R. BERGER, CONGRESS v. THE SUPREME COURT 228–36 (1969). But *cf.* 2 W. CROSSKEY, POLITICS AND THE CONSTITUTION IN THE HISTORY OF THE UNITED STATES 990–1007 (1953). That phrase in the Supremacy Clause has been invoked to support the view that the Framers intended 'judicial review'. See Ch. V, pp. 143 *et seq.*

42. See 2 FARRAND (n. 11 to Ch. I) 417; W. RAWLE, A VIEW OF THE CONSTITUTION OF THE UNITED STATES 66–7 (2d edn. 1829). See *Reid* v. *Covert,* 354 U.S. 1, 16 (1957), p. 187 above.

43. That indeed was the purpose of the phrase 'made or which shall be made', 2 FARRAND (n. 11 to Ch. I) 417, and that phrase alone achieves that meaning in Art. III, sec. 2. Compare *Worcester* v. *Georgia,* 31 U.S. (6 Pet.) 515, 558 (1832).

44. As an original matter, the Constitution might have been interpreted as recognizing the supremacy of international law to all U.S. law, including the Constitution itself. See Ch. VIII. From that perspective, since international law requires that nations respect their treaty obligations, constitutional jurisprudence might have developed so at to require giving effect to U.S. treaty obligations even if they were otherwise in conflict with provisions in the Constitution. Perhaps that was the view reflected in Holmes's dictum, though Holmes seemed to derive it not from theory but by construction of constitutional text.

45. It may be urged that in view of the possible international consequences of declaring a treaty provision unconstitutional, courts should not consider the validity of a treaty provision but treat that as a political question not for judicial determination. See Ch. V, p. 143. One commentator has said: 'It is difficult to imagine anything more anomalous than a lawsuit between private litigants becoming the means of upsetting an international engagement.' W. McCLURE,

INTERNATIONAL EXECUTIVE AGREEMENTS 223 (1941). *Cf. United States* v. *Reid,* n. 40 to this chapter. Compare Justice Chase, in *Ware* v. *Hylton,* 3 U.S. (3 Dall.) 199, 237 (1796): 'If the court possesses a power to declare treaties void, I shall never exercise it, but in a very clear case indeed.'

It has been argued that since it is established that for domestic purposes Congress can 'repeal' treaty provisions (p. 209 above), there is a safeguard against abuse of the Treaty Power making it unnecessary to rely on judicial invalidation; if a treaty is to be nullified, with possible serious consequences to the nation, let it be done by Congress which is the supreme political body (and has authority to court and make war). Some may see conceptual difficulties in a constitutional system under which treaties are not subject to constitutional limitations and judicial invalidation but can be 'repealed' by acts of Congress which are subject to judicial invalidation. See Justice Black, p. 187 above, and n. 51 to this chapter.

Private suits to invalidate international agreements are justiciable but have not in fact succeeded. See n. 51 below; see also *Dames & Moore* v. *Regan,* discussed at p. 221, upholding the settlement of the Iran Hostage Agreement against private challenges on various constitutional grounds.

46. See *Geofroy* v. *Riggs,* 133 U.S. 258, 267 (1890) quoted p. 188, this chapter; *The Cherokee Tobacco,* 78 U.S. (11 Wall.) 616, 620–1 (1871) ('It need hardly be said that a treaty cannot change the Constitution or be held valid if it be in violation of that instrument'); *Doe* v. *Braden,* 57 U.S. (16 How.) 635, 657 (1853); *Asakura* v. *Seattle,* 265 U.S. 332, 341 (1924). And see Calhoun, quoted in n. 54 to this chapter.

47. 252 U.S. at 433.

48. Judiciary Act of 1789, Ch. 20, 1 Stat. 73, 85–7. But Congress may have referred to a claim of procedural invalidity, that a treaty was not properly made by the President with the consent of two-thirds of the Senators present. Or Congress may have had in mind only limitations on the subject matter of treaties, discussed below. On the other hand, the cases dealing with this phrase in the Judiciary Act, long after it was settled that federal statutes could be declared invalid, gave no indication that the validity of a treaty was to be tested in ways different from those for testing the validity of a statute. See, e.g., *Erie R. R.* v. *Hamilton,* 248 U.S. 369 (1919).

49. For example, Secretary of State Hamilton Fish declined invitations for the United States to participate in international conferences on the enforcement of foreign judgments, in part because of supposed constitutional difficulties. Nadelmann, *Ignored State Interests: the Federal Government and International Efforts to Unify Rules of Private Law,* 102 U. PA. L. REV. 323–7 (1954). The State Department, U.S. negotiators, and the Senate, have all asserted that there are constitutional limitations on the treaty power, nn. 63, 67, 68 to this chapter; and see the reservations appended by the United States to its ratification of the International Covenant on Civil and Political Rights, particularly to Article 20, reprinted in 31 I.L.M. 645 (1992).

50. Compare, e.g., the statement of Manion supporting the amendment, *Bricker Hearings,* 1955, n. 40 to this chapter, with the statement of Perlman opposing the amendment, *id.*

51. *Reid* v. *Covert*, 354 U.S. 1, 16–17 (1957). That opinion also states: 'It would be manifestly contrary to the objectives of those who created the Constitution, as well as those who were responsible for the Bill of Rights—let alone alien to our entire constitutional history and tradition—to construe Article VI [the Supremacy Clause] as permitting the United States to exercise power under an international agreement without observing constitutional prohibitions. In effect, such construction would permit amendment of that document in a manner not sanctioned by Article V.' *Id.* at 17. Justice Black was writing for himself and three other Justices, but none of those who would have decided the case differently suggested that they disagreed with the views quoted. The Justices were fully aware of the recent Bricker Amendment, n. 40 to this chapter, and perhaps they seized an occasion to allay the fears that supported it.

    Justice Black continued: 'This Court has repeatedly taken the position that an Act of Congress, which must comply with the Constitution, is on a full parity with a treaty, and that when a statute which is subsequent in time is inconsistent with a treaty, the statute to the extent of conflict renders the treaty null. It would be completely anomalous to say that a treaty need not comply with the Constitution when such an agreement can be overridden by a statute that must conform to that instrument.' *Id.* at 18 (footnotes omitted). One might argue, however, that the anomaly is not as complete as Black said. A later inconsistent statute does not nullify a treaty but only prevents its implementation as domestic law; the doctrine Black cites, then, does not suggest that the Constitution limits also the international obligations that can be assumed. In fact, even as regards the domestic effect of treaties—to which, in general, the Bill of Rights is relevant—one might argue that although a treaty can be frustrated when the national legislature deems it desirable, it should not be invalidated by the courts at the behest of a private person to vindicate a private interest, even an interest that is protected by the Constitution in domestic contexts.

    A few months later the Supreme Court considered a claim that the Bill of Rights prohibited carrying out an agreement pursuant to the Japanese Security Treaty but found no violation. *Wilson* v. *Girard*, 354 U.S. 524 (1957).

52. See Ch. III, p. 80. Some of the prohibitions in Art. 1, sec. 9, were clearly not addressed to Congress, for example, that no officer of the United States may accept foreign office or employment without consent of Congress (*Cf.* 40 Op. Att'y Gen. 513 (1947)); or that 'No Money shall be drawn from the Treasury, but in Consequence of Appropriations made by Law'. Treaties are subject to the latter, p. 203 above; see Calhoun quoted in nn. 54, 78 to this chapter. Presumably, too, before 1808, a treaty could not have prohibited the 'Migration or Importation of such Persons as any of the States now existing shall think proper to admit'. Calhoun expressly concedes this (in language omitted from the quotation in n. 54).

53. Various statements going back to our early history are collected in H. Tucker, Limitations on the Treaty-Making Powers §§ 2–51 (1915), and Mikell, *The Extent of the Treaty-Making Power of the President and Senate of the United States,* 57 U.Pa.L.Rev. 435, 436–8 n. 1 (1909). Views of publicists on possible

limitations on the treaty power are collected in BUTLER, THE TREATY POWER
(n. 10 to Ch. I) Ch. IX; for those who believed there were limitations, see particularly 1 *id.* at 409, 413–15.

The debates on limitations do not distinguish between authority to make
treaties or to give them effect as law in the United States. As regards treaties
designed to have legal consequences in the United States, the distinction is academic. Presumably a treaty made in violation of any constitutional limitations
would still bind the United States internationally, since other states are not
bound to know our constitutional restrictions in detail. See p. 188 note, this
chapter.

54.   133 U.S. 258, 267 (1890). Compare John C. Calhoun: 'There appeared to him
but two restrictions on its exercise; the one derived from the nature of our
Government, and the other from that of the power itself. Most certainly all
grants of power under the Constitution must be controlled by that instrument;
for, having their existence from it, they must of necessity assume that form
which the Constitution has imposed. This is acknowledged to be true of the
legislative power, and it is doubtless equally so of the power to make treaties.
The limits of the former are exactly marked; it was necessary to prevent collision with similar co-existing State powers. This country is divided into many
distinct sovereignties. Exact enumeration here is necessary to prevent the most
dangerous consequences. The enumeration of legislative powers in the
Constitution has relation then, not to the treaty-power, but to the powers of
the State. In our relation to the rest of the world the case is reversed. Here the
States disappear. Divided within, we present the exterior of undivided sovereignty. The wisdom of the Constitution appears conspicuous. When enumeration was needed, there we find the powers enumerated and exactly defined;
when not, we do not find what would be vain and pernicious. Whatever, then,
concerns our foreign relations; whatever requires the consent of another
nation, belongs to the treaty power; can only be regulated by it; and it is competent to regulate all such subjects; provided, and here are its true limits, such
regulations are not inconsistent with the Constitution. If so they are void. No
treaty can alter the fabric of our Government, nor can it do that which the
Constitution has expressly forbad to be done; nor can it do that differently
which is directed to be done in a given mode, and all other modes prohibited.
For instance, the Constitution of the United States says, no money "shall be
drawn out of the Treasury but by an appropriation made by law". Of course
no subsidy can be granted without an act of law and a treaty of alliance could
not involve the country in war without the consent of this House . . . Besides
these Constitutional limits, the treaty power, like all powers, has others derived
from its object and nature. It has for its object contracts with foreign nations,
as the powers of Congress have for their object whatever can be done in relation to the powers delegated to it without the consent of foreign nations. Each
in its proper sphere operates with general influence; but when they became
erratic, then they were portentous and dangerous. A treaty never can legitimately do that which can be done by law; and the converse is also true. Suppose
the discriminating duties repealed on both sides by law, yet what is

effected by this treaty would not even then be done; the pledged faith would be wanting. . .' 29 ANNALS OF CONGRESS 531–2 (1816) [1815–1816]. And see n. 83 to this chapter.

55. See, e.g., *Holden* v. *Joy*, 4 U.S. (17 Wall.) 211, 243 (1872) ('all those objects which in the intercourse of nations, had usually been regarded as the proper subject of negotiation and treaty'); *Asakura* v. *Seattle*, 265 U.S. 332, 341 (1924) ('all proper subjects of negotiation between our government and other nations'); *Santovincenzo* v. *Egan*, 284 U.S. 30, 40 (1931) ('all subjects that properly pertain to our foreign relations'). Some general dicta suggesting limitations on the treaty power appear also in Taney's opinion in *The Passenger Cases*, 48 U.S. (7 How.) 283, 465 (1849), and in Daniel's opinion in *The License Cases*, 46 U.S. (5 How.) 504, 613 (1847). But compare Calhoun, nn. 54, 78 to this chapter.

56. In his Manual, quoted p. 189 note. By his final clause, a treaty cannot deal with matters that are within the enumerated powers of Congress (as to which the Constitution 'gave a participation to the House of Representatives'). By the third limitation, the treaty power could not deal with matters reserved to the states—presumably, those not expressly conferred upon the national government or some branch of it, principally upon Congress by the enumeration, in Art. I, sec. 8. If a treaty cannot deal with matters delegated to Congress, nor with matters not delegated to Congress, it can deal with very little, presumably only with matters that are in the President's sole domain apart from treaty. Joseph Story said: 'Mr. Jefferson seems at one time to have thought, that the constitution only meant to authorize the president and senate to carry into effect, by way of treaty, any power they might *constitutionally exercise.* At the same time, he admits, that he was sensible of the weak points of this position. 4 Jefferson's Corresp. 498. What are such powers given to the president and senate? Could they make appointments by treaty?' 2 STORY, COMMENTARIES (n. 3 to Ch. I) § 1508, at 376 n. 3 (emphasis in original). See n. 2 to this chapter.

57. This is the common interpretation of Jefferson's dictum, p. 189. Of course, if one recognizes that the Treaty Power is one of the powers delegated to the federal government, and that what comes within it is therefore not reserved to the states, one could accept Jefferson's statement to mean that there may be some areas specially reserved to the states even as regards the Treaty Power, for example, that a treaty cannot cede territory of a state without its consent. See pp. 188, 193.

Some—e.g., Finch, *The Need to Restrain the Treaty-Making Power of the United States Within Constitutional Limits,* 48 AM.J.INT'L L 57, 61 (1954)—contend that the majority of the Founding Fathers held the Jeffersonian view on this issue. Hayden, *The States' Rights Doctrine and the Treaty-Making Power,* 22 AM.HIST.REV. 556 (1917), presents evidence that the executive and legislative branches of the government in the period 1830–60 believed that treaties could not deal with matters not otherwise in the federal domain. A few commentators also adopted this narrow view of the Treaty Power. 5 MOORE DIGEST (n. 50 to Ch. II) 736; Mikell, *The Extent of the Treaty-Making Power of the President and Senate of the United States,* 57 U.PA.L.REV 435, 528, 535 (1909).

Even before the Supreme Court settled the issue, in *Missouri* v. *Holland*, pp. 189 *et seq.*, these authorities represented a minority view. Compilations of commentators may be found in Wright, *The Constitutionality of Treaties*, 13 Am.J.Int'l L. 242, 256 and n. 51, 257 (1919), and Wright (n. 3 to Ch. I) 92 and n. 97; see also 1 Butler, The Treaty Power (n. 10 to Ch. I) 4–6.

In general, those who claimed limitations implied in federalism did not claim that the states were intended to have a voice or a veto in regard to foreign relations. Their view, or feeling, was that although the states had no part in the conduct of foreign relations, treaties, *in their capacity as law of the land*, like other federal law, could not 'legislate' on matters reserved to the states. Strictly, the argument would not deny the treaty-makers power to incur international obligations on such matters, but they could not be made domestic law unless the states consented, or themselves acted to legislate them. (Compare the argument in *Ware* v. *Hylton*, 3 U.S. (3 Dall.) 199, 244–5 (1796).). Theoretically, then, such treaties could still be made by the United States with the consent of all of the states. Effectively, of course—especially as the nation grew and states multiplied—no one seriously suggested that procedure, and states' rights were asserted as obstacles to the Treaty Power in order to bar certain treaties from being made at all. It is noteworthy that these views found no support in Calhoun, a principal champion of states' rights. See nn. 54, 78 to this chapter.

58. 252 U.S. 416 (1920).
59. Ch. 145, 37 Stat. 847 (1913).
60. *United States* v. *Shauver*, 214 F. 154 (E.D. Ark.1914); *United States* v. *McCullagh*, 221 F. 288 (D.C.Kan. 1915). The courts also found that the birds were the property of the state and therefore immune to federal regulation.
    At the time, the Supreme Court was taking a narrow view of the powers of Congress, including its power to regulate commerce with foreign nations and among the several states. Compare, e.g., *Hammer* v. *Dagenhart*, 247 U.S. 251 (1918); Holmes, J. (and others) dissented. See Ch. III, p. 65.
61. With Great Britain, then responsible for Canada's foreign relations. See Treaty of Aug. 16, 1916, 39 Stat. 1702. Congress implemented it in ch. 128, 40 Stat. 755 (1918), as amended, 16 U.S.C. § 703 (1994).
62. 252 U.S. at 432. See also *Neely* v. *Henkel*, 180 U.S. 109, 121 (1901). Compare *Keller* v. *United States*, 213 U.S. 138, 147 (1909). See n. 111 to this chapter. Some implementations of treaties can be based also on the 'Offences clause', Ch. III, p. 68.
63. 252 U.S. at 432–434. I have omitted here, among other things, Holmes's reading of the Supremacy Clause, quoted p. 185 above. Holmes also rejected the argument that the treaty could not constitutionally deal with the birds because they were property of the state. 252 U.S. at 434. Compare the Treaty of 1854 with Great Britain, Article IV, which provided: 'The Government of the United States further engages to urge upon the State Government to secure to the subjects of Her Britannic Majesty the use of the several State canals on terms of equality with the inhabitants of the United States.' 1 Malloy, Treaties (n. 10 to Ch. I) 668, 671. Presumably the U.S. negotiators assumed that the United States could not promise such equal treatment because these were canals

belonging to the state and therefore could only 'urge upon the State Government'. Compare WRIGHT (n. 3 to Ch. I) 90. The 'property rights' of the state in its canals are no doubt different from its 'rights' in migratory birds (cf. Holmes, 252 U.S. at 434), but the Court would today doubtless approve a treaty dealing with state canals as well. See the cases approving federal regulation of state properties and activities, n. 44 to Ch. VI. The alleged limitation on ceding state territory, p. 188, above, is different, since that involves state territorial sovereignty, not its property.

64. I draw here on my article, *The Treaty Makers and the Law Makers: The Law of the Land and Foreign Relations*, 107 U.PA.L.REV. 903, 905–13 (1959).

65. The basic principles of *Missouri* v. *Holland* were laid down in the early years of the Republic. In 1796, in *Ware* v. *Hylton*, the Supreme Court held that a treaty with Great Britain reaffirming debts to British creditors superseded a Virginia statute (enacted during the War of Independence and valid when made) that canceled debts owed by its citizens to British subjects if they paid the sums into the state treasury. 3 U.S. (3 Dall.) 199 (1796). See Ch. IX, p. 298. John Marshall appeared as counsel; this was apparently Marshall's only appearance before the Supreme Court, and he lost the case. *Cf. Georgia* v. *Brailsford*, 3 U.S. (3 Dall.) 1 (1794).

66. See, e.g., *Hauenstein* v. *Lynham*, 100 U.S. 483 (1880); *Asakura* v. *Seattle*, 265 U.S. 332 (1924); and see the cases collected in 2 BUTLER, TREATY POWER (n. 10 to Ch. I) 11–13 nn. 1 and 2.

Treaties of Friendship, Commerce, and Navigation have conferred on nationals of another country even the right to practice some professions, although those professions are normally regulated by the states. See, e.g., the treaties with: Honduras, Dec. 7, 1927, Art. 1, 45 STAT. 2618, T.S. No. 764; Italy, Feb. 2, 1948, Art. I, 63 STAT. 2255, T.I.A.S. No. 1965 (all professions except law). In later treaties, however, there was a tendency to limit such reciprocal grants of national treatment for professionals. Thus, for example, although the treaty with Israel, Aug. 23, 1951, Art. VIII(2), [1954] 5 U.S.T. 550, T.I.A.S. No. 2948, as signed, provided that nationals of either party may not be barred from practicing the professions solely on account of alienage; and the treaty with Greece, Aug. 3, 1951, Art. XII(1), [1954] 5 U.S.T. 1829, T.I.A.S. No. 3057, would have guaranteed national and 'most favored nation' treatment to professions (with some exceptions), the Senate, in consenting to those treaties, declared these provisions inapplicable to 'professions which, because they involve the performance of functions in a public capacity, or in the interest of public health and safety, are state-licensed and reserved by statute or constitution exclusively to citizens of the country'. [1954] 5 U.S.T. at 603, 1918. It was not claimed, however, that such reservations were required by states' rights under the Constitution. The treaty with the Federal Republic of Germany, Oct. 29, 1954, Art. VIII(2), [1956] 7 U.S.T. 1839, T.I.A.S. No. 3593, extends the national treatment guarantee to 'scientific, educational, religious and philanthropic activities', but does not mention the professions.

Resident aliens may have a right under the U.S. Constitution to engage in at least some of these activities apart from treaty. See Ch. IX, pp. 293 *et seq.*

67. See, e.g., LEAGUE OF NATIONS DOC. No. C. 219 M. 142 (1927) IX, at 13; *id.* at
    No. C.F.A./2 Sess./P.V. 1 (1928), at 12; *id.* at No. A. 30 (1929) IX, at 7. This
    position was officially abandoned by the Department of State in 1932. BUREAU
    OF THE DISARMAMENT CONFERENCE, MINUTES OF THE 30TH MEETING, Nov. 18,
    1932, I, at 100. Of course, the notion that, apart from the treaty, manufacture
    even for interstate or foreign commerce is reserved to the states has long been
    exploded. See *United States* v. *Darby*, 312 U.S. 100 (1941); *Wickard* v. *Filburn*,
    317 U.S. 111 (1942). See generally Ch. III, pp. 65–7.

    Even early Attorneys-General apparently misconceived the supremacy of the
    Treaty Power to state laws. *Cf.* 1 OP.ATT'Y GEN. 275 (1819), 2 *id.* at 426, 431–2,
    436–7 (1831).

68. A United States reservation to the Charter of the OAS provided that nothing
    in the Charter should be considered as enlarging the powers of the federal gov-
    ernment or limiting the powers of the states with respect to any matter recog-
    nized under the Constitution as being within the reserved powers of the states.
    See [1951] 2 U.S.T. 2394, 2484, T.I.A.S. No. 2361. Whether this effectively
    reserved anything is open to question.

    The federal–state clause had early antecedents. Especially before the Civil
    War, the United States often made treaties dependent on state law: e.g., Article
    VII of the Treaty of 1853 with France, 10 Stat. 992, 1 MALLOY, TREATIES (n. 10
    to Ch. I) 528, 531, allowing French citizens to possess land equally with
    American citizens '[i]n all states of the Union whose existing laws permit it, so
    long and to the same extent as the said laws shall remain in force'. *Id.* at 996.
    As to other states 'the President engages to recommend to them the passage of
    such laws as may be necessary for conferring the right'. *Ibid.* But such defer-
    ence to state law was not constitutionally required, and increasingly other
    countries refused to accord it. For earlier discussions see, generally E. CORWIN,
    NATIONAL SUPREMACY: TREATY POWER v. STATE POWER (1913), and
    N. MITCHELL, STATE INTERESTS IN AMERICAN TREATIES, Chapter IV (1936).

    Compare the federal–state clause proposed by the United States in 1950 for
    the draft covenant on human rights: 'With respect to articles which are deter-
    mined in accordance with the constitutional processes of that State to be
    appropriate in whole or in part for action by the constituent states, provinces,
    or cantons, the federal government shall bring such articles, with favorable re-
    commendations to the notice of the authorities of the states, provinces or can-
    tons at the earliest possible moment.' Report of the Commission on Human
    Rights 6th Sess. at 59 (U.N.Doc.E/1681) (1950). The key word 'appropriate'
    was doubtless purposely ambiguous. The United States proposal was rejected.
    More recent federal–state clauses have admitted that they aim at a political
    rather than a constitutional obstacle.

    In ratifying the International Covenant on Civil and Political Rights, for
    example, the U.S. instrument of ratification declared, 'that the United States
    understands that this Covenant shall be implemented by the Federal
    Government to the extent that it exercises legislative and judicial jurisdiction
    over the matters covered therein and otherwise by the state and local govern-
    ments. The Federal Government shall take measures appropriate to the

Federal system to the end that the competent authorities of the state or local governments may take appropriate measures for the fulfillment of the Covenant.' International Covenant on Civil and Political Rights, Senate Treaty Doc. No. 95-2, Executive E, 999 U.N.T.S. 71. Adopted by U.N. General Assembly on Dec. 16, 1966; signed by United States on Oct. 5, 1977, transmitted to Senate Feb. 23, 1978, ratified by the United States on Sept. 8, 1992. See generally the reservations suggested by the Carter Administration and those attached by later Administrations to human rights covenants and conventions, p. 198 and n. 101 to this chapter.

69. See S.J.Res. 1, 83d Cong., 1st Sess., 99 CONG. REC. 6777 (1953). See the extended arguments on both sides in the various Bricker Hearings, n. 40 to this chapter, *1952 Hearings* 121, 132, 256, 313–16, 364, 413, 484, 486, 530; 1953 Hearings 924, 959, 994, 999, 1010, 1070, 1123, 1130, 1136; 1955 Hearings 185–6, 281–2, 297, 581–2. For articles supporting and opposing the amendment, see W. BISHOP, INTERNATIONAL LAW 112 n. 39 (3d edn. 1971). The Bricker Amendment would not have directly denied the treaty-makers the power to make such treaties but would have prevented their implementation in the United States; of course, responsible treaty-makers would not assume obligations that could not be carried out. See n. 40 to this chapter.

70. See, e.g., Henkin, *The Treaty Makers and the Law Makers: The Law of the Land and Foreign Relations,* 107 U.PA.L.REV. 903, 913 *et seq.* (1959).

71. See, e.g., *Jones* v. *Alfred H. Mayer Co.,* 392 U.S. 409 (1968); *Runyon* v. *McCrary,* 427 U.S. 160 (1976); *Patterson* v. *McLean Credit Union,* 491 U.S. 164 (1989); also *Katzenbach* v. *Morgan,* 384 U.S. 641 (1966); *South Carolina* v. *Katzenbach,* 383 U.S. 301 (1966).

72. See, e.g., *Geofroy* v. *Riggs,* quoted p. 188 above. Some may see support for that view by analogy from Art. IV, sec. 3, forbidding the alienation of state territory without its consent for the purpose of creating a new state. Compare also the provision in Art. I, sec. 8, cl. 17, requiring state cession of the territory to become the capital of the United States, and the consent of state legislatures to the purchase of places for the erection of various 'needful buildings'.

The 'Field view' has not been unanimously accepted and the issue has never been authoritatively resolved. Hamilton and Jefferson disagreed about it; Webster took the position later expressed by Justice Field, but Chancellor Kent disagreed. 'The better opinion would seem to be that such a power of cession does reside exclusively in the treaty-making power under the Constitution of the United States, although a sound discretion would forbid the exercise of it without the consent' of any state. (Quoted in T. WOOLSEY, INTERNATIONAL LAW 161 (6th edn. 1899). See also KENT COMMENTARIES (14th edn. 1896) 166–7, and note; 1 WILLOUGHBY (n. 3 to Ch. I) 576; CRANDALL, TREATIES (n. 1 above) § 99; 5 MOORE, DIGEST (n. 50 to Ch. II) 171–5. *Cf. Downes* v. *Bidwell,* 182 U.S. 244, 316 (1901) (opinion of White, C. J.). But compare *Worcester* v. *Georgia,* 31 U.S. (6 Pet.) 515 (1832) (upholding grant to Indian tribes of exclusive rights in reservations within state borders); 27 OP.ATT'Y GEN. 327 (1909) (consent of Minnesota not needed to treaty granting easement for dam). *Cf. United States*

v. *Rice*, 17 U.S. (4 Wheat.) 246 (1819) (while occupied by the British, Maine ceased to be part of the United States).

There would seem to be little doubt that in case of necessity, e.g., if the United States lost a war, a peace treaty ceding state territory could not be challenged on constitutional grounds. Letter of Jefferson, 1 AMERICAN STATE PAPERS: FOREIGN RELATIONS 252 (Gales and Seaton eds. 1833). (But international law since the U.N. Charter does not recognize title acquired by cession to an aggressor state. See CHARTER OF THE UNITED NATIONS, ART. 2(4), and Resolution on the Definition of Aggression, G.A.Res. 3314 (XXIX) 1974, Art. 5(3).)

In the only two cases in which the United States in fact ceded territory, the settlement of the Northeast boundary, and the 1842 treaty with Mexico, the consent of the relevant states was obtained. In the Webster–Ashburton Treaty, Aug. 9, 1842, (8 Stat. 572 (1846); T.S. No. 119), the consent of Massachusetts and Maine was obtained to a boundary settlement and a provision to compensate them was included in the treaty, but the settlement of a boundary dispute is not strictly a cession of territory, there being doubt whether the states in question had ever had title to it. *Cf. Lattimer* v. *Poteet*, 39 U.S. (14 Pet.) 4 (1840). The consent of Texas was not sought when the United States and Mexico settled the Chamizal dispute, though Senator Tower would have delayed until such consent was obtained. 109 CONG.REC. 24851 (1963). The legislature of New York authorized the Governor to cede to the United States jurisdiction over the territory of the U.N. headquarters, presumably in the expectation that the United States might in turn cede jurisdiction to the United Nations. N.Y. STATE LAW § 59–i—59–l, (McKinney 1995). Neither the governor nor the United States has executed such cession. To the extent that some cession by the United States is implicit in the terms of the U.N. Headquarters Agreement, June 26, 1947 (61 Stat. 3416 (1947); T.I.A.S. No. 1676; 11 U.N.T.S. 11), the consent of New York was in effect obtained through the act of its legislature.

73. See Field, J., p. 188 above. Compare Calhoun nn. 54, 78 to this chapter. But what is essential to a republican form of government is hardly agreed, and the Supreme Court has considered that to be a political question not for judicial determination or review. *Luther* v. *Borden*, 48 U.S. (7 How.) 1 (1849); also, e.g., *Pacific Telephone Co.* v. *Oregon*, 223 U.S. 118 (1912); *Ohio ex rel. Bryant* v. *Akron Metropolitan Park District*, 281 U.S. 74, 79–80 (1930); *cf. Baker* v. *Carr*, 369 U.S. 186 (1962), n. 76 to Ch. VI.

74. See HENKIN, ARMS CONTROL (n. 3 to Ch. VI) 34–6.

75. See Ch. VI, p. 166. HENKIN, ARMS CONTROL (n. 3 to Ch. VI) 33–7, 60–1.

In 1976, the Supreme Court held that Congress could not, under its Commerce Power, regulate the wages and hours of state employees because that invaded traditional powers of state government. *National League of Cities* v. *Usery*, 426 U.S. 833 (1976). It is not clear whether that limitation, a kind of 'invisible radiation' from the Tenth Amendment, would have been held to limit also the Treaty Power, but the Supreme Court reversed itself and overruled that decision. *Garcia* v. *San Antonio Metropolitan Transit Authority*, 469 U.S. 528 (1985).

In *New York* v. *United States*, 504 U.S. 144 (1992), however, the Supreme Court held that Congress could not direct state legislatures or state officials to act (though it could induce them to do so by grants of federal funds). Compare *F.E.R.C.* v. *Mississippi*, 456 U.S. 742 (1982). Presumably, the United States could not command state legislatures, or 'coopt' state officials by treaty, say a human rights convention that required state legislatures, as distinguished from Congress, to enact state procedures or provide state remedies, or an agreement that required state officials to participate in international peace-keeping operations.

The Headquarters Agreement with the United Nations seems to impose duties on both state and local officials. See Agreement Between the United States of America and the United Nations Regarding the Headquarters of the United Nations, June 26, 1947, §§ 3, 4(c), 11, 14, 16, 17, 18, 25, 61 STAT. 3416, T.I.A.S. No. 1676. International law, in effect, imposes duties on state officials to carry out the obligations of the United States that are in their care, for example, the responsibility to accord justice to aliens, but the international responsibility is on the United States, not on the states.

76. Jefferson's second clause would limit treaties to subjects 'which are usually regulated by treaty, and can not be otherwise regulated'. Later, perhaps echoing Jefferson, Chief Justice Taney said: 'The power to make treaties is given by the Constitution in general terms, without any description of the objects intended to be embraced by it; and, consequently, it was designed to include all those subjects, which in the ordinary intercourse of nations had usually been made subjects of negotiations and treaty; and which are consistent with the nature of our institutions, and the distribution of powers between the general and state governments.'

Holmes v. *Jennison*, 39 U.S. (14 Pet.) 540, 569 (1840). And compare *Holden* v. *Joy*, 84 U.S. (17 Wall.) 211, 243 (1872). See also Calhoun nn. 54, 78 to this chapter. We do not know whether Jefferson's or Taney's 'subjects' refer to the particular thing dealt with in the treaty (wheat, nuclear weapons), the rights or duties it establishes (quotas and prices, non-use of weapons), or its objective (trade, friendly relations, peace). Are human rights, for example, a new subject of international negotiation and agreement or the same subject that is involved in the principle of international law that a state may not deny justice to a foreign national? Or is the alleged object of new human rights covenants—friendly relations, international peace—as old as treaties? Taney's ambiguous tense is particularly troubling for it would seem to limit treaties of the United States to matters that had been the subject of treaty before 1787. It is difficult to find any basis for limiting the Treaty Power to eighteenth century needs, and the United States has in fact negotiated about subjects and for objectives not dreamed of by the Constitutional Fathers—e.g., the United Nations Charter and the Nuclear Test Ban. Nor is there any reason for reading the Constitution as limiting the Treaty Power to matters 'usually' regulated by treaty today. In any event, since the United States is hardly in the forefront seeking new subjects for international regulation, such a limitation would not in fact hamper the conduct of foreign affairs. It would not bar, in particular, U.S. accession to international human rights treaties: nations have been 'usually' regulating human rights by treaty at least since the 'minorities treaties' of a half century ago, surely in the U.N. Charter, in the various regional human rights arrangements now in effect, and in the human rights covenants and the numerous human rights conventions widely ratified. See COMPILATION OF HUMAN RIGHTS INSTRUMENTS, n. 92 to this chapter; and see my articles, *Rights: American and Human,* 79 COLUM.L.REV.. 405, 422–3 (1979), and *The Constitution, Treaties, and International Human Rights,* 116 U.PA.L.REV. 1012, 1019–22 (1968). See also p. 198 this chapter.

Like many issues about the treaty power this one, too, arose with the Jay Treaty, the first treaty concluded under the Constitution. See 1 BUTLER, THE TREATY POWER (n. 10 to Ch. I) 422 *et seq.*

77. See n. 48 to Ch. IV.

78. See Ch. III, p. 65. Calhoun made the point more than 150 years ago: 'If this be the true view of the treaty-making power, it may be truly said that its exercise has been one continual series of habitual and uninterrupted infringements of the Constitution. From the beginning and throughout the whole existence of the Federal Government it has been exercised constantly on commerce, navigation, and other delegated powers.' Letter of Secretary of State Calhoun to Wheaton, our minister to Prussia, June 28, 1844, reprinted in 5 MOORE, DIGEST (n. 50 to Ch. II) 164, WRIGHT (n. 3 to Ch. I) 344. He also stressed that a treaty could commit the United States to pay money, though he thought Congress could withhold the appropriation. See WRIGHT (n. 3 to Ch. I) 121–2. Earlier Calhoun had said: 'A treaty never can legitimately do that which can be done by law; and the converse is also true' (n. 54 to this chapter), but by that he apparently meant that treaties cannot legislate directly, they act only through international obligation.

Early in our history some treaties were rejected by the Senate because they dealt with matters deemed to belong exclusively to Congress. The Senate refused consent to a commercial treaty with the German States in 1844 because of lack of 'constitutional competency'. Senate Committee on Foreign Relations, *On The Convention With Prussia,* 8 REPORTS OF SENATE COMMITTEE ON FOREIGN RELATIONS, 28th Cong., 1st Sess. 36, 38 (1844), CRANDALL, TREATIES (n. 1 above) 189–90. There were questions in Congress about the validity of treaties that required an appropriation of funds. See, e.g., Speech of Albert Gallatin in the House of Representatives, March 9, 1796, 5 ANNALS OF CONG. 464, 467 (1796); see CRANDALL, TREATIES (n. 1 above) 164–82. Since then, treaties on these and other subjects as to which questions were raised have been made frequently by the United States.

79. See *Edwards* v. *Carter,* 580 F.2d 1055 (D.C. Cir.), *cert. denied,* 436 U.S. 907 (1978), upholding the Panama Canal Treaty over the objection that the Treaty disposed of property of the United States, a power given to Congress by Art. IV, sec. 3. See RESTATEMENT (n. 2 to Preface) § 303, Reporters' Note 2. See also *Curtis* v. *Carter,* Civil Action No. 77–2069, D.D.C., *aff'd,* No. 77–2105, D.C. Cir. Dec. 19, 1977, cited in *Dole* v. *Carter,* 569 F.2d 1109, 1110 (D.C. Cir. 1977), holding that the controversy regarding an executive agreement to return the Crown of St. Stephen to Hungary was non-justiciable.

80. Though wars are declared by Congress, and can be ended by Congress, no one has questioned the right to terminate war by treaty. The Wars of 1812 with England, of 1846 with Mexico, of 1898 with Spain were declared by Congress but terminated by treaty. Indeed, it has been argued that only a treaty (not an Act of Congress) can end war, presumably because international agreement is needed to end a war. That argument has not prevailed either. See Ch. III, p. 67, Ch. IV, p. 103 and n. 49 to Ch. IV.

   Jefferson privately considered his purchase of Louisiana 'an act beyond the Constitution' but hoped Congress would overlook 'metaphysical subtleties'. See T. BAILEY, A DIPLOMATIC HISTORY OF THE AMERICAN PEOPLE 111–12 (8th edn. 1968). It is not clear whether the constitutional difficulty was that Jefferson had agreed to buy it before he obtained Senate consent; that he thought the treaty-makers could not agree to spend money until Congress appropriated it; or that he doubted the power of the United States to acquire new territory. Compare HAYDEN, TREATIES (n. 8 above) 143; Deutsch, Constitutional Controversy over the Louisiana Purchase, 53 A.B.A.J. 50 (1967). The last two doubts, at least, seem unwarranted today. See n. 52 to Ch. III.

81. During more than 200 years Congress, and the House of Representatives in particular, has sought to offset its exclusion from treaty-making in various ways. Sometimes it was content to support the treaty-makers, often purporting to 'authorize' the negotiation of a treaty that would come to the Senate. For an early example, see Act of March 3, 1815, 13th Cong., 3d Sess., 3 Stat. 224, authorizing conventions to provide for reciprocal termination of alien discriminations. Compare ch. 1079, § 4, 32 Stat. 373 (1902); ch. 3621, § 4, 34 Stat. 28 (1906); WRIGHT (n. 3 to Ch. I) 281–2. In 1925 the House of Representatives resolved that it 'desires to express its cordial approval of the [World Court] and an earnest desire that the United States give early adherence' to it with certain reservations. The House also expressed 'its readiness to participate in the enactment of such legislation as will necessarily follow such approval'. H.R.Res. 426, 68 Cong., 2d Sess., 66 CONG.REC. 5404–05 (1925). Sometimes it sought to forestall a treaty by legislating: to preserve its authority over commerce it sought to enact the provisions of a treaty with Great Britain. See 5 MOORE, DIGEST (n. 50 to Ch. II) 223. On occasion it purported to prescribe that international agreements should go to Congress for approval rather than as a treaty to the Senate alone for its consent. Compare the United Nations Participation Act of 1945, 22 U.S.C. § 287d (1994), in regard to agreements under Article 43 of the U.N. Charter.

   That Congress cannot prevent the President from making a treaty, see, e.g., the famous remarks of Benjamin Curtis in his defense of Andrew Johnson at his impeachment trial. CONG.GLOBE (Supp.), 40th Cong., 2d Sess. 126–7 (1868).

82. See pp. 215 *et seq.*, and notes. Congress has also established for itself special procedures, notably 'fast track' consideration for trade agreements, to make approval by both Houses more expeditious and less onerous. See Trade Act of 1974, § 151. See Koh, *Congressional Controls on Presidential Trade*

Policymaking after INS v. *Chadha*, 18 N.Y.U. J. Int'l L. & Pol. 1191 (1986); Leebron, n. 185 to this chapter. But trade is still governed also by special provisions in treaties, such as 'most favored nation' clauses in Treaties of Friendship, Commerce, and Navigation. In 1961, Congress even directed the President to 'accelerate a program of negotiating treaties for commerce and trade, including tax treaties, which shall include provisions to encourage and facilitate the flow of private investment'. Foreign Assistance Act of 1961 § 601(b) (2), 75 Stat. 424, 438, as amended, 22 U.S.C. § 2351(b)(3) (1994).

83. See Justice Field, quoted p. 188 above. In fighting for ratification of the U.S. Constitution at the Virginia Convention, Madison responded to Patrick Henry's fears by saying of the Treaty Power: 'I do not conceive that power is given to the President and Senate to dismember the empire, or to alienate any great, essential right. I do not think the whole legislative authority have this power; the exercise of the power must be consistent with the object of the delegation.' 3 Elliot's Debates (n. 2 above) 501, 514. Also: 'A treaty to change the organization of the government, or to annihilate its sovereignty, to overturn its republican form, or to deprive it of its constitutional powers, would be void.' Story, Commentaries (n. 3 to Ch. I) § 1508. Calhoun said: 'It can enter into no stipulation calculated to change the character of the government; or to do that which can only be done by the constitution-making power; or which is inconsistent with the nature and structure of the government.' Discourse on Constitutional Government of the United States, 1 Works 203, quoted in 5 Moore, Digest (n. 50 to Ch. II) 166, Wright (n. 3 to Ch. I) 121–2. He also said: 'No treaty can alter the fabric of our Government, nor can it do that which the Constitution has expressly forbad to be done; nor can it do that differently which is directed to be done in a given mode, and all other modes prohibited', quoted in nn. 54, 78 to this chapter. Compare Willoughby quoted in n. 87 to this chapter, but he found that limitation not in the separation of powers but in a requirement of 'international concern', assuming apparently that no foreign government could possibly be interested in the distribution of our political powers or functions.

It has been assumed that constitutional limitations on delegation of legislative power apply as well to delegation by treaty. See Wright (n. 3 to Ch. I) 104 n. 48.

84. See n. 57 to this chapter.

85. International law and practice know no such limitations. See 1 Oppenheim, International Law § 588 (Jennings & Watts, 9th edn. 1992). The only subject matter 'limitation' now accepted lies in the principle of *jus cogens*. The Vienna Convention on the Law of Treaties provides: a treaty is void if, at the time of its conclusion, it conflicts with a peremptory norm of general international law (Article 53); also Article 64; see 63 Am.J.Int'l L. at 891. See also Restatement (n. 2 to Preface) § 331(2)(b). The U.N. Charter itself provides that its provisions shall prevail over any other treaty. Charter of the United Nations, Article 103.

86. See Bricker Hearings, 1953, nn. 40 and 69 to this chapter; *American Bar Association, Report of the Standing Committee on Peace and Law Through*

United Nations: Human Rights Conventions and Recommendations, 1 INT'L LAWYER 600 (1967); *Hearings on Human Rights Conventions Before a Subcommittee of the Senate Committee on Foreign Relations*, 90th Cong., 1st Sess. (1967).

87. The antecedents of the 'doctrine' are not wholly clear, but its modern underpinnings are remarks that sprang full-grown from the mouth and mind of Charles Evans Hughes in 1929: 'I should not care to voice any opinion as to an implied limitation on the treaty-making power. The Supreme Court has expressed a doubt whether there could be any such. That is, the doubt has been expressed in one of its opinions. But if there is a limitation to be implied, I should say it might be found in the nature of the treaty-making power. What is the power to make a treaty? What is the object of the power? The normal scope of the power can be found in the appropriate object of the power. The power is to deal with foreign nations with regard to matters of international concern. It is not a power intended to be exercised, it may be assumed, with respect to matters that have no relation to international concerns. . . . So I come back to the suggestion I made at the start, that this is a sovereign nation; from my point of view the nation has the power to make any agreement whatever in a constitutional manner that relates to the conduct of our international relations, unless there can be found some express prohibition in the Constitution, and I am not aware of any which would in any way detract from the power as I have defined it in connection with our relations with other governments. But if we attempted to use the treaty-making power to deal with matters which did not pertain to our external relations but to control matters which normally and appropriately were within the local jurisdictions of the states, then I again say there might be ground for implying a limitation upon the treaty-making power that it is intended for the purpose of having treaties made relating to foreign affairs and not to make laws for the people of the United States in their internal concerns through the exercise of the asserted treaty-making power.' 23 PROC.AM.SOC'Y INT'L L. 194–6 (1929).

Hughes spoke to the annual meeting of the American Society of International Law, apparently attempting to justify a position taken earlier by the U.S. Delegation (which he had headed) to the Sixth International Conference of American States, that, in part on constitutional grounds, the United States 'could not join' in a treaty to establish uniform principles of private international law. A year earlier he had attempted to justify that position in words that smacked of the Tenth Amendment, which suggests that he had not assimilated or accepted the implications of *Missouri* v. *Holland*. See Hughes, *The Outlook for Pan Americanism—Some Observations on the Sixth International Conference of American States*, 22 PROC.AM.SOC'Y INT'L L. 1, 12 (1928). His 1929 statement also had some such undertones but this time he suggested that there might be a different constitutional limitation: a treaty is valid only if it deals with a matter of 'international concern'.

Surely the case that inspired Hughes's remarks hardly affords a realistic basis for his expressed concern. Today, few would accept—on any theory—the conclusion he was justifying, that the United States could not adhere to a convention establishing uniform principles of private international law. Congress authorized the United States to join the Hague Conference on Private International Law in 1963, Pub. L. 88–244, §1, Dec. 30, 1963, 77 Stat. 775, codified at 22 U.S.C. § 269g (1994). Today, principles of conflicts of law between nations are probably subject to federal, not state, law, precisely because they affect the foreign relations of the United States. See *Banco Nacional de Cuba* v. *Sabbatino*, 376 U.S. 398, 425–6 (1964); Henkin, *The Foreign Affairs Power of the Federal Courts: Sabbatino*, 64 COLUM.L.REV. 805, 820–1 n. 51 (1964).

Hughes was not speaking *ex cathedra,* either as Secretary of State (which he had long ceased to be) or as Chief Justice (which he had been designated but had not yet become). Much of his argument dealt with the political advisability of making treaties on some subjects rather than with constitutional power to make them. But, perhaps because he became Chief Justice shortly thereafter; perhaps because the constitutional law of foreign relations has so little authoritative, hard, 'case' law and is driven to rely on other 'authority'; perhaps because some were eagerly seeking constitutional limitations on the Treaty Power—the Hughes address was quickly and uncritically seized, shorn of Hughes's own *caveats* and limitations, and accepted as authority. It was incorporated in the case books, taught to students, invoked in a lower court opinion (*Power Authority* v. *Federal Power Commission,* n. 29 to this chapter), enshrined, in first place and in black letters, in the Restatement (Second) of the Law of United States Foreign Relations, Section 117(1). That position was reversed and abandoned in the latest Restatement. See RESTATEMENT (n. 2 to Preface) § 302, Comment *c* and Reporters' Note 2.

One might perhaps consider Jefferson one of the ancestors of that doctrine. Limitations on the subject matter of treaties are implied in Jefferson's suggestion that treaties can properly deal only with matters 'usually regulated by treaty', or Taney's statement that they can deal only with subjects 'which in the ordinary intercourse of nations had usually been made subjects of negotiations and treaty'. See n. 76 above. But Jefferson's requirement that a treaty 'concern the other nation' seems to imply only that there must be a bona fide contract, not that it must deal with a subject that is 'the other nation's business'. See, generally, Henkin, *The Constitution, Treaties, and International Human Rights,* 116 U.PA.L.REV. 1012, 1024–30 (1968).

Willoughby might also be authority for the Hughes view. See WILLOUGHBY (n. 3 to Ch. I) § 314. Some of the examples Willoughby lists as inappropriate for treaties have in fact been the subject of bona fide treaties: for example, the treatment of aliens in another country is the subject of the minority treaties of post-First World War, of the 1951 Convention relating to the Status of Refugees, of the numerous human rights covenants and conventions. And governments have long sought to determine the political character of other governments, not only in peace treaties: for example, the International Covenant on Civil and Political Rights, Article 25, in effect obligates states to establish democracy and democratic institutions.

88. Some have confused the 'doctrine' of 'international concern' and 'relation to

American foreign policy', with a very different concept, claiming, in effect, that a treaty cannot deal with matters that are 'essentially within the domestic jurisdiction of the United States'. See American Bar Association, Report of the Standing Committee on Peace and Law Through United Nations: Human Rights Conventions and Recommendations, 1 Int'l Lawyer 600, 601 (1967). (Compare the U.S. reservation to its acceptance of the compulsory jurisdiction of the International Court of Justice, 61 Stat. 1218 (1946), T.I.A.S. No. 1598, n. 24 to Ch. VII; cf. U.N. Charter Art. 2(7).) 'Domestic jurisdiction' is unknown to U.S. constitutional doctrine but it is well known to international law. Under international law, a matter is deemed to be within a country's domestic jurisdiction if it is not governed by customary international law or by any treaty obligation. What is within the domestic jurisdiction of a state in the absence of treaty ceases to be so when that state enters into an international agreement on the subject. See Advisory Opinion on Nationality Decrees Issued in Tunis and Morocco, [1923] P.C.I.J. ser. B, No. 4. To suggest that the Constitution forbids treaties as to matters that are 'essentially within the domestic jurisdiction of the United States', is to bar any treaty on any matter not already governed by customary international law or previous agreement. That would invalidate common provisions in common treaties of commerce, friendship and navigation, in treaties on disarmament, extradition, nationality, the prevention of double taxation and a host of other subjects. It would prevent the United States from participating in the development of new law by multilateral convention—the principal form of international legislation today. It seems patently absurd. In any event, it is a limitation which no one has suggested before, and has no basis anywhere, surely not in Hughes's 'international concern'. It cannot be derived from the character and purpose of the Treaty Power as an instrument of foreign relations; it has no support even in the early writings about the Constitution; it is contradicted by the history of U.S. treaty practice. In the absence of treaty, this country's armaments, its nationality laws, its immigration policies, all lie within its domestic jurisdiction; the United States has had agreements on these subjects of international concern from the beginning of its history.

In part, responsibility for this confusion may be traced to old 'Circular 175' promulgated by Secretary of State Dulles, apparently in an effort to console the Bricker forces after the defeat of their efforts to amend the Constitution. The Circular—an instruction to the officers of the State Department—provided: 'Treaties should be designed to promote United States interests by securing action by foreign governments in a way deemed advantageous to the United States. Treaties are not to be used as a device for the purposes of affecting internal social changes or to try to circumvent the constitutional procedures established in relation to what are essentially matters of domestic concern.'

The Circular, it should be noted, spoke not of 'domestic jurisdiction' but of 'domestic concern'. The Circular may have used 'domestic concern' in contradistinction to Hughes's 'international concern', but that is a misleading play on words. 'Domestic concern' and 'international concern' are not closed, exclusive categories. To say that something is essentially a matter of domestic concern may be merely a way of expressing a determination not to negotiate about it. But what is essentially a matter of 'domestic concern' becomes a matter of 'international concern' if nations do, in fact, decide to bargain about it. In any event the Circular announced policy, not constitutional doctrine. Indeed, it was probably designed to impose as policy what the Bricker Amendment would have written into the Constitution, but which, it was realized, was not the law of the Constitution unamended. The quoted language in the Circular has since been eliminated. Compare Dulles, *Bricker Hearings,* 1953, 824–5; see n. 40 to this chapter.

89.   See RESTATEMENT (n. 2 to Preface) § 302, Comment *c* and Reporters' Note 2.

90.   Compare the Convention between the American Republics Regarding the Status of Aliens in their Respective Territories, Feb. 20, 1928, 46 Stat. 2753, T.S.No.815. Even when United States law already conforms to the treaty obligation, the treaty makes the domestic law a matter of international concern and subjects it to international scrutiny; the United States will not henceforth be free to modify its domestic law at will.

91.   The lack of 'international concern' was also raised as an objection to the Senate Reservation to the Niagara treaty, n. 29 above.

92.   There are now substantial volumes of such international agreements, e.g., I. BROWNLIE (ed.), BASIC DOCUMENTS ON HUMAN RIGHTS (3d edn. 1993); COUNCIL OF EUROPE, HUMAN RIGHTS IN INTERNATIONAL LAW: BASIC TEXTS (1985); R. LILLICH (ed.), INTERNATIONAL HUMAN RIGHTS INSTRUMENTS: A COMPILATION, (1983, with periodic supplements); United Nations, COMPILATION OF HUMAN RIGHTS INSTRUMENTS, Publication Sales No. E-88, ST/HR/1. Geneva: United Nations, 1988; U.S. Congress, Committee on Foreign Affairs. HUMAN RIGHTS DOCUMENTS, Washington D.C.; Government Printing Office (1983).

Modern multilateral treaties sometimes deal with matters that are not the concern of other nations in some narrow sense; even the U.N. Charter can be said to make many once domestic or bilateral matters into everybody's business, for example, threats to peace in some distant place, or colonialism in Asia or Africa, or apartheid in South Africa.

93.   International agreements, like private contracts, may be parallel as well as reciprocal: parties may bind themselves to do, or not to do, for each other; or a nation may undertake to do or not to do in its own land and to its own people, in consideration of a similar (or some other) undertaking by the other party. Such agreements are not novel phenomena or made only by other countries; the United States, too, has undertaken obligations in regard to its own citizens or inhabitants and to domestic activities. When we acquired Louisiana, Florida, Mexico, Alaska, we promised the ceding country that we would continue to give the inhabitants, after they become ours, rights of citizenship and other personal liberties. See, e.g., CRANDALL, TREATIES (n. 1 above) 210–12. The United States adhered to ILO Conventions establishing minimum labor standards for some of its citizens, e.g., the conventions relating to masters and seamen. (Conventions with Members of the International Labor Organization, Oct. 24, 1936, 54 Stat. 1683, 1693, 1705, T.S.No.950, 951, 952.) It agreed to

control opium within the United States. Convention for the Suppression of the Abuse of Opium, Jan. 23, 1912, 38 Stat. 1912, T.S.No.612, and Convention for Limiting the Manufacture and Regulating the Distribution of Narcotic Drugs, July 13, 1931, 48 Stat. 1543, T.S.No.863, implemented by the Opium Poppy Control Act, 56 Stat. 1045 (1942), 21 U.S.C. § 188 (1970)); to apply to its own vessels accepted load lines and common standards for safety at sea (International Load Line Convention, July 5, 1930, 47 Stat. 2228, T.S.No.858; International Convention and Regulation for Promoting Safety of Life at Sea, June 10, 1948 [1952] 3 U.S.T. & O.I.A. 3450, T.I.A.S.No.2495, replacing the Convention of May 31, 1929, 50 Stat. 1121, T.S.No.910); not to bring to trial an American soldier if he had been tried for the same offense by the courts of an allied NATO country (NATO Status of Forces Agreement, June 19, 1951, art. VII, para. 8 [1953] 2 U.S.T. & O.I.A. 1792, T.I.A.S.No.2846); to limit its taxes on U.S. citizens. (See, e.g., Convention with France about Double Taxation and Fiscal Assistance, Oct. 18, 1946, Supplementary Protocol, May 17, 1948, art. 5, 64 Stat. B3, T.I.A.S.No.1982.) And the United States has agreed to limit its own armaments; it continues to strive for far-reaching controls on arms and armies, which would impose strict limitations on activities by U.S. inhabitants within the United States; it sought, for years, agreement for the control of atomic energy that would have governed strictly many domestic activities by U.S. inhabitants in the United States. See HENKIN, ARMS CONTROL (n. 3 to Ch. VI) 4–9, 104, 161–2 n. 5.

In part, the United States adheres to human rights conventions because it is concerned to maintain leadership in international affairs by proving that it deserves it, by its behavior at home and by its willingness to join in cooperative international efforts to promote respect for human rights elsewhere. In larger part, the United States is concerned to see minimum standards of constitutionalism, democracy, and human rights observed in other countries in order to safeguard our own standards, to promote conditions that are conducive to U.S. prosperity and to U.S. interests in international peace and security. Of obvious 'international concern' to this country, for example, would be an international convention fixing high labor standards or outlawing slavery, or forced labor, or child labor, if it were adopted by the nations with which the United States competes to sell manufactured goods in the world markets. The condition of human rights in other countries and contexts is also of authentic international concern for the United States, witness the struggle by all states to bring an end to apartheid in South Africa, events not long ago in Communist countries, at various times in Argentina, in Cambodia, in Haiti, in Uganda under Idi Amin, in Iraq after the Gulf War, in the former Yugoslavia, in other actual or potential situations where the treatment of individuals or of minority groups is relevant to war and peace, international order, and stability.

The United States does not adhere to human rights covenants and conventions in order to distort or circumvent our constitutional system, to legislate larger guarantees of human rights for its own citizens by treaty rather than by act of Congress, or to take additional matters from the states into the federal domain; the United States adheres to such treaties in order to modify the behavior of other governments in ways that further U.S. interests. To have other nations undertake to observe higher standards and to give the United States the right to request and help monitor compliance with those standards, the United States undertakes to apply similar standards in the United States and to recognize the right of other nations to request and observe U.S. compliance.

94. *Foster* v. *Neilson*, 27 U.S. (2 Pet.) 253, 314 (1829). Compare Justice Miller in *Head Money Cases*, 112 U.S. 580, 598 (1884): 'A treaty is primarily a compact between independent nations . . . But a treaty may also contain provisions which confer certain rights upon the citizens or subjects of one of the nations residing in the territorial limits of the other, which partake of the nature of municipal law, and which are capable of enforcement as between private parties in the courts of the country. An illustration of this character is found in treaties which regulate the mutual rights of citizens and subjects of the contracting nations in regard to rights of property by descent or inheritance, when the individuals concerned are aliens.'

95. A treaty is not law of the land until proclaimed and the persons affected given notice of it. See REV.STAT. § 210; cf. *Haver* v. *Yaker*, 76 U.S. (9 Wall.) 32 (1869). Hence, a secret treaty cannot be law of the land while it is secret. Compare nn. 9, 10 to this chapter. A self-executing treaty when proclaimed, or a non-self-executing treaty when implemented by Congress, supersedes state law automatically, without awaiting its repeal or other action by the states. Compare *Ware* v. *Hylton*, 3 U.S. (3 Dall.) 199, 236–7 (1796) (Chase, J.)

It has sometimes been suggested that the obligations assumed by other nations in a treaty with the United States are also the law of this land and therefore enforceable against them by claimants in U.S. courts. That interpretation of the Supremacy Clause is not supported by its history, and I know of no authority for it. But compare the cases suggesting that there is an exception to the Act of State doctrine for acts of a foreign state inconsistent with a treaty obligation to the United States, e.g., *Kalamazoo Spice Extraction Co.* v. *Government of Socialist Ethiopia*, 729 F.2d 422 (6th Cir. 1984), upholding a counterclaim for compensation for expropriation by the Ethiopian government, pursuant to a Treaty of Friendship, Commerce, and Navigation between Ethiopia and the United States. See n. 21 to Ch. V.

96. The Bricker Amendment, p. 192 above, would have rendered all treaties non-self-executing and denied Congress the power to implement certain treaties in domestic law; that would have effectively prevented the federal government from making them.

97. That was the purpose of the provision in Article IV that the treaty should be 'carried out by the Parties in accordance with their respective constitutional processes'. North Atlantic Treaty, April 4, 1949, 63 Stat. 2241, 2246, T.I.A.S. No. 1964.

98. See C. Vazquez, *The Four Doctrines of Self-Executing Treaties*, 89 AM. J. INT'L L. 695 (1995).

99. See Damrosch, *The Role of the United States Senate Concerning 'Self-*

Executing' and 'Non-Self-Executing' Treaties, 67 CHI.-KENT L. REV. 515 (1991). And see n. 101 to this chapter.

100. See, e.g., RESTATEMENT (n. 2 to Preface) § 114(4). In an article I wrote in 1956, *The Treaty Makers and the Law Makers: The Niagara Power Reservation,* 56 COLUM. L. REV. 1151, I argued for the validity and propriety of a provision with that consequence in the Niagara Power Treaty. I adhere to that view as regards that case, or any other special case where giving effect to a treaty as law might complicate the legislative process or have other highly undesirable consequences. But if what I wrote can be read to support a general policy of declaring all treaties, or a category of treaties, to be non-self-executing, I do not hold that view.

It has been suggested that in the absence of a clear intention to that effect, a multilateral treaty should not readily be held to be self-executing in view of the lack of mutuality between the United States and countries that do not recognize treaties as self-executing. *U.S.* v. *Postal,* 589 F.2d 862, 878 (5th Cir. 1979). The Reporters to the Restatement said: 'That suggestion seems misconceived. A treaty is generally binding on states parties from the time it comes into force for them, whether or not it is self-executing. If a treaty is not self-executing for a state party, that state is obliged to implement it promptly, and failure to do so would render it in default on its treaty obligations. The purpose of having a treaty self-executing is to make it easier for the United States to carry out its international undertakings. It is not clear why the fact that some other states do not consider treaties as self-executing should govern United States practice. In fact, few other states distinguish between self-executing and non-self-executing treaties; and whether or not a treaty or provision will be self-executing for a particular state party, and any lack of mutuality in this respect, have generally not been considerations when states enter into treaty obligations, whether multilateral or bilateral. If, in some instance, a state party fails to take any necessary steps to implement a treaty, and as a result comes into material default in its obligations to the United States, the United States may suspend or terminate its obligation under the treaty, whether or not the treaty is self-executing in the United States. RESTATEMENT (n. 2 to Preface) § 111, Reporters' Note 5.

101. See, generally, Henkin, *Niagara* (n. 29 above) 1169 *et seq.*

To help defeat the Bricker Amendment, the Eisenhower Administration announced that it would not seek Senate action on the Genocide Convention that had languished in the Senate since 1949, and that it would not ratify other human rights covenants. 32 DEP'T STATE BULL. 820, 822 (1955). (Compare also U.S. DEP'T OF STATE, DEP'T CIR. No. 175 (1955), reprinted in 50 AM.J.INT'L L. 784 (1956), since revised.) When the Kennedy Administration, reversing the Eisenhower policy, sent up three modest covenants (on slavery, forced labor, political rights of women), the Senate acted only on the first, the last two remaining on the shelf of the Foreign Relations Committee. *Cf.* 113 CONG.REC. 8332 (1967). (Inexplicably, in 1968 the United States, with unanimous Senate consent, ratified a protocol and thereby in effect adhered to the Convention Relating to the Status of Refugees

[1968] 19 U.S.T. 6223; T.I.A.S. No. 6577; perhaps this was seen as relating largely to aliens, and requiring nothing that the United States was not already doing.) The Nixon Administration requested consent to ratification of the Genocide Convention (Convention on the Prevention and Punishment of the Crime of Genocide, Dec. 9, 1948, 78 U.N.T.S. 277) and the Senate Foreign Relations Committee recommended it, S.Exec.Rep. No. 92–6, 92nd Cong., 1st Sess. (1971), but the Senate did not act. The Carter Administration sent to the Senate five major human rights agreements, and did so recommending major reservations, understandings, and declarations ; nevertheless, the Senate failed to act on those treaties and Presidents did not press for action. During the Reagan Presidency, the Genocide Convention was finally approved by the Senate, with several reservations and declarations. In 1990, the Senate consented to ratification of the Convention against Torture and Other Cruel, Inhuman or Degrading Treatment or Punishment, Dec. 10 1984, G.A.Res. 39/46, 39 U.N. GAOR Supp. (No. 51) at 197, U.N. Doc. A/39/51 (1985) reprinted in 23 I.L.M. 1027 (1984), and in 1992 to the International Covenant on Civil and Political Rights, Dec. 16, 1966, 999 U.N.T.S. 171, both with reservations, understandings, and declarations, not unlike those the Carter Administration had suggested. The Senate gave consent to the International Convention on the Elimination of all Forms of Racial Discrimination, Dec. 21, 1965, 660 U.N.T.S. 195, and the United States ratified it in 1994. The United States also ratified the Convention against Torture in 1994. Other conventions await Senate consent.

Ratification of the International Covenant on Civil and Political Rights and the Racial Convention include declarations that they should not be self-executing; such a declaration is expected to be attached also to the Convention on Discrimination against Women and the American Convention. In consenting to the ratification of the Genocide and the Torture Conventions, the Senate declared that the President should not deposit the instrument of ratification until Congress had enacted the legislation rendering genocide (or torture) criminal violations in the United States.

Once the House sought to treat a treaty as non-self-executing but the Senate disagreed. 29 Annals of Congress 1022, 1057 [1815–1816].

102. See, e.g., Henkin, *U.S. Ratification of Human Rights Conventions: the Ghost of Senator Bricker,* 89 Am. J. Int'l L. 341 (1995). See Human Rights Committee, General Comment No. 24, U.N. Doc. CCPR/C/21/Rev. 1/Add. 6 (1994).

103. It was once suggested that treaties that deal with matters on which Congress could legislate cannot be self-executing. Compare Corwin, The President (n. 5 to Intro. to Pt. II) 225. There is no basis for that view, and it does not reflect constitutional practice. In the numerous instances in which acts of Congress were held to supersede treaty provisions (pp. 209–10 below), there was no suggestion that the treaty was not law anyhow since it could not be self-executing. (The doctrine that statutes and self-executing treaties have equal stature, and the later in time prevails, itself contradicts this suggestion.) Today, since any subject of a treaty is probably also within Congressional power (p. 198 above), the suggestion would virtually eliminate self-executing treaties. But Congress has often insisted that treaties modifying tariffs are not

self-executing and require Congressional implementation, and the Executive has generally acquiesced. CRANDALL, TREATIES (n. 1 above) 195–200; see n. 116 to this chapter. In recent years, tariffs have been the subject of executive agreements authorized by Congress or requiring Congressional implementation. See below, p. 215.

104. *Turner* v. *American Baptist Missionary Union*, 24 F.Cas. 344 (No. 14251) (C.C.Mich.1852). But the treaty can apparently serve as legislation authorizing the subsequent appropriation. See n. 109 to this chapter.

105. Before the Constitution, a Philadelphia court convicted a person for assaulting the French Consul-General, on the ground that he had violated the law of nations which was part of the municipal law of Philadelphia. *Respublica* v. *De Longchamps*, 1 Dall. 111 (Pa. O. & T. 1784). It is now accepted that there is no federal common law of crimes, and such an offense could not be punished in the federal courts unless defined by Congress. Compare *United States* v. *Hudson & Goodwin*, 11 U.S. (7 Cranch) 32 (1812); *United States* v. *Coolidge*, 14 U.S. (1 Wheat.) 415 (1816); *cf. The Estrella*, 17 U.S. (4 Wheat.) 298 (1819). But see Warren, *New Light on the History of the Federal Judiciary Act of 1789*, 37 HARV.L.REV. 49, 73 (1923); also 2 MOORE, DIGEST (n. 50 to Ch. II) 978.

In *Cotzbausen* v. *Nazro*, 107 U.S. 215 (1882), a provision in the Treaty of Berne that certain articles 'shall not be admitted for conveyance by the post' was said to constitute law of the United States prohibiting such importation, within the meaning of a statute providing criminal penalties and forfeiture for bringing articles into the United States 'contrary to law'. But the case did not involve criminal prosecution of the importer; it only affirmed dismissal of a suit for conversion brought by the importer against the customs officer who had forfeited the article.

106. In his testimony before the Senate Foreign Relations Committee on the North Atlantic Treaty, Secretary of State Acheson asserted that the treaty would not put the United States automatically into war. 'Under our Constitution, the Congress alone has the power to declare war.' Hearings on the North Atlantic Treaty Before the Senate Committee on Foreign Relations, 81st Cong., 1st Sess., pt. 1 at 11 (1949). *Cf.* D. ACHESON, PRESENT AT THE CREATION (1969) 2823. See Calhoun, n. 54 above. The War Powers Resolution, Ch. IV, p. 105, includes a provision that 'authority to introduce the Armed Forces of the United States in hostilities or in any such situation shall not be inferred . . . from any treaty heretofore or hereafter ratified unless such treaty is implemented by legislation specifically authorizing the introduction of the Armed Forces . . . and specifically exempting the introduction of such Armed Forces from compliance with the provisions of this Act. . . No treaty in force at the time of the enactment of this Act shall be construed as specific statutory authorization for, or a specific exemption permitting, the introduction of the Armed Forces of the United States in hostilities or in any such situation.'

In *Edwards* v. *Carter*, n. 79 above, the Court of Appeals rejected the argument that the treaty-makers could not dispose of U.S. property by self-executing treaty. Compare *Curtis* v. *Carter*, cited there.

107. Parties to a treaty are presumably masters as to what they wish to agree to

and what they consider an obligation: undertakings that might seem illusory in a private contract might yet serve the purposes of states and constitute a treaty 'undertaking'. See Henkin, *Niagara* (n. 29 above) 1164–9. Compare the provisions in older extradition treaties of the United States that 'the executive authority of each shall have the power to deliver [their own nationals] up, if in its discretion, it be deemed proper to do so'. The Supreme Court has implied that though that language contained no binding obligation, such a provision gave the President power to extradite U.S. citizens which he would not otherwise have. See *Valentine* v. *United States ex rel. Neidecker*, 299 U.S. 5, 12–16 (1936); (In *Neidecker*, however, the Court denied the President's power because the treaty in question in the case did not contain such a provision but provided only that 'Neither of the contracting parties shall be bound to deliver up its own citizens'.)

108. Apparently the question has never been raised, but in principle legislation to implement a treaty might cease to be valid if the treaty lost its effect, unless the legislation found support in other powers of Congress. *Cf. United States* v. *Chambers*, 291 U.S. 217, 222–6 (1934), and *United States* v. *Constantine*, 296 U.S. 287 (1935), holding the National Prohibition Act and related taxes inoperative when the Eighteenth Amendment which supported them was repealed. Today, other powers of Congress would be ample for any such situation (see generally Ch. III), but even where the legislation is not in terms dependent on an effective treaty, an argument might be made that the statute should fall because Congress intended to legislate only on the basis of a treaty obligation.

A treaty that is contrary to a principle of international law that has the character of *jus cogens*—a superior, peremptory norm—is void under international law. RESTATEMENT (n. 2 to Preface) § 331(2)(b). Therefore, such a treaty is not the law of the United States and would not be given effect by the courts. See n. 136 to this chapter.

That there are principles of customary law that are *jus cogens* is accepted, but there has been no agreement as to which principles of international law have that character. It is commonly accepted that the law of the Charter outlawing the use of force is *jus cogens*, and a treaty of the United States contrary to that Charter would therefore be void. See RESTATEMENT (n. 2 to Preface) § 102, comment *k*. By its own terms, moreover, the Charter declares that it supersedes any treaty contrary to its terms. See U.N. Charter, Article 103. I am aware of no case in the United States that has given effect to the doctrine of *jus cogens*.

109. Such provisions have rarely come to court, but it is commonly accepted that they will be given effect. The provision in the Webster–Ashburton Treaty that money shall be paid to Massachusetts and Maine (for their consent to a boundary settlement), n. 72 to this chapter, was apparently treated as an authorization to appropriate, and money was later appropriated. 5 Stat. 623 (1850). See Henkin, *Niagara* (n. 29 above) 1166–7, n. 104 above. Compare Calhoun, n. 54 to this chapter. Other non-contractual provisions—e.g., that particular arbitration agreements pursuant to a general arbitration conven-

tion shall require the consent of the Senate, pp. 160–7 above, or that officials appointed pursuant to a treaty shall require Senate confirmation (n. 29 to this chapter), have also been honored by the Executive, but it is not clear whether because they were treated as law of the land or as conditions to Senate consent which had to be complied with. But *cf. Power Authority* v. *Federal Power Comm.*, n. 29, this chapter.

110.   *Downes* v. *Bidwell*, 182 U.S. 244 (1901); *Dorr* v. *United States*, 195 U.S. 138, 143 (1904); see Henkin, *Niagara* (n. 29 above) 1174–5. See Ch. IX, p. 297. See the Senate reservations providing that nothing in the treaties shall be deemed to increase the powers of the President or Congress, n. 31 to this chapter.

111.   See p. 192 above. The 'necessary and proper' clause originally contained expressly the power 'to enforce treaties' but it was stricken as superfluous. See 2 FARRAND (n. 11 to Ch. I) 382; 1 BUTLER, THE TREATY POWER (n. 10 to Ch. I) 318. Earlier, Story had said that the power of Congress to implement treaties 'has been supposed to result from the duty of the national government to fulfill all the obligations of treaties'. *Prigg* v. *Pennsylvania*, 41 U.S. (16 Pet.) 539, 619 (1842).

   Only a constitutionally valid treaty would support implementing legislation by Congress. In *Missouri* v. *Holland*, for example, whether the act of Congress implementing the Migratory Bird Treaty was valid law in the United States turned on whether the treaty itself was within the Treaty Power. See p. 189 above. Presumably a treaty must be valid and binding under international law to support legislation as necessary and proper to implement it. See n. 108 to this chapter.

112.   The issue arose even before the Jay Treaty when Washington contemplated ransoming Americans captured by the Barbary Pirates and making a treaty with Algiers. Since money would have had to be appropriated for the ransom, Jefferson advised getting advance sanction of the House as well as the Senate, but the Senate objected that it would give the House 'a handle always to claim it', and 'would let them into a participation of the power to make treaties'. Jefferson agreed that if a treaty were made it would be the duty of the House to furnish the money, but feared that it might decline to do its duty. His fears proved unfounded. 1 WRITINGS OF THOMAS JEFFERSON 183–4, 190–2 (Ford ed. 1892). In accordance with his advice to Washington, Jefferson later considered putting the treaties consummating the Louisiana Purchase before both houses of Congress, but he was dissuaded by members of his cabinet lest he offend the Senate. See HAYDEN, TREATIES, (n. 8 above) 141–5; 1 RICHARDSON (n. 27 to Ch. II) 357.

113.   Works of Alexander Hamilton 566 (J.C. Hamilton ed. 1851), quoted in CRANDALL, TREATIES (n. 1 above) 170–1. See also 6 OP.ATT'Y GEN. 291 (1854); WRIGHT (n. 3 to Ch. I) 353–6.

   The arguments against Congressional discretion might seem even stronger where it is required to do something which it can do only because it is necessary and proper to implement a treaty (*Missouri* v. *Holland*), than when the implementing legislation is within some enumerated power of Congress.

Whatever merits such a distinction might have had, it has virtually disappeared now that Congress can legislate independently on all matters which might also appear in treaties.

114.   4 ANNALS OF CONGRESS 519 (1796); also CORWIN, THE PRESIDENT (n. 5 to Intro. to Pt. II) 469–70. Compare also Calhoun, n. 54 to this chapter.

115.   5 ANNALS OF CONGRESS 771 (1796) [1795–1796]. (The resolution was reaffirmed in 1871, CONG.GLOBE, 42d Cong., 1st Sess. 835 (1871).) On the day it adopted that resolution, the House passed another maintaining its 'constitutional right to deliberate and determine the propriety or impropriety of passing such laws, and to act thereon, as the public good shall require'. 5 ANNALS OF CONGRESS 769 (1796) [1795–1796]. For contemporary views not unlike Madison's, see Ch. IV, pp. 112–15.

Language to similar effect was adopted by the House when it appropriated funds to implement the treaty acquiring Alaska. CONG.GLOBE, 40th Cong., 2d Sess. 4055 (1868). But a phrase expressing 'the assent of Congress' to the treaty was stricken in conference. Language denying the power of the treaty-makers to acquire territory before Congress appropriated the funds therefore failed by two votes. See CRANDALL, TREATIES (n. 1 above) 175–7.

116.   In 1925, a Report of the House Foreign Affairs Committee lined up the champions on each side of the issue and concluded: 'There have been numerous collisions over this matter between the Senate and the House and the question cannot be regarded as definitely settled.' H.R.REP.NO.1569, 68th Cong., 2d Sess. 8 (1925). The Report noted that the House had always appropriated funds to implement treaties: 'While it would be in the power of the House to refuse, that comity which exists between the respective departments of Government and the delicate nature of our foreign relations have led to the prompt enactment of legislation carrying appropriations.' *Id.* at 9. In regard to treaties affecting revenue legislation and tariffs, the House has often insisted on the need of its concurrence and the Senate has acquiesced; such treaties have often provided for the concurrence of the Congress to make them effective. *Ibid.* The Report also lists occasions on which the House took initiative in foreign affairs matters, usually by resolution, including several expressions of views, and requests for Presidential action. *Id.* at 11–16.

117.   In a well known case early in the twentieth century, Congress, in passing the Panama Canal Act of 1912, apparently interpreted the Hay–Pauncefote Treaty as exempting U.S. vessels engaged in coastwise trade from paying canal tolls, as did President Taft. Wilson later interpreted the Treaty differently and induced Congress to repeal the statutory exemption. See 37 Stat. 560 (1912), 51 CONG.REC. 4313 (1914), 38 Stat. 385 (1914).

118.   See, e.g., *Factor* v. *Laubenheimer*, 290 U.S. 276 (1933). In early cases the Court seemed to consider itself bound by Executive interpretation of a treaty. *Foster & Elam* v. *Neilson*, 27 U.S. (2 Pet.) 253, 307 (1829). A Congressional 'misinterpretation' might of course be binding as U.S. law because Congress can legislate regardless of what the treaty-makers intended. Compare *United States* v. *Lynde*, 78 U.S. (11 Wall.) 632 (1870). But in a case involving rights under an Indian Treaty, the Court said that interpretation of treaties is 'the

peculiar province of the judiciary', and not of Congress or the Secretary of the Interior. *Jones* v. *Meehan*, 175 U.S. 1 (1899). The Court interpreted a treaty differently than did the Executive branch in a case in which the United States was party, *Perkins* v. *Elg*, 307 U.S. 325 (1939), but there was no issue with a foreign government in the case. Compare *Pearcy* v. *Stranahan*, 205 U.S. 257 (1907). It seems unlikely that a court would feel free to interpret a treaty differently if the Executive has taken a formal position on its meaning. Compare the deference to the Executive in the immunity cases, Ch. II, pp. 54 *et seq.* and the discussion of political questions, Ch. V p. 143.

Of course, later interpretations, whether by the President or the courts, do not have the consent of the Senate. Judicial 'misinterpretation' of a treaty, of course, compels the Executive to adopt that interpretation internationally, and it can be rectified presumably by a new treaty or even by a less formal agreement.

119. See *Valentine* v. *United States ex rel. Neidecker*, 299 U.S. 5 (1936), n. 14 to Ch. IV, p. 90, which held that the President could not extradite a U.S. national on his own authority, but suggested that he could do so if authorized by treaty or act of Congress. *Cf. In re Metzger*, 46 U.S. (5 How.) 176, 188–9 (1847). Compare also the authority once asserted by the President to 'govern' in the Panama Canal Zone, pursuant to 'sovereignty' acquired by treaty, in the absence of an act of Congress. 26 OP.ATT'Y GEN. 113 (1907).

120. Theodore Roosevelt stated that he had planned to use troops to protect treaty rights of Japanese in San Francisco. T. BAILEY, THEODORE ROOSEVELT AND THE JAPANESE-AMERICAN CRISES 28–9, 45, 80–4, 100–1 (1934). But *cf.* CORWIN, THE PRESIDENT (n. 5 to Intro. to Pt. II) 408 n. 106. Compare the authority of the President to use armed force to enforce federal laws in any state; 10 U.S.C. §§ 332–34 (1994); 41 OP.ATT'Y GEN. 313 (1957); *In re Debs*, 158 U.S. 564 (1895); *Alabama* v. *United States*, 373 U.S. 545 (1963).

121. The need for a federal judiciary for the purpose, *inter alia*, of enforcing treaties is a theme of THE FEDERALIST NO. 22 at 197–8 (Hamilton). Courts have given effect to intervening treaties even in a pending case. *The Schooner Peggy*, 5 U.S. (1 Cranch) 103 (1801).

The federal district courts have jurisdiction 'of all civil actions arising under the Constitution, laws, or treaties of the United States'. 28 U.S.C. § 1331 (1994). A suit to enjoin a state official from enforcing an act violating a treaty might be said to arise under the Constitution as well as under 'treaties', since the state action would violate the Supremacy Clause. Such a suit is not barred as a suit against the state (under the Eleventh Amendment), but is considered a suit against the officer only. *Ex parte Young*, 209 U.S. 123 (1908). As regards some treaty obligations implemented by Congress, a suit to enjoin state violation might qualify as one to 'redress the deprivation, under color of any State law . . . of any right, privilege or immunity secured by the Constitution of the United States or by any Act of Congress providing for equal rights of citizens of all persons within the jurisdiction of the United States'. 28 U.S.C. § 1343(3)(1994). In addition to many state provisions for declaratory judgments, the Federal Declaratory Judgment Act provides for relief '[i]n a case of actual controversy within its [the district court's] jurisdiction', 28 U.S.C. § 2201 (1994).

Sometimes, however, the Executive Branch has seemed to doubt its authority and standing to seek a judicial remedy—by mandamus or injunction—to order state authorities as well as private persons to respect U.S. obligations under international law.

122. *United States* v. *Alvarez-Machain*, 504 U.S. 655 (1992).

123. 3 U.S. (3 Dall.) 199 (1796). See also *Martin* v. *Hunter's Lessee*, 14 U.S. (1 Wheat.) 304 (1816).

124. See, e.g., *Hauenstein* v. *Lynham*, 100 U.S. 483 (1880); *Nielsen* v. *Johnson*, 279 U.S. 47 (1929); *cf. Kolovrat* v. *Oregon*, 366 U.S. 187 (1961); also *Chirac* v. *Chirac*, 15 U.S. (2 Wheat.) 259 (1817).

125. *Asakura* v. *Seattle*, 265 U.S. 332, 341 (1924).

126. See, 34 DEP'T STATE BULL. 728 (1956). The Department of State was apparently of the opinion that the Government could not seek a judicial remedy against the states. But see nn. 96, 127, 128 to this chapter.

127. Congress could authorize the Attorney General (or the Secretary of State) to seek injunctive or other relief against treaty violations by state officials or others. See HART AND WECHSLER'S, THE FEDERAL COURTS AND THE FEDERAL SYSTEM, 3d ed, by BATOR, MELTZER, MISHKIN and SHAPIRO (1988) 906, 912–13. Presidents have repeatedly asked Congress to make it a federal crime to violate treaty rights of aliens. See W.H. TAFT, THE UNITED STATES AND PEACE 74 (1914); see generally, 6 MOORE, DIGEST (n. 50 to Ch. II) 810, 837–41; compare *Baldwin* v. *Franks*, 120 U.S. 678 (1887). See n. 36 to Ch. VIII, for legislation and cases allowing aliens to bring suit in the federal courts for a tort 'committed in violation of the law of nations or a treaty of the United States'. 28 U.S.C. §1350 (1994).

128. In a suit by the United States against a state agency to enforce treaty limitations on the amount of water to be diverted from Lake Michigan, the Court said that the United States Government 'has a standing in this suit not only to remove obstruction to interstate and foreign commerce, the main ground . . . but also to carry out treaty obligations to a foreign power'. *Sanitary Dist.* v. *United States*, 266 U.S. 405, 425 (1925). See also *United States* v. *Minnesota*, 270 U.S. 181 (1926), involving a suit to obtain return to Indian tribes of title to certain lands alleged to have been mistakenly granted to Minnesota. The tribes claimed title to the land pursuant to a treaty with the United States. The Court said that the United States had 'the right to invoke the aid of a court of equity in removing unlawful obstacles to the fulfillment of its obligations'. *Id.* at 194–5.

The Court has upheld suits by the United States, or in its behalf, to enjoin state violations of various laws of the United States, e.g., voting laws. *Katzenbach* v. *Morgan*, 384 U.S. 641 (1966). Compare *In re Debs*, 158 U.S. 564 (1895); *New York Times Co.* v. *United States*, 403 U.S. 713 (1971); *United States* v. *California*, 332 U.S. 19 (1947); also *United Steelworkers* v. *United States*, 361 U.S. 39, 4344 (1960); *United States* v. *Raines*, 362 U.S. 17, 27 (1960). *Cf. South Carolina* v. *Katzenbach*, 383 U.S. 301 (1966) (original proceeding by a state in the Supreme Court to enjoin the Attorney General from enforcing the Voting Act of 1965). See generally, 32 N.Y.U. L. REV. 870 (1957); 42 CORNELL L.Q. 418 (1957).

Private interests in a foreign country aggrieved by an alleged treaty violation might also have standing to seek relief in U.S. courts; the foreign government itself might have standing to sue to protect an economic interest, but there is some question whether it could sue to vindicate political interests only. Compare *Massachusetts* v. *Mellon*, 262 U.S. 447 (1923); *Stanton* v. *Georgia*, 73 U.S. (6 Wall.) 50, 64 (1868). Foreign governments might also be reluctant to appear as suitors in U.S. courts for this purpose. See RESTATEMENT (n. 2 to Preface) § 907.

129. *Whitney* v. *Robertson*, 124 U.S. 190, 194 (1888). This view of the relation between the legislative power and the treaty power has been explained as an application of the maxim *leges posteriores priores contraries abrogant* ('later laws abrogate earlier contrary ones', sometimes paraphrased as 'the last expression of the sovereign will must control'). *The Chinese Exclusion Case*, 130 U.S. 581, 600 (1889). Implicit is the view that, in the area of jurisdiction common to both, the treaty power and the legislative power are distinct but equal. Either may enter the field but may be superseded by the other.

In other contexts it has been suggested that multilateral treaties are different because they are not primarily contracts among the parties. See *Reservations to the Genocide Convention*, 1951 ICJ Reports 15, 22. See Szasz *The Palestine Liberation Organization Mission Controversy*, 82 A.S.I.L. Proceedings 534, 538 (1988).

130. Prior treaty provisions have been held to have been superseded in numerous cases: in addition to *The Chinese Exclusion Case*, and *Whitney* v. *Robertson*, see, e.g., *Head Money Cases*, 112 U.S. 580 (1884); *The Cherokee Tobacco*, 78 U.S. (11 Wall.) 616 (1871); and see *Moser* v. *United States*, 341 U.S. 41 (1951). Also *Foster & Elam* v. *Neilson*, 27 U.S. (2 Pet.) 253 (1829). But *cf. Reichert* v. *Felps*, 73 U.S. (6 Wall.) 160, 165–6 (1868). That giving effect to later legislation results in a violation of international law by the United States is constitutionally irrelevant. See p. 210 above.

In the *Head Money Cases*, 112 U.S. at 599, Justice Miller said: 'The Constitution gives [a treaty] no superiority over an act of Congress in this respect, which maybe repealed or modified by an act of a later date. Nor is there anything in its essential character, or in the branches of the government by which the treaty is made, which gives it this superior sanctity.

A treaty is made by the President and the Senate. Statutes are made by the President, the Senate and the House of Representatives. The addition of the latter body to the other two in making a law certainly does not render it less entitled to respect in the matter of its repeal or modification than a treaty made by the other two. If there be any difference in this regard, it would seem to be in favor of an act in which all three of the bodies participate. And such is, in fact, the case in a declaration of war, which must be made by Congress, and which, when made, usually suspends or destroys existing treaties between the nations thus at war.

In short, we are of opinion that, so far as a treaty made by the United

States with any foreign nation can become the subject of judicial cognizance in the courts of this country, it is subject to such acts as Congress may pass for its enforcement, modification, or repeal.'

Where fairly possible, courts will construe an act of Congress so as not to conflict with a treaty of the United States. *Alexander Murray, Esq.* v. *Schooner Charming Betsy,* 6 U.S. (2 Cranch) 64, 118 (1804); RESTATEMENT (n. 2 to Preface) § 114. In *Baker* v. *Carr,* the Court said that 'a court will not undertake to construe a treaty in a manner inconsistent with a subsequent federal statute'. 369 U.S. 186, 212 (1962). But 'the meaning of treaty provisions so construed is not restricted by any necessity of avoiding possible conflict with state legislation . . .' *Nielsen* v. *Johnson,* 279 U.S. 47, 52 (1929).

As to some subjects at least, the Court has seemed to treat law-making by treaty as at best concurrent and inferior to Congressional legislation. Rights granted to aliens by treaty, for example, were not permanent but only at the sufferance of the legislature. *Fong Yue Ting* v. *United States,* 149 U.S. 698, 720 (1893). In *The Chinese Exclusion Case,* too, the Supreme Court spoke of the power to exclude aliens as a sovereign power that cannot be abandoned or surrendered. 130 U.S. at 609. But all treaty undertakings 'surrender' the right to do what the United States could otherwise do as a 'sovereign right'.

An unusual provision in the Internal Revenue Code of 1986 requires a taxpayer who takes the position that a treaty of the United States overrules or modifies an internal revenue tax of the United States to disclose that position on his tax return, I.R.C. § 6114 (1994). Failure to do so is punishable by fine. *Id.* § 6712(1). The requirement of disclosure applies whether the law purported to be modified or overruled was enacted before or after the treaty, but it was apparently designed to identify cases in which a taxpayer might be relying on an earlier treaty provision superseded by a provision in the Code. An explicit undertaking in a treaty that Congress would not legislate contrary to its provisions would, of course, change nothing, since Congress could disregard that provision as well. It might, however, have some psychological effect as a further deterrent to Congress and as an earnest of U.S. sincerity. Such provisions are generally hypothetical. See HENKIN, ARMS CONTROL (n. 3 to Ch. VI) 31–2. But, in GATT, for example, the United States has in effect agreed not to adopt certain legislation and the agreement indicates the international consequences if Congress should do so. See General Agreement on Tariffs and Trade and the Uruguay Round Agreements, pp. 217n., 218n., and n. 185 to this chapter.

131.   Even the Supreme Court has written—I think loosely—of Congress 'repealing' a treaty: *Head Money Cases,* 112 U.S. 580, 599 (1884), n. 130 to this chapter ('subject to such acts as Congress may pass for its enforcement, modification, or repeal'). See also *La Abra Silver Mining Co.* v. *United States,* 175 U.S. 423, 460 (1899) ('Congress by legislation, and so far as the people and authorities of the United States are concerned, could abrogate a treaty'). The Court was more careful (and more accurate) in *Pigeon River Co.* v. *Cox Co.,* 291 U.S. 138, 160 (1934).

There is a different kind of inaccuracy in saying even that Congress has power to repeal any treaty provision in its capacity as law of the land. More carefully, in a famous opinion approved by the Supreme Court, Justice Curtis, sitting in the circuit court, said that Congress can repeal a treaty provision so far as it is domestic law *provided the subject matter were within the legislative power of Congress. Taylor v. Morton*, 23 F.Cas. 784, 786 (No. 13,799) (C.C.Mass.1855), *aff'd*, 67 U.S. (2 Black) 481 (1862). In *The Chinese Exclusion Case*, Justice Field, too, recognized the power of Congress to repeal a treaty provision only when it 'relates to a subject within the powers of Congress'. 130 U.S. at 600.

If, as *Missouri v. Holland* and the Bricker Amendment (p. 192, above) both assumed, treaties can deal with matters that are not within the domain of Congress apart from the treaty, where would Congress get the power to repeal such a treaty? Under *Missouri v. Holland*, Congress has the power to implement such treaties by legislation 'necessary and proper for carrying [it] into execution', but surely repealing a treaty is not necessary and proper for carrying it into execution. Congress would have the power to repeal any treaty only if one assumes that under the sum of its various powers it can legislate on any matter which might be the subject of a treaty. See Ch. III, pp. 72 *et seq.* Or, perhaps, the power to enact a law implies an inherent power to repeal it.

132. See, e.g., E. CORWIN (ed)., THE CONSTITUTION OF THE UNITED STATES OF AMERICA, S. DOC. No. 170, 82d Cong., 2d Sess. 422–3 (1953); 1 WILLOUGHBY (n. 3 to Ch. I) § 306 at 555. Compare Justice Miller, n. 130 to this chapter.

133. *Cook v. United States*, 288 U.S. 102 (1933). Compare *United States v. The Schooner Peggy*, 5 U.S. (1 Cranch) 103 (1801), where the Court gave effect to a treaty requiring the restoration of captured property not definitively condemned, although it had been seized as prize under a commission issued pursuant to an act of Congress authorizing such seizures. The relation between the act of Congress and the treaty was not discussed. Compare also *La Ninfa*, 75 F. 513 (5th Cir.1896); see also 23 OP.ATT'Y GEN. 545 (1901); 21 OP.ATT'Y GEN. 68 (1894), and 21 OP.ATT'Y GEN. 347 (1896), ruling that a treaty with China superseded a statute requiring Chinese laborers returning to the United States to present certain certificates. Cf. 6 OP.ATT'Y GEN. 291 (1854). Several lower court cases have given effect to a subsequent treaty. *In re Fotochrome*, 377 F. Supp. 26 (E.D.N.Y. 1974), *aff'd sub nom. Fotochrome, Inc. v. Copal Co., Ltd.*, 517 F.2d 512 (2d Cir. 1975); *Vorhees v. Fischer & Krecke*, 697 F.2d 574 (4th Cir. 1983). Some cases accepted the principle that treaties supersede earlier inconsistent statutes, but found no inconsistency between statute and treaty in the particular instance. *United States v. Ray*, 423 F.2d 16, 21 (5th Cir. 1970); *Treasure Salvors v. Unidentified Wrecked and Abandoned Sailing Vessel*, 569 F.2d 330, 340 (5th Cir. 1978); *Zenith Radio Corporation v. Matsushita Electric Industrial Co., Ltd.*, 494 F. Sup. 1263, 1266 (E.D. Pa. 1980).

The principle announced in *Whitney v. Robertson* is generally accepted. See RESTATEMENT (n. 2 to Preface) § 115(2).

134. That, generally, is the result prescribed by Article 55 of the French Constitution of 1958, and Articles 65–6 of the Constitution of the

488   *Notes, Chapter VII Treaties and Executive Agreements*

Netherlands. See Sasse, *The Common Market: Between International and Municipal Law*, 75 YALE L.J. 695, 705–14 (1966). See NATIONAL TREATY LAW AND PRACTICE (M. Leigh & M. Blakeslee, eds. 1995); also Y. Iwasawa, *The Relationship Between International Law and National Law: Japanese Experiences*, 64 BRITISH YEARBOOK OF INTERNATIONAL LAW 333 (1993). As regards statutes inconsistent with customary international law, see Ch. VIII.

135.   See THE FEDERALIST No. 64 (at 424) in which Jay said: 'a treaty is only another name for a bargain, and that it would be impossible to find a nation who would make any bargain with us, which should be binding on them absolutely, but on us only so long and so far as we may think proper to be bound by it. They who make laws may without doubt, amend or repeal them; and it will not be disputed that they who make treaties may alter or cancel them; but still let us not forget that treaties are made, not by only one of the contracting parties, but by both; and consequently, that as the consent of both was essential to their formation at first, so must it ever afterwards be to alter or cancel them. The proposed Constitution, therefore, has not in the least extended the obligation of treaties. They are just as binding, and just as far beyond the lawful reach of legislative acts now, as they will be at any future period, or under any form of government.'

Hamilton's statement declaring the obligation of Congress to implement treaties, p. 205 above, has been interpreted as asserting the supremacy of treaties over statutes. See E. CORWIN, THE CONSTITUTION AND WORLD ORGANIZATION 27–8 (1944); compare, generally, W. MCCLURE, WORLD LEGAL ORDER 81–132 (1960).

That Congress can join with the President to make international agreements fully equivalent to a treaty does not suggest that Congress ought to be able unilaterally to undo what the treaty-makers have done. Even if one accepted a concurrent power in Congress to abrogate treaties in their international effect, the power to repeal their domestic character as law would not necessarily follow: Congress might have power to affect our international obligations, but not necessarily to undercut or chip away at them piecemeal by indirection.

136.   See, e.g., Vienna Convention on the Law of Treaties, Arts. 48 (error), 49 (fraud), 50 (corruption of a representative of the state), 51 (coercion of a representative of the state), 52 (coercion by threat or use of force), 60 (material breach), 61 (supervening impossibility of performance), 62 (fundamental change in circumstances), 64 (emergence of a new peremptory norm of general international law); reprinted in 63 AM.J.INT'L L 875, 894–5 (1969). See also RESTATEMENT (n. 2 to Preface) §§ 331 (invalidity), 335 (material breach), 336 (fundamental change of circumstances).

137.   See 5 HACKWORTH, DIGEST OF INTERNATIONAL LAW (1943) 330; WRIGHT (n. 3 to Ch. I) 258–60. Compare Riesenfeld, *The Power of Congress and the President in International Relations*, 25 CALIF.L.REV. 643, 658–65 (1937); Nelson, *The Termination of Treaties and Executive Agreements by the United States*, 42 MINN L. REV. 879 (1958). *Cf. Van der Weyde* v. *Ocean Transport*

Co., Ltd., 297 U.S. 114, 117 (1936), discussed by Riesenfeld, above, at 663–5. The RESTATEMENT (n. 2 to Preface) § 339 declares:

Under the law of the United States, the President has the power

(a) to suspend or terminate an agreement in accordance with its terms;

(b) to make the determination that would justify the United States in terminating or suspending an agreement because of its violation by another party or because of supervening events, and to proceed to terminate or suspend the agreement on behalf of the United States; or

(c) to elect in a particular case not to suspend or terminate an agreement.

See also RESTATEMENT (n. 2 to Preface) § 339, Comment *a* and Reporters' Notes 1, 2, and 3.

138. See 9 STATE DEPT. PRESS RELEASES 257–8 (1933); letter from the Secretary of State to Japanese Ambassador [1931–41] 2 FOREIGN REL. U.S.: JAPAN 189 (1943), DEPT.STATE BULL. 81 (1939). At the time, Congress was considering resolutions to the same effect. Compare Franklin Roosevelt's suspensions of the International Load Line Convention, in 1941, 'for the duration of the present emergency'. 6 FED.REG. 3999 (1941), relying on 40 OP.ATT'Y GEN. 119 (1941).

President Lincoln was apparently the first President to terminate a treaty without prior Congressional endorsement, although he subsequently received its approval. See 5 MOORE, DIGEST (n. 50 to Ch. II) 323. Hamilton (Pacificus), n. 10 to Ch. II, noted that, by his power to recognize or not recognize governments, the President can continue or suspend treaty relations with that country. President Carter's power to terminate the Defense Treaty with the Republic of China was upheld in the Court of Appeals but the Supreme Court did not decide the substantive issue. *Goldwater* v. *Carter*, 617 F.2d 697 (D.C. Cir.), *vacated*, 444 U.S. 996 (1979).

139. In *Techt* v. *Hughes*, 229 N.Y. 222, 243, 128 N.E. 185, 192 (1920), *cert. denied*, 254 U.S. 643 (1920), Judge Cardozo said in a dictum: 'President and senate may denounce the treaty, and thus terminate its life.' John Jay said that 'they who make treaties may alter or cancel them'. THE FEDERALIST NO. 64 at 424. Compare, 'the obligations of the treaty could not be changed or varied, but by the same formalities with which they were introduced; or, at least, by some act of as high in import, and of as unequivocal an authority'. *The Amiable Isabella*, 19 U.S. (6 Wheat.) 1, 75 (1821) (Story, J.). Compare *Presidential Amendment and Termination of Treaties: The Case of the Warsaw Convention*, 34 U.CHI.L.REV. 580 (1967), for the view that the President cannot terminate a treaty alone where private rights are affected. Compare also Riggs, *Termination of Treaties by the Executive Without Congressional Approval*, 32 J. AIR L. & COM. 526, 533–4 (1966) (courts should require 'some Congressional approval' for Executive termination of treaty that is law of the land). See also PARLIAMENTARY PARTICIPATION IN THE MAKING AND OPERATION OF TREATIES: A COMPARATIVE STUDY (S. Riesenfeld and F. Abbot eds., 1994).

140. See 'The Role of the Senate in Treaty Ratification', Staff Memorandum to the Committee on Foreign Relations, U.S. Senate (1977). In 1919 the Senate

entered a reservation to the Versailles Treaty that would have authorized its denunciation by concurrent resolution. 59 CONG.REC. 5423 (1919).

141. For older U.S. practice as regards the effect of war on treaties, see 2 C.C. HYDE, INTERNATIONAL LAW 547 *et seq.* (2d edn. 1945). Compare, for example, Cardozo, J., in *Techt* v. *Hughes,* 229 N.Y. 222, 128 N.E. 185 (1920), *cert. denied,* 254 U.S. 643 (1920); also *Society for the Propagation of the Gospel in Foreign Parts* v. *New Haven,* 21 U.S. (8 Wheat.) 464 (1823); *Clark* v. *Allen,* 331 U.S. 503 (1947); *Karnuth* v. *United States ex rel. Albro,* 279 U.S. 231 (1929). See Rank, *Modern War and the Validity of Treaties,* 38 CORNELL L.Q. 321, 511 (1953); S. MCINTYRE, LEGAL EFFECT OF WORLD WAR II ON TREATIES OF THE UNITED STATES (1958); Arts. 62, 73, Vienna Convention on the Law of Treaties, 63 AM.J.INT'L L. 875, 894–5, 896 (1969). Some multilateral treaties specifically provide for their continued effect in time of war, e.g., Art. 89 of the Convention on International Civil Aviation, December 7, 1944, 61 Stat. 1180, T.I.A.S. No. 1591, 15 U.N.T.S. 295, 356. See, generally, H. TOBIN, TERMINATION OF MULTIPARTITE TREATIES 85–7, 122 (1933). The effect of the U.N. Charter outlawing war is uncertain. *Cf.* Articles 73 and 75 of the Vienna Convention on the Law of Treaties, 63 AM.J.INT'L L. 875, 898 (1969).

On the other hand, of course, war brings into play the laws of war and treaties applicable between belligerents, for example, the Geneva Conventions on treatment of prisoners, on civilian populations, on forbidden weapons. Compare also the Nuremberg principles, unanimously affirmed by the U.N. General Assembly, G.A.Res. 95(I) U.N.Doc. A/236 (1946).

For the view that since the U.N. Charter, war has been outlawed, see Ch. III, p. 75. But Congress can presumably declare war if the United States is the victim of an armed attack. See U.N. Charter, Article 51.

The U.N. Charter doubtless intended to abolish war, but its effect on the status of war in international law is uncertain. The effect of hostilities on the law of treaties is also uncertain. See Vienna Convention, Article 73, and RESTATEMENT (n. 2 to Preface) § 336, and Reporters' Note 4.

142. See Ch. III, pp. 75–76. Jefferson said that since treaties are supreme law of the land equally with laws, 'an act of the legislature alone can declare them infringed and rescinded'. Manual of Parliamentary Practice, See c. LII, p. 189n., this chapter; compare Iredell, J., n. 148 to this chapter. Individual members of Congress have recurrently asserted Congressional authority, e.g., Senator Austin's statement that only Congress, not the President, can denounce treaties, 86 CONG.REC. 3574 (1940). Compare: 'It is the right and province of the legislative power of this country to repeal treaties where they are found to contravene the best interests or the general welfare of the people.' Senator Morgan, 13 CONG.REC. 3268 (1882). That statement, like many others, is ambiguous, it not being clear whether it asserts a right to abrogate a treaty on behalf of the United States, or merely to adopt domestic legislation inconsistent with the treaty, p. 209 above.

143. Congress abrogated treaties with France, 1 Stat. 578 (1798), 2 Stat. 7 (1800). In context, those acts, with others, were seen as constituting a declaration of war. *Bas* v. *Tingy,* 4 U.S. (4 Dall.) 37 (1800). See 5 MOORE, DIGEST (n. 50 to

Ch. II) 356–8. Later, French claims against the United States on account of such unilateral abrogations were in effect set-off against the claims of the United States and of American citizens arising out of French spoilation. The story is told in *Gray* v. *United States*, 21 Ct.Cl. 340, 367 *et seq.* (1886). See n. 63 to Ch. IX.

Later in the nineteenth century Congress also denounced treaties with Great Britain and with Belgium, apparently at Presidential request or with his concurrence. Lincoln ignored Congressional directions to terminate the Rush–Bagot Agreement disarming the Great Lakes; Wilson ignored a directive in the Jones Act to terminate certain conventions on customs and tonnage duties. Earlier he had complied with a similar directive contained in the LaFollette Seaman's Act of 1915. See Reeves, *The Jones Act and the Denunciation of Treaties*, 15 AM.J.INT'L L. 331 (1921); CORWIN, THE PRESIDENT (n. 5 to Intro. to Pt. II) 190–1. See, generally, WRIGHT (n. 3 to Ch. I) 258–9; CRANDALL, TREATIES (n. 1 above) 458–65. For a case involving Presidential compliance with a direction to terminate a treaty, see *Van Der Weyde* v. *Ocean Transport Co. Ltd.*, 297 U.S. 114 (1936). See also the President's renunciation of treaty rights of extraterritoriality in Morocco, pursuant to a Congressional resolution probably inspired by the Executive branch. 70 Stat. 773 (1956), 35 DEP'T STATE BULL. 844 (1956).

144. 100 F.2d 533 (D.C. Cir. 1979).
145. *Goldwater* v. *Carter*, 444 U.S. 996 (1979). See n. 60 to Ch. V.
146. Compare: 'Or the Chief Executive or the Congress may have formulated a national policy quite inconsistent with the enforcement of a treaty in whole or in part.' *Clark* v. *Allen*, 331 U.S. 503, 508–9 (1947).
147. In upholding a statute inconsistent with a treaty, the Court said: 'This court is not a censor of the morals of the other departments of the government.' *The Chinese Exclusion Case*, 130 U.S. 581, 602–3 (1887).
148. See *Charlton* v. *Kelly*, 229 U.S. 447 (1913). Breach by a foreign government may render a treaty voidable at the option of the United States to be exercised by the President; if he chooses not to void it, the courts will give it effect. *Ibid.* Compare Marshall's opinions in *The Nereide*, 13 U.S. (9 Cranch) 388, 422–3 (1815); see *Terlinden* v. *Ames*, 184 U.S. 270, 289 (1902); *The Schooner Exchange* v. *McFaddon*, 11 U.S. (7 Cranch) 116, 146 (1812); *Foster & Elam* v. *Neilson*, 27 U.S. (2 Pet.) 253, 307 (1829); *Clark* v. *Allen*, 331 U.S. 503, 514 (1947); *Taylor* v. *Morton*, 23 F.Cas. 784, 787 (No. 13,799) (C.C.Mass. 1855), *aff'd.*, 67 U.S. (2 Black) 481 (1862).
    Iredell, J., in an opinion delivered in the court below in *Ware* v. *Hylton*, set forth in 3 U.S. at 256, thought Congress alone had the power to declare a treaty 'vacated' by breach of the other party, but that view is not widely held.
149. The number of executive agreements to which the United States has been party depends on how an executive agreement is defined and whether it includes informal, even oral agreements. One writer counted 'well over 1,250' as of February, 1941. MCCLURE, INTERNATIONAL EXECUTIVE AGREEMENTS: DEMOCRATIC PROCEDURE UNDER THE CONSTITUTION OF THE UNITED STATES xii–xiii (1941). In 1953, Secretary of State Dulles, applying a more liberal

definition, said at the Bricker Amendment hearings that 'every time we open a new privy, we have to have an executive agreement'. Pointing out that with every treaty or agreement listed in the Executive Agreement Series there were numerous concomitant unlisted agreements, he estimated that about 10,000 such informal agreements accompanied the North Atlantic Treaty alone. Probably the number was picked out of the air, but Dulles was doubtless including informal understandings in letters, notes, even oral conversations, and routine transactions reflecting some element of consensus. See *Bricker Hearings* 1953, at 877; also *id.* at 828, 866, n. 40 to this chapter.

A Congressional Research Report finds that, as of 1989, the United States was party to 890 treaties and 5,117 executive agreements then in force. Between 1930 and 1992 the United States made 891 treaties and 13,178 other international agreements. Since 1939, more than 90% of international agreements of the United States were executive agreements. S. Prt. 103–5, TREATIES AND OTHER INTERNATIONAL AGREEMENTS, Study prepared by the Congressional Research Service (1993).

150. See, e.g., Pub. L. No. 91–375, Aug. 12, 1970, 84 Stat. 724, codified at 39 U.S.C. § 407 (1994) (authority to the Postal Service 'with the consent of the President' to make international postal arrangements); Law of June 17, 1930, c. 497, Title III § 350, codified as amended at 19 U.S.C. § 1351(a)(1)(A) (1994) (foreign trade agreements); Pub. L. No. 87–195, Pt. III, § 635, Sept. 4, 1961, 75 Stat. 465, codified as amended at 22 U.S.C. § 2395(b) (1994) (President may make 'agreements and contracts' relating to foreign assistance); and Pub. L. No. 94–553, Title I, § 101, Oct. 19, 1976, 90 Stat. 2545, codified at 17 U.S.C. § 104(b)(5) (1994) (international copyrights).

151. See the joint resolution authorizing conclusion of the Headquarters Agreement with the United Nations, ch. 482, 61 Stat. 756 (1947) (text of agreement included in resolution); Bretton Woods Agreement Act (providing for participation in the International Monetary Fund and the International Bank for Reconstruction and Development), ch. 339, 59 Stat. 512 (1945); F.A.O., ch. 342, 59 Stat. 529 (1945); U.N.E.S.C.O., ch. 700, 60 Stat. 712 (1946); W.H.O., ch. 469, 62 Stat. 441 (1948); also U.N.R.R.A., Act of March 28, 1944, ch. 135, 58 Stat. 122; joint resolutions providing for membership and participation in the International Refugee Organization, ch. 185, 61 Stat. 214 (1947). Earlier, Congress had approved United States adherence to that part of the Versailles Treaty that established the International Labor Office, ch. 676, 48 Stat. 1182, 1183 (1934).

The UN Charter was approved as a treaty, but implementation was left largely to Congressional–Executive cooperation. See the United Nations Participation Act of 1945, ch. 583, 59 Stat. 619 (1945), as amended, 22 U.S.C. §§ 287–287e (1994); 'Article 43 agreements' to put forces at the disposal of the Security Council were to be approved by Congress, not consented to by the Senate only. See § 6, 59 Stat. 621, 22 U.S.C. 287d. See Ch. VIII.

152. For example, U.S. participation in the Pan American Union. See ch. 104, 48 Stat. 534 (1934), and subsequent Congressional appropriations; see 25 Stat. 155 (1888); *id.* at 957 (1889); 26 Stat. 272, 275 (1890), and others. An uncon-

ditional 'most favored nation' clause was included in an agreement with Albania before Congress in effect approved that agreement. See MCCLURE, INTERNATIONAL EXECUTIVE AGREEMENTS (n. 149 above) 176.

153. The argument that the Constitution permits international agreements by treaty only was long ago rejected. See, for example, as to postal agreements, 19 OP.ATT'Y GEN. 513 (1890); *cf.* 29 OP.ATT'Y GEN. 380 (1912); see, generally, 19 OP.ATT'Y GEN. 513 (1890). During the Bricker Amendment controversy, a report of the Senate Judiciary Committee said: 'The Committee on the Judiciary cannot agree that the President acting alone, or the Congress and the President acting together, should bypass the treaty procedure whenever the approval of two-thirds of the Senators present and voting appears doubtful. The treaty clause is an integral part of the Constitution, which both Senators and Representatives have taken an oath to protect and defend. The committee does realize, however, that the exact line of demarcation between treaties and executive agreements has always been undefined, but existence of such a line does not seem to have been seriously questioned.' S. Rept. 1716, 84–2, 2, (1956).

For an extended debate of the constitutionality of executive agreements a half a century ago, see Borchard, *Shall the Executive Agreement Replace the Treaty?,* 53 YALE L.J. 664 (1944); McDougal and Lans, *Treaties and Congressional–Executive or Presidential Agreements: Interchangeable Instruments of National Policy,* 54 YALE L.J. 181, 534 (1945); Borchard, *Treaties and Executive Agreements—A Reply, id.* at 616. The debate occasionally resumed. E.g., R. Berger, *The Presidential Monopoly of Foreign Relations,* 71 MICH. L. REV. 1 (1972) (treaty clause bars executive agreements); Rovine, *Separation of Powers and International Executive Agreements,* 52 IND.L.J. 397, 401 (1977); Sparkman, *Checks and Balances in American Foreign Policy, id.* at 433; E. BYRD, TREATIES AND EXECUTIVE AGREEMENTS IN THE UNITED STATES 152, 155 (1960) (rejecting notion of absolute interchangeability as 'untenable'); K. Randall, *The Treaty Power,* 51 OHIO ST. L.J. 1089 (1990). The question was revived briefly during the 1994–95 Uruguay Round talks (n. 157 to this chapter).

The RESTATEMENT (n. 2 to Preface) § 303, Comment *e,* states firmly that a Congressional–Executive agreement is the equivalent of a treaty. See also L.TRIBE, AMERICAN CONSTITUTIONAL LAW, (2d edn., 1988), p. 228, n. 4: 'But it does appear settled that a hybrid form of international agreement—that in which the President is supported by a Joint Resolution of Congress—is coextensive with the treaty power. Such Congressional-Executive agreements are the law of the land, superseding inconsistent state or federal laws.'
But see n. 157 to this chapter.

154. J. B. MOORE, 60 *Proceedings of The American Philosophical Society, Minutes* XV–XVI (1921), quoted in WRIGHT (n. 3 to Ch. I) 375: 'As Congress possesses no power whatever to make international agreements, it has no such power to delegate.' If seen as delegation of Congressional authority, the absence of guidelines might also raise issues. See Ch. IV, p. 123. But Moore saw Congress as implementing the President's agreements, often in advance.

155. *Cf.* WRIGHT (n. 3 to Ch. I) at 105, 375. See also MCCLURE, INTERNATIONAL EXECUTIVE AGREEMENTS (n. 149 above) 371–2.

156. Compare *United States* v. *Curtiss-Wright Export Corp.*, 299 U.S. 304 (1936); n. 1 to Intro. to Pt. II, and p. 25, and Ch. IV. There are also arguments to support joint Executive–Congressional authority based on the history of the treaty-making power. Before the Constitution all international agreements were made by Congress. The Constitutional Convention considered proposals to require the advice and consent of both houses to the making of treaties, and rejected them largely because that would have made the process too difficult and cumbersome. The requirement of consent of the Senate alone can be seen, then, as 'settling for less', and the two-thirds requirement in the Senate as a lesser substitute for the consent of the House of Representatives also. If so, the consent of both houses (even if only by simple majority) is an even greater safeguard and should surely be no less effective than the consent of the Senate alone (even by two-thirds). Compare especially *Head Money Cases*, 112 U.S. 580, 599 (1884), quoted n. 130 to this chapter. For this suggestion that Congress was really the preferred 'treaty-maker' there is some support in that Congress, not the President, nor the President-and-Senate, was given authority to authorize agreements (other than treaties) by the states with foreign powers. Art. I, sec. 10, cl. 2. See Ch. VI.

Often an agreement approved or authorized by Congress in fact obtains the consent of two-thirds of the Senate, but the Trade Agreements Act of 1934, for an important example, passed the Senate by 57–33, thus less than the two-thirds required for consent to a treaty. 78 CONG.REC. 10395 (1934). See n. 185 to this chapter.

Of course, those who find a broad power in the President to make international agreements on his own authority (n. 164 to this chapter) might see Congressional approval as politically welcome (and disarming Senate resentment) but constitutionally unnecessary; or perhaps as needed only to give legal effect to the agreement in the United States. See p. 226, this chapter.

It has been argued that all Presidential agreements are essentially Congressional–Executive agreements, since, in effect, they have the acquiescence of Congress, if only in that Congress does not legislate to supersede them. That suggestion does not take account of the realities of the legislative process; in any event, it could not apply where Congress does not know of the agreement, or when the agreement does not deal with a matter of domestic import as to which Congress could legislate. See the RESTATEMENT (n. 2 to Preface) and Professor Tribe, n. 153 to this chapter.

157. See n. 153 above. But in 1995 Professor Tribe reopened the debate in an exchange with Professor Ackerman. Compare B. Ackerman, *Is NAFTA Constitutional?*, 108 HARV. L. REV. 801 (1995), with Tribe, *Taking Text and Structure Seriously: Reflections on Free-Form Method in Constitutional Interpretation*, 108 HARV. L. REV. 1221 (1995). See also S. Charnovitz, *The Nafta Environmental Side Agreement: Implications for Environmental Cooperation, Trade Policy, and American Treatymaking*, 8 TEMP. INT'L &

COMP. L. J. 257 (1994) See generally L. HENKIN, CONSTITUTIONALISM, DEMOCRACY AND FOREIGN AFFAIRS 60–1, 66–7 (1990).

158. See, e.g., President Truman's message to Congress in regard to the agreement for the Trust Territory of the Pacific Islands: 'I have given special consideration to whether the attached trusteeship agreement should be submitted to the Congress for action by joint resolution or by the treaty process. I am satisfied that either method is constitutionally permissible and that the agreement resulting will be of the same effect internationally and under the supremacy clause of the Constitution whether advised and consented to by the Senate or whether approval is authorized by a joint resolution. The interest of both Houses of Congress in the execution of this agreement is such, however, that I think it would be appropriate for the Congress, in this instance, to take action by joint resolution authorizing the Government to bring the agreement into effect.' Message of the President to Congress, H.Doc.No. 378, 80th Cong., 1st Sess. (July 3, 1947).

The legislative branch has also recognized Congressional–Executive agreements as alternatives to treaties. After the First World War, a House Committee Report asserted the propriety of adherence to the World Court by Congressional resolution instead of treaty, citing precedents. H.R.REP.NO. 1569, 68th Cong., 2nd Sess. 16 (1925). The Executive had apparently planned to conclude the UNRRA agreement on his own authority rather than seek Senate consent to it as a treaty, but 'compromised' with a subcommittee of the Senate Foreign Relations Committee which agreed to support approval of the agreement by a joint resolution of Congress. See *Hearings on H.R.J. Res. 192 Before the House Comm. on Foreign Affairs*, 78th Cong., 1st and 2d Sess., at 158–9 (1943–44) (remarks of Mr. Sayre of Department of State). See, generally, 90 CONG.REC. 1727–53 (1944).

The courts have approved Congressional–Executive agreements in a few cases involving matters within the delegated powers of Congress. In 1882, the Supreme Court held that postal conventions have equal status with treaties as part of the law of the land. *Cotzhausen v. Nazro*, 107 U.S. 215 (1882). (See comments, S.Doc. No. 244, SEN.MISC.DOC., 78th Cong., 2d Sess. (1944); 19 OP.ATT'Y GEN. 513 (1882).) See also *B. Altman & Co. v. United States*, 224 U.S. 583 (1912), where the Supreme Court considered a Congressional–Executive agreement to be a 'treaty' within the meaning of a federal statute.

In 1943, Representative Fulbright argued the full equality, and the inherent superiority, of Congressional–Executive agreements in *The New York Herald-Tribune* Nov. 3, 1943, reprinted in CORWIN, THE CONSTITUTION AND WORLD ORGANIZATION 49–50 (1944). Corwin supported that position generally, and in effect favored a constitutional amendment to replace Senate consent to treaties with approval by Congress. *Id.* at 49, 54. There have been innumerable bills to amend the Constitution to give the House a voice in treaties, and many to replace the treaty power with Congressional–Executive agreement.

An agreement may be approved by resolution of Congress although it bears the description 'treaty' internationally. Congress has itself referred to 'any treaty or convention' approved by the President on the authorization of Congress. Pub. L. No. 91–375, Aug. 12, 1970, 84 Stat. 724, codified at 39 U.S.C. § 407 (1994).

159. When the Executive branch decided to seek approval of the U.N. Headquarters Agreement by joint resolution, it provided to concerned foreign governments an opinion of the Attorney General assuring them that the Congressional–Executive agreement would be the equivalent of a treaty and supreme law of the land. 40 OP.ATT'Y GEN. 469 (1946). His opinion purported to speak only for the agreement in question, but the arguments and authorities cited would seem to apply as well to any agreement.

   A Congressional–Executive agreement would supersede an earlier statute, and a later statute would supersede an earlier Congressional–Executive agreement as it does a treaty, p. 209 this chapter.

   The control of Congress over such executive agreements is at least as strong as that of the Senate over treaties. In 1962, Congress required the inclusion of members of designated Congressional committees on delegations for trade agreement negotiations. See Trade Expansion Act of 1962, Pub.L. No. 87–794, § 243, 76 Stat. 878, now repealed. Similar provision were carried over into the Trade Expansion Act of 1979, P.L. 96–39 § 3(e), 93 Stat. 150, and the Omnibus Trade and Competitiveness Act of 1988, Pub.L. No. 100–418, 102 Stat 1269, codified in 19 U.S.C. § 2211 (1994). In approving agreements by joint resolution, Congress has sometimes entered conditions or reservations; see, e.g., the resolution approving U.S. adherence to the International Refugee Organization, ch. 185, 61 Stat. 214 (1947); also the resolution authorizing the U.N. Headquarters Agreement, ch. 482, 61 Stat. 756, 758, 767–8 (1947), cited in n. 27 to this chapter.

   The question as to who has the power to terminate a Congressional–Executive agreement is unresolved, but the President's authority seems no weaker than in regard to treaties. In some cases, Congress purported to reserve for itself an equal right to annul authorized arrangements independently of the President. See, e.g., The Postal Service Act of 1960, Pub.L. No. 860–682, § 6103, 74 Stat. 688. The Postal Reorganization Act of 1970 does not contain such a provision. Pub.L. No. 91–375, ch 50, § 5002, 84 Stat. 719, 766, 39 U.S.C. § 5002 (1988).

160. See nn. 12, 13, 14 to this chapter.

161. See generally my essay on 'Treaty-making in a Democracy', in CONSTITU-TIONALISM, DEMOCRACY AND FOREIGN AFFAIRS (1990), Ch. 2.

162. See n. 4 to this chapter.

163. See the agreements cited in n. 166 to this chapter; also e.g., The Conferences at Malta and Yalta, [1945] FOREIGN REL. U.S. 549, 968–87 (1955), E.A.S. No. 498; 2 Conference of Berlin (Potsdam), [1945] FOREIGN REL. U.S. 1462–99 (1960).

   In the past, some executive agreements were communicated to the Senate for information: e.g., Secretary of State Root offered to apprise the Senate of the substance and effect of the Root–Takahira Agreement, 1908; see P. JESSUP, 2 ELIHU ROOT 43 (1964). Since 1972, the Executive is required to transmit all executive agreements to Congress. See n. 181 to this chapter.

164. Senators have often accused Presidents of usurping the Treaty Power. See, for example, Senator Teller's attack on Theodore Roosevelt, 40 CONG.REC. 1475–80 (1906). When it became clear that the Senate would not consent to a protocol whereby the United States would take over the customs houses of the Dominican Republic, Roosevelt concluded it as an executive agreement 'pending the action of the United States Senate upon the treaty'. [1905] FOREIGN REL. U.S. 360 (1906); see HOLT (n. 4 above) 212 *et seq.* The issue produced a famous constitutional debate. See, for example, 40 CONG.REC. 433–6, 1173–80, 1417–31, 2125–48 (1905–06).

An executive agreement with Panama supplementing the Hay–Varilla Treaty and establishing a *modus vivendi* for the co-occupation of the Zone was 'attacked vigorously in the Senate as a usurpation of the treaty-making power'. W.H. TAFT, OUR CHIEF MAGISTRATE AND HIS POWERS 112 (1916). See also Senator Robert Taft's admonition that an 'important matter' such as then-pending agreements with Panama is inappropriate for executive agreements and they should be submitted for Senate approval as treaties. 88 CONG.REC. 9276–7 (1942). On the anniversary of the Yalta agreement in 1952, several Senators excoriated that agreement as 'shameful', 'infamous', and a Presidential usurpation of power. See, e.g., Sen. Ives, 98 CONG.REC. 900 (1952). For a later example, see *Hearings on H.R. 9042 Before the Senate Comm. on Finance on the United States–Canadian Automobile Agreement*, 89th Cong., 1st Sess., 85–6 (1965). President Lincoln was severely criticized when, without support in statute or treaty, he agreed to extradite to Spain a man named Arguelles accused of illegitimate slave trading. See, e.g., 9 NICOLAY AND HAY, ABRAHAM LINCOLN 45–7 (1890). In 1972, the Senate adopted the Case Resolution urging the President to submit the Azores and the Bahrain base agreements for Senate consent. S.Res. 214, 92d Cong., 1st Sess., 118 CONG.REC. 3290 (daily edn. March 3, 1972). See 1 U.S.C. § 112(b) (1994). When the Executive did not comply, Senator Case proposed that Congress refuse to appropriate for the aid provided in these agreements. See *New York Times*, April 3, 1972 at A7. Earlier Senator Fulbright had sought to compel disclosure, discussion, and submission for Senate consent of the extension of the military-base agreement with Spain. 116 CONG.REC. 26968–72 (1970). Compare n. 27 to this chapter. For an extended discussion of the events surrounding the Spanish Bases Agreements, see Murphy, *Treaties and International Agreements Other Than Treaties: Constitutional Allocation of Power and Responsibility Among the President, the House of Representatives, and the Senate*, 23 U. KAN. L. REV. 221, 224–7 (1975).

And see *Dole* v. *Carter*, 569 F.2d. 1109 (1977), a suit to enjoin the President from agreeing to return the Crown of St. Stephen to Hungary, on the ground that it required Senate consent.

165. In *Wilson* v. *Girard*, 354 U.S. 524, 528–9 (1957), the Supreme Court said: 'In light of the Senate's ratification of the Security Treaty after consideration of the Administrative Agreement, which had already been signed, and its subsequent ratification of the NATO Agreement, with knowledge of the commitment to Japan under the Administrative Agreement, we are satisfied that the

approval of Article II of the Security Treaty authorized the making of the Administrative Agreement and the subsequent Protocol embodying the NATO Agreement provisions governing jurisdiction to try criminal offenses.'

Numerous executive agreements have been made pursuant to NATO. In view of the important consequences and obligations new members entail, however, it was assumed that the addition of new members to NATO required consent of the Senate. *Hearings on the North Atlantic Treaty Before the Senate Comm. on Foreign Relations,* 81st Cong., 1st Sess. 26 (1949). There has been no practice of seeking Senate consent in regard to membership in organizations like the United Nations, the Specialized Agencies, or other multilateral organizations in which additional members would not importantly modify U.S. obligations, and which have 'parliamentary' procedures for admission of new members and contemplate 'open membership'. Senate consent to the original treaty can be deemed to imply consent to the procedures for admitting new members.

166. Some of the examples that follow are derived from a long series listed in CRANDALL, TREATIES (n. 1 above) Ch. VIII. The agreements mentioned in the text are: Rush–Bagot Agreement, 8 Stat. 231 (1817), T.S. No. 110½; Root–Takahira Agreement, [1908] FOREIGN REL. U.S. 510–12 (1912), T.S. No. 511½; Lansing–Ishii Agreement, 3 MALLOY, TREATIES (n. 10 to Ch. I) 2720–2, T.S. No. 630; Gentlemen's Agreement with Japan, 1907 (substance of this agreement, never published verbatim, is in a letter from the Japanese Ambassador to the United States to Secretary of State Hughes, April 10, 1924, 63 CONG.REC. 6073–74 (1924)); Correspondence Relating to the Protocol of Agreement with the Dominican Republic Providing for the Collection and Disbursement of Customs Revenues in that Republic, [1905], FOREIGN REL. U.S. 298–391 (1906) n. 162 above; for McKinley's Agreement to provide troops during the Boxer Rebellion see generally 13 RICHARDSON (n. 27 to Ch. II) 6417–25 (1897); Boxer Indemnity Protocol, 1901, 2 MALLOY, TREATIES (n. 10 to Ch. I) 2006, [1901] FOREIGN REL.U.S., App. 312 (1902); Destroyer Exchange with England, 1940, E.A.S. No. 181, n. 164 to this chapter.

167. The President's authority to conclude agreements to implement or supplement a treaty is not difficult to justify. See, e.g., the executive agreement to lease the Guantanamo base, concluded pursuant to the 1903 treaty with Cuba, 1 MALLOY, TREATIES (n. 10 to Ch. I) 358, 360 (1938). For other examples, see CRANDALL, TREATIES (n. 1 above) 117. An executive agreement pursuant to a security treaty with Japan was given effect by the Supreme Court in *Wilson v. Girard*, 354 U.S. 524 (1957); see n. 165 above. The peace treaty with Italy was also supplemented by executive agreements; e.g., Memorandum Agreement with Italy on Financial and Economic Relations, August 14, 1947, T.I.A.S. No. 1757.

It is difficult to see why there was ever any doubt as to the power by general arbitration treaty to authorize the President later to submit claims to arbitration. See WRIGHT (n. 3 to Ch. I) 108–9. Probably he could submit claims to arbitration on his own authority even without an antecedent treaty; *ibid* and n. 186 to this chapter; compare Ch. II, p. 43. But where the Senate has insisted otherwise, the President, by accepting their consent on that condition, is presumably bound by it. Compare the Hague Convention of 1907, 2 MALLOY, TREATIES (n. 10 to Ch. I) at 2247–8, and the General Arbitration Treaty of 1908, Art. II, 1 MALLOY, TREATIES (n. 10 to Ch. I) at 814.

168. 301 U.S. 324, 330–1 (1937); the facts of the case are given above at pp. 220–1. See also *United States* v. *Pink*, 315 U.S. 203 (1942).

169. For lists of such agreements, see, e.g., CRANDALL, TREATIES (n. 1 above) 109–11; FOREIGN CLAIMS SETTLEMENT COMMISSION OF THE UNITED STATES: DECISIONS AND ANNOTATIONS 731–64 (1968). Compare n. 60 to Ch. IX.

170. 453 U.S. 654 (1981).

The Iran–U.S. Claims Tribunal has had many years of successful activity. See, generally, D. Caron, *The Nature of the Iran-United States Claims Tribunal and the Evolving Structure of International Dispute Resolution,* 84 AM. J. INT'L L. 14 (1990).

171. In *Curtiss-Wright*, Sutherland included 'the power to make such international agreements as do not constitute treaties in the constitutional sense' as one of those powers which, though not expressly affirmed by the Constitution, nevertheless exist as inherent in national sovereignty. *United States* v. *Curtiss-Wright Export Corp.*, 299 U.S. 304, 318 (1936).

172. See, e.g., McCLURE, INTERNATIONAL EXECUTIVE AGREEMENTS (n. 149 above) 330, 363, 371; Matthews, *The Constitutional Power of the President to Conclude International Agreements,* 64 YALE L.J. 345, 370 *et seq.,* (1955); Wright, *The United States and International Agreements,* 38 AM. J. INT'L L. 341, 348 (1944); *cf.* McDougal and Lans, 54 YALE L.J. at 246. Theodore Roosevelt's discussion of his action in regard to the San Domingo customs houses (n. 164 to this chapter) implies a view that the Constitution does not limit the President's power to make executive agreements. T. ROOSEVELT, AUTOBIOGRAPHY 551–2 (1912). Note, *The Executive Claims Settlement Power: Constitutional Authority and Foreign Affairs Applications,* 85 COLUM. L. REV. 155 (1985); Rovine, n. 153 to this chapter; L. MARGOLIS, EXECUTIVE AGREEMENTS AND PRESIDENTIAL POWER IN FOREIGN POLICY 30–46, 78–94 (1986).

173. In The Federalist, Hamilton makes much of the fact that whereas the King of Great Britain could himself make treaties, the President could not. 'In this respect, therefore, there is no comparison between the intended power of the president and the actual power of the British sovereign.' THE FEDERALIST No. 69, at 448. Recall also the view that the President makes treaties essentially as an agent of the Senate.

174. A different issue is whether under international law the United States could ever claim it was not bound by an agreement because it was made without Senate consent. Whether a state can escape obligation on the ground that those who incurred it in her behalf acted *ultra vires* under the national constitution is not wholly agreed. See H. BLIX, THE TREATY-MAKING POWER 370–4 (1960). Compare Art. 46(1) of the Vienna Convention on the Law of Treaties, 63 AM.J. INT'L L. 875, 890 (1969), which provides that a state cannot invoke failure to comply with its internal law as a defense 'unless that violation was

manifest and concerned a rule of its internal law of fundamental importance'. Senate consent in the United States has been cited as an example of a fundamental requirement. A. McNair, The Law of Treaties 63 (1961). But the power of the President to make many agreements without the Senate casts some doubt on the 'fundamental importance' of Senate consent; in any event, failure to obtain such consent cannot be a 'manifest' violation of the Constitution since no one can say with certainty when it is required. See also Glennon, *Treaty Process Reform: Saving Constitutionalism Without Destroying Diplomacy*, 52 U.Cin.L.Rev. 84 (1983).

175. In the language quoted p. 220, Sutherland might leave the impression that what matters is whether an agreement is called a treaty, or something else, but surely constitutional power does not hang on those labels. Even international practice is hardly firm and clear about them: there is nothing to prevent nations from calling an agreement a treaty instead of a *modus vivendi*, or vice versa, and international law accords all these agreements the same binding effect. See Restatement (n. 2 to Preface) § 301.

On the difficulty of distinguishing executive agreements from treaties, see, e.g., Dulles, *Bricker Hearings*, 1953, at 866. It does not seem unreasonable to suggest that the Bricker Amendment might have succeeded in limiting or regulating executive agreements if its proponents had been able effectively to define them and distinguish their scope clearly from that of treaties.

176. See Senator Taft, n. 164 to this chapter. But compare: 'In some instances we have come close to reversing the traditional distinction between the treaty as the instrument of a major commitment and the executive agreement as the instrument of a minor one.' Senate Comm. on Foreign Relations, National Commitments, S.Rep. No. 129, 91st Cong., 1st Sess. 28 (1969).

In 1939 an Assistant Secretary of State wrote: 'International agreements involving political issues or changes of national policy and those involving international arrangements of a permanent character usually take the form of treaties. But international agreements embodying adjustments of detail carrying out well-established national policies and traditions and those involving arrangements of a more or less temporary nature usually take the form of executive agreements.' Sayre, *The Constitutionality of the Trade Agreements Act*, 39 Colum.L.Rev. 751, 755 (1939). That distinction, too, is not consistently reflected in practice.

177. Compare nn. 9, 10 to this chapter. Senate committees or individual Senators are sometimes informed of confidential agreements privately. Sometimes constitutional formalities are satisfied by making an unclassified covering treaty to which the Senate's consent is obtained, and classified executive agreements pursuant to the treaty.

178. See S.Res. 85, 90th Cong. 1st Sess., 115 Cong.Rec. 2603 (1969). The same resolution was originally introduced in 1967 (S.Res. 151, 113 Cong.Rec. 20702), and was modified by the Senate Foreign Relations Committee after extensive hearings. See S.Rep. No. 797, 90th Cong., 1st Sess. (1967); *Hearings on S.Res. 151 Before the Senate Comm. on Foreign Relations*, 90th Cong., 1st Sess. (1967). Senator Fulbright reintroduced his original resolution in 1969, and

this time it was approved by the Senate Foreign Relations Committee without modification. S.Rep. No. 129, 91st Cong., 1st Sess. (1969). The Senate also sought to require the President to obtain its consent to all base agreements but in conference the House of Representatives refused to accede.

In December, 1950, while Prime Minister Attlee was visiting in the United States, twenty-four Republican senators introduced and debated a resolution to require Senate advice and consent to any agreement that might be made by President Truman and the Prime Minister. See 96 Cong.Rec. 16173 (1950).

179. See 115 Cong.Rec. 17245 (1969).

180. See Ch. IV, p. 55.

181. The President is required to transmit to Congress all international agreements other than treaties, within 60 days after their execution. If the President deemed public disclosure of an agreement to be prejudicial to national security, he shall transmit it instead to the foreign affairs committees of both houses of Congress under injunction of secrecy to be removed only upon due notice from the President. Case Act of 1972, Pub. L. No. 92–403, 86 Stat. 619, codified as amended at 1 U.S.C. § 112b (1994). In 1978 Congress amended the Case Act to extend the definition of international agreement to include 'the text of any oral international agreement, which agreement shall be reduced to writing'. See Pub. L. No. 95–426 § 708(1).

Pub. L. No. 100–204, Title I, § 139, Dec. 22, 1987, 101 Stat. 1347 added: '(a) Restriction on use of funds. If any international agreement, whose text is required to be transmitted to the Congress pursuant to the first sentence of subsection (a) of section 112b of Title I, United States Code (commonly referred to as the "Case–Zablocki Act") is not so transmitted within the 60–day period specified in that sentence, then no funds authorized to be appropriated by this or any other Act shall be available after the end of that 60–day period to implement that agreement until the text of that agreement has been so transmitted.'

182. See the legislation regarding oral executive agreements n. 181 above. The regulation listing criteria to be applied as to whether an undertaking constitutes an international agreement within the meaning of the Case Act specifically includes agency-level agreements and oral agreements. 22 C.F.R. § 181.2.

183. *United States* v. *Guy W. Capps, Inc.*, 204 F.2d 655 (4th Cir. 1953), *aff'd on other grounds*, 348 U.S. 296 (1955). The Acting Secretary of State and the Canadian Ambassador had exchanged notes in which it was agreed that Canada would permit the export of potatoes into the United States only if the importer agreed that they would be used exclusively for seed. The Capps Company gave such assurances but later sold the potatoes to a grocery chain. The United States sued for damages and the lower court directed a verdict for the Company on the ground that the United States had shown no breach of contract and no damage. The Court of Appeals affirmed on the ground that the executive agreement was void; the Supreme Court affirmed the judgments below but did so on the grounds relied on by the trial court.

184. 204 F.2d at 659.

Lower courts have held that 'orderly marketing arrangements', whereby the

Executive branch negotiates voluntary restraints on exporting to and from the United States, are within the Executive power since they are not legally binding agreements. See *Consumers Union of the United States, Inc.* v. *Kissinger*, 506 F.2d 136 (D.C.Cir. 1974) *cert. denied*, 421 U.S. 1004 (1975).

185. e.g., the International Antidumping Code. See *Hearings on the International Antidumping Code Before the Senate Comm. on Finance*, 90th Cong., 2d Sess. 13 (1969). At the beginning, United States participation in G.A.T.T. (Oct. 30, 1947, 61 Stat. A3, T.I.A.S.No.1700), may also have been wholly on Presidential authority: compare the provision in the Trade Agreements Extension Act, Ch. IV, pp. 97–8. In recent years, U.S. participation in G.A.T.T. has been supported by legislation, which also authorized the President to negotiate additional trade agreements. See the Trade Act of 1974, the Trade Agreements Act of 1979, and the Trade and Tariff Act of 1984. The Omnibus Trade and Competitiveness Act of 1988 authorized the negotiations leading to the Uruguay Round Agreements, by which G.A.T.T. was reconstituted into the World Trade Organization and which Congress approved in the Uruguay Round Agreements Act of 1994, Pub.L.No. 103–465, 108 Stat. 4809 (1994). But that Act did not purport to deprive the President of authority to negotiate other agreements on his own authority. See generally IMPLEMENTING THE URUGUAY ROUND (1996) (J.Jackson & A.Sykes, eds. 1996) and, in particular, Leebron, *Implementation of the Uruguay Round Results in the United States, ibid.*

In 1965 the Acting Legal Adviser of the State Department took the position that trade agreements may be concluded either by executive agreement or by treaty, and that Congressional authorization is clearly needed only when the agreement is inconsistent with prior legislation. Letter from Leonard C. Meeker to Senator Fulbright, Feb. 24, 1965, in *Hearings on the United States—Canada Automotive Products Agreement Before the House Comm. on Ways and Means*, 89th Cong., 1st Sess. 226–7 (1965); compare *id.* at 227–30.

186. See, e.g., T. Roosevelt, note 164 this chapter; Borchard, n. 153 to this chapter, at 678–9; *cf.* 88 CONG.REC. 9276 (1942) (remarks of Senator Taft). A related suggestion would have it that agreements that can be consummated immediately and do not require legislative implementation need not be submitted for Senate approval. 39 OP. ATT'Y GEN. 484, 487 (1940). Such alleged limitations have been widely criticized. See, e.g., Levitan, *Executive Agreements,* 35 ILL.L.REV. at 376–8; McDougal and Lans, 54 YALE L.J. at 331–48 (n. 153 to this chapter); CORWIN, THE PRESIDENT (n. 5 to Intro. to Pt. II) 214; Lissitzyn, *Duration of Executive Agreements,* 54 AM.J.INT'L L. 860–70 (1960).

It has also been suggested that Senate consent is not necessary for agreements that involve only obligations or concessions by the other side. See 30 OP.ATT'Y GEN. 484, 487 (1940). Compare, e.g., *Smallwood* v. *Clifford*, 286 F.Supp. 97, 100 (D.C.D.C. 1968). That case upheld an executive agreement establishing the status of U.S. forces in Korea; a basis for that executive agreement might be found in a treaty between the United States and the Republic of Korea. See Korean Mutual Defense Treaty of 1953, art. IV, [1954] 5 U.S.T. 2368, T.I.A.S. No. 3097.

Some other assumed limitations on the President's agreement-making authority have also not survived. It was suggested that while the President could arbitrate claims by the United States on his own authority, an agreement to arbitrate claims against the United States required Senate consent. 5 MOORE, DIGEST (n. 50 to Ch. II) 211. Presidents in fact have agreed to arbitrate claims against the United States. See WRIGHT (n. 3 to Ch. I) 108–9. Compare the Algiers Accord, p. 221 and n. 191 to this chapter.

187. The suggestion has been made frequently. See, e.g., Morse, *Hearings, Separation of Powers* 75; see also *id.* at 63. Compare Attorney General Jackson's statement that agreements requiring Congressional implementation 'are customarily submitted' for Senate approval as treaties. 39 OP.ATT'Y GEN. 484, 487 (1940).

188. See, e.g., *Russian Socialist Federated Soviet Republic* v. *Cibrario*, 235 N.Y. 255, 263, 139 N.E. 259, 262 (1923); *James & Co.* v. *Second Russian Ins. Co.*, 239 N.Y. 248, 257, 146 N.E. 369, 371 (1925); *Vladikavkazsky Ry. Co.* v. *New York Trust Co.*, 263 N.Y. 369, 378, 189 N.E. 456, 460 (1934); *Moscow Fire Ins. Co.* v. *Bank of New York & Trust Co.*, 280 N.Y. 286, 20 N.E.2d 758 (1939), *aff'd by an equally divided court*, 309 U.S. 624 (1940). The Act of State doctrine, Ch. V, p. 137, does not apply where the assets confiscated by a foreign government are situated here. See, e.g., *Republic of Iraq* v. *First National City Bank*, 353 F.2d 47 (2d Cir. 1965), *cert. denied*, 382 U.S. 1027 (1966).

Earlier the Soviet Government had tried to recover these claims in court, but the New York courts held that it was against the policy of the State of New York to give effect to confiscations of assets situated in the state.

189. 301 U.S. at 331.

190. *United States* v. *Pink*, 315 U.S. 203 (1942).

A California Court invalidated California Buy-American provisions as inconsistent with G.A.T.T. *Baldwin-Lima-Hamilton Corp.* v. *Superior Court*, 25 Cal.Rptr. 798, 208 Cal.App.2d 803 (D.Ct.App.1962). GATT may have been a sole executive agreement. See n. 185 to this chapter. Other courts have held that such Buy American acts violate the Commerce Clause. See Ch. VI.

191. The Iran Hostage Agreement would bar suits in state courts as well. See the Algiers Accord, art. VII, in 20 I.L.M. 230–3 (1981).

192. *Valentine* v. *United States ex rel. Neidecker*, 299 U.S. 5 (1936), n. 13 to Ch. IV.

193. A century earlier several Justices held that when the Governor of Vermont sought to extradite one Holmes to Canada, he was entering into an agreement with Canada which Vermont could not do without Congressional consent. *Holmes* v. *Jennison*, 34 U.S. (14 Pet.) 540 (1840), discussed in Ch. VI, p. 153.

194. In 1883, the Attorney General concluded that the President could not, on his own authority, extend to the German Government the privilege of taking testimony of prisoners in state prisons. 17 OP.ATT'Y GEN. 565 (1883). It is questionable whether that opinion survives *Belmont* and *Pink*.

Whether an agreement is self-executing is considered a matter of interpretation, first for the President then for the courts. See p. 200, this chapter. As a matter of interpretation, however, *ad hoc* agreements governing some single instance would rarely be intended to await congressional action, especially if the agreement is to be carried out immediately; indeed some agreements exist solely by implication in the President's act of executing them.

195. See 204 F.2d. 655, 660. For criticism of *Capps*, see Matthews, *The Constitutional Power of the President to Conclude International Agreements*, 64 YALE L.J. 345, 386–87 (1955). Compare *South Puerto Rico Sugar Co. Trading Corp.* v. *United States*, 334 F.2d 622, 634 (Ct.Cl. 1963), where the Court of Claims suggested that the Supreme Court's affirmance of *Capps* on other grounds 'neutralized' the views of the Court of Appeals on executive agreements. See also Note, *The Executive Claims Settlement Power: Constitutional Authority and Foreign Affairs Applications*, 85 COLUM.L.REV. 155, 183 (1985) (*Capps* was followed in *Swearingen* v. *United States*, 565 F.Supp. 1019 (D. Colo. 1983). But see *United States* v. *Walczak*, 783 F. 2d 852 (9th Cir 1986); *Guerra* v. *Guajardo*, 466 F.Supp. 1046 (S.D. Tex. 1978) *aff'd*, 597 F. 2d 769 (5th Cir. 1979).

196. Of course, those who argue that a treaty should not be law in the face of an earlier statute, would hold that view as to executive agreements, *a fortiori*. It has been argued that a power in the President to 'overrule' Congressional legislation is irreconcilable with the 'entire tenor' of the Constitution. See MCCLURE, INTERNATIONAL EXECUTIVE AGREEMENTS 343. Compare *United States* v. *Clarke*, 87 U.S. (20 Wall.) 92, 112–13 (1874) ('No power was ever vested in the President to repeal an act of Congress').

197. In *Harris* v. *United States*, 768 F. 2d 124 (1985), the court held that executive agreements could not supersede provisions in the Federal Tax Code. But such agreements would seem to partake of the authority of the underlying treaty and would seem to be within the later-in-time principle.

198. *Cf.* THE FEDERALIST No. 64 (Jay) quoted in *Pink*: 'All constitutional acts of power, whether in the executive or in the judicial department, have as much legal validity and obligation as if they proceeded from the legislature.' 315 U.S. at 230. An argument can be made that even if unilateral acts of the President do not have effect as law, sole executive agreements stand better. Like a treaty, an executive agreement has the 'seriousness' of an international act and an international obligation, clearly engaging international interests of the United States. For a judicial suggestion that, like a treaty, an executive agreement might supersede an earlier act of Congress, see *Etlimar Société Anonyme of Casablanca* v. *United States*, 106 F. Supp. 191 (Ct. Cl. 1952). And see an early case from the Territory of Washington that appears to give effect to an executive agreement to modify the government of the territory as earlier provided by Congress. *Watts* v. *United States*, 1 Wash.Terr. 288 (1870).

It has been suggested that F.D.R'.s destroyer agreement with Great Britain (p. 219 this chapter), was inconsistent with existing statutes and represents an assertion of the power to supersede an act of Congress by sole executive agreement. See E. CORWIN, THE CONSTITUTION AND WORLD ORGANIZATION 42 (1944); also CORWIN, THE PRESIDENT (n. 5 to Intro. to Pt. II) 238. But Attorney General Jackson did not hold that view: he thought that the agreement was not inconsistent with any statute, and indeed expressed the opinion that the

President could not transfer certain mosquito boats because that was forbidden by statute. 39 Op.Att'y Gen. 484, 494 (1940).

Franklin Roosevelt also entered into agreements to station troops in Greenland and Iceland apparently in disregard of Congressional legislation limiting conscripted troops to service in the Western Hemisphere and the territorial possessions of the United States. See Defense of Iceland by United States Forces, July 1, 1941, 55 Stat. 1547 (1941), E.A.S. No. 232; Defense of Greenland, April 9, 1941, 55 Stat. 1245 (1941), E.A.S. No. 204. Compare the Selective Training and Service Act of 1940, ch. 720, § 3(e), 54 Stat. 885, 896 (1940). See Ch. IV, p. 100. Perhaps the President believed that agreements under this power as Commander in Chief could disregard Congressional limitations, even if executive agreements generally could not.

Another instance is cited in a Congressional committee report in 1969: 'This was illustrated in 1968, in the course of a controversy between the Senate and the President over the International Anti-Dumping Code agreed to by the President as an adjunct to the Kennedy round of negotiations on reciprocal trade. The conflict arose because of congressional expressions of opinion against the negotiation and signature of such a code during the Paris meetings, the execution of such an agreement by the President, the alleged conflict between the terms of the code and preexisting statutory law, and the suggestion by the executive branch that executive agreements, like treaties were superior in law to prior, inconsistent statutes.' *Separation of Powers,* S.Rep.No. 549, 91st Cong., 1st Sess. 16 (1969).

NOTES, CHAPTER VIII. INTERNATIONAL LAW AND INTERNATIONAL
ORGANIZATIONS: CONSTITUTIONAL ISSUES FOR THE UNITED STATES,
pp. 231 to 273

1. In addition to customary law and treaties, the 'sources' of international law
   include rules that have been accepted by the international community by deriva-
   tion from 'general principles common to the major legal systems of the world',
   RESTATEMENT (n. 2 to Preface) § 102(1)(c). The Statute of the International
   Court of Justice, Article 38(1)(c), includes 'the general principles of law recognized by civilized nations' among the law which the Court shall apply.

   For constitutional purposes, 'general principles' can ordinarily be assimilated
   to customary law.
2. See generally HENKIN, INTERNATIONAL LAW: POLITICS AND VALUES (1995) Ch. II;
   O. SCHACHTER, INTERNATIONAL LAW IN THEORY AND PRACTICE (1991). See also
   R. HIGGINS, PROBLEMS AND PROCESS, INTERNATIONAL LAW AND HOW WE USE IT.
   (1994). Some of this customary law has been codified and developed since the
   Second World War by multilateral treaty, principally under the auspices of the
   United Nations General Assembly, many of them through the efforts of the
   International Law Commission. See, e.g., the 1958 conventions adopted April
   28, 1958, which codified, clarified, and somewhat modified the law of the seas.
   Convention on the High Seas, 450 U.N.T.S. 82, T.I.A.S. No. 5200; Convention
   on the Continental Shelf, 499 U.N.T.S. 311, T.I.A.S. No. 5578; Convention on
   the Territorial Sea and the Contiguous Zone, 516 U.N.T.S. 205, T.I.A.S. No.
   5639; Convention on Fishing and Conservation of the Living Resources of the
   High Seas, 599 U.N.T.S. 285, T.I.A.S. No. 5969. The 1982 Convention on the
   Law of the Sea, concluded by the Third U.N. Conference on the Law of the Sea,
   entered into force on Nov. 16, 1994. See 33 I.L.M. 309 (1994).

   Other treaties that largely codified customary law include the Vienna
   Convention on Diplomatic Relations, done April 18, 1961, 500 U.N.T.S. 95;
   Vienna Convention on the Law of Treaties, 1155 U.N.T.S. 331, printed in 63
   AM.J.INT'L L. 875 (1969); the International Convention Against the Taking of
   Hostages, Dec. 4, 1979, 18 I.L.M. 1456, United Nations Doc. A/C.6/34/1.23
   (1979); Convention on the Prevention and Punishment of Crimes Against
   Internationally Protected Persons, Including Diplomatic Agents, Dec. 14, 1973,
   28 U.S.T. 1975, T.I.A.S. No. 8532, 1035 U.N.T.S. 167 (1974); Convention for
   the Suppression of Unlawful Acts Against the Safety of Civil Aviation, Sept. 23,
   1971, 24 U.S.T. 564, T.I.A.S. No. 7570, 974 U.N.T.S. 177 (entered into force
   Jan. 26, 1973), reprinted in 10 I.L.M. 1151 (1971); and Convention Against
   Torture and Other Cruel, Inhuman or Degrading Treatment or Punishment,
   adopted Dec. 10, 1984, United Nations Doc. A/Res/39/46 (1985), reprinted in
   23 I.L.M. 1027 (1984). See generally n. 101 to Ch. VII.

   Some multilateral treaties have contributed to development of customary law
   on their subject. See generally RESTATEMENT (n. 2 to Preface) § 102, Comment *i*.
3. *Chisholm* v. *Georgia*, 2 U.S. (2 Dall.) 419, 474 (1793). Compare: 'When the
   United States declared their independence they were bound to receive the law

of nations, in its modern state of purity and refinement', Wilson, J., in *Ware v. Hylton*, 3 U.S. (3 Dall.) 199, 281 (1796).

4. For the suggestion that for our Constitutional Fathers 'the law of nations' included also private international law, see n. 22 to Ch. III. Today the rules of conflicts are largely domestic law except insofar as they may be modified by treaty. See Ch. VII.

5. SEE L. HENKIN, HOW NATIONS BEHAVE: LAW AND FOREIGN POLICY (2d edn. 1979) Ch. II.

6. For example, in 1779 the Continental Congress resolved that the United States would cause the 'law of nations to be strictly observed'. 14 J. CONT. CONG. 635. In 1781, it recommended that the states adopt laws to punish offenses against the law of nations, 21 J. CONT. CONG. 1136–7. See also THE FEDERALIST No. 3 (John Jay). Art. I, sec. 8 of the Constitution gives Congress the power to define and punish offenses against the law of nations. And see the constitutional provisions on the jurisdiction of the courts in respect of treaties, Art. III, and the provision declaring treaties to be law of the land, Art. VI.

7. The United States accepted the compulsory jurisdiction of the International Court of Justice in 1946, but terminated its acceptance in 1986. It remains subject to the jurisdiction of the Court for disputes arising under many treaties.

8. The statute of the International Criminal Tribunal for the Former Yugoslavia, approved by the United Nations Security Council under U.S. leadership, requires states to 'cooperate fully with the International Tribunal and its organs'. See U.N.S.C. Res. 827 (1993), 'Resolution on Establishing an International Tribunal for the Prosecution of Persons Responsible for Serious Violations of International Law Committed in the Territory of the Former Yugoslavia', reprinted in 32 I.L.M. 1203 (1993).

9. See generally HENKIN, HOW NATIONS BEHAVE, (n. 5 above) Ch. III, and INTERNATIONAL LAW: POLITICS AND VALUES, (n. 10 below) Ch. III. International law gives 'specific performance' or restitution as a remedy only in limited cases. And political enforcement of international law is available in principle only through the United Nations Security Council (subject to veto), and only for violations that threaten international peace and security. See RESTATEMENT (n. 2 to Preface) § 901, Comment *d,* and Reporters' Note 4.

10. But states differ as to whether courts will give effect to legislation that is inconsistent with a treaty or with customary law. Compare Article 94 of the Netherlands Constitution of 1983, and Article 55 of the Constitution of France, with Germany's *Grundgesetz* Article 32, and the Italian Constitution Article 10. See THE EFFECT OF TREATIES IN DOMESTIC LAW (F. JACOB AND S. ROBERTS, (eds.) 1987); also Wildhaber and Breitenmoser 'The Relationship between Customary International Law and Municipal Law in Western European Countries', 48 *Zeitschrift für Ausländisches Offentliches Recht und Völkerrecht* 163 (1988), excerpted in INTERNATIONAL LAW, CASES AND MATERIALS (HENKIN, PUGH, SCHACHTER & SMIT eds., 3d edn. 1993) pp. 154 *et. seq.*; NATIONAL TREATY LAW AND PRACTICE (LEIGH & BLAKESLEE, eds. 1995). See also HENKIN, INTERNATIONAL LAW: POLITICS AND VALUES (1995), p. 73.

Compare *The Chinese Exclusion Case*, 130 U.S. 581, 602 (1889): 'This court is not a censor of the morals of other departments of the government: it is not invested with any authority to pass judgment on the motives of their conduct.'

11. *Whitney* v. *Robertson*, 124 U.S. 190 (1888), discussed in n. 129 to Ch. VII. See RESTATEMENT (n. 2 to Preface) § 115.

12. See n. 6 above.

13. *The Paquete Habana*, 175 U.S. 677, 700, 708 (1899), discussed p. 239 below; *The Nereide*, 13 U.S. (9 Cranch) 338, 423 (1815).

14. For a strongly held view to the contrary, see Paust, *Is the President Bound by the Supreme Law of the Land?*, 9 HASTINGS CON. L. Q. 719 (1982). See also his contribution to the symposium, and the symposium generally, in *Agora: May the President Violate Customary Law?*, 81 AM. J. INT'L L. 371 (1987). Also, Leigh, *Is the President Above Customary International Law?*, 86 AM. J. INT'L L. 757 (1992); GLENNON, CONSTITUTIONAL DIPLOMACY, 232–48 (1990).

15. 175 U.S. 677 at 700.

16. As a textual matter, the reference in the Supremacy Clause to 'the laws of the United States which shall be made in pursuance' of the Constitution, does not easily include international law. Customary international law, it will be argued, is the law of the international community of which the United States is a member, not the law of the United States directly. Strictly, customary international law is not 'made'; it *results* from the practice of states. If it is 'made', not all of it was made 'pursuant' to the Constitution, since much of it antedated the Constitution. If it is made, it is not made by the United States and through its governmental institutions alone but by them together with many foreign governments in a process to which the United States contributes only in an uncertain way and to an indeterminate degree.

Treaties do not have to qualify as 'Laws of the United States' since they are expressly mentioned in the Supremacy Clause and in Art. III. Compare Ch. VII.

Congress has implemented obligations under international law by statute. See, e.g., WRIGHT (n. 3 to Ch. I) 179–86 for various old statutes punishing offenses against foreign governments or persons protected by international law, or those committed on the high seas, or violations of neutrality laws or international boundaries or treaties. International law is sometimes incorporated by reference in federal law. See, e.g., Act of April 10, 1806, ch. 20, § 2, 2 Stat. 359, 371; Act of March 3, 1819, ch. 76, § 5, 3 Stat. 510, 513–14; for a more recent example, see 18 U.S.C. § 1651 (1994) which addresses 'piracy under the law of nations'. See also WRIGHT (n. 3 to Ch. I) 179–83. Compare *United States* v. *Repentigny*, 72 U.S. (5 Wall.) 211 (1866); *United States* v. *Smith*, 18 U.S. (5 Wheat.) 153 (1820); *Ex parte Quirin*, 317 U.S. 1 (1942).

Since 1789 the federal courts have had jurisdiction 'where an alien sues for a tort only in violation of the law of nations or a treaty of the United States'. 1 Stat. 73, 77 (1789), as amended, 28 U.S.C. § 1350 (1994). See n. 35 to this chapter. This grant was independent of the diversity jurisdiction of the federal courts and suggests that the first Congress took the view that the law of nations was part of the laws of the United States (not of the states) for purposes of Art. III. See Note, *Federal Common Law and Article III: A Jurisdictional*

Approach to Erie, 74 YALE L.J. 325, 335–7 (1965). For a recent exercise of that jurisdiction in the case of a violation of international law of human rights, see, e.g., *Filartiga* v. *Pena-Irala*, 630 F.2d 876 (2d Cir. 1987) and subsequent cases, n. 36 below.

In a number of instances, Congress has left it to the state courts to enforce sanctions for violations of international law, even after it had enacted laws to punish such offenses. Thus, at one time at least, it was assumed that treason and sedition against a foreign government might be punished by the states. See 2 MOORE, DIGEST (n. 50 to Ch. II) 432. Perhaps that would now be an impermissible intrusion in foreign relations under *Zschernig* v. *Miller*, Chapter VI, pp. 162–5.

17. American judges followed their British ancestors who had earlier said that the law of nations was part of the law of England. See, e.g., Lord Mansfield in *Triquet and Others* v. *Bath*, 97 Eng.Rep. 936, 938, 3 Burr. 1478 (K.B.1764). Numerous statements speak of the law of nations as being part of the common law received in the United States from England, e.g., Iredell, J., in *Talbot* v. *Jansen*, 3 U.S. (3 Dall.) 133, 161 (1795). See generally, Sprout, *Theories as to the Applicability of International Law in the Federal Courts of the United States*, 26 AM.J.INT'L L. 280 (1932). See generally Henkin, *International Law as the Law of the United States*, 88 MICH. L. REV. 155 (1984); Henkin, *The Chinese Exclusion Case and Its Progeny*, 100 HARV.L.REV. 853 (1987).

Even without state legislation to that effect, some states treated violations of international law as violations of state law: e.g., in 1784, in *Respublica* v. *De Longchamps*, see n. 105 to Ch. VII, a Philadelphia court found the accused guilty of assault on the Secretary of the French legation, 'a crime against the whole world'. (*Id.* at 116.) States can continue to enforce international law unless barred by federal law. Compare *Fox* v. *Ohio*, 46 U.S. (5 How.) 410, 417 (1847). Compare Washington's first neutrality proclamation of April 22, 1793, in which he announced that he had given instructions to prosecute persons who violate the law of nations, 11 Stat. 753 (App.1859). It is now established that the federal courts can punish violations only pursuant to statute. See *United States* v. *Hudson & Goodwin*, 11 U.S. (7 Cranch) 32 (1812).

18. At one time, the Supreme Court denied review of state determinations of customary international law on the ground that they did not raise federal questions. *New York Life Ins. Co.* v. *Hendren*, 92 U.S. 286 (1875); *Oliver American Trading Co.* v. *Mexico*, 264 U.S. 440 (1924); *Wulfsohn* v. *Russian Socialist Federated Soviet Republic*, 266 U.S. 580 (1924) *(semble), per curiam* dismissing a writ of error for want of jurisdiction, 234 N.Y. 372, 138 N.E. 24 (1923), *rev'g* 202 App.Div. 421, 195 N.Y.S. 472 (1922), *aff'g* 118 Misc. 28, 192 N.Y.S. 282 (1922). Compare Wright: 'A state constitution or legislative provision in violation of customary international law is valid unless in conflict with a Federal constitutional provision or an act of Congress as would usually be the case.' WRIGHT (n. 3 to Ch. I) 161.

As regards international 'comity', international conflicts of laws, and related subjects, see Ch. V.

19. *Erie R.R.* v. *Tompkins*, 304 U.S. 64 (1938). The *Erie* doctrine, however, applies

to questions of local law: on federal questions, federal courts, like state courts, must apply federal law, including federal law made by the federal courts. See Friendly, *In Praise of* Erie—*And of the New Federal Common Law,* 39 N.Y.U.L.REV. 383 (1964), reprinted in BENCHMARKS (1967) Ch. 9.

In *Bergman* v. *De Sieyes,* 170 F.2d 360 (2d Cir. 1948), Judge Learned Hand held that in cases based on diversity of citizenship, the state court's interpretation of international law is binding on the federal courts. He said that he did not consider whether an avowed refusal to accept a well-established doctrine of international law or a plain misapprehension of it would also be binding on the federal court. Perhaps Judge Hand felt bound by the cases holding that international law did not raise a federal question. See n. 18 above. Perhaps he thought that if a question of international law was sufficiently uncertain there was obviously no uniform or federal view and until one was achieved, it was important that the parties to a particular case should not be able to achieve a different result by 'forum shopping', by going to a federal rather than a state court.

20.   376 U.S. 398. The discussion of the federal character of international law was incidental to the Court's treatment of the Act of State Doctrine. See n. 16 to Ch. V. In *Sabbatino,* Justice Harlan said: '[W]e are constrained to make it clear that an issue concerned with a basic choice regarding the competence and function of the Judiciary and the National Executive in ordering our relationships with other members of the international community must be treated exclusively as an aspect of federal law. It seems fair to assume that the Court did not have rules like the act of state doctrine in mind when it decided were *Erie R. Co.* v. *Tompkins.* Soon thereafter, Professor Philip C. Jessup, now a judge of the International Court of Justice, recognized the potential dangers were *Erie* extended to legal problems affecting international relations. . . . He cautioned that rules of international law should not be left to divergent and perhaps parochial state interpretations.' 376 U.S. 398, 425 (1964).

See Hill, n. 16 to Ch. V. Henkin, note 17 this chapter, 82 MICH. L. REV. at 1558–1560. For earlier suggestions to similar effect, see Jessup, *The Doctrine of Erie Railroad* v. *Tompkins Applied to International Law,* 33 AM.J.INT'L L. 740, 742–3 (1939). See Bradley, J., dissenting in *New York Life Ins. Co.* v. *Hendren,* 92 U.S. 286, 287–8.

In *Chisholm* v. *Georgia,* 2 U.S. (2 Dall.) 419, 474 (1793), Chief Justice Jay said that the 'United States were responsible to foreign nations for the conduct of each state, relative to the laws of nations, and the performance of treaties', that it would be inexpedient to leave such issues to state courts, particularly the courts of the delinquent state, and it was the proper responsibility of a national judiciary. That the Framers expected federal courts to enforce state observance of the law of nations, see THE FEDERALIST No. 3 (Jay) and No. 80 (Hamilton). See also Dickinson, *The Law of Nations as Part of the National Law of the United States,* 101 U.PA.L.REV. 26, 792 (1952) especially at 34–46, 55–65; 1 W. CROSSKEY, POLITICS AND THE CONSTITUTION IN THE HISTORY OF THE UNITED STATES 651–2 (1953). Compare Note, *The Federal Common Law and Article III,* 74 YALE L.J. 325, 335–6 (1964). See generally RESTATEMENT (n. 2 to Preface) § 112(2), Comment *a.*

It has been suggested that principles of international conflicts of law also raise federal questions and those developed by the federal courts should be binding on the states.

Consider the Supreme Court's holding that, even where the federal government has taken no relevant action, the states and their courts may not intrude in matters affecting the foreign relations of the United States. *Zschernig* v. *Miller*, 389 U.S. 429 (1968), Ch. VI, pp. 162–5.

21. See RESTATEMENT (n. 2 to Preface) § 112. There is confusion, too, as to the obligation of the courts to follow the Executive on questions of customary international law. See Hill, n. 16 to Ch. V. See also Note, *The Relationship Between Executive and Judiciary: The State Department as the Supreme Court of International Law*, 53 MINN.L.REV. 389 (1968). It would seem that the courts ought to follow the Executive at least when it has taken an international position on an issue of international law, not only for the obvious practical reasons, but because the practices and policies of executives, including our own, are major ingredients of customary international law, and Executive statements on international law make foreign policy and are legislative in some measure. Compare: 'When articulating principles of international law in its relations with other states, the Executive branch speaks not only as an interpreter of generally accepted and traditional rules, as would the courts, but also as an advocate of standards it believes desirable for the community of nations and protective of national concerns.' *Banco Nacional de Cuba* v. *Sabbatino*, 376 U.S. 398, 432–3 (1964). See RESTATEMENT (n. 2 to Preface) § 112, Comment *c*.

22. 175 U.S. 677, 700 (1900).

23. See, e.g., *Berizzi Bros. Co.* v. *S.S. Pesaro*, 271 U.S. 562 (1926); see Ch. II, p. 54. See also, *The Nereide*, 13 U.S. (9 Cranch) 388 (1815); *The Schooner Exchange* v. *McFaddon*, 11 U.S. (7 Cranch) 116 (1812); *Argentine Republic* v. *Amerada Hess Shipping Corp.*, 488 U.S. 428 (1989); *Saudi Arabia* v. *Nelson*, 113 S.Ct. 1471 (1993). See Ch. II, pp. 54–5.

24. 175 U.S. 677, 700 (1899). See also *Hilton* v. *Guyot*, 159 U.S. 113, 163 (1895).

25. *Id.*, at 708.

26. See RESTATEMENT (n. 2 to Preface) § 115, Reporters' Note 3. See *Tag* v. *Rogers*, 267 F.2d 664 (App.D.C. 1959), *cert. denied*, 362 U.S. 904 (1960); *The Over the Top*, 5 F.2d 838 (D.Conn. 1925).

27. See Henkin, n. 17 above, 100 HARV. L. REV. at 872–8.

28. *The Paquete Habana*, 175 U.S. 677, 700 (1900). The Court did not define or justify that exception, and in intervening years no court has explained which executive acts qualify as public acts to supersede international law, or which executive acts are 'controlling'. Compare the power of the President to denounce or terminate treaties even in violation of their terms, or to act under other constitutional power inconsistently with treaty obligations. See p. 242, and Ch. VII, pp. 211–14. The 'exceptions' do not appear in the court's opinion in *Hilton* v. *Guyot*, n. 24.

29. *Garcia-Mir* v. *Meese*, 788 F.2d 1446 (11th Cir. 1986), *rev'g Fernandez-Roque* v. *Smith*, 622 F. Supp. 887 (N.D. Ga. 1985), *cert. denied*, 479 U.S. 1886 (1986).

The distinction I suggest—that courts must give effect to Presidential acts under their independent constitutional authority that have the effect of law,

512 *Notes, Chapter VIII International Law and Organizations*

but, in the absence of such Presidential legislation, they should enjoin the Executive branch to obey international law—was not recognized in *Garcia-Mir*. In that case, the lower courts accepted that the prolonged detention of Cuban nationals not lawfully admitted to the United States was a violation of international law but refused to enjoin the Attorney General from ordering their detention.

In testimony before the House Judiciary Committee Subcommittee on Civil and Constitutional Rights, Abraham Sofaer, then the Legal Adviser to the Department of State, testified that '[f]orcible abductions from a foreign state clearly violate' the principle of sovereignty, and that 'the United States has repeatedly associated itself with the view that unconsented arrests violate the principle of territorial integrity'. *FBI Authority to Seize Suspects Abroad: Hearings Before the Subcomm. on Civil and Constitutional Rights of the House Jud. Comm.*, 101st Cong. 1st Sess. 31 (1989). See also *Authority of the Federal Bureau of Investigation to Override Customary or Other International Law in the Course of Extraterritorial Law Enforcement Activities*, 13 Op. Off. Legal Counsel 195 (June 21, 1989) and *Extraterritorial Apprehension by the Federal Bureau of Investigation*, 4B Op. Off. Legal Counsel 543 (1980).

30. 788 F.2d at 1455. But see Sweeney, n. 35 below.
31. See Henkin, *The Constitution and United States Sovereignty: A Century of Chinese Exclusion and its Progeny*, 100 HARV. L. REV. 853 (1987); also, *Correspondence*, 87 AM. J. INT'L L. 100 (1993).
32. See, e.g., *The Effect to be Given in the United States to Foreign Nationalization Decrees: Banco Nacional de Cuba v. Sabbatino*, 19 RECORD OF THE ASS'N OF THE BAR OF THE CITY OF N.Y., Report by the Committee on International Law, No. 1, at 12–14 (Supp., Jan. 1964). Compare the lower court opinion in *Sabbatino*, 193 F.Supp. 375, 381–2 (S.D.N.Y.1961). But *cf.* generally Henkin, *Act of State Today: Recollections in Tranquility*, 6 COLUM.J.TRANSNAT'L L. 175, 181–2 (1967); and see L. Collins, *Foreign Relations and the Conflict of Laws*, 6 KING'S COL. L.J. 20 (1995).
33. Compare *Banco Nacional de Cuba v. Sabbatino*, 376 U.S. 398, 42 (1964); *Charlton v. Kelly*, 229 U.S. 447, 474, 476 (1913). That the courts of the United States will not apply international law to acts of foreign governments was held in *Sabbatino* and in other Act of State cases: *Oetjen v. Central Leather Co.*, 246 U.S. 297, 304 (1918); *Ricaud v. American Metal Co.*, 246 U.S. 304, 310 (1918); *Shapleigh v. Mier*, 299 U.S. 468, 471 (1937). Compare *Williams v. Armroyd (The Fortitude)*, 11 U.S. (7 Cranch) 423, 432 (1813).
34. As in the Second Hickenlooper Amendment. See Henkin, n. 32 above. Of course, the federal courts might themselves, perhaps, venture to legislate remedies, under the authority to make law in foreign relations matters established in *Sabbatino*. See Ch. V, pp. 138–40.
35. Judiciary Act of 1789, ch. 20 § 9, 1 Stat. 73, 77. That provision was later amended, 62 Stat. 934 (1948), and as now codified (28 U.S.C. § 1350 (1994)) gives the district courts 'original jurisdiction of any civil action by an alien for a tort only, committed in violation of the law of nations or a treaty of the United States'. This provision would presumably permit an alien to seek an

injunction or money damages for a violation of a treaty that constitutes a 'tort'.

It has been suggested that the Alien Tort Claims Act was designed to give to federal district courts jurisdiction, concurrent with the jurisdiction of the state courts, in 'prize cases', for injury to aliens or their property aboard ships intercepted by U.S. war vessels. See Sweeney, *A Tort Only in Violation of the Law of Nations,* 18 HAST. INT'L. & COMP. L. REV. 445 (1995). If so, the statute may not have intended to provide federal jurisdiction for torts arising out of violations of international law or treaty other than prize law. Of course, by the terms it used, the statute may have conferred more jurisdiction than necessary to meet its immediate purpose. See Dodge, *The Historical Origins of the Alien Tort Statute: A Response to the Originalists,* 19 HAST. INT'L & COMP. L. REV. 221 (1996). Also, in 'Filartiga-type' cases, the court may have jurisdiction as well under 18 U.S.C. § 1331, jurisdiction which may not be limited to suits by aliens. See n. 36 to this chapter.

Professor Sweeney also points out that in *The Paquete Habana,* U.S. courts were sitting as prize courts, and the language of the Supreme Court suggesting that U.S. courts should apply international law only when not governed by controlling legislation or executive act applies only to prize cases where the President has particular authority to declare the applicable prize law. Professor Sweeney concludes that the reading of the Supreme Court's language by the court in *Garcia-Mir,* n. 29 to this chapter, as warranting the Executive in disregarding international law generally was 'nothing but nonsensical construction of what the Supreme Court was actually saying in the case'. *Id.* at 483–4. Compare *Hilton v. Guyot,* n. 24, this chapter.

36. In a series of cases, beginning in *Filartiga v. Pena-Irala,* 630 F.2d 876 (2d Cir. 1980) *on remand,* 57 F.Supp. 860 (E.D.N.Y. 1984), federal courts have given remedies to alien plaintiffs against foreign officials found responsible for acts of torture, on the ground that torture constitutes a violation of the law of nations. See also *Forti v. Suarez-Mason,* 672 F.Supp. 1531 (N.D.Cal. 1987), *reconsidered in part,* 694 F.Supp. 707; *Paul v. Avril,* 812 F.Supp. 207 (S.D.Fla. 1993); *In re Estate of Ferdinand Marcos, Human Rights Litigation,* 978 F.2d 493 (9th Cir. 1994), 25 F.3d 1467 (1994). *Xuncax v. Gramajo,* 886 F.Supp. 162 (D.Mass 1995); *Kadic v. Karadzic,* 70 F.3d 232 (2d Cir. 1995). See RESTATEMENT (n. 2 to Preface) § 702, Reporters' Note 5. These and other cases sought remedies for aliens who alleged violation of international law, but the Alien Tort Claims Act is available also for claims of violation of a treaty. In 1991, Congress enacted the Torture Victims Protection Act giving the federal courts jurisdiction of suits by victims, aliens or citizens, against persons acting under color of foreign law, for torture or extrajudicial killing, 102 Pub.L.No. 256, 106 Stat. 73 (1992).

37. That multilateral 'organization' was established in 1865 to direct, administer, and financially support the lighthouse that had been built by the Moroccan government at Cape Spartel. See Convention Concerning the Cape Spartel Lighthouse, May 31, 1865, 14 Stat. 679–81 (1868), T.S. No. 245. The Convention was terminated by protocol on March 31, 1958 [1958] 9 U.S.T. 527,

T.I.A.S. No. 4029; 320 U.N.T.S. 103. Control was returned to the government of Morocco.

38. U.N. Charter, June 26, 1945, 59 Stat. 1031, T.S. No. 993; U.N. Participation Act of 1945, ch. 583, 59 Stat. 619, *as amended*, 22 U.S.C. §§ 287–287*l* (1994). See also the International Organizations Immunities Act, ch. 652, 59 Stat. 669 (1945), *as amended*, 22 U.S.C. § 288 (1994).

No one pressed constitutional objections to U.S. adherence to the United Nations Charter, whereas proposals for participation in the League of Nations had run into many such objections. See WRIGHT, (n. 3 to Ch. I) 113–15; also, Wright, *Validity of the Proposed Reservations to the Peace Treaty,* 20 COLUM.L.REV. 121 (1920). Political change apart, major constitutional change (or clarification) had intervened, e.g., *Curtiss-Wright, Missouri* v. *Holland* and the New Deal Commerce clause and Due Process cases. See nn. 6–8 to Chapter III, and n. 28 to Chapter IX. See CORWIN, THE PRESIDENT (n. 5 to Intro. to Pt. II) 217 *et seq.*

39. U.N. Charter, Articles 23, 27; see generally *id.,* Chs. V–VII.

40. *Id.* Article 2(4); compare Article 51. Article 2 is a treaty undertaking independent of the U.N. Organization established elsewhere in the Charter. See several of my writings: HOW NATIONS BEHAVE: LAW AND FOREIGN POLICY (2d edn. 1979) Chs. 7 and 8; *Force, Intervention, and Neutrality in Contemporary International Law,* (1963) PROC.AM.SOC.INT'L L. 147–53; HENKIN ET AL., RIGHT V. MIGHT (2d edn. 1991) pp. 37–60; INTERNATIONAL LAW, POLITICS AND VALUES (1995) Chs. VII and VIII.

41. U.N. Charter, Articles 55, 56.

42. It has been urged, indeed, that the legal concept of war and traditional laws of war have been abolished. See, e.g., Henkin, *Force, Intervention, and Neutrality in Contemporary International Law,* (1963) PROC.AM.SOC.INT'L L., 159–61. But *cf.* Deák, *Neutrality Revisited* in TRANSNATIONAL LAW IN A CHANGING SOCIETY (Friedmann, Henkin, & Lissitzyn, eds.) 137 (1972); see also Norton, *Between the Ideology and the Reality: The Shadow Land of Neutrality,* 17 HARV.J. INT'L L. 249 (1976).

43. Compare: 'The powers of government are delegated in trust to the United States, and are incapable of transfer to any other parties. They cannot be abandoned or surrendered.' *The Chinese Exclusion Case,* 130 U.S. 581, 609 (1889).

44. U.S. Const. Art. II, sec. 3.

45. U.N. Charter, Article 43, para. 3.

46. U.N. Participation Act of 1945, n. 38 above, requires the consent of Congress, not of the Senate alone, but if the Senate gave consent to an Article 43 agreement concluded as a treaty, that treaty would no doubt be valid.

47. See U.N. Charter, Articles 42–7. See Henkin, *Congress, the President and the United Nations,* 3 PACE Y.B. INT'L L. 1 (1991).

48. See n. 8 to this chapter.

49. Article 27(3), *as amended,* 1965, 16 U.S.T. 1134, T.I.A.S. No. 5857, 557 U.N.T.S. 143: 'Decisions of the Security Council on all other matters shall be made by an affirmative vote of nine members including the concurring votes of the permanent members . . .'

The General Assembly, in which resolutions can be adopted by majority vote, or by two-thirds vote on 'important questions' (art. 18(2)), can only recommend action, not command it. See U.N. Charter, Ch. IV. Compare the Uniting for Peace Resolution, November 3, 1950, G.A.Res. 377 A, 5 U.N. GAOR, Supp. 20 (A/1775), at 10.

50. The United Nations Participation Act, n. 38 above, confirms the power of the President to act for the United States in the Security Council, thus lending the support of Congressional authority to his own. The Act requires Congressional approval for Article 43 agreements and expressly supports the President's authority (without further approval by Congress) to act for the United States in determining their use by the Council. See 22 U.S.C. §§ 287a, 287d (1994).

Compare the decision of Congress to flout United Nations sanctions against Rhodesia by requiring the President to permit the importation of Rhodesian chrome. See Pub.L.No. 92–156 § 503, 85 Stat. 423 (1971). U.S. courts upheld the Act of Congress. *Diggs* v. *Shultz*, 470 F.2d. 461 (D.C. Cir. 1972), *cert. denied*, 411 U.S. 931 (1973).

51. U.N. S.C.Res. 83,84 (1950).

52. U.N. S.C.Res. 661, 665, 678 (1990).

53. See 96 Cong. Rec. 9228–33, 9268–9, 9320–3, 9327–9, 9538–9, 9647–9 (1950).

54. That power, which the President might have claimed by virtue of his power to execute the treaty, was in fact expressly confirmed by Congress in Section 5(a) of the United Nations Participation Act, n. 38 above. In the Persian Gulf crisis, the President claimed authority also from the International Emergency Economic Act, Sec. 204(b), 50 U.S.C. § 1703(b) (1988), and the National Emergency Act, 50 U.S.C. § 1621 (1991).

55. U.N. S.C.Res. 665, 678 (1991).

56. 22 U.S.C. § 287c (1994).

57. Section 7 of the United Nations Participation Act declares '[t]hat nothing herein contained shall be construed as an authorization to the President by the Congress to make available to the Security Council for such purpose armed forces, facilities, or assistance. . .' other than those provided pursuant to Article 43. Congress apparently did not consider that the President might wish to send forces for collective self-defense pursuant to Article 51 of the Charter. It is arguable that such forces, too, are made available to the Security Council for its purposes under Article 42, and that Congress was refusing the President that authority also.

58. See 2 H. R. J. Res. 77, 102nd Cong., 1st Sess., 137 Cong. Rec. 443 (1991). See n. 60 to Ch. IV. On Korea, compare Fisher, *The Korean War: On what Legal Basis did Truman Act?* 89 Am. J. Int'l. L. 21 1995.

59. Congress refrained from authorizing or approving the invasion, but authorized funds for a limited operation. See Publ. L. 103–423 (1994). See generally Damrosch, *Agora: The 1994 U.S. Action in Haiti*, 89 Am. J. Int'l L. 58 (1995).

60. See, e.g., *Diggs* v. *Shultz*, 470 F.2d 461 (D.C. Cir. 1972), *cert denied,* 411 U.S. 931 (1973). See generally, *The Chinese Exclusion Case*, 130 U.S. 581 (1889); *Whitney* v. *Robertson*, 124 U.S. 190 (1887).

61. Compare *Garcia-Mir* v. *Meese*, 788 F.2d 1446 (11th Cir.), *cert. denied*, 479 U.S. 1022 (1986) discussed at pp. 244–5.

62. See, e.g., 'A Bill to impose limitations on the placing of United States Armed Forces under the operational control of a foreign national acting on behalf of the United Nations', H.R. 631, 104th Cong., 1st Sess. (1995) and the proposed 'Peace Powers Act of 1995', S. 5, 104th Cong., 1st Sess. (1995) (which would have repealed the War Powers Act and forbidden the President to place U.S. troops under United Nations command).
63. 'Certain Expenses of the United Nations', 1962 I.C.J. 151 (July 20).
64. North Atlantic Treaty, April 4, 1949, 63 Stat. 2241, T.I.A.S. No. 1964, 34 U.N.T.S. 243. The United States later accepted additional member (Greece, Turkey, the Federal Republic of Germany) with Senate consent. [1951] T.I.A.S. No. 2390, 126 U.N.T.S. 350; [1955] T.I.A.S. No. 3428, 243 U.N.T.S. 308.
65. North Atlantic Treaty, Articles 5 and 11.
66. Constitutional 'niceties' were met also by a two-hat arrangement: the NATO Council asked the United States to make available a U.S. officer as Supreme Commander; the President designated General Eisenhower, whom he also appointed Commander of U.S. Forces in Europe. In this way, the President in effect commanded U.S. forces assigned to NATO through his appointee, a U.S. officer. See D.ACHESON, PRESENT AT THE CREATION 486 (1969).
67. I draw here on HENKIN, ARMS CONTROL (n. 3 to Ch. VI) Ch. VII; see also Henkin, *International Organization and the Rule of Law*, 23 INTERNATIONAL ORGANIZATION 656 (1969).
68. U.N. Charter, Articles 83, 85.
69. See International Monetary Fund Articles of Agreement, art. IV, 60 Stat. 1401, T.I.A.S. No. 1501. Under the Bretton Woods Agreement Act of 1945, c. 339, § 2, 59 Stat 512, codified as amended at 22 U.S.C. § 286c (1994): neither the President nor any person shall, on behalf of the United States 'request or consent to any change in the quota of the United States under article III, section 2(a), of the Articles of Agreement of the Fund. . . .' unless Congress 'by law authorizes such action'.
70. Convention on International Civil Aviation, 1944, Art. 37, 61 Stat. 1180, 1190, T.I.A.S. No. 1591.
71. Wheat Trade Convention, London, March 14, 1986. Entered into force July 1, 1986. Senate Treaty Doc. 100–1. Ratified, U.S. January 27, 1988. International Sugar Agreement, 1987. Done at London, September 11, 1987. Entered into force provisionally March 24, 1988. The World Health Organization and the Universal Postal Union also develop rules and practices in their respective fields, and international officials have propounded cooperative practices for the international control of narcotics. There is regulation also by regional, even by bilateral bodies, especially of fishing. See, e.g., Whaling Convention Act of 1949, ch. 653, 64 Stat. 421 (1950), 16 U.S.C. §§ 916–916l (1994). See HENKIN, ARMS CONTROL (n. 3 to Ch. VI) 107–8 and notes, and *International Organization and the Rule of Law*, n. 67 to this chapter, at 657–61.
    States are bound to conform to 'generally accepted international standards and rules' to prevent injury to the environment, many of which are adopted by international organizations pursuant to Conventions. See RESTATEMENT (n. 2

to Preface) Part VI, Introduction, and § 601, Reporters' Notes and Comment *b*.

72. Uruguay Round Agreements Act, Pub. L. No. 103–465, 108 Stat. 4809 (1994).

73. These are the conclusions of my book ARMS CONTROL (n. 3 to Ch. VI), as summed up in its Ch. IX. I have not been persuaded of the need to change them in important respects.

74. See, for example, the arms control agreements between the United States and the USSR during the 1970s and 1980s, and the Conventions outlawing biological and chemical weapons; e.g., Treaty on the Limitation of Anti-Ballistic Missile Systems, May 26, 1972, U.S.–Soviet Union, 23 U.S.T. 3435, T.I.A.S. 7503, 944 U.N.T.S. 13; Memorandum of Understanding Regarding Bilateral Verification Experiment and Data Exchange Related to Prohibition of Chemical Weapons, Sept. 23, 1989, U.S.–Soviet Union, T.I.A.S. 11460. See generally PRESIDENTS AND ARMS CONTROL (K. Thompson, ed., 1994).

75. U.S. Dep't of State Special Committee on Atomic Energy, *A Report on the International Control of Atomic Energy*, U.S.DEP'T OF STATE PUB.NO. 2498 (1946). See also *International Control of Atomic Energy*, U.S.DEP'T OF STATE PUB.NOS. 2702 (1946), 3161 (1948). *Cf.* 'Findings on the Safeguards to Ensure the Use of Atomic Energy Only for Peaceful Purposes', in *The International Control of Atomic Energy: First Report of the United Nations Atomic Energy Commission to the Security Council*, U.N. DOC.NO. AEC/18 REV.1 (1947). This plan substantially embodied the United States proposal known as the 'Baruch Plan', which, in turn, was based on the proposals of the Acheson–Lilienthal Report.

76. I draw here on HENKIN, ARMS CONTROL (n. 3 to Ch. VI), Ch. VIII.

77. See DEP'T STATE PUB. NO. 2420 (1945), 39 AM.J.INT'L L. (Supp.) 257 (1945). The Nuremberg Charter established a tribunal for the trial of war criminals; it did not commit the United States to submit to the jurisdiction of similar tribunals in the future. The principles of international law recognized by the Nuremberg Charter were unanimously affirmed by the U.N. G.A., Res. 95(I) December 11, 1946, 1 UN GAOR, 2d pt., Verbatim Record 1144 (1946).

78. 'All members of the United Nations are *ipso facto* parties to the Statute of the International Court of Justice'. U.N. Charter, articles 93(1). The jurisdiction of the Court depends on consent of the parties in each case unless the parties had committed themselves to accept its jurisdiction for the solution of disputes in particular treaties or conventions. I.C.J. Statute, Article 36(1). Parties may also accept compulsory jurisdiction of the Court by declaration under Article 36(2) of the Statute. In numerous instances, the United States has accepted the jurisdiction of the Court for issues arising out of particular treaties. See 106 CONG.REC. 11184 (1960); Bishop and Myers, *Unwarranted Extension of Connally Amendment Thinking*, 55 AM.J.INT'L L. 135 (1961).

In 1946, the United States also filed a declaration under Article 36(2), but the reservation imposed by the Senate (including the 'Connally Amendment'), as later interpreted, may have rendered it largely illusory. See 61 Stat. 1218 (1946). But *cf.* Henkin, *The Connally Reservation Revisited and, Hopefully,*

Contained, 65 AM.J.INT'L L. 374 (1971). In 1985, President Reagan terminated the U.S. declaration under Article 36(2). See Dept. of State Letter and Statement concerning Termination of Acceptance of I.C.J. Compulsory Jurisdiction, 24 I.L.M. 1742 (1985). Some anticipate that the United States will file a new declaration but probably subject to limitations and exclusions. Compare generally THE INTERNATIONAL COURT OF JUSTICE AT A CROSS ROADS, (L. Damrosch, ed. 1987).

79. See, for example, the International Covenant on Civil and Political Rights, Article 41, and the optional protocol to the Covenant, Annex to G.A. Res. 2200 (XXI), Dec. 16, 1966; the International Convention on the Elimination of all Forms of Racial Discrimination, Annex to G.A.Res. 2106–A (XX), Jan. 19, 1965; the European Convention for the Protection of Human Rights and Fundamental Freedoms, Nov. 4, 1950, 213 U.N.T.S. 221, and its subsequent protocols; the American Convention on Human Rights, OAS Official Records, OEA/Ser. K/XVI/I.I, Doc. 65, Rev. 1, Corr. 2, Jan. 7, 1970. See n. 83 below.

80. See the International Law Commission report on the establishment of a permanent international court, p. 268 and n. 87 to this chapter.

81. That in some circumstances suits between the United States and another power might come before U.S. courts as well is immaterial; such suits might be concurrently within the judicial power of one or more particular countries as well as of extra-national bodies established by agreement. Nor does it matter that the International Court itself decides whether it has jurisdiction (Statute of the International Court of Justice, Article 36(6), 59 Stat. 1055, 1060 (1945); T.S. No. 933), though at one time a Senate Committee considered it to be unconstitutional to give to a joint commission authority to determine whether a dispute is subject to arbitration under a treaty. S.Doc.No.98, 62d Cong., 1st Sess. 6 (1911), 47 CONG.REC.3935 (1911); see WRIGHT (n. 3 to Ch. I) 111–12. In *Nicaragua* v. *United States*, the International Court of Justice rejected U.S. objections to its jurisdiction, 1984 I.C.J. 392.

82. Compare *Hirota* v. *MacArthur*, 338 U.S. 197 (1948), n. 97 to this chapter.

83. See the American Convention, n. 79 to this chapter; compare the European Convention, *ibid.*, which provides for proceedings against a state brought by the European Commission or by another state, but not by the individual victims. 213 U.N.T.S. 221, Article 48; but compare Article 25. Compare also the Optional Protocol to the International Covenant on Civil and Political Rights, n. 79 to this chapter. The United States is not eligible to become a party to the European Convention, but having adhered to the International Covenant on Civil and Political Rights (see Ch. VII, n. 101) it is eligible to adhere to the Optional Protocol. It has not done so. The United States has declared its willingness, under Article 41 of the Covenant, to be the 'target' of complaints by other states, on a reciprocal basis.

84. Proposals for international tribunals superimposed on national judicial systems are no longer seriously considered, but, hypothetically, they would raise different issues. In the days of the Hague Conferences at the turn of the twentieth century, when international arbitration and adjudication were a principal focus of hopes for a better world, one proposed convention would have estab-

lished an international prize court to hear appeals from national prize courts. The United States, some argued, could not adhere to such arrangements: appeals to the international court directly from lower federal courts would deny the appellate jurisdiction of the Supreme Court; appeals from the Supreme Court to the international court would be inconsistent with the U.S. court being 'the Supreme Court'. To meet such objections the Convention was modified to provide for a new action in the international court instead of appeal from the national courts. Other proposals for appeal from national courts to international tribunals were also modified to avoid constitutional issues for the United States: national courts would be required instead to certify questions of international law or treaty interpretation to an international tribunal, with final decision of the whole case left to the domestic court; then, should United States courts fail to accept the international court's answer in some case, the United States would be in violation of the treaty and be required to compensate those aggrieved. See HENKIN, ARMS CONTROL (n. 3 to Ch. VI). It seems highly unlikely that such arrangements would be given serious consideration in the foreseeable future. See the first edition of the present work p. 197 and accompanying notes.

85. For earlier efforts, see the United Nations Committee on International Criminal Jurisdiction, *Draft Statute for an International Criminal Court*, UN Doc. A/AC.48/4 (1951), reprinted in 46 AM.J.INT'L L. (Supp.) 1 (1952); Wright, *Proposal for an International Criminal Court*, 46 AM.J.INT'L L. 60 (1952). And see HENKIN, ARMS CONTROL (n. 3 to Ch. VI), Ch. VIII and corresponding notes.

   The Convention on the Prevention and Punishment of the Crime of Genocide, December 9, 1948, 78 U.N.T.S. 578, is directed at individual offenders (Art. 4), and provides that persons charged with genocide may be tried by 'such international penal tribunal as may have jurisdiction with respect to those Contracting Parties which shall have accepted its jurisdiction'. (Art. 6). The United States ratified the Convention in 1988. See n. 101 to Ch. VII. The Yugoslavia and Rwanda Tribunals (n. 86 below) may be seen as partial implementation of the Genocide Convention.

86. In 1993, the U.N. Security Council established 'The International Tribunal for the Prosecution of Persons Responsible for Serious Violations of International Humanitarian Law Committed in the Territory of of the Former Yugoslavia', S.C.Res. 808, Feb. 22, 1993; the Council adopted the statute of the Tribunal by S.C.Res. 827, May 25, 1993. The Council declared that it was acting under Chapter VII of the U.N. Charter, and that establishing the Tribunal was a measure necessary to maintain international peace and security. Resolution 827, and Article 29(2) of the Statute of the Tribunal require states to comply with 'any request for assistance or an order of the Tribunal', including arrest, detention and transfer of an accused person. There appears to be a legal obligation on states to comply. See, generally J. O'Brien, *Current Developments, The International Tribunal for Violations of International Humanitarian Law in the Former Yugoslavia*, 87 AM.J.INT'L L. 639 (1993).

   In 1994, the Security Council created another *ad hoc* tribunal, The International Tribunal for Rwanda, S.C. Res. 955, Nov. 8, 1994.

87. The International Law Commission completed a draft statute for a permanent
International Criminal Court and recommended that the General Assembly
convene a diplomatic conference to conclude a treaty and a statute for the
establishment of such a court. See Report of the International Law
Commission on the work of its 46th Session, UN GAOR, 49th Sess., Supp.
No. 10, U.N. Doc. A/49/10 (1994). Since such a court would be established by
treaty, the United States would be bound by it only if it adhered to the treaty
and according to its terms. The proposed court would have jurisdiction to try
violators of the crime of genocide and other crimes to be agreed. It might be
provided that when the Security Council is taking action under Chapter VII of
the U.N. Charter, a prosecution arising from the situation could not be commenced without the Council's authorization. See essays by McCaffrey and by
Crawford, in *Current Developments*, 89 AM. J. INT'L L. 390, 404 (1995).

88. See *Valentine* v. *United States ex rel. Neidecker*, 299 U.S. 5 (1936); *Charlton* v.
Kelly, 229 U.S. 447 (1913); compare 18 U.S.C. § 3184 (1994). The power to
extradite U.S. citizens under a treaty was upheld in an early case that aroused
wide public interest. *United States* v. *Robbins*, 27 F.Cas. 825, No. 16,175 (D.S.C.
1799). (There is some doubt as to whether Robins was in fact an American citizen, but it was apparently assumed that he was.) See n. 19 to Ch. II.

89. For the view that only courts ordained and established by Congress can exercise
the judicial power of the United States, see *Martin* v. *Hunter's Lessee*, 14 U.S.
(1 Wheat.) 304, 330–1 (1816); *Ex parte Milligan*, 71 U.S. (4 Wall.) 2, 121 (1866);
Williams v. *United States*, 289 U.S. 553, 566 (1933); *cf. Robertson* v. *Baldwin*, 165
U.S. 275, 278–9 (1897). It is accepted that federal criminal law can be enacted
only by Congress, not by treaty. See n. 105 to Ch. VII and p. 203.

90. For the suggestion that a person accused of a crime in the United States has a
constitutional right to a trial by a judge enjoying the independence that comes
with life tenure and assured compensation, see *United States ex rel. Toth* v.
Quarles, 350 U.S. 11, 15–17 (1955); *Ex parte Milligan*, 71 U.S. (4 Wall.) 2,
121–2 (1866); compare the court-martial cases, n. 44 to Ch. III.

   One of the grievances in the Declaration of Independence was that the King
had 'made Judges dependent on his Will alone, for the tenure of their offices,
and the amount and payment of their salaries'. Compare THE FEDERALIST NO.
78 (Hamilton).

91. To meet these objections, there had been suggestions in the past that the
United States agree instead to a system that provides trial in U.S. courts with
appeal to an international tribunal. That would raise questions as difficult as
those it would eliminate. It would involve appeal from U.S. courts to a body
other than the Supreme Court, n. 84 above. And if an appeal by the prosecution were permitted after an acquittal in a U.S. court, there would a serious
issue under the double jeopardy clause of the Fifth Amendment. *United States*
v. *Ball*, 163 U.S. 662, 671 (1896); *Peters* v. *Hobby*, 349 U.S. 331, 344–5 (1955);
Green v. *United States*, 355 U.S. 184, 188 (1957); *cf. Kepner* v. *United States*,
195 U.S. 100 (1914); *United States* v. *Sanges*, 144 U.S. 310 (1892); *Benton* v.
Maryland, 395 U.S. 784 (1969); *Price* v. *Georgia*, 398 U.S. 323 (1970).

   If trial by a U.S. court is constitutionally required, trial by an international court with appeal to a U.S. court might not satisfy the requirement, perhaps even if the U.S. court gave the accused a trial *de novo.* Compare *Callan* v. *Wilson*, 127 U.S. 540, 556–7 (1888); but *cf. Crowell* v. *Benson*, 285 U.S. 22 (1932), and Brandeis, J., dissenting *id.* at 86–7; *Ng Fung Ho* v. *White*, 259 U.S. 276, 283 (1922); *Colten* v. *Kentucky*, 407 U.S. 104 (1972).

For an unusual instance, in extraordinary circumstances, of a treaty providing judicial review in U.S. courts of determinations by an international body, see *Abrey* v. *Reusch*, 153 F.Supp. 337 (S.D.N.Y.1957).

92. Indeed, foreign consuls have had the right to call upon officials and courts of the United States for assistance in arresting, interrogating, and imprisoning persons subject to their jurisdiction. See, e.g., Convention Between the United States of America and Greece Defining the Rights, Privileges and Immunities of Consular Officers in the Two Countries, Nov. 19, 1902, arts. II, IX, XII, 33 Stat. 2122, T.S. No. 424; Consular Convention between the United States of America and Ireland, May 1, 1950, arts. 21–7, [1954] 5 U.S.T. 949, T.I.A.S. No. 2984; and the enabling legislation in 22 U.S.C. §§ 256–58a (1994). 22 U.S.C. § 256 confers jurisdiction on a consul only where by treaty the nation he represents gives reciprocal rights to United States consuls in its territory. 22 U.S.C. § 258a provides for enforcement by federal courts or magistrates of consular awards and decrees in differences between captains and crews of the vessels of the nation the consul represents.

Lower federal courts have given effect to foreign consular jurisdiction: *The Koenigin Luise*, 184 F. 170 (D.N.J.1910) (denying court's jurisdiction of alien seaman's libel against vessel, because of exclusive jurisdiction of consul); but *cf. The Neck*, 138 F. 144 (W.D.Wash.1905) (refusing to dismiss suit for wages by U.S. citizen who had served as seaman under flag of country whose consul claimed exclusive jurisdiction under a treaty). See also *Glass* v. *The Betsey*, 3 U.S. (3 Dall.) 6 (1794) (implying that the United States has the power by treaty to permit foreign countries to establish courts in the United States); *cf. The Belgenland*, 114 U.S. 355, 364 (1884).

93. North Atlantic Treaty Status of Forces Agreement, June 19, 1951, Art.VII, [1953] 4 U.S.T. 1792, T.I.A.S. No. 2846, 199 U.N.T.S. 67.

94. Service Courts of Friendly Foreign Forces Act, ch. 326, 58 Stat. 643 (1944), 22 U.S.C. §§ 701–6 (1994). The statute also authorized U.S. military officials to arrest members of the foreign forces at the request of their commanding officer. These sections of the law depend upon activation by the President.

95. The disposition of claims of U.S. citizens by international claims commissions affords some analogy. Although judicial or quasi-judicial in character, and deciding cases that might be decided by U.S. courts, they are *ad hoc* tribunals of a special bi-national authority created by international agreement, and are exercising only its 'judicial power'. See, e.g., Convention Between the United States of America and the Republic of Mexico for Adjustment of Claims, July 4, 1868, art. II, 15 Stat. 679, 681–2, T.S. No. 212; Agreement Between the United States and Germany for a Mixed Commission, Aug. 10, 1922, 42 Stat. 2200, T.S. No. 665. Professor Hudson, writing in 1944, stated that the United States had participated in twenty-six such tribunals in the past 100 years.

M. HUDSON, INTERNATIONAL TRIBUNALS 196 (1944). There have been a number of them since, prominently the Iran–U.S. Claims Tribunal. See Caron, *The Nature of the Iran-United States Claims Tribunal and the Evolving Structure of International Dispute Resolution,* 84 AM. J. INT'L. L. 104 (1990).

Congress has also authorized international and foreign officials to act within this country and to use American courts and processes to support their activities. For example, the United States–Canadian International Joint Commission, under a treaty with Canada as implemented by Congress, is authorized to administer oaths and take evidence in the United States in proceedings within the Commission's jurisdiction. Treaty between the United States and Great Britain Relating to Boundary Waters Between the United States and Canada, Jan.11, 1909, 36 Stat. 2448, T.S. No. 548, *as implemented,* 22 U.S.C. § 268 (1994), and 22 C.F.R. §§ 401.1 (1994). By application to the U.S. court in the district within which the Commission is sitting, the Commission may compel the attendance of witnesses and the production of evidence and invoke the court's contempt power to insure compliance (FED.R.CIV.P. 45(e); 18 U.S.C. § 401 (1994)).

Congress once gave even broader authority to any international tribunal or commission to which the United States is party, considering a claim in which the United States or any of its nationals is interested, to administer oaths under penalty of perjury and to require the attendance of witnesses and the production of evidence, enforceable by contempt proceedings. Ch. 851, § 1, 46 Stat. 1005 (1930). Subsequent amendment permitted the United States agent before such tribunals to invoke the aid of federal court to order witnesses to appear before the court for examination by the agent. Ch. 50, 48 Stat. 117 (1933). The legislation was repealed in 1964, Pub.L.No. 88–619, § 3, 78 Stat. 995 (1964), but federal district courts may order testimony for use in a proceeding in a foreign or international tribunal. *Id.* at 997, 28 U.S.C. § 1782 (1994).

96. United States 'services' to such tribunals would also seem constitutionally acceptable, although difficulties might be further attenuated if convicted individuals were imprisoned in some international facility rather than in one under the authority of the United States. Seamen convicted by foreign consuls, n. 92 to this chapter, may be confined in U.S. prisons, 22 U.S.C. § 258 (1994). Compare also Art. VII, § 7(b) of the NATO Status of Forces Treaty, n. 40 to this chapter. And see n. 100 to this chapter.

97. In *Hirota* v. *MacArthur,* 338 U.S. 197 (1948), the Supreme Court was asked to review on habeas corpus the constitutionality of the trial of several Japanese for 'war crimes' before an international commission which the Allied military commander, who was also United States commander, had established on behalf of the Allied Powers. The Court held *per curiam* that the military tribunal was not a 'tribunal of the United States' whose judgments could be subject to review by the Supreme Court or by other federal courts. Justice Douglas, concurring in the result, was of the opinion that there was no power of review because the military tribunal 'was solely an instrument of political power' as to which the President, spokesman for the United States in its foreign affairs, had the final say. *Id.* at 199, 215.

Even if these arguments were accepted in principle, it is unlikely that the courts would tolerate any exercise in the United States of a foreign criminal jurisdiction that entailed violations of fundamental fairness or 'shocked the conscience'. Compare Ch. IX.

98. The Statute of the International Tribunal for the Prosecution of Persons Responsible for Serious Violations of International Humanitarian Law Committed in the Territory of the Former Yugoslavia Since 1991 (the International Tribunal), Adopted by Security Council Resolution 827 of 25 May 1993, directs in Article 29 that:

1. States shall cooperate with the International Tribunal in the investigation and prosecution of persons accused of committing serious violations of international humanitarian law.

2. States shall comply without undue delay with any request for assistance or an order issued by a Trial Chamber, including, but not limited to:

(a) the identification and location of persons;

(b) the taking of testimony and the production of evidence;

(c) the service of documents;

(d) the arrest of persons;

(e) the surrender or the transfer of the accused to the International Tribunal.

99. See, for example, *Fernandez* v. *Phillips*, 268 U.S. 311 (1925); *Ahmad* v. *Wigen*, 910 F.2d 1063 (2d Cir. 1990). See also RESTATEMENT (n. 2 to Preface) sec. 478 Reporters' Note 2.

100. Compare the Treaty on the Execution of Penal Sentences with Mexico, 1976, 28 U.S.T. 7399, T.I.A.S. No. 8718, and similar arrangements with other countries. Also see generally, the multilateral Convention on Transfer of Sentenced Persons, 1983, T.I.A.S. No. 10824, 1985. The constitutionality of such arrangements was upheld in a number of cases, e.g., *Pfeifer* v. *United States Bureau of Prisons*, 615 F.2d 873 (9th Cir. 1980).

101. Uruguay Round Agreements Act § 102(c), Pub. L. No. 103–465, 108 Stat. 4809 (1994). See also W.M. Reisman and W. Wiedman, *Contextual Imperatives of Dispute Resolution Mechanisms—Some Hypotheses and Their Applications in the Uruguay Round and NAFTA*, 29 J.W.T. 3 (1995).

102. See the U.S.–Canada Free Trade Agreement, 1989, Ch. 19; North American Free Trade Agreement, Article 1904, and Annex 1904.13.

NOTES, INTRODUCTION TO PART IV, pp. 277 to 281

1. See generally my essays, *The Idea of Rights and the United States Constitution, Constitutional Rights—Two Hundred Years Later, and Rights: American and Human,* in THE AGE OF RIGHTS (1990), Chs. 6, 7 and 9. See also N. Dorsen, *Foreign Affairs and Civil Liberties,* in FOREIGN AFFAIRS AND THE U.S. CONSTITUTION (Henkin, Glennon & Rogers, eds. 1990).

2. Only the prohibitions on *ex post facto* laws and bills of attainder (Art. I, secs. 9, 10), the provision that the writ of habeas corpus shall not be suspended (Art. I, sec. 9); the local jury trial for those accused of crime (Art. III, sec. 2); and the special safeguards for those accused of treason (Art. III, sec. 3). One might include also the prohibition on impairment of contract obligations by the states (Art. I, sec. 10), and the limitation on direct taxes (Art. I, sec. 9). The provision for jury trial in criminal cases is largely duplicated in the Sixth Amendment, and other safeguards—e.g., those against *ex post facto* laws—are probably also subsumed in the due process clauses of the Fifth and Fourteenth Amendments. See also the suggestion that trial before a judge assured of life tenure and guaranteed compensation is also a 'right' of the accused. See n. 90 to Ch. VIII.

3. The Bill of Rights did not abolish slavery or require the Government to afford the equal protection of the laws. It did not apply to the states. See n. 97 to Ch. IX.

4. See, e.g., *Martin* v. *Hunter's Lessee,* 14 U.S. (1 Wheat.) 304 (1816); *McCulloch* v. *Maryland,* 17 U.S. (4 Wheat.) 316 (1819); *Gibbons* v. *Ogden,* 22 U.S. (9 Wheat.) 1 (1824).

5. See Ch. V.

6. See the cases collected by Frankfurter, J., concurring in *Kovacs* v. *Cooper,* 336 U.S. 77, 90–7 (1949), and Justice Cardozo in *Palko,* n. 7 to Ch. IX.

7. As of 1995, the United States had become party to the Genocide Convention, the Convention against Torture, the International Covenant on Civil and Political Rights, the Convention on the Elimination of All Forms of Racial Discrimination, the Convention on the Political Rights of Women, and older conventions against slavery and slave trade. It has signed but not ratified the International Covenant on Economic, Social and Cultural Rights, the Convention on the Elimination of All forms of Discrimination against Women, and the Convention on the Rights of the Child. The United States has adhered to very few of the conventions sponsored by the International Labour Organization. See n. 101 to Ch. VII.

NOTES, CHAPTER IX. INDIVIDUAL RIGHTS AND FOREIGN AFFAIRS,
pp. 283 to 310

1. That indeed was one of the objections raised by Sutherland's critics. See Levitan, (n. 6 to Ch. I); *cf.* WRIGHT (n. 3 to Ch. I) 134 n. 13.

   Hamilton perhaps implied that national defense and 'the public peace' ought to know no constitutional limitations: 'As the duties of superintending the national defence and of securing the public peace against foreign or domestic violence involve a provision for casualties and dangers to which no possible limits can be assigned, the power of making that provision ought to know no other bounds than the exigencies of the nation and the resources of the community.' THE FEDERALIST No. 31.

   There was a view that the powers deriving from sovereignty were limited 'not by Constitutional provisions, but by those fundamental principles upon which the Government of the United States, and of its people, is based'. See discussion and authorities cited in 1 BUTLER, THE TREATY POWER (n. 10 to Ch. I) 62 *et seq.* The Supreme Court cases he cites, however, referred to fundamental principles in addressing limitations on the authority of the United States in governing acquired territory, and even those were derived 'by inference and the general spirit of the Constitution'. *Mormon Church* v. *United States*, 136 U.S. 1, 42–4 (1890). They do not suggest that only these implied limitations govern powers inherent in sovereignty exercised within the United States. Later cases found limitations akin to 'fundamental principles' implied in 'due process of law', but these were in addition to other rights enumerated in the Bill of Rights. For what courts have poured into substantive due process, see p. 289 above.

2. 299 U.S. at 320.

3. *Perez* v. *Brownell*, 356 U.S. 44, 58 (1958). Although the Court later overruled that case in *Afroyim* v. *Rusk*, n. 5 below, not even the sharp dissent suggested that legislation relating to foreign affairs is not subject to constitutional limitations. A later case, *Rogers* v. *Bellei*, n. 5 below , narrowed *Afroyim* somewhat, but that case, too, does not deny that such statutes are subject to the full panoply of constitutional safeguards.

4. This is now generally assumed, although there appears to be no clear Supreme Court holding to that effect, and no discussion of the issue as it relates to foreign affairs. The First Amendment was one of a number of constitutional provisions invoked in *Joint Anti-Fascist Refugee Comm.* v. *McGrath*, 341 U.S. 123 (1951), but the Court's judgment did not necessarily rest on it, and the opinions did not examine the applicability of the Amendment to the Executive. In his concurring opinion, however, Justice Black said: '[I]n my judgment the executive has no constitutional authority, with or without a hearing, officially to prepare and publish the lists challenged by petitioners. . . This cannot be reconciled with the First Amendment as I interpret it.' *Id.* at 143. Justice Reed's dissent dealt with the First Amendment so as to imply that in a proper case it would limit the powers of the Executive. *Id.* at 199. That the First Amendment was in play was not questioned by any of the parties or any of the Justices in the

Pentagon Papers Case, n. 17 to this chapter. And compare the references to the First Amendment in *United States* v. *U. S. District Court, Eastern Michigan,* 407 U.S. 297 (1972); also *Laird* v. *Tatum,* 408 U.S. 1 (1972). Compare Justice Jackson: 'If there is any fixed star in our constitutional constellation, it is that no official, high or petty, can prescribe what shall be orthodox in politics, nationalism, religion, or other matters of opinion or force citizens to confess by word or act their faith therein.' *West Virginia State Bd. of Educ.* v. *Barnette,* 319 U.S. 624, 642 (1943). (The case itself involved state action, not action by the federal Executive, but, in addition to the Fourteenth, the First Amendment is much mentioned in the opinion.) Also Justice Douglas dissenting, in *Beauharnais* v. *Illinois,* 343 U.S. 250, 284, 286 (1952): 'The First Amendment says that freedom of speech, freedom of press, and the free exercise of religion shall not be abridged. That is a negation of power on the part of each and every department of government.' Compare also Justice Black, in *Reid* v. *Covert,* 354 U.S. 1 (1957); Justice Douglas dissenting in *Gravel* v. *United States,* 408 U.S. 606, 633 (1972). See also *United States* v. *Schmucker,* 721 F.2d 1046 (6th Cir. 1984), *vacated,* 471 U.S. 1001 (1985). The plaintiff, a Mennonite, violated President Carter's Proclamation 4711, requiring all males 21 or older to register for the draft. Since this plaintiff was prosecuted only because he *publicly* disagreed with the law, it was a 'violation of the first amendment for the Executive branch to give the draft registration law this construction . . .' *Id.* at 1050. See generally Maslow, 'Is the President Bound by the First Amendment?' *Hearings on S.J.Res. 1 and 43 Before a Subcomm. on Treaties and Executive Agreements of the Senate Comm. on the Judiciary,* 83rd Cong., 1st Sess., at 314 (1953).

   The other provisions in the Bill of Rights are not in terms addressed to Congress only, and the provision in the Fifth Amendment that no person may be deprived of liberty without due process of law applies to all branches of government and would doubtless be held to include the freedoms specified in the First Amendment. See e.g., *Bullfrog Films, Inc.* v. *Wick,* 847 F.2d 502 (9th Cir. 1988), holding that the U.S. Information Agency's actions under the Beirut Agreement, a multilateral treaty controlling circulation of audio-visual materials, violated the First and Fifth Amendments.

   On remedies for violations of individual rights that impinge on U.S. foreign relations, see, e.g., RESTATEMENT (n. 2 to Preface) § 721, Reporters' Note 13.

5. In 1967, the Court overruled *Perez,* n. 3 above, holding that the Constitution prohibits deprivation of citizenship. *Afroyim* v. *Rusk,* 387 U.S. 253 (1967). *Afroyim* was narrowed somewhat in *Rogers* v. *Bellei,* 401 U.S. 815 (1971), which held that Congress can take away 'derivative citizenship' granted by statute. *Afroyim* was followed in *Vance* v. *Terrazas,* 444 U.S. 252 (1980). See also *Reid* v. *Covert,* 354 U.S. 1, 16–17 (1957); compare *Burnet* v. *Brooks,* 288 U.S. 378 (1933); Justice Brewer dissenting in *Fong Yue Ting* v. *United States,* 149 U.S. 698, 737–8 (1893). And compare the decision by a three-judge court invalidating a requirement that a naturalized citizen have been a citizen for ten years to be eligible for the Foreign Service. See *Faruki* v. *Rogers,* 349 F.Supp 723 (D.D.C. 1972). But where naturalization is obtained on the basis of misrepresentation, it can be nullified and the citizenship terminated. *Fedorenko* v. *United*

States, 449 U.S. 490 (1981) (Nazi concentration camp guard concealed his past on naturalization application).

6. See the discussion in the *Slaughter-House Cases*, 83 U.S. (16 Wall.) 36, 79–80 (1884), quoted on p. 309, this chapter.

7. Justice Cardozo in *Palko* v. *Connecticut*, 302 U.S. 319, 326 (1937).

8. See, e.g., *New York Times* v. *Sullivan*, 376 U.S. 254 (1964); also *The Pentagon Papers* case, n. 17 to this chapter.

9. The First Amendment has not precluded punishment for violation—by speech or publication—of military censorship or other security regulations, *Schenck* v. *United States*, 249 U.S. 47 (1919); unlawful picketing, *Giboney* v. *Empire Storage & Ice Co.*, 336 U.S. 490 (1949); individual or group libel, *Beauharnais* v. *Illinois*, 343 U.S. 250 (1952); public obscenity, *Roth* v. *United States*, 354 U.S. 476 (1957); disrupting the Selective Service System by 'symbolic speech' such as burning a draft card in protest against the Vietnam War, *United States* v. *O'Brien*, 391 U.S. 367 (1968); child pornography, *Miller* v. *California*, 413 U.S. 15 (1973); using treasury funds for political advertising, *Austin* v. *Michigan Chamber of Commerce*, 494 U.S. 652 (1990). Compare *Dennis* v. *United States*, 341 U.S. 494 (1951); also the various opinions in *New York Times* v. *United States*, n. 17 to this chapter. The Supreme Court also gave short shrift to First Amendment claims of persons in the United States who had invited a lecturer to the United States whom the immigration authorities held to be excludable under the Immigration Laws. *Kleindienst* v. *Mandel*, 408 U.S. 753 (1972), p. 288 and n. 15 to this chapter.

10. See, e.g., International Convention on the Elimination of All Forms of Racial Discrimination (1966), cited in Introduction to Part IV, note 7, and the International Covenant on Civil and Political Rights (ICCPR), articles 19 and 20, *ibid*. In adhering to the ICCPR, the United States entered a reservation to Article 20 of the Covenant which requires states to prohibit war propaganda and 'hate speech', on the ground that the United States could not assume such obligations in view of the First Amendment. The Supreme Court has ruled that the First Amendment draws a line between speech that is directed to inciting or producing 'imminent lawless action' and expression that merely advocates it or teaches its desirability. *Brandenburg* v. *Ohio*, 395 U.S. 444 (1969); *cf. Scales* v. *United States*, 367 U.S. 203 (1961). See also *NAACP* v. *Claiborne Hardware, Inc.*, 458 U.S. 886 (1982). That distinction might well have governed interpretation of treaty provisions such as Article 20 of the Covenant if the U.S. had made no reservation.

First Amendment issues were argued also in a case challenging the Mexico City Policy banning foreign aid to clinics that counsel the availability of abortion as an option. See *Planned Parenthood Fed'n of Am., Inc.* v. *Agency for Int'l Dev.*, 838 F.2d 649 (2d Cir. 1988), *cert. denied*, 500 U.S. 952 (1991).

11. See *United States* v. *Edler Industries, Inc.*, 579 F.2d 516 (9th Cir. 1978), upholding the Mutual Security Act of 1954, 22 U.S.C. § 2778 (1994), which prohibits export of technical data without government approval. Earlier, Justice Frankfurter suggested that research and scholarship cannot be barred 'except for reasons that are exigent and obviously compelling'. *Sweezy* v. *New*

Hampshire, 354 U.S. 234, 262 (1957); see HENKIN, ARMS CONTROL (n. 3 to Ch. VI) 45, 185–6. See also discussion in n. 17 to this chapter.

12. See, e.g., *Police Dept.* v. *Mosley*, 408 U.S. 92 (1972); *Carey* v. *Brown*, 447 U.S. 455 (1980). For a discussion of the distinction between content-based and content-neutral speech, see Stone, *Content Regulation and the First Amendment*, 25 WM. & MARY L.REV. 189 (1983).

13. See e.g., *National Broadcasting Co.* v. *United States*, 319 U.S. 190 (1943). Compare *Red Lion Broadcasting Co.* v. *FCC*, 395 U.S. 367 (1969), and *FCC* v. *League of Women Voters*, 468 U.S. 364 (1984), with *Miami Herald Publishing Co.* v. *Tornillo*, 418 U.S. 241 (1974), and *City of Lakewood* v. *Plain Dealer Publishing Co.*, 486 U.S. 750 (1988).

14. *Haig* v. *Agee*, 453 U.S. 280 (1981). See pp. 286n., 288 and n. 35 to this chapter.

15. *Kleindienst* v. *Mandel*, 408 U.S. 753 (1972).

16. *Meese* v. *Keene*, 481 U.S. 465 (1987); *Attorney General of the United States* v. *Irish Northern Aid Committee*, 688 F.2d 159 (2d Cir. 1982), *cert. denied*, 409 U.S. 1080 (1982) (dissenting opinion). See Roth, *The First Amendment in the Foreign Affairs Realm: 'Domesticating' the Restrictions on Citizen Participation*, 2 TEMP. POL. & CIV. RTS. L. REV. 255, 258–65 (1993).

    A provision in the Export Administration Act that prohibits responding to questionnaires by the Arab Boycott Office was held not to violate the First Amendment. *Briggs & Stratton Corp.* v. *Baldrige*, 728 F.2d 915 (7th Cir. 1984).

    The threat of prosecution under the Logan Act, entitled 'An Act to Prevent Usurpation of Executive Functions', making it a crime for any person to correspond with a foreign nation with an intent to influence its conduct in relation to a controversy with the United States, also raises First Amendment issues, but the courts have never had the opportunity to adjudicate the Act's constitutionality. Act of January 30, 1799, c. 1, 1 Stat. 613 (now 18 U.S.C. §§ 953 *et seq.* (1994)). See the Roth article, above, at 265–71.

17. *New York Times Co.* v. *United States*, 403 U.S. 713 (1971). In a brief *per curiam* opinion, the Court held that the Government had failed to sustain its burden of overcoming a heavy presumption against the constitutional validity of 'prior restraints of expression'. Some of the concurring opinions, however, suggest that there was a majority of the Court for only a very narrow doctrine. Three of the concurring Justices seemed to imply that the injunction might have issued if Congress had authorized it. Stewart and White, JJ., thought that it was the constitutional duty of the Executive 'to protect the confidentiality necessary to carry out its responsibilities in the fields of international relations and national defense'; but in the absence of an act of Congress authorizing an injunction (or even of specific Executive regulations), the First Amendment bars the injunction at least when the courts are not persuaded that disclosure 'will surely result in direct, immediate and irreparable damage to our Nation or its people'. *Id.* at 727–30. Marshall, J., considered it would 'be utterly inconsistent with the concept of separation of powers for this Court to use its power of contempt to prevent behavior that Congress has specifically declined to prohibit'. *Id.* at 742. Justice White, in an opinion which Stewart, J., joined, stressed that Congress had apparently been satisfied to rely on criminal sanctions and

their deterrent effect, implied that criminal statutes in effect were here relevant, and asserted that he 'would have no difficulty in sustaining convictions under these sections on facts that would not justify the intervention of equity and the imposition of a prior restraint'. *Id.* at 737. Harlan, J., dissenting in an opinion joined by Burger, C. J., and Blackmun, J., would apparently grant an injunction where the Court was satisfied that 'the subject matter of the dispute does lie within the proper compass of the President's foreign relations power', and if the determination that disclosure would 'irreparably impair the national security be made by the head of the Executive Department concerned—here the Secretary of State or the Secretary of Defense—after actual personal consideration by that officer'. *Id.* at 757. See, generally, Henkin, *The Right to Know and the Duty to Withhold: The Case of the Pentagon Papers,* 120 U.PA.L.REV. 271 (1971). See also RESTATEMENT (n. 2 to Preface) § 721, Comment *d* and Reporters' Note 4.

In recent cases, courts have weakened the heavy presumption against prior restraint in instances involving national security. See *United States* v. *Morison,* 844 F.2d 1057 (4th Cir. 1988), *cert. denied,* 488 U.S. 908 (1988) (providing stolen files to the press not protected by First Amendment); *Snepp* v. *United States,* 445 U.S. 507 (1980) (CIA agent must abide by written agreement not to publish information about the agency); *United States* v. *Marchetti,* 466 F.2d 1309 (4th Cir. 1972), *cert. denied,* 409 U.S. 1063 (1972) (affirming an injunction prohibiting a former CIA agent from publishing information); *United States* v. *Progressive, Inc.,* 467 F.Supp. 990 (W.D. Wis. 1979) (issuing a temporary restraining order and preliminary injunction to prevent publication of an article explaining hydrogen bomb manufacture). See also RESTATEMENT (n. 2 to Preface) § 721, Comment *d* and Reporters' Note 4.

18. See, e.g., D.C. Code § 22–1115, upheld in *Frend* v. *United States,* 100 F.2d 691 (D.C. Cir. 1938), *cert. denied,* 306 U.S. 640 (1939). The D.C. Circuit Court of Appeals upheld this statute again in *Finzer* v. *Barry,* 798 F.2d 1450 (D.C. Cir. 1986), but the Supreme Court affirmed only in part. It held that the clause prohibiting signs that bring a foreign government into 'public disrepute' is a content-based restriction and violates the First Amendment, but the Court upheld the statute's 'congregation clause', prohibiting demonstrations within 500 feet of any embassy. *Boos* v. *Barry,* 485 U.S. 312 (1988).

The Courts of Appeal for the Second and Fifth Circuits have upheld a similar federal provision, 18 U.S.C. § 112 (b) (1994). See *Concerned Jewish Youth* v. *McGuire,* 621 F.2d 471 (2d Cir. 1980), *cert. denied,* 450 U.S. 913 (1981); *Committee in Solidarity with the People of El Salvador* v. *F.B.I.,* 770 F.2d 468 (5th Cir. 1985).

See RESTATEMENT (n. 2 to Preface) § 721, Comment *d.* See also n. 28 to Ch. III.

19. I have explored such issues more fully in respect of hypothetical arms control agreements, see HENKIN, ARMS CONTROL (n. 3 to Ch. VI) c. IV. The privilege against self-incrimination (the Fifth Amendment) would also be relevant to such a disarmament inspection system, especially if it involved interrogation of persons. See *id.* at 59–63, 79–81 and notes. Inspection systems became less

hypothetical during the extended arms control negotiations between the U.S. and the USSR. See Leich, *Contemporary Practice of the United States Relating to International Law*, 85 AM.J.INT'LL. 539, 548–51 (1991).

Generally, a search is not unreasonable if pursuant to a warrant meeting the requirements of the Fourth Amendment—'upon probable cause, supported by Oath or affirmation, and particularly describing the place to be searched, and the persons or things to be seized'. In some cases a search may be valid even without a warrant. *United States* v. *Montoya de Hernandez*, 473 U.S. 531 (1985) (border searches); *United States* v. *Villamonte-Marquez*, 462 U.S. 579 (1983) (searches on the high seas); *Michigan* v. *de Fillippo*, 443 U.S. 31 (1979) (searches incident to a valid arrest); *South Dakota* v. *Opperman*, 428 U.S. 364 (1976) (inventory searches); compare *Coolidge* v. *New Hampshire*, 403 U.S. 443 (1971), with *Arizona* v. *Hicks*, 480 U.S. 321 (1987) (item in plain view); compare *Carroll* v. *United States*, 267 U.S. 132 (1925), and *Henry* v. *United States*, 361 U.S. 98 (1959) (moving vehicle); compare *Terry* v. *Ohio*, 392 U.S. 1 (1968), with *Sibron* v. *New York*, 392 U.S. 40 (1968), and *Adams* v. *Williams*, 407 U.S. 143 (1972) ('stop and frisk'); *Warden* v. *Hayden*, 387 U.S. 294 (1967) ('hot pursuit'); *cf. Schmerber* v. *California*, 384 U.S. 757 (1966) (compulsory blood test). *Cf. Vale* v. *Louisiana*, 399 U.S. 30 (1970); *United States* v. *Ross*, 456 U.S. 798 (1982). Evidence seized during a search of a vessel on the high seas in violation of international law need not be excluded. *United States* v. *Hensel*, 699 F.2d 18 (1st Cir. 1983).

The Fourth Amendment is particularly important in criminal cases since the courts will exclude evidence obtained in violation of the Amendment. *Weeks* v. *United States*, 232 U.S. 383 (1914). See *Mapp* v. *Ohio*, 367 U.S. 643 (1961), but *cf. Stone* v. *Powell*, 428 U.S. 465, 486 (1976). The Amendment can also be the basis for civil suit against officials who violate it. 42 U.S.C. § 1983 (1988 & Supp. III 1991). See *Monroe* v. *Pape*, 365 U.S. 167 (1961) (city police officers); *Monell* v. *Dept. of Social Services of City of New York*, 436 U.S. 658 (1978) (city official); *Bivens* v. *Six Unknown Named Agents*, 403 U.S. 388 (1971) (judicially created remedy against federal officials); but *cf. Schweiker* v. *Chilicky*, 487 U.S. 412 (1988); *Bush* v. *Lucas*, 462 U.S. 367 (1983); *Chappel* v. *Wallace*, 462 U.S. 296 (1983). The Supreme Court refused to allow a *Bivens* cause of action against a federal agency. *F.D.I.C.* v. *Meyer*, 114 S.Ct. 996 (1994). Willful violation of the Amendment could also be a criminal offense under 18 U.S.C. § 242 (1994); *cf. Screws* v. *United States*, 325 U.S. 91 (1945) (state official); the language of the statute would seem to cover federal officials as well. But see the attack on the exclusionary rule by Burger, C.J., in his dissent in *Bivens*, above. See also RESTATEMENT (n. 2 to Preface) § 721, Comment *e*.

See generally, W. LaFave, CRIMINAL PROCEDURE (2nd edn., 1992); J. WEINSTEIN, WEINSTEIN'S EVIDENCE MANUAL (1987).

20. Compare *United States* v. *Butenko*, 494 F.2d 593 (3d Cir. 1974), in which the court held that in national security cases, the Fourth Amendment does not require prior judicial approval of electronic surveillance if conducted to gather foreign intelligence information. But wiretapping might infringe rights of the other party to a conversation with a foreign embassy. *Katz* v. *United States*, 389 U.S. 347 (1967). A warrant is required before a wiretap can be used against

an organization that is not affiliated with a foreign state. *Zweibon* v. *Mitchell*, 516 F.2d 594 (D.C. Cir. 1975). See also *United States* v. *Brown*, 484 F.2d 418 (5th Cir. 1973), *cert. denied*, 415 U.S. 960 (1974); *United States* v. *Clay*, 430 F.2d 165 (5th Cir. 1970), *rev'd on other grounds*, 403 U.S. 698 (1971), both holding that warrantless wiretapping is permissible in cases involving national security. See generally the Foreign Intelligence Surveillance Act of 1978 (FISA), 50 U.S.C.A. §§ 1801 *et seq.* (1988) (amended 1994). For cases on warrants under FISA, see *United States* v. *Truong Dinh Hung*, 629 F.2d 908 (4th Cir. 1980), *cert. denied*, 454 U.S.1144 (1982); *United States* v. *Belfield*, 692 F.2d 141 (D.C. Cir. 1982); *United States* v. *Duggan*, 743 F.2d 59 (2d Cir. 1984). On foreign states under the Constitution, see Damnosch, p. 285n., above.

21. Border patrols may search a vehicle or its occupants without probable cause, *Almeida-Sanchez* v. *United States*, 413 U.S. 266 (1973), but not without a reasonable basis for suspicion. Stopping a vehicle near the Mexican border merely because its occupants appear to be of Mexican ancestry is not a search based on reasonable suspicion. *United States* v. *Brignoni-Ponce*, 422 U.S. 873 (1975).

22. *Cf. Abel* v. *United States*, 362 U.S. 217, 219–20 (1960).

The prohibition of 'cruel and unusual punishments' precludes punishment grossly disproportionate in relation to the offense. *Weems* v. *United States*, 217 U.S. 349 (1910); see also *Coker* v. *Georgia*, 433 U.S. 584 (1977); *Enmund* v. *Florida*, 458 U.S. 782 (1982). It requires extraordinary justification and safeguards for the imposition of capital punishment. *Furman* v. *Georgia*, 408 U.S. 238 (1972); *Gregg* v. *Georgia*, 428 U.S. 153 (1976); *Woodson* v. *North Carolina*, 428 U.S. 280 (1976); *Roberts* v. *Louisiana*, 428 U.S. 325 (1976); *Coker* and *Enmund*, above; *Sumner* v. *Schuman*, 483 U.S. 66 (1987).

Compare *Soering* v. *United Kingdom*, European Ct. Hum. Rts., Judgment of 7 July 1989, Ser.A No. 161, 11 Eur. Hum. Rts. Rep. 439, in which the European Court of Human Rights declared that to extradite a person likely to remain on 'death row' for an extended period would violate Article 3 of the European Convention for the Protection of Human Rights and Fundamental Freedoms, which provides 'No one shall be subjected to torture or to inhuman or degrading treatment of punishment'.

23. See *Wong Wing* v. *United States*, 163 U.S. 228 (1896); *Consolidated Edison Co.* v. *National Labor Relations Bd.*, 305 U.S. 197 (1938); *Gonzales* v. *United States*, 348 U.S. 407, 417–18 (1955); *cf. Goldberg* v. *Kelly*, 397 U.S. 254 (1970); *Bell* v. *Burson*, 402 U.S. 535 (1971); *Fuentes* v. *Shevin*, 407 U.S. 67 (1972); *Morrissey* v. *Brewer*, 408 U.S. 471 (1972). Compare *Mitchell* v. *W.T. Grant Co.*, 416 U.S. 600 (1974); *North Georgia Finishing, Inc.* v. *Di-Chem, Inc.*, 419 U.S. 601 (1975). But due process is not available to alien enemies abroad in time of war. *Johnson* v. *Eisentrager*, 339 U.S. 763, 771 (1950); compare *In re Yamashita*, 327 U.S. 1 (1946), with dissenting opinion *id.* at 26, 42.

Generally, but not universally, due process 'implies and includes *actor, reus, judex,* regular allegations, opportunity to answer, and a trial according to some settled course of judicial proceedings . . .' *cf. Murray's Lessee* v. *Hoboken Land & Improvement Co.*, 59 U.S. (18 How.) 272, 280 (1856); see also *Ex parte Wall*, 107 U.S. 265, 289 (1883).

But not all administrative actions require similar procedures. 'The procedures the Due Process Clause requires prior to administrative action . . . can vary, depending upon the precise nature of the government function involved, the importance of the private interests that have been affected by governmental action, and the nature of subsequent proceedings.' *Brock* v. *Roadway Express, Inc.*, 481 U.S. 252, 271–2 (1987) (White, J., dissenting). See also *Opp Cotton Mills* v. *Administrator*, 312 U.S. 126, 152–3 (1949); *cf. Bowles* v. *Willingham*, 321 U.S. 503, 519–21 (1944) (upholding war-time orders without hearing since judicial review available); *Richardson* v. *Perales*, 402 U.S. 389 (1971); *Cleveland Bd. of Education* v. *Loudermill*, 470 U.S. 532 (1985). See also RESTATEMENT (n. 2 to Preface) § 721, Comment *f*.

24. See, e.g., *United States* v. *Florida East Coast R. Co.*, 410 U.S. 224, 244–5 (1973); *Bowles* v. *Willingham*, 321 U.S. 503, 519 (1944); *Bi-Metallic Investment Co.* v. *Colorado*, 239 U.S. 441, 445 (1915); *Bragg* v. *Weaver*, 251 U.S. 57, 58 (1919).

25. See, for example, the 'Tate letter' declaring the restrictive theory of sovereign immunity as Executive policy and the Executive determinations on immunity in *Peru* and *Hoffman,* discussed in Ch. II; some might consider the latter more 'judicial' than 'legislative' in character. In *First National City Bank* v. *Banco Nacional de Cuba*, 406 U.S. 759 (1972), the State Department letter was issued in the context of a particular case but purported to establish a general principle. Compare the provision for *ad hoc* Presidential intervention in the Second Hickenlooper Amendment, n. 86 to Ch. II.

For suggestions urging a right to a hearing, see Leigh and Atkeson, *Due Process in the Emerging Foreign Relations Law of the United States,* 21 Bus. Law. 853 (1966); 22 Bus. Law. 3 (1966); compare Timberg, *Wanted: Administrative Safeguards for the Protection of the Individual in International Economic Regulation,* 17 ADMIN.L.REV. 159 (1965). See also Cardozo, *Sovereign Immunity: The Plaintiff Deserves a Day in Court,* 67 HARV.L.REV. 608 (1954); Note, *Notice-and-Comment Rights for Administrative Decisions Affecting International Trade: Heightened Need, No Response,* 99 YALE L.J. 669 (1989). The claim to a hearing may be stronger if the State Department intervenes in a particular case with a 'suggestion' that is conclusive on the courts. Ch. II, p. 54. In cases that fall within the Foreign Sovereign Immunities Act, the parties now receive a judicial hearing on the issue of immunity.

26. That day is epitomized by *Lochner* v. *New York*, 198 U.S. 45 (1905), and *Adkins* v. *Children's Hospital*, 261 U.S. 525 (1923), and had its last gasps in *Morehead* v. *New York ex rel. Tipaldo*, 298 U.S. 587 (1935). The doctrine grew primarily in Fourteenth Amendment jurisprudence, and has been invoked more frequently in regard to action by the states, but substantive due process had been frequently invoked and applied under the Fifth Amendment in regard to acts of Congress. A single famous instance, before the Fourteenth Amendment, was *Scott* v. *Sandford*, 60 U.S (19 How.) 393 (1857), p. 278, footnote, Introduction to Part IV. See also *Adair* v. *United States*, 208 U.S. 161 (1908); and *Adkins,* above, as applied to an act of Congress for the District of Columbia. The doctrine was laid to rest in *West Coast Hotel Co.* v. *Parrish,* 300 U.S. 379 (1937).

27. *Nebbia* v. *New York*, 291 U.S. 502, 525 (1934). It became established doctrine with *Parrish*, n. 26 above.
28. The contemporary judicial attitude is represented by *Nebbia*, perhaps even more by *Williamson* v. *Lee Optical, Inc.*, 348 U.S. 483 (1955), and *Day-Brite Lighting, Inc.* v. *Missouri*, 342 U.S. 421 (1952). The 1980s experienced a movement among scholars to revive substantive due process in economic areas. See, e.g., SIEGAN, ECONOMIC LIBERTIES AND THE CONSTITUTION (1980); Phillips, *Another Look at Economic Substantive Due Process*, 1987 WIS.L.REV. 265. The Court, however, has continued to reject substantive due process challenges to economic regulation. See, e.g., *Exxon Corp.* v. *Governor of Maryland*, 437 U.S. 117 (1978); *Duke Power Co.* v. *Carolina Environmental Study Group, Inc.*, 438 U.S. 59 (1978); *Texaco* v. *Short*, 454 U.S. 516 (1982); *Pruneyard Shopping Center* v. *Robins*, 447 U.S. 74 (1980). For a while it appeared that the economic rights of the poor, in welfare or consumer-protection cases, might yet receive a measure of protection by substantive due process. See Henkin, *Foreword: On Drawing Lines*, 82 HARV.L.REV. 63, 91 n. 92 (1968). Compare the limited development of new 'equal protection' for the poor, n. 43 to this chapter.

    For the special attitude requiring 'reasonableness' in fixing the rates of public utilities, compare *Power Commission* v. *Hope Gas Co.*, 320 U.S. 591 (1944); *Duquesne Light Co.* v. *Barasch*, 488 U.S. 299 (1989).
29. See HENKIN, ARMS CONTROL (n. 3 to Ch. VI) 39–43.
30. For a discussion of the 'double standard' of substantive due process as applied to political or economic liberty, see G. GUNTHER, CASES AND MATERIALS ON CONSTITUTIONAL LAW 462–5, 505–6 (12th edn. 1991); Henkin, *Some Reflections on Current Constitutional Controversy*, 109 U.PA. L. REV. 637, 658–60 (1961).

    The Supreme Court sought to mitigate the conceptual difficulties of its double standard by finding additional rights implied in the 'specifics' of the Bill of Rights, some also in their 'penumbra'. Compare *Griswold* v. *Connecticut*, 381 U.S. 479 (1965). The Court's opinion, and particularly Justice Goldberg concurring, also invoked the 'retained' rights referred to in the Ninth Amendment. As regards the states, it sought to avoid substantive due process by finding most of the provisions of the Bill of Rights (and their penumbra) 'incorporated' in the Fourteenth Amendment and therefore applicable to the states exactly as the Bill of Rights governs the federal government. See p. 309, this chapter. In *Roe* v. *Wade,* however, the court found the right of privacy, in the sense of autonomy in private intimate matters, to be within 'liberty' in the Fifth and Fourteenth Amendments and protected as such by substantive due process. See *Roe* v. *Wade*, 410 U.S. 113 (1973), relying on earlier cases, *Pierce* v. *Society of Sisters*, 268 U.S. 510 (1925), and *Meyer* v. *Nebraska*, 262 U.S. 390 (1923).
31. For example, the Mexico City Policy, n. 10 above.

    Roe v. *Wade* was under heavy attack but was not overruled. See *Planned Parenthood of Southeastern Pennsylvania* v. *Casey*, 505 U.S. 833 (1992). A right of privacy in other contexts is even sturdier and will probably prevail. See *Zablocki* v. *Redhail*, 434 U.S. 574 (1978) (right to marry); *Moore* v. *East Cleveland*, 431 U.S. 494 (1977) (right to live with extended family). But the

Supreme Court has rejected challenges to statutes prohibiting male homosexual relations. *Bowers* v. *Hardwick*, 478 U.S. 186 (1986).

32. *Kent* v. *Dulles*, 357 U.S. 116, 129 (1958). *Cf. United States* v. *Laub*, 385 U.S. 475 (1967). The Supreme Court has not considered the validity of additional restrictions on the departure of aliens. See 8 U.S.C. § 1185(a) (1994). The Court has distinguished the 'unqualified' right of interstate travel, n. 43, with the more limited due process freedom of international travel. See, e.g., *Califano* v. *Torres*, 435 U.S. 1, 4 n.6 (1978); *Memorial Hosp.* v. *Maricopa County*, 415 U.S. 250, 254–62 (1974). See also RESTATEMENT (n. 2 to Preface) § 721, Reporters' Note 12.

33. *Aptheker* v. *Secretary of State*, 378 U.S. 500, 505 (1964).

34. *Zemel* v. *Rusk*, 381 U.S. 1 (1965). See also *Califano* v. *Aznavorian*, 439 U.S. 170 (1978); *Regan* v. *Wald*, 468 U.S. 222, 240–3 (1984). See also RESTATEMENT (n. 2 to Preface) § 721, Reporters' Note 12.

35. 453 U.S. 280 (1981). Philip Agee, an American citizen and former CIA official, announced in 1974 that he had begun a campaign to fight the CIA by exposing its personnel around the world. Over the next 5 years, he traveled extensively, exposing hundreds of persons as CIA personnel. In December 1979, Secretary of State Haig revoked Agee's passport, pursuant to 22 C.F.R. § 51.70(b)(4). This statute does not expressly give the Secretary of State this power, but, as in *Kent* and *Zemel*, the Secretary claimed such power by implication.

In upholding the action, the majority of the Court distinguished this case from *Kent*, n. 32 to this chapter, in that in *Kent* the individual was denied the right to travel because of his political *beliefs*. The Court also distinguished the right to travel abroad which it characterized as an ordinary liberty protected only by substantive due process, from the freedom to travel in the United States, a right more fundamental and rooted. A constitutional right to travel freely within the United States has been long accepted, although the Justices were not agreed as to whence it derives. See *Edwards* v. *California*, 314 U.S. 160 (1941); *United States* v. *Guest*, 383 U.S. 745, 757 (1966); *Shapiro* v. *Thompson*, 394 U.S. 618, 629–31 (1969); *Oregon* v. *Mitchell*, 400 U.S. 112, 237–8 (1970) (opinion of Brennan, J.); *Dunn* v. *Blumstein*, 405 U.S. 330 (1972); *Griffin* v. *Breckinridge*, 403 U.S. 88, 105–6 (1971); *Memorial Hosp.* v. *Maricopa County*, 415 U.S. 250 (1974); *Attorney General of New York* v. *Soto-Lopez*, 476 U.S. 898 (1986) (plurality opinion). For a discussion of different sources suggested for this right, see *Lutz* v. *City of York*, 899 F.2d 255 (3rd Cir. 1990). The court rejects six arguments and finds that the right is based on substantive due process.

Compare *Snepp* v. *United States*, 445 U.S. 507 (1980), where the Court enforced a contract by a former C.I.A. agent not to publish without clearance with the Agency, rejecting his First Amendment claims.

36. *Korematsu* v. *United States*, 323 U.S. 214 (1944). Compare the interesting dissent by Justice Jackson refusing to approve the action but asserting a kind of 'political question' doctrine for military decisions in time of war. 'A military commander may overstep the bounds of constitutionality, and it is an incident.

But if we review and approve, that passing incident becomes the doctrine of the Constitution.' *Id.* at 246. Compare *Ex parte Quirin*, 317 U.S. 1 (1942). See CORWIN, THE PRESIDENT (n. 5 to Intro. to Pt. II) 287–93.

While he was still a Senator, Justice Sutherland said that the War Power is subject only to express prohibitions 'and such fundamental restraints upon governmental action, as are obviously and clearly intended to apply at all times and under all conditions'. CONSTITUTIONAL POWER AND WORLD AFFAIRS 94 (1919). Compare Hamilton, quoted in n. 1 to this chapter.

37. The Fifth Amendment contains no explicit guarantee of the equal protection of the laws, but 'discrimination may be so unjustifiable as to be violative of due process'. *Bolling* v. *Sharpe*, 347 U.S. 497, 499 (1954) (outlawing segregation in the schools of the District of Columbia). *Cf. Hurd* v. *Hodge*, 334 U.S. 24 (1948); *Thiel* v. *Southern Pacific Co.*, 328 U.S. 217 (1946). 'Equal protection analysis in the Fifth Amendment area is the same as that under the Fourteenth Amendment.' *Buckley* v. *Valeo*, 424 U.S. 1, 93 (1976). Compare RESTATEMENT (n. 2 to Preface) § 721, Reporters' Note 6. See also Justice Jackson, concurring, in *Railway Express Agency, Inc.* v. *New York*, 336 U.S. 106, 112 (1949). It is generally accepted that, despite its aversion to 'substantive due process', p. 290 above, the Supreme Court will now strike down under the due process clause federal discriminations which it would have invalidated under an equal protection clause if one were contained in the Bill of Rights.

38. Holmes, J., in *Buck* v. *Bell*, 274 U.S. 200, 208 (1927).

39. See, e.g., *Railway Express Agency* v. *New York*, 336 U.S. 106 (1949); Jackson, J., concurring, *id.* at 111; *Williamson* v. *Lee Optical Inc.*, 348 U.S. 483 (1955); *McGowan* v. *Maryland*, 366 U.S. 420, 426 (1961); *Dandridge* v. *Williams*, 397 U.S. 471 (1970). See, generally, GUNTHER, CONSTITUTIONAL LAW, Ch. 9, n. 30 above.

At no time was equal protection without importance for protecting against racial discrimination. See, e.g., *Strauder* v. *West Virginia*, 100 U.S. 303 (1880); *Yick Wo* v. *Hopkins*, 118 U.S. 356 (1886). But see *Plessy* v. *Ferguson*, 163 U.S. 537 (1896), *overruled, Brown* v. *Board of Education*, 347 U.S. 483 (1954).

40. Ironically, the principle that racial classifications were suspect, required strict scrutiny, and could be upheld only if they served a compelling public interest, derives from *Korematsu*, n. 36 above, where the Court articulated the doctrine, but despite suspicion, and after strict scrutiny, the Court upheld the relocation of citizens of Japanese ancestry because it served a compelling public interest during the Second World War. See also *United States* v. *Carolene Products Co.*, 304 U.S. 144, 152 n. 4 (1938).

Racial classifications were treated as suspect in numerous cases, e.g., *Loving* v. *Virginia*, 388 U.S. 1 (1967); *Hunter* v. *Erickson*, 393 U.S. 385 (1969); *Palmore* v. *Sidoti*, 466 U.S. 429 (1984). And a majority of the Court applied strict scrutiny even for classifications for benign purposes, such as 'affirmative action'. *Adarand Constructors, Inc.* v. *Pena*, 115 S.Ct. 2097 (1995).

41. A majority of the Court refused to declare 'gender' a suspect classification, but gender distinctions were given extraordinary scrutiny and invalidated because they did not serve an important interest. *Frontiero* v. *Richardson*, 411 U.S. 677 (1973). The Court has treated gender distinctions similarly in cases when the

objection was raised by males. *Craig* v. *Boren*, 429 U.S. 190 (1976); *Mississippi University for Women* v. *Hogan*, 458 U.S. 718 (1982).

42. See *Levy* v. *Louisiana*, 391 U.S. 68 (1968); *Trimble* v. *Gordon*, 430 U.S. 762 (1977); *Massachusetts Board of Retirement* v. *Murgia*, 427 U.S. 307 (1976). As to alienage as suspect classification, see pp. 295–6.

43. The Court early included voting and interstate travel as 'fundamental' rights as to which distinctions required strict scrutiny and could be justified only for a compelling interest. See *Shapiro* v. *Thompson*, 394 U.S. 618 (1969); see the development of the doctrine which Justice Harlan traces (and rejects) in his dissent, *id.* at 658–63. On voting, see *Storer* v. *Brown*, 415 U.S. 724 (1974); *American Party of Texas* v. *White*, 415 U.S. 767 (1974); *Kramer* v. *Union Free School District No. 15*, 395 U.S. 621 (1969); *Harper* v. *Virginia Board of Elections*, 383 U.S. 663 (1966). On interstate travel, see cases, n. 32 to this chapter. At one time the Court scrutinized social regulation or spending that had a prejudicial effect on the poor or minority groups. Compare *Shapiro*, above; *Harper* v. *Virginia Board of Elections*, 383 U.S. 663 (1966); *James* v. *Strange*, 407 U.S. 128 (1972). But the Court soon began to retreat from the sweep of its new equal protection doctrine. See *Dandridge* v. *Williams*, 397 U.S. 471 (1970); *James* v. *Valtierra*, 402 U.S. 137 (1971); *Jefferson* v. *Hackney*, 406 U.S. 535 (1972); *Salyer Land Co.* v. *Tulare Lake Basin Water Storage District*, 410 U.S. 719 (1973); *Richardson* v. *Ramirez*, 418 U.S. 24 (1974). Compare *Labine* v. *Vincent*, 401 U.S. 532 (1971), *overruled*, *Trimble* v. *Gordon*, 430 U.S. 762 (1977). In *Shapiro*, the Court suggested in dicta that strict scrutiny might apply to welfare support as well; it has since rejected that analysis. See *Dandridge*; cf. *Lindsey* v. *Normet*, 405 U.S. 56 (1972). See generally GUNTHER, CONSTITUTIONAL LAW (n. 39 above) at 875–7.

44. *Yick Wo* v. *Hopkins*, 118 U.S. 356 (1886); *Truax* v. *Raich*, 239 U.S. 33 (1915); *Graham* v. *Richardson*, 403 U.S. 365 (1971). *In re Griffiths*, 413 U.S. 717 (1973); *Sugarman* v. *Dougall*, 413 U.S. 634 (1973); *Bernal* v. *Fainter*, 467 U.S. 216 (1984). '[A]n alien in the United States may not be denied the equal protection of the laws, but equal protection does not preclude reasonable distinctions between aliens and citizens, or between different categories of aliens.' RESTATEMENT (n. 2 to Preface) § 722(2). See also § 721, Comment *f*, and § 722, Comments *c, d*. See *United States* v. *Duggan*, 743 F.2d 59 (1984). See generally Aleinikoff, *Federal Regulation of Aliens and the Constitution*, 83 AM.J.INT'LL. 862 (1989).

The Bill of Rights protects aliens as well. *Hampton* v. *Mow Sun Wong*, 426 U.S. 88, 100 (1976); *Wong Wing* v. *United States*, 163 U.S. 228 (1896); *Yick Wo* v. *Hopkins*, 118 U.S. 356 (1886). For the application of safeguards in the criminal process as they apply to aliens, see n. 78 to this chapter. 'An alien in the United States is entitled to the guarantees of the United States Constitution other than those expressly reserved for citizens.' RESTATEMENT (n. 2 to Preface) § 722(1) and Comment *a*. An alien, of course, is not entitled to the rights, privileges and immunities of citizenship under the Fourteenth Amendment, but what these are is still highly uncertain. Compare the *Slaughter-House Cases*, n. 6 above. Art. IV, sec. 2 would also seem not to guarantee rights to persons not 'citizens' of any state. See generally MUTHARIKA, THE ALIEN UNDER AMERICAN LAW (1980); Henkin, *The Constitution as Compact and as Conscience: Individual Rights Abroad and At Our Gates*, 27 WM. & MARY L. REV. 11, 15–17 (1985).

Does a restriction against foreign ownership of electronic media in the United States violate the First Amendment? See Note, *Barring Foreigners from the Airwaves: An Anachronistic Pothole on the Global Information Highway*, 95 COLUM. L.REV. 1188 (1995). Federal limitations on foreign ownership exist in regulations of banking, 12 U.S.C. § 619 (1994), public utilities, 15 U.S.C. § 79z-5b (1994), energy sources, 15 U.S.C. § 785 (1994), foreign direct investment, 22 U.S.C. § 3103 (1994). See generally, RESTATEMENT (n. 2 to Preface) § 722, Comment *e, f*; S. GORDON AND F. LEES, FOREIGN MULTINATIONAL INVESTMENT IN THE UNITED STATES: INDUSTRIAL SUPREMACY (1986). On state restrictions on alien companies and foreign ownership of land, see RESTATEMENT (n. 2 to Preface) § 722, Reporters' Notes 8 and 9; MUTHARIKA, above; J. Huizinga, *Alien Land Laws: Constitutional Limitations on State Power to Regulate*, 32 HASTINGS L.J. 251 (1980).

Corporations are entitled to the protections of the Bill of Rights, but with some differences. Security against search and seizure may be different, for 'corporations can claim no equality with individuals in the enjoyment of a right to privacy'. *United States* v. *Morton Salt Co.*, 338 U.S. 632, 652 (1950). Corporations do not enjoy the privilege against self-incrimination, and corporate officers may not refuse to surrender corporate books or documents on the ground that they might incriminate the corporation or its officers. *United States* v. *Kordel*, 397 U.S. 1, 7 n.9 (1970); *United States* v. *Bausch & Lomb Optical*, 321 U.S. 707, 726–7 (1944); *Hale* v. *Henkel*, 201 U.S. 43 (1906). In recent years, corporations have invoked the Bill of Rights to greater success. See Mayer, *Personalizing the Impersonal: Corporations and the Bill of Rights*, 41 HASTINGS L.J. 577 (1990); see the appendices for a list of cases considering corporate rights under the Constitution, *id.*, at 664.

45. See, generally, H. Walker, *Modern Treaties of Friendship, Commerce, and Navigation*, 42 MINN. L.REV. 805 (1958). To a large extent, traditional provisions in FCN treaties relating to trade were superseded or subsumed in the General Agreement on Tariffs and Trade (GATT), and in 1994 by the Uruguay Round Agreements establishing the World Trade Organization. But many FCN treaties remain in effect and their provisions giving rights to individuals generally continue and are U.S. law.

46. See n. 37 above. Earlier Supreme Court cases refused to apply concepts of equal protection to federal acts, sometimes stating expressly that principles of equal protection did not apply (since the equal protection clause in the Fourteenth Amendment was addressed only to the states). *Truax* v. *Corrigan*, 257 U.S. 312, 332 (1921); *Steward Machine Co.* v. *Davis*, 301 U.S. 548, 584 (1936); *Sunshine Anthracite Coal Co.* v. *Adkins*, 310 U.S. 381, 401 (1940); *Detroit Bank* v. *United States*, 317 U.S. 329 (1943). Since the relevant source of limitations on U.S. actions was the due process clause, a court might have asked whether the federal regulation was rational as applied to either of the

categories distinguished; it was less likely to ask whether the distinction or classification was itself rational and reasonable. Equal protection principles became fully applicable to federal law with *Bolling* v. *Sharpe*, 347 U.S. 497 (1954), n. 37, above.

47.   In *Hampton* v. *Mow Sun Wong*, 426 U.S. 88 (1976), the Supreme Court struck down a ruling excluding resident aliens from the U.S. Civil Service, in large part because it had not been authorized by Congress. President Ford's Executive Order No. 11, 935, 41 Fed. Reg. 37301 (1976) excluding aliens except under limited circumstances was upheld in *Hampton* v. *Mow Sun Wong*, 435 F.Supp. 37 (D.D.C. 1973); *Vergara* v. *Hampton*, 581 F. 2d 1281 (7th Cir. 1978), *cert. denied*, 441 U.S. 905 (1979). And compare the limitations in Public Works Appropriation Act, Pub.L.No. 91–144, 93 Stat. 1336–7 (1970), and in cases dealing with state discrimination against aliens, nn. 44, 99, 100, 101 to this chapter. In *Mathews* v. *Diaz*, 426 U.S. 67 (1976), the Court upheld a provision conditioning participation in a federal Medicare program on permanent residency status and continuous residence in the United States for 5 years. See also *Narenji* v. *Civiletti*, 617 F.2d 745 (D.C.Cir. 1979); RESTATEMENT (n. 2 to Preface) § 722.

The right to vote is now denied to non-citizens. See generally, Neuman, *'We are the People': Alien Suffrage in German and American Perspective*, 13 MICH J. INT'L L 259 (1992).

48.   The property of an alien, like that of a U.S. citizen, can be taken only for a public use and subject to just compensation, even if the government of the alien's nationality does not reciprocate. *Russian Volunteer Fleet* v. *United States*, 282 U.S. 481 (1931).

Marshall had 'no doubt' that, in time of war, the United States could confiscate property of alien enemies. See *Brown* v. *United States*, 12 U.S. (8 Cranch) 110, 122 *et seq.* (1814). See also *United States* v. *Chemical Foundation*, 272 U.S. 1, 11 (1926); *Miller* v. *United States*, 78 U.S. (11 Wall.) 268 (1870). For the legality of blockade and capture of neutral ships that run the blockade, see *The Prize Cases*, 67 U.S. (2 Black) 635 (1862). Alien enemy properties were sequestered or confiscated during both World Wars without any constitutional doubts. See *Clark* v. *Uebersee Finanz-Korporation*, 332 U.S. 480 (1947); *Clark* v. *Allen*, 331 U.S. 503 (1947) (Trading with the Enemy Act not incompatible with treaty rights of German aliens to inherit realty, rights to which the United States had succeeded); see RESTATEMENT (n. 2 to Preface) § 721, Comment *g* and Reporters' Note 8, § 722, Comment *g*.

49.   'That provision [in the Fifth Amendment] has always been understood as referring only to a direct appropriation, and not to consequential injuries resulting from the exercise of lawful power. It has never been supposed to have any bearing upon, or to inhibit laws that indirectly work harm or loss to individuals.' *Legal Tender Cases*, 79 U.S. (12 Wall.) 457, 551 (1870). Holmes has called such laws 'the petty larceny of the police power'. 1 HOLMES-LASKI LETTERS 457 (Howe ed. 1953). See also Holmes's dissent in *Tyson and Brother* v. *Banton*, 273 U.S. 418, 445–6 (1927). Compare generally the opinions of Holmes and Brandeis on opposing sides in *Pennsylvania Coal Co.* v. *Mahon*, 260 U.S. 393, 412, 416 (1922). And see nn. 52 and 53 to this chapter.

50. *Causby* v. *United States*, 328 U.S. 256 (1946). Later cases extended the principle to other 'takings' by aviation. *Griggs* v. *County of Allegheny*, 369 U.S. 84 (1962). But *cf. Laird* v. *Nelms*, 406 U.S. 797 (1972).

51. *United States* v. *Caltex, Inc.*, 344 U.S. 149 (1952). Compare *Juragua Iron Co.* v. *United States*, 212 U.S. 297 (1909). On takings during wartime, see also *Hohri* v. *United States*, 782 F.2d 227 (D.C.Cir. 1986), *vacated*, 482 U.S. 64 (1987) (compensation granted to Japanese-Americans relocated during the Second World War for 'taking' of their property). The Court also found no compensable 'taking' by the United States when the War Production Board ordered the closing of non-essential gold mines to release personnel, equipment, and materials for essential defense production. *United States* v. *Central Eureka Mining Co.*, 357 U.S. 155 (1958). Compare also *National Board of YMCA* v. *United States*, 395 U.S. 85 (1969) (rejecting suit for damage inflicted by rioters after U.S. troops retreated into buildings).

52. See, e.g., *Goldblatt* v. *Hempstead*, 369 U.S. 590 (1962) (town ban against certain types of mining was not a 'taking' of plaintiff's mining pit property); *Penn Central Transportation Co.* v. *New York City*, 438 U.S. 104 (1978) (prohibition against building atop Grand Central Terminal under New York City's Landmarks Preservation Act was not a 'taking'); *Keystone Bituminous Coal Assn* v. *DeBenedictis*, 480 U.S. 470 (1987) (prohibition against mining under public buildings is not a 'taking').

53. See, e.g., *Loretto* v. *Teleprompter Manhattan CATV Corp.*, 458 U.S. 419 (1982) (law requiring landlords to permit cable television installation in rental properties is a compensable taking); *Lucas* v. *South Carolina Coastal Council*, 505 U.S. 1003 (1992) (prohibition against building homes on beach property, enacted after purchase of property, is a taking). Conditions on property development, e.g., setting aside land for public easements, have been ruled takings. *Nollan* v. *California Coastal Comm'n*, 483 U.S. 825 (1987); *Dolan* v. *City of Tigard*, 114 S.Ct. 2309 (1994). But *cf. Shanghai Power Co.* v. *United States*, n. 61 to this chapter. A court of appeals held that a deduction by the United States of 2% from an individual recovery in a judgment of the U.S.–Iran Tribunal constitutes a taking. *United Stated* v. *Sperry Corp.*, 493 U.S. 52 (1989). See n. 66 to this chapter.

Freezing of assets does not deprive the alien of property without due process of law nor does it constitute a taking requiring compensation. *Miranda* v. *Secretary of the Treasury*, 766 F.2d 1 (1st Cir. 1985). See Executive Order 12947, Prohibiting Transactions with Terrorists who Threaten to Disrupt the Middle East Peace Process, Jan. 23, 1995, promulgated under authority of the International Emergency Economic Powers Act (IEEPA), 50 U.S.C. § 1702 (1988), as amended, Pub.L.No. 103–236, Title V § 525(c)(1), 108 Stat. 474 (1994).

54. 3 U.S. (3 Dall.) 199 (1796).

55. 3 U.S. (3 Dall.) at 281, 283.

56. *Id.* at 245 (emphasis in original). Chase continued: 'Although Virginia is not bound to make compensation to the debtors, yet it is evident that they ought to be indemnified, and it is not to be supposed, that those whose duty it may

be to make the compensation, will permit the rights of our citizens to be sacrificed to a public object, without the fullest indemnity'.

Compare W. Cowles, Treaties and Constitutional Law 292–5 (1941), suggesting that this case would not be followed today. His argument, however, does not lead to the conclusion that the treaty is invalid, but rather that to bring it into effect domestically in the United States, Congress would have to meet the requirements of the Fifth Amendment and provide compensation. A court, therefore, might well follow *Ware* v. *Hylton* and give effect to the treaty, leaving the debtor to an action in the Court of Claims on a claim 'founded upon the Constitution'. *Cf. Cities Serv. Co.* v. *McGrath*, 342 U.S. 330 (1952), discussed this chapter, p. 299. See also Henkin, Arms Control (n. 3 to Ch. VI) 230–1 n. 20.

If, in a situation such as that in *Ware* v. *Hylton,* the courts were to decide in favor of the U.S. citizen whose property rights are involved, the United States might fulfill its international obligations by itself compensating the foreign claimant.

57. Compare the treaty exception in the Tucker Act (codified in scattered sections of 28 U.S.C.), 28 U.S.C. § 1491 (1994), and the reference to it in *Dames & Moore* v. *Regan*, 453 U.S. 654, 689 (1981).

58. *Cities Service Co.* v. *McGrath*, 342 U.S. 330 (1952).

59. 342 U.S. at 336. *Cf. Yearsley* v. *W. A. Ross Constr. Co.*, 309 U.S. 18, 21 (1940); *Hurley* v. *Kincaid*, 285 U.S. 95 (1932).

60. See generally M. Hudson, International Tribunals 196 (1944). In some cases private claims were adjudicated by joint claims commissions. See, e.g., Convention Between the United States of America and the Republic of Mexico for the Adjustment of Claims, July 4, 1868, Art. II, 15 Stat. 682, T.S.No. 212; compare the Agreement Between the United States and Canada Concerning the Establishment of an International Arbitral Tribunal to Dispose of United States Claims Relating to Gut Dam, March 25, 1965, [1966] 17 U.S.T. 1566, T.I.A.S. No. 6114, 52 Dep't State Bull. 643 (1965); Iran-United States Claims Tribunal (implemented by Exec. Orders Nos. 12276–12285, 46 Fed. Reg. 7913–7932), established pursuant to the 1981 Algiers Accord which provided also for the release of the U.S. nationals held hostage in Iran. Many claims settlements have been by executive agreement. See n. 172 to Ch. VII.

In 1949, Congress authorized the establishment of the Foreign Claims Settlement Commission to adjudicate American claims and determine their validity and amount. International Claims Settlement Act of 1949, ch. 54, 64 Stat. 12 (1950), 22 U.S.C. § 1621 *et seq.* (1994), as amended, Foreign Claims Settlement Commission Act, ch. 645, 69 Stat. 562 (1955), pursuant to Reorganization Plan No. 1 of 1954, 68 Stat. 1279 (1954). See also the Cuban Claims Act [also applicable to Communist China], Pub.L.No.88–666, 78 Stat. 1110 (1964), as amended, 22 U.S.C. § 1643 *et seq.* (1994). There is no appeal from the Commission to the courts. 22 U.S.C. § 1623h (1994).

Recent cases have upheld the authority of the President to make such agreements. See Ch. VII. If a foreign government reneges on a debt, 'a claimant's only hope of obtaining any payment at all might lie in having his government negotiate a diplomatic settlement on his behalf'. *Dames & Moore* v. *Regan*, 453 U.S. 654, 679 (1981). See also *Shanghai Power Co.* v. *United States*, 4 Cl.Ct. 237 (1983), *aff'd*, 765 F.2d 159 (Fed. Cir. 1985), *cert. denied*, 474 U.S. 909 (1985), for a discussion of the policy reasons behind such agreements. See generally Lillich and Weston, *Lump Sum Agreements: Their Continuing Contribution to the Law of International Claims*, 82 AM.J.INT'L L. 69 (1988); Note, *The U.S.-Iran Accords and the Taking Clause of the Fifth Amendment*, 68 VA.L.REV. 1537 (1982).

61. Courts have consistently upheld such claims settlements as not violating the Fifth Amendment rights of claimants. See, e.g., *Shanghai Power Co.*, v. *United States*, 4 Cl.Ct. 237 (1983), *aff'd*, 765 F.2d 159 (Fed. Cir. 1985), *cert. denied*, 474 U.S. 909 (1985), upholding President Carter's settlement with the People's Republic of China. But *cf. Meade* v. *United States*, 76 U.S. (9 Wall.) 691 (1869), where the Court struggled with whether the claimant had authorized the United States to deal with his claim. See generally HENKIN, ARMS CONTROL (n. 3 to Ch. VI) 109–10 and notes.

62. See Article V, Convention of Peace, Commerce and Navigation, Sept. 30, 1800, 1 MALLOY TREATIES (n. 10 to Ch. I) 496, 498.

63. Congress adopted three bills to provide for payment, but the first two were vetoed, one by President Polk, another by President Pierce. The whole story is told at length in *Gray* v. *United States*, 21 Ct.Cl. 340 (1886). In that case, the Court of Claims dismissed the claim because any award of compensation was not enforceable without Congressional legislation. See also *Buchanan* v. *United States*, 24 Ct.Cl. 74, 82 (1889). Congress later paid, no doubt partly in response to the pleas of the Court of Claims, quoted p. 301–2.

64. The Constitutional provision prohibiting impairment of the obligation of contracts (Art. I, sec. 10) is directed to the states, but similar limitations have been held to apply to the federal government by virtue of the due process clause of the Fifth Amendment. *Lynch* v. *United States*, 292 U.S. 571 (1934); *Perry* v. *United States*, 294 U.S. 330 (1935). But compare *National Railroad Co.* v. *Atchison, Topeka, and Santa Fe Railway Co.*, 470 U.S. 451 (1985).

65. Compare *Meade* v. *United States*, 76 U.S. (9 Wall.) 691 (1869); *Comegys* v. *Vasse*, 26 U.S. (1 Pet.) 193 (1828); *Alling* v. *United States*, 114 U.S. 562 (1885). See also *Dames & Moore* v. *Regan*, 453 U.S. 654 (1981), the Iranian Hostages Settlement Case, where the Supreme Court found that a claim that private interests had been sacrificed or depreciated and were taken for the public use of obtaining the release of hostages was not ripe for consideration. Compare *In re Aircrash in Bali*, 684 F.2d 1301 (9th Cir. 1982), *cert. denied*, 493 U.S. 917 (1989), in which the court said that plaintiffs had a right to compensation if their claims had been unreasonably impaired by the Warsaw Convention. See also *Ramirez de Arellano* v. *Weinberger*, 568 F.Supp. 1236 (1983), *rev'd*, 724 F.2d 1500 (D.C. Cir. 1984) (en banc), *vacated*, 471 U.S. 1113 (1985), *on remand*, 788 F.2d 762 (D.C. Cir. 1986).

66. The Supreme Court has referred to Congressional payments in such a case 'as of grace and not of right'. *Blagge* v. *Balch*, 162 U.S. 439, 457 (1896). Compare *Aris Gloves, Inc.* v. *United States*, 420 F.2d 1386 (Ct.Cl. 1970). The Supreme

Court held also that even payments received 'on behalf of' a U.S. claimant do not legally belong to him, and the Executive branch could refuse to remit payments received from the Mexican Government (allegedly because it suspected the claimants of fraud). *La Abra Silver Mining Co.* v. *United States*, 175 U.S. 423 (1899); *United States ex rel. Boynton* v. *Blaine*, 139 U.S. 306 (1891); *Frelinghuysen* v. *Key*, 110 U.S. 63 (1884). *Cf. Z. & F. Assets Realization Corp.* v. *Hull*, 311 U.S. 470 (1941). See also *Shanghai Power Co.* v. *United States*, 4 Cl.Ct. 237 (1983), *aff'd*, 765 F.2d 159 (Fed. Cir. 1985), *cert. denied*, 474 U.S. 909 (1985). In recent years the Supreme Court has not been reflecting that doctrine, but it has rejected particular constitutional objections to particular aspects of particular claims settlements. See, for example, objections to applications of the Algiers Accord settling the Iranian Hostages crisis: *Dames & Moore* v. *Regan*, 453 U.S. 654 (1981), which provided, *inter alia*, for the revocation of licenses, suspension of claims, termination and preclusion of suits in U.S. courts (discussed also in Chapter VII, p. 220); compare *United States* v. *Sperry Corp.*, 493 U.S. 52 (1989); *Belk* v. *United States*, 858 F.2d 706 (Fed.Cir. 1988). See also *Belk* v. *United States*, 858 F.2d 706 (Fed. Cir. 1988), holding that the Algiers Accord, which extinguished former Iranian hostages' causes of action for false imprisonment, assault and battery, did not constitute a taking.

67. Compare Chief Justice Marshall: '.[B]ut in great national concerns, where individual rights, acquired by war, are sacrificed for national purposes, the contract making the sacrifice ought always to receive a construction conforming to its manifest import; and if the nation has given up the vested rights of its citizens, it is not for the court, but for the government, to consider whether it be a case proper for compensation.' *United States* v. *Schooner Peggy*, 5 U.S. (1 Cranch) 103, 110 (1801).

68. *Gray* v. *United States*, 21 Ct.Cl. 340, 392–3 (1886).

69. For the jurisdiction of the United States Court of Federal Claims, see 28 U.S.C. §§ 1491 *et seq.* (1988 and Supp. V 1993). There is, however, an ambiguous limitation barring the court from hearing any claim against the United States 'growing out of or dependent upon any treaty'. 28 U.S.C. § 1502. See Magraw, *Jurisdiction of Cases Related to Treaties: The Claims Court's Treaty Exception*, 26 VA.J.INT'L L. 1 (1985). The treaty exception was held inapplicable in *Dames & Moore* v. *Regan*, 453 U.S. 654 (1981). *Cf. Alling* v. *United States*, 114 U.S. 562 (1885) (treaty exception applies to claims arising out of a treaty stipulation where Congress has legislated a remedy for such claims).

70. See Leigh and Atkeson, *Due Process in the Emerging Foreign Relations Law of the United States*, 22 BUS. LAW. 3, 23–6 (1966), suggesting that there may be a substantive right to compensation when, in the interests of achieving national foreign policy objectives, one's property rights are abridged, one's foreign claim is settled over his (her) objection, or one is compelled to release an attachment of property of a foreign sovereign. These authors have also proposed that future claims settlements go to the Senate for ratification, thus affording private claimants an opportunity to be heard there. 21 BUS. LAW. at 875–6. Compare n. 25 to this chapter.

71. *Dames & Moore* v. *Regan*, 453 U.S. 654, 673–4 (1981).

72. International organizations and their officials generally enjoy only 'functional immunity', those privileges and immunities needed for carrying out their official functions. See the Convention on the Privileges and Immunities of the United Nations, 1 U.N.T.S. 15 (1946); see also the International Organizations Immunities Act, 22 U.S.C. § 288 *et seq.* (1994). Member Representatives of the United Nations enjoy full diplomatic privileges and immunities (but may be subject to removal for abuse of their privileges of residence). See Agreement between the United States of America and the United Nations regarding the Headquarters of the United Nations, June 26, 1947, 61 Stat. 3416, T.I.A.S. No. 1676. See also the Diplomatic Relations Act, 22 U.S.C.A. § 254e (1994).

73. Diplomatic immunity might raise other questions. For example, an accused is entitled 'to have compulsory process for obtaining witnesses in his favor' (the Sixth Amendment), but international law denies the United States the right to compel a diplomat to testify. The international immunity has been considered a historical exception to the constitutional requirement, and presumably recent extensions of immunity to new categories (e.g., international officials or member representatives to the U.N., n. 72 to this chapter) would also prevail, I think, despite the constitutional language. In 1854, Secretary of State Marcy said that the constitutional right to compulsory testimony was at its inception limited by diplomatic immunity to subpoena and other compulsory process, but consuls had no such immunity under international law and therefore a grant of immunity by treaty was unconstitutional. See 5 MOORE, DIGEST (n. 50 to Ch. II) § 736 at 167. A lower federal court, however, held the treaty exemption for consuls valid, interpreting the Sixth Amendment as satisfied when both the prosecution and the defendant are subject to the same limitations. See *In re Dillon*, 7 F.Cas. 710 (No. 3914) (N.D.Cal.1854). (The United States has long discontinued such consular exemptions.) Compare the Supreme Court's view that the United States may have to choose between making 'privileged' evidence available to an accused or foregoing the prosecution. *Jencks* v. *United States*, 353 U.S. 657 (1957), n. 73 to Ch. IV. Congress promptly superseded that decision by the Jencks Act, 18 U.S.C. § 3500 (1994).

74. *Fong Yue Ting* v. *United States*, 149 U.S. 698 (1893); *Wong Wing* v. *United States*, 163 U.S. 228 (1896); *United States ex rel. Knauff* v. *Shaughnessy*, 338 U.S. 537 (1950); *Shaughnessy* v. *U.S. ex rel. Mezei*, 345 U.S. 206 (1953); *Galvan* v. *Press*, 347 U.S. 522 (1954). Recent Equal Protection clause challenges to immigration rules have generally failed. See, e.g., *Fiallo* v. *Bell*, 430 U.S. 787 (1977). For a rare exception, see *Francis* v. *I.N.S.*, 532 F.2d 268 (2d Cir. 1976). See generally Aleinikoff, *Federal Regulation of Aliens and the Constitution*, 83 AM.J.INT'L L. 862 (1989).

75. *Harisiades* v. *Shaughnessy*, 342 U.S. 580 (1952); *Galvan* v. *Press*, 347 U.S. 522, 529–32 (1954). In *Augustin* v. *Sava*, 735 F.2d 32 (2d Cir. 1984), the court held that an alien has the right to effective translation in a deportation hearing. Also, see Bullitt, *Deportation as a Denial of Substantive Due Process*, 28 GEO. WASH.L.REV. 205 (1953), and Hesse, *The Constitutional Status of the Lawfully Admtited Permanent Resident Alien: The Pre-1917 Cases*, 68 YALE L.J. 1578 (1959), 69 YALE L.J. 262 (1959); they suggest that there ought to be and are constitutional limitations on the power of Congress to expel lawfully admitted

resident aliens. See Henkin, *The Constitution and U.S. Sovereignty: A Century of Chinese Exclusion and its Progeny*, 100 HARV.L.REV. 853 (1987); Scharpf, *Judicial Review and the Political Question: A Functional Analysis*, 75 YALE L.J. 517 (1966) at 580–3, who treats the cases upholding expulsion as asserting an unreviewable political question. See also Rosberg, *The Protection of Aliens From Discriminatory Treatment By the National Government*, 1977 SUP.CT.REV. 275; Note, *The Indefinite Detention of Excluded Aliens: Statutory and Constitutional Justifications and Limitations*, 82 MICH.L.REV. 61 (1983); *Due Process and the Treatment of Aliens* (symposium issue), 44 U.PITT.L.REV. 163 (1983); S. Legomsky, *Immigration Law and the Principle of Plenary Congressional Power*, 1984 SUP. CT. REV. 255, cited in Legomsky, *Ten More Years of Plenary Power: Immigration, Congress, and the Courts*, 22 HASTINGS CONST. L.Q. 1087 (1995); Comment, *Petitioning on Behalf of an Alien Spouse: Due Process Under the Immigration Laws*, 74 CALIF.L.REV. 1747 (1986); CHOPER, KAMISAR, and TRIBE, DISCRIMINATION AGAINST ALIENS, THE SUPREME COURT: TRENDS AND DEVELOPMENTS 1981–82 (1983); RESTATEMENT (n. 2 to Preface) § 722, Comment *i* and Reporters' Note 12.

See also *American-Arab Anti-Discrimination Comm.* v. *Meese*, 714 F.Supp. 1060 (C.D. Cal. 1989), invalidating a provision of the McCarran–Walker Act of 1952. The court found that the provision, which permits deportation of aliens for exercising free speech, is a violation of the First Amendment test of *Brandenburg* v. *Ohio*, 395 U.S. 444 (1969). In a later case involving the same plaintiffs, the Ninth Circuit held that aliens 'enjoy full First Amendment Rights'. *American-Arab Anti-Discrimination Comm.* v. *Reno*, 70 F.3d 1045 (9th Cir. 1995). (On the argument that exclusion of an invited alien denies United States citizens' First Amendment rights, see n. 15 to this chapter.) See also Comment, *Immigration and the First Amendment*, 73 CALIF.L.REV. 1889 (1985).

The Kentucky Resolutions of November 10, 1798, drafted by Jefferson, notorious as a vain attempt by a state to 'nullify' national action, were directed against the alien and sedition laws and include an attack on the constitutionality of the provisions giving the President authority to expel aliens. See H.R.REP, No. 43, 21st Cong., 2d Sess. (1831).

76. *Nishimura Ekiu* v. *United States*, 142 U.S. 651 (1892); *U.S. ex rel. Knauff* v. *Shaughnessy*, 338 U.S. 537 (1950). The Supreme Court has held that under general statutory authority to exclude aliens in the national interest (formerly 22 U.S.C. § 223, now 8 U.S.C. § 1185(a) (1994)), even a resident alien who leaves the United States can be excluded upon return without a hearing and on undisclosed evidence and could be detained if there is no country that will accept him. *Shaughnessy* v. *U.S. ex rel. Mezei*, 345 U.S. 206 (1953); but see *Landon* v. *Plasencia*, 459 U.S. 21, 32 (1982) (alien who returns after a few days is entitled to due process). See *Due Process and the Treatment of Aliens* (symposium issue), 44 U. PITT. L. REV. 163 ff. (1983). Excluded aliens have no standing to sue to challenge their exclusion. *Kleindienst* v. *Mandel*, 408 U.S. 753, 762 (1972). But the entrant is entitled to a fair hearing on his claim that he is a citizen. *Kwock Jan Fat* v. *White*, 253 U.S. 454, 457 (1920). Congress has enacted special procedures, including judicial review, for those with a substantial, *bona*

fide claim that they are U.S. nationals. C. 477, Title III, Ch. 3, § 360, 66 Stat. 273 (1952), 8 U.S.C. § 1503 (1994).

77. See, e.g., *Fernandez-Roque* v. *Smith*, 734 F.2d 576, 582 (11th Cir. 1982); *Jean* v. *Nelson*, 727 F.2d 957 (11th Cir. 1984) *en banc, aff'd on other grounds*, 472 U.S. 846 (1985). Both decisions relied upon *Shaughnessy* v. *United States ex rel. Mezei*, 345 U.S. 206 (1953). See n. 80 to this chapter.

78. The Supreme Court confirmed Congress's right to deport aliens in *Harisiades* v. *Shaughnessy*, 342 U.S. 580 (1952). An alien in the United States, however, is entitled to a fair administrative hearing and the Government must prove by clear, unequivocal and convincing evidence that he is deportable on the grounds provided by Congress. *Woodby* v. *Immigration and Naturalization Service*, 385 U.S. 276 (1966). The standard of proof is higher than in ordinary civil cases but not as high as that required in criminal cases (which require proof 'beyond a reasonable doubt'; see *In re Winship*, 397 U.S. 358, 361–4 (1970)). He (she) has the right to effective translation at the deportation hearing. *Augustin* v. *Sava*, 735 F.2d 32 (2d. Cir 1984). He (she) can bring habeas corpus to challenge a deportation order for lack of fair hearing or of any supporting evidence. *U.S. ex rel. Vajtauer* v. *Comm'r of Immigration*, 273 U.S. 103, 106 (1927). For cases involving due process claims in exclusion and deportation hearings, see n. 76 above.

Since deportation is deemed not to be a criminal punishment, the alien is not denied due process because the immigration officers are not given power to compel witnesses in his behalf. *Low Wah Suey* v. *Backus*, 225 U.S. 460 (1912). Search and seizure pursuant to an administrative arrest by immigration officials do not violate the Fourth or Fifth Amendments, and the use in evidence of an article seized does not invalidate the petitioner's conviction. *Abel* v. *United States*, 362 U.S. 217 (1960); *I.N.S.* v. *Lopez-Mendoza*, 468 U.S. 1032 (1984). Several lower courts have held that an alien arrested pursuant to an immigration order is not entitled to '*Miranda*' warnings. *Jolley* v. *Immigration and Naturalization Service*, 441 F.2d 1245 (1971), *cert. denied*, 404 U.S. 946 (1971); *Chavez-Raya* v. *I.N.S.*, 519 F.2d 397 (7th Cir. 1975); *Trias-Hernandez* v. *United States*, 528 F.2d 366, 368 (9th Cir. 1975); *Lavoie* v. *I.N.S.*, 418 F.2d 732, 734 (9th Cir. 1969), *cert. denied*, 400 U.S. 854 (1970); *United States* v. *Alderete-Deras*, 743 F.2d 645, 648 (9th Cir. 1984). Aliens subject to criminal proceedings, however, must be advised of their *Miranda* rights. See e.g., *United States* v. *Henry*, 604 F.2d 908, 914 (5th Cir. 1979). The government need not supply an attorney for an indigent alien in deportation proceedings. *Cf.* 8 U.S.C. § 1252(b) (1994).

'When the Constitution requires a hearing, it requires a fair one, one before a tribunal which meets at least currently prevailing standards of impartiality.' *Wong Yang Sung* v. *McGrath*, 339 U.S. 33, 50 (1950). To avoid the constitutional question, the Court interpreted the law as precluding a deportation hearing presided over by an immigration inspector. But a divided court held that an enemy alien in time of war is not entitled to any hearing and cannot complain of the inadequacy of one he is given gratuitously. *Ludecke* v. *Watkins*, 335 U.S. 160 (1948). See RESTATEMENT (n. 2 to Preface) § 722, Comment *i* and Reporters' Note 12.

79. *Galvan* v. *Press*, 347 U.S. 522, 530–1 (1954).
80. See ALEINIKOFF AND MARTIN, IMMIGRATION: PROCESS AND POLICY 7–39 (2d edn., 1991). It is not unlikely that in less fearful days, at least, Justice Jackson's eloquent dissent in *Mezei* requiring procedural due process will prevail.

To date, efforts to have *Mezei* and *Galvan* reconsidered have not succeeded. Compare *Fernandez* v. *Wilkinson*, 505 F.Supp 787 (D.Kan.1980), *aff'd*, 654 F.2d 1382 (10th Cir. 1981). See Henkin, *The Constitution and United States Sovereignty*, n. 75 to this chapter.
81. *In re Ross*, 140 U.S. 453, 464 (1891).

Consular courts exercised jurisdiction over offenses by U.S. citizens in many 'uncivilized' countries under treaties that granted exclusive jurisdiction to the United States. *Ross* upheld the constitutionality of such trials. A brief history of these consular courts can be found in Justice Frankfurter's concurring opinion in *Reid* v. *Covert*, 354 U.S. 1, 56–64 (1957).
82. 354 U.S. 1 (1957).
83. *Id.* at 12; also at 1. Justice Black used other language suggesting that the Constitution might govern almost all acts of the United States anywhere. Justice Frankfurter also emphasized the historical context of *Ross,* but said only that the Constitution applied in some situations, leaving further refinement of that doctrine to the future. *Id.* at 41, 64. Justice Harlan found that *Ross* did not apply to the case before him but emphasized that the applicability of constitutional requirements to United States action abroad would depend on the 'particular circumstances, the practical necessities, and the possible alternatives which Congress had before it'. *Id.* at 65, 75. The implications of *Reid* v. *Covert* were confirmed and extended in other cases invalidating U.S. court-martial jurisdiction over civilians abroad, n. 44 to Ch. III.

The Insular Cases, and U.S. occupation courts, pp. 47, 307 above, were distinguished by Justice Black in his *Reid* opinion. The Status of Forces Agreements distributing jurisdiction over visiting forces between the host and the sending state do not raise these issues. See n. 93 to Ch. VIII. As regards a member of the U.S. armed forces in an allied country, it is not the Agreement that subjects him (her) to the jurisdiction of foreign courts where he does not enjoy the protections of the Bill of Rights; he is subject to foreign jurisdiction because he is in foreign territory, by virtue of the domestic laws of that country and the accepted international principle of territorial sovereignty. The Agreement merely confirms that principle and modifies it to the extent that the host country agrees that in some circumstances a visiting soldier will not be subject to local jurisdiction, but only, or primarily, to that of his military authorities.

The argument that the United States cannot constitutionally send troops abroad against their will and thereby expose them to foreign laws and lesser safeguards than they enjoy under the Constitution was unanimously rejected a few months after *Reid* v. *Covert. Wilson* v. *Girard*, 354 U.S. 524 (1957). One might note that members of the armed forces do not enjoy the particular constitutional rights in question—jury trial and other elements of due process— even in the United States, since military justice does not provide them. In

O'Callahan v. Parker, 395 U.S. 258 (1969), the Court held that a soldier cannot be tried by court-martial for non-service-connected crimes committed in the United States in time of peace, but that case was overruled in *Solorio* v. *United States*, 483 U.S. 435 (1987).

84. 354 U.S. at 6. The opinions in *Reid*, n. 83 to this chapter, left doubt as to whether in respect of U.S. actions abroad the Bill of Rights protects all who are subject to an exercise of U.S. authority, as in the United States, or whether it protects only the U.S. citizen. There is language in Justice Black's opinion implying that the United States can never act free of constitutional limitations, but he stressed that U.S. citizens were involved in the case before him. For the Justices who took a more limited view of constitutional rights abroad, the citizenship of the claimant was perhaps a critical factor. The Restatement concludes that 'the Constitution governs the exercise of authority by the United States government over United States citizens outside United States territory. . .' RESTATEMENT (n. 2 to Preface) § 721 Comment *b*.

See *Ramirez de Arellano* v. *Weinberger*, 568 F.Supp. 1236 (1983), *rev'd*, 724 F.2d 1500 (D.C. Cir. 1984) (en banc), *vacated*, 471 U.S. 1113 (1985), on remand, 788 F.2d 762 (D.C. Cir. 1986). The U.S. government stationed troops on the land of a U.S. citizen living in Honduras, as part of its foreign policy relating to the situation in El Salvador. The case was finally dismissed when, after 3 years, all U.S. personnel had withdrawn from the property. See also *Committee of U.S. Citizens Living in Nicaragua* v. *Reagan*, 859 F.2d 929 (D.C. Cir 1988) (dismissing Fifth Amendment claim against U.S. actions in Nicaragua for failing to state a claim on which relief can be granted).

No one has suggested that it is a denial of due process for the United States to apply its laws to acts of U.S. nationals abroad or to others whom it can reach under one of the bases of prescriptive jurisdiction accepted under international law. See RESTATEMENT (n. 2 to Preface) § 721; see also n. 57 to Ch. II. 'Extra-territorial' legislation by one of the states of the United States would probably violate due process. Compare *Pennoyer* v. *Neff*, 95 U.S. 714 (1878); *Union Refrigerator Transit Co.* v. *Kentucky*, 199 U.S. 194, 204 (1905); *United States* v. *Bevans*, 16 U.S. (3 Wheat.) 336, 386–7 (1818); but *cf. Skiriotes* v. *Florida*, 313 U.S. 69 (1941).

85. See, e.g., *United States* v. *Hilton*, 469 F.Supp. 94 (D.Me. 1979), *aff'd*, 619 F.2d 127 (1st Cir. 1980), *cert. denied*, 449 U.S. 887 (1980); *United States* v. *Demanett*, 629 F.2d 862, 866 (3d Cir. 1980), *cert. denied*, 450 U.S. 910 (1981); *United States* v. *Hensel*, 509 F.Supp. 1264 (D.Me. 1981), *aff'd*, 699 F.2d 18 (1st Cir. 1983) *cert. denied*, 461 U.S. 958 (1983); compare *United States* v. *Villamonte-Marquez*, 462 U.S. 579 (1983). See Henkin, *The Constitution at Sea*, 36 MAINE L. REV. 201 (1984). In 1992, a foreign national successfully presented a substantive due process claim arising out of events occurring overseas. In *Wang Zong Xiao* v. *Reno*, 837 F.Supp. 1506 (N.D.Cal. 1993), the plaintiff, awaiting criminal charges in a Chinese prison but temporarily paroled into the United States to testify in a heroin conspiracy case, sought asylum in the United States against deportation to China. The district court held that the U.S. officials had violated Wang's substantive due process rights by ignoring evidence that

Wang's testimony was coerced by Chinese officials. 837 F.Supp. at 1547–59. For a lower court holding that the Constitution protects the Swiss bank accounts of a U.S. citizen against unreasonable search and seizure, see n. 39 to Ch. VII. See generally Henkin, *The Constitution as Compact and Conscience: Individual Rights Abroad and at Our Gates*, 27 Wm. & Mary L. Rev. 11, 23 (1985), reprinted in L. Henkin, The Age of Rights (1989), Ch. 8.

86. In *United States* v. *Tiede*, 86 F.R.D. 227, a United States court sitting in Berlin held that a Polish national tried in that court has a constitutional right to a jury trial. See also *United States* v. *Yunis*, 681 F.Supp. 909 (D.D.C. 1988), *rev'd on other grounds*, 859 F.2d 953 (D.C. Cir. 1988). These cases imply that a foreign national held under United States authority abroad could seek release on habeas corpus in an American court. See generally, Henkin, n. 85 above, at 11, 24. In *United States* v. *Toscanino*, 500 F.2d 267 (2d Cir. 1974), federal officials had allegedly kidnapped and tortured an alien abroad and brought him to the United States for criminal proceedings. The court held that the alien's constitutional rights had been violated and invalidated his trial. That case was later sharply limited. *United States ex rel. Lujan* v. *Gengler*, 510 F.2d 62 (2d Cir.), *cert. denied*, 421 U.S. 1001 (1975); *United States* v. *Lira*, 515 F.2d 68 (2d Cir. 1975), *cert. denied*, 423 U.S. 847 (1975); *United States* v. *Reed*, 639 F.2d 896 (2d Cir. 1981). See the discussion of the 'supervisory jurisdiction' of the federal courts, Ch. V, p. 140.

87. *United States* v. *Verdugo-Urquidez*, 494 U.S. 259 (1990). Justice Stevens, concurring, joined the judgment of the Court because, though he thought that the Fourth Amendment protected Verdugo, he found that the search and seizure were not unreasonable in the circumstances. See 494 U.S. at 279. The constitutionality of 'remote sensing' by satellite has not been adjudicated, but it is assumed that the practice does not violate the privacy rights of the targets of the practice. See DeSaussure, *Remote Sensing by Satellite*, 71 Am. J. Int'l L. 707 (1977). For a Department of Justice Report on the reading of mail by the CIA, see 71 Am. J. Int'l L. 520 (1977).

88. See, e.g., Henkin, note 85 above.

89. *The Chinese Exclusion Case* and *Ker* v. *Illinois* were decided in 1886; *In re Ross* in 1891. See Henkin, *The Constitution and U.S. Sovereignty*, n. 75 above.

90. 119 U.S. 436 (1886). *Ker* was followed later in *Frisbee* v. *Collins*, 432 U.S. 519 (1952).

91. *United States* v. *Alvarez-Machain*, 504 U.S. 655, 662 (1992).

In 1993, in *Sale* v. *Haitian Centers Council, Inc.*, 113 S.Ct. 2549 (1993), the Court rejected the claims of persons on vessels interdicted by the United States Coast Guard and forcibly returned to Haiti. The Court held that the U.S. action did not violate U.S. law or the provision of the Refugee Convention against *non-refoulement*, which the Court said was not intended to apply outside the territory of the state party to the Convention. The Court did not address rights under the Constitution, e.g., whether the action deprived the refugees of liberty without due process of law, or under customary international law.

92. The courts of the United States have not been available to foreign nationals

abroad for raising such claims, despite the general language of the statutes establishing the courts' jurisdiction. See, e.g., *Johnson* v. *Eisentrager*, 339 U.S. 763 (1950), where a national of an enemy nation was denied access to the courts in time of war. In *Berlin Democratic Club* v. *Rumsfeld*, 410 F.Supp. 144 (D.D.C. 1976), the court denied foreign plaintiffs standing to sue because of insufficient contact with the United States: the plaintiff had not been thrust into U.S. courts nor had he been denied a benefit under a U.S. statute, *id.*, at 153. But compare *Greenham Women Against Cruise Missiles* v. *Reagan*, 591 F.Supp. 1332 (S.D.N.Y. 1984), *aff'd*, 755 F.2d 34 (2d Cir. 1985); Henkin, *The Constitution as Compact and as Conscience*, n. 85 to this chapter, at 24, 32 n.127. See p. 304, above.

93. *Dorr* v. *United States*, 195 U.S. 138 (1904); *Balzac* v. *Puerto Rico*, 258 U.S. 298 (1922); *Hawaii* v. *Mankichi*, 190 U.S. 197 (1903); *cf. Downes* v. *Bidwell*, 182 U.S. 244 (1901). But compare *Torres* v. *Puerto Rico*, 442 U.S. 465 (1979).

94. Or the Mariana Islands. See *Wabol* v. *Villacrusis*, 958 F.2d 1450 (9th Cir. 1992), *cert. denied*, 113 S.Ct. 675 (1992).

On the ambiguous status of Puerto Rico, see *Torres* v. *Puerto Rico*, 442 U.S. 465 (1979); *Califano* v. *Torres*, 435 U.S. 1 (1978); *Harris* v. *Rosario*, 446 U.S. 651 (1980).

95. See *Palko* v. *Connecticut*, 302 U.S. 319 (1937); *Snyder* v. *Massachusetts*, 291 U.S. 97 (1934); *Rochin* v. *California*, 342 U.S. 165 (1952). See n. 97 to this chapter. See also *Examining Bd. of Engineers* v. *Flores de Otero*, 426 U.S. 572, 599, n.30 (1976). In *United States* v. *Verdugo-Urquidez*, 494 U.S. 259 (1990), the Supreme Court relied in part on the fact that residents of unincorporated territories have only limited constitutional rights as a reason for rejecting the Fourth Amendment claims of aliens.

96. *Barron* v. *Baltimore*, 32 U.S. (7 Pet.) 243 (1833).

97. As regards the states, the liberty protected by the due process clause long included all the 'preferred freedoms' which the First Amendment safeguards against undue federal encroachment. See n. 26 to this chapter. Until the 1960s, however, the Court eschewed the doctrine propounded by Justice Black in his dissent in *Adamson* v. *California*, 332 U.S. 46, 68, 92 (1947), that the Fourteenth Amendment 'incorporated' all of the Bill of Rights and made it applicable to the states. Instead, the Court was deciding case by case whether the procedure in a state case was basically unfair; that the same procedure if applied by the federal government would have violated one of the specific provisions of the Bill of Rights was not determinative. See *Palko* v. *Connecticut*, n. 95 above. In the 1960's, however, the Court adopted a modified version of Black's doctrine, 'selective incorporation': those provisions of the Bill of Rights that are 'fundamental' are incorporated in the Fourteenth Amendment and applicable to the states exactly as to the federal government. See Henkin, *'Selective Incorporation' in the Fourteenth Amendment*, 73 YALE L.J. 74 (1963). By 1969 all the provisions governing criminal procedure except the grand jury requirement (the Fifth Amendment) had been held fundamental and incorporated. *Mapp* v. *Ohio*, 367 U.S. 643 (1961) (exclusion of evidence obtained by unlawful search and seizure); *Malloy* v. *Hogan*, 378 U.S. 1 (1964)

(privilege against self-incrimination); *Gideon* v. *Wainwright,* 372 U.S. 335 (1965) (right to counsel); *Klopfer* v. *North Carolina,* 386 U.S. 213 (1967) (speedy trial); *Pointer* v. *Texas,* 380 U.S. 400 (1965) (confrontation of witnesses); *Washington* v. *Texas,* 388 U.S. 14 (1967) (compulsory process for obtaining witnesses); *Duncan* v. *Louisiana,* 391 U.S. 145 (1968) (jury trial in criminal cases); *Benton* v. *Maryland,* 395 U.S. 784 (1969) (double jeopardy); *Robinson* v. *California,* 370 U.S. 660 (1962) (protection from cruel and unusual punishment); *In re Oliver,* 333 U.S. 257 (1948) (public trial). Perhaps because these provisions had been extended to the states, however, the Court was later moved to reduce their content. See, e.g., *Apodaca* v. *Oregon,* 406 U.S. 404 (1972) (jury verdict need not be unanimous); *Colten* v. *Kentucky,* 407 U.S. 104 (1972) (double jeopardy); *Schilb* v. *Kuebel,* 404 U.S. 357 (1971); *cf. Kastigar,* v. *United States,* 406 U.S. 441 (1972) (grant of immunity need not provide greater immunity than that of the privilege against compulsory self-incrimination).

During the heyday of selective incorporation, the Court looked to the Bill of Rights (as incorporated) to protect rights against state infringement. It went to great lengths to find safeguards in the Bill of Rights rather than invoke 'substantive due process' (p. 291 above): compare *Griswold* v. *Connecticut,* 381 U.S. 479 (1965), where a majority of the Court found a right of marital privacy in the 'penumbra' of several provisions of the Bill of Rights and incorporated it in the Fourteenth Amendment. It also revitalized the equal protection clause, p. 292 above. But some fundamental rights not explicit in the Bill of Rights continue to find protection in substantive due process. See *Rochin* v. *California,* n. 95 above. Then, in 1973, in *Roe* v. *Wade* n. 30 to this chapter, the Court, through Justice Blackmun, revitalized liberty and substantive due process in order to protect 'privacy' in personal matters.

The 'Rehnquist Court' of the 1980s and 1990s has shown no disposition to reopen or modify the doctrine of incorporation. As a result, with small exceptions, the individual enjoys essentially the same constitutional safeguards against the state as against the federal government. The provisions of the Bill of Rights apply to the states as to the federal government; the provisions originally applicable only to the states—the prohibition against impairing the obligation of contracts, the equal protection clause of the Fourteenth Amendment—apply to the federal government as well.

98. *Slaughter-House Cases,* 83 U.S. (16 Wall.) 36, 79–80 (1873).
99. *Yick Wo* v. *Hopkins,* 118 U.S. 356 (1886); *Truax* v. *Raich,* 239 U.S. 33 (1915); *Wong Wing* v. *United States,* 163 U.S. 228 (1896); *Takahashi* v. *Fish and Game Commission,* 334 U.S. 410 (1948); see also the concurring opinions in *Oyama* v. *California,* 332 U.S. 633, 647, 650 (1948).

A state cannot bar an immigrant alien from common employment, but the United States can, and an alien has no right to work in the face of restrictions imposed by the United States as conditions of his entry in non-immigrant status. *Pilapil* v. *Immigration and Naturalization Service,* 424 F.2d 6 (10th Cir. 1970), *cert. denied,* 400 U.S. 908 (1970); *Wei* v. *Robinson,* 246 F.2d 739 (7th Cir. 1957), *cert. denied,* 355 U.S. 879 (1957).

Aliens are protected against state discrimination also by federal law superseding or preempting state laws, or by the *Zschernig* principle, Ch. VI, pp. 163, 164. The Civil Rights Act of 1870 granted basic rights to aliens as well as citizens, ch. 114, 16 Stat. 144 (1870). Earlier cases upholding some state discriminations against aliens (*Ohio ex rel. Clarke* v. *Deckebach*, 274 U.S. 392 (1927); *Terrace* v. *Thompson*, 263 U.S. 197 (1923); *Heim* v. *McCall*, 239 U.S. 175 (1915)), are now of dubious validity, for 'the power of a state to apply its laws exclusively to its alien inhabitants as a class is confined within narrow limits'. *Takahashi*, above, at 420. That power has been further narrowed, no doubt, by *Hines* v. *Davidowitz*, 312 U.S. 52 (1941) (Congressional preemption), and *Zschernig* v. *Miller*, 389 U.S. 429 (1968).

100. See, e.g., *Sugarman* v. *Dougall*, 413 U.S. 634 (1973); *Graham* v. *Richardson*, 403 U.S. 365 (1971); *Plyer* v. *Doe*, 457 U.S. 202 (1982); *Nyquist* v. *Mauclet*, 432 U.S. 1 (1977). Alienage triggers strict scrutiny when aliens as a class are treated differently solely because of alienage, but not when classifications are made among aliens. *Dunn* v. *I.N.S.*, 499 F.2d 856 (9th Cir. 1974), *cert. denied*, 419 U.S. 1106 (1975); *Alvarez* v. *I.N.S.*, 539 F.2d 1220 (9th Cir. 1976), *cert. denied*, 430 U.S. 918 (1977).

101. See e.g., *Crane* v. *New York*, 239 U.S. 195 (1915), upholding the exclusion of aliens from employment on public works.

102. *In re Griffiths*, 413 U.S. 717 (1973) (admission to state Bar); *Surmeli* v. *State of N.Y.*, 556 F.2d 560 (2d Cir. 1976), *cert. denied*, 436 U.S. 903 (1978) (medical practice); *Examining Bd. of Engineers, Architects and Surveyors* v. *Flores de Otero*, 426 U.S. 572 (1976) (engineers).

103. *Foley* v. *Connelie*, 435 U.S. 291, 295–6 (1978), quoting from *Sugarman* v. *Dougall*, 413 U.S. 634, 647–8 (1973). Compare *Mathews* v. *Diaz*, 426 U.S. 67 (1976), discussed at n. 47 to this chapter.

104. *Foley* v. *Connelie*, previous note; *Ambach* v. *Norwick*, 441 U.S. 68 (1979); *Cabell* v. *Chavez-Salido*, 454 U.S. 432 (1982); *Perkins* v. *Smith*, 370 F.Supp. 134 (D.Md. 1974), *aff'd*, 426 U.S. 913 (1976). But compare *Bernal* v. *Fainter*, 467 U.S. 216 (1984) (notary public).

NOTES, CHAPTER X. AN EIGHTEENTH CENTURY CONSTITUTION
FOR THE TWENTY-FIRST CENTURY, pp. 313 to 323

1. Letter to H. S. Randall, May 23, 1857, in 2 G.O. TREVELYAN, THE LIFE AND LETTERS OF LORD MACAULAY 409–10 (1875).
2. Holmes, J., *Missouri* v. *Holland*, 252 U.S. 416, 433 (1920).
3. As on Vietnam in 1970. Compare the state statutes designed to circumvent the Supreme Court's discretion on certiorari and 'compel' it to hear objections to the constitutionality of the Vietnam War. The Massachusetts statute (1970 Laws, c. 174), for example, authorized the Attorney General to bring a proceeding in the name of the State alleging Presidential usurpation of Congressional power. (It sought, in effect, to persuade the Court to overrule *Massachusetts* v. *Mellon*, 262 U.S. 447 (1923), which held that a state's objection to alleged Congressional usurpation was not justiciable.) Of course, the original jurisdiction of the Supreme Court is also, in fact, optional and the Supreme Court refused the case. *Massachusetts* v. *Laird*, 400 U.S. 886 (1970). See n. 45 to Ch. V.

    These statutes and proceedings were, in my view, misguided. They rang of the eighteenth century Kentucky and Virginia Resolutions and invoked reactionary and hopeless arguments of 'States rights' to challenge federal policy. If the Court wished to consider the questions raised, it had had ample opportunity to do so. See nn. 10, 51 to Ch. V. If impelled to hear the issues, it might have held them to be political questions, see Ch. V, p. 143. If it decided the issues on the merits, it would almost surely have upheld the legality of the President's action because it had been authorized by Congress. See Ch. IV, pp. 101–2. Possibly the proponents did not wish to have the issues decided and indeed hoped the Court would not decide them, but sought to publicize and dramatize the issues in order to mobilize public support in opposition to the war.
4. 'Great cases like hard cases make bad law.' Holmes, J., dissenting in *Northern Securities Co.* v. *United States*, 193 U.S. 197, 400–1 (1904).
5. Compare Senator Fulbright's earlier view that 'for the existing requirements of American foreign policy we have hobbled the President by too niggardly a grant of power', Fulbright, *American Foreign Policy in the 20th Century under an 18th Century Constitution*, 47 CORNELL L.J. 1, 2 (1961), and Fulbright, *Foreign Policy—Old Myths and New Realities*, 53 KY.L.J. 13, 33 (1964–65), with his later views as expressed in *Hearings, Separation of Powers* (n. 40 to Ch. IV), and *Hearings, National Commitments* (n. 38 to Ch. IV), n. 74 to Ch. III.
6. For example, the suggestion for a Congressional Force Committee that would share with the President any decision to use force short of war. See *Hearings, Separation of Powers* (n. 40 to Ch. IV) at 164; Ch. IV, p. 110n.
7. Justice Jackson concurring in *Youngstown Sheet & Tube Co.* v. *Sawyer*, 343 U.S. 579, 654 (1952).
8. For reflections by a contemporary, renowned Secretary of State on relations between President and Congress in foreign relations, and on bipartisan and non-partisan foreign policy, see D. ACHESON, PRESENT AT THE CREATION (1969)

especially at 95–101, 318. Note in particular his report of Senator Taft's view that the purpose of an Opposition is to oppose. *Id.* at 95–7.

Compare President Truman: 'I've always said that the President who didn't have a fight with the Congress wasn't any good anyhow. And that's no reflection on the Congress. They are always looking after their rights. You needn't doubt that.' Speech, May 8, 1954 reprinted in R. HIRSCHFELD, THE POWER OF THE PRESIDENCY 111, 113 (1968).

9. Chancellor Kent, quoted in *Myers* v. *United States*, 272 U.S. 52, 149 (1926).
10. Holmes, J., dissenting in *Tyson & Brother* v. *Banton*, 273 U.S. 418, 445 (1927).
11. *The Treaty Makers and the Law Makers: The Law of the Land in Foreign Relations*, 107 U.PA.L.REV. 903, 936 (1959).
12. Gladstone, *Kin Beyond Sea,* 127 NORTH AMERICAN REVIEW 185 (1878).

APPENDIX

THE CONSTITUTION
OF THE UNITED STATES OF AMERICA

We the People of the United States, in Order to form a more perfect Union, establish Justice, insure domestic Tranquility, provide for the common defence, promote the general Welfare, and secure the Blessings of Liberty to ourselves and our Posterity, do ordain and establish this Constitution for the United States of America.

ARTICLE I.

SECTION 1. All legislative Powers herein granted shall be vested in a Congress of the United States, which shall consist of a Senate and House of Representatives.

SECTION 2. The House of Representatives shall be composed of Members chosen every second Year by the People of the several States, and the Electors in each State shall have the Qualifications requisite for Electors of the most numerous Branch of the State Legislature.

No Person shall be a Representative who shall not have attained to the Age of twenty five Years, and been seven Years a Citizen of the United States, and who shall not, when elected, be an Inhabitant of that State in which he shall be chosen.

Representatives and direct Taxes shall be apportioned among the several States which may be included within this Union, according to their respective Numbers, which shall be determined by adding to the whole Number of free Persons, including those bound to Service for a Term of Years, and excluding Indians not taxed, three fifths of all other Persons. The actual Enumeration shall be made within three Years after the first Meeting of the Congress of the United States, and within every subsequent Term of ten Years, in such Manner as they shall by Law direct. The Number of Representatives shall not exceed one for every thirty Thousand, but each State shall have at Least one Representative; and until such enumeration shall be made, the State of New Hampshire shall be entitled to chuse three, Massachusetts eight, Rhode Island and Providence Plantations one, Connecticut five, New-York six, New Jersey four, Pennsylvania eight, Delaware one, Maryland six, Virginia ten, North Carolina five, South Carolina five, and Georgia three.

When vacancies happen in the Representation from any State, the Executive Authority thereof shall issue Writs of Election to fill such Vacancies.

The House of Representatives shall chuse their Speaker and other Officers; and shall have the sole Power of Impeachment.

SECTION 3. The Senate of the United States shall be composed of two Senators from each State, chosen by the Legislature thereof, for six Years; and each Senator shall have one Vote.

Immediately after they shall be assembled in Consequence of the first Election, they shall be divided as equally as may be into three Classes. The Seats of the Senators of the first Class shall be vacated at the Expiration of the second Year, of the second Class at the Expiration of the fourth Year, and of the third Class at the Expiration of the sixth Year, so that one third may be chosen every second Year; and if Vacancies happen by Resignation, or otherwise, during the Recess of the Legislature of any State, the Executive thereof may make temporary Appointments until the next Meeting of the Legislature, which shall then fill such Vacancies.

No Person shall be a Senator who shall not have attained to the Age of thirty Years, and been nine Years a Citizen of the United States, and who shall not, when elected, be an Inhabitant of that State for which he shall be chosen.

The Vice President of the United States shall be President of the Senate, but shall have no Vote, unless they be equally divided.

The Senate shall chuse their other Officers, and also a President pro tempore, in the Absence of the Vice President, or when he shall exercise the Office of President of the United States.

The Senate shall have the sole Power to try all Impeachments. When sitting for that Purpose, they shall be on Oath or Affirmation. When the President of the United States is tried the Chief Justice shall preside: And no Person shall be convicted without the Concurrence of two thirds of the Members present.

Judgment in Cases of Impeachment shall not extend further than to removal from Office, and disqualification to hold and enjoy any Office of honor, Trust or Profit under the United States: but the Party convicted shall nevertheless be liable and subject to Indictment, Trial, Judgment and Punishment, according to Law.

SECTION 4. The Times, Places and Manner of holding Elections for Senators and Representatives, shall be prescribed in each State by the Legislature thereof; but the Congress may at any time by Law make or alter such Regulations, except as to the Places of chusing Senators.

The Congress shall assemble at least once in every Year, and such Meeting shall be on the first Monday in December, unless they shall by Law appoint a different Day.

SECTION 5. Each House shall be the Judge of the Elections, Returns and Qualifications of its own Members, and a Majority of each shall constitute a Quorum to do Business; but a smaller Number may adjourn from day to day, and may be authorized to compel the Attendance of absent Members, in such Manner, and under such penalties as each House may provide.

Each House may determine the Rules of its Proceedings, punish its Members for disorderly Behaviour, and, with the Concurrence of two thirds, expel a Member.

Each House shall keep a Journal of its Proceedings, and from time to time publish the same, excepting such Parts as may in their Judgment require Secrecy; and the Yeas and Nays of the Members of either House on any question shall, at the Desire of one fifth of those Present, be entered on the Journal.

Neither House, during the Session of Congress, shall, without the Consent of the other, adjourn for more than three days, nor to any other Place than that in which the two Houses shall be sitting.

SECTION 6. The Senators and Representatives shall receive a Compensation for their Services, to be ascertained by Law, and paid out of the Treasury of the United States. They shall in all Cases, except Treason, Felony and Breach of the Peace, be privileged from Arrest during their Attendance at the Session of their respective Houses, and in going to and returning from the same; and for any Speech or Debate in either House, they shall not be questioned in any other Place.

No Senator or Representative shall, during the Time for which he was elected, be appointed to any civil Office under the Authority of the United States, which shall have been created, or the Emoluments whereof shall have been encreased during such time; and no Person holding any Office under the United States, shall be a Member of either House during his Continuance in Office.

SECTION 7. All Bills for raising Revenue shall originate in the House of Representatives; but the Senate may propose or concur with amendments as on other Bills.

Every Bill which shall have passed the House of Representatives and the Senate, shall, before it become a Law, be presented to the President of the United States; If he approve he shall sign it, but if not he shall return it, with his Objections to that House in which it shall have originated, who shall enter the Objections at large on their Journal, and proceed to reconsider it. If after such Reconsideration two thirds of that House shall agree to pass the Bill, it shall be sent, together with the Objections, to the other House, by which it shall likewise be reconsidered, and if approved by two thirds of that House, it shall become a Law. But in all such Cases the Votes of both Houses shall be determined by Yeas and Nays, and the Names of the Persons voting for and against the Bill shall be entered on the Journal of each House respectively. If any Bill shall not be returned by the President within ten Days (Sunday excepted) after it shall have been presented to him, the Same shall be a Law, in like Manner as if he had signed it, unless the Congress by their Adjournment prevent its Return, in which Case it shall not be a Law.

Every Order, Resolution, or Vote to which the Concurrence of the Senate and House of Representatives may be necessary (except on a question of Adjournment) shall be presented to the President of the United States; and before the Same shall take Effect, shall be approved by him, or being disapproved by him, shall be repassed by two thirds of the Senate and House of Representatives, according to the Rules and Limitations prescribed in the Case of a Bill.

SECTION 8. The Congress shall have Power To lay and collect Taxes, Duties, Imposts and Excises, to pay the Debts and provide for the common Defence and general Welfare of the United States; but all Duties, Imposts and Excises shall be uniform throughout the United States;

To borrow Money on the credit of the United States;

To regulate Commerce with foreign Nations, and among the several States, and with the Indian Tribes;

To establish an uniform Rule of Naturalization, and uniform Laws on the subject of Bankruptcies throughout the United States;

To coin Money, regulate the Value thereof, and of foreign Coin, and fix the Standard of Weights and Measures;

To provide for the Punishment of counterfeiting the Securities and current Coin of the United States;

To establish Post Offices and post Roads;

To promote the Progress of Science and useful Arts, by securing for limited Times to Authors and Inventors the exclusive Right to their respective Writings and Discoveries;

To constitute Tribunals inferior to the supreme Court;

To define and punish Piracies and Felonies committed on the high Seas, and Offences against the Law of Nations;

To declare War, grant Letters of Marque and Reprisal, and make Rules concerning Captures on Land and Water;

To raise the support Armies, but no Appropriation of Money to that Use shall be for a longer Term than two Years;

To provide and maintain a Navy;

To make Rules for the Government and Regulation of the land and naval Forces;

To provide for calling forth the Militia to execute the Laws of the Union, suppress Insurrections and repel Invasions;

To provide for organizing, arming, and disciplining, the Militia, and for governing such Part of them as may be employed in the Service of the United States, reserving to the States respectively, the Appointment of the Officers, and the Authority of training the Militia according to the discipline prescribed by Congress;

To exercise exclusive Legislation in all Cases whatsoever, over such District (not exceeding ten Miles square) as may, by Cession of particular States, and the Acceptance of Congress, become the seat of the Government of the United States, and to exercise like Authority over all Places purchased by the Consent of the Legislature of the State in which the Same shall be, for the Erection of Forts, Magazines, Arsenals, dock-Yards, and other needful Buildings;—And

To make all Laws which shall be necessary and proper for carrying into Execution and foregoing Powers, and all other Powers vested by this Constitution in the Government of the United States, or in any Department or Officer thereof.

SECTION 9. The Migration or Importation of such Persons as any of the States now existing shall think proper to admit, shall not be prohibited by the Congress prior to the Year one thousand eight hundred and eight, but a Tax or duty may be imposed on such Importation, not exceeding ten dollars for each Person.

The Privilege of the Writ of Habeas Corpus shall not be suspended, unless when in Cases of Rebellion or Invasion the public Safety may require it.

No Bill of Attainder or ex post facto Law shall be passed.

No Capitation, or other direct, Tax shall be laid, unless in Proportion to the Census or Enumeration herein before directed to be taken.

No Tax or Duty shall be laid on Articles exported from any State.

No Preference shall be given by any Regulation of Commerce or Revenue to the Ports of one State over those of another; nor shall Vessels bound to, or from, one

State, be obliged to enter, clear or pay Duties in another.

No Money shall be drawn from the Treasury, but in Consequence of Appropriations made by Law; and a regular Statement and Account of the Receipts and Expenditures of all public Money shall be published from time to time.

No Title of Nobility shall be granted by the United States: And no Person holding any Office of Profit or Trust under them, shall, without the Consent of the Congress, accept of any present, Emolument, Office, or Title, of any kind whatever, from any King, Prince or foreign State.

SECTION 10. No State shall enter into any Treaty, alliance, or Confederation; grant Letters of Marque and Reprisal; coin Money; emit Bills of Credit; make any Thing but gold and silver Coin a Tender in Payment of Debts; pass any Bill of Attainder, ex post facto Law, or Law impairing the Obligation of Contracts, or grant any Title of Nobility.

No State shall, without the Consent of the Congress, lay any Imposts or Duties on Imports or Exports, except what may be absolutely necessary for executing its inspection Laws: and the net Produce of all Duties and Imposts, laid by any State on Imports or Exports, shall be for the Use of the Treasury of the United States; and all such Laws shall be subject to the Revision and Controul of the Congress.

No State shall, without the Consent of Congress, lay any Duty of Tonnage, keep Troops, or Ships of War in time of Peace, enter into any Agreement or Compact with another State, or with a foreign Power, or engage in War, unless actually invaded, or in such imminent Danger as will not admit of delay.

ARTICLE II.

SECTION 1. The executive Power shall be vested in a President of the United States of America. He shall hold his Office during the Term of four Years, and, together with the Vice President, chosen for the same Term, be elected, as follows

Each State shall appoint, in such Manner as the Legislature thereof may direct, a Number of Electors, equal to the whole Number of Senators and Representatives to which the state may be entitled in the Congress: but no Senator or Representative, or Person holding an Office of Trust or Profit under the United States, shall be appointed an Elector.

The Electors shall meet in their respective States, and vote by ballot for two Persons, of whom one at least shall not be an Inhabitant of the same State with themselves. And they shall make a List of all the Persons voted for, and of the Number of Votes for each; which List they shall sign and certify, and transmit sealed to the Seat of the Government of the United States, directed to the President of the Senate. The President of the Senate shall, in the Presence of the Senate and House of Representatives, open all the Certificates, and the Votes shall then be counted. The Person having the greatest Number of Votes shall be the President, if such Number be a Majority of the whole Number of Electors appointed; and if there be more than one who have such Majority, and have an equal Number of Votes, then the House of Representatives shall immediately chuse by Ballot one of them for President; and if no Person have a Majority, then from the five highest on the List the said House shall in like Manner chuse the President. But in chusing the President, the Votes shall be taken by States, the Representation from each State having one Vote; a quorum for this Purpose shall consist of a Member or Members from two thirds of the States, and a Majority of all the States shall be necessary to a Choice. In every Case, after the Choice of the President, the Person having the greatest Number of Votes of the Electors shall be the Vice President. But if there should remain two or more who have equal Votes, the Senate shall chuse from them by Ballot the Vice President.

The Congress may determine the Time of chusing the Electors, and the Day on which they shall give their Votes; which Day shall be the same throughout the United States.

No Person except a natural born Citizen, or a Citizen of the United States, at the time of the Adoption of this Constitution, shall be eligible to the Office of President; neither shall any Person be eligible to that Office who shall not have attained to the Age of thirty five Years, and been fourteen Years a Resident within the United States.

In Case of the Removal of the President from Office, or of his Death, Resignation, or Inability to discharge the Powers and Duties of the said Office, the Same shall devolve on the Vice president, and the Congress may by Law provide for the Case of Removal, Death, Resignation or Inability, both of the President and Vice President, declaring what Officer shall then act as President, and such Officer shall act accordingly, until the Disability be removed, or a President shall be elected.

The President shall, at stated Times, receive for his Services, a Compensation, which shall neither be encreased nor diminished during the period for which he shall have been elected, and he shall not receive within that Period any other Emolument from the United States, or any of them.

Before he enter on the Execution of his Office, he shall take the following Oath or Affirmation:—"I do solemnly swear (or affirm) that I will faithfully execute the Office of President of the United States, and will to the best of my Ability, preserve, protect and defend the Constitution of the United States."

SECTION 2. The President shall be Commander in Chief of the Army and Navy of the United States, and of the Militia of the several States, when called into the actual Service of the United States; he may require the Opinion, in writing, of the principal Officer in each of the executive Departments, upon any Subject relating to the duties of their respective Offices, and he shall have Power to grant Reprieves and Pardons for Offences against the United States, except in Cases of Impeachment.

He shall have Power, by and with the Advice and Consent of the Senate, to make Treaties, provided two thirds of the Senators present concur; and he shall nominate, and by and with the Advice and Consent of the Senate, shall appoint Ambassadors, other public Ministers and Consuls, Judges of the supreme Court, and all other Officers of the United States, whose Appointments are not herein otherwise provided for, and which shall be established by Law: but the Congress may by Law vest the Appointment of such inferior Officers, as they think proper, in the President alone, in the Courts of Law, or in the Heads of Departments.

The President shall have Power to fill up all Vacancies that may happen during the Recess of the Senate, by granting Commissions which shall expire at the End of their next Session.

SECTION 3. He shall from time to time give to the Congress Information of the State of the Union, and recommend to their Consideration such Measures as he shall judge necessary and expedient; he may, on extraordinary Occasions, convene both Houses, or either of them, and in Case of Disagreement between them, with Respect to the Time of adjournment, he may adjourn them to such Time as he shall think proper; he shall receive Ambassadors and other public Ministers; he shall take Care that the Laws be faithfully executed, and shall Commission all the Officers of the United states.

SECTION 4. The President, Vice President and all Civil Officers of the United States, shall be removed from Office on Impeachment for, and Conviction of, Treason, Bribery, or other high Crimes and Misdemeanours.

ARTICLE III.

SECTION 1. The judicial Power of the United States, shall be vested in one supreme Court, and in such inferior Courts as the Congress may from time to time ordain and establish. The Judges, both of the supreme and inferior Courts, shall hold their Offices during good Behaviour, and shall, at stated Times, receive for their Services, a Compensation, which shall not be diminished during their Continuance in Office.

SECTION 2. The judicial Power shall extend to all Cases, in Law and Equity, arising under this Constitution, the Laws of the United States, and Treaties made, or which shall be made, under their Authority;—to all Cases affecting Ambassadors, other public Ministers and Consuls;—to all Cases of admiralty and maritime Jurisdiction;—to Controversies to which the United States shall be a Party;—to Controversies between two or more States;—between a State and Citizens of another State;—between Citizens of different States;—between Citizens of the same State claiming Lands under Grants of different States, and between a State, or the Citizens thereof, and foreign States, Citizens or Subjects.

In all Cases affecting Ambassadors, other public Ministers and Consuls, and those in which a State shall be Party, the Supreme Court shall have original Jurisdiction. In all the other Cases before mentioned, the supreme Court shall have appellate Jurisdiction, both as to Law and Fact, with such Exceptions, and under such Regulations as the Congress shall make.

The Trial of all Crimes, except in Cases of Impeachment, shall be by Jury; and such Trial shall be held in the State where the said Crimes shall have been committed; but when not committed within any State, the Trial shall be at such Place or Places as the Congress may by Law have directed.

SECTION 3. Treason against the United States, shall consist only in levying War against them, or in adhering to their Enemies, giving them Aid and Comfort. No Person shall be convicted of Treason unless on the Testimony of two Witnesses to the same overt Act, or on Confession in open Court.

The Congress shall have Power to declare the Punishment of Treason, but no Attainder of Treason shall work Corruption of Blood, or Forfeiture except during the Life of the Person attainted.

ARTICLE IV.

SECTION 1. Full Faith and Credit shall be given in each State to the public Acts, Records, and judicial Proceedings of every other State. And the Congress may by general Laws prescribe the Manner in which such Acts, Records and Proceedings shall be proved, and the Effect thereof.

SECTION 2. The Citizens of each State shall be entitled to all Privileges and Immunities of Citizens in the several States.

A Person charged in any State with Treason, Felony, or other Crime, who shall flee from Justice, and be found in another State, shall on Demand of the executive Authority of the State from which he fled, be delivered up, to be removed to the State having Jurisdiction of the Crime.

No Person held to Service or Labour in one State, under the Laws thereof, escaping into another, shall, in Consequence of any Law or Regulation therein, be discharged from such Service or Labour, but shall be delivered up on Claim of the Party to whom such Service or Labour may be due.

SECTION 3. New States may be admitted by the Congress into this Union; but no new State shall be formed or erected within the Jurisdiction of any other State; nor any State be formed by the Junction of two or more States, or Parts of States, without the Consent of the Legislature of the States concerned as well as of the Congress.

The Congress shall have Power to dispose of and make all needful Rules and Regulations respecting the Territory or other Property belonging to the United States; and nothing in this Constitution shall be so construed as to Prejudice any Claims of the United States, or of any particular State.

SECTION 4. The United States shall guarantee to every State in this Union a Republican Form of Government, and shall protect each of them against Invasion; and on Application of the Legislature, or of the Executive (when the Legislature cannot be convened) against domestic Violence.

ARTICLE V.

The Congress, whenever two thirds of both Houses shall deem it necessary, shall propose Amendments to this Constitution, or, on the Application of the Legislatures of two thirds of the several States, shall call a Convention for proposing Amendments, which, in either Case, shall be valid to all Intents and Purposes, as Part of this Constitution, when ratified by the Legislatures of three fourths of the several States, or by Conventions in three fourths thereof, as the one or the other Mode of Ratification may be proposed by the Congress; Provided that no Amendment which may be made prior to the Year One thousand eight hundred and eight shall in any Manner affect the first and fourth Clauses in the Ninth Section of the first Article; and that no State, without its Consent, shall be deprived of its equal Suffrage in the Senate.

ARTICLE VI.

All Debts contracted and Engagements entered into, before the Adoption of this Constitution, shall be as valid against the United States under this Constitution, as under the Confederation.

This Constitution, and the Laws of the United States which shall be made in Pursuance thereof; and all Treaties made, or which shall be made, under the Authority of the United States, shall be the supreme Law of the Land; and the Judges in every State shall be bound thereby, any Thing in the Constitution or Laws of any State to the Contrary notwithstanding.

The Senators and Representatives before mentioned, and the Members of the several State Legislatures, and all executive and judicial Officers, both of the United States and of the several States, shall be bound by Oath or Affirmation, to support this Constitution; but no religious Test shall ever be required as a Qualification to any Office or public Trust under the United States.

ARTICLE VII.

The Ratification of the Conventions of nine States, shall be sufficient for the Establishment of this Constitution between the States so ratifying the Same.

* * *

ARTICLES IN ADDITION TO, AND AMENDMENT OF, THE CONSTITUTION OF THE UNITED STATES OF AMERICA, PROPOSED BY CONGRESS, AND RATIFIED BY THE SEVERAL STATES, PURSUANT TO THE FIFTH ARTICLE OF THE ORIGINAL CONSTITUTION.

AMENDMENT I [1791].

Congress shall make no law respecting an establishment of religion, or prohibiting the free exercise thereof; or abridging the freedom of speech, or of the press; or the right of the people peaceably to assemble, and to petition the Government for a redress of grievances.

AMENDMENT II [1791].

A well regulated Militia, being necessary to the security of a free State, the right of the people to keep and bear Arms, shall not be infringed.

AMENDMENT III [1791].

No Soldier shall, in time of peace be quartered in any house, without the consent of the Owner, nor in time of war, but in a manner to be prescribed by law.

AMENDMENT IV. [1791].

The right of the people to be secure in their persons, houses, papers, and effects, against unreasonable searches and seizures, shall not be violated, and no Warrants shall issue, but upon probable cause, supported by Oath or affirmation, and particularly describing the place to be searched, and the persons or things to be seized.

AMENDMENT V [1791].

No person shall be held to answer for a capital, or otherwise infamous crime, unless on a presentment or indictment of a Grand Jury, except in cases arising in the land or naval forces, or in the Militia, when in actual service in time of War or public danger; nor shall any person be subject for the same offence to be twice put in jeopardy of life or limb; nor shall be compelled in any criminal case to be a witness against himself, nor be deprived of life, liberty, or property, without due process of law; nor shall private property be taken for public use, without just compensation.

AMENDMENT VI [1791].

In all criminal prosecutions, the accused shall enjoy the right to a speedy and public trial, by an impartial jury of the State and district wherein the crime shall have been committed, which district shall have been previously ascertained by law, and to be informed of the nature and cause of the accusation; to be confronted with the witnesses against him; to have compulsory process for obtaining Witnesses in his favor, and to have the Assistance of Counsel for his defence.

AMENDMENT VII [1791].

In Suits at common law, where the value in controversy shall exceed twenty dollars, the right of trial by jury shall be preserved, and no fact tried by a jury, shall be otherwise re-examined in any Court of the United States, than according to the rules of the common law.

AMENDMENT VIII [1791].

Excessive bail shall not be required, nor excessive fines imposed, nor cruel and unusual punishments inflicted.

AMENDMENT IX [1791].

The enumeration in the Constitution, of certain rights, shall not be construed to deny or disparage others retained by the people.

AMENDMENT X [1791].

The powers not delegated to the United States by the Constitution, nor prohibited by it to the States, are reserved to the States respectively, or to the people.

AMENDMENT XI [1798].

The Judicial power of the United States shall not be construed to extend to any suit in law or equity, commenced or prosecuted against one of the United States by Citizens of another State, or by Citizens or Subjects of any Foreign State.

AMENDMENT XII [1804].

The Electors shall meet in their respective states and vote by ballot for President and Vice-President, one of whom, at least, shall not be an inhabitant of the same state with themselves; they shall name in their ballots the person voted for as President, and in distinct ballots the person voted for as Vice-President, and they shall make distinct lists of all persons voted for as President, and of all persons voted for as Vice-President, and of the number of votes for each, which lists they shall sign and certify, and transmit sealed to the seat of the government of the United States, directed to the President of the Senate;—The President of the Senate shall, in the presence of the Senate and House of Representatives, open all the certificates and the votes shall then be counted;—The person having the greatest number of votes for President, shall be the President, if such number be a majority of the whole number of Electors appointed; and if no person have such majority, then from the persons having the highest numbers not exceeding three on the list of those voted for as President, the House of Representatives shall choose immediately, by ballot, the President. But in choosing the President, the votes shall be taken by states, the representation from each state having one vote; a quorum for this purpose shall consist of a member or members from two-thirds of the states, and a majority of all the states shall be necessary to a choice. And if the House of Representatives shall not choose a President whenever the right of choice shall devolve upon them, before the fourth day of March next following, then the Vice-President shall act as President, as in the case of the death or other constitutional disability of the President—The person having the greatest number of votes as Vice-President, shall be the Vice-President, if such number be a majority of the whole number of Electors appointed, and if no person have a majority, then from the two highest numbers on the list, the Senate shall choose the Vice-President; a quorum for the purpose shall consist of two-thirds of the whole number of Senators, and a majority of the whole number shall be necessary to a choice. But no person constitutionally ineligible to the office of President shall be eligible to that of Vice-President of the United States.

AMENDMENT XIII [1865]

SECTION 1. Neither slavery nor involuntary servitude, except as a punishment for crime whereof the party shall have been duly convicted, shall exist within the United States, or any place subject to their jurisdiction.

SECTION 2. Congress shall have power to enforce this article by appropriate legislation.

AMENDMENT XIV [1868].

SECTION 1. All persons born or naturalized in the United States and subject to the jurisdiction thereof, are citizens of the United States and of the State wherein they reside. No State shall make or enforce any law which shall abridge the privileges or immunities of citizens of the United States; nor shall any State deprive any person of life, liberty, or property, without due process of law; nor deny to any person within its jurisdiction the equal protection of the laws.

SECTION 2. Representatives shall be apportioned among the several States according to their respective numbers, counting the whole number of persons in each State, excluding Indians not taxed. But when the right to vote at any election for the choice of electors for President and Vice President of the United States, Representatives in Congress, the Executive and Judicial officers of a State, or the members of the Legislature thereof, is denied to any of the male inhabitants of such State, being twenty-one years of age, and citizens of the United States, or in any way abridged, except for participation in rebellion, or other crime, the basis of representation therein shall be reduced in the proportion which the number of such male citizens shall bear to the whole number of male citizens twenty-one years of age in such State.

SECTION 3. No person shall be a Senator or Representative in Congress, or elector of President and Vice President, or hold any office, civil or military, under the United States, or under any State, who, having previously taken an oath, as a member of Congress, or as an officer of the United States, or as a member of any State legislature, or as an executive or judicial officer of any State, to support the Constitution of the United States, shall have engaged in insurrection or rebellion against the same, or given aid or comfort to the enemies thereof. But Congress may by a vote of two-thirds of each House, remove such disability.

SECTION 4. The validity of the public debt of the United States, authorized by law, including debts incurred for payment of pensions and bounties for services in suppressing insurrection or rebellion, shall not be questioned. But neither the United States nor any State shall assume or pay any debt or obligation incurred in aid of insurrection or rebellion against the United States, or any claim for the loss of emancipation of any slave; but all such debts, obligations and claims shall be held illegal and void.

SECTION 5. The Congress shall have power to enforce, by appropriate legislation, the provisions of this article.

AMENDMENT XV [1870].

SECTION 1. The right of citizens of the United States to vote shall not be denied or abridged by the United States or by any State on account of race, color, or previous condition of servitude.

SECTION 2. The Congress shall have power to enforce this article by appropriate legislation.

AMENDMENT XVI [1913].

The Congress shall have power to lay and collect taxes on incomes, from whatever source derived, without apportionment among the several States, and without regard to any census or enumeration.

AMENDMENT XVII [1913].

The Senate of the United States shall be composed of two Senators from each State, elected by the people thereof, for six years; and each Senator shall have one vote. The electors in each State shall have the qualifications requisite for electors of the most numerous branch of the State legislatures.

When vacancies happen in the representation of any State in the Senate, the executive authority of such State shall issue writs of election to fill such vacancies: *Provided*, That the legislature of any State may empower the executive thereof to make temporary appointments until the people fill the vacancies by election as the legislature may direct.

This amendment shall not be so construed as to affect the election or term of any Senator chosen before it becomes valid as part of the Constitution.

AMENDMENT XVIII [1919].

SECTION 1. After one year from the ratification of this article the manufacture, sale, or transportation of intoxicating liquors within, the importation thereof into, or the exportation thereof from the United States and all territory subject to the jurisdiction thereof for beverage purposes is hereby prohibited.

SECTION 2. The Congress and the several States shall have concurrent power to enforce this article by appropriate legislation.

SECTION 3. This article shall be inoperative unless it shall have been ratified as an amendment to the Constitution, by the legislatures of the several States, as provided in the Constitution, within seven years from the date of the submission hereof to the States by the Congress.

AMENDMENT XIX [1920].

The right of citizens of the United States to vote shall not be denied or abridged by the United States or by any State on account of sex.

Congress shall have power to enforce this article by appropriate legislation.

AMENDMENT XX [1933].

SECTION 1. The terms of the President and Vice President shall end at noon on the 20th day of January, and the terms of Senators and Representatives at noon on the 3d day of January, of the years in which such terms would have ended if this article had not been ratified; and the terms of their successors shall then begin.

SECTION 2. The Congress shall assemble at least once in every year, and such meeting shall begin at noon on the 3d day of January, unless they shall by law appoint a different day.

SECTION 3. If, at the time fixed for the beginning of the term of the President, the President elect shall have died, the Vice President elect shall become President. If a President shall not have been chosen before the time fixed for the beginning of his term, or if the President elect shall have failed to qualify, then the Vice President elect shall act as President until a President shall have qualified; and the Congress may by law provide for the case wherein neither a President elect nor a Vice President elect shall have qualified, declaring who shall then act as President, or the manner in which one who is to act shall be selected, and such person shall act accordingly until a President or Vice President shall have qualified.

SECTION 4. The Congress may by law provide for the case of the death of any of the persons from whom the House of Representatives may choose a President whenever the right of choice shall have devolved upon them, and for the case of the death of any of the persons from whom the Senate may choose a Vice President whenever the right of choice shall have devolved upon them.

SECTION 5. Sections 1 and 2 shall take effect on the 15th day of October following the ratification of this article.

SECTION 6. This article shall be inoperative unless it shall have been ratified as an amendment to the Constitution by the legislatures of three-fourths of the several States within seven years from the date of its submission.

AMENDMENT XXI [1933].

SECTION 1. The eighteenth article of amendment to the Constitution of the United States is hereby repealed.

SECTION 2. The transportation or importation into any State, Territory, or possession of the United States for delivery or use therein of intoxicating liquors, in violation of the laws thereof, is hereby prohibited.

SECTION 3. This article shall be inoperative unless it shall have been ratified as an amendment to the Constitution by conventions in the several States, as provided in the Constitution, within seven years from the date of the submission hereof to the States by the Congress.

AMENDMENT XXII [1951].

SECTION 1. No person shall be elected to the office of the President more than twice, and no person who has held the office of President, or acted as President, for more than two years of a term to which some other person was elected President shall be elected to the office of the President more than once. But this Article shall not apply to any person holding the office of President when this Article was proposed by the Congress, and shall not prevent any person who may be holding the office of President, or acting as President, during the term within which this Article becomes operative from holding the office of President or acting as President during the remainder of such term.

SECTION 2. This article shall be inoperative unless it shall have been ratified as an amendment to the Constitution by the legislatures of three-fourths of the several States within seven years from the date of its submission to the States by the Congress.

AMENDMENT XXIII [1961].

SECTION 1. The District constituting the seat of Government of the United States shall appoint in such manner as the Congress may direct:
A number of electors of President and Vice President equal to the whole number of Senators and Representatives in Congress to which the District would be entitled if it were a State, but in no event more than the least populous State; they shall be in addition to those appointed by the States, but they shall be considered, for the purposes of the election of President and Vice President, to be electors appointed by a State; and they shall meet in the District and perform such duties as provided by the twelfth article of amendment.

SECTION 2. The Congress shall have power to enforce this article by appropriate legislation.

AMENDMENT XXIV [1964].

SECTION 1. The right of citizens of the United States to vote in any primary or other election for President or Vice President, for electors for President or Vice

President, or for Senator or Representative in Congress, shall not be denied or abridged by the United States or any State by reason of failure to pay any poll tax or other tax.

SECTION 2. The Congress shall have power to enforce this article by appropriate legislation.

AMENDMENT XXV [1967].

SECTION 1. In case of the removal of the President from office or of his death or resignation, the Vice President shall become President.

SECTION 2. Whenever there is a vacancy in the office of the Vice President, the President shall nominate a Vice President who shall take office upon confirmation by a majority vote of both Houses of Congress.

SECTION 3. Whenever the President transmits to the President pro tempore of the Senate and the Speaker of the House of Representatives his written declaration that he is unable to discharge the powers and duties of his office, and until he transmits to them a written declaration to the contrary, such powers and duties shall be discharged by the Vice President as Acting President.

SECTION 4. Whenever the Vice President and a majority of either the principal officers of the executive departments or of such other body as Congress may by law provide, transmit to the President pro tempore of the Senate and the Speaker of the House of Representatives their written declaration that the President is unable to discharge the powers and duties of his office, the Vice President shall immediately assume the powers and duties of the office as Acting President.

Thereafter, when the President transmits to the President pro tempore of the Senate and the Speaker of the House of Representatives his written declaration that no inability exists, he shall resume the powers and duties of his office unless the Vice President and a majority of either the principal officers of the executive department or of such other body as Congress may by law provide, transmit within four days to the President pro tempore of the Senate and the Speaker of the House of Representatives their written declaration that the President is unable to discharge the powers and duties of his office. Thereupon Congress shall decide the issue, assembling within forty-eight hours for that purpose if not in session. If the Congress, within twenty-one days after receipt of the latter written declaration, or, if Congress is not in session, within twenty-one days after Congress is required to assemble, determines by two-thirds vote of both Houses that the President is unable to discharge the powers and duties of his office, the Vice President shall continue to discharge the same as Acting President; otherwise, the President shall resume the powers and duties of his office.

AMENDMENT XXVI [1971].

SECTION 1. The right of citizens of the United States, who are eighteen years of age or older, to vote shall not be denied or abridged by the United States or by any State on account of age.

SECTION 2. The Congress shall have power to enforce this article by appropriate legislation.

AMENDMENT XXVII [1992].

No law varying the compensation for the services of the Senators and Representatives shall take effect until an election of Representatives shall have intervened.

INDEX